Modern American Religion

Modern American Religion

Volume 2

The Noise of Conflict

1919–1941

Martin E. Marty

The University of Chicago Press
Chicago and London

Frontispiece: Lucas Cranach (1472–1553), *War in Heaven* (Collection of William H. Scheide, Princeton University Library)

Martin E. Marty is Fairfax M. Cone Distinguished Service Professor of the History of Modern Christianity at the University of Chicago. He is the author of numerous books, including *A Nation of Behavers*, also published by the University of Chicago Press.

The University of Chicago Press, Chicago 60637
The University of Chicago Press, Ltd., London
© 1991 by The University of Chicago
All rights reserved. Published 1991
Printed in the United States of America

99 98 97 96 95 94 93 92 91 54321

Library of Congress Cataloging-in-Publication Data
(Revised for vol. 2)

Marty, Martin E., 1928–
  Modern American religion.

  Includes bibliographical references and indexes.
  Contents: v. 1. The irony of it all, 1893–1919—
v 2. The noise of conflict, 1919–1941.
    1. United States—Religion—1901–1945.   2. United
States—Religion—1945–   .   3. United States—
Church history—20th century.   I. Title.
  BL2525.M37   1986   291′.0973′0904   85-16524
  ISBN 0-226-50893-5 (v. 1)
        0-226-50895-1 (v. 2)

To Franklin I. Gamwell

The aims of scientific thought are to see the general in the particular and the eternal in the transitory.
—Alfred North Whitehead

. . . now storming fury rose
And clamor such as heard in Heav'n till now
Was never, Arms on Armor clashing bray'd
Horrible discord, and the madding Wheels
Of brazen Chariots rag'd; dire was the noise
Of conflict . . .
John Milton, *Paradise Lost,* VI, 207–12

Contents

Acknowledgments

Students in seminars at the University of Chicago made the most critical contributions to the substance of this work, and they know how dependent upon them I am. Audiences at lectureships also contributed more than the questioners among them could know. Authors of what scholars often condescendingly call "secondary sources" make primary bestowals on those who benefit from their research, and they certainly did on me. American citizens who spoke and wrote between the world wars provided rhetoric and engaged in actions that became the stuff of history and of this volume, and without them I would have nothing to say.

By name, now, I thank the following: Franklin I. Gamwell, to whom this work is dedicated, has been my Dean through the years of its evolution, and has provided every kind of support, not least of all intellectual, to the venture. His assistants, the late Mrs. Delores Smith and more recently Mrs. Sandra Peppers, went out of their way to give encouragement to its production. Professor Jay Dolan and some thirty Upper Midwest historians of American religion who met at the Cushwa Center at the University of Notre Dame for a session we called "Fricasseed Marty," then and before and after offered helpful criticisms. Four historians—colleague Jerald C. Brauer, brother Myron A. Marty, associate James P. Wind, and son Pastor Peter Marty—read the manuscript and helped me reshape it. Another, Professor Grant Wacker of the University of North Carolina at Chapel Hill made exceptionally valuable suggestions in the late stages of writing, and I have tried to respond to them.

At the University of Chicago Judith Lawrence by both daylight and moonlight on weekdays and weekends made heroic accomplishments as typist and editor through numerous drafts. She also brought into a pattern my originally chaotic footnotes. Finally, she served as picture editor, performing many imaginative tasks in selecting and getting permissions for reproductions. Let me at this point also thank the various publishers and agencies for such permissions. Kenner Swain-Harmon served as a copy editor who brought to his work extensive knowledge of the subject. Stephen Graham was research assistant in the early years of this work. In later stages Peter D'Agostino took over, assuring succession in work so important to historians. As doctoral candidates they capably and generously did far more than the locating of sources and checking of references which was hoped for from them, strenuous as that work was. They made constant informed suggestions concerning the subject matter, narrative, and argument, and they more than other students know how deep is my debt to them. In later editing and proofreading stages, Gilson Waldkoenig made substantial contributions, even as he set out to assist in research on volume 3 in this series.

Harriet Julia Marty did all the things for which spouses conventionally get thanked and, during an Australian winter, patiently listened and responded to a reading of the whole manuscript before the American summer, a year later, in which she made final editorial suggestions and helped read proof. While "the noise of conflict" sounded in the sources I was studying, all those named here provided cooperative and congenial climates for the author who acknowledges their partnership.

1

Dire Was the Noise

Guns explode in murderous religious encounters only four times in this narrative. The dire noise of conflict in America during the years between the two World Wars, the conflict which is the topic of this book, instead came mostly from the sound of human voices, of applause and jeers, of crowds and conventions. This arena was not in most ways like the "Intestine War in Heav'n" which produced the clamor in John Milton's *Paradise Lost*, whose lines provide our title. Our story tells of a more mundane intestine or civil combat over the shape and destiny of America, the role of various religions and peoples in the nation, and the part faith should play in personal destinies.

One of the many curious features of Milton's Book VI is the fact that the "War in Heav'n" could produce "spiritual" wounds and pain and agony, but never death. Immortal Angels were contending on all sides; ". . . strange to us it seem'd / At first, that Angel should with Angel war. . . ." The rhetorical warriors in American religion, on the other hand and obviously, were not Arch-angels and Arch-foes, Michaels or Satans, though all thought they were on the side of the angels. Their battles instead had one feature in common with the War in Heaven: no one, or almost no one, was killed in them. Their armies, much like those in Milton's poem, lived on to continue their warfare in the years to come. They influence the daily lives of Americans still.

1:1

1:2

1:3   My assertion that conflict between peoples and among people
was the most important public religious theme in the period between the two World Wars grows out of acquaintance with a vast
array of documents from those times. The interwar years originally gave more difficulty than any others in the half-millennium
covered in my *Pilgrims in Their Own Land: 500 Years of Religion
in America*. Gradually the obvious theme and a chapter title
emerged. This was "A Season of Conflicts." One sentence indicates a resistance I had felt about this topic: "Such conflicts do
not represent the most pleasant phases of American religious history." Since writing that chapter and while doing research for this
book, however, I concluded that something positive was being
worked out in these conflicts and deserved my full attention now.

1:4   The more one focuses on the period from 1919 to 1941 the
more clear it becomes that a complex religious event was occurring on a scale that matched earlier diffuse movements and events
in America. These had included the story of religion in the settlement of colonies, the establishment and disestablishment of religion, the effort to convert people on the frontier and in the cities,
the use of religion to justify the removal of Native Americans or
the enslavement of blacks, or, conversely, to help abolish slavery
and promote various freedoms. Now, in the interwar period, one
conflict predominated and tended to inform the others: the one
between the original-stock Anglo-Saxon Protestant peoples and
"everyone else." Through a career I had been tracing the fortunes
of that stock, beginning with *The New Shape of American Religion* thirty years ago; through the tractarian *Second Chance for
American Protestants* (after their displacement); to the most sustained pursuit in *Righteous Empire: The Protestant Experience in
America* in 1970. Then, after a study of world *Protestantism* it
seemed in place, through several books, to talk about the era after
Protestantism ruled until in *Modern American Religion*, volume
1, *The Irony of It All, 1893–1919*, American Protestantism was
seen to be surrounded by other religious forces bidding for equal
national attention.

1:5   Now in *Modern American Religion*, volume 2, *The Noise of
Conflict, 1919–1941*, it becomes apparent that a climactic struggle over the role of the once imperial Protestantism provided the
main drama. In volume 1 the themes related to the word *Modern*:
how did the various agents conceive of and relate to what they
thought of as modern assaults and opportunities? In this second
book the second word, *American*, is central: how did the same

actors struggle to define and deal religiously with what they considered the national experience to be about? A third volume, on the years from 1941 to 1965, will concentrate on the third word, *Religion*: how did modern American people of diverse faiths interact in efforts to promote religion itself? A final volume will revisit all the themes through much of the last third of the century. For now: the years between the two World Wars became decisive in the destiny of the people I had been tracking for so long; the story of their divisions had once seemed "unpleasant"; now I felt called to tell it with positive purposes also in mind.

The period between the two World Wars: reference to it calls   1:6
forth a comparison of those times with more recent days. The present book was written in a time when many citizens wanted to be told a pleasant story. They were turning nostalgic about that world of their grandfathers and grandmothers. Millions were seeking simplicity in life and bemoaning the factionalism of the new times. Urbanites invoked the lost world of towns almost forgotten. They remembered each of these as having found its center in a single white church and a nearby red schoolhouse. These were symbols of a harmony many associated with life earlier in this century. Once upon a time, it was argued, the pacific Americans agreed with each other on issues of faith and morals, values and ideals. Since then, the new imagery suggested, the nation had fallen, and the discord of contending factions had replaced the concord once known. This book shows how false that mythic image is.

Instead of harmony and simplicity, conflict ruled. We will   1:7
see that not since the Civil War had America been more torn. In matters specifically religious the nation had never seemed more divided than it was in these interwar years. Here are some enemies we shall be meeting: original-stock Protestants vs. everyone else; "100 percent Americans" vs. Communists and Slavs in the Red Scare; old-stock Anglo-Saxons vs. Catholic or Jewish or Asian immigrants; the Ku Klux Klan vs. the same, plus liberals and blacks; white Christians vs. black Christians; conventional black churches vs. "back to Africa" movements; Zionists vs. anti-Zionists; prolabor Catholics vs. antilabor Catholics; Protestant Fundamentalists vs. Modernists; pro-Peace Pact movements vs. anti-League of Nations sorts; pro-Repeal wets vs. anti-Repeal drys; Protestants against a Catholic president vs. Catholics for a Catholic president; supporters of birth control vs. enemies of birth control; Depression demagogues of the Right vs.

left-wing firebrands; Protestant liberals vs. Protestant realists; Catholic Workers vs. capitalists; pro-New Deal religionists vs. anti-New Dealers; pacifists vs. "preparedness for war" partisans; and more.

1:8   All of these conflicts were based in religious beliefs and passions or else included profound religious motivations. This feature may cause some surprise among readers who think of America as a secular society which makes room for religion only in sequestered churches or as a private affair in individual lives. Most histories of the times, those which have focused on the Harlem Renaissance, the literary exiles, alienated Jewish writers, university agnostics, the administrative sides of the New Deal, or debates over the economics of military preparedness, tend to neglect or suppress the story of religion in a society which instead fairly reeked of religion.

1:9   The other occasion for evoking surprise in this story is the virtual absence of dead bodies as a result of these intense conflicts. Americans take for granted that their own religious controversies should be verbal and bloodless, that it is too late in history for religious wars. Yet near the end of the twentieth century television daily and newsmagazines weekly depict ways in which religion is a key element in conflicts which take enormous tolls in lives and property. In Northern Ireland, Iran, Iraq, Indonesia, Israel, India, the murderous parties bear names like Catholic, Protestant, Shi'ite, Sunni, Jew, Sikh, Hindu, and more, and their conflicts issue in death. Not so in America. While telling the story of these two decades we shall be especially alert to finding reasons why interreligious conflict has taken a different character here.

1:10   Revising the history and revisioning the events that nostalgia miscasts can be an aesthetic diversion. The story told in *The Noise of Conflict* also anticipates, and, one hopes, throws light on a controversy over a substantive issue which continues to divide Americans. Fifty and sixty years after the events here remembered, citizens and leaders debated whether America had or needed a single center, a dominant influence, a privileged philosophy, a specified religion, if it was to promote morals, engender good values, and encourage civic virtue in the populace. One side advocated homogeneity: America, it was said, must find its center and define who was "in" and who was "out." Depending on who was making the point, the dominance, it was said, must belong variously to Western ideals, the Judeo-Christian tradition, the cause of the Christian nation, or even Born-Again America.

On the other side were those who argued that America must come to terms with the diversity that was growing each year, with the pluralism evident and evidently increasing in a free society.

The debate was an old one, and notable people have argued   1:11
their cases during it. At the birth of the nation, John Jay, in *The Federalist*, spoke for one side: Providence had been pleased to give this "one connected country to one united people—a people descended from the same ancestors, speaking the same language, professing the same religion, attached to the same principles of government, very similar in manner and customs." From within the Protestant empire, Princeton's noted Charles Hodge in 1829 was pleased to see the United States becoming one people, "having one language, one literature, essentially one religion, and one common soul."

Now during the interwar years expatriate poet T. S. Eliot lec-   1:12
tured in Virginia, speaking to and for many who stayed in America when he exalted tradition as "all those habitual actions, habits and customs, from the most significant religious rite to our conventional way of greeting a stranger, which represent the blood kinship of 'the same people living in the same place.' " To pursue this, said Eliot, the advocate of a Christian culture, "the population should be homogeneous; where two or more cultures exist in the same place they are likely to be either fiercely self-conscious or both to become adulterate. What is still more important is unity of religious background; . . ." He then went on to illustrate with a notorious example not often invoked by those who promoted a homogeneous America fifty years after he spoke: "What is still more important is unity of religious background; and reasons of race and religion combine to make any large number of free-thinking Jews undesirable." With rare pathological exceptions, most of the recent advocates of a Christian America were not anti-Semitic. They focused more readily on "the secular humanists" or some other vague opponent who was destroying morals, values, and virtues.

I have sided with the pluralists; indeed, more so since having   1:13
read the kinds of documents which are the base of *The Noise of Conflict*. Such an identification does not mean that I see no basis for the homogenizers' case: both the expression of religious convictions and the national pursuit of consensus seem easier when there is a dominant or central force, even for the sake of reaction against it. A less centered society lacking a "main line" presents a more confusing scene. Nor is the alternative a simple advocacy

of mere or utter or mindless pluralism, but rather of what I call civic pluralism. This style of support for an America which recognizes diverse sources of values is born of realism and asks, "How are we all to deal with an increasingly heterogeneous America?" It is inspired, in part negatively, by a view of the horrors of conflict when one group aspires to "run the show" and then at best to tolerate dissenters and outsiders. Such a pluralism shows positive concern for a republic in which citizens aspire to some measure of common conversation and even a basic consensus, but sees this aspiration better fed on common stories and intentions than on privileging one religious complex, for example a Christian America or a "Judeo-Christian society."

1:14   If this book is to advance the story and aid reflection, its author has to have clearly in mind its potential audience. This narrative, I hope, will attract one general and several particular readerships. Generally: it is the second freestanding volume in a large work whose ambition it is for the first time to treat on a large canvas the epic of American religion in the fifth "American century." I have confidence in this story and hope it finds a continuing and enlarging readership of such books, people who simply want to know more American history and enjoy what I hope is a good story. Particularly: it lifts up the religious element for those who have cared about American history but may not always have recognized the role of religion in that history. At the same time, it aims for the attention of those who have cared about religion but may not usually seek understandings of present discontents and hopes in the historical record.

1:15   That readership will be curious as to how the author conceives of the genre of *The Noise of Conflict*. This is not pure intellectual history, though it gives consistent attention to ideas. While there are extended encounters with formal works of theology—sometimes for pages at a time we will listen to one or another articulate thinker's voice—the interest here is in locating religious and other beliefs within the patterns and ways of daily life. Second, though heavily influenced by social historians and marked by several close-up looks at the daily life they favor, it does not aspire to be an original contribution to social history. More nearly it is a form of political history in that its topic is power and influence in the *polis*, the human city, the republic, though its first preoccupation is not with political events. It is best described as an essay in *cultural* history.

Necessarily, cultural history must imply some definition of cul-   1:16
ture. In an important chapter on such history Michael Kammen
cites an illuminating sentence by James Axtell. His thoughts are
compressed and demanding, but they can easily be unpacked:
"Culture is an idealized pattern of meanings, values, and norms
differentially shared by the members of a society, which can be
inferred from the non-instinctive behavior of the group and from
the symbolic products of their actions, including material artifacts, language, and social institutions." The historian sees which
patterns dominate in a particular society, how the parts of society
add up to some sort of whole, and what part actions, beliefs, and
artifacts play in the story of change in the course of the years.

Cultural historians have to be aware, as Kammen is, that theirs   1:17
is an inexact discipline. He cites an essay from 1956 by a master,
Jacques Barzun, to press the point: the historian must depend on
"the gift of seeing a quantity of fine points in a given relation
without ever being able to demonstrate it. The historian in general
can only show, not prove; persuade, not convince; and the cultural
historian more than any other occupies that characteristic position."

Within the cultural history genre, *The Noise of Conflict* pays   1:18
particular attention to one kind of noise, *rhetoric*: that is, to per-
suasive speech transcribed, or to writing which intends to persuade. We will follow events by paying very close attention to the
rhetoric of leaders and would-be leaders as they set out to gather
or hold followerships. In *The Irony of It All*, volume 1 of the
present work, a citation from Paul Crawford addressed the issue,
and it will be economical to quote him again. First, the rhetorical
critic "must so absorb the realities of conflict and the climate of
opinion and audience attitudes of the time under consideration
that he can mentally place himself in the past under study, yet
must not pretend to divorce himself from the advantages that recent scholarship has given to hindsight." Second, he or she must
try to identify and distinguish ideas and attitudes of rank-and-file
members of a movement from the views of its leaders, "particularly as embodied in their private expressions or in remarks to
relatively sophisticated hearers who may not be typical of ordinary members." Third, such a critic must be alert to whether written or oral discourse or other forms of symbolic behavior were
being used, and what their intention was. As one example: some
rhetoric may be used with an intent to be overheard by the press

as well as merely to be heard. Finally, such a critic must be aware that rank-and-file members and spokespersons may have been identified with only one or two phases or aspects of a movement, without a concern for the long-range historical movement or context.

1:19   More recently Dominick LaCapra has contributed to the understanding of rhetoric and cultural history, particularly by pointing to the emphasis on the "conversation" or dialogue which goes on between the historian and the documents from the past. "Historians generally recognize that they begin not with a 'virgin' historical record but with a record processed by the accounts of other historians." But they are to do more than merely "revise" standard accounts. Their encounter with texts, which otherwise would seem to represent a "dialogue with the dead," comes to life when one conceives that the writer of history is also a rhetorician, a persuader, someone who is being changed by a conversation with the past which "involves the historian in argument and even polemic—both with others and within the self—over approaches to understanding that are bound up with institutional and political issues." To make possible a hearing of these past voices, I have again generously quoted many characters. (Since this means that someone talks and is to be cited in almost all paragraphs, I have continued using an endnoting system which many readers have found convenient and attractive.)

1:20   Two more points relating to approach remain. First is the matter of *conflict theory* itself. In the modern world almost all writing on conflict positively or negatively adduces Karl Marx, who had so much to say about social class and religion. Of course, there were classes in interwar America, so class analysis plays some part in the present treatment. It will be clear that something like Marx's concept of ideology also connects with the way various peoples or denominations legitimated their attempts to hold or gain power. Yet, despite occasional references to "elites" or "the business class," questions concerning the forms religious conflict took in this period are better informed by other than Marxian theories of conflict. In this case, the German Georg Simmel has been most provocative and to the point. Since after the story begins we rely almost exclusively on writings from the interwar American time and place, this is the place to hear Simmel.

1:21   Several of his motifs will be most helpful as we listen to the violent rhetoric used by Protestants and others in this period. First, social conflict helps groups take form and endure. "A certain amount of discord, inner divergence and outer controversy, is organically tied up with the very elements that ultimately hold the group together." For example, after mainstream American Protestants eventually ceased fighting Catholics, they found more difficulty holding loyalties than when they had been militant and hateful. Next, wrote Simmel, hostility reinforces group ties: "It is *expedient* to hate the adversary with whom one fights . . . , just as it is expedient to love a person whom one is tied to." This book, it will become clear, is a story of strange bedfellows, of acquired hatreds and hit-or-miss coalitions. Simmel adds, third, that conflict close to home is always most intense, as we shall also see in Fundamentalist-Modernist or Protestant Liberal-Realist controversies. "Typical of this is the way the renegade hates and is hated." Conflict helps groups define themselves and probably forces their overdefinition; therefore, fourth, "Groups in any sort of war situation are not tolerant." We shall see a growth in rigidity in various camps through these years of conflict.

In the crazy-quilt of denominational allegiances within a vol-   1:22
untary society where it is easy to drop out of a religious group, as is the case with America, churches and peoples acted out more patterns that had been anticipated by Simmel. Thus he showed how groups have to keep hunting for enemies in order to hold themselves together. Of course, they do not do it self-consciously. Such hunting activity is almost instinctive. The groups do not often try to annihilate each other; the parties live symbiotically. Both sides all but have a covenant to keep on fighting. "One *unites* in order to fight, and one fights under the mutually recognized control of norms and rules." To advance these causes, groups form coalitions; conflict, Simmel argues, "may also bring persons and groups together which have otherwise nothing to do with each other." For instance, Zionist and anti-Zionist Jews could link to fight against anti-Semitism. Fundamentalists and Modernists could coalesce as Protestants against a wet Catholic candidate for president, even if their common action looks bizarre on any other terms. Simmel would have found interwar American religions to be copybook examples of his theories.

The last major question is: *what was at issue* at the heart of the   1:23
public religious conflicts of the period? The answer which unfolds in the narrative is: the power to influence. The partisans all loved America, and they loved both their own people and the religions of their people. They wanted a claim on the past and a role in the future of these religions. Today scholars would no doubt phrase

all this as a debate over "cultural hegemony," but the more common word then was "dominance." A different kind of book than this, one which aspired to be a full story of private and congregational American religion, would deal more than this book does with prayer, devotion, mysticism, worship, meditation, and parochial activity. This instead is a story of *public* religion, of the various faiths as they vied to shape the nation, of the rhetoric of leaders and the kinds of actions their followers undertook.

1:24   Decades later, Americans have to deal with the aftereffects of the conflicts which occurred in the interwar period. In the eyes of many, the legacy takes the form of apparent cultural chaos, since the dominant group which had set so many of the terms for the society in that period is no longer dominant in the same way. It now has to share influence with many others. The term for the heirs of that formerly privileged group is Mainline Protestant. In the twenties and thirties, when people referred to those who made up this group, the characteristic words were original-stock Americans or old-stock Protestants. Sometimes there were variations in institutional references such as "churches of the early American emphasis" or "normal" churches. Sometimes I refer to them as "mainstream," "privileged," or "culturally established." Many analysts now date the loss of dominance by this cluster and its sometimes merely nominal adherents to the 1970s, but it is clear from this story that its progressive yielding of a place at the center of American life and some decline date from soon after World War I. The fateful internal schism that goes by the name of Fundamentalism vs. Modernism had effects which color all Protestant activities decades later.

1:25   At first glance this brand of Protestantism may seem to be receiving proportionately too much attention in this volume, especially in contrast to its role in the earlier book. That predecessor, which dealt with the immigration period between 1893 and 1919, necessarily included such an expansive cast of characters—Native American, Hispanic, black, schools of philosophy and therapy, and more—that it may have looked like a modern affirmative action platform. Almost all of these peoples and faiths do appear again in the present story. They will also return to center stage in the next volume, where there will be an accounting of American pluralism after mid-century. This present more mainstream Protestant-accented work gives a fair apportioning of space to the groups which had the greatest public impact. The purpose of these volumes is not to provide almanacs, yearbooks, encyclopedias, or catalogs of denominations and peoples but to try to assess what was the public focus of American religious life in a particular period.

The nearer this narrative comes to the present-day, the fewer   1:26
are the secondary sources on which one can rely. Yet those which exist have been of immeasurable help; I shall single out two and note others. Robert T. Handy's *A Christian America: Protestant Hopes and Historical Realities* is a brief pioneering work; its chapter on this period, "The Second Disestablishment" of mainstream Protestantism, in many ways parallels part of the thesis of this book. His essay on religion and the Depression also set the terms for inquiries by many others, though it has been partly countered or balanced by an essay on Fundamentalism in the period by Joel Carpenter; I have taken both articles into reckoning. Also William R. Hutchison and his colleagues in *Between the Times: The Travail of the Protestant Establishment in America, 1900–1960* have shown how crucial the interwar years were for this "establishment" and have influenced my work in its later phases.

Those who have been students in my seminars or readers of   1:27
my essays may be surprised to see how "canonical" this history appears to be. They are used to discussions of how history is written by winners and how an informal canon of American religious history needs analysis, criticism, and re-formation. In class and in articles we focus on the outsiders, the religious groups considered marginal, the overlooked classes and sorts of people. But the point of the present work is to show how for one last time the winners from previous centuries were hanging on, trying to keep the outsiders outside and the ones they considered marginal at the margins. So it contributes to the contemporary debates by showing the trauma of those in the center of the older canon.

Who specifically appears to be slighted in such a telling? The   1:28
half of American religious people who were women, admittedly, do not often appear. Certainly any historian of religion writing late in the century will be aware of such an apparent omission and will have made efforts to do justice to the role of women. In social history they would also certainly be prime. However, this book concentrates on public history, on the rhetoric of pulpit and pamphlet. Women were excluded from most pulpits, seminaries, and positions of public influence. One might even argue therefore that when they are absent, this absence is making its own point as to how power was bartered in the twenties and thirties. At the same

time, at numerous points in the story where they play a public part, women do appear.

1:29   Judaism, of course, receives considerable attention here because of its centrality in major national conflicts. Yet one of the best recent books on American Judaism introduces a chapter on this era thus: "The years between the world wars were not an exciting time for American religion." (After stating that, author Michael A. Meyer went on to present an almost forty-page treatment of real excitements in Judaism.) I believe that I have addressed the main public Jewish issues. Islam, today a strong force, then numbered in the lower thousands of adherents, and they were not in position to have public impact. The story of Eastern Orthodoxy has not been told and is little referred to here; this again is a fair comment on the public role. Orthodoxy almost does not show up in the periodical literature and national news media dealing with the conflicts of the times, however important its churches may have been for adherents in local communities. Asian religions counted few adherents and new Asians were not allowed to immigrate. It was not a fertile period for new eruptions of intense religious groups of the sort later called cults. Therefore, the fight over dominance at the center of the culture in two contrasting decades provides the engrossing plot.

1:30   One chapter here quotes a Catholic figure who complained that attention to conflict in religion could be distorting; it always focused on what was "picturesque." Conflict is the main theme in this book because it was the main theme of American public religion in that period. But I have tried also to do justice to the healing, consoling, and gentle features that led people to be loyal to their faiths in times of troubles.

1:31   Regarding the dominant Anglo-Saxon Protestant peoples in this story: in recent times, some of their enemies have enjoyed their downfall and scorned their later follies. The heirs of past victims of a once-dominant group may be excused for displaying some *Schadenfreude*, some joy in others' misfortune. A measure of self-hate even appears in some editorials or accounts by members of what is left of the Protestant mainstream. But such emotions have little place here. I believe that those dominant Anglo-Saxon Protestant peoples, for all the evidences of racism and attachment to privilege they showed, yielded their hegemonic place in the culture more gracefully than one could have expected as they gradually learned to share space and power. This story is a long chapter in the positive history of their adjustment. One need not be a chauvinist to suggest that in most places in the world, in times of twentieth-century change, mixed populations did not have the good fortune to encounter such adaptable groups as these. Americans were also fortunate to have inherited a polity which helped make adjustment feasible. It strikes me that attention to keeping that polity healthy remains a good civil and religious investment.

In the first volume of *Modern American Religion*, Reinhold   1:32
Niebuhr's philosophy of history, one colored by "humane irony," had a privileged place. The actors in that story were constantly seeing outcomes which frustrated what they intended, and this frustrating occurred partly because of the illusions, pretensions, and miscalculations of these actors themselves. Yet the purpose of seeing events through the prism of "humane irony," I noted, was not to lead people of later times to see nothing but futility and then to say "What fools these mortals be!" Instead, while this approach focuses on human history under a "divine judge who laughs at human pretensions," it also reflects the view of "an observer who is not so hostile to the victim of irony as to deny the element of virtue which must constitute a part of the ironic situation." For in this philosophy, the divine judge is also not "hostile to human aspirations," holds them responsible, and calls them to be co-creators.

This amounts to a philosophy of history which resists both   1:33
cynicism or despair on the one hand and utopianism on the other. The theological realism described in chapter 8 is quite congenial to me. Reinhold and H. Richard Niebuhr, who gave voice to it, were of mixed Reformed and Lutheran background. Some colleagues have detected in my approach, too, an understanding of history informed by a Lutheran outlook. To develop that observation into some sort of creedal statement would be irrelevant. Suffice it to say that my instincts and intellect lead me to concur with a view of history which, with Luther, stresses the hiddenness, the self-concealment of God, in human events. Yet God uses *larvae* or masks in history, and is active through the human actor seen as *cooperator Dei* in two interactive realms, *politia* and *religio*, which are fatefully webbed in this work. This means that since histories "describe nothing other than God's work," as Luther contended, "they should certainly be written with the greatest diligence, faithfulness, and truth." One tries.

Such an approach leaves a religious historian working at the   1:34
side of the secular historian. They both stare at the chaos of his-

tory and see the self-centeredness of people who surprise us by their mixtures of nobility and baseness, generosity and greed, vision and blindness. Yet the story overall adds up to something worthwhile; as Luther says somewhere, against both the nihilists and the perfectionists, and with a theological insight that could sustain one through these narratives: "God carves the rotten wood; God rides the lame horse."

2

Religious America's Search for Steadiness

President Harding's Call for Triumphant Nationality

To an American living between the two World Wars, religion would suggest the least likely field in which to seek excitements or to expect disruptions. Citizens passing churches or synagogues anticipated something like the quiet of hospital zones, not the din of combat. Tranquillity, the great goal in postwar public life, was also supposed to mark American religious existence. On May 14, 1920, barely three weeks before the Republican National Convention nominated him for the presidency of the United States, Warren G. Harding assessed the public mood in a speech at Boston's Home Market Club. People remembered him there listing the national needs of the hour, especially through his call for "not nostrums but normalcy." Less noticed were his other contrasts. According to Harding, some citizen needs were for "not heroics, but healing"; "not revolution, but restoration"; most characteristically, America needed "not surgery, but serenity." Europe, Harding observed, was viewing the world "through a vision impaired in a cataclysmal war." The postwar United States felt only the reflex, not the hurting wound. America desired

2:1

15

"not experiment, but equipoise." Senator Harding hoped for his country a "sustainment in triumphant nationality."

2:2   At the end of the decade, halfway between the World Wars, popular writer Frederick Lewis Allen reminisced about what all had happened *Only Yesterday*. For Allen and many others, the eleven years between the end of the First World War, November 11, 1918, and the beginning of the Depression after the crash on Wall Street on October 29, 1929, became one intact period, "the nineteen-twenties." Allen framed that decade between his second chapter which recalled the goal of Harding's time, "Back to Normalcy," and his next-to-last chapter with its reference to changed times, "Crash!" On the pages between he showed how Americans all along also pursued another Harding theme. They consistently wanted not "revolution, but restoration."

2:3   Candidate and later failed president Harding could well have been "Sage Warren" or "Saint Warren," so closely did churches seem at first to follow his descriptions and prescriptions for their nation. Thus by normalcy, Mr. Harding once explained, he meant a regular steady order of things, normal procedure, the natural way, normal order. Religious America also had an aversion to conflict and disorder, and the churches were crucial supporters of natural and normal ways of doing things. Millions stayed with religion in their search for steadiness. The president did not define what restoring meant. Regular worshipers needed no one to spell that out for them. Like habitually religious or spiritually hungry people in any age, they looked for personal healing to match the national healing for which Harding appealed. While in the White House Harding also never precisely described for them what serenity meant when he contrasted it to surgery. Churchgoing Americans also did not need such exact description. Throughout history, they knew religious speech and action had often cut and hurt. The story of crusades, jihads, inquisitions, and persecutions laid bare the horrific side of religion. Yet it was the prospect of serenity that so warmly attracted people in spiritual life. It is paradoxical and astonishing, therefore, to discover how American religion after World War I turned out to reinforce a threatening tribalism. By tribalism I mean aggressive and self-centered group behavior as it showed itself in the decade historians often call "the tribal twenties." In those years, perhaps despite themselves, citizens in their religious clusterings often lived out what philosopher Thomas Hobbes considered the human circumstance: "a condition of war of every one against every one."

Had serenity ruled, few would have noticed or remarked on   2:4
religion in America. Believers did not become members of religious groups in order to engage in battles for reporters or historians to notice. The steepled churches and domed synagogues
reposed in the tranquil landscape of those times. They represented
refuges from upheaval, hostels of normalcy. Restless young writers and intellectuals who so consistently turned against worship
and church in the twenties emphasized that they did so because
religion was too restful, too ordered—in short, boring. The fa-
bled kinds of "experiment" which the bland President Harding
shunned went on elsewhere: in New York's Greenwich Village, in
Parisian exile, or in American universities, where an antireligious
ethos prevailed as never before. Worshipers who turned to the
churches, however, made clear by their choice that they were doing so to find peace with God and with each other. They were at
home in the house of the Lord, in the company of their fellows.
They were serving and saving their nation. Let the surrounding
public world be filled with conflict, if it must. Religion was to
provide nothing but calm away from public disorder because for
millions religion was, as they liked to say, a private affair.

Local Churches: Middletown *as the Nation Writ Small*

Religion, to most Americans between the World Wars, meant   2:5
first the easy-to-overlook local churches in the local communities.
All measurements begin from these places. Congregations and
communities, of course, differ vastly from each other. The reporter on Jewish Harlem as it was turning into black Harlem in
New York would discover very different worlds than would the
chronicler of doings in an Iowa Quaker town or in largely Mormon Salt Lake City. Baptist sharecroppers in Mississippi seemed
to have little in common with the Eastern Orthodox in Pennsylvania coal country or the wealthy Episcopalians in Hyde Park,
New York. But one stop-action portrait of a community where
there seemed little action to stop stands out clearly. Its authors,
Robert and Helen Lynd, called this place and their book *Middletown.* A *New York Times* reviewer spoke of their chosen small
city as the whole nation writ small: "Despite some local and
sectional peculiarities, Middletown is the country in miniature,
almost the world in miniature." It was not that, any more than
a comparable classic referring to a selected *Middlecountry* or

Middlecity could be a perfect miniature of the world of all farms or all metropolises. Yet this portrayal of Muncie, Indiana, which the Lynds studied for their pioneering and classic work, can stand for thousands of other places where the citizens supported religion and wanted it to help provide serenity and normalcy. The Lynds lived in Muncie in 1924 and 1925 and published their work in 1929. They followed it up in 1937 with *Middletown Revisited.*

2:6   The Lynds wanted to know what it meant for traditional citizens to be turning modern, for religious people to become secular. Robert had trained at New York's Union Theological Seminary to be a Presbyterian minister, but when he dropped out he brought negative angles of vision to his subsequent research on religion. He and his wife, Helen, set out to prove how secular small-town America had become, how irrelevant religion and the churches were. Their bias is an asset. A pro-church prejudice on their part could skew our purpose if it made church life appear more vital than it was.

2:7   In the second of two reports, in 1937, Lynd and Lynd quoted a leading minister as he spoke to the Kiwanis Club. "In the old days," he opined, the "people went to preachers for consolation, information, and inspiration. They still come to us for consolation, but go to the newspapers for information and inspiration." Significantly, there as elsewhere it was the soothing element in faith and congregational life that was surviving. The Lynds commented only a bit too summarily that this ministerial speech "expresses succinctly the apparent role of religion in Middletown as an emotionally stabilizing agent, relinquishing to other agencies leadership in the defining of values." One minister and two social scientists need not stand for all Americans. But whoever reads widely in other literature of the period is certain to find thousands of parallels to this idea that religion, while declining, was still a stabilizer. The churches relinquished some influence but tried to hold their ground enough to define values for their members, for Middletown, for America itself. That is why so many advertisements claimed that religion advanced the nurture of the young, appropriate training in morality, and the desirable normalcy of natural order.

2:8   Where observe the churches? The Lynds dropped in at Sunday schools, where so much religious activity began. The visitors found middle-class citizens supporting them out of a hunger for continuity and nostalgia: "When business class people send their children to Sunday School in the effort to conserve and pass on

Paul Sample, *Church Supper* (1933), is a contemporary depiction of "ordinary" church life in the interwar period. (The James Philip Gray Collection, Museum of Fine Arts, Springfield, Massachusetts.)

what they feel has been an essential foundation of their own lives or to recapture something lost and wistfully remembered, no mere piling up of verbal descriptions of the services can set forth the thing they seek." So it was, other documents suggest, in a thousand Middletowns. The Lynds stayed around to find that the Protestant majority favored four additional forms of religious observance: Sunday morning and evening preaching services, mid-week prayer meeting, and Sunday evening young people's meeting. These all had survived fundamentally unchanged since the 1890s, there as in other Middletowns. Whoever wanted to revolutionize America's values would have stiff competition from these round-the-week, sometimes round-the-clock, lifelong and life-encircling activities.

The churches had no monopoly on the attention of the citizens.   2:9 The Lynds did find plenty of competition to them in what they called "other centers of 'spiritual' activity" which were then

springing up. The Rotary and other service clubs provided
sources of religious loyalty and zeal. The authors contended, no
doubt to the shock of many, that " 'civic loyalty,' 'magic Middletown,' as a religion, appears to be the greatest power for some
Middletown citizens." Their footnote to this line tells how some
Muncie business people even classified the church itself among
"civic responsibilities." Robert and Helen Lynd made a thesis of
all this and showed how the local church connected with the nation: "National patriotism is civic pride writ large." Middletowners supported this set of loyalties religiously.

2:10   Muncie citizens invented a useful scheme which Americans
elsewhere were also discovering. They devised "a multiplication
of groups performing often criss-crossing activities," a pattern
that served to reduce competition between rival agencies. How
might inhabitants minimize the potential for conflict? Overworked
business people resolved the problem by accepting what the
Lynds called a "blanket pattern solution." This meant a kind of
straight-ticket voting with their energies. Such people linked several loyalties: to church, party, fraternal order, country club, local
charities, and the like. What the two sociologists called a stan-
dardizing and fusing pattern of loyalties thus developed. Jesus,
the central figure of the Middletown believers' religion, became
as well Jesus "the first Rotarian." Their approach bred conformity and safety. The old freethinkers' Ethical Society by then was
gone, just as the Progressive party there had all but disappeared.
Middletown, like so many other safe havens, frowned on "strong
heretics—religious, economic, political, social." Dissent had become so quiet that indifference alone marked the passively dissenting minority. Oldtimers advised wavemaking newcomers to
" 'sit steady in the boat.' " The goal of such counsel was to produce for the middle classes at least some cohesion. People must
retain a sense of belonging, of fitting into the existing world.

2:11   The Lynds appropriately found these Indianans observing religion on this local scale mainly because it helped them to "understand and to cope with the too-bigness of life." These visitors
found Muncieites agreeing that all their beliefs simply came
handed down from the Bible. On that foundation, believers were
quite content to give assent to the basic Christian doctrines. Once
upon a time people had killed, empires had fallen, over these very
doctrines. Now townsfolk regarded them as necessary supports of
civilized life. Oh, there was always a bit of improvising. In the
mood of the twenties some people tried to avoid harsh realities or

particularly shocking dogmas. For just one example, "belief in Hell," the Lynds noticed, was "apparently dying out somewhat." But the survey showed that belief in Heaven survived, if with less intensity of conviction than before.

While some of these scrutinized Indianans were indifferent to   2:12
the organized church, few rejected it outright. One equation that spiritual rebels then and thereafter would reject was still valid in 1924 in Muncie: "There is a strong disposition to identify the church with religion and church-going with being religious." Slight warning signals were only beginning to be apparent. Minor doubts and uneasinesses among otherwise conforming individuals had grown slightly respectable and somewhat more visible than before. But these did not threaten civil life. Nor did the presence of a few small nonconforming groups such as Jews, Christian Scientists, or Spiritualists disturb the surface peace. The Protestant majority, anxious to hold its place, expressed only some impassioned anti-Catholicism, uninformed anti-Semitism, and a desire for rigid segregation of blacks by whites. Since there were fifteen Protestants to every Catholic in the city, the Lynds drew most of their conclusions from this overwhelming majority. But they had to notice that the suspect Catholics also fit perfectly the described civic and patriotic patterns, however much their formal dogmas differed from those doctrines so casually professed and then neglected by the Protestant majority.

So it was that serenity reigned on the surface. Two hate orga-   2:13
nizations, versions of the Ku Klux Klan, had recently spurted but then declined by the mid-twenties. Among the Protestant denominations, the Lynds could find only some increase of passionless and genteel rivalries which seemed beside the point. Their thesis: "There is more subtle church rivalry today than formerly, as financial and social competition, particularly among the business class, have tended to replace earlier doctrinal differences as lines of cleavage." Most people remained at least nominally faithful to the church in which they had been born. Nationally, advocates of new-fashioned church federation talked increasingly in favor of cooperation. In towns like this, however, "the interdenominational mingling of an earlier day [had] apparently declined somewhat."

Why? Most people already had firm religious preferences, so   2:14
the leadership had to invent reasons for people to choose one religious group over another. The churches engaged in competitive building programs so that each could put on the best possible face.

Everyone, therefore, had to deal with financial demands resulting from such competition. No antagonism over dogma resulted. No citizen was physically hurt. The Lynds heard only harmless regret, as voiced by a typical housewife: " 'When I was a girl here in Middletown people used to go about to the Christmas entertainments and other special services at the Methodist, Presbyterian, and other churches. People rarely do that sort of thing today.' " Let denominations federate nationally and announce their concords elsewhere, the local congregations more than before would serve their own eggnog under their separate mistletoes. The view from Middletown was impressively different from that at the Federal Council of Churches headquarters in New York. The Lynds puzzled over ways to connect what they saw locally with what they knew of the larger scene: "This apparent tightening of denominational lines, despite much talk of inter-church unity, is possibly not unrelated to national denominational organization." Denominations also had to compete for the limited market, while at the same time giving assent to the ideal of Christian and national cooperation.

2:15   Robert and Helen Lynd took time also to glimpse the small Catholic and tiny Jewish communities in largely Protestant Middletown, and saw them doing pretty much what the Protestant churches were doing. They too, perhaps more than they knew, helped people fuse religious and civil loyalties on the local level with the national culture that Catholics and Jews were not yet decisively helping shape. Most of the time the Catholic parish, for instance, spent its energies addressing people who were seeking mystery or company or opportunities to carry on the works of love. Their churches were reassuring presences to passersby who saw that all of them fit into a complex environment. They served as secure havens for quiet American loyalists who were not picking fights.

2:16   While the two visitors had come to sneer, they finally sounded eloquent about the place left for religion. To be fair to local sentiment they quoted a Muncie editorial on " 'Why Attend the Church?' " The answer: " 'In the church of the right kind there is an atmosphere of soul peace and contentment that comes more nearly meeting human needs and longings for better things than anything the week days hold.' " Then came the Lynd coda linking the local with the national, the patriotic with the spiritual: "As in the case of civic loyalty and patriotism, in church question marks straighten out into exclamation points, the baffling day-by-day complexity of things becomes simple, the stubborn world falls into step with man and his aspirations, his individual efforts become significant as part of a larger plan." President Harding or his two successors, Calvin Coolidge and Herbert Hoover, could not have said this so well, but what they did say concurred with the sentiment.

The Year Book: Denominations as the Nation's Churches

If the local churches were like precincts, then national bodies—denominations and federations—served as religious parties in the spiritual politics of America between the World Wars. These too resemble a sea of superficial tranquillity under whose surface and at whose edges conflict churned. It is hard to picture directing the attention of the literary exiles—the Gertrude Steins and Ernest Hemingways and Ezra Pounds—to any drama in the local institutions on which they were turning their backs. It also demands a willing and drastic suspension of disbelief on the part of readers who are seeking to understand America decades later, if they are to find historic denominations interesting. At first glance such agencies seemed determined to be uninteresting, politically safe inventions designed to suppress the conflict that threatened all of them and tore some apart. To make sense of the subsurface roiling, we must first do justice to appearances, to the face church bodies wanted to present. A guided tour of guidebooks will serve best—fortunately excellent ones survive. Three belong in the pack of any visitor to the scene: the *Year Book of the Churches 1924–25*, the *Federal Census of the Religious Bodies* taken in 1926, and *Twenty Years of Church Federation*, subtitled *Report of the Federal Council of the Churches of Christ in America 1924–1928*.

2:17

It makes sense to begin the denominational survey the way the Lynds looked at the local churches in order to speculate about the future: with the Sunday schools. The *Year Book* editor boasted that in a nation with 100 million religious members and adherents, there were over 26 million Sunday school students attending almost 200,000 Sunday schools. Anyone who might otherwise forget could easily be reminded by a one-hour visit to any of these schools that they did not exist for revolution but for support of order and restoration along lines which first President Harding's and now President Calvin Coolidge's citizens would regularly ob-

2:18

serve. Nothing much ever happened in Sunday school that would draw public notice. It was not supposed to. Weekly, the parents of a score of millions of children must have scrubbed their off-spring's faces, jammed Bibles or leaflets into their hands, and pushed these children out the door on the trail to religious educa-tion. Many adults joined them, to teach or to learn at the same hour, perhaps in drab green or dark wainscoted classrooms down the church corridors from the rooms of the tiny ones. In such settings well-meaning, often quite able, but ordinarily amateur teachers drilled the little scholars with Bible stories. They taught the commands of God and set out to instil the moral habits of a nation even as they induced ennui in thousands of adolescents who grew up rebelling against Sunday school.

2:19   The surviving documents of denominational culture show that the teachers in Sunday schools honored birthdays and rhymed the ways of God, gathered pennies in collections for foreign mission-aries, prayed for the absent, inspired some pupils and benumbed others, but never, never made news. A reporter who might peek from behind a tree to get material for a front-page story by watch-ing a cross-burning at a Ku Klux Klan rally would always come away from any Sunday school with a noteless pad. A journalist in 1925 might watch the perennial presidential candidate William Jennings Bryan perspire and persuade in a hot Tennessee court-room where the teaching of evolution versus biblical creation was at issue. She could then cool off by finding nothing to report in vacation church schools, where the teaching of divine creation endured. Along the way, such a casual reporter would have slighted a subtle story of success: in one year these church schools had added a million new pupils.

2:20   Those little Sunday school children often grew up to become adult members of congregations which normally worked together in denominations, the standard American form of organizing re-ligion nationally. What would politicians make of inventions such as these denominations? The government could not tax them. No citizens were required to belong to them, and about half the people did not. Being ejected from a denomination brought no civil disability and little stigma. These church bodies raised no armies. Their members were not as easy to mobilize as voters. The denominations could not levy taxes. Much of what they talked about and stood for seemed beside the point in the world surrounding them. When denominations fought, their issues were hard to explain to anyone a few inches removed from particular battles. Most of the time, they did not use denominational lines as instruments when fighting. It was no longer good manners or very satisfying for people in a group named Presbyterian to look for trouble with those called Episcopalian or Lutheran. Instead, Presbyterians now fought other Presbyterians over who-knew-what small spoils.

What sense, next, could a newcomer to the doctrinal scene   2:21
make of the chaos in a *Year Book* which signaled that it took seventeen church bodies with, variously, black or white majority constituencies, to make up the largest Protestant cluster, the Methodists; or eighteen entities for the Baptists? What about the record-breaking Lutherans, whose twenty-three then current denominations resulted from the fact that their ancestors had come to America as immigrants in different boats from different shores at different times? Why ask members to fight about the legacy of old boat schedules and antique European differences, this late and this far away in America? And why should any non-Lutheran care about any of this, if most Lutherans themselves had trouble making rational sense of their own boundaries and issues? How even locate all these groups? One virtually needed a microscope to spot the Lutherans' tiny Jehovah Conference, with its six congregations and 925 members, or the Eielsen Synod with its thirty congregations and 700 adherents. Only a hobbyist or collector could love such miniatures. But, one asks, must not the politician or advertiser then pay attention to the larger United Lutheran Church with its over 800,000 members and the Missouri Synod with its vaunted 600,000-plus adherents? If the leaders of these two bodies fought, and they did, and if their pastors competed and spoke ill of each other, as some did, no one outside these bodies got hurt. In any case, people belonged to their 7,500 Lutheran congregations in order to praise the God who justified and forgave sinners in Jesus Christ; they belonged not in order to do battle but to find serenity and restoration.

The careful reader, however, can begin to find even in year-   2:22
book and almanac pages some hints of fault lines running under the landscape of denominations. One table in the *Year Book* suggested the kind of competition that would spell conflict in tense times, for it assessed spiritual armies as heirs of ancient hostilities. In that table, editor E. O. Watson scrupulously compared how rival Catholics and Protestants were faring while they vied for the loyalty of Americans. His chart demonstrated that Catholicism had grown from 7,343,186 members in 1890 to 18,260,793

in 1923. But if in that period the Catholic population grew by eleven million, Protestants, admittedly starting from a larger base, also surged by fifteen million. Some years, editor Watson seemed happy to note, Protestant denominations even led in the numbers game with slightly larger percentages of growth than Catholicism boasted.

2:23   Protestants, alas for them, could also find reason to lose their calm when they looked at the membership figures for the entire third of the century. Catholicism during that time had grown by 4.5 percent every year, or 148.6 percent, while Protestantism lagged with only 3.26 percent growth annually or 107.8 percent. Let it be noted, however, that the *Year Book* did not exist to raise fears about such a trend. It chronicled what still seemed to be boom times in religion. Millions were loyal to institutions which provided care and offered prayer. Members counted on pastors to be at their side, rabbis to counsel and teach them, preachers to preach reassuring words about God, and fellow members to be friends. It is almost inconceivable that it would occur to people in the denominations to see themselves as agents who were preparing cannon fodder for spiritual conflicts which were to sunder America through the decade.

2:24   Often the traditional categories disguised untraditional conflicts. These seemed to have little to do with contemporary national themes. For example, near the beginning of the list one finds the African Orthodox Church. This new body spun off from Marcus Garvey's highly controversial "Back to Africa" movement. The Right Reverend George Alexander McGuire had organized it on September 1, 1921. Its 2,500 members, according to the descriptions, held to the ancient faith that was "essentially that of all Orthodox churches." Had the members been seeking spiritual surgery, they might instead have constituted themselves around current debates that concerned American blacks as blacks. Instead they evidently looked for serenity and therefore revisited centuries-old and thus now-safe battle zones. These believers adopted the "historic Nicene Creed without the Filioque, . . . and the so-called Aethanasian [sic] Creed, also without the Filioque." That word "Filioque" signalled arcane but once not unimportant nuances. Disputes over these had helped divide Eastern and Western Christianity into empire-sized blocs a thousand years before. The "Back to Africa" theme in such a denomination now instead meant turning from turmoil and threat into "Back to Nicaea," and thus to solace.

A few pages later one comes across another niche in the   2:25
churchly landscape, the Assyrian Jacobite Apostolic Church. It
also evidently felt safer with Old World imports. Its *Year Book*
notice announced that this church used a slight variation on that
"Filioque" clause (which referred to the way Jesus Christ the Son
related to God the Father and the Holy Spirit). Also, an impressively exclusive clergy served it: "Very Reverend Hanna Koorie
is the only priest in America." Turning to the "B's," one finds
immediately a pacific movement, the Bahá'í's. Its soothing notice
reads: "There is no regular organization of Bahais [sic]. One may
be a Bahai and still retain active membership in another religious
body." By the time one comes down the listing to "E" as in the
Evangelical Synod of North America, there is one tiny clue which
suggests the responsible way a certain denomination provided
some repose for the church leader who was to make a name for
himself as a contentious public Protestant between the World
Wars. The secretary of that synod was "Rev. R. [Reinhold] Niebuhr, Detroit, Mich.," of whom much more, much later.

The *Year Book* editor seemed to be hiding or ignoring signs of   2:26
nationally significant conflict. For instance, where was race in all
this? The Baptists, the second-largest Protestant cluster, included
the largest group of African-Americans. White and black Baptists
lived completely separate denominational lives. While both were
often engaged in religiously reinforced racial conflicts, no sign
of that fighting is apparent in the *Year Book*'s serenities. A second example: the Northern Baptist Convention, which had a liberal faction, stood apart from the more conservative Southern
Baptist Convention giant, but their differences were flattened
out smoothly in the *Year Book*. "The Northern and Southern
churches interchange membership and ministry on terms of perfect equality, and their separation is administrative in character,
not doctrinal or ecclesiastical," wrote the Southern reporter. He
chose not to comment on the warfare of styles and accents that
was current between the rival groups.

One looks to the smaller "separating" or "come outer" Bap-   2:27
tists for signs of battle, because leaders of these bodies sounded
militant. Their controversies, however, did not immediately
threaten civil peace or national security. The fighters did not dig
in along battlelines which matched those of Republicans and
Democrats or capitalists and socialists. Their names dazzle with
references to issues only they could care about: the Six-Principle
Baptists, Seventh-Day Baptists, Free-Will Baptists, Colored Free-

Will Baptists, Free-Will Baptists (Bullockites—or "Buzzellites," who have "practically disappeared as a distinct body, though a few remain in Maine"), General Baptists, Separate Baptists, Regular Baptists, Duck River and Kindred Associations of Baptists (Baptist Church of Christ), Primitive Baptists, Primitive Baptists (Progressive), Two-Seed-in-the-Spirit Predestinarian Baptists, and more.

2:28   It is tempting to deride these groups merely by citing their names. Yet this list is here not for the sake of demeaning Baptists of the twenties but to show how apparently irrelevant to the common civic world seemed the issues which drew people to houses of God several times a week. Why pay attention to such private concerns? I propose a thesis: the people in these churches and their churches themselves were part of a complex national ecosystem. Within the denominations, issues which originally appeared to be of interest only to fellow members eventually emerged transformed in conflicts of national import. Thus debates over the inerrancy of the Bible, the prospect of seeing a new nation of Israel forming in Palestine, what was licit in birth and population control, the portents of Armageddon, the threat of the pope in American politics, all of which began as mere tempests in denominational teapots, years later had geopolitical significance. Under the humble steeples of churches and in the musty basements of synagogues people made up their minds concerning topics on which voters voted, about which demagogues preached, and around which millions rallied.

2:29   If some citizens used denominations to hide from the surrounding culture, others chose only polite ways to help shape it, and the *Year Book* displays some of these. They aimed at the life of the mind. For almost three centuries the churches had been establishing colleges where national elites were formed and nurtured. The religious auspices and ties of many of these schools had sometimes been obscured, severed, or forgotten, but the listings still referred to many. A Congregational roll call included prestigious Amherst and Carleton, Dartmouth and Grinnell, Mount Holyoke and Smith, Oberlin and Wellesley, Williams and Yale, and dozens more. Northern Methodists, long in the business of college-planting, claimed universities like Boston and Northwestern, Syracuse and Southern California, while the tell-tale name "Wesleyan" for colleges and universities was prefixed by words like Central, Dakota, Illinois, Iowa, Kansas, Missouri, Nebraska, Ohio, and West Virginia. Presbyterians, Episcopalians, Lutherans, and many other established denominations listed notable schools whose agendas did not, at least not intentionally, include providing grist for religious or civil conflict.

Only near the *Year Book* borderlines, beyond denominations,   2:30
were there agencies whose programs could suggest designs to create unrest. In their efforts to do justice and love mercy, these sometimes ran into opposing forces. The inventors of these organizations did not all intend to stir up trouble. Faithful to a century-old pattern, they simply pooled volunteer resources and energies to promote the faiths or to help their members serve other people. What, one asks, could be more harmless than the groups with "American" prefixes? The American Bible Society was effective because it was so noncontroversial. Its stated purpose was to translate, publish, and circulate the Holy Scriptures "without note or comment." The society's partisans knew that the slightest note or mildest comment about the biblical text could lead to open spiritual warfare, for the Bible was a controversial book. The American Tract Society also continued in its purposes after exactly a century: to "diffuse a knowledge of our Lord Jesus Christ and to promote the interests of vital Godliness, sound morality and good citizenship by the distribution of Christian literature." What citizen could grumble about such purposes? Should either of these "American" giants turn out to be inefficient, the Gideons or "The Christian Commercial Travelers' Association of America" stood by "to supply every hotel in America with a Bible for each guest room." Their goals sounded safe enough.

The agency listings in the *Year Book* which edged nearest to   2:31
the acknowledged world of conflict had to do directly with the public and only by generous definition belonged in a yearbook of American *churches*. Thus the "Peace and Patriotism" column included two organizations whose leaders could not have lived well with each other. One was the American Committee for the Outlawry of War. The other was the American Legion, which was designed "to foster and perpetuate a 100 per cent Americanism" in ways that the Outlawry people could never have understood or liked. Also, the "Sabbath-Day" category was headed by the Lord's Day Alliance of the United States, which was seeking "to defend and preserve the Lord's Day as a day of rest and worship." It knew little rest because its demand for legislation and law enforcement necessarily created public reaction. So, potentially, did numbers of "Social Service" causes and agencies.

To go the one step further toward zones of conflict which the   2:32

Year Book faintly signaled: in the mid-twenties the temperance and prohibition groups wandered most riskily into the realm of conflict. Among these were the Flying Squadron Foundation, the World League Against Alcoholism, and sixteen other listed groups. They supplemented the enduring Women's Christian Temperance Union (National) that had done so much before 1917 to promote passage of the prohibitionist Eighteenth Amendment to the Constitution. The league predictably professed that it wanted to stay clear of politics through its "attitude of strict neutrality" *except*, it warned, where Prohibition was concerned. Its members would totally suppress alcoholic beverages, since alcoholism was "the poison of body-plasm, mind, conduct and society." Some reformers were looking for trouble and, as we shall see, they found or induced it.

The U. S. Census: Counting Churchly Citizens

2:33   The churches did their own accounting in the *Year Book*, but between the wars the decennial United States Census still gathered religious data. C. Luther Fry, an expert on rural church life, interpreted the statistics in *The U. S. Looks at Its Churches*. Later historians have envied Fry for having been able to rely one last time on census data, for the figures gathered in 1926 and 1936. While Fry claimed that census information about the number of churches was virtually 100 percent complete in respect to earlier censuses, in 1926 he had to recognize some shortcomings. Many leaders were beginning to drag their feet or to resist governmental numbering efforts. He was aware that scholars were suspicious of records kept by churchly organizations; that some clerics distorted statistics for various purposes; that diverse church bodies used differing definitions of membership. For all their flaws, however, the censuses gathered data with which people like Fry could make some intelligent calculations about church life in America.

2:34   The religious organizations looked healthy to Fry. There were 232,000 church buildings to compete with the 256,000 public school edifices in America. The more than 21,000,000 Sunday school pupils numbered only 3,700,000 fewer than the total number of pupils enrolled in public schools. Church expenditures were themselves 40 percent as large as those of public schools. In all, the census showed, 55 percent of the country's adult population was signed up on church or synagogue rolls. While growth rates in Sunday schools had slowed by 1926, 44 percent of the under-nineteen-year-old set were still registered in them.

Fry made much of the way national religion was marked by   2:35
regionalism. If peace between churches was desirable, the fact that one religious group tended to dominate in a certain region while another was powerful elsewhere helped keep large potentially warring parties at some distance from each other. Thus Fry called the South "the stronghold of Protestantism," for in that region were eleven states reporting nine out of ten of their church members as Protestant. Jews were particularly numerous in New York City, while Mormons claimed nine-tenths of the church members in Utah. In no state did Jews or Catholics make up a majority of the population in the way that Protestants did in those nine southern states. Only three denominations could boast three or more of their congregations in every state.

In the twenties, many citizens thought of men as fighters and   2:36
women as reconcilers. On those terms, religion contributed to tranquillity. Nationally, religious membership was predominantly a women's affair, since women registered 125 members to every 100 male members. Yet the cast of characters in public religion and thus necessarily in our present story of that form of faith was largely male. No woman was a theological professor in any major seminary in those decades. Few women's names were on the mastheads of religious periodicals directed at the public. Almost no mainstream denomination permitted women to be active in ordained ministry, though women did hold many leadership posts in religious voluntary organizations. Fry also noted that "Negro women are particularly attracted to the churches," since 73 percent of black women were members, while only 46 percent of all adult Negro men belonged to churches. Overall, however, "these findings," added Fry, "tend to explode the idea that the church has a peculiar hold upon the Negro temperament." Still, wherever Negroes congregated, in both rural South and northern urban slum, religion was a powerful force among men and women.

There was in census findings also a signal of serenity on the   2:37
interdenominational front. Aware of the sad history of religious warfare, churchly pundits took increasing delight in finding some signs that for the good of God's cause and the country's, denominations were cooperating, federating, and uniting. Here their views differed from those seen in Middletown, where people gave lip service to interchurch activity but then went back to life in

rival churches. Fry saw signs that amity between churches was coming to be in vogue in the twenties. Between 1916 and 1926 he counted eighteen church bodies merging, while only two had split. He was embarrassed that because of sectarian inventiveness the number of denominations kept growing despite mergers, but he set out to minimize the effects of that fact on citizens who read the merger statistics. Fry did have to recognize that, as he recorded it, "exclusive of Buddhist temples and Mohammedan mosques," the number of separate denominations had grown from 186 two decades earlier through 200 in 1916 and then to 212 in 1926.

2:38   Fry hastened to say that the appearance of increasing sectarianism was exaggerated, partly as a result of new ways of enumerating and recording. He insisted, however, that "in reality there has been no very great increase in the number of denominations" in the new century. Overall, denominations were tending to combine. When Fry cited the combinations, however, he came up with little drama, for they chiefly represented mergers within the Presbyterian, Lutheran, and similar families. As for raw schisms, he took pride in the fact that the split of a small American Baptist Association from the Southern Baptist Convention was the unique example in his years. The churches seemed to be pleasingly coexistent. Adult membership, according to the Census, had grown from approximately 32 million in 1906 through 38 million ten years later to more than 44 million in 1926.

2:39   Fry and others could see signs of shifts in the power relations among the nation's churches as some grew more rapidly than others. The burgeoning denominations were no longer those which had borne the standard brands of American church life through the previous two centuries. Instead the militant, culturally out-of-step minority and immigrant churches tended now to be gaining. Fry wrote but five years after the celebrated Scopes trial of 1925 in Tennessee. That event posed defenders of evolutionary theory against those who wanted public schools to teach literalist biblical views of the world's creation. Sophisticates thought that this incident should have disgraced hill-country religion and driven people from it. Yet Fry observed that Mississippi and Tennessee, "in the 'Scopes trial' region," along with always-unsettling Mormon Utah, were three of the five states in which church increase was twice as rapid as population growth overall.

2:40   The author of *The U.S. Looks at Its Churches* mused further, if not in extensive ways that would give himself or us a single clear sense of trend. The religions that had once looked marginal now attracted more new members than did the mainstream ones. Fry eyed four major denominations which had doubled in size in the previous twenty years. These were the Church of Christ, Scientist; the Church of Jesus Christ of Latter-day Saints; the African Methodist Episcopal Church, and the Churches of Christ. Only Catholics, Episcopalians, and a Norwegian Lutheran group among the longer-established, largely white denominations had stepped up their growth rate in the previous ten years. Otherwise—and here Fry was anticipating a long-term trend—"the rapid growth of such non-traditional sects as the Mormons and the Christian Scientists would seem to demonstrate fundamental changes in the religious thinking of large groups of Americans."

No one asked Fry to favor one set of churches over another.   2:41
Yet he pointed to one categorical split between "traditional" and "non-traditional" bodies. Most of the chroniclers between the wars saw the churches in such terms. Fry, along with other informed people, whether hostile or friendly to religion—unless they were members of "outsider" religions—tended to speak of one set of churches as being central to national life and definition. Others, like the Mormons and Christian Scientists, were definitely at the periphery. On the boundary between the center and the periphery in standard analyses were several very large groups: Roman Catholic, Southern Baptist, Missouri Synod Lutheran, and Jewish in particular. When conflict came, it seemed to make no difference whether the census interpreters had these located as traditional, nontraditional, or on the borderline. There was to be no place to hide.

Federating Churches: To Influence the Nation

If the local churches, the denominations, and most agencies   2:42
reflected serenity, the interdenominational Federal Council of Churches of Christ in America promoted calm. The council had been formed in 1908 to help the churches of the nation overcome conflict and to urge cooperation. Most standard-brand churches that someone of President Harding's outlook would have called "normal" belonged to the council. These normal denominations made up a kind of "federal nucleus" of churches. Together they aspired to speak to and for the larger culture in matters religious. If a newspaper of record or a general newsmagazine covered

church life, its editors instinctively extended a sense of privilege to such bodies. Reporters regarded these as a kind of establishment. Signs of trauma or promise within any of them would have more bearing on national life than would changes in Pentecostal, Holiness, or other sectarian kinds of Protestant churches which were presumably off somewhere in the cultural backwoods or backwaters.

2:43   Samuel McCrea Cavert's edited report on the mid-decade years (1924–28) of the Federal Council of Churches, *Twenty Years of Church Federation*, opens a window on council activities. Up front, where epigraphs in books ought to be, Cavert reprinted the words which stated the council's original goal. It existed "more fully to manifest the essential oneness of the Christian Churches of America in Jesus Christ as their divine Lord and Saviour and to promote the spirit of fellowship, service and cooperation among them."

2:44   By the twenties such a statement sounded like boilerplate church-union language. It also accurately represented the dreams of many who hoped that the quietly coexistent churches might cooperate to effect their purposes. Cavert listed the member bodies as of 1924. In addition to three black Methodist groups and a few small bodies, most member churches were predictably there. First were the heirs of the colonial big three: Presbyterians, now of two sorts, plus the Episcopalians and Congregationalists. Then came the heirs of the frontier movements, including northern and southern Methodists, three kinds of Baptists, and the Disciples of Christ. These were the kinds of denominations to which presidents of the United States and leaders of business or education belonged. There were also a few legatees of various groups with non-English-speaking ancestries: Lutheran, Reformed, and the like. Some of the connections to the council were tentative and cautious: italicized words after the Episcopal and Lutheran listings described such churches as only a "*Cooperating Agency*" or a "*Consultative Body*." Still, the Federal Council represented an achievement: these denominations, born and developed to promote the integrity of competing doctrinal visions, were no longer interested in fighting each other. The denominations were becoming in some respects dysfunctional, yet all lived on. Not a single one ever surrendered any of its autonomy to any other or to the Federal Council as a whole.

2:45   Samuel McCrea Cavert, who held high positions in the Federal Council of Churches, thought much about federalism and union.

He cited the central theme associated with Jesus' prayer for his disciples, "that they may be one." Cavert used this prayer as a prospect or goad for the still divided churches, but he also provided other and more practical reasons for federating. For one thing, he argued, if churches wished to convert anyone, they must do so by drawing new members to what Christians had in common, not to their peculiarities. He did not notice that already then the most belligerent and fanatically standoffish denominations grew more rapidly than did these cooperative ones. But the idea of unity for the sake both of effective convert-making and shaping the nation was still new, popular, and privileged in the twenties.

Second, argued Cavert, the churches must therefore act together if they were to have a mighty influence on public opinion in behalf of social righteousness. Power and influence were very much on the minds of council leaders and advocates. At this point enemies of churchly power in public and political life had good reason to prick up their ears. Jewish, Catholic, and Mormon rivals had similar reason to be skeptical. What to the federalizers looked like social righteousness, seemed to outsiders efforts to hold a claim to dominion under the American sun. But Cavert did not worry about how the movement looked from the outside. His task was to rally the forces within, to spread the federal vision. He made no secret of his goal, citing layman Glenn Frank on a theme which dominated the federating churches in the twenties: "Protestantism must attain an increasing unity or it will exert a decreasing influence." This fear of decreased influence haunted Frank, Cavert, and even the most apparently self-assured Protestant empire-builders, because they were used to asserting power in national life.

The council federalists were proud of their concept, and looked for examples of it everywhere. When they looked around the nation they even found it in enemy camps. In a chapter designed to rally the churches to common action, General Secretary Charles S. Macfarland of the Federal Council bemoaned the fact that competitive churches were losing to federated enemies. These included "federated vice, the federated saloon, federated corruption in political life, federated human exploitation, and then all these together multiplied in one strong federation, the federation of commercialized iniquity." Macfarland's language did not echo biblical ways of talking about the organization of evil, but it seemed appropriate for the present purpose. In their "solemn league and covenant" these forces of evil still faced a church

2:46

2:47

which, said the general secretary, was derided because it was divided. Like so many advocates of church unity in his time, Macfarland did not leave off without spreading some compensatory cheer. In church federation, he wrote, "the common people are beginning to realize the unity in spirit and in service of our Protestant forces," forces which, he contended, had indeed become an influence in the moral life of the nation.

2:48   The theme of Protestant power organized for national influence was captivating. Cavert counted twenty-eight denominations working together in the council, but the federal idea was spreading to lower, more provincial strata. In most cities, local federations were active. They were busy converting people, doing research, and "making their influence felt" in the cause of peace and against racial prejudice. No wonder the council enthusiast could conclude his summing up with the thought that this federating achievement meant "a new stage in the history of the Church."

2:49   When his turn came to speak up in Cavert's report, Methodist bishop Francis J. McConnell, the council's president-elect, was most blunt about the importance of *size* in the modern United States. "When we think of God we think of a sort of capaciousness in quality, and that calls for the largest terms." There was no secret as to what McConnell was about: "I do not misrepresent the churches in the Federal Council when I say that by the sheer magnitude of our enterprise we may take a new place, and make possible a more adequate revelation of God." At his side the only slightly less exuberant and equally practical-minded current federation president, the notable pulpiteer S. Parkes Cadman, defined the "genius" of the federal approach. The founders, Cadman wrote, "thoroughly understood the futility of attempting the reconciliation of denominational differences solely by theological discussion," so they "wisely concentrated upon those joint activities which emphasize Christianity's social and humanitarian benefits."

2:50   God and country both were on the minds of Federal Council pioneers when they celebrated their first generation of life together. They made a point of anchoring their present endeavors in patriotic national contexts. In defining council work, the pioneer secretary Elias Sanford recalled a bishop's speech delivered in 1908 at the council's opening. He had tied the whole venture to the quest for American empire. The bishop pointed to "one flag over all." The cross and the flag were thus bonded: "Let it be ours to sustain that flag and to see to it that wherever that flag goes our holy religion goes, in every part of the world."

Theological Support for a National Church

Not only bureaucrats and conciliar leaders promoted the idea   2:51
of a national church. In the years immediately after the First World War, theologians, trained to be critical, joined them. While they often kept their critical guard up, they too advocated some sort of federated and cooperative church for the nation. To make sense of religion in American culture between the wars, it is urgent to understand how theological leaders reasoned as they were poised on the narrow lines between cooperation and conflict, organic union and federation, the cosmopolitan and the local, the divinely transcendent and the immediately national. The most eloquent representative, William Adams Brown, stated the case with the discernment of an artist and with a faithfulness to what I find in similar if less convincing documents by scores of his peers. Readers who might weary of *Year Book* statistics will find it valuable to encounter a single voice, his voice, on stage long enough for him to state a case. The New York-born Presbyterian who taught at Union Seminary in Manhattan was a Protestant blue blood, born also to the blue of Yale University, which he later served in numerous advisory posts. He began his career by undertaking the then requisite graduate studies in Germany under prime liberal theologians. Brown did a stint in the slums and worked for reform in New York. A friend of labor unions and an early civil libertarian, he gave his best years and thoughts to the movements for church union. Brown also led American delegations to Europe for the two most promising international conferences promoting unity. The names of these indicated his interests. In 1925 the delegation went to the Universal Christian Council for Life and Work. In 1927 the World Conference on Faith and Order beckoned. Life and Work plus Faith and Order: these indicated where Protestants directed their energies for Christian concord, and Brown was a pioneer with both.

Early in the decade Brown began to write long tracts for the   2:52
times. These stated his positions with clarity and symmetry. Most notable was the rationale in his *The Church in America*. Brown wrote of the commonplace that "the present movement for unity takes two forms: that for organic and that for federal unity." The

Union professor then displayed the "equipoise" President Harding praised. He wrote of these two forms that "the former takes its departure from the nature of the Church, the latter from the need of the world," which, in the present case, meant also the need of the nation. Organic unity dealt with issues of truth and integrity. The church, in this vision, had to take a particular shape because God wanted it so, because Christ chartered it that way. The revealed nature of the church evidenced the demand that the separated groups be brought together in "a single visible and corporate body." Federation, on the other hand, meant that in the meantime churches could "pool their resources." Brown put the best light on the distinction, insisting that the two models need not be in simple competition with each other. "Federal union may be a step toward organic union. Organic union when it comes, in church as in state, may prove to be federal."

2:53   In true Presbyterian style, Brown also dealt with the problem of human limits, whether he spoke of the churches or the republic. This meant that he had a realistic view of why it was hard to unify churches in a democracy. Brown could see below the surface serenity in religious life. His awareness of self-interest in the church reflected the ambivalent spirit of James Madison in affairs of state. Thus Brown could be glum: "When we appeal to men on the basis of their present aspirations we find these aspirations working for division rather than for unity." Under his liberally optimistic exterior there beat a Calvinist heart and a pulse alert to theories of conflict. The impulse to disunity, Brown thought, was evident in the "intensified group consciousness which expresses itself in the desire of different bodies of men to break away from the larger units of which they form a part and to live their own lives in independence."

2:54   Not only did the New York professor have a view of human nature and society which led him to *fore*see conflict, he could also *see* it—if still under the surface of serenity, if still in ill-defined parties that were tearing at denominational unities. One side of him would have agreed with Harding's description of and prescription for postwar America. The other side of him forced Brown in honesty to express reservations that were rare among his company in the early twenties. He worried less about conflict between churches than conflict within churches. Such conflicts distracted Christians from forming a national church. He saw that, within denominations, sets of self-interests worked most dangerously against the spirit of Christian unity. There was a "division of sentiment among the present members" of church bodies. The Union professor offered illustrations to make his point: "each church has its high and its low churchmen, its liberals and its conservatives." Brown found psychological elements in the forming of these hardened battle lines. "The conservatives fear any movement which would seem to justify the liberals in their position. The liberals hesitate to assent to action which might increase the power of the conservatives."

Would a national church blend Catholic and Protestant interests? Visionary though he was, Brown could not yet extend his hopes for eventual organic union to Catholics, though he wanted to be friendly to them. Meanwhile, there could be some cooperation for local and national purposes. When the hopeful theologian looked for good signs, he had to be content to notice that Protestants and Catholics did work together on causes of moral and social reform, on temperance fronts, against vice, and for industrial justice. For a close-up view Brown pointed to Detroit, where Catholics had pleased Protestants by helping them urge the mayor to close businesses at noon on Good Friday. Brown could not resist recognizing the fact that a strong Protestant church federation was in place and active in the Motor City and that it stimulated such programs. He dared not rest content with small steps such as those taken in Detroit. "Beside the general desire for social betterment our fellow-citizens of other religious faiths share with us our interest in the spiritual interpretation of the universe." Professor Brown had to let it go at that. His remained necessarily only a Protestant vision for America.

Professor Brown had a keen sense of the moment, an instinct for spotting trends, and an ability to locate the life of the churches on the largest possible landscape. To project Protestant power, he had to begin at the beginning, at least the beginning of the present age and stage. That meant dealing with the disillusion that came to the nation after World War I. "The war," Brown wrote just a few years after it ended, "has shaken us out of our easy satisfaction with things as they are." That war had also forced citizens to produce a new agenda. America had learned from the war's devastation that modern conflict was a specific kind of competition; it was "not an affair of armies, but of peoples and civilizations." That being the case, there was no humane choice now but to lead "competitions of peace." Few instruments seemed more important for such efforts than did the churches, however contentious they were. Brown was a somewhat realistic person who could

2:55

2:56

look out at scores if not hundreds of internally torn denominations and still proclaim, in the spirit of countless colleagues: "*Democracy has a right to expect of the Church a unifying spiritual influence, springing from a common faith, and issuing in common action.*"

2:57   In the meantime Brown wanted the churches, plagued though they were, to be resources offering common faith and action. This meant that religion was to be to their members a matter of public life, not a mere private affair. Brown thought there were reasons to locate churches of the federating sort near the strategic centers of American life. He saw the institutional church as a subject of curiosity and hope in the America of the twenties and advertised its vast financial resources. The bill of particulars included other assets. Here he sounded like Robert and Helen Lynd with a Middletown writ large: the church was staffed with millions of voluntary workers. It touched the life of citizens at moments of their great crises and inspired works of charity and patterns of education. In it people came "face to face with the unseen realities with which religion has always been concerned." These were issues that, as Brown saw them, were "in essence spiritual." While neither Brown nor any other American could discern anywhere what he called in classic terms "a revival of religion," yet religion could serve as the "unifying and steadying influence in the realm of the spirit."

2:58   Brown said that the church "has still a hold upon public sentiment and respect." His book and his lifework were designed to rally church people to use that hold to godly and civil effect while they could. When people use the word "still" as Brown did, they may give away a whole philosophy of history. With it they reveal their unconscious but cosmic hunch about the future, a tucked-in pessimism about the institution with which they connect that word. So Brown may have signaled more and other than he wished to when he used it, but for the moment it would serve.

2:59   One undeveloped asset, in Brown's view, was the presence of women in religious life. Even to include reference to them was a rare act in a time when most male analysts—and male analysts almost alone left accountings—did not call them to mind. He wrote when leadership in the federating churches was almost entirely in the hands of men. In this period so soon after the arrival of Woman Suffrage, when the feminist movement was presumably in a slump, he spoke up for an increased churchly role for women. Yet the index to his book included few references to women. Indeed, it is hard to write about women on the basis of documents when dealing, as he was and we are, with manifest power in the privileged and well-established churches of the time. Women were excluded from high-status positions, were rarely given a forum, and were absent from public argument unless the topic was something like prohibition or birth control. Their great effectiveness came in auxiliary and voluntary organizations in and alongside denominations.

Brown's expansive scope did include women, but only at the margins. Against the trend of even many liberal male clerics, he commented favorably on the emancipation of women from household drudgery and their freedom for action in social, economic, political, and religious fields. He cited Rhoda McCulloch's pamphlet of 1920 on *The War and the Woman Point of View*. McCulloch led Brown to believe that the consciousness of women would change as they applied their religious experience to new conditions. No longer would they do simply what men told them to do, but they would use the "modern religion of freedom and responsibility" to pose questions and seek answers. She said and he reported that women were finding a new sense of comradeship outside their homes and, being less sheltered than before, they would now meet new problems "with peculiar freshness and power." 2:60

Ahead of his time within male church culture, Brown asked next: "Is it conceivable that woman . . . will be content to remain a mere spectator, a runner of errands in the Church?" Then, returning quickly to the spirit of his times, he did not seem to envision women's ordination to ministry and he certainly did not advocate that they in any way abandon their special sphere, the home and the nurturing of children. Still, Brown thought, it must be essential and possible for churches "to use the wider training and insight which women are gaining through their entrance into the world of affairs." Thus they could make their work as homemakers both efficient and successful—two good words in the liberal Protestant dictionary. They would thereby fit themselves "to become in the new age what they have been so conspicuously in the past," the character-builders of society, the custodians of the future. These words sound tame and timid in retrospect, but many other books on church and national life overlooked women entirely or formally restricted them in the world of affairs. 2:61

One theme brought together the whole vision of church and society that Brown held along with almost all the leaders of the 2:62

federating churches, a theme whose importance it is hard to over-emphasize. This was the notion that sects or denominations were not only elements of a world church. They also were part of what Brown called the ideal of "a national church, conscious of its aim and its power." He feared that this was an ideal that was as yet cherished only occasionally, by some exceptional spirits. But now the citizenry as a whole must support a national church. Remarkably, this call did not mean that he hoped for a religion of nationalism, of uncritical support for the United States in any chauvinist fashion. During World War I the hypernationalist style had predominated. Now, however, Brown tempered his nationalism with a postwar recognition that the twenties also needed the internationalism of the gospel. In the face of such need, this advocate of a national church therefore had to speak also of "the problem of nationality," which was to him more baffling than issues of either class or race.

2:63   What about America's historic concept of the separation of church and state? Brown drew fine lines and took high risks with his concept of a national church and a critical patriotism. He argued that one could retain and balance both the idea of a national church and the distinction between civil and religious life. He took pains to articulate a position which reappeared in so many of the religious writings of the twenties. "While jealously guarding the principle of the separation of state and church, the American people are equally insistent upon the fact that their country is a Christian nation." *A Christian nation.* The idea, which died or dies hard, was very much alive in the 1920s. Already then there were problems with the notion. Jews were not the only Americans who by their presence and argument in the United States were beginning to challenge that claim in formal ways, but such efforts must not have registered with the otherwise well-aware and generous Professor Brown. And while many articulate Catholics shared the "Christian nation" thesis, they of course could not enjoy the often unspoken and sometimes explicit equation, in things national, of Christian with Protestant.

A National Religion: Lay Support for the Business Creed

2:64   The undertone of realism and the sense of limits which pervaded the work of William Adams Brown were not representative of the popular religious climate early in the 1920s. The sense of the churchly federationists that they could not accomplish all that they would like to, because of the federated forces of evil arrayed against them, also helped create a somewhat false impression of the surface of American spiritual life in the twenties. Neither bureaucrats nor theologians, from whom we have heard so far, speak for all American religion. The laity who were at home in the culture and friendly to religion spoke up in different terms. The moderate to liberal Protestant churches blended in well with the culture around them to create an aura of complacency. Certain extremely popular figures, often authors of religious best-sellers, offered virtually uncritical affirmations of the world as it was. For everyone who ever heard of even the best-known representatives of church culture, scores or hundreds would know of entrepreneurs like Russell Conwell, Roger Babson, and Bruce Barton. They earned a permanent place in surveys of the American religious landscape in the twenties.

Russell Conwell was ending his career in the twenties. He had   2:65 already made his mark and was by now repeating himself, but in a climate that was newly congenial. This Baptist minister demonstrated that he had a high threshold of boredom by preaching the same sermon over six thousand times. He converted it to a book, *Acres of Diamonds*. Conwell not only built up the Baptist Temple in Philadelphia, he founded Temple University there in 1888 from sermon proceeds. While he was only repeating himself, huge audiences kept hungering for his uplift, his advice on how others could lift up themselves.

Only after Conwell's death in 1925 were critics ready to do   2:66 surgery on his approach. In 1928 one of these critics, W. S. Crosby, recalled how on the Chautauqua circuit Conwell had always appeared "to the hallelujahs of the local clergy." Crosby went on to remind readers how Conwell would pour forth Pollyanna economics and saccharine sentiments. His clienteles of farmers and townsmen would converge in good cheer and then would sniff self-righteously on their way to the Conwell tent as they passed the beer-drinking corner loafers. Then they would go home "assured that it was the Lord's will that they should succeed in the world and make piles of money." Conwell scored best in a culture Crosby described as "smug, thrifty, tightly moral American middle-class, rustic and urban."

As Conwell's force and fame receded, younger replicas took   2:67 his place. One of the two most prominent lay people was Congregationalist Roger Babson. His version of Pollyanna economics and saccharine sentiments drew millions of readers for his columns and books. A man without evident guile, Babson gained a constituency both for his reputed canniness in talking about markets and his sincerity in offering tips for investing in the prosperous economy of the decade. But he was more chary about praising the principle of raw competition, on which the socialists said the capitalist order was built. At times he could even sound like an advocate of mild surgery to effect limited reforms.

2:68   People in any case were not paying him for surgery. They sought serenity in spiritually based economic security. Babson argued that only a moral, prudent, churchgoing, prayerful nation could pile up the spiritual capital which would make financial investment valid. He was an economic individualist, an exemplar of what Max Weber had called the Protestant ethic. Work hard and long, for God's sake. Do not waste. Be honest. Save. Use time well. Be inventive. Babson's book titles, such as *Religion and Business* and *New Tasks for Old Churches*, in 1921 and 1922, kept repeating Babsonian themes which supported the individual person in the business culture which Babson wanted to help humanize.

2:69   In *Religion and Business* Babson, fearing conflict, was preoccupied with ways to make Americans more prosperous and at the same time less selfishly competitive, for he feared conflict. His approach was a mix that most capitalists might have found puzzling. Babson offered many kinds of nostrums in support of normalcy, always with the backing of his own version of Christianity. "Jesus was plainly an individualist. Public charities never appealed to Him." In Babson's popular world, religion was always basic. "It appears that religion is intrinsically stronger than politics, because it deals immediately with the forces of nature and of life, while politics must deal with these things at second hand." Babson also invested faith in the practicality of religion. "Statistics teach that a business man will be happiest by following the teachings of Jesus; statistics teach that the Golden Rule is practical; statistics teach that prayer is a real force with unlimited possibilities; and statistics teach that religion is the greatest of undeveloped resources."

2:70   Babson, a supporter of the Interchurch World Movement and the Federal Council of Churches, insisted on going no further than the federating model on the path to cooperation. The culture necessarily, he noted, made available differing denominations for the various dispositions of people. Like Brown, he also had to notice denominational fights—and fights is exactly what Babson kept calling them—but he went on to remind readers that these were "very repugnant to the business man." Businessmen, he insisted, would support churches which promoted pure religion and business; they were "not interested in theology or denominational fights."

Pure religion did not mean that churches were to be unspotted   2:71
by the world, to have no influence in Washington and state capitals. Babson had the shape of the nation very much on his mind. He headed a section of his book: "BACK THE CHURCH-MEN IN POLITICS." He was bold: "One of the saddest things connected with the church is to see church people divided as to politics and putting their politics ahead of their religion." He estimated that church people were about 50 percent Republicans, 40 percent Democrats. "Such a division does not speak well for the church people. If we are followers of Jesus and have the same interests, it seems as if we ought to be in one united political party," a newly organized one. Then believers could have proper influence to assert Jesus' way. Babson and his readers had no doubts about what that way was.

Nor did Bruce Barton, who was even more popular than the   2:72
aged Conwell or the specialist Babson. Barton chose to be a generalizer. The son of a Congregationalist minister, he was a troubled advertising man who invented formulas for promoting success within a business culture. He disguised from public view his own inner tumults while he tried to unite business ethics with his inherited religious vision and then to transmit this to millions. He used the example of Jesus to show how to combine self-centered success with service to fellows. Three books in three successive years—*The Man Nobody Knows* (1925), *The Book Nobody Knows* (1926), and *What Can a Man Believe?* (1927)—represented Barton's reduction of the gospel to advertising-copy prose. Jesus' religion, Barton claimed, "conquered not because there was any demand for another religion," but because Jesus knew, and taught others, how to "translate a great spiritual conception into terms of practical self-concern."

Frederick Lewis Allen in *Only Yesterday* was among the first   2:73
to see Barton as having been a prime embodiment of the spirit of the twenties. Allen here, as so often, pointed to the nether side of national life obscured by those he saw to be hucksters, including religious ones. Was it not strange, Allen asked, that in the very years the "Barton Gospel" was circulating most vigorously,

America's selling and advertising campaigns were becoming more cynical, and there were constant exposures of American business corruption, such as the Teapot Dome scandal and the Continental Trading Company crimes? Allen answered: "Perhaps; but it must be remembered that in all religion there is likely to be a gap between faith and works."

2:74   Barton succeeded, thought Allen, because he blended his Christianity with business, which was "almost the national religion of America." Business as a national religion: the Lynds had found it so in the business class in Middletown, and many a foreign visitor in the twenties came to agree with them and Allen. According to Allen, Barton had discovered that business people could lead tranquil lives if they could be reassured that this religion was altogether right and proper, and that in the rules for making big money lay all the law and the prophets. To that end, Barton fashioned Jesus as the greatest business executive. His parables were the most powerful advertisements of all time. Jesus, the "founder of modern business," would have been an advertiser in the twenties, thought Barton. Allen correctly concluded that "the association of business with religion was one of the most significant phenomena of the day." Barton was a custodian of values that the middle-class churches of the day nurtured for the nation.

2:75   Barton was also a custodian of values that the churches of the federating cluster habitually promoted when they were not being self-critical. After all, he did not teach *mere* selfishness. He contended that Jesus' nineteen-centuries-old anticipation of "the spirit of modern business" included three main points: "1. Whoever will be great must render great service. 2. Whoever will find himself at the top must be willing to lose himself at the bottom. 3. The rewards come to those who travel the second, undemanded mile." These motifs sounded something like the gospel of many churches, though such a message would displace the creeds of many centuries. Barton acknowledged that. "Let us forget all creed for the time being, and take the story just as the simple narratives give it. . . . Stripped of all dogma, this is the grandest achievement story of all!"

2:76   As with creed and dogma, so with the details of the Protestant history on which Barton relied: he never disguised his background in the parsonage and could even playfully make it part of his autobiography. Forgetting the daughters, he boasted: "We preachers' sons have an unfair advantage over the rest of the world." A thou-

sand of the 12,000 names in *Who's Who*, he pointed out, belonged to sons of clerics. "In fact, we show up so well that any
unprejudiced man will agree that all the money given to the
church would have been well invested had it done nothing more
than enable preachers to raise sons." To show that in lighthearted
moments he kept some perspective, Barton qualified his compliment to parsons' households: "Not all of us make good, of
course. A third of us go to the devil; another third float around in
between; but another third rule the world." There was no doubt
that Barton saw himself among such rulers.

Barton could also collapse the austere otherworldliness of his   2:77
Congregational and Puritan background into his modern business
gospel. "Great progress will be made in the world when we rid
ourselves of the idea that there is a difference between *work* and
religious work." To be bald: "Ask any ten people what Jesus
meant by his 'Father's business,' and nine of them will answer
'preaching.' " But Jesus, argued Barton, did not come to preach
or teach or heal, though each of these tasks did belong to his
Father's business. No, there had to be a wider scope: "Thus *all*
business is his Father's business." Barton's book was a best-seller
a year after the controversial Scopes trial. But it reflected no trace
of America's religious tumult. From the business center of the
religious culture, all seemed serene; motives for keeping it quiet,
Barton thought, should have been strong enough to give leaders
the impulse to suppress disruption and conflict at the core. Such
suppression would need the collusion of the clergy.

The Nation's Ministers: Charged to Avoid Conflict

Where were the clergy in all this? The spiritual ideals of a   2:78
serene-surfaced culture are carried not only by presidents who
wish things to be quiet, by business people who would avoid criticism, or by advertising people who make Jesus their hero, but
also by ministers. To suggest that the Protestant clergy of a certain
sort were then still custodians or bearers of cultural norms may
awaken a sense of incredulity among many. It may be hard to
picture that "still" within this century Protestant clergy of Federal
Council stripe had such influence. Yet we have seen Bruce Barton
pointing simply to the role of the parsonage by saying that it produced one out of twelve *Who's Who* personalities.

Not all clergy of all denominations were equal, especially   2:79

when it came to national power and influence. One could infer something about their standing by checking the status of their laity. One way to do that was to look with C. Luther Fry at *Who's Who*. In 1931 he included in his survey the reckoning that among the 16,600 people who listed their religious preference in that reference work, a startlingly high 7,000 were Episcopalian or Presbyterian, while Congregationalism and (chiefly Northern) Baptist churches added, in turn, 2,000 and 1,500 more. Unitarians, growing out of the old Congregational culture, took pride in 1,000 listings. That left the others, from 750 Catholics, down through Lutherans, Disciples of Christ, Jews, and 180 Quakers, to share much of the remainder. Some of these entries may have been clergy and many were no doubt merely nominal members, but Fry's analysis did show how people of influence clustered in a few denominations. The fact that at least some influential citizens bothered to cite their church tie indicates that they wanted to signal some level of attachment to the institutions of religion.

2:80   Just as they filled *Who's Who*, members of a few denominations, including heirs of the colonial Congregationalists, Presbyterians, and Episcopalians; the frontier northern Methodists, Baptists, and Disciples, and the acclimatized United Lutherans, dominated the Federal Council actions. When international Christian gatherings occurred, these seven churches were dominant. Those who noticed the rising Fundamentalist ranks did so to scorn these dissenters, or to depict their eccentricity and marginal character. Both clerical and lay church leadership in these groups knew each other and interacted with each other. They vacationed together, retired near each other, held common memberships in uncommon clubs, and corresponded across denominational lines. William Adams Brown, for instance, was related to the presidential Adamses and the banking Browns. He vacationed in Maine with university presidents and professors named Eliot, Gilman, Dana, Peabody, and Low, and could drop names like Rockefeller, Morgan, and Ford with ease and credibility. Such people could hardly complain that they were marginal. They had much at stake, both as defenders and critics, in the serene culture under whose surface conflict was impending and from whose edges and near whose center challenges were rising.

2:81   Every group of people has castes, and many of these consist of members of professions. In the case of a religious people, these professionals are largely clergy. They had to lead the fund-raising efforts of churches, keep laypersons happy and involved, attract growing congregations, administer complex institutions, and use rhetoric to persuade constituencies to follow. Measuring their status is one way of seeing how the custodianship of a people's covenants and destiny is prospering. On such terms, the Protestant clergy in the federating denominations were well-positioned. In 1924 the undenominational weekly, the *Christian Century,* a persistent advocate of Protestant mainstream interests, undertook a poll to determine "the twenty-five most influential and representative living preachers of our time." No Catholics need vote in the poll or apply for it, since few of them read this journal and few were known for preaching or cultural leadership. The magazine forwarded 90,000 ballots and received an amazing 20,000 in return. The response, the variety of nominations, and the strong support for the winners in the poll suggest something about the morale of the Protestant community and the place preachers, and thus clerical leaders in a preaching culture, occupied.

The most obvious feature of the selection in retrospect but un-   2:82
noticed in its own time was the total absence of women. The clerical leadership was all male, but we have seen that even when generous types like William Adams Brown pictured a broadened role for women and an enlarged scope for ministry, they envisioned women only in other than preacherly posts. Education was their field. Second, geographically most of the well-knowns came from the Northeast and the Great Lakes area. Only two were from the South, the heartland of the strongest but less nationally visible Protestantism. Two others were from the West Coast. Denominationally, the choices came from the churches we have called nuclear: Presbyterians, Methodists, Congregationalists, and Baptists predominated, with one Episcopalian being represented. Two of the seven or eight central church bodies, the Lutherans and the Disciples of Christ, registered no celebrity leaders, and not a single person outside the central cluster made the top twenty-five. The *Christian Century* editors, needless to say, seemed unaware of the inevitable bias of their sample. An editor of a Catholic or a Pentecostal magazine would have come up with other notables. But their lists would have gone unrecognized in the larger culture.

That these preachers contributed to serenity more than surgery   2:83
becomes clear from a scrutiny of their own choices of the sermons they wanted published to represent themselves. No one ventured to do what Union Seminary theologian Reinhold Niebuhr later said he thought preachers should do: question the assumptions of the age and the way of life. All of them dealt with the tranquil

surface of their members' worlds. Few remembered the Red Scare
or were alert to the Ku Klux Klan or race riots. Few mentioned
that Americans were divided by classes or interest groups. Almost
none took on denominational civil wars. Few touched controversial themes, though the most conservative of the group, Seattle's
Mark A. Matthews, dealt with the Virgin Birth of Jesus and one
of the most liberal, the Evanston, Illinois, minister Ernest F. Tittle, tackled evolution. Virtually all gave attention to private religion and character development, legitimate themes for Christian
preaching, but indicative of the posture of moderate Protestantism. Warren G. Harding would have been happy with the performance of the best-known preachers. None set out to disturb. Only
later, when in the 1930s more and more preachers under the influence of critics like Reinhold and his brother H. Richard Niebuhr
began calling into question the assumptions of the time and place
and giving less solace to self-helpers, did preachers of this school
of thought begin to lose support of congregations and perhaps
thus contribute to the decline of their caste.

2:84   Ministers generally won favor for accepting their supportive
role, and some laity advocated more of the same. Thus when the
Methodist *Christian Advocate* gave space for a layperson to provide critique and counsel, he typified the settled and serene orientation: "An excellent way to choose a minister . . . would be
to send him down on Main Street and around to the school buildings to chat with the business men and the children about politics,
civic affairs, football, and geography, and then let the business
men and children vote on him." Community acceptance is important in a Protestant polity, where the tie between pulpit and pew
is strong and where it empowers the clergy. Business people and
children made up much of the constituency that clergy had to
serve and satisfy. But letting the laity set all the norms for preaching entirely in the terms of the serene culture, away from conflict,
was dangerously limiting.

2:85   In ways no longer easily imaginable, then, the clergy from the
federating nucleus of denominations were visible, had the ear of
many who set the terms for life in American culture, and aimed
at remaining in the spotlight and in hearing range. Not yet displaced from their centrality, the clergy seemed decisive in the
custodianship of America in a decade of normalcy. This did not
mean that all was well within the elite. Some clergy were articulate about the low quality of ministerial leadership. Ellis J.
Hough, a prestigious pastor himself, observed in 1930 that it was

"a fairly safe generalization to say that no profession among men is so thoroughly empty of dignity and grace as that of the Protestant ministry today."

Self-deprecation may be a ministerial trait and hazard, and one statement by a Hough is not the equipment of a scientific social survey. But there were some troubling signs. The clergy were underpaid to the point that the secular press often bewailed their demeaning situation. Ministers might confess that they were not in the religious office to make money, but in a money culture they had children to send to college, costs that went with professional status, appearances to keep up, and tastes bred in their middle-class backgrounds, in college life, and in the company of the cultured. A quotable observer in 1929, Glenn Frank, president of the University of Wisconsin, was dour: on $30 a week the minister was expected to be "a medieval saint, a carelessly courageous agitator, an expert in mental hygiene, and the hustling head of a business corporation." 2:86

More formally, a study chartered early in the 1920s produced data-confirming problems in ministerial custodianship. Robert L. Kelly's *Theological Education in America*, a major analysis published in 1924, concluded that "with rare exceptions" seminaries were "not conspicuous as centers of scholarly pursuits." Few seminaries kept up with standards in law, medicine, and other business schools. A regular procession of secular critics did still pay the clergy the compliment of noticing them. Thus author Heywood Broun sneered: "The ministry is the only learned profession in which a man may close his mind forever at the moment of ordination." 2:87

Pastor and later Yale professor Halford Luccock, as so often, was ready to appraise ministry in its delicate posture, where it had to please the seekers of serenity in order to survive but while it was supposed to engage in criticism to be faithful. Threatening the keepers of normalcy, Luccock counseled: "Our most urgent task is not the extension of Christianity as a conventional majority faith; it is rather the preservation of its essentially Christian quality and purpose." Extending Christianity as a conventional majority faith was the more attractive half of the bargain, and to it the majority of leaders in the mid-twenties devoted themselves with skill and passion. They had much to lose. They knew that under the tranquil surface there were troubles and threats. They may often have sounded complacent, but there was a certain nervous defensiveness in much of what they preached and did. 2:88

2:89   Now and then a clash would surface on the issue of business as a sort of national religion. Some clergy did have the courage to contradict the lay preachers of the gospel of success. It was easier to do this from the professorial chair or the editorial post than from the pulpit, whose occupants transacted directly with the people who supported and took hope from the positive-thinking clerics. Two figures, a Yale professor and a New York preacher, illustrate the difference in approaches. First, the professor, whom we have just met, Halford Luccock. No match for Barton in popularity, but reasonably well known in church circles, the Methodist editor and budding professor uttered reservations about complacency that went almost unnoticed beyond the readership of a denominational periodical.

2:90   Barton's "church" was to Luccock "just exactly the kind of church that every reactionary and Grand Duke of special privilege would like to see." The advertising man was selling a very pretty religion, but not a profound or true one, because it omitted the "harsh words of Jesus against the lust of greed which spoils and mangles life." Luccock proclaimed a Jesus who, dying on a cross, issued a gospel which "must work through the lives of men and women who will go to the Cross in sacrificial warfare against the malignant powers of evil and exploitation." The gospel which would redeem the world, he advised, must be a stout gospel, not the sound of "blowing on a penny whistle or a few moments of silence." Luccock was listening to the voice of disillusionment which he heard in the twenties. It never sounded so loudly, however, as did the drums which beat for the gospel of serenity and success.

2:91   Less comfortable than a layperson like Barton and less surgical than an editor like Luccock was the most notable pastoral minister of the generation, if not the century, in the Protestant mainstream, Harry Emerson Fosdick. A gifted liberal who drew and returned Fundamentalist fire, he led in the merger of two Manhattan congregations, one Baptist and one Presbyterian. Out of this union came Riverside Church on Morningside Heights. From this Gothic fortress adjacent to Union Seminary, where he also taught preaching, Fosdick for decades issued pronouncements on the Christian gospel and culture. He had the delicate task of mediating between influential congregants such as the Rockefeller family and critics like Union's Reinhold Niebuhr, who frequently attended the church. Niebuhr regarded Fosdick as a colleague, often admired him, sometimes reviewed his books, and, from his

own tenured professorial vantage, always showed a tinge of uneasiness over the apparent compromises such a parish minister
had to make.

To business people who wanted to benumb the critical church,   2:92
Fosdick could shout, for "multitudes of my brethren . . . , *Before
high God, not for sale!*" In spite of such prophetic stabs by Fosdick, Niebuhr still thought that the preacher was too soothing, too
compromising. When in 1926 he reviewed Fosdick's *Adventurous
Religion*, Niebuhr handed the author some garlands before he
passed out the thorns. Niebuhr thought that "like all great leaders,
Dr. Fosdick is as typical as he is unique, and the whole liberal
evangelical movement may be tested in the pages of his book."
Fosdick was not the articulator of a unique theological position
but was "modern evangelical liberalism personified." It was precisely this feature that makes Fosdick attractive to historians who
comb records to identify exemplars, models, and typifiers.

Niebuhr felt that Fosdick took too seriously the merely intel-   2:93
lectual attacks on religion; it was the moral failure of the churches
that repelled thoughtful people. Niebuhr argued that for all its
efforts to be prophetic or critical, modern religion had "on the
whole been no more successful than traditional religion in chal-
lenging or in changing the fundamental immoralities of modern
civilization, its immoral nationalism, its lust for power, and its
accentuated greed."

To Niebuhr's eye, Fosdick and his type did not with sufficient   2:94
rigor question America's modes of being: "America regards herself as both honest and pious, but the world declares that we are
selfish and that our selfishness is becoming more and more insufferable." Friend Niebuhr therefore had to conclude that *Adventurous Religion* portrayed "adventure like that of the knights in
the age of chivalry. It develops within the limits of the age and
does not challenge the age itself." Niebuhr wanted to be charitable to evangelical liberals like Fosdick for having done half the
work. But the cleric's entire preachment seemed too given over to
serenity about the shape and spirit of the age.

Fosdick, in turn, thought he was addressing the problem of the   2:95
age through his concept of stewardship, of care for the culture by
people of his own sort. Thus he mitigated what a later time would
see as racism coming from a pastor who worked hard for reconciliation between races. Fosdick said in a sermon in 1920 that
there was no use in blinking at plain facts: "You put the Anglo-
Saxon people almost anywhere on earth, and before very long

they will be running the government." He later tempered this slightly: "The strong and the weak, side by side, in individuals and races; we must somehow live together on this earth." While Fosdick would modify such statements in later decades, they typified the self-satisfaction of whites in power in 1920. Then came the appeal to stewardship: "Our strength does not belong to us in fee simple to possess and to use as we will. We are custodians of the gains of the whole race for the sake of mankind."

2:96   Such custodians, though they ministered to elites and wore pulpit robes, could yet at least mildly question the American way of their time. In 1927 John D. Rockefeller, Jr., criticized his pastor for a sermon that raised questions about the business world. In a letter of reply, Fosdick admitted that on that particular day when he dealt compensatorily with labor he had tramped but lightly. Yet the preacher sneaked in the point that he had to notice an "appalling contrast between luxury and poverty" in America. That contrast needed denouncing. Fosdick addressed his wealthy supporter in the pew: "You say that the business man is sensitive to public criticism." Hardly so, thought Fosdick. "I say far more critical things about my own realm, the ecclesiastical, than I ever dream of saying about the industrial realm." No one in the church or among lawyers was as touchy as business people. "And yet they would surely confess that some of the most serious problems of modern life lie in their realm."

2:97   Fosdick must have been aware that tougher-minded Union Seminary professors from across the street were monitoring him. He went on in his letter to say that he, Fosdick, was "very occasionally and bitterly criticized because, being in a powerful church with powerful men," critics thought that their pastor did not deal as frankly with industrial problems as he did with international, ecclesiastical, and theological problems. When Rockefeller responded to the letter with a booklet of his own speeches, Fosdick wrote back to say that he found them "interesting." The pastor insisted, however, that he had always felt free to take Rockefeller's liberalism for granted. "I never would have dreamed of taking the pastorate of a church in which you were so prominent and powerful a member," wrote Fosdick, had he feared prejudice or sniping from the magnate. Fosdick had mastered the art of combining the supportive with the critical, the pastoral with the prophetic. Not all his colleagues practiced this art so well, and Fosdick himself, as we shall see, was responsible for crossfire, in

which he was caught, when ministers came into conflict with each
other. Such conflict was almost impossible to escape.

Public Religion: The Language of Three Presidents

All this talk about the public influence of church religion and   2:98
the churchly influence of denominational religion in the early
twenties pulls us back to where we began: with the United States
president who called for "triumphant nationality," Warren G.
Harding, and then to his two Republican successors. The concept
of serenity, not surgery, and even the naming of the time of "normalcy," came from the figure who stood above all the Fosdicks
and Bartons by the mere fact of his having held highest office:
President Warren G. Harding. He and his successors demand attention in any assessment of spiritual tranquilities in the twenties.
One could make the case, as some have done, for seeing the twenties merely as a time of calm by using nothing but the careers of
its three presidents to make the point. They spoke for and presided
at the rites of civil or public religion in America. Students of that
religious context, which wraps around the churches or is a canopy
above them, regularly turn to the letters, papers, and speeches of
decisive and charismatic presidents. The canon of such leaders
includes Washington, Jefferson, Lincoln, Wilson, and Kennedy.
Overlooked are inhabitants of the White House who lacked rhetorical gifts and who did not lead America through new turns,
men such as Warren G. Harding, Calvin Coolidge, and Herbert
Hoover. Such overlooking is understandable, but it obscures
the fact that, religiously speaking, the three do typify something
about the character of the period and the state of citizen expectation.

Harding, of course, was a Protestant. He was the son of a Sev-   2:99
enth-day Adventist mother, whose faith if transferred to him
would have put him outside the religious establishment fold. But
he came to be a member of Trinity Baptist Church, and thus was
a nominal and casual insider. Harding, who had sound instincts
for reading the signs of the times, said he would not enter the
political arena like an armed gladiator spoiling for combat. He
was not involved with a crusade, though he was ready to be custodian of a republic he was sure God had shaped. A biography of
Harding written in the thirties by Samuel Hopkins Adams located

Peers of the American pulpit: *Christian Century* readers select the notable preachers when mainstream Protestantism dominated. (*The Christian Century*.)

precisely the hapless president who went down in scandal and died prematurely while in office: "Harding was not innately nor profoundly religious. He supported and attended the church of his faith; that was the seemly thing for a man in his position." He was a believer, but not a follower of the code imposed by his creed. Adams presumed that "Presidents of the United States were, *ex officio*, so to speak, under divine guidance." So was the nation itself.

2:100   After the president's death and before the exposure of the moral flaws in the Harding administration, Vice-President Calvin Coolidge finished out Harding's term and was then elected in 1924 to serve a full term of his own. Anthologies of his writings show why Coolidge was no contributor to the canon of civil religion, yet why he filled so well the need of the citizens to find peace and quiet at the administrative center of the nation. His successor, Herbert Hoover, slightly mislocated Coolidge with one misapplied term, but it connoted something of what people saw in the predecessor: Coolidge was "a fundamentalist in religion, in the economic and social order, and in fishing."

2:101   Coolidge also, of course, was a Protestant. When young he attended the Congregational church in Northampton, Massachusetts, where colonial America's most notable theologian, Jonathan Edwards, had once held forth. Little of the Edwardsean outlook survived in Coolidge, for whom religion was as vague and formless as it was real. On occasion he could rise to religious themes, as he did in 1924 when he dedicated a monument in Washington to Francis Asbury, the Methodist pioneer. "On the foundation of a religious civilization which [people like Asbury] sought to build our country has enjoyed greater blessings of liberty and prosperity than were ever before the lot of man." Now, many decades later, "no tumult has been loud enough to prevent [the people's] hearing the still, small voice. No storm has been violent enough to divert inspired men from constantly carrying the Word of Truth." A stability of action, Coolidge hoped and thought, resulted from America's religious sense. Still, small, stable: these were the words and themes that sustained Coolidge, who became a Congregational communicant in his White House years, but who gave voice to the spirit of pacific mainstream Protestantism as well when he was not near Washington.

Herbert Hoover, elected in 1928, was, of course, a Protestant. 2:102 His Quaker roots connected him with colonial dissent and with a relatively small modern religious movement, but his outlook was very much that of mainstream Protestantism. He had the good taste not to regard requests to endorse Bible sales or promotions, but occasionally was caught in sectarian crossfire. Thus in 1930 when the Lutherans celebrated the four hundredth anniversary of their own uniting document, the Augsburg Confession, the president sent them a letter. In it he recognized, he said, that new views of religion and government, American style, resulted from the fact that "the predominant numbers of adherents to the Protestant faith" had produced the separation of church and state and the new order.

Catholics thought Hoover's was an inaccurate rendering of 2:103 both Lutheran and Catholic attitudes. The flap resulted from a gaffe made by French Strother, a Hoover assistant. It was uncharacteristic of Hoover, but it did some damage and momentarily disrupted the tranquil scene. More consistently the humanitarian president supported acts of mercy by the churches and avoided forays into controverted church history. "I come of Quaker stock," said Hoover just before he took office. He was reportedly to have admitted on one occasion: "I never worked very hard at [Quakerism]." If Hoover did say it, this did not represent the way he worked out his humanitarian Quaker commitments. Yet these were utterly unobtrusive, and never stood in the way of his representing in broad outline the outlook of standard-brand Protestantism. Like his two predecessors, Hoover did not significantly expand the presidential civil religion canon. That he would not have wished to, perhaps best describes his religious approach. "Triumphant nationality" had enough supporters in the church; they needed no more than congeniality from the bully pulpit that was the White House in their efforts to keep America serene. Such friendly intentions turned out to be insufficient to keep the peace.

3

The "100 Percent Americans" Attack

Red Scare, Yellow Peril, White Hoods

The first and most abrupt disturbance after the First World 3:1
War was the Red Scare. This was a brief and intense attack on
Bolshevism abroad and Communism at home, quickened when
bomb blasts by Reds, or anarchists, or somebody, were heard on
May Day, 1919. Someone blasted the rectory of Philadelphia's
Our Lady of Victory church. Another explosion hit the home of
Cleveland's mayor. But most aftershocks followed one in front of
the home of Attorney General A. Mitchell Palmer in Washington.
The Palmer family escaped the bombing without injuries except
to their nervous systems. The bomber, though, was exploded to
bits. His clothing remnants identified him as an Italian alien, an
anarchist, who thus well matched the public's image of the radical. And the rhetoric of the bomber's tract, left at the door, stimulated fears, as well it might have: "There will have to be
bloodshed; we will not dodge; there will have to be murder; we
will kill . . . there will have to be destruction; we will destroy. . . . We are ready to do anything and everything to suppress the capitalist class." Reflexively, presidential candidate

Warren G. Harding, one year later, would describe America's need as "not revolution, but restoration."

3:2   The second disruption was occasioned by fear of the Yellow Peril. This was the code name for white Americans' horror of immigration by Asian hordes. It inspired language which blended racial and religious antagonisms. In 1924, during debates preceding the vote to exclude Asian immigrants, a congressman from Arkansas elicited applause when he described a vision of Christian America which ruled out yellow races and other unwelcome people. "We have admitted the dregs of Europe until America has been orientalized, Europeanized, Africanized, and mongrelized to that insidious degree that our genius, stability, greatness, and promise of advancement and achievement are actually menaced." More congressional words, from Maine, seconded those: America was "God-intended to be the home of a great people. English-speaking—a white race with great ideals, the Christian religion, one race, one country, one destiny. [Applause]." America, the speaker went on, was "a mighty land, settled by northern Europeans "from the United Kingdom, the Norsemen, and the Saxon, the people of a mixed blood." The Africans, the Orientals, the Mongolians, and all the other yellow races of Europe and Asia should never have been allowed to help people the great land. They could never become "true Americans"; they were a menace. Again, "[Applause]" greeted the assertions. "Triumphant nationality," which the late President Harding called for four years earlier, now did dominate. But what had happened to the "adjustment" and "serenity" he had also evoked?

3:3   The third concurrent tumult came with the white hoods and robes of the reborn Ku Klux Klan. This secret organization spread terror in the North as well as the South in the first half of the twenties. Its presence was a sign that many fearful Americans would go to extremes to promote what they and others called "100 Percent Americanism." The Klansmen consistently blended racial with religious passion in their attacks. No one would think of the Klan then or now as representative of the best ideals of Protestantism in the 1920s, but it was representative of the ideals of many Protestants in that tribal time. The noise it made belongs in the history of conflict in churchgoing America. One Klan infiltrator accurately assessed that the group's "spirituality is, that they should hold rigidly to the fundamental idea of Protestantism." According to him, they felt that "the Klan is the power by which they, Klansmen, can do their best work for America and

Protestantism itself." Warren G. Harding had called for "not the
dramatic, but the dispassionate." The Klan and its kin and kind
were expert at drama but knew nothing of dispassion.

The Red Scare, the Yellow Peril, and the white hoods dis-   3:4
played something of the color in passion-inflamed sectors of
America. The extremists in these sectors disrupted the surface
serenity that religious America kept seeking and offering. What
sense do we make of such extremes, which suggested anything
but Hardingesque "equipoise?" Ex-Presbyterian sociologist E. A.
Ross, himself an academic racist, thought he knew. He was well-
read in the work of Europeans, such as Georg Simmel, who offered plausible theories of conflict. Ross wrote at length on conflict in 1920, in his influential text, *The Principles of Sociology*.
He was especially observant of religious roles and provides here
a necessary state-of-the-art guide to understanding conflict after
World War I.

Ross proposed a psychologically informed thesis which helped   3:5
explain the Red Scare, immigration restriction, and the Klan. He
knew that in all such cases resentment inspires the aggressive
party in conflict and was psychologically astute when he wrote:
"Resentment is a species of hostility springing from menace to
the mirrored self." The members of one party in each of these
three conflicts, usually then called the "hundred-percenters," saw
themselves representing what they called original-stock Protestant
America against real or presumed threats by those they considered
alien. Ross also drew on another American social theorist familiar
with religion, Charles Horton Cooley. Resentment, Cooley had
said, rests upon "a feeling that the other person harbors ideas
injurious to us; so that the thought of him is an attack upon ourself." Ross knew that conflict in the form of competition could be
creative. But deep resentment by one party demanded the elimi-
nation of the other. He labeled that "the utterly evil element in
conflict."

Ross could be eloquent, and was, when he denounced this ele-   3:6
ment. "It is a pit into which heedless man is precipitated by his
aggressive and self-assertive instincts. It is the lurking devil
which all glorifiers of war and struggle overlook. It is the Adversary baffling, betraying and tormenting a too-pugnacious and too-
sanguine race." Continuing in tones recalling the old Presbyterian
language about the demonic on which Ross had grown up, he
added that "it devastates society as its counterpart, hatred, devastates the soul." No wonder then, he wrote, that all the seers,

prophets and founders of religion worked "to draw mankind away from hatred and strife into the paths of amity and peace." But while such seers and founders dreamed of reconciliation, Ross noticed that most of their followers in the religious traditions were warlike. He spoke very much to the America of the twenties when he said that religion heated up the instinctive hostilities. In those years it led groups to what he termed "altogether bad and deplorable" antagonisms. Ross was not looking into his own mirror, for he harbored notions of Anglo-Saxon superiority through the twenties. Yet he was somehow aware of the dangers in such attitudes and, paradoxically, in *The Principles of Sociology*, set forth as America's rule number one: "No invidious discriminations. In all save private and domestic relations let a man's color, race, ancestry, *religion* and politics be ignored."

3:7   Ross added an observation about strategy which applied to these three incidents. It should be clear to anyone who studied conflict, he wrote, that deep antagonisms often had led throughout history to wars of attrition. These battles wore down the belligerents until both sides were prostrate. For that reason, those who believed they had superior power often attempted what Ross, borrowing appropriate language from boxing, called a " 'knockout' blow," to avoid prolonged and exhausting conflict. Take the present three efforts: First, the Red Scare in that context was an attempt to rid religious America of godless Communists immediately, finally, and totally. Second, immigration restriction would at once limit the entry into America of many more people who came from what the old majority thought was the wrong stock, people who were jeopardizing America's free institutions. The Ku Klux Klan, finally, was an urgent extremist effort to intimidate people of such stock who were already here.

3:8   Thus a struggle over power in America, over the soul and mission of the nation, was evident in the antagonisms of the twenties. The "superior power," though itself internally divided, was made up of self-described original-stock Protestant Americans. It would be misleading to depict all such Middletowners spending the decade doing nothing but fighting bare-fanged in "bad and deplorable" battles. Most of the churches as churches were not directly stirred to combat. Members generally kept doing at worship what they also did in more pacific eras. We have observed them quietly minding their own business in congregations and denominations. It would be distorting to picture three out of five Americans, the tens of millions of Protestants, forming a phalanx against 13 mil-

lion united Catholics, 2.9 million Jews, a half-million Eastern
Orthodox, and scatterings of Buddhists. The lines separating parties were much more confusing than such a portrayal suggests.
First, Catholics and other non-Protestant Americans, some un-
moved by religion, joined in action against Communists during
and after the Red Scare. Second, many well-settled Catholics also
favored immigration restriction. Third, blacks, historic victims of
the Ku Klux Klan, made up millions in the cohorts of American
Protestantism. Even so, it was Protestants who were or fancied
that they were of the original British Isles stock in America who
were central in the aggressions.

A Visitor's Portrait of "100 Percent Americans"

"Will America Remain Protestant and Anglo-Saxon?" This   3:9
question appears in isolation against the empty white space on
page one of André Siegfried's *America Comes of Age*, which appeared in 1927. The French visitor then began his full text on page
three with words which directly countered the tone of Warren G.
Harding's famed speech of 1920. Siegfried: "The essential characteristic of the post-war period in the United States is the nervous
reaction of the original American stock against an insidious sub-
jugation by foreign blood." Today's readers know, and Siegfried
could say already then: "As every one knows, there is no real
American race." But, he went on, "the Americans as a whole
pride themselves on their original stock, which was Anglo-Saxon
and inherently Protestant." Because Native Americans or Indians
were the true original stock, this self-designation was ironic, but
not then noticed.

Siegfried's discerning question about the American future   3:10
frames the plot for this and the next two parts of this book. The
presence of a foreign visitor helps give perspective on a subject
hard to grasp decades later: that original-stock Protestants could
still credibly dream of keeping their cultural dominance. André
Siegfried was an economist, political scientist, traveler, historian,
and journalist who repeatedly visited the United States and twice
reflected on the country at book length. He was not a genius, as
his predecessor Alexis de Tocqueville a century earlier had been,
but he had an instinct for discerning and elaborating the central
plot of American spiritual life. His visits and his book, taken together, were an important event of the decade.

3:11   Siegfried regarded the nation in the Harding and Coolidge years as being in a late adolescent stage; it was "coming of age." Now, the Frenchman noted, original-stock Americans were beginning to have doubts about the growing "heterogeneous elements," Catholic, Jew, and Oriental, who seemed out of sympathy with their traditions. The old American majority promoted "unity of spirit by insisting impatiently that their centre of gravity still lies in the Anglo-Saxon and Puritan stock." But now: "They have a vague uneasy fear of being overwhelmed from within, and of suddenly finding one day that they are no longer themselves."

3:12   Those who reduce the theme of American peoplehood simply to race or ethnicity need correcting by the likes of Siegfried, who always saw the blending ("Anglo-Saxon and Puritan") of this with religion. Of the new times he wrote that "from the religious point of view the change was even more striking, for the majority of the immigrants were no longer Protestant." For the moment he was not talking about blacks, no longer newcomers, who were of the wrong race but the right religion. They numbered only 10 percent of the total 105.5 million citizens in 1920. Of the 95 million whites, however, only a shockingly low 58 million had been born of American parents in the United States. This meant, Siegfried added, that the number of "real Americans, or '100 per cent Americans,' as they call themselves" had dropped to only 55% of the total. With ten million blacks and 36 million foreigners already present, he heard the survivors asking, "What is the country coming to?"

3:13   Siegfried elaborated on the theme of the bitter questions original-stock Americans asked in a time of what he called a new nationalism. Blacks and Jews and all the other peoples remained undissolved in their presence like a layer of silt. Those who saw themselves as originals were asking whether there was any hope of preserving intact the Protestant spirit and British traditions they were convinced had produced the moral and political character of the country. Siegfried noticed that such critics were particularly irritated that whole sections of the population remained impervious to Protestant thought and to the social and political concepts that proceeded from it. These other peoples, for instance, opposed traditional Protestant causes such as the presence of religion in public schools and prohibition of alcoholic beverages. "The menace of alien influences" around them induced old-style Protestant Americans to adopt what Siegfried called a "new nationalism, narrow and sectarian."

The French visitor played the historian, with a perceptive eye   3:14
on the Puritan and Calvinist past and present. "No one can possibly understand the United States without a profound, almost innate appreciation of their Puritanism." Here was a people
conscious of a covenant that gave them a privileged relationship
with God. With that map in hand, Siegfried then took the reader
on an imaginary tour with an imaginary befuddled immigrant
through the maze of American peoples and religions. In his most-
quoted line Siegfried set out to get at the heart of all the impressions: "Protestantism is the only national religion, and to ignore
that fact is to view the country from a false angle."

The immigrant or the reader needed more finesse than merely   3:15
to think of Protestantism as a bloc, reasoned Siegfried. Americans, first off, never favored otherworldly Lutheranism but built
upon this-worldly Calvinism. Observing and writing in the
America of Russell Conwell, Roger Babson, Bruce Barton, and
business-minded President Calvin Coolidge, he joined others in
claiming, not without good warrant I believe, that America's real
religion was a mixture of efficiency and materialism seen as
Christian virtues. The influence of this new lay religion was not
to be located and observed in the "confusion of sects," the group
of organized churches themselves. Siegfried suppressed any interest in statistics of religious institutions. Indeed, he could even
watch Protestant Fundamentalists fight Modernists at mid-decade
and claim that both sides kept respecting the mysticism of success, which had become perhaps their nation's genuine religion.
"An essentially American viewpoint on religion does exist."

One of their root notions, Siegfried accurately observed, led a   3:16
certain set of citizens to see themselves as an elite, a "moral aristocracy." Its members thought that they must live out their calling in domestic politics and must be missionaries to the world.
From these impulses came their moral crusades, which Siegfried
catalogued and which we shall visit later: *against* cigarettes, alcohol, slums; *for* feminism, pacifism, antivivisectionism, Americanization of immigrants, and even the gospel of eugenics and
birth control. Protestantized Americans who supported such causes
could never leave other people alone; their self-sanctification
as members of God's elect seemed to him almost insufferable.

In fairness, Siegfried admitted that not everyone and not even   3:17
all Protestants embraced the materialist faith. Some chose what
he termed not too appropriately the mysticism of the faith healer
over the practicality of the business-minded moralists. Some

Episcopalians were of mystical and sacramental bent. Lutherans, of German stock, seemed never fully at home or completely accepted. However, it was the Catholics who were most left out and who in response became the chief menace of the mirrored self to original-stock American Protestantism. "The Catholic Church is thus a thing apart in the heart of the American body politic." Siegfried did not even bother to list the godless secularists as being apart. "Neither Protestantism nor Catholicism is threatened from without by aggressive disbelief, for the agnostics, though numerous, maintain the Protestant vocabulary and the Protestant outlook on moral problems. They like its background and are not hostile in any way."

3:18   The struggle, as *America Comes of Age* depicted it, had recently come to its center in efforts by the old majority to restrict immigration, a policy which the Frenchman called "literally a case of political eugenics." These attempts were the logical outcome, Siegfried said, of the instinctive fears and beliefs of the generation. The legislation represented what he termed the primitive reaction of the genuine American. It was primitive because there was no practical reason to close the doors in a still underpopulated nation. Siegfried thought, however, that the door-closing had come too late. The most recent newcomers threatened the "100 percenters," because "they will not be Anglo-Saxons." Protestant America would never assimilate them. That was why the nation's majority was so profoundly anxious. So empathic was Siegfried that he almost sounded like one of these "genuine" Americans: "Is it possible to contemplate a United States that is neither Protestant nor Anglo-Saxon?" He had to leave the subject in resignation and with an implied question: "The final destiny of the country is still in suspense, and it is unable to foretell what tomorrow will be its very soul."

The Red Scare as a Religious Event

3:19   The first postwar struggle for America's very soul was codenamed the Red Scare (of 1919–20). It posed Christian America against Communism abroad and at home. In the eyes of the religious, Reds posed a religious issue which involved people and organizations occupied with religion. This first of the three encounters in the twenties was distinctive because it drew, along with the Protestants at the center, many Jews, Orthodox, Catholics, the nonreligious, blacks, and whites into a common front. Their two sets of enemies were Russian Bolsheviks overseas and their suspected allies in America. The targets were not always easy to define. People of Anglo-Saxon background, for instance, often focused on the Slavic roots of Soviet Communism. But they also had to deal with presumed apostates from their own Anglo ranks. Even the economic aspects of the conflict received theological treatment. Many Americans regarded their free-enterprise-based economic system as God-given; Communism as a polity was then looked on as being anti-God. Also, because the Russian revolutionaries professed Marxist atheism, the churched naturally opposed them. Since a few American advocates of Communism tried to blend their ideology with necessarily reinterpreted religion, the more conventional believers fought them as heretics. This meant that for two years one regularly heard agitation against a foreign foe and saw passion for a purge in the house of the American majority. The Red Scare, as people called it then and ever after, was to be a decisive act. Citizens wanted Communism to be over with so they could establish the way of life that future president Harding was hailing: not revolution but restoration.

To revisit E. A. Ross's apt boxing metaphor, the "knockout   3:20
blow" in this first conflict came late in the first round, during the period of slightly more than a year after World War I ended. Following the Armistice in late 1918, many citizens experienced disillusionment and restlessness. Industry had overexpanded to meet the demands for armaments. Consequently workers, then needed for new manufactures, had joined labor unions in record numbers and now wanted to fight in order to retain their recently acquired rights. Returning military personnel also needed jobs back home, and their numbers added to tensions. Inflation threatened economic stability. Much of non-Germanic America had practiced scapegoat hunting during the war by hounding German-Americans, but such action had become irrelevant now. Citizens were therefore ready to use their techniques in new forays against a presumed foe. Those who felt besieged wanted to associate radical American movements with Slavic subversions of society. They needed scapegoat theories to explain what was going wrong in America.

Three main factions were at hand which their enemies could   3:21
use to create a sense of threat on this front in 1919. Most noteworthy was the Socialist party. Though it had never known much success in the polls, it still often served as a symbol of subversion

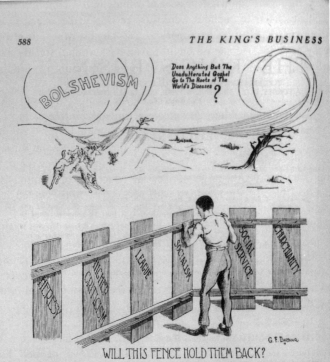

WILL THIS FENCE HOLD THEM BACK?

What means this strange unrest, this foreboding of the future? The war is over, but we are not at rest. There are strange, significant sounds; a rumbling of discontent; and he is far from wise who does not recognize it and its significance.

※ ※ ※

WHAT ARE THE SIGNS of the Schools?

Our nation is the greatest in the history of the world. Founded upon the Bible, it has had the favor of God in an unusual degree. Prosperity has filled us with pride. We have drifted far from our moorings. In the early days, the Bible was read and taught in our public schools, and children were taught to revere and respect it as God's Word. The Roman Catholic Church, ever on the alert for supremacy, played well the political game until the Bible was eliminated from the schools, and then taught her own children in her parochial schools. This departure from the Book was the beginning of the downfall of a great people. Now the Bible is not permitted in our schools, but teachers are permitted to under-

In this cartoon, conservative Protestants, soon to be called Fundamentalists, combine images of the Red Scare with fears of the loss of spiritual integrity because of Modernists. (From *The King's Business*, Biola University Archives.)

in the eyes of conservative capitalists. The second and more notorious element, but less noteworthy, was the Industrial Workers
of the World, sometimes called the IWW or, more often, the
Wobblies. A bit of prehistory will provide background to the religious and later antireligious tonality of the Wobblies. Respectable church people had already made up their minds about this
radical labor force before the war. The Wobblies union that made
the first strike headlines in 1919 and 1920 was started in 1905 by,
among others, "Mother Jones," the Irish-born Mary Harris
Jones, whose spirit the IWW embodied in the twenties. This eloquent agitator, who lost all four of her children to an epidemic in
1867, became a compassionate friend of miners and textile workers. She appeared on the scene wherever she could, identifying
with labor wherever agitation and passion were in place.

Mother Jones, although of Catholic background, expected lit-   3:22
tle of the church. Along with another organizer, Terence Pow-
derly, she liked to call Jesus Christ the friend of labor and the
"greatest agitator of all time." Jones once turned down an invitation to join a nonreligious workers' commune: "Only religion
can make a colony successful and labor doesn't have religion."
She had helped the lead miners in bitter Colorado strikes in 1913
and 1914, engagements so violent that forty-three women and
children were among the sixty-five persons killed. John D. Rockefeller, Jr., one of her steadfast opponents in the Colorado incident, told a congressional committee that he would kill for the
principle of "open camps"—nonunion mining stations. But even
Rockefeller came to have grudging respect for Mother Jones. At
one time he all but tried to buy her off, and he did send greetings
to friends and family when she died, seven years after her retire-
ment in 1923, and thus past her hundredth birthday.

By 1919 the widely hated and now aged Mother Jones had   3:23
yielded most of the IWW leadership to other, less religious, indeed, overtly antireligious organizers who would perpetuate other
elements of her legacy. During a strike one year to the day after
the end of the war, military veterans in the American Legion
fought IWW members in Centralia, Washington. After an incident in which four veterans were killed and one Wobbly was
lynched, eight Wobblies received sentences to Walla Walla Peni-
tentiary. Protestant opinion at this stage was quite divided. Much
of the Protestant press laid all the blame for the carnage on the
Wobblies. "Reds Murder Former Soldiers," headlined the North-

ern Presbyterian *Continent*. Yet some denominations, including the Northern Baptist Convention, were more discriminating. The Baptists daringly opposed what they labeled "'Red' hysteria which indiscriminately classes all foreigners as Bolshevists." Some church leaders helped gain pardons for the Centralia Wobblies. The Federal Council of Churches also tried to cool things off, but won few friends for doing so. In the spirit of the Presbyterian *Continent*, on the other hand, after the Centralia event several denominations and other sorts of religious jurisdictions in the state of Washington called for investigations. In the Red Scare years it was easy to inflame the churches whenever the Wobblies in the heritage of Mother Jones would strike.

3:24   After the effects of the Bolshevik Revolution spread, a third domestic force appeared. This American Communist party made the Socialist party and even the Wobblies look pale by comparison. In 1919 when someone calculated that the American Communist movement had 70,000 members, 60,000 of them in the party, Red-hunting became a profession. It was important for the hunters to link the Communist party at home to the Russian Bolsheviks. Fortunately for the conspiracy hunters, a few American Reds became visible. Among these were journalist John Reed and Albert Rhys Williams, a Congregationalist minister. Williams, who spent some time in Russia, was such a negligible figure in history that he would have been simply forgotten had he not turned up when searchers for domestic Communists used fine nets.

3:25   The Reverend Mr. Williams was that extreme rarity, the bona fide idealist turned Communist. It was his name that antiradicals would always adduce when called upon to produce the names of American clerics who might be engaged in subversion of Christianity and the nation. The Reverend Mr. Williams had made his move at a time when he was under the influence of the socialist novelist Upton Sinclair, who also was becoming disillusioned about the church. Whether or not Williams was ever a member of the party, his books did express fervor for the Bolshevik cause. While many other idealistic sympathizers tended to give up on the Soviets fairly soon, he never departed from the dream of transforming the world through Soviet-style revolution and polity. Williams for a time lived in Russia and served the Soviet Commissariat for Foreign Affairs through its Bureau of International Propaganda. He was a translator and supplier of Communist materials to the English-speaking world. At one time he was said to have been assigned by Russians to an office in the United States.

However, because there were no diplomatic relations between Moscow and Washington, the stranded Williams had to undertake his efforts from a distance.

While loners like Reed and Williams threatened only from half   3:26
a world away in Russia, domestic labor strikes served as specters at hand. Thus two months after the war the failure of a Seattle general strike led a church periodical to give thanks for "the overthrow of the Bolsheviki" in Seattle. Seven months later the Boston police strike of 1919 frightened the nation. The editor of the *Presbyterian Advance* saw that strike as "the nearest approach to Bolshevism which we have had in this country." Then came the worst of the furies set loose on May Day, 1919, in the bombings at Philadelphia, Cleveland, and Washington, including the home of Attorney General Palmer.

Religion helped fire the zeal of Mitchell Palmer, the galvaniz-   3:27
ing agent in the brief Red Scare. A progressive reformer, he was a Quaker who seven years earlier as a religious pacifist had declined President Wilson's request that he become secretary of war. But by 1919 Palmer had turned ambitious and militant. He evidently even dreamed of succeeding Wilson as president. Palmer's personal predilections, his religious antipathy to Bolshevist atheism and radicalism, much understandable shock over the home bombing, and his ambition together helped spur Palmer to step up surveillance of leftists.

The attorney general authorized arbitrary raids on suspects and   3:28
threw fear into those who were testing the postwar consensus from the Left. He found Reds almost everywhere he looked, and he looked almost everywhere. Palmer claimed that the public, including the preachers, had egged him on to such actions. "I was shouted at from every editorial sanctum in America from sea to sea; I was preached upon from every pulpit; I was urged—I could feel it dinned into my ears—throughout the country to do something and do it now and do it quick." Then he used knockout-blow language; he would "do it in a way that would bring results to stop this sort of thing in the United States." The most notable of his raids occurred in November of 1919 at the headquarters of the Union of Russian Workers in New York. This was a union self-described as made up of "atheists, communists and anarchists." Palmer followed with raids on the union outposts in eleven more cities.

Supporting Palmer in the months that followed was presiden-   3:29
tial secretary Joseph Tumulty, no old-stock Protestant but a

Catholic who, like Palmer, discovered atheistic Reds almost everywhere he turned. In consequence of efforts by such national leaders as these, the government sent 249 deportees from New York toward Soviet Russia on the liner *Buford*. This expulsion was a popular act. The *New York Evening Mail* proposed a provocative analogy that was frequently quoted: "Just as the sailing of the Ark that Noah built was a pledge for the preservation of the human race, so the sailing of the Ark of the Soviet is a pledge for the preservation of America." The *Saturday Evening Post* chose another image rooted in Puritan America: "The *Mayflower* brought the first of the builders of this country; the *Buford* has taken away the first destroyers." As the waves closed behind the ship on December 21, anti-radical America was ready for a new year with, Palmer evidently thought, even more popular support of himself and his actions.

3:30   The attorney general opened 1920 with expanded activities on January 2. Palmer raids, as they came to be known, occurred in New York, Chicago, and dozens of smaller cities. There were indiscriminate arrests, some questionable and cruel imprisonments, and numerous suspensions of civil liberties. The " 'Fighting Quaker' of the Cabinet" momentarily became a national hero. He played on nativist fears and appealed to 100 percent Americanism. "Fully 90 percent of Communist and anarchist agitation is traceable to aliens," Palmer reported in his annual accounting. Colorado Senator Charles S. Thomas went along, publishing an article that also described the attacked leftists as aliens or descendants of aliens. But Thomas was reassuring: "the ark of Democracy's covenant was committed to Anglo-Saxon keeping long ago."

3:31   Palmer invoked anti-Semitic feelings through familiar code language when he charged that "a small clique of autocrats from the East Side of New York" were the disreputable aliens who were responsible for the subversion. Yet as quickly as the shadow of anti-Semitism became usable the whole scare began to diminish. Before long it was apparent to the public that all this nativist reaction was disproportionate to alien threat. The 100 percent Americans had zero percent citizen conspirators to attack. For all the strikes and the bombings, it became clear that little of the domestic unrest was directly connected with the Soviet Union. Bolshevism was never a popular movement among Americans, nor one with any prospects in the American labor movement.

3:32   When early in 1920 some civil libertarians and judges began to speak up for the accused, the hysteria had begun to pass.

Palmer was now no longer seen as the popular Fighting Quaker. He acquired new names such as the Quaking Fighter or the Faking Fighter and came to be seen as a foolish alarmist. His presidential ambitions were irrelevant henceforth. Palmer's successful rival for the Republican nomination, Senator Warren G. Harding, in May put in a terse word: "Too much has been said about Bolshevism in America." Perhaps he had something of the Red Scare in mind when later that month in the famed Boston speech Harding pointed to America's need: "not revolution, but restoration." Harding would be a restorer. Four years later in 1924 the *Saturday Evening Post* could treat the incident and its accompanying passions all rather lightly, as "nothing but the last symptom of war fever."

What of the churches through this incident? Since this cause   3:33
united all faiths, there are reasons to look to Catholicism first for reaction. Some fierce anti-Catholics, notably in the Ku Klux Klan, had futilely tried to associate Catholicism with radicalism because some of the deported aliens had been forced to return to countries in Europe that were predominantly Catholic. Though world Catholicism was a reflexive and mortal foe of atheistic Communism, the fact that so many American Catholics were members of the suspect labor movement also led to suspicion of them for radically leftist tendencies.

An event which unnecessarily and improperly fed the suspi-   3:34
cions occurred in 1919, when Catholic leadership approved a mild, but for its time obtrusive, "Bishops' Program." This measure favored progressive social legislation. The program, whose chief agent was Monsignor John A. Ryan, appeared in pamphlet form with emphases that were unattractive to economic conservatives: *Social Reconstruction: A General Review of the Problems and Surveys of Remedies*. The program provoked instant reaction, divided the Catholic community, and thoroughly confused anti-Catholics.

The personal secretary of Stephen C. Mason, president of the   3:35
National Association of Manufacturers, wrote a letter of complaint to the aged but still influential James Cardinal Gibbons. He was puzzled and angered. He joined those who had generally assumed that the Roman Catholic Church of the United States was, and always had been, unalterable in its antagonism to all forms of socialism. How then explain this program? The manufacturers' man thought the booklet might prove to be a covert effort to disseminate "partisan, pro-labor union, socialistic propaganda under

the official insignia of the Roman Catholic Church in America."
Mason wanted an answer but never received satisfaction.

3:36   The *National Civic Federation Review* also attacked the bishops' program and Ryan. A celebrated two-volume memorandum called the "Lusk Report" on *Revolutionary Radicalism* included a note by Ralph M. Easley, a federation leader. Easley claimed to be trying to separate the conservative Catholicism he had known from the emergent and progressive Catholicism. He consoled himself or dismissed the bishops' program by cutting it off from the larger Catholic body: "But it must be remembered that this 'manifesto' is not the view of the Catholic Church; it is only the expression of the gentlemen signing the document and has no official sanction."

3:37   On another Protestant front, that of mass evangelism, there was also response to the Red Scare. Evangelists took advantage of anxieties and made good use of the minuscule presence of Communism. From their rhetoric and from the fact that they held support we can deduce that there had been some market for extreme reaction. Thus invokers of the Red specter included evangelists like the then fading Billy Sunday, the preeminent popular evangelist of the period, who still remained a crowd-pleaser. During the Palmer raids Sunday told the attorney general just what he would do to purify America. Deporting radical aliens was insufficient. The evangelist said he needed no arks like the *Buford* to purify America at citizen expense. "I would stand every one of the ornery, wild-eyed I.W.W.'s, Anarchists, crazy Socialists, and other types of Reds up before a firing squad and save space on our ships." Sunday called for citizens who would never dream of being tempted, who would turn their backs instead and join "the party of Grand moral ideas," which the evangelist found exemplified by Presidents Harding and Coolidge. America, he shouted, was "not a country for a dissenter to live in."

3:38   Billy Sunday offered alternative standards of his own. "No man who swerves in the slightest degree from absolute loyalty should be called an American citizen." The evangelist also constantly reworked themes of Protestant America's world mission: "It so happens that America is placed in a position where the fate of the world depends largely on our conduct." He tied the fate of the world to that of the nation: "If we lose our heads down goes Civilization. Woe to the world if this nation wabbles [sic] out of the orbit of Liberty." Nor was Sunday above including a bit of churchly sniping, to further his cause against Federal Council of

Churches types with whom he always feuded. "Atheism marches with Communism—Bolshevism—Socialism," and he then added to that unholy trio, Protestant Modernism. In fact, the revivalist claimed that he had "more respect for the gang of cut-throates [sic] [in] Russia in their attitude toward religion than for these Modernists."

One finds in Sunday a militant representative of populist Prot-   3:39
estantism, not an agent of analytic finesse or faithful reporting. In his representativeness and because of the way he spoke for a huge cohort of 100 percenters, the evangelist could and did articulate in the folk-Protestant style some calls for return to "the old time religion of our fathers." He beckoned America back "to the Bible—back to God" and asked for a tidal wave of old-time religion. On the other side of these good things Sunday posed Red anarchists, agents of Communism, and members of two specific organizations, the Christian Social Order Conference and the Fellowship of Reconciliation. The evangelist named names of radicals, a few of whom belonged on the list and others of whom were as respectable as future United States Supreme Court justice Felix Frankfurter. Of course, Sunday was by no means alone when he invoked the threat of radicals during the Red Scare. To take one example out of scores, the Southern Baptist *Western Reporter*, a couple of months after the quieting of the Red Scare, was still calling for alleged Reds to be put to death: "Better a million perish than a nation."

With so few Reds to scare the nation, one must ask: were there   3:40
Communists *at all* in the churches? The 100 percent Americans conventionally attacked people who might better be thought of as misguided idealists, romantics, or critics of capitalism who readily bought alternatives to the system they considered corrupt; Social Gospel liberals who simply hoped to maintain ties with Russia; or dreamers of differing ways to organize life who chose to overlook the violence of the Bolshevik Revolution. Methodist editor Lewis O. Hartman was mild enough in *Zion's Herald* when he used the pages of his journal to claim that "Marxian theory has many similarities to Christian teaching," and urged Christians to be patient with the Soviet experiment. More typical was Methodist bishop Edgar Blake, who could turn attacks on himself and his kind into counterattacks on other denominations. In 1923 in a gesture of good will and support while Blake and some colleagues were visiting Russia, they offered a church gift of $50,000 to Orthodox clerics. What these Methodists naively thought would

be credited as a Christian good work instead left them vulnerable to scorn when they returned. Yes, Blake admitted, Soviet leaders made no secret of their atheism. But he could not let the issue merely lie there with such an admission. Instead, he went on, "there is undoubtedly a larger measure of religious tolerance in Russia than in any other country of Europe or in America, that is dominated by the Roman Catholic Church." The Protestant outlook on occasion could thus be capacious enough to include Soviet Russia before it could embrace Catholic polities.

3:41   Most Protestant liberals within the federating churches were antirevolutionaries. They had no taste for violence or atheism and thus little sympathy for Bolshevism. For a variety of reasons, which included discontent with some aspects of the American economic system and a pragmatic need to deal with Russia, they often remained both open to and critical of the Soviet experiment at the same time. All through the decade, for instance, the undenominational *Christian Century* kept its eye on Russia, not always condemning everything in it, but never wavering in its opposition to Communism and atheism. Some of its writers came back from visits to Russia with comment not sufficiently measured to satisfy critics of the Billy Sunday type, but the editors were undeterred.

3:42   In 1927, long after the Red Scare, these editors argued that since "red Russia, bristling with propaganda, is and will probably continue to be," America had no choice but to reckon with it. With some prescience they declared that they would see whether philosopher Bertrand Russell might be right. He had uttered what the editors called a sad prophecy: "Russia and America will become world focal points for two conflicting and intolerant creeds." The editors hoped that "by an unexampled exercise of intelligent forbearance such a catastrophe can be averted." They called for normal relations with Russia, from "a purely practical and even antagonistic point of view." From this dual stance, they thought, there would be far greater opportunity to affect the policies of the Bolsheviki. Attitudes expressed by a fearful and hostile neighbor seeking refuge behind a stone wall would not be as productive as those that came with friendliness. Such positive if wary approaches, counseled the editors, were preferable to a devastating death struggle between the two systems.

3:43   Some of the denominational press agreed. Thus from the Northern Baptist Convention's weekly, the *Baptist*, came similar counsel: "let none but friends venture counsel." Why did they speak with uncharacteristic tentativeness on the Soviet subject?

They admitted that it was hard to get facts on the basis of which to speak at all. And they wanted to note that they had waited to hear first what their sponsoring convention had to say. Now it had spoken. Along with their body of Baptists, a denomination committed to religious freedom, they hoped for Russian citizens to be free, united, prosperous, and happy. What was the alternative to being open? "A protest in the name of religious freedom from persons who are already committed to an implacable political hostility toward the existing regime would add fuel to fire." In Russian eyes, such a protest would be resented as a political attack masquerading in the guise of religion.

The *Baptist*, expressing a characteristically Baptist hope, also   3:44
thought that the Soviet Union could not have its way around the world if it continued to suffer the embarrassment of religious intolerance at home. On practical grounds the Soviets must allow for more freedom. As for the Baptists in Russia: "all that we have heard concerning them indicates that they are of the sort that Baptist martyrs have always been." This meant to the editors that as Baptists these dissenters pursued only the right to hold and propagate the simple, free faith of the gospel.

Some independent Protestant magazines were far to the left of   3:45
these two. Thus the avowedly pro-socialist *World Tomorrow*, could and did go further than papers like the *Baptist*. Sometimes its editors would use incidents in Russia to goad the American churches into positive action. Thus during the height of the Red Scare in January 1920, as Western nations continued blockades and policies dedicated to "starving Russia," the editors expressed the wish that Americans would all admit that the game was up, that the starvation policy was not successful. They claimed that in both Washington and London some capitalists were urging a change in policy because they spotted a potentially large market in Russia. Labor union leadership could see opportunities and was demanding peace with Russia. "It is all very well to fight 'Bolshevism' at home," wrote the editors, "but it's a pity to lose a chance to do profitable business with peacefully inclined Bolsheviki thousands of miles away." What had the churches to do with all this? Because of their support for the "starving Russia" policy, wrote the editors, "the churches are still silent, and by their silence they crucify Christ afresh."

Norman Thomas, formerly a Presbyterian minister but now   3:46
and henceforth a well-recognized socialist partisan, responded to one letter writer who feared that Thomas was in danger of leaning

over backwards in his desire to be fair to the Bolsheviki. What, the correspondent asked, did Thomas then think about widely reported atrocities and violence in Russia? "How can you reconcile Bolshevik policy in confiscating land and other property with the ethics of Christianity?" Thomas replied that it was necessary to be patient with Russia, "very patient, for it is a slow business leavening that old Czardom with the leaven of brotherhood and justice." The socialist went on to emphasize that still "*the so-called Red Terror in all its worst excesses has not cost the lives of a tithe—nay of a thousandth part, of the unnumbered conscripts who were slaughtered in that vast holocaust we call the European war.*" When, therefore, the average man who supported war condemned the Bolsheviki, he must first recognize the wanton violence of militarism itself. Thomas cited recent visitors to Russia in his effort to moderate the charges that mere violence prevailed there. He called as witnesses Jerome Davis of the YMCA and sociologist E. A. Ross, but was clearly most impressed by the testimony of Quakers in the Friends' Reconstruction Unit.

3:47   While Christian advocates of 100 percent Americanism (the National Association of Manufacturers, the American Legion, and others), would classify Bishop Blake or Norman Thomas as fellow travelers, they came up with extremely few bona fide church-related Communists in the early 1920s. Of course, there was always the Reverend Williams. But to illustrate the pathos of their quest and to point to the quick quieting of the Red Scare as a result of the exposure of its follies, it is appropriate to focus on the self-parodying figure of real live Communist ex-bishop William Montgomery Brown. For fifteen years Brown had been Episcopal bishop of Arkansas; in the twenties he held membership in the Communist party. But what did the baggers of Brown as a prize Red captive have to show for their catch? He was an evolutionist, a pacifist, a self-described heretic, who also embarrassed Communist friends by being a simple racist. The bishop was eccentric, unrepresentative of anyone but his own and his wife's egomaniacal pretensions. In 1920 the two published a small book, *Communism and Christianism*. Before any believers could take it seriously, they would have to get past the weirdness of Brown's self-awarded title: "Episcopus impartibus Bolshevikium et Infidelium." His summons was to "Banish Gods from Skies and Capitalists from Earth." The accompanying call was to "Aban-

don Christian Socialism for Marxian Communism." One title
page claims that its edition included a "Fortieth Thousand" copy
in print. One suspects that the Browns had given away more than
thirty-nine thousand.

This booklet termed the Bolshevik Revolution "the greatest   3:48
event in the history of the world." Brown was himself its American apostle, even though he gained no following. The American
Communist party had no idea what to do with the bishop, who
posed in offensive clerical garb for his frontispiece. It would be
frivolous even to mention Brown here, had he not become a footnote to Russian and American Episcopalian history. The Soviet
government came across the booklet, had it translated, and found
use for it against the Russian Orthodox Church. Brown's fellow
bishops in America thereupon had not much choice but to depose
him in 1925. With him went one of the few traces of Communist
party membership by anyone called "Reverend." If the proponents of the Red Scare were to deliver a knockout punch, its
objects, when they were like Bishop Brown, demonstrated that
self-inflicted blows were most devastating.

Race and Religion in Immigration Restriction

Catholics, who were among the agents in the Red Scare, re-   3:49
verted to being among the victims of immigration restriction.
After the great tide of European immigration in the previous half-
century and fearing more of the same from Europe and now Asia
in the next half-century, the majority of Americans moved to exclude most of those who wanted to immigrate in the years after
World War I. There is no need here to detail the obvious economic
aspects of debates over exclusion; the racial or ethnic and religious arguments make up a sufficiently revealing story. This time
the 100 percent Americans attracted the broadest support and
eventually won their way in Congress.

During the nineteenth century the United States, needing farm-   3:50
ers to fill frontier lands and laborers to build cities, provided an
Open Door or Golden Door policy through which immigrants
were made more or less welcome. As the nineteenth century
turned to the twentieth it became ever more clear to original-stock
settlers that most of the newcomers were not of their kind, and
they put out the unwelcome mat. Still, they hoped that old and

Immigration restriction measures, passed in 1924, were designed in part to end the Japanese traffic, symbolized by this scene of immigrants and returning Japanese visitors. They are aboard ship, waiting to be processed at the Angel Island U. S. Quarantine Station in San Francisco Bay. (National Archives.)

new peoples would assimilate. The favored image of the melting pot in which the newcoming peoples would blend signaled some of that hope.

3:51   Against such a background, laws passed in 1921 and 1924 to effect an almost Closed Door policy represented an epochal shift, even if the events are not often listed among the most decisive in American history. In brief: after excluding the Chinese in 1902, restrictionists wanted more victories. In 1910 a commission headed by Vermont senator William P. Dillingham turned in an alarmist 42-volume report on the frightening effects of immigration. The Immigration Act of 1917 demanded literacy and clamped down further on Asians. Still, too many southern and eastern Europeans learned to read their way through the Golden Door, and original-stock Americans had to take more steps to keep out their kind. The Quota Act or Johnson Act of 1921 invented a new formula. Now the yearly numbers of newcomers of each "admissible" nationality was to be 3 percent of the foreign-born of that nationality who had arrived in 1910, according to the census. Western Hemisphereans had more open access. Senator Albert Johnson led the fight of more extreme restrictionists until the Johnson-Reed Act or Immigration Act of 1924 changed the formula from 3 to 2 percent and used 1890 instead of 1910 as a base year, meanwhile cutting down the overall number of entrants. The choice of 1890 was obvious: not so many people of the wrong stock had been coming back then. For the next forty years, northern and western Europeans, the right stock, were favored.

How did Americans interpret their action religiously? One 3:52 turns instinctively to the White House, where the presidents as priests of public religion translate the symbols of national change. A particularly uncharismatic president, Calvin Coolidge, was in office in 1924. He had made immigration policy a specialty ever since he was running for vice president in 1920. When he signed the Johnson-Reed Act on May 26, 1924, the president squirmed, since the Japanese were outraged and he knew there would be new complications in foreign policy. On other days he spoke less grudgingly. Thus in his annual message to Congress on December 6, 1923, Coolidge asserted, "America must be kept American." New arrivals had to come in numbers that the nation could absorb and with features that would help them be assimilated. He added: "those who do not want to be partakers of the American spirit ought not to settle in America."

Yet when foreign-born citizens came to visit Coolidge at the 3:53 White House on October 16, 1924, he took the occasion to sound more open. Not long ago, he admitted to himself and reminded his guests, "all of us were alien to this soil." Americans, in Coolidge's reading of history, had successfully transcended the fate of Europe, always a battleground of warring peoples. There, not here, differences in race, in religion, and the like were what he called "invitations to contest by battle." Since the peaceful people in the United States had once been provincial warriors in Europe, they must have found something in the character of American institutions that made change possible. Chief among these expressions, Coolidge urged, was the tolerance of religious opinion alongside other expressions of tolerance. Speaking for the moment against the formulas of the quota bill, Coolidge then argued that, when Americans thought it best to exclude so many, they were not reflecting negatively on any race or creed but merely had in mind the interests of both those who were already here and those who were to come. This was an evasion, of course, for race and creed were prime considerations in the formula. But Coolidge chose his own topics, as presidents are free to do. He urged citizens especially to keep up their devotion to religion. They should not fall away from the religion of their fathers. In what seems to be an oversupply of words from quiet Coolidge, he went on to urge that his hearers leave behind Old World prejudices, be loyal to American institutions, and thus leave the nation "internally harmonious, making it externally powerful in promoting a reign of justice and mercy throughout the earth."

3:54   On levels below the presidential, original-stock religious people found a variety of strategies open to them. They had always been free to try to convert uncongenial newcomers to their religion and their ways. While it was impossible to alter the ethnic backgrounds of others, their religions were at least theoretically replaceable. A few Protestants had made efforts to proselytize and assimilate those who were not of their stock. But in 1933 Columbia University professor Theodore Abel, head of a commission that was charged to look at the record, admitted that almost nothing had ever come of such efforts. Three denominations, Presbyterian, Baptist, and Methodist, worked hardest to talk Catholics into changing their religion. The goal, he wrote, was "promoting Americanization and breaking down the isolation of immigrants from American society by bringing them into the fellowship of the Protestant church." In such rhetoric, Americanization equalled Protestantization.

3:55   Abel elaborated on his theme. The Protestants based their outreach toward Catholic immigrants, he declared, on the belief that "the ideals and principles of government and social life in America were derived from and supported by the spirit of Protestantism." Yet, Abel added, the venture had failed in its main purpose. It certainly produced no churchgoing Protestants out of ex-Catholics. Also, it did not help Protestants achieve the control they wanted, that of "directing the process of their adaptation to American life." The conclusion was bald: "No movement toward Protestantism has taken place as a result of these missionary ef-

forts." Abel had the advantage of writing with the hindsight of
twelve years after legislation ruled out the wrong kinds of people.
He was describing policy behind immigration restriction: if you
cannot trust those who will not change, and you cannot change
them, then rule them out from coming to America in the first
place.

Sometimes Jews were the targets of restriction. The U.S.   3:56
House Committee on Immigration hearings include testimonies
by people who feared that America might soon be overrun by
"abnormally twisted," "unassimilable," "filthy, un-American"
Jews who were "often dangerous in their habits." But with respect to European immigrants, the issue of Catholicism was more
consistently on the Protestant mind. While support for restriction
often resulted from the simple fears of simple people, some self-
interested church leaders could exploit bewilderments through efforts to advance their own causes. For example, celebrated New
York Episcopal rector Leighton Parks in 1922 published concerns
which represented his caste and kind. If immigration continued
on the present pattern, Parks wrote, "the Roman Catholic Church
may dominate the religious life of this country" because it was
making moves to increase power. That church was successful,
charged Parks, largely because the Protestant churches chose to
be weak. They would gain strength only if they would cooperate
against the strong and united Catholic Church. Park's apparent
generosity to denominations of Protestant stripe other than his
own, however, had its limits. He soon turned sectarian. If English-speaking peoples of the world wanted to be cooperative he
urged that they logically needed a church like the Episcopal, in
order to "influence the life of the people of this land so as to
cement the spiritual union of the great race of which we form so
important a part."

Some church people who had earlier defended the immigrants   3:57
came to have second thoughts, changing with the changing mood
of the times. Thus Howard B. Grose, who had once made a name
for himself as a reform-minded, broad-spirited Baptist editor of
Missions magazine, switched positions. Back in 1906 Grose's
The Incoming Millions was the kind of friendly book a Protestant
would write if he wanted to convert Catholic immigrants. But in
1922 the author joined those who worked for what he termed
"permanent, constructive legislation" of the restrictive sort. He
justified his turn of mind because now he too feared radicalism

and the glutting of the labor market. Grose also charged that the newer immigrants had avoided military service during the recent war, thus proving their un-Americanism.

3:58   While Howard B. Grose was himself a Baptist leader, not all of his fellow believers joined him in making a move from support of immigrants to opposition. Critiques of the tribal attitudes of the old majority kept coming from his own denomination. In 1925 the Northern Baptist Convention passed a resolution against the spirit of Congress's new restrictive act, in language that stressed racial, not religious, factors. The convention delegates also listened to a resolution which some Presbyterian, Congregationalist, and Methodist editors promoted in an effort to keep their own churches open to change. "Neither the 'Nordic' nor any other group has the ear of the Almighty to the exclusion or injury of any other race. The question of race relationship must be honestly faced." What the constituency all thought about such stands it is impossible to learn. But in the face of the general national climate, voicing such opinion was an act of courage by the editors and convention delegates.

3:59   The American Baptist Home Mission Society, meanwhile, in the very year the convention was being torn over deep doctrinal controversy, talked to its denomination at large. It reminded fellow Baptists that where "human liberty is teaching the world the truth of freedom," thence the followers of Christ would go forth. These Baptist followers must be imbued with Christ's spirit and then, by implication, they would also let other kinds of people be welcomed in their nation. The record in this and other cases demonstrates that some Protestant leadership wanted to work against the spirit of the times and at least alert the membership-at-large to think about change.

3:60   Between the bureaucracies or convention delegates and the churchgoing Protestant public at large stood the pastoral ministers. Harry Emerson Fosdick, the most prominent New York preacher, typified the ambivalence so characteristic of open-minded leaders in that decade. As a liberal, Fosdick did not want to be seen as prejudiced. The noted preacher simply worried, he said, lest America would not find resources enough for all future newcomers. Earlier America had welcomed "teeming peoples," but if its gates were now to stay open to all, no one's problems would be solved. "I am a restrictionist in immigration because I am not a sentimentalist," Fosdick stated. He wanted Americans instead to help alleviate world population problems. On the other hand, despite his own restrictive impulses, the preacher came to believe that the extreme legislation of 1924 was a wretched blunder and an appalling insult, for instance, to the Japanese. Fosdick apologized over the radio to them. He there and then attacked both the Nordic myth and the Ku Klux Klan and spoke out boldly, as if against his own earlier instincts. "The Exclusion Act stands as one of the most senseless, needless, intolerable pieces of racial prejudice ever perpetrated by a great nation."

Congress during its debates relied often on the testimony of the   3:61 nonreligious or semireligious but always blatantly racist writings of "scientific humanists" like Madison Grant, Lothrop Stoddard, and Kenneth Grant. Stoddard voiced a secular creed: Nordicism, which would replace Catholicism and Protestantism. He spread his vulgarizing opinions in popular magazines like *Collier's* and the *Saturday Evening Post* and in a score of books. He attacked southern and eastern Europeans who wanted to come to America. Among these, he charged, were "Bolshevik agitators" who whispered in the ears of "discontented colored men their gospel of hatred and revenge." Stoddard liked to reach for the most ancient and honored parallels. Quoting Gustave Le Bon, he entered into the record: " 'Cain, in the Old Testament, had the mind of a Bolshevik. But it is only in our days that this ancient mentality has met with a political doctrine to justify it.' " Senators who favored restriction were happy to have Stoddard be heard.

An even more eloquent racist was Dr. Albert E. Wiggam,   3:62 who, like Le Bon, also invoked religious parallels. He promoted his ideas in popular books and magazine articles. Wiggam drew on the views of eugenicists who wanted to perform scientific race-breeding. "Had Jesus been among us, he would have been president of the First Eugenics Congress." Jesus had been an alert and up-to-date person, so Wiggam knew that in modern times the rabbi of Nazareth would have drawn on theories of Mendel, Darwin, and other scientists. In language that the readers who kept purchasing Wiggam's books must have found directed to their needs, he wrote: "A new commandment I give unto you—the biological Golden Rule, the completed Golden Rule of science. *Do unto both the born and the unborn as you would have both the born and the unborn do unto you.*" The favor done the unborn would be to see that only the fittest would be born, to say nothing of surviving.

In the arguments of men like Wiggam, science was God's me-   3:63 dium of revelation for the moment. This revelation warned that "the advanced races of mankind are, biologically, plunging downward," while the inferiors were advancing. The message to restrictionists: keep advanced and civilized America pure. Others could work out all the details politically, as Senator Johnson did; Wiggam would stay with science and his pen. Madison Grant, a third major pseudoscientist, also kept influencing the Immigration Restriction League. In its files is a letter Grant wrote saying: "When the Bolshevists in Russia are overthrown, which is only a question of time, there will be a great massacre of Jews and I suppose we will get the overflow unless we can stop it."

3:64   While restrictionists kept their eyes on Catholic and Jewish populations, much of the impetus for legal exclusion came from the West Coast, where old-stock Americans and almost anyone who was not Asian had feared the Chinese and now opposed the Japanese. What would the coming of Asian hordes do to Christian America? Some of the language was religious, though more of it reflected classic Yellow Peril terms, which were racial and economic. In 1920 California stepped up its anti-Japanese endeavors to solve what came to be known as the "great race problem." Valentine Stuart McClatchy, retired from the *Sacramento Bee*, knew how to propagandize effectively during the campaign so soon after World War I. He began to speak of Japan as "the Germany of Asia."

3:65   The religious dimension was present but not prime. Still, when editors and politicians on the West Coast wanted to introduce particularly emotional elements into their arguments, when they wanted to exploit public fears or to engender them, they brought up the subject of Japanese Shintoism or Buddhism. Clearly, as every Sunday school child was taught to know, these were idolatries and paganisms to shun. Should American citizens like to anticipate a day when they would see Japanese temples down the block from their church? Equally clearly, Asian faiths operated far outside the consensus of biblical religion, which almost everyone in the western states agreed should shape the morals of America. Overlooked was the fact that Japanese—before coming to America or soon after arrival—often converted to Christianity, in a pattern many associated with an adaptable people. It is notoriously difficult to gather statistics on this subject, but as one example there are estimates that in 1936 1,200 of perhaps 6,000 Japanese-Americans in Seattle were Christian, as opposed to fewer than 980 Buddhists or adherents of other Eastern religions from that number. And the Buddhists adapted to American ways: it was said that one could hear Buddhist Sunday school children adapting a song from their Christian counterparts, "Buddha loves me, this I know."

Typical of the religious alarms were those of V. S. McClatchy,   3:66
who in a scholarly article in 1921 insisted that the Japanese government was intruding into Japanese-American communities and subverting American ways. Even Japanese children born in America had to attend Japanese schools after public-school hours, he said. There they were "taught the language, the ideals and the religion of Japan, with its basis of Mikado worship." McClatchy pointed out that teachers in these schools were Buddhist priests who knew no English and no patterns of American citizenship. The children they taught were good only for the faith of the Mikado and could never become good Americans.

Representative MacLafferty of California also knew how to   3:67
incite prejudice. The *Congressional Record* preserves a speech he made during debates in 1924: "Every Japanese believes that he is a child of the sun goddess, that the world belongs to Japan, and that Japan can possess any part of the world rightly by any means she may see fit to take. That is their belief." Californians, already worried about Japanese labor forces and purchases of farmland, found such appeals one more reason to keep pressure on Congress.

Senators, during their debates over restriction, used and heard   3:68
similar language. Senator Shortridge of California naturally carried the burden of some of the argument. In order to assure the stability, strength, and righteousness of the nation, he said, Americans "must strive for homogeneity among the citizenship. Therein lies the strength of the republic." And while racial homogeneity was something for which first of all to strive, "assuredly we should have homogeneity in the sense of common belief, common aspirations, common devotion." This advice meant that, more than circumstances were to allow in the early twenties, Americans should be "one people—one people, not many peoples."

Senator Shortridge even reached back to America's founders   3:69
to support his promotion of national homogeneity. These founders, he suggested, had worked to rule most races out of America. They wanted only "free white persons" to be citizens. The Japanese and others could never be racially eligible or capable of shar-

ing the common national belief patterns. Arguments like these tended to rule out other considerations. A gentleman's agreement reached in 1907, in which the Japanese agreed to abide by self-imposed restrictions on emigration, haunted a minority in the Senate and made them cautious, but did not finally deter them from taking action. A Japanese exclusion clause, it turned out, was to pass in the larger framework of restrictive legislation. Of course, the law did produce the expected anguished and bitter reactions on the part of the Japanese government and people. In the climate of 1924, however, few senators worried about quickening controversy with Pacific nations.

3:70   The Johnson-Reed bill passed and was signed in 1924. Neither the Anglo-Saxon nor the Nordic myth carried the day along with it, but the "Anglos" and "the Nordics" had delivered a "knockout blow," and the bill protected their interests. Economics, race, and religion had combined to help America, in André Siegfried's terms, "remain Protestant and Anglo-Saxon." John B. Trevor, who had done so much to help work out the approved statistical formulas, wrote an explanation of the act. His words provide the seal on the whole endeavor: "The passage of the Immigration Act of 1924 marks the close of an epoch in the history of the United States." As so often, a law expressed the spirit of an age that had just passed more than it anticipated what was coming. The late 1920s even saw some decline in nativist sentiment. But by then the immigration gates were largely closed, and those who bannered their slogans at the closing were no longer heard simply because they were no longer needed. They had done the defining when it counted, early in the tribal twenties.

The Spirituality of the Ku Klux Klan

3:71   Respectable citizens perpetrated the Red Scare and legislated against the Yellow Peril, but unrespectables donned the white hoods of the revived Ku Klux Klan in the twenties. The Klan was a third attempt at a "knockout blow" against presumed enemies by those whose resentment sprang from the "menace to the mirrored self" these posed. The Klan was obviously a disproportionate and implausible reaction to threats. Most later Americans came to regard the Klan as an irredeemable blight on the national record. The Ku Klux Klan episode was completely linked with religion or, in a term sometimes used by Klan members, with

Racial ambiguity in religious "Middletown": people of good will teach an integrated Sunday School (above) and people of ill will march in a Ku Klux Klan parade (below) in Muncie, Indiana, in 1924 and 1923. (Center for Middletown Studies, Ball State University.)

spirituality. This third form of postwar antagonism was the most closely related of the three to activities in local congregations in the first half of the decade.

3:72   To focus on the Ku Klux Klan in a work on religion and religious conflict might seem an intrusion, a side glance at something that spices up the story. The plot of a book which contented itself with reporting on sermons or church suppers and Sunday school could induce yawns. Reference to days when raiders of the Ku Klux Klan stormed the pulpits, nights when they salted the suppers, or noons when they subverted the lessons—this all enlivens the plot. Or: it is one thing to talk about conflict in never-read theological pamphlets, in shouting matches between professors, or even in demeaning speeches by senators. It is another to conjure up images of thousands of white-robed spectral figures marching through Indiana streets or riding Oklahoma plains, heirs of those who once terrorized and even lynched blacks. To follow Klan members through their secret rites, to overhear their rituals, to watch their cross-burnings: all this connotes *real*, not toy or play conflict. But has it anything to do with American religious life, with church existence?

3:73   The simple answer to such a question is yes in almost every respect. The Klan, itself an object of resentment for much of respectable America, including respectable Protestant America, turned out also to have been a "menace to the mirrored self" for many of those who would never personally don robes or burn crosses. Often the organization was a parody of more decorous and discreet secret societies, some of which even preached brotherhood and tolerance as, of course, the Klan did not. Curiously, the Klan leaders sometimes even advocated policies—among them the union of Protestants against Catholic threats—that were populist versions of the very Christian unity moves fashioned also in the middle- and higher-brow cultures of the Federal Council of Churches. Klan rituals were explicitly "Christian," its ethos was decisively Protestant, the membership was often church-going, and the leadership was sometimes clerical. As a fascinated and appalled André Siegfried reminded his readers, the Klan, whose aim was to perpetuate "100 per cent. Americanism" was "Protestant enough to satisfy the most out-and-out Fundamentalist" while also managing to sound at the same time like an uplift society.

3:74   One glimpse of Klan life in a northern city can bring focus to subsequent general comments on the organization's life in the half-decade of its revival. A trove of photographs that survived serendipitously in Muncie, Indiana, and the good or bad luck that small city had to be chosen later as *Middletown* in the classic study by Robert and Helen Lynd, make it a good candidate for such a view. From the pictures and the accounts one can get a sense of both the normalcy and the eeriness of what the Klan then meant in mid-America. The Lynds reached for metaphor: "Coming upon Middletown like a tornado, catching up many . . . latent differences into a frenzy of activity, the Ku Klux Klan has emphasized, during its brief career in Middletown, potential factors of disintegration." Disintegration: this word can refer as well to the Protestant pattern of dominance and synthesis nationally as to the thin veneer of civilization in one city among many, one that was and still is typed as typical.

The Klan was on the scene in the spring of 1922. Ostensibly   3:75
as part of a program of civic reform, townsmen organized a local Klavern of the Klan at the Chamber of Commerce; there were traces of Klan activity as early as the autumn of 1921. Through the three years of its prime, the Klan leadership was much involved in partisan mayoral and other campaigns, though the organization soon took on a life of its own as a gathering place where people could give expression to diffuse terrors. It was part of an Indiana-wide storm of activity that led to an estimated 240,000 people joining there. Indianapolis was the capital of a movement which in that state was most at home in such middle-sized cities as Muncie and Kokomo. The Klan attracted moralists who were bewailing changes in behavior, prohibitionists fighting against repeal, people hungry for clandestine ritual and bonding with brothers (and, through a parallel organization, sisters), and the Protestant preservers of 100 percent Americanism.

The "menace of the mirrored self" thesis stands up well when   3:76
one notes that the 100 percent Americans were holding up mirrors that in most cases caught few local threats to their way of life in the angle of vision. In other words, Catholics, blacks, Jews, and other undesirables were often not even in geographical range. The mirrors picked up only images of distant groups of hated "others." Who, after all, were those residents of Muncie who might jeopardize its Protestant and Anglo-Saxon purity? The population records of the city show this *Middletown* to have remained relatively homogeneous, full of original-stock people. Were southern and eastern European Catholics a real specter to local Protestantism? They were hardly surging. The 1920 census found that 92.1

percent of Muncie citizens were native-born and an astonishing 85 percent were also of native-born parentage. Yet the Klan fed and fused the anxieties of Protestants who could be convinced that the pope was being aggressive in their nation, their state, their city. As for blacks, the victims of the old-time Klan, they were also remote from the experience of most Muncieites. Only six out of a hundred dwellers were black. The 100 percent American usually kept the foreign-born immigrant of Catholic or Eastern Europe in his figurative gunsights. But there were few targets of this sort: only 2.2 percent of the inhabitants were foreign-born whites of any sort. And Jews, nationally and often in local rhetoric, were seen as enemies of Protestant America. Muncie could count less than 0.1 percent of its citizens in the Jewish camp. Yet in a city where only seven out of a hundred citizens were Catholic, it is estimated that 3,500 persons joined the Klan.

3:77   The Klan liked to demonstrate its power by staging parades down the main street. Martin E. Schwartz, who was part of that 0.1 percent Jewish minority, recalled one of these occasions for the Lynds. "Oh God, yes!" he remembered the parades down Walnut Street. Not only did Jews not have to go into hiding on such occasions; the Schwartzes were even present, little Martin poised on his father's shoulders to see above the crowd. "The Klan was anti-Catholic, and anti-black. There weren't enough Jews, you see around Muncie, to make much of a target. . . . " Schwartz brought a visual image to mind: "You know, the Klan idea of Americanism was to have this big fat gal seated on a white draft horse with the American flag draped over its rump, with her sitting on it." Should non-Klan members salute the flag when it came with such associations? Or should they shun the fat lady and thus neglect the flag? On the night of June 2, 1923, as 2,000 robed and hooded Klansmen marched, many bystanders, some of them notables, refused to salute. Klan members were offended at their refusals, demanding that their neighbors doff their hats and pay respects. Arguments and scuffles followed. After that event the Klan, now exposed to view in a different light, began to face reaction and decline.

3:78   Meanwhile, off the street and in the closed meeting rooms, dissension within the ranks of the local movement itself broke out, in the classic pattern of American tribalism. After March 1924, a schismatic group called itself the Independent Klan of America. Lawyers, judges, civil officials, and a Methodist minister named J. Walter Gibson were in the elite of this faction.

These people, one might say, became the resenters of the resenters. In their distorting mirror, the traditional Klan itself came to be viewed as part of a Catholic conspiracy. An interviewer for the Lynds heard a virtual lecture from a woman who differentiated between the two Klans. "The Pope is trying to get control of this country, and in order to do it, he started the old Klan to stir up trouble among the Protestants." Instead, this action only "opened their eyes to the situation." Now, therefore, "all the Protestants are getting together in the new Klan to overcome the Catholic menace."

Momentarily, Klan faction fought Klan faction in Muncie politics, and thus the organization spent much of its energy attacking its own hooded kin. But things were falling apart for both sects as Muncie came to its senses. Mayor (and Klan member) John Hampton got into increasing trouble for public intoxication. Notoriety based on such events did not help the Klan make its moral claims. Soon the secret order's white hoods were put into mothballs or on trash heaps, and Muncie survived the episode. The souvenirs left behind included a residue of mistrust and hate and a collection of photographs which serve to show later generations that not all was good in the good old days.   3:79

Muncie was not the whole world, but the American world of the twenties laid bare enough fears and resentments to assure that the Klan spirit found a large home. The Klan everywhere saw itself as the potential deliverer of a knockout blow by citizens who did not want to exhaust themselves with protracted battles against those they regarded as less than 100 percent Americans. To see the larger picture, one must try to imagine the beginnings of this capacious Klan. It was invented or reborn from residues of the nineteenth-century racist movement, in the dark of Thanksgiving night in 1915 atop Atlanta's Stone Mountain. Ex-Klan member Edgar J. Fuller described the ritual of that reincarnation in terms that ought to convince any doubters about the religious character of the doings. A rock served as an altar. A Bible lay next to the requisite sword and flag. The worshipers and oath-takers looked on by the light of a burning cross, which they also used to keep warm. William Joseph Simmons, who claimed once to have been a try-out for Methodist ministry but whose real love was fraternally ordered life, led the proceedings. Growth after that ceremony was slow at first. Not until June 7, 1920, when Simmons signed a contract with a promoter named Edward Young Clarke, did the Klan begin to prosper. Clarke and his live-in friend, wid-   3:80

owed Mrs. Elizabeth Tyler, helped Simmons convince people with latent Klan ideals to sign up and then to pay up. Much Klan activity was frankly designed for the personal profit of leaders who took advantage of the public.

3:81   Oaths and catechisms survive. In one popularly used ritual there were ten questions, including: "Are you a native-born white, Gentile, American citizen?" "Do you believe in the tenets of the Christian religion?" "Do you believe in and will you faithfully strive for the eternal maintenance of white supremacy?" Two of the questions left the opening for anti-Catholic action: "Are you absolutely opposed to and free of any allegiance of any nature to any cause, government, people, sect or ruler that is foreign to the U.S.A.?" And: "Do you esteem the U.S.A. and its institutions above any other government, civil, political, or ecclesiastical in the whole world?" Words like "sect" and "ecclesiastical" did not refer to the Baptist or Methodist churches; only one "sect" was supposed to fit the description. Hooded Americans would ward off its influence.

3:82   A section on the "Character of the Organization" in *Ideals of the Ku Klux Klan*, published in 1923, used the language of the primer to spell out the genius of the movement. "1. This is a white man's organization. 2. This is a gentile organization. 3. It is an American organization. 4. It is a Protestant organization." The Jew, said Klan leader Hiram Wesley Evans, did not fit because for two millennia he "rigidly adhered to a racial limitation of intermarriage which makes it impossible for him to be assimilated into American life wholly and unreservedly." The same Imperial Wizard could go further: not in a thousand years more could a Jew "form basic attachments comparable to those the older type of immigrant would form within a year." This mythical Jew had gotten the wandering habit in part thanks to the experience of persecutions. "He does not tie himself to the land," as the good American must.

3:83   Evans spoke formally for the Klan at its purest when he attacked immigrants, as he regularly did in the *Forum*. The pioneers who built America bequeathed to their own children a prior right to it, wrote Evans, so "no one on earth can claim any part of this inheritance except through our generosity." The mission of America "under Almighty God" was to perpetuate and develop just the kind of nation and civilization the forefathers created. "The American stock, which was bred under highly selective surroundings," should not be mongrelized.

Catholics as Catholics were the worst candidates for American   3:84
life, to be forever barred from becoming "100 per cent American
standard." They followed the pope, not the president; the Vatican,
not the White House. The priests taught "supreme loyalty to a
religious oligarchy that is not even of American domicile." In a
1923 Dallas speech, Evans became most pointed: "The real objection to Romanism in America is not that it is a religion—which
is no objection at all,—but that it is a church in politics; an organized, disciplined, powerful rival to every political government."
The Klansman offered a maxim which deliberately overlooked
Protestantism's own involvements: "A religion in politics is serious; a church in politics is deadly to free institutions."

Handbills were less genteel than these tracts and speeches. In   3:85
Indiana a popular broadside spelled out the Klan's moral program.
"Remember, every criminal, every gambler, every thug, every
libertine, every girl ruiner, every home wrecker, every wife
beater, every dope peddler, every moonshiner, every crooked
politician, every pagan Papist priest, every shyster lawyer, every
K. of C. [Knight of Columbus], every white slaver, every brothel
madam, every Rome controlled newspaper, every black spi-
der—is fighting the Klan. Think it over. Which side are you on?"

Blaine Mast in *K.K.K. Friend or Foe: Which?* wrote a Klan   3:86
defense using the menace theme. "A nation's greatest enemy is
never without—*It is always within*! The worse political enemy is
he who stirs up civil strife." Mast showed that he knew what the
events of the twentieth century keep teaching. A religious war, a
holy war, would make an ordinary civil war seem tame: "intolerant, lopsided, radical leaders are never safe to follow." His
counsel: follow instead the tolerant, balanced, moderate leaders
of the Klan.

While one Klan spokesman claimed wildly that 40,000 Prot-   3:87
estant ministers were members and that there were many fellow
travelers, Klansmen antagonized preachers of good sense. There
were reports that Klan members would enter church services,
make some threats or deliver their own sermons, and sometimes
try to win over congregations. Bare-knuckle brawls in some
Texas churches followed when anti-Klan churchgoers reacted. A
Shreveport, Louisiana, reporter in 1924 had to notice that "feeling concerning the Klan has been so intense for more than a year
that many of the churches have been divided in their congregations," and that "very little work has been done along religious
lines." The divisions sometimes worked to the benefit of the Klan

on occasions when clerics did take off their pulpit gowns and don Klan robes. A Houston Klan writer counted "the preachers of the Protestant faith almost solid for the Klan and its ideals" in Texas. Only here and there, he claimed, an isolated minister would "line up with the Catholics in their fight on Protestantism," but that kind of preacher was persona non grata almost anywhere in Texas.

3:88   As for Catholic response to it all, Michael Williams, editor of *Commonweal*, made use of Stanley Frost's *The Challenge of the Klan* to explain the Klan. Frost had quoted an unnamed correspondent with an insider's view, a man who concentrated on "the spiritual aspects of the Klan movement." Williams reported at second hand that this spirituality was closely allied with what he called orthodox fundamentalist American Protestantism. This faith was "firmly adhered to by millions of Anglo-Saxon Americans, particularly in the rural regions in the South and Midwest." These Americans felt menaced by Roman Catholicism, Judaism, and—here Williams and Frost and the observer added a proper twist—by "the growing liberalism within American Protestantism." Unlike these liberals, Klan members would "not change the 'faith' and the 'semblance of symbolism' " of Protestantism, but they "would change the machinery of government of the church itself."

3:89   Williams speculated as to whether the Klan represented rebellion in the Protestant church and saw signs to indicate that it did. Thus the secret organization would do to Protestantism what it hoped to do to the American government: capture it and hold control. The Klan, in Frost's reading, helped lessen the intolerance of one denomination toward another. Klansmen did attend church, and they boosted attendance. They gave financial aid to churches. Williams agreed with Frost's closing assessment. Klan members "believe that the danger to Protestantism lies in Catholic encroachments" and that Protestants who were themselves freed from creeds and denominationalism must stoutly resist Catholicism in America or be driven from the field. Protestantism as a religion must become militant. As for the rank and file members: "They feel the Klan is the power by which they, Klansmen, can do their best work for America and Protestantism itself."

3:90   Grand Wizard Hiram Wesley Evans knew his constituency well. They made up, he expounded, "a movement of the plain people, very weak in the matter of culture, intellectual support, and trained leadership." But Evans recognized that these people

were experiencing a sense of loss. They demanded what he called
"a return of power into the hands of the everyday, not highly
cultured, not overly intellectualized, but entirely unspoiled and
not de-Americanized, average citizen of the old stock." Evans,
who was momentarily being provided a forum in the respectable
North American Review, almost took pride in his humility among
the "hicks" and "rubes" and "drivers of second hand Fords."
Together this company would persist in opposing "the intellectuals and liberals who held the leadership, [and] betrayed Americanism"; they were people "from whom we expect to wrest
control."

The division within churches that led the public to see the   3:91
Klansman as the Protestant conservative fighting the Protestant
liberal helped keep the Klan from exerting even more influence
than it did. The liberal was seen as too compromising; amazingly,
too friendly to Catholics and, less amazingly, to Jews; too open
to Communism and radicalism, but, most of all, insufficiently
moral. A Klan leader put the case for the Klan's own vision well.
Toleration, he complained, was a luxury available to Catholics,
Jews, secularists, and certain sorts of Protestants. However, that
tolerance "becomes a vice when fundamentals are in danger."
American liberals, he thought, even extended their liberality so
far that they were apparently willing "to help the aliens tear at the
foundation of the nation." Evans moved such liberals within Protestantism toward a tie for first place in villainy: they had become
"one of the chief menaces of the country" themselves and,
against much evidence, he charged that they gave "an almost joyous welcome to alien criticism of everything American." While
he charged that they represented an unopposed attack on the Puritan conscience, sometimes, he thought, these liberals seemed
ashamed of having any conscience at all. Liberals favored tolerance more than conviction, and that was fatal.

Some of the denominational papers were timid at first, not   3:92
knowing how to assess the degree of Klan sympathy within the
churches, but when some editors did speak up, they became emphatic. The Methodist *Northwestern Christian Advocate* turned a
Klan claim against itself: "the K.K.K. No Per Cent American."
The *Baptist*, at the end of the Red Scare, used Northern Baptist
voices to turn the rhetoric of the era against the Klan. "White
Faces, but Red Hands" bannered an editorial. The editor was
wary: "In the name of liberty, humanity, Christianity and the
principles of Americanism, we must denounce this order as crimi-

nal and dangerous. No communist conspiracy could be more so." And Northern Methodist bishop Edwin Holt Hughes gave a good sample of theologically rich reply: "It is not Anglo-Saxon blood, but the blood of Jesus Christ that has made us what we are." Decades later it may strike some as strange to recall that such mild examples reflected courage on the part of those who spoke thus in the twenties.

3:93   Catholics fought back. Two direct confrontations occurred in the period. The first had to do with what came to be called the "bogus oath" of the Knights of Columbus. No one knows quite how the purported "Fourth Degree" oath of the Knights came to be invented, but plenty of these Knights had occasion to become aware of its circulation in 1921. The *New York World* gave it publicity. Eighteen other newspapers took up the Rowland Thomas exposé from the *World*, and there were additional serious calls for examination of the background to the hoax. Soon both the Klan and the Knights were calling for congressional investigations of each other's patriotism. But when Simmons testified for the Klan, he stressed the organization's law-abiding character so strenuously that no follow-up investigation occurred; he almost succeeded in getting the Knights investigated instead.

3:94   The bogus-oath issue was too bizarre to serve as an enduring front for anti-Catholic action. Catholic parochial schools therefore provided a second and better target. These schools had sometimes been suspect during World War I as un-American, especially because in some communities their instruction occurred in German, the language of the current enemy. The best chance the Klan had to perpetuate the suspicions in the twenties was in Oregon, where a nativist climate prevailed. Major Luther I. Powell, a Kleagle from Louisiana, in 1921 invaded the state to exploit the negative ethos. Powell wanted to unite all the existing anti-Catholic groups against parochial schools and for "one hundred percent Americanism." He would regularly feature someone billed as an "escaped nun" or someone else who could lure Protestant ministers in order to bring their sympathy to the Klan cause.

3:95   The new coalition, concentrating on the University of Oregon, kept Catholics there from organizing a Newman Club. As such activities spread, Governor Ben Olcott stood up to the Klan for its "fanaticism, race hatred, religious prejudice, and all of those evil influences which tend toward factional strife and terror." The governor thereby picked up enemies who helped unseat him in the election of 1922. A bill requiring public education for all Oregon-

ian children subsequently passed, with the support of the Klan
and some fraternal orders. Catholics, fronted by the Knights, had
only four years to appeal before the threatened phase-out of their
schools.

The Klan program against the governor and against Catholic   3:96
schools was based on a familiar strategy, one set forth by Exalted
Cyclops J. R. Johnson against the governor. Johnson listed some
"generally recognized facts." First, "the United States was
founded by Protestants of the white race, mainly Anglo-Saxons."
Second, "every race predominantly Protestant has been and is a
progressive free people." And third, the Klan "presupposes its
right to establish and carry on an organization exclusively American," which Catholics were not.

The Catholic hierarchy and the Knights of Columbus wasted   3:97
some time arguing over who should fund, fight, and take credit
for any achievements against the Klan. The Knights even complained that the bishops were not militant enough in protecting
their own interests. But the Klan, with internal scandals plaguing
it, had overstepped, and cooler heads among non-Catholics in
Oregon sensed this. Then on June 1, 1925, Justice James C.
McReynolds of the United States Supreme Court ruled the Oregon act unconstitutional. Significantly, he did not cite the First
Amendment, which assured religious freedom. Instead he talked
about property interests of the Catholic sisters who owned the
schools and of parents who invested in them. The Act, said the
court, "unreasonably interferes with the liberty of parents and
guardians to direct the upbringing and education of children under
their control."

One question haunts: what led ordinary Americans to be be-   3:98
guiled into channeling their resentments through a hate organization like the Klan? Some observers from the time offered clues.
An obscure citizen named Aldrich Blake understood Klan psychology: "When a man joins the Ku Klux Klan, a sensation seems
to come over him as definite as falling in love. He simply drops
out of society and enters a new world." Such a recruit henceforth
knew where he stood. A million members on any day could have
agreed with Imperial Klokard William James Mahoney's summary: "We magnify the Bible—as the basis of our Constitution,
the foundation of our government, the source of our laws." Members, he said, honored Christ "as the Klansman's only *criterion
of character.*" Members had to be "moved by unselfish motives,
such as characterized our Lord the Christ."

3:99   The testimonies are consistent: the Klan had a churchly character or one which rivaled that of churches. After the 1924 Klan
convention, a Pennsylvania Exalted Cyclops captured the ethos:
"I've attended a lot of church gatherings and conventions, . . .
but I never attended one where the revival spirit was as pronounced as it was at the Klan Klonvocation." He exulted: "The
Klan stood for the same things as the Church, but we did the
things the Church wouldn't do." Sociologist John Mecklin
grasped the moral sense of it all. He watched how "men joined
the Klan because it appealed to their patriotism and their moral
idealism more than to their hates and prejudices." Thus, he said,
the Klan gained community footholds "in the role of moral reformer, unearthing the bootlegger or chastising criminals and disreputable characters that have escaped the law." Mecklin
accurately located some of the appeal of the Klan. The people
saw themselves as elites, as members of an aristocracy of morals.

3:100   Millions of Americans, including Protestant ministers who resisted and faced threat of assassination, abhorred the Klan. But it
would be an underestimation of tribalism in the twenties to minimize the place the Klan found in the American fit of the times.
Mecklin, on the scene to report as early as 1924, observed: "If
the Klan were utterly un-American it could never have succeeded
as it has. The Klan was not alien to American society. If it were,
the problem would be much simpler." Mecklin had read in the
New York World that the Klan was alien, destructive, "'tunnel-
ing, molelike, under the whole structure of American institutions'." After reading that, he responded. The Klan, he thought,
instead drew inspiration from above-ground "ancient prejudice,
classical hatreds, and ingrained social habits." And Mecklin used
an appropriate medical metaphor: "The germs of the disease of
the Klan, like germs in the human body, have long been present
in the social organism and needed only the weakening of the social tissue to become malignant." In the decades to come, few
improved on his discernment of the social tissue of the times.

3:101   While more nearly respectable anti-Catholics, anti-Semites,
anti-blacks, and anti-immigrants could find discreet organizations
and moderate-sounding language to protect the America they
loved and would guard, the resenters who made up the Klan had
access to a bold and offensive vocabulary, ritual, and costumery.
Plenty of such recruits were temporarily available. Estimates suggest that in the early 1920s the Klan probably had four million
members. Since the hooded citizens had to be male, white, and

native-born Protestant adults, they were thus drawn from a cohort
of limited size. The Klan controlled decisive political forces in at
least Indiana and Ohio and had influence in California, Oklahoma, Kansas, Texas, Arkansas, and Oregon—none of these being states in the heart of Dixie, where the Reconstruction-era Klan
had triumphed.

Shortly after its greatest successes, the Klan fell into sudden   3:102
decline. Tornados go as they come. Frenzies quiet even as they
rise to fury. As the true colors of the Klan showed, many moderates backed off. Good sense prevailed. Other fraternal orders or
churches filled again the need people had for association. Resentments that are disproportionate to threats do not always last. But
enemies of the Klan got their greatest help from the Klan leadership, which was corrupt to the core. It advertised itself as moralist
but was immoral. Promoter Ed Clarke, who was said for a time
to have netted $40,000 per month by extracting personal funds
from each new membership, had to share a cut with Mrs. Tyler,
and he also had high liquor bills. Then the drunkenness of Simmons became public knowledge, and that shocked the prohibitionist members. Ed Clarke and Bessie Tyler had been arrested
back in 1916 for being drunk and half-clad, and word of it finally
spread. Such scandals undercut the Klan.

Dentist Hiram Wesley Evans was an exception. He was too   3:103
respectable and outraged to let disgraced rivals escape with their
reputations intact. He made a point of Clarke's being known as a
wife-deserter, a man who consorted with a major black leader
(Marcus Garvey), and an indicted person who had to face trial for
shipping whisky and for white slavery. Yet in Clarke's prime he
had done most for the Klan. Simmons also survived attacks for a
time. But in state after state the Klan overreached. There were
beatings, floggings, fights, and threats which, taken together, vio-
lated the sensibilities of too many Americans, including the simpler folk who might be described as the half-innocent Klan rank
and file. Attendance at meetings dropped off. The Klan rallied a
bit to help oppose Catholic Alfred E. Smith for the presidency of
the United States in 1928, but more credible Protestants and prohibitionists were fighting him, and the Klan was becoming irrelevant to such causes.

Our Hobbesian observation that in the twenties there seemed   3:104
to be "a condition of war of everyone against everyone" in
America but that almost no one was killed finds a rare exception
in the Klan experience. Charles P. Sweeney, writing in the *Na-*

tion, told a story from the summer of 1921. According to this account, E. R. Stephenson, a former Methodist minister, seethed with anti-Catholicism. Indeed, his daughter told the *Birmingham News* he particularly hated Father James E. Coyle, pastor of St. Paul's Roman Catholic Church in Birmingham. The daughter, it turns out, was in love with a Catholic, and she eventually turned Catholic. Father Coyle also officiated at her wedding. The Reverend Mr. Stephenson later acknowledged that for those reasons he went to Coyle's porch on August 14 and shot the priest to death.

3:105   Sweeney editorialized about the climate in which the murderer was set free on bond. "The sign is up. No Catholics are wanted in Birmingham and those now there are desired to leave." In popular fancy, to be a Catholic was to be a soldier of a secret army, sworn at the pope's command to "burn the nation, slaughter the Protestant men, outrage the Protestant women, and flog the Protestant children into being obedient little Catholics." Stephenson, according to Sweeney, believed all that. The Methodists had dropped him as a kind of clerical shyster, so he had found new outlets in the Ku Klux Klan. His daughter remembered that her father "had a robe of one of the organizations at home and on Hallowe'en night I wore it."

3:106   The northern liberal writer in the *Nation* decried the climate in which the Coyle murder took place at the biggest Catholic church in the Alabama city. Overlooking the fact that the Klan was also at home in the North and the West, he wrote of the southern Klan, "It is all very well for us of the North or West to dismiss its manifestations with a shrug or a shudder. Bigotry is as much a product of a considerable section of the South as is cotton. Both are therefore essentially American products and as such the concern of every decent American." But the Birmingham press, Sweeney thought, was ill-serving the nation. It gave no clue that "behind what was apparently the isolated act of a madman were marshaled the sinister forces of a great militant movement." It would take some time before the militancy would be countered, the sinister force exposed to view, or the mad acts would disappear. Surviving them meanwhile were apparently milder attempts to keep Protestant America "100 percent American."

4

The Challenges
of the Other
Americans

Native Americans: The Quiet Exceptions on the Reservations

Will America remain Protestant and Anglo-Saxon?" An- 4:1
dré Siegfried's question serves a second time to frame the discussion of "the essential characteristic of the post-war period in the
United States." What this European visitor had diagnosed as a
"nervous reaction of the original American stock" persisted beyond the Red Scare incident, debates about immigration restrictions, or the storms caused by the Ku Klux Klan.

How should the people who were or thought they were of the 4:2
original American stock relate to millions of alien types who were
already citizens? This question haunted many Americans. These
challengers were people who were minding their business, but
whose very presence threatened the majority group and might one
day surround or displace it. What would soon happen to Protestant dominance, to the claim that the old-stock Americans should
have the privilege of being custodians of culture? What part
should the clergy play? Siegfried singled them out: "It is largely
due to the Protestant minister, *whose influence has been growing
since the War*, that the well-meaning but timorous middle class
has been awakened to certain fears." Among these were "the fear

of Catholicism, atheism, and evolution; of wine and European immorality; of radicals, Bolshevists, and revolutionaries; of invasion by *blacks, yellows, and Latin-Slavs*; and of the mongrelizing of the race." Where in this list, where among their fears, were to be found the *real* original-stock Americans, the Native Americans, then called Indians? As contemporaries, they were not in Siegfried's book, just as they were out of sight and out of mind so far as most American citizens were concerned.

4:3   As Siegfried wrote for foreign consumption, E. A. Ross addressed domestic readers. He knew that the mere "nervous reaction" of which Siegfried spoke could easily turn violent when anyone thwarted the purposes of the fearful. "Interference of interests is likely to engender hatred," Ross wrote, "for our innate pugnacity is stirred against those who continually come between us and our goal." His list of obstructors more or less matched

Missionary efforts by Christians among Native Americans persist in the 1920s: Jesuit missionary Father Cataldo speaks at the old Sacred Heart Mission at Cataldo, Idaho, to a thousand Spokane people who formed a caravan to greet him. (Jesuit Province of Oregon.)

Siegfried's: "the masses," emotional as they were, he said, hated *immigrant Chinese, Slavs, negroes from the south*; "we come to hate supplanters." As with Siegfried, so with Ross and the other analysts on the scene: the Native American had vanished. Five times in one book Ross showed an awareness of the Indians, but never as contemporary threats.

After three hundred years and for the first time, Native Ameri- 4:4 cans evidently were not on the public agenda of European-Americans. Georg Simmel, a European theorist of conflict who was read by at least one American, Ross, had explained that "a certain amount of discord, inner divergence and outer controversy, is organically tied up with the very elements that ultimately hold a group together." Then came his informing insight: "It is *expedient* to hate the adversary with whom one fights (for any reason), just as it is expedient to love a person whom one is tied to and has to get along with." Native Americans were so far removed that it was no longer expedient to hate them. They had few functions in the white American world. But they were also making their adjustments to the assaults of American modernity; Native Americans were religious, and they had lives of their own to live.

From the English arrival in 1607 until the immediate past, Na- 4:5 tive Americans had served as one of the most effective binders of European-American life. But back at Wounded Knee, South Dakota, in 1890 their threat and their trail had come to a bloody end. For three decades thereafter, whites had become ever more efficient at keeping them remote on their reservations. They played a part in the lives of the few white Americans who lived on the borders of their reservations, in the files of Washington's Bureau of Indian Affairs, in the Western films in vogue in the twenties, and in the mythic world of the American past.

The United States Constitution had set the original terms for 4:6 what was still being worked out legally 150 years later. It authorized Congress "to regulate Commerce with foreign Nations, . . . and with the Indian Tribes," thus in effect treating natives as foreigners. Chief Justice John Marshall, in an 1831 decision, furthered this defining. He talked of Indians as "domestic dependent nations." In Marshall's ruling, "they occupy a territory to which we assert a title independent of their will." Thenceforth they looked for protection to what the justice then called "our" government. Marshall declared that Indians relied upon this government's kindness and its power, as when they addressed the president as their great father.

4:7   The next stage of defining occurred with the passage of the General Allotment Act, often called the Dawes Act, which took effect in 1887 near the end of the Indian trail. This Act looked like a fair economic and political resolution of difficulties. But it also heralded a new kind of attack on tribal life, culture, and religion that was still going on in the 1920s. After Dawes, if an Indian—now officially regarded as an independent citizen and not a part of the tribe—adopted what the Dawes Act called "the habits of civilized life" and met certain other terms, he or she could thereby be "declared to be a citizen of the United States." During the time this policy lasted, Indians lost 90,000,000 acres of land, largely to white purchasers.

4:8   One glance ahead: in 1934, just after policy changes effectually revoked the force of the Dawes Act, a report for the Office of Indian Affairs reviewed the ways the allotment policy had achieved what old treaties and wars had failed to do. It had broken down the internal organization and culture of the Indian tribes. The report said that after the Act, agents, white superintendents, and missionaries often superseded Indian leaders and to a large extent succeeded in destroying Indian culture. This report also admitted that during what it called an "autocratic phase of the Federal policy," the guiding concepts of United States policy *intended* the destruction of all Indian tribal bonds. This policy would efface Indian languages and cultural heritages and blend the Native Americans, separated from their tribal bonds, into the larger white culture. Of course, Indians put up resistance, if often of a silent sort. They found ways to uphold the integrity of tribes and to perpetuate many forms of their worship and ritual. Thus Native Americans remained at least potentially a theoretical problem for a nation whose citizens devoted little energy to the issue.

4:9   Curiously, it was in 1924, the very year which saw immigration restriction laws work against the possibilities of citizenship for many other peoples, that citizenship rights were enhanced for the one-third of the Indian population which had not yet met the terms of the franchise. The Indian Citizenship Act (43 Stat. 1255) included as its key passage the declaration "that all noncitizen Indians born within the territorial limits of the United States be, and they are hereby, declared to be citizens of the United States." The follow-up Indian Reorganization Bill of 1934 was designed to "stabilize the tribal organization of Indian tribes by vesting such tribal organizations with real, though limited, authority." By then it was almost too late for them to recover.

Ordinary life went on, of course, on the reservations, whether   4:10
or not the rest of America noticed much of it. Anthropologists
focused close-up on such life. But our concern is with the *public*
dimensions of the lives of peoples, those aspects that came to be
a part of the political agenda. On that scene, the Indian, as we
have said, was rarely visible. Theologians paid almost no attention to native North American religion. In 500 pages of reference
to hundreds of organizations, the *Year Book of the Churches* listed
only two which touched on Indians. One was a paternalistic, nonpolitical, nonsectarian, and noneffective Indian Rights Association. The other was the National Indian Association. Its stated
main concern was to direct undenominational teaching of religious truths where no Christian instruction was being given by
any other agency.

The religious census of 1926 did not even set out to assess the   4:11
statistical strength of Indian religion. The Federal Council of
Churches, while it was the most effective and alert religious so-
cial-service agency, in its report on the twenty years past devoted
barely one and a half pages out of over 300 to Native Americans.
The drafters of the report only pointed to the desperate situation
of reservation Indians and the need for better missionary activity
among them. They concluded by stating that now the goal of well-
intentioned people must be "integrating the Indians into the surrounding civilization" or helping them cope along the way. That
was all. Such treatment makes very clear that there was no longer
any danger that Indians would be supplanters of white culture,
that they could block or interfere with the interests of citizens who
lived far from them, or that Indians would be, as they had been
for centuries before, the most useful objects of hate. If religiously
based conflict over Indian affairs did in fact endure, the documents from the time suggest that it was largely noiseless.

Now and again, however, controversies of religious import be-   4:12
tween the chief governmental agents, the successive commissioners of the Bureau of Indian Affairs, were sufficiently visible to
warrant inclusion in the record though they were never vivid
enough to produce front-page news. Most of their battles dealt
with competing views about government treatment of Native
Americans and of the values of Indian ritual. In 1920 an amateur
authority, Walter M. Camp, filed a typed report on "The Condition of Reservation Indians" with the United States Board of Indian Commissioners. His work exposed to view the polarities
with which the board and its agents worked. During seventeen

years of Indian-watching in the West, Camp came to see what he termed a "difference of mental attitude as between the two races," because the Indians were savage or primitive. He charged that they suffered from an "excess of hospitality" and communistic ideas. Camp urged that in the future they have more association, including intermarriage, with white people. The well-meaning reviewer concluded: "We should do all that is within our power to elevate [the Indian]."

4:13   How to elevate the Indian became the central theme of attentive leaders. The opinions of Charles Henry Burke, commissioner from 1921 to 1929, and his notable successor once removed, John Collier, displayed opposing views of Indian life. Burke thought Indian religion was nothing more than degrading ceremonialism. He wanted to keep Native Americans under the age of fifty even from observing tribal dances, which he thought were orgiastic, lascivious, and immoral. Also during this period the controversial Native American Church was developing its cultus, which included the sacramental chewing of peyote by participants. True, its observers had to note, the worshipers in this sect gained from their rites what mainstream fellow Christians did from theirs: a sense of meaning and belonging along with heightened morale and incentive for moral action. The hallucinogenic plant, however, was legally, medically, and morally suspect. Burke's enforcement officers therefore hounded the chewers when they celebrated their sacrament.

4:14   Some Indians fought back against such policing. They had not received help in this cause from older defense organizations. The Society of American Indians, which held its last meeting in 1923, had itself opposed the use of peyote. In 1926 its replacement, the National Council of American Indians, continued the opposition. Yet some new agents and organizations helped legitimate these tribal practices and the existence of the suspect Native American Church itself. Their most durable champion, the social worker but future commissioner John Collier, helped form the American Indian Defense Association in 1923. With the assistance of well-placed friends, this reformer began to win gains for Native Americans at the expense of the older and compromising Indian Rights Association. Collier argued that the criticized dances and ceremonies were integral to Indian religion. To ban them was to violate the constitutional rights of these new citizens. Finally in 1933, a year after he became commissioner of Indian affairs, Collier successfully removed the prohibitions against tribal customs.

Native Americans did experience selective gains. In open en-   4:15
counter with Burke, Collier gradually prevailed while his enemy
increasingly tired. For example, in earlier stages Burke had tried
to force Taos Pueblo Indians to forgo a traditional eighteen-month
initiation period into the tribal ways and to promote instead com-
pulsory day-school education. Collier defended the initiation.
Burke eventually came to see that reports from Christian missionaries had been exaggerating tribal excesses. Still, as long as he
could, he held his ground, considering Collier a "notorious Indian agitator."

Religious issues were thus still at stake among the first   4:16
Americans on their reservations. Years after the controversy the
empathic Collier in his autobiography looked back on his experiences in what he called the Red Atlantis which had been Indian
culture. He was quick to point out in pioneering literature that
Native Americans long opposed the impulse simply to become
consumers. They remained in rebellion against the merely secular
but culturally dominant styles of life in much of surrounding
America.

In the pueblos especially, Collier saw the continuance of what   4:17
he called "the power of art—of life-making art." The friend of
Indians turned eloquent as he described to the white world the
"solitary vigils which carried the individual out into the cosmos." He remembered "communal rituals whose grave, tranquil
yet earth-shaking intensity," as he put it, "is not adequately
suggested by anything outside the music of Bach." Collier saw
that the significance of the ceremonies was never merely local
but also universal. Yet few whites knew or cared about any of
this. He complained that non-Indians never did bother to learn
enough from these "possessors and users of the fundamental
secret of human life," and that this ignorance meant a loss for
white America. Yet in respect to peoplehood, politics, and the
defining of Protestant America, it was clear that despite his defenses of their separateness, the Indians had become virtually
useless. It was no longer expedient to hate the Native Americans.
Collier ended his recollections pessimistically. Looking ahead
toward the future pressures on Native American community and
ritual, he added one gloomy prospect to all the others: "It might
be, as well, that the Indian life would not survive." In any case,
it had cruelly come to be beside the point for the non–Native
Americans who were defining themselves and trying to hold or
gain power.

African-Americans: "The Colour Problem as an Abyss"

4:18   Inexpedient though it was to hate a second people, black Americans or African-Americans, much of white America still found reasons to do so. This hate was expensive. For example, in 1919 a young Chicago black swam across a line that the community had drawn figuratively to prevent mixing of races along the beaches on the Lake Michigan shore. Probably as a result of some rock-throwing by whites, the boy drowned. An angered black community reacted, and conflict broke out. A week of riots followed during Chicago's "Red Summer," leaving 38 dead and 537 injured citizens. While religion played no part in this unholy war and while the churches were neither agents of conflict nor major contributors to reconciliation, they thereafter did have to face a nation in which race rioting became a constant urban threat in black communities where the churches were the most stable institutions. In a "race war" in Tulsa, Oklahoma, thirty people, twenty-one of them black, were killed. There were other traumas. By 1919 the era of lynchings had not yet ended. And the renewed Ku Klux Klan, though it no longer concentrated principally on blacks, still reflexively stirred hatred against them.

4:19   "Will America Remain Protestant and Anglo-Saxon?" From 1619 to 1919 blacks were constantly on the minds of Americans, particularly in the South. If they turned Christian, they almost always became Protestant, but still they remained a threat to Anglo-Saxonism. What was new in the twenties was their increasing presence in the North and thus as a national influence. In these years in New York a celebrated Harlem Renaissance took secular form, but it did not displace the churches from their central roles in the lives of African-Americans. Blacks in segregation as in slavery before it were religious and provoked religious issues. They could not be out of sight and out of mind as Indians were. Precisely the opposite: they were coming more and more into the field of vision and into ever more neighborhoods of northern whites, whose ways of life these internal migrants jostled and threatened. Conflict seemed inevitable.

4:20   In the formal sense, it is true that religion had little to do with the bloodier moments of the conflict and may on occasion even have served slightly to moderate it. The clash was usually over racial and sexual fears, threats to property values and the economic status quo, taboos and jobs, territory, and peace of mind. Yet white Americans then as before used the language of faith to justify the way they handled their anxieties while blacks similarly used their religion to provide rationales for their ways of life. So long as blacks remained in Methodist or Baptist churches, as most of them did, white counterparts in such movements respected their loyalty to Jesus Christ and their church—but not next door. That is, the northern churches grew increasingly segregated, adopting southern patterns of church life as more of the black South moved north.

Northerners expressed increasing appreciation for the bibli-   4:21
cally based forms of black worship, however unacceptable these expressions would have been in most white churches. Northern white congregations regularly took up offerings for the black spiritual singers whose choirs toured suburban strongholds. They gave some money for missions and education among the southern poor. If once upon a time Christian theology had been used to legitimate slavery and then suppression, now it was more rare to make the case against blacks on such spiritual grounds. Despite moderating signs, however, it is still more appropriate to assess the distance than the nearness between the races and also to notice the tension that arose when some blacks turned their backs on conventional Christianity.

While conflict between whites and blacks was therefore not a   4:22
crusade, not holy war, this did not mean that it was not grave. What American, white or black, could possess enough emotional distance to appraise the problems fairly? A foreigner with a clear eye best provides perspective: for a third time, André Siegfried. When he cast a visitor's eye on this "colour problem," he spoke in a rare apocalyptic voice. "No matter which way we turn in the North or the South, there seems to be no solution. The colour problem is an abyss into which we can look only with terror." In respect to the South, the French writer almost mourned: "Every-thing is poisoned, even religion." Where the color question was concerned, the white race had lost all sense of justice. Everything in respect to it, even crime, was permissible. To a man in search of conscience, this observation was most telling: "Religion has no restraining influence, for the churches are divided into black and white; and the conscience of the Christian no longer suggests that he is doing wrong in maltreating the inferior race."

It was not yet clear to Siegfried in 1927 just how the Baptist   4:23
and Methodist ministers among the southern black majority would react to all the changes, but he saw they were born leaders and even when they looked illiterate and undeserving they had

great influence among black masses. In the North, he noted that it took courage for churches to face the race issue. He credited the YMCA and the Federal Council of Churches of Christ with having adopted the Christian viewpoint without hesitation or reserve. Siegfried discerned no ulterior motive in their attempts, but even as he recognized purity in their motives he knew that they had had to make a thousand compromises to hold the loyalty of their supporters as they ventured into controversial territory.

4:24   As for the traditional black churches, scholars Benjamin Mays and Joseph Nicholson chronicled their status in these crisis years. In *The Negro's Church* these coauthors accounted for more than a million Negroes who moved during the twenties from the southern rural districts; 650,000 to southern cities and 450,000 to northern cities. They observed thus that in the five years after 1920 the southern Negro farm population dropped by 789,736 people. Henceforth, then, the southern story became also increasingly urban. In both cases, the black congregations arrived in a zone where more interaction was possible between races than there had been in the hollows, swamps, and rural areas of the old South. The new situation meant that leadership would be tested as never before. Clergy still constituted the main elite in the black community, though they increasingly shared status with those intellectuals in the Harlem Renaissance and with the organizers in the Urban League, the National Association for the Advancement of Colored People, and some labor unions.

4:25   The Methodist and Baptist churches produced the most impressive statistics. In 1926, for instance, the pioneer African Methodist Episcopal Church claimed 750,000 adherents while the rival African Methodist Episcopal Zion church numbered 500,000 and the Colored Methodist Episcopal 350,000. Together these figures showed that this non-Anglo-Saxon form of Methodism was one of the largest clusters among all Protestant bodies in America. It was harder to count the Baptists, since they were fiercely congregational and, because usually unconnected with each other and unmonitored, they were unnumbered. Certainly millions were members. Their congregations could be found in small storefronts or sizable churches. Thus Olivet Baptist, near the site of the Chicago riots, claiming 8,430 members in 1919, became America's largest Protestant congregation of any race in the 1920s.

4:26   Some Christians made heroic and quite successful efforts to bridge black and white worlds. Benjamin Mays was a rare leader who could work on both sides. A University of Chicago M.A. in 1925 and Ph.D. in 1935, Mays from his Atlanta base at Morehouse College was in the forefront of religious and educational enterprises and scholarship. Equally visible as a moderator was George Edmund Haynes, who during the twenty-five years after 1922 was the Federal Council's choice to lead its Commission on Race Relations. A southerner from Pine Bluff, Arkansas, this Fisk University graduate, who studied sociology under William Graham Sumner at Yale and then received a Ph.D. from Columbia, was well suited to his task.

Haynes published *The Trend of the Races* in 1922. He reflected   4:27
the mood of the Commission on Interracial Co-operation, which two southern preachers, Methodist Will Alexander and Presbyterian John Eagan, organized in 1929. In their spirit, Haynes warned whites that blacks were losing patience and were becoming ever less docile. He served notice that white Christians had to become better-informed about blacks. To aid them, Haynes spelled out some differences between the contending camps within the black community. He located socialist labor leader A. Philip Randolph and the Garveyite "Back to Africa" people on the Left. The NAACP, the symbolic focus of the center, went about its work to secure rights on mainly secular grounds. Haynes also spotted a large right-wing among those who sought opportunity and justice but still conciliation in preference to agitation.

Haynes had to play safe. He could not too frankly promote   4:28
desegregation of races everywhere. He knew how slow the largely white denominations would be to move toward any measure of racial integration. Forming committees of concern and care, he thought, might be the best way for gradualists to build bridges. So the bridge builder in 1923 helped invent Race Relations Sunday, only to see it often derided by militants as a mere token measure. He worked to gain church support for antilynching laws. Haynes fought off Communist influence in the black community. Despite his good efforts, the Federal Council provided few funds and did not offer sufficient support to help him promote progress.

Women took the more aggressive role in race relations, though   4:29
in a limited sphere, within the mainstream Protestant churches. The Federal Council established a Woman's Committee and saw Katherine Gardner turn it vital. Against greater odds, southern women were even more active. In 1920 Methodists appointed a Women's Commission on Race Relations, led by people who also took part in National Association of Colored Women's Club meet-

ings. By 1925 the Commission on Race Relations of the Woman's Missionary Council included 1,571 local interracial committees of Methodists. Presbyterian women started similar organizations, some of which had the courage to stand in open defiance of the norms and practices of their own church body. To cite such networks seems not very exciting; the names of these organizations sound like routine committees of church bureaucracies. Yet in many local communities they were the vanguard organizations which disrupted the superficial serenity of denominational life.

4:30   Almost nothing better illustrates the difficulty of effecting racial change than does notice of the danger that befell those in the churches who supported antilynching legislation. Southern Methodist bishops often lost popularity when they named lynching "the crime of crimes." Some lower-ranking Methodist ministers were themselves members of the Klan. While the Klan in its second incarnation in the twenties did not include lynching in its program and while those ministers were not likely to have been direct partisans of lynch mobs, they contributed to a climate in which the murder of accused and hunted blacks could take place without massive disapproval. Through the decade many delegates to southern church conventions opposed the antilynching laws which southern Methodist women often promoted vigorously and courageously.

4:31   Some largely northern denominations passed resolutions favoring Negro rights, but few of these were daring. In 1916 the Northern Baptist Convention had begun boldly facing the abyss of terror. Its leaders said that the "barbarous assumption of racial superiority" needed to be faced by those who would emphasize the spirit of Christ in race relations. In 1929, when there should have been plenty of reason for reconciling activities, however, the convention's Committee on Interracial Cooperation dozed. It noted that for the previous few years it had found nothing definite to do, and asked for no appropriation for its work. Thus the nearly comatose group went on, "during the last year it has, therefore, done no work and has no report to make." The committee, its representatives said, could reiterate important principles, but thought that such activity would not be of value. This expression of resignation from a church body with a better record on race relations than others was dispiriting.

4:32   Even efforts regarded as mildly progressive in their day were based on outlooks which in a later time are seen as simply racist. Episcopal bishop Theodore D. Bratton, a sort of Social Gospel activist and reformer, provided a celebrated example of racial condescension and employed it as an instrument. In 1922 Bratton wrote *Wanted—Leaders! A Study of Negro Development*. He argued that both self-seeking whites and a bad cultural environment were responsible for what he called Negro backwardness. The time had come, Bratton argued, for Christians to use sentiment and science to bring about change.

Bratton remained cooped within the framework of the racial   4:33
assumptions of his time. He stopped far short of calling for any kind of social equality. The route of progress meant that all people should be just, but their actions never dared to begin the destruction of racial segregation. Had Bratton believed in anything more than that, or pushed further, he would have gotten no hearing at all in the climate of his day. Nor would it have occurred to the bishop to promote the cause any further. Blacks, he kept observing, followed a way of life which in the present stage of cultural development seemed to fall "little short of savage morality."

If there were mild progressives, the retrogressives in this case   4:34
were more prominent, more vocal than they. Georgia congressman William C. Lankford wanted to sound theological and did so in remarks reprinted in the *Congressional Record*. On the matter of human origins, he began orthodoxly enough: God created man of the dust of the earth and molded this into His own image. But then in the retelling there followed some free enterprise of imagination. God, Lankford went on, had made man to be "a part of God Himself; a Caucasian, a white man, and God gave that first white man dominion over all things, and . . . that first man, a white man, went forth to solve, understand, conquer, and know the universe in which he had been placed." Lankford had no way of accounting for the black man. Extremist E. H. Randle did not reach back to Adam; he needed to go only to Noah. "All Caucasian races can be traced to Noah by history, mythology, customs, language, and tradition," he wrote, conveniently forgetting that even historic racist myths had seldom gone as far as that. They had ordinarily divided the human family into three races when retelling the story of the sons of Noah.

Robert Edwin Smith attracted few readers for his work on   4:35
Christianity and Race Relations; such books are better seen as representative than individually influential. Smith assumed that both races valued separate social life, so he made his suggestions for progress within that context. For reform, Smith turned with hope to the white Christian clergy. They must, he urged, "cry

aloud against injustice, oppression, and every other evil that afflicts the land." Yet in the end all he could think to ask for was right thinking, which did not amount to much. Right thinking in what he claimed was the mind of Christ still led him to urge that "negroes must recognize the supremacy of the white man and be willing to be a good second." For now, "the Caucasian race," said this man without evident hate, "seems destined to lead all other races. Only the shifting of the now apparent purposes of the Supreme Arbiter of Nations will make it otherwise."

4:36   Moderates did not have life easy, even when they worked with such a limited and timid vision. Fire-breathers were always at hand to counter them. Thus in 1928 one George Mallison raged against efforts by such moderates to promote brotherhood. He heard that some people he called radicals were advocating eventual "commergence" of white and black races. Mallison studied the sources of such calls and found something upsetting: "The doctrine of the brotherhood of man, operating through organized religious bodies, has been, since the Negro first appeared in America, a disturbing, disorganizing influence pointing inevitably toward social equality and eventual amalgamation." Instead, he admonished, in complete accord with their Christian spirit the whites should aid all backward people by example. Believers could be helpful in every practical way consistent with preserving the white race, "with its accompanying civilization and religious faith." If, however, there was to be any eradication of the line between the white race and the black race, "in furtherance of the Middle Age [s sic] and uncritical interpretation of the Scripture in regard to the brotherhood of man," then indeed it would be time for another Reformation in America. "An exalted religion can exist only among a people of the highest type." Degenerate race-mixing would take away standards so that one could never again recover integrity through the profession of faith.

4:37   Since Protestants often discriminated against Roman Catholics, the Catholic church might well have made commoι. cause with other despised peoples. Thus Catholics could have been expected to help form a defensive alliance with other non-Anglo-Saxons or non-Protestants to wage cultural war against the dominant white Protestant majority. Yet few observers credited Catholicism with ever transcending its own boundaries of racial prejudice. W. E. B. Du Bois, the black intellectual who, having turned his back on the Protestant churches years before and who was already then turning ever further toward the political left, in

1925 focused on Catholicism. He argued that in both North and South Catholicism represented color separation and discrimination "to a degree equalled by no other church in America."

In the mid-twenties few parishes were made up of black Catholics, and Negroes were barely represented in Catholic schools. By 1926 Catholics had ordained only eight black priests in America. The tiny Federated Colored Catholics group finally got organized in 1930, but it was scarcely heard, despite its gentle cry. Their agents pleaded, "We do not wish to be treated as 'a problem,' but as a multitude of human beings, sharing a common destiny and the common privilege of the Redemption with all mankind." The federation did begin to make white Catholics aware of black communicants, against the odds created by many white ethnic groups that worked against any sort of idea which would lead them to mix with blacks. 4:38

Blacks, lacking major bridge-building efforts outside the Federal Council and these small organizations, were largely on their own. They had to see whether they could carve out a better place in American religion. As Mays and Nicholson saw them in a survey they made in the early thirties, blacks did not wait upon white churches for major or even minor breakthroughs. They were busy filling the many needs of their members and communities. Most of their efforts did not go into racial defense. For their own reasons their members were also in quest of spiritual tranquillity. They too expressed spiritual and communal needs which only the quiet routines of congregational life addressed. When Mays and Nicholson talked about white congregations at all, they mentioned these chiefly as having been previous owners of buildings sold or abandoned to blacks when urban communities experienced population shifts. The coauthors spent most of their time on issues similar to those familiar in white communities: education, neighborhood activities, effects of migration, the role of the minister, provision for self-expression, ownership, sources of support, and the like. 4:39

Most Christians of African descent tended to their own affairs. The whole agenda in black religion was manifestly *not* set then by the Ku Klux Klan or progressive women, by white southern moderates or northern churchly bureaucrats. Disruptions also came from within. Now and then someone would come along on the soil of black religion and offer a threat to the serene status quo. For a time it was Marcus Garvey who dominated public consciousness and offered the most visibly controversial alternatives. 4:40

His career suggests something of what life at the edge of terror—and hope—might mean for blacks.

4:41   Jamaica-born Garvey, one of the more colorful and inventive of black leaders in American history, devised the Universal Negro Improvement Agency on his home island in 1914. Two years later he brought it to New York. By 1919 it had spawned thirty branches. His UNIA program, which made profound use of religious symbols, intended, it said, to unite "all the Negro peoples of the world into one great body to establish a country and Government absolutely their own." Like many other radicals, Garvey responded with black self-definition to assaults moved by white hatred. Anathema to such movements of racial pride were conventional practices by some lightly colored blacks who wanted to "pass" for whites. Garvey scorned those who would attempt thus to pass, because they thus failed to identify with the 400,000,000 fellow Negroes around the world.

4:42   Garvey stressed the need for unity of blacks over against the white oppressors, the common foe. In 1919 he wrote that if blacks remained divided as they were, they would all remain oppressed. Therefore he would dedicate himself in the next decade to uniting them. "The very moment all the Negroes of this and other countries start to stand together," Garvey wrote, "that very time will see the white man standing in fear of the Negro race even as he stands in fear of the yellow race of Japan today." In this way blacks, he thought, could "match fire with hell fire." Solidarity would change everything for all. As for the present: "When you offend one white man in America, you offend ninety million of white men. When you offend one Negro, the other Negroes are unconcerned because we are not organized." That situation had to change.

4:43   The 700 local branches that Garvey claimed existed made up a movement whose size was always hard to measure. One hears figures boasting of somewhere between 100,000 and 2,000,000 supporters. Garvey's weekly, the *Negro World*, reached 200,000 circulation. The achievement in any case was impressive; historians call it the largest mass movement of African-Americans to that time. In 1919, perhaps deluded toward grandeur by his successes, in 1919 Garvey invented his most daring but ultimately foolish venture, the Black Star Shipping Line. Designed to promote movement back to Africa, it held some immediate if momentary appeal. Almost at once, the founder sold stock worth $610,000. A promoter with a sense of the grand gesture, the plumed Garvey could attract thousands along the streets as aides drove him in an open car through Harlem. He rode in that flamboyant style on his way to the opening of his International Convention of the Negro Peoples of the World. Garvey hoped to work with Liberia, the historic home of returned slaves, to build an African headquarters and community. But his moment of organizational triumph was brief. Sales of stock in his shipping line soon dropped to almost nothing, and membership dues in his organization came up short. There were painful strikes and embarrassing defections by Black Star workers.

Garvey's Sunday meetings at Liberty Hall usually began with worship. The Garveyan messages were ambiguous, though he insisted that his single purpose was to promote black pride and self-empowerment without spite. "We are not preaching propaganda of hate against anybody. We love the white man; we love all humanity, because we feel that we cannot live without the other." Garvey could also chide weak blacks. "We are the most careless and indifferent people in the world; we are shiftless and irresponsible."   4:44

Like other preachers of black consciousness and pride, a few of whom preceded and many of whom followed him, Garvey cared little for the reluctant outreaches some moderate white Christians made toward African-Americans. He insisted that he no longer relied on them for anything. In his message and thought, blacks would have to take control of their own lives if they wished to achieve democracy and justice. To promote both these claims and his own ego, in 1921 he appointed himself provisional president of another creation, the organization of the Empire of Africa. To photographers, he and his potentates, knights, and dukes were irresistible. They attracted newspaper headlines and the Garveyites became celebrities of sorts, although they were notorious in the eyes of unsympathetic blacks, like the secular-minded Du Bois, and most whites.   4:45

Strong criticism by whites bred strong reaction from radical blacks. While Garvey scorned conventional politics, much of what he worked for was rich in political implications. In 1920 his movement had agreed upon a "Declaration of the Rights of the Negro Peoples of the World." The document criticized segregation in public places and discrimination in education, reasonably daring but by no means unheard-of reaches for that decade. The Declaration asked for economic opportunity and legal justice. The Universal Negro Improvement Association also affirmed self-   4:46

defense. It justified war between races when a minority was being consistently victimized. Some militant black Baptist and Methodist pastors welcomed such emphases. So did some leaders in autonomous storefront churches. Garvey's theology may have put some off, but they found it expedient to form alliances with him and invest in his passion. When Garvey could take their side, working for black self-assertion in the world as opposed to deferred benefits in a life to come, he welcomed their support.

4:47   The more conventionally orthodox black Christian clergy had difficulty keeping Garvey in focus. His provocative approach was unwelcome to most of them. In 1924 Garvey's leaders at the Fourth International Convention of Negroes found that they could no longer fail to speak clearly on the issue of religion. After both clergy and lay people voiced their views and when they had heard from both the pious and the "worldlian," the delegates decided that "as there are Moslems and other Non-Christians who are Garveyites, it was not wise to declare Christianity the state Religion of the Organization."

4:48   Instead, they determined, the Universal Negro Improvement Association would establish the Temple of God in each heart. Then all would find what they called "inner Serenity so as to enable us to establish on earth the Fatherhood of God and the Brotherhood of Man—a belief which is the basis of recognized religions." As for Christians, if they were as yet members of no church, they were encouraged to join the new African Orthodox Church. But all church members should realize that God was everywhere, not "just in Churches on Sundays." Such a vision made it possible for many venturesome ministers to be Garveyites, but it drove off some of the more doctrinally orthodox. Garvey himself was cautious when he said he would never desert the black religion of his mother, though he repudiated the white religion. Blacks, he insisted, would not advance unless they worshiped a black God.

4:49   Garvey's personal moment was relatively brief, his empire short-lived, his very movement foredoomed. In 1923, while raising funds for the steamship line, he was arrested and sent to jail for mail fraud. Much of the opposition that led to the pressure on him came from rival or disillusioned blacks. In due course Liberia broke relations with him and called his organization seditious. In 1927 President Coolidge pardoned Garvey, but by then most of his movement had collapsed. Negro Zionism, as he sometimes called it, the first really broad-based organization of its sort in

America, came to lose its importance. But by then Garvey had served to unsettle the white American majority as well as the complacent blacks, some of whom were jostled to the point that they looked with hope to his movement for a better future.

Before this demise, gifted black leaders of the day who as-   4:50
sessed what Garveyism had meant stressed its religious style. Thus poet James Weldon Johnson saw it as a transcending of mere politics: "The movement became more than a movement, it became a religion, its members were zealots. Meetings at Liberty Hall were conducted with an elaborate liturgy," including a new hymn, "God Save Our President." Johnson found it all noteworthy if for no other reason than for the way in which it regularly impressed the throngs. Garvey readily used religious rhetoric. In a typical speech at Liberty Hall in 1921 he asked hearers to "go out as missionaries and preach this doctrine of the Universal Negro Improvement Association. Let all the world know that this is the hour; this is the time of our salvation."

One of the legacies of Garveyism was an enduring church   4:51
body, a partly schismatic movement that resulted from a sectarian challenge by George Alexander McGuire. This chaplain general of the Garvey movement was an aggressive Episcopal priest. For a time he successfully urged an order of worship on the association and promoted the role of clergy within it. Then in July of 1921 McGuire became a bishop in what he called the Independent Episcopal Church. That autumn a Russian Orthodox bishop agreed to install McGuire in his new inspiration, the African Orthodox Church. Garvey immediately sensed that there would be rivalry here with existing churches and that standard-brand black Protestant clergy would flee and shun his association. For that reason the calculating Garvey did not grant McGuire the monopoly he sought. Hence the schism followed. As the two parted, Garvey spoke in what were for him moderate terms when he averred that McGuire was "not as perverse as Judas Iscariot, Alcibiades and Benedict Arnold." McGuire eventually returned to the fold and, somewhat sheepishly, again served the association as a chaplain of sorts.

One bizarre twist remains to Garvey's tale; it illustrates how   4:52
beleaguered aggressors can go looking for strange alliances in times of upset. It is hard in those circumstances to develop permanently hardened lines between two huge factions. In what looked like and had to be an act of bold opportunism, Garvey eventually took his organization south. In the peak years of the

new Ku Klux Klan, which had been the terror of blacks for decades, he made overtures toward what everyone would have called his movement's soul enemy. In the South Garvey's actions confused everyone. While he himself suffered under the segregating Jim Crow policies, and though his rallies were often disrupted by thugs, he praised Jim Crow and spoke disparagingly of many blacks. "Social equality," he said, was no longer his goal. Such equality would have cut into the appeal of his strident "Back to Africa" movement.

4:53   In this climate and circumstance, on June 25, 1922, Garvey held a two-hour meeting in which he sought detente with and help from Klan leader Edward Clarke. It seemed to be advantageous to Clarke to ally with a confusing but powerful black who supported Jim Crow separatism. Clarke also could use the moment, he thought, to show that the new Klan could be respectable and that it would not always use violence against all blacks. But both Garvey and Clarke overstepped bounds, underestimating the perduring hostility of their backers. Clarke quickly had to retreat from contact with Garvey under Kleagle pressure. These other Klan leaders wanted no contact, even of advantageous sorts, with Negroes. Partly as a result of this venture, Clarke eventually was to be unseated in a Klan coup and finally expelled.

4:54   Garvey also failed when, back in New York, he tried to put the best possible face on the Klan and his contacts with it. He portrayed the Klan as being a plausible bargaining agent. After all, it represented what he called the "spirit, the feeling, the attitude of every white man in the United States." Couldn't affiliation with the Klan be used to advantage against whites? His notion met with hisses. Followers recalled that not too long before the fateful meeting Garvey himself had said that the Klan's real object was to crush the Negro. Now he came back to say that in dealing with Clarke, "I was speaking to a man who was brutally a white man and I was speaking to him as a man who was brutally a Negro." But even what these two "brutallys" symbolized could not save him.

4:55   Garvey's rivals exploited the moment of the fall. A. Philip Randolph's newspaper headlined: *MARCUS GARVEY! THE BLACK IMPERIAL WIZARD BECOMES MESSENGER BOY OF THE WHITE KU KLUX KLEAGLE.* Randolph announced that he would "drive Garvey and Garveyism in all its sinister viciousness from the American soil." By now more and more religious leaders were finding a voice to criticize Garvey as despotic, con-

niving, and even treacherous. Rivals thwarted his efforts at conciliation. When the Universal Negro Improvement Association
leadership wanted to give an award to the National Association
for the Advancement of Colored People, that respectable organization turned it down. One-time supporter William Pickens spoke
eloquently for many, "You say in effect to the Ku Klux: All right!
Give us Africa and we in turn concede you America as a 'white
man's country!' In that you make a poor deal; for twelve million people you give up EVERYTHING and in exchange get
NOTHING."

Now for a second time we register violent death on the scene   4:56
of religious conflict in the twenties. On January 1, 1923, James
Eason, a minister who had been expelled at the 1922 convention
of the UNIA and who continued to oppose Garvey, was shot and
killed. As Eason lay dying he whispered that he believed three
Garveyites had done the shooting. No one ever implicated Garvey
legally in the matter, but the leader clearly took delight in both
the fact of the killing and the rumors.

It was in such a vulnerable moment that Garvey's black antago-   4:57
nists played into the hands of the white police by pressing Attorney General Harry Daugherty to act. In the event, as we have
seen, a fraud charge finally cornered Garvey in 1923. He was
deported after President Coolidge pardoned him in 1927. Garvey
lived on in Jamaica and London, but died without ever having
seen Africa. Black religious extremists had come to oppose others
of their kind in the tense climate of the times. The pattern of such
conflict should have seemed simply futile and incomprehensible.
It made some sense, however, in a decade when there were few
options for blacks, against the background of true despair and
false hopes in the tribal twenties.

The Jews: More American Than the Americans Themselves

"Will America Remain Protestant and Anglo-Saxon?" Jews   4:58
gave a third set of answers to the question in the twenties, the
decade when public anti-Semitism became a public issue in the
United States. André Siegfried blended racial stereotypes with
acute and original observation as he set the stage. He noticed that
most Jews gave the surface impression of being Americanized and
adapted. Why? America respected money, success, and worldli-
ness. So did Jews, in their restlessness and with an ambition that

was marked with "a certain vengefulness for centuries of hatred and oppression." More accurately as well as more to the present point, Siegfried recognized that "in moral origin, [the Jew] is closely allied to the Puritan—the same biblical tradition, the same belief that his is the chosen race, the same easy step from religious mysticism to the conquest of power and riches." Not a few Jews happily connected colonial New England, its images and its laws, with the Hebrew Scriptures and Jewish tradition. They were at home. All seemed well.

4:59   Why, then, should the Jew also not be at home; why should Anglo-Saxon America find any reason for nervousness? Because most Jews, as Siegfried put it, wanted to be "more American than the Americans themselves" and were guilty of overadapting. The individual Jew " 'passes,' as the Negroes say; that is, he moves among the Christians without being remarked." In the very restlessness and ambition that so impressed the author, his prototypical Jew made light of his own religious tradition. After a first generation of faithfulness to the Sabbath, this adaptive Jew became content with halfway measures in the second. Many Jews simply disappeared into what the Frenchman called the ocean of America, leaving the Orthodox to remain faithful to their synagogue. The majority of the rest were busy "making it" in universities, clubs, hotels, where, in a repulsive but common metaphor, they "wormed their way." So they remained finally unassimilated pseudo-Americans, a sort of residue, in Siegfried's view, at the bottom of the melting pot.

4:60   At this point Siegfried, touching that bottom with the Jews, moved beyond stereotypes and again revealed himself to be a perceptive observer. He discerned a Jewish difference. On the one hand, Jews may be willing to sacrifice everything, even their mysticism, to adopt "that dreary social pragmatism which is the real religion of modern America." Yet as children of Abraham they could not escape the spirit of their ancestors, Siegfried thought, for "they are infinitely more religious than the Americans." Only momentarily or superficially could the outlook of Jews coincide with that of Protestants, against whose materialism and love of business success Siegfried had a special grievance. The soul of Jewish religion, he thought, somehow survived untouched.

4:61   Presciently, Siegfried was noting the beginning of a partial return on the part of some adapted Jews to more traditional religion within the Conservative and Reform movements. While many immigrants had earlier thrown off all traces of religion, now, to re-

Promoting pioneer interfaith efforts through what became the National
Conference of Christians and Jews were a major Jewish, Catholic, and
Protestant leader: Rabbi Morris Lazaron, Father John Elliot Ross, and the
Reverend Everett R. Clinchy. (The National Conference of Christians and Jews.)

tain their identity and coherence as a people, some were being
drawn back to it. He even discovered leaders who were reimpos-
ing mystical traditions of orthodoxy in modern form on Jews
whose religion had evidently become bitter and dry through the
taint of their contact with Christians. Even in the lowest grades of
society, he noticed, one came across such irreconcilable folk who
had first attempted to become a part of Western civilization and
then repudiated much of it in the end to go their own ways.

The phenomenon which, unfortunately, confronted this kind of   4:62
neo-Judaism was the new and ominous anti-Semitism. Some conflict arose for nonreligious reasons, because of the competition
Jews gave Protestants in business and in the sphere of the intellect. As for the old-stock Protestant nationalist, "left to himself,
the 100 per center is not given to brain-work." The Jew, on the
other hand, had an intellect ever alert, a mind never tamed or
disciplined as it asked questions. "This [character] is just what
the Americans do not want."

4:63   So the Protestant and Jew soon diverged. "In spite of the great value of Jewish collaboration, the Protestant American has adopted a hostile attitude which has developed into an anti-Semitic movement." In just a few paragraphs Siegfried thus framed the social scene of the twenties, detected the ambiguities of the Jewish presence, and defined the interweaving of religion with peoplehood and with stereotypes of personality traits.

4:64   This mix confused Protestants. First, they were Americans. Second, in their own communities, they saw themselves as Anglo-Saxons, or Scotch-Irish, or possibly German-Scandinavians. That took care of their peoplehood. Third, they then regarded themselves as Methodists or Baptists or Episcopalians. That part was their religious reckoning. What could they do to make sense of Jews, who seemed in their Jewishness to fuse their peoplehood with religion? People thus puzzled did not seem to realize that in the ordinary course of life Indians, Japanese, black Protestants, Catholics, and Jews in their turns saw these original-stock or 100 percent Americans as *also* combining the three elements.

4:65   We must spend a moment with this confusion because it complicated Jewish-Gentile relations before and after the twenties, when many were beginning to try to clear it up. The best systematic attempt to sort things out then was a still helpful book by Claris Edwin Silcox and Galen M. Fisher, who worked for the Institute of Social and Religious Research. In a notable work of the early thirties on *Catholics, Jews and Protestants*, they had to come to terms with the fusions of nationhood, ethnicity, and denomination during the interwar decades. While many social analysts were seeing religion as a private affair, something one could pick up and drop, these coauthors introduced and reinforced a different notion they discerned in the documents from the period. Silcox and Fisher knew that "the religious differences which separate the various groups in a community tend to color their whole existence." These differences between peoples determined individual life, from baptism, circumcision, or some other rite, through education and mate selection to the choice of pictures on the home wall and the institutions which minister to human need. "Thus, religious affiliation may affect all of life," and even the ceremonies of death. "Religious issues divide us in various ways from the cradle to the grave."

4:66   Why not frankly face the issues created by such distinctions and why not ask what the two scholars called "that solemn sociological question: What about it?" Admittedly, religious differ-

ences were not as unyielding as racial differences, because the
former were modifiable through conversion. Still, most of us, said
Silcox and Fisher, inherit our religion as we inherit nationality
and mother tongue. Most religious groups try to immunize their
youth against any possible defection later. So religion was not
purely a personal matter, as some maintained that it was. Religious citizens did *not* ask thirteen-year-olds to make their own
choice "from the menu-card of available religious delicacies."
Instead they saw religion as a method of social control and social
discipline. Except among the rootless, defection was then still a
form of high treason.

Their essay on fusion, so important for understanding the as-   4:67
sumptions behind our story of conflict in religion, bears most directly on the question Silcox and Fisher and their contemporaries
posed in respect to American Jews. For that matter they asked, in
strict categorical classification, were Protestant, Catholic, and
Jew the names of *genera* or of *species*? Did the Jew cease to be a
Jew when he or she became a Christian Scientist or a Two-Seed-
in-the-Spirit Baptist? This was the point: "In all his criticism of
the discrimination to which he is often subjected, the Jew usually
speaks of religious discrimination, but the Gentile almost univer-
sally repudiates the allegation and claims that religion has little,
if anything, to do with it."

Scholars at large and the community of Jews often located the   4:68
roots of anti-Semitism in the religious struggles of the first eight
centuries of Christianity. Most anti-Semites, however, said with
great emphasis that their controversy with the Jews had nothing to
do with Jewish faith, "of which they know little or nothing, and
care less," said the authors, but only with the manners and habits
of Jews. "The bitterest comments against the Jews come, not
from the people who are the most intimately associated with the
churches, but from those on the periphery, if not entirely outside
church life altogether." Exactly. In their expressed antipathies,
they distinguished among Jews but almost never used religious
principles of differentiation.

So the question of the twenties persisted in the thirties: *What*   4:69
are the Jews? "Do they constitute a racial group, a religious
group, a national group, or just *a* group?" Even Jewish writers
did not always agree on answers to the question. Silcox and Fisher
knew of many varieties. Thus Zionist Jews, who were becoming
stronger in these two decades, insisted that the essential unity of
Jewry was neither racial nor religious; it was national, and de-

manded a political state of Israel. The non-Zionist Jews disagreed, while the Gentiles asked: "If you insist on identifying religion and nationhood, why should you blame us if we do likewise?" This issue *was* the sticking-point between anti-Zionist Gentiles and Zionists, one on which anti-Zionist Jews constantly seized to make their case against Zionism.

4:70   To all this, Silcox and Fisher added still other nuances. They reported on Reform Jews who insisted, against Zionists, that "the Jews are a religious community, not a nation." True, there were "Hebrew Christians" as well as aggressively nonreligious Jews, yet the vast majority did wish to be included as Jews in religious censuses. The Jewish community therefore still seemed essentially religious, but it was far from a unity, because it displayed everything "from unadulterated humanism to unadulterated fundamentalism and orthodoxy." The patterns crisscrossed or made crazy quilts. Liberal Christians cooperated freely with liberal Jews on many projects, yet Reform and Orthodox Jews cooperated little with each other. Orthodox Christians who wanted to convert Jews despised the Christian liberals and were more comfortable with the definiteness of Jewish Orthodoxy.

4:71   Experts Silcox and Fisher admitted that they ended their mapping with only a better-informed confusion than that of the people on whom they reported. That is why they provided a plausible context for a narrative about Jews and anti-Semitism in the twenties. There were good reasons for the confusion. As its consequence, in the Gentile mind the Jew emerged as an international irritant, "resisting assimilation and finding ever-shifting grounds on which to found his right to a separate existence." The two observers all but threw up their own hands as they launched a well-regarded 350-page study: "In short, the whole situation is a frightful mess, and by his strange dexterity in playing the triple role of a racial, religious and national group, the modern Jew brings down upon his head a triple type of antipathy."

4:72   What, one might fairly ask, were Jews doing to evoke anti-Jewish responses as never before in America in the twenties? The simplest answer could be: they were perceived as growing in numbers and rising in status. Silcox and Fisher recalled that in 1877, before the European pogroms, there had been only 229,087 Jews in America. Two decades later there were still fewer than a million. But by 1917, with the great East European immigrant influx—many of them the kinds of Jews who would least assimilate and be least ready and able to adopt Protestant styles—the number had grown to 3,288,951. And then, even though the door closed on almost all Jews with the immigration restriction legislation of 1924, the population kept growing so that by 1927 it numbered 4,228,029. Jews were by no means thinly spread around the country; they were at most symbolic presences in small-town Protestant America, the Muncies of the land. But the New York Jewish community especially was becoming a center of publishing, editing, opinion-making, entertainment, business, and intellectual life, and it sent signals to the whole country. New York housed 1,765,000 of those Jews in the late 1920s. Seven out of ten Jews lived in only ten cities. These were also America's new power centers, mistrusted by backcountry 100 percent Americans but, of course, influential also among them.

Something had to be done. The period between the wars was not a time of *mere* tribalism, mere antagonism and conflict. Numerous Americans wanted to reduce the noise of conflict and eliminate the reasons for it. Just as the Federal Council member churches worked for Christian unity among their Protestant selves, so Christians and Jews often tried to do something together about the triple type of antipathy Jews felt and the counter-antipathy of some Jews toward all Christians. They wanted to change the whole context of Jewish-Christian relations. Some henceforth began to speak not of Anglo-Saxon Protestant, or Protestant, or Christian America, but invented the notion of a Judeo-Christian America. They were motivated by a desire to make a genuine gesture of amity and an effort to display the true Hebrew-Puritan roots of the United States. Others organized interfaith groups, the necessity of whose presence indicated the reality of conflict and a need to address it, along with the sign of the founders' humane regard for citizens across boundaries of religion and race. An organization which was at first called the National Conference of Jews and Christians did the pioneering.   4:73

Jews often had difficulty knowing how to regard friendly approaches. The most generous of these seemed to come from the very set of denominations composed of original-stock Americans, the kind of citizens who wanted to do the defining of who really belonged in the United States and who did not. The inviters did not do their excluding of unacceptables while wearing Ku Klux Klan hoods. They did not use paint brushes to desecrate synagogues or engage in overt anti-Semitism. Their elites instead imposed quotas at prestigious universities, closed their clubs to Jews, and found refined ways to define them out. Yet, in their   4:74

federated church activities they also kept looking for certain kinds of Jews with whom to ally on many programs, and in their agendas and through their energies they indicated a desire for better relations. Thus the Federal Council worked with the Social Justice Department of the Central Conference of American Rabbis, the Reform group, on numerous causes—just as both of them sometimes linked with the National Catholic Welfare Conference in public causes.

4:75   Roger Straus, a wealthy Jew who often bankrolled and helped lead the organization which later changed its name to the National Conference of Christians and Jews, once noted that most interfaith overtures came from Protestants. On occasion, however, Jews did the initiating. Sometimes these Jews built on ties developed during the emergencies of World War I, often as the result of friendliness between chaplains of differing faiths. At other times the cooperators linked their endeavors to the pro-peace causes of the twenties. Both wanted to set a good example of concord at home in order to be credible when talking about peace abroad. Many of these early interfaith efforts were merely civic. Sooner or later, however, conciliators had to face up to specifically religious ideas and ideals. Which should prevail? How far could the Jewish minority go within overwhelmingly Protestant America, when efforts by Christians to convert Jews were so standard?

4:76   Interfaith activities in the twenties drew on mixed sources. The founders of the nation had preached tolerance on the grounds of reason, and liberal Protestantism increasingly stressed a similar note. Reform and Conservative Jews drew on their own resources to promote similar ideas of tolerance. The leading National Conference of Jews and Christians organizer and enthusiast, Everett R. Clinchy—a stalwart Protestant—often deftly suggested a kind of trifaith unity which would be available for national purposes. Clinchy treated Jews, Catholics, and Protestants as culture groups. He tried to synthesize their separate contributions to American life. Finally, Clinchy found it important to call off attempts by one group to convert members of another, which meant practically that Christians should stop proselytizing Jews. The traffic was largely one way. Jews were not active in passing tracts or buttonholing possible converts.

4:77   Needless to say, the mere mention of a cease-fire on the evangelizing front led to tensions within the Protestant communities. The majority were still clearly in favor of trying to convert Jews (and Catholics), even if they put few energies into the activity and expected a low yield. The idea of formally deserting all attempts to convert others would mean in their eyes a denial of the truth of the Protestant interpretation of the Christian gospel. This message impelled believers to help draw unbelievers or people of other and thus wrong faiths to the evangelical Protestant cause or, as they would put it, to the cross of Jesus Christ. When liberal Protestants said that they did not try to convert Jews, fundamentalist and conservative Protestants accused them of the heresy of universalism. This was a notion that a loving God would save all people, regardless of the doctrines they held. Such universalism, the critics claimed, represented a sapping of Christian energies and was a final treason; it became therefore still another element of tensions within Protestantism.

Conrad Hoffman, who led the International Missionary Council's campaign called a "Christian Approach to the Jews," said that the interfaith endeavors were based on what looked to him like a very compromising "uncompromising good-will approach." These efforts, he thought, would inevitably have an unfortunate effect. What the rabbis formally called a goodwill approach was paralyzing the participating Christian leaders because it robbed them of motives to save the souls of Jews. Federal Council leaders were reluctant to formalize any decision *not* to evangelize just as in practice they had little zest for conversion efforts. The Federal Council of Churches Committee on Goodwill Between Jews and Christians thus had to live a cautious life and walk a careful, defensive line for years. Now and then a notable Christian leader would be caught in ambiguity and crossfire. Thus the March 1931 *B'nai B'rith Magazine* focused on John R. Mott. Mott was the major ecumenical figure of the decades, the leader of the International Missionary Council and always an agent of goodwill. Jewish editors aware of his work complained that Mott consistently sent out confusing signals. He kept saying on the one hand that Christians must missionize the Jews and on the other he also kept urging that there should be a deeper understanding between Christians and Jews. His critics insisted that Mott had to make up his mind.

While Mott was indeed an active missionary, many of the other Federal Council and establishment denominational leaders did not have their hearts in aggressive evangelizing of any sort. But Jews were not equipped to sort out the various Protestantisms on the basis of the temperature of their commitments. All they could do

4:78

4:79

was to read the Federal Council's continuing call to lead people to Christ and the church. Communications failed on both sides, given their vastly different perspectives. Many Christians who wanted to convert Jews thought that through conversion Jews would be fulfilling their Judaism, while the vast majority of resistant Jews saw conversion to Christianity as simple betrayal. In 1929, therefore, the Synagogue Council of America announced that it almost despaired of the goodwill movements, in view, they said, of "the sanction which the proselytizing program receives at the hands of the leaders of that movement." To Jews, Protestants were simply Protestants. They did not realize how an effort to overcome one conflict with Jews led to increasing conflict of another sort, that is, with other Protestants who tried to convert Jews. What came to be called goodwill encounters, of course, also resulted in new tensions within Judaism. For instance, some of the goodwill-minded Christians and Jews were explicit anti-Zionists. Those who wanted to see the founding of the state of Israel rejected any ententes that might exclude hopes for the birth of such a political Zion. Other goodwill leaders, both liberal Christians and reform Jews, however, opposed Zionism.

4:80   For all the evident caution and tension shown by leaders, the Federal Council-type of engagement had a measurable effect on the way some Protestant elites who favored the interfaith movement began to conceive of a changing America. "Will America remain Protestant and Anglo-Saxon?" This minority answered "No." Clinchy's trifaith view made headway, particularly as Jews supported it. The National Broadcasting System, for instance, began to allot radio broadcasting time on an equal basis to Jews, Catholics, and Protestants. In higher education, at a time when religion was being introduced or reintroduced into curricula, the three-group approach was also increasingly supported.

4:81   The National Conference had emerged gradually from the diverse goodwill organizations and began to become formal only with Clinchy's arrival in 1928. It stands here as a signal that not everyone wanted conflict and that some pioneers saw the need for concord, a need born out of agony over the new anti-Jewish episodes that were intensifying in the early twenties. Two of these, neither explicitly religious in content, provide the necessary background to the religious responses. The most notorious case came from an unexpected source, one of the true celebrities of the era, industrialist Henry Ford. In 1920 the automaker, for reasons never completely clear, embarked on an anti-Jewish crusade. He promoted his nostalgic version of a simpler America, one which he thought alien Jews complicated. Somehow along the way Ford was also gulled into accepting the authenticity of the fake *Protocols of the Elders of Zion*. This hoax document had made its way around Europe and the American racist underground for some decades. It purported to reveal plans by Jews to take over international economic life. Ford gave the *Protocols* publicity through the eight years from 1920 to 1927. He even founded a newspaper, the *Dearborn Independent*, to spread word about the existence of the *Protocols* and other Jewish conspiracies.

Ford's inability or lack of need to turn the anti-Jewish case into   4:82
one with a substantively religious theme might make one omit him from a religious history. Yet just as the Ku Klux Klan attracted lowbrow America, Ford now gave credibility and sanction to middlebrow hate campaigns that exacerbated religious tensions. His newspaper, aware of the radicalism of some Jewish labor leaders, accused Jews of being Bolsheviks during the latter stages of the Red Scare. This accusation led him in turn via arcane conspiracy theories to connect Jews with old-style Masons and Illuminati and to see modern Jews as heirs of eighteenth-century atheistic and revolutionary causes. So powerful was Ford that Jewish leadership had to make him their own public enemy number one. Louis Marshall, president of the American Jewish Committee and one of the best-known Jews in public life in 1925, saw Ford as "the intellectual brother of the Ku Klux Klan." Marshall also cited two new names on the horizon of terror. Ford was "the inspirer of Hitler and Ludendorf."

When the Detroit automaker's activity came to be a public   4:83
scandal, Federal Council leaders tried to talk him out of his bizarre, almost paranoid attacks against Jews. So did political leaders, including former presidents William Howard Taft and the mortally ill Woodrow Wilson. They did not prevail. In 1921, when Ford's editors published a third volume of collected writings from the *Dearborn Independent*, calling it *Jewish Influences in American Life*, they went looking for respectability by seeking other notables to quote, not a hard task at that time. More and more they found what they called a notable discussion of the Jewish question in magazines of quality. They liked the highbrow magazines, *Century Magazine* and *Atlantic Monthly*, for example, because of some of their features dealing with the question.

After quoting such secular press outlets, the anthologists then   4:84

turned to the religious press. They were cheered to find it "freer of control than the secular." It was unburdened by market ties and thus able to be honest, according to Ford standards, about the Jewish question. Ford and his editors found helpful such magazines as the conservative *Christian Standard* or the *Moody Monthly* and, because it was anti-Zionist, the liberal *Christian Century*. What would eventually turn Ford from his anti-Semitic course? Goodwill movement arguments had little effect on him during his crusade. Economics did. Lawsuits, boycotts, threats to the future of the Ford firm—all these finally led the industrialist to have second thoughts and a change of heart. When he was finally reached and convinced to change, after much damage had been done, Ford acted upon what gave every evidence of being a profoundly and permanently new outlook. He allied himself henceforth with Jewish causes, as if in penitence, and went so far as to urge Jews to turn his huge Brazilian rubber plantations into a Fordlandia for resettling Jewish refugees from Hitler. All this, however, occurred half a generation after he first took his strange tack defending 100 percent Americanism against Semites.

4:85   Business and intellect were the two apparently secular zones wherein Jews were challengers. Thus the presence of anti-Jewish policies in citadels of secularity demonstrates that not all racism or ethnocentrism issued from the churches, and thus provides perspective in a story of religion. In the most notable instance, some non-Jewish alumni and administrators expressed fear that Harvard University, 11 percent of whose student body was Jewish in 1921, was coming to look like "New Jerusalem." Harvard, in turn, came to be the target for Jews who wished to abolish the informal quotas that President A. Lawrence Lowell was imposing there. Responding unguardedly while overlooking the many Jews already in the alumni association and at Harvard, Lowell spoke critically of the desire by Jews to stay together as being one factor that worked against them. As did so many Gentile leaders at that time, Lowell both faulted Jews for not assimilating and helped prevent their doing so with any ease.

4:86   Meanwhile, in the *Nation* Lewis Gannett observed that "anti-Semitism, as it manifests itself in America, is essentially a part of a long Anglo-Saxon tradition of dislike of the newer arrival." Lowell, said the redoubtable Louis Marshall, had made his bed; Jews would let him lie in it. Marshall could not resist adding a telling swipe: Lowell's position "could not have been worse had

it been written by the advocates of what the late Dr. Schechter
called the Higher Anti-Semitism of Germany."

Reacting to Marshall's charges, Harvard formed a committee   4:87
which recommended equal opportunity for all, regardless of race
or religion. Still, Harvard and other front-rank schools kept finding sub rosa ways to limit Jewish enrollment. The university's
practices and causes, as mentioned, were not rooted in religion;
they did represent one more part of the consistent effort by the
old-stock majority to keep America more nearly 100 percent pure.

If commerce led Ford and alumni-influenced Lowell to change   4:88
their approaches, on the third or theological front Jewish leaders
also worked to change attitudes. Some of the inherited Christian
talk about Jews as "Christ-killers" lived on, particularly in the
populist backwoods. While such views may have added to the
color and passion of some anti-Semitism, they do not seem to
have been central in the acts against Jews in the decade. Early in
the 1930s, for instance, efforts were already being made to assess
the amount of theological anti-Judaism extant in Protestant educational literature. The Methodists' Drew Theological Seminary
undertook a study financed by the American Jewish Committee to
pursue the same subject. Hostility to ancient Jews was, of course,
evident in some retellings of New Testament stories. Yet James V.
Thompson, who published findings in 1934 and 1935, found that
Sunday school lessons made few connections between ancient
Jews and contemporaries. Given the climate of the times, it is
surprising to find that only 12 percent of the surveyed teachers
thought Jews were responsible for the death of Jesus. One must
look elsewhere than among these texts to find the roots of the
postwar anti-Semitism. It had most to do with efforts to keep
America Protestant, Anglo-Saxon and old-stock Christian, as opposed to new-style heterogeneous.

The Jews: Zionism, Cultural Pluralism, Reconstructionism

The noise of conflict between Gentiles and Jews would have   4:89
been much louder from the Jewish side had there not been a major
neutralizing conflict within Judaism. The issue was Zionism versus anti-Zionism: should American Jews support a Jewish state of
Israel or not? Jews thus were also involved in the debates over
"triumphant nationality," and had to guard against the notion that

they might be less than fully patriotic if they showed interest in supporting a Jewish state in Palestine. Had all Jews been Zionists, most Christians could have massed forces against a single foe. Similarly, Jews would have been undistracted and thus free to put all their energies into defense against Christians. As it was, Judaism in both interwar decades was torn by profound differences over the issue of Zionism. This originally European movement, usually secular in outlook, often took socialist forms there and in the Lower East Side ghettos of New York. American Jewish leaders in the synagogues, however, increasingly turned the hoped-for founding of the state of Israel into a religious cause.

4:90   Curiously, the idea of founding a modern political state of Israel had already been promoted before the turn of the century by "Christian Zionists" in America. These Zionists were premillennialist Christians whose vision of the future demanded such a state of Israel. They foresaw the gathering of all Jews before Jesus could return to begin a thousand-year reign. Jews, of course, could not accept their proposition, but Zionists welcomed their practical support. Yet these premillennialists were not well known outside their own circle, and most Jews had frequent intercourse only with Christians suspicious of a reborn Israel. If Jews were already too unassimilated, too clannish, the interfaith advocates argued, would they not only become more so if they had to give dual loyalty to an Israel where their heart was and to an America where they housed their bodies and paid their taxes?

4:91   Many Jews of Reform and German background simply and emphatically rejected Zionism when it first appeared in American Judaism. They dismissed it as a Russian-Jewish fervor, one that would poison the climate at a time when the Reform movement was trying to show that it was much like the rest of America. The vast majority of Reform rabbis opposed Zionism all through the twenties. Yet the movement gradually picked up some vocal following, often of important sorts. Most notable was the turning of some secular Jews to the cause. Louis Brandeis, the great jurist who joined the Supreme Court in 1916, turned Zionist during the war. The assimilated Jew was explicit: his approach to Zionism was, as he put it, through Americanism. Practical experience and observation convinced him that "Jews were by reason of their traditions and their character peculiarly fitted to the attainment of American ideals." And it was precisely these ideas that Brandeis found in Zionism and in the founders of the future State of Israel. Of course, after Brandeis became a Supreme Court justice he could no longer remain visible in such a cause because of its political contexts. Yet his sanction for a time greatly benefited Zionism.

The strategically placed Protestant clergy of New York, Chicago, Philadelphia, Boston, and Cleveland rarely had social or civic interaction with Orthodox rabbis, who seemed to them too isolated and clannish. Nor did they or those in the second five of the ten most Jewish cities, Los Angeles, Newark, Baltimore, St. Louis, and Detroit, have many encounters with Conservative Judaism. Conservatism was a historically conscious version of Judaism that criticized Reform for having overadapted to pluralistic American styles. Belonging as it did to what had earlier been called the "Historical School," its pioneers cherished Jewish tradition and thought they could survive and energize Judaism in America. It was largely Reform leadership, educated, often Germanic in background, urbane, and full of goodwill energies, with which Protestant opinion-makers dealt. 4:92

Reform leadership, almost to a rabbi—there were a couple of very important early exceptions—was suspicious of American Jewish commitment to Jewish nationalism and the Zionist cause. Therefore this leadership found congenial company with those Protestants who respected Jewish belief but wanted all Americans, including all Jews, to be like themselves in style and habit. In their eyes, Zionism was certainly an offense, but it did not seem to be prospering or threatening. Nor did it seem to be gaining, in the eyes of impatient Reform rabbis such as that rare Zionist among them, Stephen S. Wise of New York. At the end of the decade Wise mourned: "There is a complete lull in things Zionist in America." He could even speak of the way "the killing of Zionism as a mass democratic movement" had all but robbed him of his faith. That faith had to wait for the 1930s to spread in Reform circles, as news of the Hitler demonry reached the synagogue world. 4:93

Conservative Judaism, half-obscured from old-stock Protestant view but increasingly influential, was more warm to Zionism. In fact, Rabbi Israel Goldstein of New York could say in 1927 that the Zionist Organization of America had turned to the Conservative rabbinate as the bulwark of American Zionism. Most of the Orthodox also advocated Zionism, except for certain literalists who thought Israel could be refounded only when the Messiah came. Zionists called these "our brothers—our foes." In an early anti-Zionist pamphlet, *Sha'alu Sh'lom Yerushalayim*, Rabbi Ba- 4:94

ruch Meir Klein regretted the religious turn Zionism was taking. "So long as the Zionists were from the non-religious Jews, they were less harmful, and we kept our silence." But recently, he wrote, Zionists had begun to put on a pious face, so the time had come to undertake battle. "I hope for the redemption," Klein wrote, but the Balfour promise of 1918, which chartered a modern Israel, "and which deniers of the Torah, scoffers and rebels demand"—this had to be faced with a "No, no!" And by his kind of Orthodox it was, consistently.

4:95   One looks for the drama, then, in the developing Reform arguments. These best illustrate how religious conflict within a family could be more intense than clashes between groups. The Central Conference of American Rabbis refused each year to effect ties with the Zionist Organization. In 1919 Julian Morgenstern, who two years later would head Reform's flagship Hebrew Union College in Cincinnati, led the anti-Zionist appeals. He advocated that Jews integrate themselves completely into the American nation and culture. In that respect, Reform and Morgenstern believed that "Zionism is altogether foreign to and incompatible with Americanism and American Judaism."

4:96   The next year Detroit's Rabbi Leo Franklin, by then president of the Central Conference, again displayed the Reform's anti-Zionist mind-set. He reminded hearers that Americanization had progressed during the recent war. In Christian circles, he said, people came to identify Americanization with Christianization. Strategically, this linking meant that Jews must break the connection. To do this it was unwise to let anyone suggest, as Franklin put it, that "Jews, or people of other religions and races, are not good Americans." Zionist commitment, he warned, could breed such sentiment.

4:97   As passions *for* Zionism cooled during the decade to the point that Stephen Wise mourned its virtual death, so did Reform energies *against* it dissipate. Fewer and fewer anti-Zionist resolutions marked annual conference meetings. In the cooled-off climate, meanwhile, the occasional conversions by Reform rabbis to the Zionist cause became less controversial. By 1927 over 10 percent of the Reform leadership had shifted allegiance to it. Joining Wise were notables like the outspoken New York rabbi Judah Magnes and Abba Hillel Silver, a Cleveland rabbi of great influence. That year, however, New York rabbi Louis Newman, speaking at Stephen S. Wise's Jewish Institute of Religion, still felt a need to attack laggards: "The most flagrant blunder of Reform

Judaism is its opposition to Zionism. If it continues to be 'dead against' Zionism it will soon be entirely dead." As late as 1929 Rabbi Hyman Enelow in his presidential address confessed: "there is no denying that as a whole Reform Judaism has been opposed to [political Zionism] and our Conference, representing Reform Judaism, has been opposed to it."

The fulfillment of the Zionist story awaited the advent of Na-   4:98
zism in Europe half a decade later. Meanwhile, if Zionism could not serve to define all American Jews, it was urgent that leaders in public life work out strategies for dealing with their new situations. Jews of the twenties experimented with numbers of these and developed a variety of ideologies by which to revise concepts of America and make them congenial to Jews. Two of these representative proposals stood out; we might call both "anti-assimilationist." The first approach, which bore considerable similarity to Everett Clinchy's outlook, came from free-lance scholar Horace Kallen. Mordecai Kaplan, who started a movement that almost became a denomination, promoted the other.

First, Kallen's patent, "cultural pluralism." If we consider it   4:99
as a distinctive formal proposal, we make too much of it. Very few people adopted it by saying in so many words, "I am going to follow Horace Kallen." It is important instead because it clarified somewhat what many Jews (and other Americans) were coming to support instinctively, or without much definition. Nor was it necessarily as benign as it looks: Kallen worked with romantic racial or racist notions which assigned to the groups that would make up a "federation of nationalities" in America some inborn features or character. These to him had an inalienable, inevitable, and ineradicable character.

German-born Kallen, whose father was an Orthodox rabbi,   4:100
grew up in Boston, where he repudiated synagogue Judaism and ingratiated himself with Yankees and Harvard men. But at Harvard he was guided back into Jewish studies. There he became convinced that the Hebrew Bible had helped shape America and that out of a reaffirmation of Judaism he could help reshape the nation now. Kallen never did come back to his father's faith in the God of Israel, was never a believer, and one day would even write a book with the lively title *Secularism Is the Will of God*. But he did affirm Jewish peoplehood and its heritage; he also became a Zionist.

Zionism did not always mean that its devotees wanted to re-   4:101
found Israel as a modern political state. Kallen promoted only

cultural Zionism, arguing that part of what Zion meant could be found in America. Anti-Semitic persecutions were not the great threats to such a Zionist ideal. The greater danger was that Jews would be dissolved in the melting pot, that they would come to be absorbed into the culture. Far from worrying about not fitting into Protestant America, Jews, Kallen thought, *should* be misfits so that they could help recut the nation in a new pattern. Israel in Palestine could help Jews elsewhere remain identifiable, could help them stay together and find focus. Kallen also discovered along the way that Jews were not the only misfits. He therefore came to celebrate the many ethnic groups in the upper Midwest, finding among them people who kept something of the old country in their minds and hearts and habits. Yet the closer Kallen approached the rest of them the more he detected on their part a common mark in both subtle and unsubtle forms of anti-Semitism. This discernment helped motivate him to develop his own vision.

4:102   For a time Kallen taught at the University of Wisconsin. This brought him into the precincts of E. A. Ross, whose racist viewpoint inspired Kallen to respond with his first major essay, in 1915, which he expanded into a book during the twenties. Ross was also developing a model of cultural pluralism, but his version was made up of groups who struggled on Darwinian lines until only the fittest survived. Such a vision, with its threat to Judaism, was precisely what Kallen feared. He had a positive, more benign view of the coexistence of such particular communities. "Nature is naturally pluralistic; her unities are eventual, not primary; mutual adjustments, not regimentations of superior force." Human institutions, Kallen thought, possessed characteristics similar to those of nature. Within the larger cultural context, he discovered that peoples possessed some measure, but only some measure, of choice about their identity and purpose. Of course, since in bald terms race and nationality obtained once and forever, it had to be culture that was adaptable. "So an Irishman is always an Irishman, a Jew always a Jew. Irishman or Jew is born; citizen, lawyer, or church-member is made." Therefore natural groups like the Irish or the Jews could not be destroyed without destroying their members themselves. However, Kallen thought, "artificial groups, like states, churches, professions, castes, can." Their interplay offered society the best prospects.

4:103   "Will America Remain Protestant and Anglo-Saxon?" For Kallen the answer was clear: it had better not. His other answer by this time was: America already was no longer simply Protestant and Anglo-Saxon. Countering a recently expressed popular view, he insisted that there was no melting pot of peoples. There *should* be no original-stock American Protestant norm. People could not entirely shed their old culture even if they wanted to; why should they want to? Why should they be taught to cherish the nation as One more than the nation as Many? Both outlooks, he proposed, had their place. In the tradition of James Madison, Kallen believed that the American polity was based on the notion of group interests. Kallen thought it should remain so. He worked out more details in 1924 in his *Culture and Democracy in the United States*. There he plotted a notion that turned America into a kind of nation of nations. Enemies called this approach Balkanization and feared the disintegration of nationhood. Kallen's book came out in the very year of the Johnson-Reed Act for Immigration Restriction—not a good time for modeling an America which demanded emotional and spiritual ties to most old countries.

Along the way, Kallen offered a whole new vocabulary of "cultural pluralism" designed to help Jews and others resist assimilation. The political model for America—Kallen was vague about politics—would follow the character of the Swiss federal republic. Its substance was to be one of a democracy of nationalities. America would eventually demonstrate what Kallen's great teacher William James would have called a multiplicity in unity. There could then survive what he described as a "persistence of a 'Jewish separation' that shall be national, positive, dynamic and adequate." Jews would rely for their integrity not on their God but on their history, culture, art, politics, and universalizing religious outlook. As they undertook this cultural turn or return, Kallen foresaw that so would the other peoples that made up America. Kallen asked, "Do the dominant classes in America want such a society?" The alternatives to a "yes" became clear. "Can they choose wisely? Or will vanity blind them and fear constrain, turning the promise of freedom into the fact of tyranny, and once more vindicating the ancient habit of men and aborting the hope of the world?" 4:104

Since Kallen was an independent intellectual who left no institutional legacy, it is harder to measure his influence than that of the Zionists in the Central Conference of American Rabbis or the various goodwill movements. But ideas do have consequences, and he was both grasping ideas then current and formulating new ones. He elaborated his vision for a half-century and made con- 4:105

tributions to models of pluralism which many who never learned his name have adopted. Yet the limits to that vision are obvious, limits other than those which led his critics to dismiss him as a potential Balkanizer of America. Kallen seemed never able to deal with these. There is pathos in a telltale footnote he added after one of the key passages in his writings. Kallen had worked out a whole philosophy, but only for people who had come from Europe's cultural heritage. He did not talk about Asians. More important, he also had to write that the Negro issue "requires a separate analysis." Capable of moving beyond only what we shall but momentarily call Anglocentrism, he remained bound to solutions related to Europe and Europeans in America.

4:106   The third important Jewish alternative offered in these decades of troubles was the Reconstructionist movement within Conservative Judaism. Its energetic inventor, Mordecai Kaplan, lived for a century. He was thus given decades in which to shape the cause that further confused the "mess" of which Silcox and Fisher had spoken. Kaplan also complicated the life of traditionally religious Jews. For him Judaism was not so much a matter of religion, race, *or* nation, though he could be respectful of all three. Judaism instead represented a way of life, a cherished civilization. Kaplan was not devoted to traditional synagogues, with their connotations of divine worship. Instead, the New Yorker's model was "The Jewish Center," which was dedicated to many functions. "Instead of the primary purpose of congregational organizations being worship, it should be social togetherness." Such an approach had to be an affront to any Americans dreaming of a homogeneous republic. This company included Christians who favored a biblical tradition, because Kaplan's vision, like Kallen's, also did without the God of Israel, whom Christians worshiped.

4:107   Kaplan was innovating and knew that he was doing so in radical fashion. God, for Reconstructionists, was to become "the power that makes for salvation." The rabbi professor sized up his times: "When new conditions arise that threaten the life of a people or of its religion," people in a tradition must create new social agencies and concepts. Judaism, Kaplan thought, could not rely on a common faith; too many good Jews disbelieved, must disbelieve, in God. But they could all cherish the heritage and the reality of belonging to a people and that would suffice. To promote such ends, when anti-Jewish movements were already contentious, Kaplan in 1922 founded the Society for the Advancement of Judaism out of his post at the Conservative Jewish Theological Seminary.

The full exposure of Kaplan's thought did not come until 1934   4:108
with his *Judaism as a Civilization*, yet he was quite consistent and very public with his ideas through the two decades before that book appeared. Kaplan stressed the civilizational theme constantly, thus mixing both emotional factors and rational achievements. He argued that there could be room for both cultural Zionism as a movement and for a pluralist America on Kallen's model. Kaplan, after all, was also speaking in favor of continuing Jewish separateness. He too opposed the melting pot approach through a program that he argued was religious. Through the years, Kaplan taught his seminarians what his work of 1934 canonized for his movement: *"From the standpoint of the Religious-Cultural program, whatever helps to produce creative social interaction among Jews rightly belongs to the category of Jewish religion, because it contributes to the salvation of the Jew."* What an observer might call the "interestingness" of any elements in a tradition became the basic criterion of communal life. Neither the supernatural basis of religion nor its rational foundations were of much account in this reading.

As Kallen spoke of "cultural Zionism," Kaplan devised a   4:109
"spiritual Zionism," while he put but few energies into the political Israel that was then taking shape. Reconstructionist Zionism could never be content with rebuilding Palestine. Kaplan thought that while a spiritual center for the civilization must exist there, Jews had to organize vigorous communities wherever they lived. None of these communities was extraneous to Jewish religion; each community was "the very substance out of which the Jew must strive to evolve religious qualities." Jewish communalism was turning out to be more deeply rooted than Jewish religion. The Reconstructionist cause, Kaplan argued, was intended to raise the present status of Jews from what he termed a "disintegrated and fragmented mass of individuals into an organic unity." What oil and wick were to flame, organized Jewish life was to be to religion—not vice versa.

Reconstructionism's program, with its consequent "God   4:110
idea," may have been offensive to conventional theists, but in Kaplan's eyes it definitely remained religious. He needed no longer to speak of the chosenness of Jews, and thus removed one offense which bothered those who claimed to be friendly to Ju-

daism but who resisted and resented radical claims for it. Other peoples should do with their civilizations what Jews must do with their own. But Jews should not underestimate their own potential. "In the Torah Jews have a potent instrument with which to humanize and civilize the human being." They had a vocation, as did other religious civilizations.

4:111   Kaplan, keeping an eye on the overwhelming Protestantism that surrounded him, found company with the Catholics, who struck him as being the other large unassimilable camp in the nation. "In America, the non-Catholic majority will accentuate its Protestantism by keeping at arm's length not only Catholics but also Jews." Kaplan noted accurately that the formal separation of church and state meant little in the United States. Protestants already knew how to work around that factor. Church influence would remain strong, but it would largely take Protestant form in national affairs and would be Catholic only in certain locales. Despite the resultant rivalry between the two sets of Christians, he thought, they would still keep the United States sufficiently Christian to force the need for some self-definition on Jews. Compromisers would come to realize that if Jews simply wanted to merge with the general population, their gift and their vocation would soon be virtually lost. They would therefore not advance one whit the cause of democratic nationalism, nor would they help complete the integration of the American people. They would only augment the ranks of the two churches that were then already dividing the American people, thus making national life less tolerable. Judaism, Kaplan thought, should find a mission alongside the two main versions of Christian community, and thus could also further democratic nationalism.

4:112   Kaplan, though a Conservative Jew, was so radical he could not help but create civil conflict within Judaism. When he and his friends in *Tehiyyath Yisrael*, "The Society of the Jewish Renascence," issued a pamphlet that Zionists reprinted, he drew response. His former teacher, Bernard Drachman, published a line in the *Jewish Forum* that typified the criticisms. Kaplan's ideas, Drachman charged, were un-Jewish and irreligious, full of "misconceptions, half-truths, incorrect assumptions and illogical conclusions." What had happened to divine revelation, to God, in such a scheme? Kaplan, he charged, was involved with crass naturalism of a sort that had to be in utter and absolute antagonism to Judaism. Genuine Judaism would suffer extraordinary calamity if Kaplan prevailed, thought his critic.

Orthodoxy, meanwhile, did not have the last word on the sub-   4:113
ject, but it voiced continuing words of attack. Kaplan charged that
such Orthodox Jews only asserted, "I believe in believing all that
I say I believe," but he did not see how Orthodoxy could connect
that kind of dogmatic but vapid assertion about faith with anything else in life. Therefore Orthodoxy, in Kaplan's concrete
phrase, could not be "geared into the wheels of the working and
thinking world of today." In 1928 Rabbi Jacob Kohn protested in
the name of Orthodoxy that Jewish faith was not a mere segment
of Jewish civilization. Instead, it was "a phase of the Jewish universal consciousness in the sphere of the Jewish people." Kaplan
answered: "From the fact that I would have Judaism treated as a
civilization, Dr. Kohn wrongly infers that the religion in it must
necessarily be deposed from a position of primacy." Not at all.
Kaplan simply would transform religious Judaism into a not necessarily theistic faith.

To an observer of such arguments between Zionists or over   4:114
cultural pluralism and Reconstructionism, it was evident that
American Judaism, though long torn into separate and often warring factions, was now being offered options which separated
Jews into a number of competing camps. In some respects these
camps relied on religious visions that seemed further apart from
each other than were Protestant Modernism and Fundamentalism.
It seems strange that so many non-Jews could regard from without
the communities of Jews as if they were all united in a single
entity. It seems less strange that many such viewers thought the
Jewish entity was not really at home in the America of the "100
percenters." By itself Judaism could never supplant their Protestant America, but in company with other faiths such as Catholicism the beleaguered feared that it could disrupt the homogeneity
these original-stock Americans cherished.

Catholics: In Civil War with the Puritan Spirit

"Will America remain Protestant and Anglo-Saxon?" Not if   4:115
the Catholics, finally, could help it. Americanism prevailed
among them. Now and again in the twenties the church had occasion to display itself as being both powerful and fully at home
in America. The best illustration of the triumphalist impulse was
the Twenty-Eighth Eucharistic Congress, the first such congress
to meet in the United States. Over a half-million people crowded

the trains and the streets of Chicago to converge on the religious event. James M. Gillis of the *Catholic World* best perceived the character of that event. "At Chicago we came, so to speak, out of our holes and corners, out of our catacombs into a blinding light." As a result, thought the editor, Catholicism "became the cynosure of the eyes of America, and of the world, and even according to the judgment of our most exacting critics, we conducted ourselves as those 'to the manor born'." No longer were Catholics in America a *gens lucifuga*, a hunted people. Sufferance and suppression had long been the badge of what Gillis, in friendliest tones, called "all the Catholic tribe." During that long period, he noted, an inferiority complex had been creeping into the Catholic consciousness or subconscious. No more. Now everything would be different.

4:116   By standing in imagination on the curb of a Chicago street watching the parade going by, the latter-day reader can get some sense of what this turning out of crowds for the Congress meant for Catholicism. Chicago's potent George William Cardinal Mundelein and his cohorts timed the building of a new seminary—he wanted to make it a university—for the congress and attracted 600,000 visitors to this St. Mary of the Lake forty-five miles from the city. In a nation where the sight of a single Catholic cardinal could appear threatening to non-Catholics, the procession of forty-nine red-robed princes of the church on Michigan Avenue had to stun bystanders. At Soldier Field 150,000 faithful attended Mass. The magnificent pageantry of the church there unfolded before the faithful and the fearful alike.

4:117   *Le Correspondent* in France sent Bernard Fay to report his mixed impressions. Fay gaped at the "gaudy and ostentatious pomp, the purple painted train, the vast public ceremonials, the display of luxury, the ornamentation [which] surprised both Protestants and unbelievers who had previously been rather favorable to Catholicism." Fay, by no means a neutral bystander, affected a sneering style while he wrote off the event as a display of gauche Americanism. His writing showed that he saw a cloud where Gillis found blinding light. To this French journalist the whole event smacked of triumphalism. While he thought the social and political prestige of Catholicism in America might have been increased by the congress, its pomp offended. Fay feared that in certain circles the display would cause the church's intellectual prestige to suffer. He may have been using the wrong glasses, and therefore he misread the situation. American Catholicism at this time, unlike its French counterpart, had little intellectual prestige to risk. Two decades earlier, after the pope had condemned modernism, Catholic clerical intellectuals turned timid. Little reputation of the sort a French elitist would be seeking, survived.

Fay demands more than quick dismissal for his snobbery. His   4:118 analysis of the church was quite balanced. He sensed that some American Catholics were using the Eucharistic Congress to lash back at politically minded Protestant preachers who often overstepped their bounds. As he put it, they had "made the mistake of allowing themselves to preach of America as the chosen land." Many intellectuals, wrote Fay, were now finding such notions puerile. The Protestant denominations were paying the penalty for their earlier zeal. They were now too ready to popularize, too ready to vulgarize the faith. In such a setting the dignity of the partly nonpolitical Catholic church poised it well to attract Americans: "The majesty of the Church makes a profound impression on the Protestants and the unbelievers in America." Fay added that the government respected the Catholic church as a powerful and effective element in the maintenance of order. It was against the background of this optimistic assessment—that an otherwise cynical America would be attracted to the mystery, the liturgy, the aesthetics, and the stability of Catholicism—that Professor Fay was let down by what looked to him to be the vulgarity and pomp of the Eucharistic Congress.

Still, as he toured universities, Hollywood, communities, and   4:119 churches, Fay found signs of hope. He noted especially the attitude of agnostics, who displayed no such systematic hostility toward Catholicism in America as they did in Europe. At times some' of them even looked congenially at Catholicism and seemed ready to ally with it against overassertive culture-Protestantism. Eventually, he remarked without explaining himself in detail, these agnostics would allow Catholicism to make use of them. They had a common enemy in Protestantism, "as an official religion (and that is what it almost is)," as a resented social system designed too much for moral watchdoggery. As Protestantism made its way into politics, Fay thought, it annoyed and wearied agnostics. While Protestantism thus frittered itself away, Catholicism was growing stronger, often finding favor with unbelievers, Jews, some Protestants, and youth in general.

Fay deserves recognition for having sensed better than most   4:120 the reaction to a Protestantism that was overplaying its hand, indeed to an official Protestantism which others thought was overstaying its time as the guardian of a chosen people. The United States, said the journalist, was undergoing the most serious moral crisis of its history. Protestantism was concurrently showing itself powerless to inspire the whole nation. Would Catholicism at such a moment win over the leaders, intellectuals, artists, and scholars—the elites who must precede the masses into the church? Fay's hope for Catholicism was that it might move and remain beyond the simply political sphere where it was beginning to assert power. Otherwise, the Catholic goal would also be frustrated, and the church would fail.

4:121   Some American Catholics joined Fay in being ambivalent about the congress display. The Chicago archdiocesan *New World* itself seemed wary of effects, if a bit disingenuous, as it warned: "Let there be no mistaking the fact that the Eucharistic Congress is no endeavor to demonstrate strength." Mundelein also cautioned lest the display get out of hand. At the opening event the Cardinal said, "Far be it from us to look upon this congress as a demonstration of our strength and numbers." Despite appearances, the *New World* kept stressing, "there is no thought behind it of a flaunting of vast numbers before non-Catholics," and, no doubt reflecting a sincere intention, the editorial urged that the whole event was designed as a distinctly religious manifestation. Protestant reaction, of course, was generally critical, but two blocks from Michigan Avenue the liberal editors of the *Christian Century* tried to drop their guard and their aesthetic sense for a moment and stay serene: "One may criticize the taste of some of these things," said their writer, but "they are all highly effective." There seemed to be new reasons to fear Catholic power and pride of place.

4:122   If one surveys the potential challengers to the dominant forms of Protestantism, this expansive expression of Catholicism stands out as the only credible candidate. Most of the nation's new immigrants were from Catholic Europe. In the decades before World War I Catholicism also had received the greatest influx of United States immigrants and had grown to threatening size. Under astute hierarchical leadership it was increasingly involved in public life.

4:123   "Will America remain Protestant and Anglo-Saxon?" André Siegfried used eyes trained in Catholic France to appraise American Catholicism. He thought that Catholics made up the civilization which would not assimilate but would instead continue to trouble Protestant America. Siegfried wondered whether in the cases of Slavic and Latin Catholics it was actually their religion that did the offending. Could religion perhaps be only part of what appeared to other Americans to be a resistant and fundamentally different civilization from theirs? The new immigration policy of 1924, he observed with some warrant, seemed directed at preserving a different civilization from the one these Slavs and Latins had been bringing.

At the same time, Siegfried also and rightly took the Catholic challenge seriously. "The Catholic Church . . . is the chief opposition to American Protestantism, for, besides its powerful vitality, which no doubt leads to excessive ambitions, it also has great religious prestige." That was why Catholicism remained a thing apart in the heart of the American body politic. Siegfried's verdict was that it "remains distinct and does not fuse." He went on to say that of course Catholicism along the way also picked up enemies other than Protestantism. Chief among these was the everyday materialism which encroached on spiritual life but which, he feared, might engulf Protestants and Catholics alike.   4:124

Silcox and Fisher, writing several years later, thought that antagonism between non-Catholic and Catholic America was even deeper than merely a struggle over who should dominate in civilization. To deal with the subject of aversion they quoted Sir Arthur Keith: "The heart of modern man is still alive with the instinctive longings, desires and prejudices of the tribal man." Those who would seek to build a new social order, he urged, must frankly give their prejudices a place in their civilization, but then keep them under the control of reason.   4:125

Keeping reason under control was something the Ku Klux Klan never had in mind as it brought Catholicism into its focus. The proponents of immigration restriction in 1921 and 1924 were also, in Keith's terms, as tribal as they ever were reasonable, though many found occasions to adduce rational arguments for limiting the numbers and kinds of newcomers. From both sides of the interbloc conflict between Catholics and Protestants that Mordecai Kaplan had feared, tribalism often dominated. Pamphlet warriors'and street fighters then turned their scattered enemies into what looked like tribes by the simple acts of pointing at and defining *the* Jews, *the* Protestants, *the* Catholics.   4:126

It was never to the advantage of partisans and crowd-pleasers in the twenties to remind themselves and others how internally divided was the group they opposed. Silcox and Fisher showed some sophistication when they dealt with the Catholic case. They spoke in terms of "struggle," "rivalry," "complications," "in-   4:127

transigence," and the like between Catholic groups. These were grudges they inherited from earlier immigrant days. "So it goes." The authors also pointed to competitive religious orders and communities of men and women vying for place in Catholicism. Even some personalities created conflict in the church: "It is impossible to exaggerate the importance of the personal factor in considering the future cooperative adjustments between Catholics and the larger community." Yet Protestants usually overlooked these troubling varieties within Catholicism. They found it advantageous to lump their rivals together and treat them simply as "the Catholics."

4:128   A few daring souls also worked for civic peace and civil relations between Catholics and Protestants, but the church made it hard for them. No ecumenical movement yet allowed for theological conversation. Joint worship was simply ruled out. Such formal limits, however, did not prevent some Catholics from linking for practical causes with Jews and Protestants. After World War I the National Catholic War Council was converted into the National Catholic Welfare Conference. Its leaders often found company with leaders of other religions when dealing with social issues. On Christmas Eve in 1920 Catholics of the conference stripe thus joined with Jews and Protestants within an American Committee on the Rights of Religious Minorities to issue an unprecedented three-faith attack against racial prejudice and religious fanaticism. All through the decade such Catholics also joined with other faiths to promote social justice causes.

4:129   An elite of Catholics emerged as counterparts to Everett Clinchy among Protestants and Louis Marshall and Roger Straus among Jews. A Catholic historian at Columbia University, Carlton J. H. Hayes, served as co-chair of the National Conference of Jews and Christians after 1929. Monsignor John A. Ryan, the tough-minded advocate of papal policies and truth claims, was also a farseeing pragmatist who created links on social issues with non-Catholics.

4:130   Pope Pius XI, pontiff through the interwar decades, was strongly opposed to any signs of interfaith cooperation. In 1928 he put some dampers on priestly involvements when he rejected all formal discussions by Catholics with Protestants anywhere. He forbade any kind of activity which might lead people to think there was parity between faiths or that Catholics could tolerate error. Only a tireless and daring Catholic could find a way past the obstacles of the papal document. Those who did summon energies had to make clear that they were working only on civic issues, matters of justice and not of theology. Yet even so they were cautious, for the papal encyclical seemed to anticipate even such kinds of creative dodges. The document was severe: there were not to be any religious relations, it said, with "those who do not profess [Christ's] entire and uncorrupted teachings." Not all Catholics were utterly deterred from common action with their religious neighbors, but in effect they had to secularize their activities with other believers before they could participate.

Not all the failures to cooperate could be blamed on the pope   4:131 or recalcitrant stay-at-home bishops. Within Protestantism, liberals were as wary as conservatives about bartering away what they claimed were liberties imparted by Protestantism to the nation. Even the Federal Council of Churches found it easier to work through interfaith organizations that also included Jews than it did to engage Catholics alone. Meanwhile, those Catholics who did find ways to deal with Protestants resented the coverage that stories of conflict received. In 1929, at a National Conference of Jews and Christians seminar at Columbia University, Catholic apologist J. Elliot Ross insisted that in spite of the very evident surviving manifestations of bigotry, some people were making good efforts to understand Catholics. "I suppose," he sighed, "that bigotry is more picturesque, and has a greater news value." But the American heart was sound, and people of good will still were making progress; why not accent that?

One may appreciate such irenic words and still recognize that   4:132 picturesque bigotry and conflict dominated the years. The Catholicism that encountered nervous Protestants was stronger than it had been earlier in America. American Catholicism entered the postwar world in an exuberant spirit, and seemed ready to issue some challenges. In 1919 James Cardinal Gibbons was jubilant as he met with the heads of Catholicism at the Catholic University of America in Washington during his golden jubilee as priest. He cheered the forming of the National Catholic Welfare Conference, which, he thought, would promote the Catholic cause nationally. In it, he said, one could hear a divine call to summon the best Catholic thought and the maximum energy for the kindling of religion in the hearts of the American people. Gibbons could sound as cheerful as the Protestant optimists. Coming at that postwar moment the conference appeared providential; it represented, he thought, a new era in the church.

However much the *New World* stressed the purely religious   4:133

character of prime events such as the Eucharistic Congress, or visitors like Bernard Fay hoped Catholicism would stay above politics, there was no place for the huge church to hide. Even to protect its interests, the church had to accent power in public life. To define this role, a sort of two-party system was developing within the church (as it was doing in Protestantism and Judaism). As in the case of the internal rivalries in Judaism, these contentions detracted from any possibility of its challenge to Protestantism, though militant Protestants rarely let themselves notice such internal disunity in the enemy camp. It was to their advantage to misportray Catholicism as a monolith. Its parties fought each other as much as they fought Protestant outsiders. The party lines served to divide into conflicting elements some of the cardinals, archbishops, bishops, priests, sisters, and laity, most frequently in disputes over economic and political issues. The catalyst for a decade of dispute over the National Catholic Welfare Conference was the passage of what came to be called the Bishops' Program of Social Reconstruction. While the conference programs appear moderate in retrospect, what Monsignor John A. Ryan advocated at the time, as we have seen, provoked some Catholic lay leaders to smell socialism, especially when dealing with organized labor.

4:134   As events of the decade unfolded and progressivism declined, there was little danger that too much of Catholicism would remain pro-labor. Church leadership increasingly deserted the scene, while labor leaders turned cooler to Catholicism. Teamster official Daniel Tobin generally supported Gibbons and Ryan but he noticed silence elsewhere. He complained that there were few Catholic clerics who had the courage to support the trade union movement. As a Catholic, he said, he was more dissatisfied with the position of the Catholic Church toward labor than he was with many Protestant or non-Catholic churches as churches. Labor leader James Meurer was of the opinion that "the people never left the church, but that many churches have left the people for a smug seat in the clouds of self-righteous contentment, where the lowly Nazarene would most likely get his head cracked by a burly policeman if he attempted to interfere." Ryan kept promoting the labor program but had to wait for the Depression years of the thirties to have much effect.

4:135   How Protestants viewed the new self-confidence of Catholicism, divided though it was, is well captured in one of the many books written to oppose the presidential candidacy of Governor

Al Smith of New York in 1928. Winfred E. Garrison, a liberal member of the Disciples of Christ at the University of Chicago and an editor of the *Christian Century*, spoke for many of the original-stock Protestants. He offered the standard Protestant view that, while Catholics were outnumbered, their influence in mass activity was disproportionate because they were united in a single body under authoritative leadership. This posture led him to pose the question: "Is Roman Catholicism consistent with American patriotism?" Garrison laid bare his prejudices when he described himself as having been reared a Protestant of Protestants. But he pledged fairness and representativeness.

When Garrison attacked Catholics for entering political life   4:136
while he defended Protestants for being there, he had to find a way to make his case. He did so on two grounds. Catholic pressure differed from the force exerted, "say, by the Methodist church in the interest of prohibition." Garrison charged first that Catholic policies were set undemocratically by a small hierarchy and not by the common conscience of the total membership of the church, as he presumed Methodism's were. Second, Catholicism claimed unique and divine authority over its lay members—as it would over candidate Smith. Garrison also feared what he called "the Cheapest Army in the World." These were the Jesuits, who enhanced their own power by working with major Catholic organizations. Though Garrison had to admit that Catholics were making only 30,000 converts a year in the United States, he still saw their aggression as a threat.

In another critical book from the period, *Will America Become*   4:137
Catholic?, John F. Moore quoted those more notable than himself, including British Catholic polemicist Hilaire Belloc, to show how Catholicism was the aggressor. In 1924 Belloc wrote in America's *Century Magazine* that "in this fundamentally Protestant and Puritan country a conflict, approximating to civil war, is arising between the Puritan Spirit and the Catholic Church." Belloc followed up this vision elsewhere with a taunting and triumphalist word about the Catholic choice of a pattern. It would act aggressively: "It has always done so, and it always will, please God."

Moore described what a present Protestant or a future Catholic   4:138
America meant. Protestant America was not threatening because Protestantism was individualistic. Catholicism was communal, territorial, authoritarian. That is why Georgetown historian Theodore Maynard, whom Moore cited as a militant convert to Ca-

tholicism, could use military terms for the struggle: "The plain fact is that America will soon become the decisive battle ground of the Faith," Maynard had written, pointing to the issue of Catholic power. That power was taking on an America which was truly Protestant. As such it was responsive to purely voluntary influence simply because the majority of citizens were themselves Protestant. Moore did not mention that Maynard spoke only of intellectual attempts to convert individuals, which sounded very much like the Protestant goal.

4:139   Moore did not want to exaggerate Catholic threats, but he also found reasons for Protestants to stay alert. "Protestantism will be seriously mistaken if it leaves the future of religion to the Roman Catholic Church." Protestantism must be "active, evangelical, definite in its faith, its discipline, its worship," or the United States would fall not to Catholicism but to indifference and disbelief. Moore's tract for the times ended with a twist that both sides often neglected: "The issue today is not whether America is to be made Catholic but whether America, Protestant or Catholic, is to be made Christian." It was too soon to ask whether it would be "made" any one religion at all.

4:140   While Garrison and Moore and any number of apologists made the case for Protestant power, they remained aware of limits resulting from Protestant individualism and sectarian division. Both factors blunted the Protestant impact and led to confusion. Both authors overlooked the communal and social character of Protestantism. This led both of them to omit this social element from consideration when they faced those who would supplant the Protestant powers. So they did not yet realize the effect a grand and permanent doctrinal division down the middle of the Protestant camp was having on its national influence. Out of the noise of this conflict would come a schism whose story we must tell. This schism was more threatening to Protestant dominance than the assertiveness of all those rivals outside the camp. With no single and immediate outside force to supplant Protestants and Anglo-Saxons in their national house, the issue then became *which Protestants, which Anglo-Saxons* would win in that house divided.

5

The Protestant
House Divided

The Rhetoric of Denominational Violence

Will America remain Protestant and Anglo-Saxon?" For   5:1
a third time, André Siegfried's question frames the plot for public
religious conflict in the interwar years. But in the early 1920s this
plot thickened when Protestants fought one another and as a result
permanently divided their house. For once, denominational controversy made the front pages of newspapers. Whether "explaining things to each other" or merely flailing away, the two main
parties entertained and appalled a public that ordinarily paid little
attention to them. Thus a *New York Evening Post* writer said that
with "the Fundamentalists and modernists explaining things to
each other, it is getting to be more interesting to go to church than
to stay at home and read the newspapers."

While the anti-Fundamentalists included moderates and liber-   5:2
als, we shall follow the practice of the newspapers and public and
in this chapter refer to the non-Fundamentalist camp simply as
Modernist (with a capital "M" to signify party labeling). The
rhetoric of these Modernists, even when it sounded civil, barely
disguised their fury. More often, however, it was the Fundamentalists who made a point of their militancy, as if not caring

155

Just before the Fundamentalist-Modernist conflict erupted openly, the Fundamentalist party through cartoons like this posed the issues as they saw these Modernist "signs of the times." (*The King's Business*, Biola University Archives.)

who overheard it, or even taking care *that* they be heard. F. M. Goodchild, a moderate conservative, told of an incident when a Fundamentalist had counseled against overt assault on a Modernist in an open meeting. A member of the Baptist Bible Union, a Fundamentalist faction, in the face of this counsel, disclosed his own method of procedure. He drew on a maxim of his hero, Davy Crockett: "Whenever you see a head, hit it." He also cited a prayer of Herbert Parson as being applicable: "O Lord! if thou doest deem it right/Send me some enemy to fight. I haven't had a dinging row/For six long months. Lord send one now!" The Lord was generous.

Our expert on dinging rows in the twenties, sociologist E. A.   5:3
Ross, threw light on such battles. "Conflict is sharpest and most passionate when it comes between those who have been united." This had been evident in the middle of the nineteenth century when three major Protestant groups, the Baptists, Methodists, and Presbyterians, split on North-South lines before the Civil War. None had come back together by 1920. Now a churchly civil war was to bring sharp and passionate conflict within the Protestant family. Another observation of Ross was relevant: "Family quarrels are proverbial for the intensity of the bitterness they develop, and next come church quarrels." These parties were *family*, if not of blood kin, then at least of believers related through long ties of affection, shared experience, common love of the America they had created or inherited, and fear of enemies they faced in common. But now on top of these family ties and further bloodying the scene, they were also *church* quarrels; the schism in the Protestant families and soul cut deeply through their denominations.

Ever after the twenties, church leaders had to face the question   5:4
of *which* Protestantism would speak for the whole, and *why* cultural Protestantism should claim credentials to order others when it did not know how to keep its own house together. The intransigents or Fundamentalists, the apparent losers in the immediate battle, were seen eventually to slink away from the scene of defeat, to be dismissed by the winners as fossilized or as scheduled for demise. Yet their heirs were to return decades later to challenge those who had apparently won decisively over them in the twenties. The effects of their endeavors were evident a half-century later in the form of Fundamentalist political movements which reached the Supreme Court, the Congress, the White House, the mass media, and the worlds of social analysis and

opinion polling. The tearing apart of Protestantism in the twenties, then, is one of the major incidents of American religious history. Its full consequences for culture and society keep revealing themselves differently with each passing decade.

5:5   The public in the twenties might show at best mild intellectual curiosity over what separated these churches, but the distinctions seemed to have little public consequence. In 1933 Harvard philosopher Alfred North Whitehead scored with an observation which has forced subsequent historians of Protestantism to take pains with the contexts of their story. Protestant Christianity, he wrote, was "shewing all the signs of a steady decay. Its dogmas no longer dominate: its divisions no longer interest: its institutions no longer direct the patterns of life." On that set of terms, America was to be viewed about the same way, whether Methodism or Congregationalism prospered or declined. By 1920, the surviving public curiosity about organized religion was directed not to dogma but to the public stands which about half the leadership in various denominations took in respect to issues like evolution or biblical criticism, over against the stands, on these issues, of the other half in the same churches. Evolution and biblical criticism may themselves have often appeared to be doctrinally esoteric. Yet they became issues of consequence with respect to public schooling and to battles over moral authority in the culture. And if even these matters of controversy still looked too dogmatic and churchly, we can move further to say: the positions half the people in a church body took on the Red Scare, immigration restriction, and the Ku Klux Klan; to war and peace or prohibition; to birth control or labor versus management, had consequences in voting booths and the public forum.

5:6   What often originally appears to be beside the point in the culture turns out later to have been central, in this case because these churches were part of that ecosystem. Their members, one recalls, were also citizens. They gave some part of their heart to churches and other parts to the other spheres of life. What appears at first to be an act of daring on the part of any historian who promotes the notion that the churches were consequential makes eminent sense when one reassesses power relations in the twenties. Not all events in all organizations, of course, have visible direct bearing on the larger citizenry. The stories of *aggiornamento*, a shaking-up reform, in the Knights of Pythias or the Odd Fellows or any number of other fraternal orders may be, or may seem to be, an indicator of nothing more than the condition of

Pythianhood or Oddfellowship. The effects of these stories stop at the edges of the lodges themselves. Even in such cases, however, it might not take much effort to show how attitudes formed in these subgroups can affect behavior in the larger society. Back to the churches: echoes of the story of upheaval in the Northern Baptist Convention or the Presbyterian Church reverberated all the way to the halls of legislation, the libraries of intellectuals, the seats of power.

While the major battles within the Baptist and other churches   5:7
were fought between 1919 and 1925, there had been skirmishes, gatherings of armies, drawings of battle lines, and digging of trenches for some years previously. After the middle of the nineteenth century, movements of Protestant liberalism developed to adjust the faith in order to greet and embrace the modern world. In the main, such movements were part of an adaptation to Darwinism; partisans called their expressions theistic evolution. The movements also imported from Europe some measure of the higher biblical criticism. Scholars using this approach treated biblical materials much the same as they would handle other ancient literature. Out of this liberalism within many mainstream denominations there also did develop some overtly and militant modernist camps which helped lead the party we are presently capitalizing: Modernist. They gave hospitality to scholars who challenged the traditional ways of stating the faith, people who were devotees of science, reason, and progress at the expense of traditional views of revelation or dogma.

Fundamentalism in America, a complex emergence which also   5:8
inevitably eludes precise definition, was at base a reactionary movement against Protestant liberalism and the Modernist party. As such it appeared as a revanchist force, after the challenges of modernity had become too corrosive, abrasive, and threatening in the eyes of millions of believers. The pioneers of this movement first began gathering at major Bible conferences already before the turn of the century. They prospered in the circle of mass evangelists who, in order to convert people, stressed the believer's personal experience of Jesus and the full authority of the Bible.

In the second decade of the new century, conservatives, not   5:9
ready yet to form a party called Fundamentalist, anticipated the name of the movement by calling a series of pamphlets on controverted themes *The Fundamentals*. After World War I these countermodernists began to congeal in organizations including versions of that key word in their title. In July 1920 Curtis Lee

Laws, editor of the Baptist *Watchman-Examiner*, deciding that "conservative" was too pejorative a term, chose "Fundamentalist" as both a less worn and a more appropriate name. There was to be ever after no turning back on the part of those who embraced the cause associated with the name. Some opponents used it to stigmatize these militants, but the victims of such efforts in turn proudly marched under its banners. They spoiled for war, at whatever expense to their energies or good names.

5:10   When editor Laws named the movement, he set out to define its focus: "Fundamentalism, then, is a protest against that rationalistic interpretation of Christianity which seeks to discredit supernaturalism." Scholars have picked apart or supplemented every word in that original definition. For instance, Fundamentalisms can be, and the American versions often were themselves, in a special way rationalistic about divine revelation. One should therefore not be thrown off by the dismissal by Laws of the anti-supernaturalist version. Many of the groups Fundamentalists fought did not by any means engage in wholesale discrediting of supernaturalism. Other critics have thought Laws' description too negative, too defensive. Yet to see protest or reaction in the movement is a creative way to begin analysis. When Laws and his party selected their own name, many words like "conservative," "traditional," "orthodox," or "classic" could have been available. They had to coin "Fundamentalist" to indicate that a special innovative kind of response was emerging at a time when liberals were testing conservative and orthodox traditions. In the face of the testing, Fundamentalists protested. That reactive character was at the heart of this American ingathering and in the consequent drawing of permanent party lines.

5:11   Laws rejected one name which would have applied to most but by no means all in his faction. This candidate was "premillennialist," which meant that there would be great unsettlement on earth *before* Jesus came to rule for, literally, a thousand years. Laws would not wait for the battle of Armageddon which would precede such upheavals; there were battles to fight here and now, for God and country. Laws made history more than he could have foreseen on July 1, 1920, with these lines: "We suggest that those who still cling to the great fundamentals and who mean to do battle royal for the fundamentals shall be called 'Fundamentalists.' By that name the editor of the *Watchman-Examiner* is willing to be called."

The word stirred reaction at once. Laws was soon publishing   5:12
letters to the editor, one of which took exception to the notion that
safe-and-sound Baptists, who held conservative Baptist views,
should be put under suspicion and accusation unless they signed
up for Fundamentalism. That term, said the correspondent, was
"not new. It is old and well into the stage of cant, pretense, hy-
pocrisy and chronic accusation." But let such readers complain;
Laws and his colleagues would push on. For instance, William
Bell Riley, a militant pastor in Minneapolis, on enemy turf in *The
Baptist*, said that his Fundamentalists had "entered this controversy knowing that it was not a battle, but a war." They had entered it, he added, "in a union of strength that will not be broken
and that will never surrender" to religious skepticism.

Some of the intentions Laws disclosed in the choice of name   5:13
were never to be realized. He thought that Fundamentalism could
be a more neutral word than conservatism, but moderates and
liberals in the church soon made Fundamentalism a more stigmatizing term than conservatism itself had been in 1920. And in
corners of the secular world, most of the leaders who commented
were not as ready as some *New Republic* intellectuals had been to
charge liberals with evasiveness, duplicity, or compromise. They
instinctively and naturally sided against the Fundamentalists.
These believers under attack were easily caricatured as southern
hillbillies, even though leadership came from northern urbanites.
They were also just as readily dismissed as desiccated, fossilized
relics in an age of science, reason, and progress.

To set the struggle in a larger context, however, it is best to   5:14
understand Fundamentalism as a worldview among worldviews,
one mode of looking at the world alongside others. Competitors
to Fundamentalism included the modernist Christian philosophy
of history, the systematic Marxist and progressivist outlooks of
the day, or one of the humanisms current in the twenties. That is,
Fundamentalism looked implausible to everyone who stood outside it. But within the movement there were dedicated and intelligent people who provided highly informed arguments for their
case. While in their urgent spirit they often resorted to despicable
tactics, they could rightfully say that so did the other side; that
they often sacrificed more, showed more integrity, and held the
line with a sense that the stakes were higher than did many liberals
and many in the Modernist faction.

The Fundamentalists had as one purpose to stir up troubles and   5:15

engage in fights. Another Baptist fundamentalist, the militant Minneapolis cleric William B. Riley, elaborated: "A fundamentalist is a person who unreservedly believes in the fundamental doctrines of supernatural, evangelical Christianity. A modernist is a person who rejects any or all of these doctrines." Fundamentalists finally had to become, in their colloquial version of a biblical term, "come-outers." They were believers who had to follow the logic and act on the emotion which tugged at them to come out and be separate from those they saw as compromisers or tainters of their faith. These contenders soon came to form a neatly bounded and profoundly bonded group. They developed instincts to determine who was inside and who outside their circle. They decided what the fundamental doctrines were to be. The choices available to fundamentalists were many, for the dictionaries of Christian dogma or doctrine were thick with entries.

5:16   America's most noted public philosopher of the twenties, Walter Lippmann, was a humanist who often accused Modernists of pretension and equivocation. He refused to make cultural alliances with them and used his neutralist posture to critical advantage. Lippmann better than most discerned what was at stake. Despite its apparent irrelevance to him, he and his readers knew that the issue as to whether "Adam was created at nine o'clock in the morning or whether he descended from an ape" *did* have importance for millions. In a culture founded so significantly on the Bible, Lippmann saw that one set of believers thought that only an infallible, inerrant Book could serve as an absolute authority. For them, Lippmann noted, "the issue is whether there exists a Book which, because it is divinely inspired, can be regarded by men as the 'infallible rule of faith and practice,' or whether men must rely on human reason alone, and henceforth do without an infallible rule of faith and practice."

5:17   Lippmann devised a little drama to show why the levels of emotion invested by the two sides differed so radically. He heard the Modernist characteristically saying: "We can at least discuss it like gentlemen, without heat, without rancor." The Fundamentalist then would ask: "Has it ever occurred to you that this advice is easier for you to follow than for me?" The Modernist would be put off: "How so?" Then the Fundamentalist would reveal his involvement. "Because for me an eternal plan of salvation is at stake. For you there is nothing at stake but a few tentative opinions none of which means anything to your happiness." It is hard to picture either Modernists or liberals recognizing their own side in that portrait, but for Lippmann this was an accurate rendering of the circumstance. His Fundamentalist went on, revealing the emotions of at least one side. "Your request that I should be tolerant and amiable is, therefore, a suggestion that I submit the foundation of my life to the destructive effects of your skepticism, your indifference, and your good nature. You ask me to smile and commit suicide."

Of course, Fundamentalists attached other doctrines to this   5:18
root issue of biblical authority. The majority of the Christians in the world—Catholic, Orthodox, Lutheran, Anglican, and the like—would have named some additional or other teachings than those being selected as fundamental. Among these would have to be ideas about the sacraments or the doctrine of the church. Yet Fundamentalists chose the kind of doctrines on which they could unite, as they could not on the sacraments. Their selected dogmas served better for the defining of causes. Fundamentalists especially resisted what they called the impulse of liberals to spiritualize or symbolize what they thought they must take literally. Sacramental themes were too spiritual and symbolic by nature, and anyhow, to their embarrassment in case any one was noticing, Fundamentalists could not agree on these themselves. Thus Baptist and Presbyterian Fundamentalists held vastly differing views on baptism. They chose instead those themes that could be a "scandal" in the Greek New Testament sense of the term *skandalon*: these were trip-wires, traps, things to stumble or fall over, or into which one would bump. Back then, just as later, contenders and observers argued over how many fundamentals there had to be—five? fourteen? an indefinite number?—but the quality of the chosen doctrines was more important than the quantity.

Thus most Christians would say that Jesus died for them, but   5:19
Fundamentalists insisted on a literal substitutionary blood atonement. The blood, taken literally, was scandalous and thus effective as a symbol for drawing boundaries. Other Christians also said they believed that Jesus was risen from the dead, but Fundamentalists often sniffed the odor of spiritualization in the minds of these other believers. To the reactionaries, there had to have been in the raising of Jesus a physical event involving corpuscles and muscle tissue. Such insistences were offensive to other parties. The creeds others professed also talked about Jesus coming again in glory at the end of history, but many in the denominations treated that theme symbolically too. They looked for the reality to which such language pointed: that the Lord of history

controlled the outcome of history. Fundamentalists in reaction talked about a literal second coming, foreseeing a visible descent of Jesus from heaven, with clouds and the sound of trumpets, an event certainly to be followed by the thousand-year actual rule of Christ on earth. Such a picture and proposal would never do for progressive Christians.

5:20   The best illustration among the chosen doctrines was the virgin birth of Christ. The creeds stated and most Christians concurred that Jesus was "born of the Virgin Mary." But many found no reason to speculate about specifically how this all occurred. Ancient religions found virgin births commonplace, and most biblical writings did not bring up the subject in connection with Jesus. In the modern world the idea of virgin birth seemed to belong to obsolete and by now irrelevant worldviews and not to the revelation of God. Isaac M. Haldeman of New York's First Baptist Church attacked Modernists on this subject. "How can you be a friend to the man who so deals with the birth of Christ that His Mother is put in the pillory of unchastity and faithless wifehood?" In short, as Haldeman continued, this meant that one who was vague about the virgin birth had to profess that Jesus was a bastard and Mary a fornicator. Fundamentalists were not ready to yield ground to people who thought symbolically or spiritually about such issues. The battle was joined.

The Fundamentalist Loss of Denominational Machinery

5:21   The Gettysburg of this civil war was fought on the soil of the Northern Baptist Convention, which seems to be a strange locale to take people who want to understand modern American political life and culture. How many literal battles take place on landscapes seen as remarkable aside from the battle? Yet the convention was in its own way worthy of remark. True, it lived in the statistical shadow of the giant Southern Baptist Convention and the larger black Baptist churches. In the 1926 religious census it numbered only an estimated 1,230,509 adult members out of a total Baptist population among American whites of 7,859,626. Nor did Baptists as a whole amount to as much in *Who's Who* as did Episcopalians or Presbyterians. Their linking together at all in the form of the convention was itself a recent achievement. Not until 1907 had a cluster of boards and bureaus and several thousand local congregations united to form it. And yet members of this body,

themselves heirs of dissenters against churchly establishment
back in colonial times, had become secure members of the cultural establishment in the twenties. They were part of a strategically poised church body.

The location of this denomination appears ever more strategic   5:22
when one notes some of those Baptists within it who *were* in
Who's Who and who were somebodies in American culture. The
Convention could claim Charles Evans Hughes, later chief justice
of the United States Supreme Court and already governor of New
York when he gaveled the convention into being in 1907. In the
years of the controversies early in the twenties, President Warren
G. Harding was also a member of the convention, as were numerous political figures.

As for prominent Baptists involved directly with religious or-   5:23
ganizations, the most notable Protestant cleric earlier in the century, Social Gospel pioneer Walter Rauschenbusch, moved from
a small German Baptist group into the orbit of the Northern
Baptists, who were emerging as a denomination around 1907,
and remained there until his death in 1918. In the twenties, the
best-known Protestant preacher in the country, Harry Emerson
Fosdick, was a Northern Baptist, though he also picked up Presbyterian ties. George Eastman of Kodak photography fame in
Rochester was active in Baptist circles. John D. Rockefeller, Jr.,
was an enthusiastic lay Baptist who poured millions into Riverside
Church, the (once Baptist) University of Chicago, the Interchurch
World Movement, foreign missions, and many other causes. To
this roll call one could add the names of many of the nation's more
notable theologians and educators, including Brown University
president William H. P. Faunce. Perhaps the most influential systematic theologian in the Protestantism of the period had been A.
H. Strong of Rochester. As such people poured energy into the
convention, its battlegrounds and fates were not marginal to
spheres of power in the surrounding public culture.

After all this advertisement of the importance of the setting, it   5:24
may seem like a comedown to deal with the arena of battle itself
and with the modes of its prosecution. Surnames of most partisans
are not and were not then household or churchhold words: people
named Riley, Straton, and Shields for the extreme Fundamentalists; Goodchild and Massee for conservatives who ended in the
middle; Mathews battling for Modernism. While major newspapers and magazines looked on, reporting sometimes in amuse-
ment, more often in condescension, and sometimes with partisan

horror, most of the rhetoric of battle appeared in sectarian and small-circulation organs like the official *The Baptist* and the independent *Watchman-Examiner*. These journals would be utterly unremembered, did not historians have to consult them in archives where they preserve recall of the sounds of battle.

5:25   The editors of Baptist journals, especially on the Fundamentalist side, were bold to declare that theirs was to be a fight to the finish, that the other side in their family quarrels was especially despicable. They seldom wasted as much fury on infidels or Methodists as they spent on each other. When any worked for an armistice, tried to pretend the war was over, or sneered a dismissal of it, Fundamentalists reacted. In 1921, only a year after the party acquired a name, *The Baptist* editors announced that "Fundamentalism . . . if it ever was an issue in the Baptist denomination, is no longer so. It is not even an accredited candidate for consideration among us." The *Watchman-Examiner*, not wishing to take the death of Fundamentalism lying down, came back: "With a twist of mind almost serpentine *The Baptist* declares that fundamentalism is dead," it stated, simply because Fundamentalists at the annual convention in Des Moines that year refused to play along with Modernist agenda-setters. *The Baptist* then replied in the sort of tones the wounded would choose. But the *Watchman-Examiner* crusaders were not finished. Their rival editors, the journal's own article of response concluded, were "angry because they have been publicly corrected, and now like incorrigible children they bite and scratch and use ugly language."

5:26   When the undenominational *Outlook* interfered on the scene in behalf of the Modernist cause, the *Watchman-Examiner*, ever on the ramparts, was critical. Why, its editors asked, did non-Baptist editors overlook the fact that Fundamentalists, as these intransigent Baptists put it, were "thorough-going Baptists who are trying to rid our denomination of saddles and bridles and riders, too?" The *Watchman-Examiner* even took on the *New York Times*, because that paper's editors failed to comprehend what the war was about. The influential *Times* had represented Fundamentalism as "addiction to odds and ends of dogma borrowed from other religions." Nor were they happy to find secular editors placing Fundamentalists on a parity with the Modernists by uttering plagues on both houses. This is what Episcopal writer Algernon Crapsey had done in the *Nation* in 1924. Crapsey wrote that it was "difficult for anyone of ordinary intelligence and common decency to retain a shred of respect for either party in this disgraceful quarrel."

An editorial in the *Watchman-Examiner* complained that the   5:27
outside world never was able to get the true issues in focus, nor,
it went on, did secular writers properly measure the weight of the
debated points. Such misassessments, the editors charged, consistently created the impression that at stake were dead doctrines in
which only piously ignorant people were still interested. Public
editorialists, complained these Baptists, tried to see the controversy as trivial by charging that the churches were being "rent
asunder by the blind allegiance paid by zealots to antiquated, medieval dogmas."

At other times, the Fundamentalist Baptists rejoiced over the   5:28
way secular journalists could be even-handed, when they pointed
to duplicity and evasion on the part of Modernists who were trying to be the kin of humanists in the public culture. They had
reason to cheer Herbert Croly who said in the *New Republic* that
although many on one churchly side prided themselves on being
liberal, "their liberalism consists largely of applying to religion
the compromising technique of opportunist politics." Many in the
secular press then shared, and later students of the controversy
often agreed with, this judgment. Most of all, the Fundamentalist
editors resented what they considered opportunist efforts by Modernists who pretended that there was no war on at all, or when
these uttered premature calls for a cease-fire. Late in the game the
Western Recorder editors chided *The Baptist*: "Friend Baptist,
how did you do it? How did you get the hare and hounds all into
a happy love feast together?" This 1929 exchange occurred four
years after the climactic convention battle, and after the secular
press had lost interest. The militant religious editors dared not
drop the subject and could not welcome efforts at concord.

Fundamentalists organized because they thought that the   5:29
Northern Baptist Convention machinery was entirely in the hands
of compromisers and Modernists. They chose to rally both in an
interdenominational organization as well as at least one inside
their convention, the Baptist Bible Union. The larger group was
the World's Christian Fundamentals Association, which Baptist
William B. Riley led. Six thousand people showed up in Philadelphia in May of 1919 to take part in forming it. Riley billed the
founding as "an event of more historic moment than the nailing
up of Martin Luther's theses at Wittenberg cathedral," the symbolic moment of the beginning of Protestantism. So aggressive

was this movement in the trenches that some Baptist conservatives had to make clear that it did not represent their own Fundamentalism in all respects. Both for personal and strategic reasons there were cautious Baptists who for a time tried to be congenial. For one instance, the association chose to make anti-evolution a main point of its crusade in the mid-twenties. Not all Baptist Fundamentalists wanted to put their first energies into that issue.

5:30   Now, it would be wrong to side with Walter Lippmann and give the impression that all the passion and militancy on these issues came from one side. Modernists also cared greatly for their churches and their viewpoints. They were genuinely agitated by the idea that, if Fundamentalists won, Christianity would become so implausible that the faith could no longer help shape the culture or attract and "save" thoughtful individuals. The catalytic event which made these counter-Fundamentalists visible and which enraged the reactionaries was a sermon Harry Emerson Fosdick preached just before the 1922 Northern Baptist Convention meeting: "Shall the Fundamentalists Win?"

5:31   The golden-voiced pulpiteer spoke up for magnanimity, liberality, and tolerance of spirit. "What immeasurable folly," he cried, was the effort by some to drive from the Christian churches all who did not agree with their own view of the inspiration of scripture. Tragically, Fosdick went on, all this activity was occurring at a time when believers ought to be working for other sets of answers in the presence of colossal problems. Sermons may have been losing their power as major cultural events, but Fosdick had the power to influence, and his preaching produced vehement reactions. When these came in, the New York preacher quoted John Dryden against Jeremy Collier and applied the words to the typical Fundamentalist attacker: "I will not say 'The zeal of God's house hath eaten him up'; but I am sure it has devoured some part of his good manners and civility."

5:32   Manners and civility were the last things Fundamentalists dared permit distract them. While these were important to moderates, the militants took pride in their own brusqueness. In Calvary Baptist Church in New York a Fundamentalist warrior, John Roach Straton, replied to Fosdick with an anti-evolutionary sermon title which also bore a question mark and which showed how quickly the fights could descend to lower depths: "Shall the Funny-Monkeyist Win?"

5:33   Some incautious Fundamentalists simply impugned the motives of their fellow Baptists. The *Western Recorder* dealt a low blow as its editors recalled Fosdick's relation to the high and mighty, such as the Rockefellers. Their colleague, the editorial said, had preached his notorious sermon in a Presbyterian church. "It goes without saying that Presbyterian cash looks good to him, and withall covers a multitude of Baptist doctrines." Another attack, which Fosdick took the trouble to preserve in his autobiography, spoke of the famed preacher's "chameleon accomplishments." The attacker charged that Fosdick denied the fundamental truths of the faith, but then added, "it's 'dollars to doughnuts' that he has faith enough in the monthly pay check to deposit it at the bank."

The conclusive battle-scenes were to be the successive North-   5:34
ern Baptist conventions held beginning in 1919 in Denver and then through succeeding years in Buffalo, Des Moines, Indianapolis, Atlantic City, Milwaukee, and climactically in 1925 in Seattle. Ordinary citizens awakened in those metropolises on the summer mornings when these Baptists gathered, no doubt hardly noticing that conventioneers were present in their cities, and certainly not picturing anything decisive going on. Yet those who fought the battles for votes in warfare over seminaries, mission boards, and church government, did think that *their* world was at stake, and with it *the* world.

The World's Christian Fundamentals Association now paled as   5:35
an instrument compared with the denominational party itself. Fundamentalist Northern Baptists mobilized to attract the lay majority they believed was quietly with them against the minority of Modernists who ruled the schools and boards. No one can assess exactly what that membership was thinking. There were indications that the majority of them were put off by the battles and had other concerns on their minds, but they were drawn in willy-nilly because their leaders attacked each other from pitched camps. No doubt the majority were instinctively conservative, non-Modernist believers, who sided with the convention moderates when these sought peace in the time of destructive family and church quarrels. Fundamentalists, however, could never compromise, even if because of that stance they sometimes overplayed their hands, lost backing, and thus lost battles.

Many of the original skirmishes were about and against Baptist   5:36
involvement in various ecumenical ventures, such as the Interchurch World Movement, the Rockefeller-backed utopian scheme for church cooperation, which flourished for only a season after World War I. To autonomy-minded Baptists, the movement

looked too nondoctrinal, too busy and Modernist. Haldeman reacted for the Fundamentalists: "The church is not here to mend
society." Instead, its supreme purpose was to pluck brands from
the burning. The Fundamentalist party at the same time feared the
tendency to bring Baptist congregations, which historically regarded themselves as autonomous, into too formal alliances and
thus under the sway of nettling and then encroaching church bureaucracies. The very notion of church people setting out to raise
$100,000,000 back when that figure amounted to something pre-
supposed too much interconnection in a New World Movement
and a five-year plan. What would happen to Baptist local-church
independency? asked the Fundamentalist leaders.

5:37   In Buffalo in 1920 the Baptists were to debate something that
had been previously seen as very un-Baptist: should their
churches formulate and live by official creeds? Creeds in old
times had always smelled of Catholicism to Baptist dissenters
who wanted to live only by the Bible. But these were new times.
Editor Laws looked back much later on the Buffalo event and
asked in the face of the compromisers, "Having fought valiantly
for the truth through the centuries, are we now to compromise
with error in the name of tolerance, fraternity, and Christian charity? The Baptist fathers conquered error on the fields of battle.
Are their sons to compromise with error at drawing-room conferences?" Yet he and his colleagues admitted that even they had not
liked the character of the Buffalo fray, where "a sober, reveren-
tial, thoughtful body of men and women was transformed into a
shouting, hissing, applauding bedlam. The behavior was shame-
ful." During that bedlam, he had to remember, one of the stands
in the auditorium collapsed. That was the kind of religious convention news the *New York Times* thought merited reporting. That
event had indicated both the overflow size of the audience and its
passion. William B. Riley wanted to keep the proper scale. Writing in *The Baptist*, a journal not friendly to his cause, he said that
his Fundamentalists had "entered this controversy knowing that it
was not a battle, but a war." They had entered it, he added, "in a
union of strength that will not be broken and that will never surrender" to religious skepticism.

5:38   In 1922, Newton Seminary professor F. L. Anderson, in a letter to the *Watchman-Examiner*, isolated several parties. "The
fundamentalists are only a fraction of the conservatives," he reminded editors and readers. They were simply those conservatives
who were organized for the propagation of their views. He turned

the phrase properly: they mobilized "for the purpose of capturing the machinery of the denomination." Next to them were the non-Fundamentalist conservatives; they opposed the tone and personnel of the extremists. He situated accurately the next faction, the "great middle-of-the-road group, which both fundamentalists and radicals conspire to ignore, but which is the balance wheel of the denomination." Then came the liberals, followed by the largely lay, nontheological group who understood little of the controversy, thought little about it, and uttered " 'a plague on both your houses'."

And what would all the spoils be? Because of congregational   5:39 autonomy, Baptists had little power over each other's local churches. They had to seize control over the common ventures, notably in foreign missions and higher education. So apathetic have mainstream Protestants subsequently become about the idea of sending missionaries into the world that it is hard to recreate the sense of how much was at stake in the battles of the twenties. The convention itself had been more than anything else an outgrowth of the American Baptist Foreign Mission Society. Its leadership now drew Fundamentalist fire in the decade of controversy. If the large financial goals proposed by the convention in those years were to be met, critics asked, who would get to manage the funds and set the policies? The intransigents complained that bureaucracies already kept most of the dollars that were intended for missions at home, far from foreign shores. They charged that Modernists in seminaries poisoned missionary minds. When donor Milo P. Treat gave $1,750,000, with conservative creedal strings attached, to the Home Mission Society, moderates and liberals took their turns to protest the poisoning of the atmosphere, the spirit of distrust on this front.

New York pastor John Roach Straton used his Fundamentalist   5:40 League to organize for this battle. Bertha Henshaw, a member of Straton's congregation and a former employee of the Foreign Mission Society, made the charge that in the files were evidences of Modernism on the mission front. The society would not release these files, so Straton jabbed at it through 1923 and 1924. So strident and tantalizing was he that even the *New York Times* and other secular papers found it of value to report on the charges and tactics of both sides. The Board of Managers of the Society claimed that after searching the files they had found no evidence to support the attacks by Henshaw and Straton, and exonerated itself. Such summary judgment did nothing to quiet affairs, and delegates to the Milwaukee convention of 1924 ordered that the charges be investigated. The Fundamentalists then came up with some condemning material in interviews with missionaries, and found good reason to continue the battle.

5:41   During these decisive five years the other front alongside foreign missions was higher education in the form of the Baptist colleges and seminaries which Fundamentalists rightfully feared they were losing. Some were already gone. T. T. Shields of Toronto in 1923 attacked the University of Chicago, founded with Baptist money but "nurtured by the Rockefeller Trust" and now "the most gigantic corruption fund that ever cursed the Christian world." The school was a hotbed of infidelity, an accursed thing "from Hell, beyond any doubt." Fundamentalist defense also took them to the convention floor. It is hard now to suggest what a great role such church-related institutions played in the culture of the 1920s. Private schools had a larger part in the higher academic and professional-training market then, and the ministerial profession was appropriately seen as fateful for the culture. Prominent Baptists had endowed divinity schools—Colgate Rochester, Crozer, the University of Chicago—but now, said Fundamentalists, these places were turning apostate.

5:42   In 1921 a number of Fundamentalist leaders had issued a call to arms with a pamphlet called *The Denominational Situation: Should Our Schools Be Investigated?* Of course they should. Liberals warned that such probes would drive out scholars and leave Baptist leadership unprepared for the scientific age while other denominations would profit from their exodus. The Fundamentalists heard these charges, but felt the stakes were too high for them to sit quietly by and avoid risks.

5:43   The Fundamentalist challenge to the seminaries met varied responses, but neglecting to answer the attackers' mail seemed to be the prevalent practice or strategy in at least five of eight targeted institutions. Those who spoke up in the other schools defended freedom and reminded Baptists of their time-honored resistance to creedal tests. Some schools, like Newton seminary in Massachusetts, were clever enough to pose alternative fundamentals and to taunt those who appeared to be too sure of which doctrines belonged on the list. But such efforts only angered the critics more. Only one school, Northern Baptist Seminary, founded in 1913 to oppose the University of Chicago, was able to offer generally satisfying responses, but of conservative, not Fundamentalist, sorts. In 1920 at Buffalo the critics of the schools had succeeded in getting an investigation approved, but the next year a whitewashing report came back.

In December of 1921 a communication to the Fundamentals Council emphasized: "There is no place for the philosophy of modernism in Baptist schools." One almost amusing misfire occurred in 1921 when Ernest M. Hopkins, who moonlighted as a trustee at a small Baptist school, received an inquiry about his school's orthodoxy. The letter, it turned out, had been missent to him at his place of employment, Dartmouth, a non-Baptist school where Hopkins was president. Hopkins replied vehemently, angered as he was over what he termed bigotry. By the time the mail situation was cleared up, word had spread that Baptists were out to do heresy-hunting at independent colleges.   5:44

A "monstrous inquisition" by a "religious Ku Klux" was now underway, editorialized the Unitarian *Christian Register*. Soon the *Boston Herald* picked up the story, and the secular press was off and running with this occasion to provoke both horror and glee. Congregational-backed Carleton College in Minnesota had had some ties with the Baptist church, but began to distance itself and finally in 1928 broke all relations with the Minnesota Baptist Convention. W. B. Riley and his pursuers went after all the Baptist schools, and ended up publishing lists of which they considered to be safe ones. Most of the prestigious colleges and even many of the generally conservative institutions were off his approved list. The Fundamentalists then embarked on a policy of starting their own Bible colleges to perpetuate their movement. For the moment, moderates and liberals were in command of ministerial training and Baptist higher education in general. The Fundamentalists would have to fight another day.   5:45

As so often before, the theological points at issue never did get much airing in the climactic confrontation at Seattle in 1925. Parliamentary moves determined the winners and losers. The two extreme parties were obviously stalemated, and were unable to coexist. At a crucial moment a contender named J. Whitcomb Brougher sought compromise: "If every extreme modernist will resign his position and every extreme fundamentalist stop his fighting and get down to business we will be ready to go."   5:46

The convention generally followed Brougher's counsel of moderation, which meant that the members of the militant organization, the Baptist Bible Union, at the end had to trudge off unsatisfied. They even stopped coming as a group to the conventions after 1925, never having been able to outmaneuver other   5:47

parties. Four years after it was over, Riley said what had been obvious to his party after 1925: it was time to dissolve the bonds of denominational affiliation, because the other party was crucifying the Lord afresh and putting him to open shame before the world. The Fundamentalists would go where they could honor Christ in pure company.

5:48   While Modernists embraced positive views of the surrounding culture, the Fundamentalist leadership kept propounding negative views concerning most of it. Their standard metaphor was the lifeboat. Christianity, they argued, must rescue as many as possible from the flood of evil around it. Such a view was based in part in premillennialism and its belief that time for redemption of the human race was limited. It also derived from the classic evangelical desire to save souls. Such an approach changed the relation of its proponents to the world. Why devote energies to making peace between nations, management and labor, men and women, or religious groups, if Jesus' second coming would change the terms of all life? Why work thus if to do so distracted from the first work of Christians, the task of rescuing people from the world? The movement of ultraconservative Christians into this specialized work reduced the ranks of those who wanted to shape America around a particular vision of the Kingdom of God, Protestant style.

5:49   The Fundamentalists in one respect were never as good, or as bad, as their word. They made at least one great exception in their negation of the world: nationalism, and with it support of America's economic system. They never lost interest or faith in America. It remained God's last and best hope, the nation that must remain true to its calling. America was the most fruitful source of people and money for world missions, which is why its churches and seminaries needed to remain pure. Both sides of the Protestant house fought for power and influence in God's country, their United States, though with different armament toward differing ends.

5:50   On a few selective projects Fundamentalists also remained fighters for civic virtue and personal morals; they specialized in somewhat different causes than did Modernists and moderates. Staying within the nineteenth-century evangelical tradition, they concentrated on issues not dealing with structural flaws in society but with those which could fall under one's personal control: drinking, gambling, prostitution. Reform individuals, they argued, and each convert could avoid contributing to evil. A person did not need to wait for the reform of society or for the retrieving of public structures from the devil's sphere. In Minneapolis, William B. Riley was as well known for attacking vice as was John Roach Straton in New York. Yet even where such clerics were effective, they tended not to want to take much credit for their work. Straton did not believe in social service and, he said, he had "neither faith nor hope in connection with mere reform efforts and secular agencies for amelioration of the wrong conditions of human society and the redemption of the individual and the race." A review of the Baptist periodicals edited by partisans showed how Fundamentalists picked and chose their way through the culture.

The *Watchman-Examiner* showed that it cared about the American scene, always on the side of conservative law and order. It backed Massachusetts governor Calvin Coolidge when that future president put down the Boston police strike of 1919. In a spirit that went back to colonial Puritan views of the city set upon a hill, its editor wrote that "Boston is Armageddon for the Nation." The *Western Recorder* lunged verbally at striking police, who often came from immigrant, not original-stock, ranks. Many of these officers lacked Americanism and integrity; they were "raw recruits from riotous Ireland" who, said the editor, love our liquor much better than our laws."   5:51

Late in the decade the trial and execution of two anarchists in what came to be known as the Sacco-Vanzetti case revealed massive Fundamentalist distaste for the accused, who seemed to be a threat to American law and order. The *Christian Fundamentalist* joined other periodicals of its sort in attacking Modernist Christians when they spoke up for justice in the case of the accused anarchists condemned for murder. Maybe one or the other of the men was innocent, wrote the editors. Judges do make mistakes. But the radicals should not be eulogized as martyrs or saints, even if innocent: they were, after all, anarchists. Order and law were the Fundamentalist premiums for society. These partisans, argued the editorialist, were not as nonpolitical as they claimed to be or as many thought they were. They simply took part in political life in radically different ways than did moderates and Modernists.   5:52

In the Baptist churches as elsewhere, then, Fundamentalists wanted both to camp on the central Protestant tradition in America and at the same time to turn their back on the America that that tradition had helped shape. They left to others the open and positive embrace of public order. They turned negative or   5:53

they concentrated on the private dimensions of national life. Thus they began to move toward seeking a monopoly in respect to some of the concerns which ancestors of liberals had once shared, particularly, the saving of souls out of the world. And while the non-Fundamentalists kept a hold on the machinery of the denominations and the seminaries, something of the old spirit was sapped from these church bodies as Fundamentalists began to place their energies elsewhere. And there were new reasons for the nation at large not to take seriously a group which could not agree on its basic vision.

Theology: The Warfare of the World in the House of God

5:54   While the Fundamentalist conflict marked life among Southern Baptists, Northern and Southern Presbyterians, the Disciples of Christ, and some Methodist jurisdictions, we single out the Presbyterian Church in the United States, nicknamed Northern Presbyterian, as the other most engaging and illuminating battlefront. Because Presbyterian polity did connect congregations and did allow for more centralization; because Presbyterians constituted creedal and confessional bodies and could more easily define the boundaries of the permissible; because they had a somewhat more scholarly tradition than did the Baptists; because they were more central to the establishment, and were a denomination better represented in *Who's Who* among the powers who ran the country, they demand notice. They also included the most-noted Fundamentalist theologian in J. Gresham Machen and the best-known lay Fundamentalist in William Jennings Bryan. Their story informs that of Fundamentalism as an American cultural force.

5:55   Machen was to lose out in denominational warfare, but was able to live with himself, convinced as he was that he had acted with creedal and intellectual integrity. He was a match for any of the Modernists then on the scene. A bachelor from an affluent family of original-stock English and southern American heritage, he was well-nurtured on the Bible and the Presbyterian Westminster Confession, and he never reacted against the training. A Johns Hopkins Phi Beta Kappa graduate, Machen entered Princeton Seminary in 1902, in time to profit from the teaching of stalwarts like Benjamin Breckinridge Warfield, the Presbyterian dogmatist supreme in his time. Machen briefly sampled the more radical scholarship in Germany, having been awed by the scholarship and devotion of some professors just as he was put off by what looked like faithlessness in their theological positions.

After 1906 Machen stood his ground as a faculty member at   5:56
Princeton Seminary, where he lasted until 1929. Midway through the period, having resolved some momentary doubts about his own faith, Machen was ordained a minister. In 1923 he wrote a celebrated work, *Christianity and Liberalism*, and followed it in 1930 with the Fundamentalist classic *The Virgin Birth of Christ*. Through a long career Machen defended what he considered to be orthodox biblical, Reformation, Presbyterian, and Princetonian thought against all comers.

Machen did not like to call himself a Fundamentalist, but, as   5:57
he put it, he found no inherent objection to the term. He said that if someone brought up the word Modernist as its polar opposite, then he was willing to call himself "a Fundamentalist of the most pronounced type." If Machen was not a typical partisan, not a joiner on all the Fundamentalist fronts, he also seemed atypical in the forthrightness, though not in the substance, of some of his social and political stands. While many Baptists and Presbyterians claimed to be above politics, he entered frays not as a denomina-tionalist but as an inveterate letter writer to the *New York Times* and other major papers. He *looked* nonpolitical because he was not pro-Social Gospel. In fact, his stands, while generally liber-tarian, anticipated precisely the conservative forms that Funda-mentalism assumed when, decades later, its leadership took a turn and confessed to having become overtly political.

While Machen's political positions were clearly subordinate to   5:58
his doctrinal stands, they demonstrated that the schism within old-stock Protestantism did extend to the shaping of America, to the battle for its soul. In some matters of life-style he was atypical. No smoker, he did envy and enjoy the company of the "fellows" who, in their friendly circles, smoked in Princeton rooms. Ma-chen, a bachelor much devoted to his mother, was so enthralled by such company of fellows that he once said, "I have sometimes regretted that I never began to smoke." He was not much for alcoholic drink, but was less for Prohibition, chiefly because it represented a state intrusion in private life.

Machen appeared to be in the Fundamentalist political van-   5:59
guard when he defended the local governmental power over that of the state, the state over the federal government, and always the private sector over all of these. To achieve his ends, he engaged, on very predictable grounds, in political controversy. So near the

stance of libertarianism was Machen that he opposed anti-jay-walking ordinances in Philadelphia; he wanted to walk where he would, in Philadelphia as in Presbyterianism. Machen loved nature but opposed conservation action by the government because it *was* by the government. He opposed the Child Labor Amendment in 1924 not because he disliked children or would ignore their interests but because he thought that through it the state would intrude on family rights.

5:60   Position followed position with relentless political logic on the part of the Princetonian. Thus he argued in 1926 that a Department of Education would represent unification, standardization, uniformity and conformity of the governmental kind, and thus the worst sort of oppression. He would not have teachers licensed by the state because such an act could impinge on the utter freedom of parochial schools. Woman Suffrage? The professor had battled it back in 1918 because he thought women did not want it, states should decide the issue, suffragettes were unrepresentative of most women, and because ill-timed and unintelligent feminism was promoting it. He opposed the church taking stands on public issues because individuals alone should do that. In short, his was a full-dress conservative view of the social order which, he thought, secularists and now Christian liberals were bartering away in America.

5:61   Machen saved most of his fire in the era of schism for Presbyterian wars. His background was in Princeton's celebrated version of Scottish common-sense realism, the philosophy which gave intellectual Fundamentalists their permanent if not always overtly recognized grounding. This philosophy, imported by Scottish Enlightenment refugees in the era of America's formation, had been influential among national founders and came close to being an official framework of thought during much of the nineteenth century. But the rise of a new and eventually classic American philosophy at the turn of the century had called it into question and displaced it in most arenas outside of Princeton. There conservative Protestants seized on common-sense realism to defend biblical revelation. Key for them was the notion that one could trust sense experience based on access to facts. And since the Bible had a factual basis, the Christian faith in its teachings was absolutely sure, grounded in unassailable realities.

5:62   Machen refined the view. "You cannot change the facts. The modern preacher offers reflection. The Bible offers more." Thus

"Christianity depends, not upon a complex of ideas, but upon the narration of an event." This meant that Christians had to defend the notion of the Bible in its original, though now lost, manuscripts as the "infallible rule of faith and practice." What came to be at issue in Presbyterianism was the degree to which and the way in which this infallibility meant inerrancy with respect to biblical accounts of historical, geographical, natural, and scientific matters. Moderates thought that these had little to do with faith and practice. Machen argued that to yield on any such point would undercut the factual basis of the Bible and lead to liberalism and thus to loss of faith.

Curiously, one doctrine which most Fundamentalists thought was based in scriptural fact Machen did not find in the Bible at all. In the fusion of forces that made up modern Fundamentalism, we have seen that some version or other of premillennialism came to be a standard theme. Critics of Fundamentalism argued that if inerrancy were basic and if one could come to absolute grounding of faith on the basis of it, then *all* scriptural teachings should be patent and assured. Yet Fundamentalist leadership was sundered on a key question. Machen, however, thought that although many Christians believed in the idea that Jesus in bodily presence would bring about "a reign of righteousness which will last a thousand years," this was an error arrived at by a false interpretation of the Word of God. Such a view could not be justified by the words of Scripture. Other Fundamentalists were shocked by his conviction. They usually suppressed their distaste, however, because Machen on all other causes was such a doughty champion. Yet his integrity led him to part company with the partisans at key times, and in 1930 he would not even attend a World's Christian Fundamentals Association meeting. He protested because the association demanded creedal assent to this premillennial teaching. Fundamentalism, a house also divided against itself, could stand chiefly because it found the Modernist foe so abhorrent.   5:63

Machen was sure that Modernism, which he usually called liberalism, was not a Christian alternative but a sellout, treason, a separate faith that could not keep company with or share the logic of Christianity. The two faiths differed at root and thus in trunk and branch. Liberals were duplicitous when they used Christian terms to delude themselves and the faithful. The Princeton professor set forth this view in lectures through 1921 and 1922 and the next year published *Christianity and Liberalism*, which came to   5:64

be a full-length counterblast to Fosdick's famed sermon the year before. No document better preserves the Fundamentalist polemic as uttered by an intellectual.

5:65   On page 1 Machen scoffed at those who would fight the battles of the day in what Princeton president Francis L. Patton had called a "condition of low visibility." Quiet religion, Machen argued, would "never stand amid the shocks of life." In religion as elsewhere, the consensus on which people agreed was least worth holding; "the really important things are the things about which men will fight."

5:66   And fight they would, in what Machen also labeled a time of conflict, for Christianity as he interpreted it was battling against a totally diverse type of religious belief masquerading as the faith. The roots of modern liberal religion, he contended, were in philosophical naturalism. This school of thought represented a denial of any entrance of the creative power of God into the world. Naturalistic liberalism rose not by chance but as part of what the author identified as the modern lust for scientific conquest and the ruthless flinging to the winds of all tradition. Machen was not content to show that religion was separable from science, but insisted instead that Christianity was scientifically plausible. The problem for dogma in his time was what Machen called "pseudo-scientific accretions." The liberal, he charged, sought to rescue Christianity by pursuing its essence and compromising along the way, but this approach must fail. Fundamentalists had to insist: there can be no "peace without victory." One side or the other must win.

5:67   Liberalism in Machen's eyes was a return to un-Christian and sub-Christian approaches to life. Machen also took on the cultured despisers of Christianity who rejected the Bible. Those who tossed the book aside in the name of progress, he wrote, had not produced a better world. Think of the loss in the realm of art. Gone were the great poets, painters, musicians, and sculptors, replaced by producers of the bizarre. In economics and politics, he chided, think of socialism and the loss of individualism. Human life was thus impoverished. In education, statism was closing in. In America its advance was being slightly delayed by what he characterized as the remnants of Anglo-Saxon individualism, but all signs were against that, too. Materialistic paternalism, as Machen called it, would soon make of America one huge Main Street where spiritual adventure would be discouraged. Listen, André Siegfried: "God grant that there may come a reaction, and that

the great principles of Anglo-Saxon liberty may be rediscovered
before it is too late!"

With such a preface, Machen attacked every feature of liber-   5:68
alism. He had seen it make its way from seminaries to Sunday
school lessons and the lives of ordinary believers. Liberalism
therefore demanded public response. This did not mean that conservatives and liberals had to live in personal animosity. With
some poignancy he wrote: "Many ties—ties of blood, of citizenship, of ethical aims, of humanitarian endeavor—unite us to those
who have abandoned the gospel" though in the name of Christian
faith and under its banners. But there could be no compromise
with liberal teachings, nor could there be tolerance of other views
within the churches. "The greatest menace to the Christian
Church to-day comes not from the enemies outside, but from the
enemies within; it comes from the presence within the Church of
a type of faith and practice that is anti-Christian to the core."
Whether or not liberals were Christians, Machen added, "it is at
any rate perfectly clear that liberalism is not Christianity," so "a
separation between the two parties in the Church is the crying
need of the hour." He well knew how wearying churchly battles
could be when, in his phrase, "the warfare of the world [had]
entered even into the house of God." Machen then noted that in
such a time sad indeed was "the heart of the man who has come
seeking peace."

Machen opposed the idea that within a denomination Christian   5:69
union, harmony, and cooperation would solve everything. He
smelled duplicity: "But the union that is meant is often a union
with the world against the Lord, or at best a forced union of machinery and tyrannical committees." He was destined to spend
two decades fighting that machinery and those committees, at
great personal expense. But the Presbyterian professor had set the
boundaries of truth and pure church life so high and made the gate
so narrow that few could meet the terms. As a result he ended up
experiencing more than one schism in his thirst for the true center
of religious life.

Princeton Seminary was his first battleground. As often, it   5:70
takes some explaining to show why one school could be important
in an America that otherwise could generally ignore seminaries,
to say nothing of seminaries of single denominations. Princeton
was the citadel when the other schools of note had fallen to the
Modernists. On its fate depended much of the intellectual future

of ultraconservatism. Machen's enemies there were not Modernists or even true liberals but moderates who, he thought, had compromised.

5:71   When J. Ross Stevenson in 1914 succeeded Machen's admired and frequently quoted leader, President Francis L. Patton, Princeton was to begin to be more inclusive, more representative of the Presbyterian spectrum. Machen at once sensed the opening for heresy to break out. When Stevenson scorned the idea that Princeton should become what he dismissed as "an interdenominational Seminary for Bible School-premillennial-secession fundamentalism," Machen knew he had to fight back. When Stevenson followed that with the proposal that moderate evangelical denominations ought to get together to form a common front, the beleaguered professor said that he detected forthcoming compromises of a fatal sort.

5:72   Soon students took sides and ripples reached the denomination: there was trouble in the bastion. According to Machen, in the trend of the times the students were more conservative than the faculty. Stevenson had been right when he described those who now were matriculating at the school. To further his own inclusive ends, Stevenson arranged for a reorganization committee which redefined power at the school in a way that made Machenites uncomfortable. So Machen walked out in 1929 to form Westminster Seminary, which quickly distinguished itself as a school for harder-line evangelicals.

5:73   The Presbyterian denominational feud as such had come to a head already, four years before that walkout. Machen found much company when that battle began as early as 1920. There were some similarities to the lineup in other denominations. If Baptist Modernists could claim the Rockefellers, Presbyterian Fundamentalists found support in John Wanamaker, the Philadelphia supermerchant, and any number of other prominent and wealthy lay leaders. They were closer to Machen's kind of political individualism than to Social Gospel liberalism in the denomination. But they also displayed genuine concerns for faith, evangelism, and the old ways in church life. And they could count on three-time presidential candidate and former secretary of state William Jennings Bryan to keep their cause on page 1. So far as ability and fame were concerned, the man who became their pulpit champion, Philadelphia's Clarence E. Macartney, was perhaps second only to Fosdick among mainstream Protestant preachers. And this denomination had a running start with Modernist controversy, for Presbyterians had been involved in heresy trials and contests for doctrine since the 1880s.

Presbyterian conservatives could sense erosion in every cause that might lead Protestants to federate across denominational lines. They knew how to fight off the ill-fated Interchurch World Movement, which would have involved them in 1919. They then targeted a cooperative effort called the New Era Movement, a joint mission campaign over which particularist Presbyterians would not have complete control. When Harry Emerson Fosdick changed his credentials in 1918 to begin to share Presbyterian clerical orders, that Baptist heretic inspired them to be alert. His sermon of 1922 led them to organize against his intrusion and threat. In one of the notable encounters across party lines, Macartney took on Fosdick in the 1923 General Assembly. But unfortunately for both, the heads of the assembly voters were turned that year toward William Jennings Bryan's stepped-up attack on evolution. Bryan was running for the office of moderator in order to gain his own denominational ends, but the perennial candidate also lost that race. While Bryan sulked, the two parties kept hardening their battle lines, using Fosdick as foil. The anti-Fosdick forces momentarily prevailed. 5:74

In Presbyterianism as in the Northern Baptist Convention, argument over missions was less glamorous but more important than attacks on a single accused heretic. The conservative party seized upon a document called the *Auburn Affirmation*, which advocated liberal theology, to pose the issue of doctrinal standards. They wanted to test these standards on the mission front. *The Presbyterian* called the affirmation bolshevist, an advocacy of a new and antagonistic religion. In their 1924 General Assembly at Grand Rapids, meanwhile, the traditionalists, now increasingly called Fundamentalists, for the moment had their hands on what Machen had also called the machinery and committees representing denominational control. They were well-organized, squeaking Clarence E. Macartney into office as moderator in a heated contest. With a zest for battle fired by momentary apparent victory, the Fundamentalists could now go hunting up causes, and missions was the most glamorous of these. But they overpressed their suit and began to lose votes. On procedural grounds Fosdick escaped exclusion from the arrangement which allowed for a shared pulpit, though he subsequently resigned from the denomination because he resented creedal imposition on conscience. 5:75

Increasingly Fundamentalist pressure, personalities, and man- 5:76

ners offended moderate conservatives, who wanted to hold the Presbyterians together. The more extreme party lost more votes in 1926 and thereafter. Matters looked stalemated and seemed quiet during the next two conventions. In the world around that church too many critics were scorning Fundamentalism for its worldview and its behavioral excesses. It could not therefore look attractive to middle-of-the-roaders. The reorganization of Princeton Seminary and the departure of Machen in 1929 showed that, just as in the Baptist case, the Fundamentalists had not won, though it was not clear that anyone else had, either.

5:77   The last signal of complete break did not occur until 1935, when Machen established a Foreign Missions Board to challenge the denomination's own. Rebellious when disciplined, he was suspended and founded a "true church," which eventually came to be named the Orthodox Presbyterian Church, only to see it also break apart with a new schism under his antagonist Carl McIntire in 1937. McIntire thought that Machen's group was too ready to compromise with Modernism because it did not insist on premillennialism. He formed the Bible Presbyterian Synod, a schism on the right of Machen's true church. Presbyterianism survived, splintered.

Evolution: The Greatest Battle, or Rather War

5:78   The founders of the World's Christian Fundamentals Association in 1919 declared that "thousands of false teachers, many of them occupying high ecclesiastical positions, are bringing in damnable heresies." The Bible, in their use of a biblical phrase, "was wounded in the house of its friends." The fighters used militant terms in the end. "Satan himself is transformed into an angel of light." Fundamentalists commonly divided the world into two starkly opposing camps: God's versus Satan's, Christ's versus Antichrist's, Fundamentalism's versus Modernism's, America's versus its enemies'.

5:79   Thus warriors in God's cause came to be battlers for America's own. The notion of a national church tantalized both sides. In 1920 David S. Kennedy, a contributor to *The Presbyterian*, saw the whole doctrinal issue as "The American Crisis." America, he argued, had been born of moral progenitors, on an eternally moral foundation. "Her ancestors were Christian of a high order, purified by fire, and washed in blood. Her foundation is the Bible, the

One of the most memorable images of the mid-twenties finds lawyer Clarence
Darrow and politician turned anti-evolutionist William Jennings Bryan trying to
keep cool at the Scopes trial in 1925. (Wide World Photos.)

infallible Word of God." The decalogue had ruled the nation's
religious and social life. Now in an age of luxury there was evident weakening of America's moral standards. Both German biblical criticism and Red propaganda had poisoned civil and
industrial life. "The Bible and the God of the Bible is our only
hope." America, he continued, must restore the Bible to its place
in the family, the day school, the college and university, and everywhere. Otherwise, concluded the editorial writer, "she might
collapse and fail the world in this crucial age." Such rhetoric was
consistent within the camp of these putatively nonpolitical contenders throughout the twenties.

While Protestant Modernists also made the nation a battle-   5:80
ground, Fundamentalists fought for very particular versions of the
heritage. They believed that the teaching of evolution in the public
schools would destroy the moral and spiritual America they knew.
For Amzi C. Dixon, who was then rising in the Fundamentalist
ranks, evolution posed "the conflict of the ages, darkness vs.

light, Cain vs. Abel," and, significantly, "autocracy vs. civilized democracy." But such a cause needed a champion, and fortuitously, William Jennings Bryan came along. After many political defeats, Bryan was looking for victories, and found a potential in the denominational struggles for God and civilization. As a man of peace, Bryan also was genuinely convinced that ideologies based on evolution had recently motivated the German foe of civilization. Along with Machen, Bryan inhabited the thought-world of Scottish common-sense realism, though he was not formally schooled in its heritage. He wanted American life to be based on the Bible and on facts and on the Bible as fact. "Science is classified knowledge; it is the explanation of facts," he claimed, and Darwinian science to him was mere hypothesis, guesswork.

5:81   Bryan had been thrice candidate for president of the United States, briefly secretary of state, and a lay preacher. He had always shown mistrust of the suave easterners, who now seemed to be the main proponents of evolution. After Bryan's political career was over, when he was looking for new arenas, he took with zest to the anti-evolution cause in politics. In 1921 Bryan had moved to Miami, Florida, where his energies for local affairs went into teaching a Bible class, while those of his ambitions that were available for national matters he turned into a fight against evolution as well as for his winning the moderatorship of the Presbyterian Church.

5:82   Bryan was a political progressive, a supporter of liberal causes like Woman Suffrage, a federal income tax, the rights of organized labor, full disclosure of their finances by political campaigners, the League of Nations, Prohibition, and more democratic ways of electing the president. All these Bryan neglected when he led the Fundamentalist ranks in public issues in the twenties. In church politics Bryan thus sided with people who would have opposed most of his old political program. But now came the issue of evolution to help promote new coalitions. If processes of life were all determined by the survival of the fittest, who would ever work for social reform? asked the same Bryan who, though not a premillennialist, now allied himself with anti-reform premillennialists. Evolution promoted brutishness. Bryan wanted civility. He also desired to promote belief in immortality, which he thought evolutionists disbelieved. Only with such a faith, he concluded, could citizens produce public virtue, and thus help assure the survival of democracy and religion.

It was Bryan who did most to bring the evolution controversy   5:83
to the public stage. In most church bodies pro-Darwinism remained a kind of side issue, a proof of Modernism's betrayal but
seldom a test of orthodoxy that parties fought over. Evolution, it
was argued, instead tainted home and school and country. In the
public sphere Bryan found company in raucous types like the Fort
Worth Baptist preacher J. Frank Norris, the South's only front-
rank pioneering Fundamentalist. In 1923 an editorial in *Moody
Monthly* agreed with Norris that "evolution is Bolshevism in the
long run." The theory eliminated the idea of a personal God, and
"with that goes all authority and government, all law and order."
The magazine *King's Business* also connected Modernism with
Bolshevism and evolution in its campaign for a Christian
America, for that national corner of Christendom which, the editor said, reposed upon a book, the Bible. In 1925 a less well-
known southerner, M. E. Dodd of Louisiana, fired scattershot in
The Christian Index: "I would say that a modernist in government
is an anarchist and Bolshevik; in science he is an evolutionist; in
business he is a Commmunist; in art a futurist; in music his name
is jazz; and in religion an atheist and infidel."

The battles over evolution seemed out of place, out of time, in   5:84
the America of the twenties. By then Darwinism had been debated
in England and America for six decades. Long before the twenties
Protestant liberals had absorbed evolutionary thinking into their
own style. They even wanted to hurry evolution along, in the
name of God. They may have made their original accommodation
to it a bit too easily, too glibly, without having thought through
all that the concept of arbitrary natural selection meant, but they
could not now conceive of the world apart from evolutionary
thought.

Anti-evolutionist Protestants, many of whom had been friendly   5:85
to evolution before the full brunt of natural-selection theories
came to challenge divine providence, were equally clear on their
own stand against all forms of the Darwinian alternative. The informed statements on their side had already been made in the
nineteenth century. It is hard to find fresh, original thinking on
the subject in the conflicts of the twenties. What happened instead
was a delayed reaction, a new cultural unfolding, a hardening of
party lines. Evolution came to be of use by the contending groups
in Protestantism, and much of this use related to acts of defining,
name-calling, and rallying. It was one more element in the war

for the soul of Protestantism, thus of Christianity and thus of America, in the eyes of those who prosecuted the case.

5:86   The anti-evolutionists liked to pose the issue most starkly. Thus the Southern Baptist Convention in 1922 declared: "One can understand both the Bible and evolution and believe one of them, but he cannot understand both and believe both." Modernists disagreed, so the battles were joined. Harry Emerson Fosdick saw the whole fight as nothing but a red herring across the trail. At the Methodists' new School of Religion at Duke University, Dean Edmund D. Soper also was condescending about this subject when he was called a Modernist. Evolutionary fights, in his language, were "last year's bird nest."

5:87   Modernists, however, got less help than they expected from evolutionary humanists, who did not yet recognize that their classroom teaching and laboratory experiments would soon become issues of politics. From a neutral corner, science editor Watson Davis of the secular *Current History* wrote perceptively: "Evolution and the science of biology seem to have been picked upon by the fundamentalists as symbols of modernism." He said that scientists were glad that the battle had shifted from being an issue between science and religion to "an arena more nearly included within the field of religion," where it was apparently safer, more irrelevant, or less distracting. If scientists did show interest at all, Davis thought, they would consider the viewpoint of Modernists in the remaining conflict as their very own.

5:88   The anti-evolutionists, on the other hand, brought basically three concerns. First, Christian acceptance of evolution, they argued, led to denial of basic Christian doctrines. Second, two concepts of science were at issue; Fundamentalists in defense of their concept never wanted to be or be seen as antiscientific. Third, here was a battle for American civilization, culture, and morals. To further their cause, they gave their journals militant-sounding names: *The Conflict, The Crusader's Champion, Dynamite, The Defender*; their books typically were *The Great Conflict, The Bible versus Evolution, The Battlefield of Faith, War on Modernism*. The language sounded like wartime propaganda: "It is a battle royal. . . . There is no discharge in this war." Or: "The conflict is raging. The call to arms is being heard from sea to sea." Moody Bible Institute said it "was preparing for the greatest battle, or rather war, known to ecclesiastical history." And the World's Christian Fundamentals Association announced "a truceless war on the worst and most destructive forms of infidelity," in which "fundamentalists draw the weapon of their warfare from the arsenal of God's word; modernists draw theirs from evolutionary philosophy."

The two sides held what the public conceived of as their classic   5:89
encounter in the best-known religious incident of the decade, called then and since the Scopes trial. This oft-told tale belongs to folk religion, and thus is necessarily a part of the dynamics of American culture. With William Jennings Bryan as protagonist, humanist lawyer Clarence Darrow as antagonist, skeptical newspaperman Henry L. Mencken derisively reporting, and with radio covering the event, it offered color, personality, and drama. Because of Bryan's blustering performance, it was easy for reporters to caricature the anti-evolution position. Because of some mental lapses on Bryan's part, it was also easy to point to internal divisions within the Fundamentalist camp. Serious Fundamentalists regretted the forum and the form and distanced themselves from Bryan's arguments. Some may have done so prudentially, sensing it would be a lost cause. Others did so because they held more refined views of their case or sought better arenas in which to stage their attacks and defense. To the scholar who traces the Darwinian theme as an incident, intellectually the Scopes trial came a half-century late. To the observer who studies indicators of what counts in a culture, it deserves something of the place it holds in the tale of the twenties.

The story is simply told. Picture a small Tennessee town and   5:90
in it a beginning high-school teacher named John Scopes. The Tennessee legislature played its part by passing the Butler Act, a law of the sort other legislatures were also enacting. The Butler legislation was "An Act prohibiting the teaching of the Evolution Theory in all the Universities, Normals, and all other public schools of Tennessee." The American Civil Liberties Union wanted to test the law and agreed to back young Scopes if he would be willing to teach evolution. He did and they backed him. In July 1925 in Dayton, Tennessee, the case came to trial, with Bryan supporting the Tennessee law and Darrow defending Scopes. To no one's surprise, Scopes was found guilty, which should have meant that Bryan won. However, to all but Fundamentalists he had disgraced himself by his literalistic support of biblical creation accounts—the press was there in force, issuing two million words of newspaper copy and making early use of

radio—and some Fundamentalists came to despise him because he had not been literal enough about twenty-four hour days of creation in the Book of Genesis.

5:91   While evolution was the theme, the rights of citizens, especially parents, to have their own way with the topic of religion in public schools was at issue. The Fundamentalists desired the sanction of civil authority for their dogmas. "It was after all exactly what local public opinion and the authors of this law desired," observed André Siegfried after a visit from France. He saw in Bryan's world no true separation of church and state. "Power in this country," Bryan had said, "comes from the people; and if the majority of the people believe that evolution breaks down religious faith and threatens Christianity, they have the right to demand that it be suppressed or at least confined to the little group of research men, who may study it as a theory not yet proven." For Bryan and his supporters "the only morality comes from the Bible, all our institutions and our social life are founded on an implicit belief in it, and without that belief there is no ground on which moral teaching may be founded."

5:92   This was, in short, not an event in the history of science but in that of nationalism, civic morality, and religious power. Not a dispute over dead constitutions or old texts, it was a burning question to the folk who dreaded the possible contamination of their faith, as Siegfried saw. The attorney general of Tennessee wanted science not to intrude on the worldview of these folk. If what was going on that year was to be termed a battle between religion and science, then "in the name of the great God," stated the official, "I am on the side of religion." Though supporters in Europe and the Atlantic states made at best sheepish excuses for the outburst of fanaticism in Tennessee, the impression caused in the South and the West was tremendously favorable to Bryan and against evolution. The citizens were eager to use public schools to support a particular religious view of America.

5:93   In religious debate Bryan was caustic, which he had not been in his years of political controversy. He was supercilious and defensive at once against those he called that "cultured crowd," those who dismissed religion as being useful only among the "superstitious and ignorant." He retained only a rare glint of his old good humor when he said he was "trying to bring some of the honesty of politics into the church." In his best populist style, Bryan said he would "take the church out of the hands of the bosses and put it into the hands of worshippers." As for the substance at issue, theistic evolution was in his words "an anesthetic administered to your Christians to deaden the pain while their religion is being removed by materialists." In the Sprunt Lectures at Union Theological Seminary in Virginia in 1922, published as *In His Image*, Bryan had taken on Darwin with a condescension he rarely showed in politics. Darwinism represented "tommyrot," "ridiculous attempts to explain the unexplainable." It was "ludicrous"; evolution promoted the basis of Germanic "Superman" teaching and was thus responsible for the recent war. Bryan seemed on the verge of reviving the Red Scare when he argued that Darwinism was also responsible for class struggle. What could he then do, he asked himself and the public, but respond when the opportunity to fight Darwinism in the public arena came along? He accepted the challenge of this, his last battle.

As an amateur theologian, Bryan gobbled up and then replied to popular Modernist writings. He explicitly defended all the fundamentals, not least among them belief in an inerrant Bible. In one sentence he could summarize all that went wrong when opponents of the faith took over: "Give the modernist the words, 'allegorical,' 'poetical,' and 'symbolical' and he can suck the meaning out of every vital doctrine of the Christian Church and every passage of the Bible to which he objects." Bryan opposed evolution because he saw it sucking away the meaning of faith for collegians who were forced to learn that theory. "The hand that writes the paycheck rules the school," he was again to argue. The Christian writers of checks, he argued, would not and should not pay for undercutters of faith. 5:94

Fundamentalists through the years previous to the trial had applauded and always said they would support Bryan, but the major clerics left him to stand alone at Dayton, Tennessee. Some of them had better things to do as Baptists that summer at the important Seattle conference of the Northern Baptist Convention. Others took vacations or went to summer conferences. Billy Sunday sent help, but did not offer his own presence. 5:95

Sunday's was the typical cheer from the grandstand. He had written Bryan three or four years before the Dayton climax: "Every time I pick up a paper and find where you are smiting evolution, ... I feel like reaching out my hand to you and saying 'God bless you.'" Some people Sunday met were ex-evolutionists who, he said, had recanted their earlier stand, thanks to Bryan's efforts. Sometimes, it should be said, a few churchly intellectuals also found in Bryan a champion. President J. D. Eggle- 5:96

ston of Hampden-Sydney College, a prestigious southern Presbyterian School, asked Bryan to contend for him, using the standard phrase: "After all, the worst enemies of the church are inside, not outside." Former Arkansas governor Charles H. Brough connected the cause with patriotism: Bryan's "strength and continued eloquence to serve as the moral leader of America" deserved God's blessings.

5:97   Visitor André Siegfried typified the disdain of intellectuals as he set the trial in context. "Christianity in its Protestant form is so closely woven into the whole fabric of society that it is impossible to conceive of a separation, even suppose it were desired." Thus the Tennessee legislature was acting on religious grounds in a supposedly secular society. The legislative act in question was not a relic of past intolerance but a present expression of sentiments and of what Siegfried called a "type of nationalism that cannot distinguish between patriotism and religion."

5:98   Siegfried was snide about "the stubbornly insular State of Tennessee," its most backward people, its "honest, frugal farmers of pure Anglo-Saxon origin who have preserved their Protestant faith on ice." He knew, however, that these people were anything but fools. Millions of other Americans followed their example. Siegfried could not resist emphasizing that in Dayton there were no Catholics, no Jews, and no Anglicans. All the social life of the town was in the original-stock churches, which also addressed the cultural needs of citizens. The Fundamentalist ministers there, he claimed, "preached mediaeval dogmas with the fervour of the Inquisition" and shielded the town from contamination with modern ideas or foreign influences. The eastern states with their Catholics, Jews, and foreigners were almost as abominable to the pious in such strongholds as was decadent Europe. The old stock must at all costs avoid contagion. "Now at long last they hear tell in Tennessee of the doctrine of evolution, and they consider it dangerous to their faith."

5:99   Bryan also attracted important foes alongside Darrow and Mencken. Modernist Shailer Mathews saw him as one who wanted to "rehabilitate the theology of a pre-democratic, pre-industrial, pre-scientific society," and even went so far as to call the tireless progressive a Tory who kept company with conservative premillennialists. Philosopher John Dewey acknowledged the importance of the democratic implications in Bryan's crusade "against science and in favor of obscurantism and intolerance." Dewey regretted the obvious personal decline that the old progressive stumper was now manifesting. And when Bryan pushed for legislation banning evolution in schools, the public press reacted violently. The *New York Times Book Review and Magazine* scorned what it labeled Bryan's "curious revival of medieval prejudice" and his "curious essay in prejudice." Therewith, the whole press seemed to Bryan to be representing the very world against which he must fight. The *New York Times* on July 8, 1925, saw Bryan off to Tennessee with his own words setting the terms: "The contest between evolution and Christianity is a duel to the death." Bryan argued that "if evolution wins in Dayton Christianity goes." The two could not stand together. So they faced off in the trial which Scopes lost, and then, while winning legally, Bryan also, and in the end, lost. He died one week after his Pyrrhic victory at Dayton. After the Scopes trial, which in so many ways was an incident that exemplified cultural lag, the cleavage between evolutionary scientists and Fundamentalists was completed. The scientists could henceforth largely ignore their antagonists. The breaches between evolutionist Christians and their opponents were just as deep, and those who wanted to speak up for a Protestant culture and nation could never again ignore the profound division. The mid-twenties, in this case as in so many others, produced a permanent schism between Protestantisms and within the culture at large.

Premillennial Apocalypse versus Modernist Apostasy

While Fundamentalists debated about the beginning of the   5:100 world and of life, they also reckoned with the end of history. Leaders like J. Gresham Machen and William Jennings Bryan were not premillennialists, but those who were saw Modernism itself as a sign of apostasy, the sort of signal Jesus said would occur before the end. Some used their apocalyptic vision to sustain themselves during the Fundamentalist controversy. Thus Arno C. Gaebelein, a leader in the conflict in 1925, claimed that "the modernistic cancer is too far gone. There is no more hope." In fact, he continued, "the apostasy is on," and after 1925 "it will be worse than when the year began. God help us all to be faithful, loyal, and uncompromising." In that mood, some even made premillennialism serve as a test of other doctrines. Texas Baptist J. Frank Norris could smell heresies at a distance, but he said that "when a man tells me he believes in the literal, personal, bodily, visible, imminent return of the Lord to this earth as King, I know what he believes on every other question." Most of all, claimed Norris, "I know he is not a Modernist, and I know that he does not believe in the evolutionary hypothesis."

5:101   Politically, premillennialism was to have a fateful role in the decline and subsequent revivals of Fundamentalism in these decades, because of the obsessive way its proponents promoted the rise of a modern Jewish political state. As they read the Bible, the prophets and Jesus had foreseen such a nation, and Jesus connected his return with its establishment. There were other political and social consequences. If Christ was to return soon, Christians must hurry to rescue people from the world. If the same Christ was thereby to bring in a reign of righteousness, then the church did not need to establish the Kingdom of God through reformed social structures. Individual Christians must always be moral and merciful and just, but they need not transform the world. To try to do so was what the enemy, postmillennialists, had long worked for, believing as they did that Christ would return to rule only after the world had been readied for him.

5:102   Premillennialism, then, was a philosophy of history designed to match and to counter Marxism, progressivism, and Darwinism, with all of which it was in open competition. Its propagators had views about the beginning and the end of history; they could thus learn much about the meaning of it, something full-blown philosophies of history must always set out to do. Those who held to this teaching were in command in 1919 at the forming of the World's Christian Fundamentals Association. They thereupon challenged all comers with whom they had to coexist through the twenties. But precisely because they thus had to coexist for the purpose of forming their faction, they also had to surrender their general designation as premillennialist and replace it with the more inclusive organizational name, Fundamentalism.

5:103   While not all Fundamentalists believed in premillennialism, those who did were most energetic about organizing the movement nationally. While Fundamentalism acquired the image of being most at home in the southern Bible Belt, much of the leadership had come from the North: from Niagara Bible conferences; from pulpits in Boston and New York, Philadelphia and Chicago; from Bible institutes in Chicago and Minneapolis. Yet the natural evangelistic and conservative Protestant base in the South made that a fertile region for many reactionaries who came to call themselves Fundamentalists. We have already seen how much of the controversy over evolution in the schools was fought in the South. The South produced only one of the founding fathers of militant premillennialist Fundamentalism, but his career informs the whole movement.

Fort Worth's Pastor J. Frank Norris, who made premillennial-   5:104
ism the mark of the movement, seldom paled in comparison with anyone else. He more than anyone else helped form or reinforce stereotypes of the rough-hewn Fundamentalist. Norris was an American original, one of the best-known clerics of his period. If Machen was a political conservative, Norris was a raging ultra whose version of 100 percent Americanism had measurable popular appeal. Norris in effect was holding regular referendums to determine interest in the larger cause, since he did not depend merely upon his Fort Worth Baptist church but on a larger constituency for support. Subscriptions and financial contributions from across the land enhanced his power. Somehow he was also able to commute as a pastor between two large congregations which were located a thousand miles apart in Fort Worth and Detroit, while he was taking part in radio broadcasts, newspaper publishing, political campaigns, and self-help programs for the poor. Norris attracted thousands. In retrospect on Norris's career, Ralph McGill, editor of the *Atlanta Constitution*, was also sure that he alienated more. "The Rev. J. Frank Norris, and others like him, is one good, sound reason why there are 50,000,000 Americans who do not belong to any church at all."

Shot and seriously injured by horse thieves when he was a   5:105
fifteen-year-old, Norris nursed at least psychic wounds all his life. Somehow along the way he also learned how to inflict them. In 1909 he came to head what was to become in his prime the largest white Protestant church in the United States and one of the most prosperous of all churches in the South, Fort Worth's First Baptist. It remained his base through all his travels and storms. He also needed enemies in order to prosper. Lacking homegrown Modernists among Texas Baptists, he had to invent some in the form of mildly pro-evolutionary Southern Baptists, with whom he constantly feuded. His weapon, as in the case of so many in his faction, was the notion of biblical inerrancy. He stated in crude terms what intellectuals like Machen could argue delicately: "Whenever you find a preacher who takes the Bible allegorically and figuratively," he charged, "that preacher is preaching an allegorical gospel which is no gospel." "Literal" became the favorite adjective of a man who may have known little about fancy

philosophical grounds, such as Scottish common-sense realism's view of factuality. He thought that premillennialism was literally taught in the Bible, but did not recognize how many complex interpretations came into play with texts from Ezekiel, Daniel, and Revelation to produce premillennialism. When Jesus comes to rule for a thousand years, Norris preached, there will come "the overthrow of the beast and his armies, the conversion of the Jews," and other signs prophesied in the Bible.

5:106   While Norris the political figure saw himself as an enemy of all who threatened the ways of the 100 percent Americans, theologically he claimed he did not want to make anything earthly, even American nationalism, central to his cause. "Our motive is not to redeem America, China, or Russia, it is to get ready the Body of Christ." In the meantime, he preached, all Christians of the right stripe must rescue sinners out of the world. Such views inevitably did push him into politics, however, and turned him into a precedent for belligerent political Fundamentalists who would take full rise to power decades later. For example, though not personally close to Jews, Norris was, for reasons other than theirs, a Zionist. He announced that he therefore foresaw an alliance between God's two peoples, Anglo-Saxons and Jews. Thus developed another one of those crisscrossing sets of loyalties which kept blocs of Americans from simply massing against other blocs: why mass, when you may have allies across the boundary?

5:107   The busy preacher's main energies went into the family quarrels that made up denominational politics, so he joined the World's Christian Fundamentals Association and the Baptist Bible Union when they formed in 1919 and 1923, respectively, even though he was not able to bring many Southern Baptists with him into either. He certainly tried. Norris speculated: "I believe with all my soul that future generations will write about this Fundamentalist Movement as historians now write up the Reformation" and other great awakenings. "What if the present-day denominations are smashed to smithereens?" They ought to be, he answered his own question. "They are unscriptural."

5:108   Still, Norris found time in 1928 as a Protestant to oppose Catholic Al Smith's presidential campaign and then to support Herbert Hoover as a Christian gentleman. Hoover returned the favor by inviting Norris to be his personal guest at the presidential inauguration. Smith was a "wet," while the preacher was a strong enemy of the repeal of prohibition and a crowd-pleaser for his sermons against liquor. His anti-Catholicism, expressed on doctrinal and nativist grounds alike, was legendary. In 1926 Norris claimed to have discovered a kind of plot to elect a Catholic president who would overthrow the Constitution and thus control American government for Rome. His own ambitions were so great and his threat to other parties so strong that one Texas legislator promoted a bill which would have kept clergy out of office. To Norris, on the other hand, the existing politicians were "simlin-headed, sawdust-brained grafters."

In the Southern Baptist Convention Norris carried old grudges   5:109
into the battles of the twenties, beginning with his opposition to the "Seventy-five Million Campaign," a convention fund-raiser. The campaign, he said, was dictatorial and unscriptural, a waste of evangelical energies. He opposed hierarchy in the convention ("The Sanhedrin"), the Baptist World Alliance, the Federal Council of Churches, and wherever else he claimed to find it. In 1924 the General Baptist Convention, to which he also belonged, eventually lost patience and finally removed him and his church from the denominational lists. As their charges put it, Norris was "unBaptistic and non-cooperative." All such attacks only boosted the size of his crowds and congregation, but he eventually tired of fighting the Southern Baptist Convention at every step. In 1931, after the pattern of any number of disgruntled and ambitious Fundamentalists, Norris went on his own to invent a "Premillennial, Fundamental, Missionary Fellowship" church body, a denomination whose name was predestined to be shortened several times in several ways in the years to come.

The most notorious moment in his highly visible career came   5:110
in 1926. Norris was feuding with Fort Worth's Catholic mayor, H. C. Meacham, who made his living running a large department store. During the feud the First Baptist preacher devoted one Sunday sermon in July to alleging that Meacham was siphoning city funds into Catholic causes. Norris also attacked the mayor's personal morals. Then he brought on stage six First Baptist Church members who, Norris said, had been fired from Meacham's store simply because they were members at Norris's church. Norris spread word of this feud all over Fort Worth. At the end of an unsettling week, a friend of Meacham's named D. E. Chipps threatened Norris by phone and then made a personal call on the pastor at the church. During an overheard shouting match, Norris picked up his own gun and killed Chipps with four shots.

Police apprehended Norris; he told his story to the district at-   5:111
torney, and then went home to do some sermon writing. A grand

jury indicted Norris for murder. His plea: self-defense against a drunk who had been a danger to the preacher. The Austin jury dispensed what its critics called Texas justice, spending only forty minutes deciding that shooting an unarmed man was not an offense. It found the preacher innocent. Back at his church, Norris magnanimously asked the huge crowds not to hold any malice against his persecutors. We score this as a third killing in a decade when, as we have argued, almost everyone seemed angry at every one else in religion, but almost no one was killed. The violence was ordinarily verbal, but it had devastating effects on original-stock Protestantism, which was trying to remain credible as the shaper and interpreter of American culture.

The Faith of Modernism

5:112   Across the great divide, non-Fundamentalist Protestantism approached life in the 1920s in anything but an apocalyptic mood. "There never was an hour in the history of the world when the Christian Church has had such occasion for confidence and joy as just now." A liberal Methodist bishop was doing this exulting on May 27, 1920, in the postwar season when everyone was supposed to have been disillusioned. Unbowed liberal Protestantism lived on. Certainly the speaker could not have been thinking of or foreseeing the challenges to moderation and liberalism just ahead. There were, he said, no reasons to listen to "the dismal croakings of the chronic pessimist," because this was "the best hour of the best day of the best week of the best month of the best year of the best decade of the best century that this world has ever seen." And, of course, "tomorrow will be every way better." Such misreading of the signs of the time was what helped lead nonchurched humanists to dismiss the church as trivial, just as premillennialist Fundamentalists came to dismiss this kind of church as simply wrong.

5:113   The enlightened leadership of original-stock churches was sure of one thing: faithfulness to God and Christ called them to adopt a new line. As Modernist Robert Leet Patterson also wrote in 1920, the continued rebuilding of the postwar world demanded liberation from confining creeds. "If we go on stifling the living breath of freedom within the walls of ancient creed, then there is scant hope of swift betterment in the future." Those who were looking to Roman Catholicism to spread the catholicism of tomorrow, warned Patterson, were building not on a rock but on a foundation of sand. Only a united Christendom, one which had not declared war on science and history or upon human reason, stood a chance of fulfilling its vocation.

So far as the dream of Protestant unity was concerned, the best   5:114 decade turned out to be one of the worst. The Modernists, for all their energy and imagination, lacked the ability to formulate versions of faith which satisfied the longings of the traditionalists, who had their own reasons in any case to thwart any kind of compromise or even outreach to them. New York's pastor Harry Emerson Fosdick was typical of those who tried. He was anything but a simple optimist in the mode of the just-cited Methodist bishop. Fosdick always warned against superficial views of progress and modernity. Throughout his adult life he sensed the shadow of human evil. "All we need to do is to open our eyes to facts," the preacher said when accounting for the presence of sin. "This is no fool-proof universe automatically progressive"; instead, moral evil was still the central human problem. Fosdick could and did even sound like the conservative evangelicals when he assailed "the amiable idiocies of evolution popularly misinterpreted," and praised the "fresh sense of personal and social sin."

Fosdick was the most eloquent speaker for Modernist Protes-   5:115 tantism between the wars, but even he could not stretch Modernism to serve the whole Protestant spectrum. Of course, viewpoints such as his were anathema to Fundamentalists and problematic for conservatives. But all along, these Modernists experienced a squeeze from the left as well. Thus throughout the controversy Unitarians liked to call attention to what they saw as Fundamentalism's integrity; many Unitarian leaders were themselves exiles from repressive conservatisms. They looked back on such forms of Protestantism as normative, as if these expressed the only way the old orthodox faith ever should have sounded and looked. In their eyes the Modernists, because they adjusted to modernity while remaining in the context of conventional Protestantism, looked compromising and cheap. Thus Unitarian editor A. C. Dieffenbach: "I have the profoundest respect for a man who is consistently a Roman Catholic, or for a man who is consistently a fundamentalist, but I have no respect for the attitude of Dr. Fosdick." Fundamentalists could cheer when men like Dieffenbach would agree with Machen: "An evangelical Christian is not a liberal, in the accepted use of both words. They are mutually exclusive terms."

5:116   Similarly, at the University of Chicago, the naturalist religious philosopher Henry Nelson Wieman heaped scorn on Fosdick, claiming that evangelical liberalism of Fosdick's sort was an unsatisfying religion of illusion. Wieman and his school of thought described their own approach as scientific, realistic, empirical. The professor gave no comfort to Fundamentalists but provided discomfort to Modernism when he said that he was battling "not against either fundamentalism or modernism as such," but "against all religion of illusion wherever it may be found." Fundamentalism was so far beyond his scope that he spent little time on it; in practice, naturalists like Wieman spent most of their energy sniping at the Modernist Christianity positioned nearer them. They spoke up, at least Wieman did, for an understanding "that this is not a nice world and God is not a nice God." The implication: Modernist Christians were nice, and thus unrealistic and eventually ineffectual.

5:117   The Fundamentalist schism, however, occurred not in opposition to Unitarianism or naturalism but over against the conservative-to-moderate coalition of leaders who controlled much of the machinery of the Northern Baptist Convention, the Presbyterian Church in the U.S.A., and other Protestant denominations. They used the word Modernist to attack almost anyone who would not join them, however moderate they were. There were plenty of "evangelical liberals" around to quote. But when Fundamentalists wanted to argue, they chose to oppose the language of self-declared Modernists.

5:118   They focused their attacks, with good reason, on Shailer Mathews, theologian at and dean of the University of Chicago Divinity School from 1908 to 1933. He was evangelical in that Christ was central to his thought, and he was churchly—as the naturalists like Wieman were not. As a teacher of New Testament, Mathews dealt with the origins of Christianity and thus touched at the heart of all the controverted fundamentals. Mathews brought to his work a Baptist theological education, some influence of German theology picked up in Berlin in 1890–91, a zest for Baptist church life, a hulking figure, and a kindly disposition. He enjoyed a bully pulpit at a citadel of modernism, and a love for the emerging scientific world. Chastened by World War I, Mathews in 1936 could also recall how it had shattered all optimism. He wrote: "It is easy now to be contemptuous of the optimism of pre-war liberalism but when one recalls the elements of the world situation it is not strange that we should have suffered illusion."

The war did more than excite horror for itself. "It argued a break-down of forces which we believed were shaping up a new world order."

Mathews sounded evasive on the "fundamentals" in his *The Faith of Modernism*. For example, on Jesus' virgin birth he could sound prim: "Indelicacy attends any discussion of the biological difficulties involved in the parthenogenesis of a human being." Christians simply did not need to believe in such a birth. Jesus meets human needs; that was what mattered in *The Faith of Modernism*. These needs, argued the theologian, did focus in some form on the resurrection of Jesus, an event which was attested to consistently in the basic historical documents just as the virgin birth was not. As to the precise nature of the event in question, said Mathews, the Modernist had nothing to say. "Whether his body came out of the tomb or his appearances to his disciples are explicable only by abnormal psychology, he is still living person-ally in whatever may be the conditions in which the dead now are." A sentence less satisfying to Fundamentalists than that is hard to picture. They would not stay around to hear, from Ma-thews, that Modernists "share in the deep conviction of the Christians of all the past that Jesus survived death and made himself known to his disciples . . . . If Christ lives we shall live also."

Modernists believed, argued Mathews, that biblical picturings of apocalypse indicated that "the final outcome of human experience and history is to be the triumph of that which has been once outgrown." As long as God operated in human life, there would be growth. "To no other consummation do we dare look forward." Thus, over against premillennialism, what Mathews called the Modernist's eschatology was an "uplifting hope for a social order in which economic, political and all other institutions will embody the cosmic good will which Jesus taught and revealed; and of an advance through death of those possessed of Christ-like attitudes to a complete and joyous individuality." Here the breach with the Fundamentalist party was unmistakable, even to those who could not always make their way past ambiguity or evasion in other Modernist teachings.

What bothered Fundamentalists like Machen was that Mathews refused to see the two Protestant camps as holders of different faiths. Some liberals and modernists, however, did. Thus Charles Clayton Morrison, editor of the *Christian Century*, argued that two worlds had clashed, "the world of tradition and the world of modernism. One is scholastic, static, authoritarian, individualis-

5:119

5:120

5:121

tic; the other is vital, dynamic, free, social." Yes, these rivals were "two religions," and Morrison saw the clash between them being "as profound and as grim as that between Christianity and Confucianism." In language that echoed Jesus and Abraham Lincoln, Morrison spoke of the American Protestant house divided: "Christianity is hardly likely to last much longer half fundamentalist and half modernist."

5:122   The primary content of theology for Modernists was not that of definition, but, as Mathews described it, "of a group's power to perpetuate itself by reproducing similar institutions, attitudes and beliefs in successive but genetically related groups." Hence the evolution of Christianity but also the continuity within it. At the center of the whole vision was loyalty to Jesus. But this Jesus came without dogma. "He did not demand belief in the inerrant Bible, his virgin birth, his atoning death (in the medieval sense of the term), his physical resurrection, or his physical return." Jesus never proposed or enforced tests of orthodoxy. This does not mean that the church doctrines were untrue; they simply were not to be used as tests, and they dared not hinder development.

5:123   The debate over theology in the present stage of development was not itself arcane or irrelevant. "No one can fail to see that the alternative views of Christianity are more than the debates of theologians. A world, a civilization, the welfare of humanity itself are at stake." With those lines alone among all those cited here from Mathews could Fundamentalists have agreed with that prime Modernist. But they disagreed with his beliefs that "*inherited patterns*" would fail the new world, and that only "*Christian attitudes and convictions embodied and expressed in the Christian group's life*" would serve in a new day.

5:124   Where the various parties fighting for control of Protestant denominations did agree was in the conviction that more was at stake than the destiny of their little church bodies. They saw the conflict of their day as a battle over the soul of the civilization they had informed and wanted still to address if not control. The rise of democracy in Europe and America, the generating of what Mathews called our "new social mind seeking new knowledge of reality, liberty, and justice in all social relations" made the present age creative. Once again as often before in such moments, Mathews argued, a new Modernism had arisen to greet the age and only Modernism could help in such emergences. "Society has grown irreligious where Christians have opposed religious progress. Social inertia has bred religious decline."

Democracy by itself, science by itself—these were not saviors. 5:125
"But can Christianity meet those needs and change human life?
That is the supreme question of the hour." Mathews was sure that
unnamed premillennialists declared it could not. The world could
only grow worse. Could any attack on Machen and Fundamentalists have been more systematic than Mathews' listing of false options? "The world needs new control of nature and society and is
told that the Bible is verbally inerrant." When it needs a means
of composing class strife, it "is told to believe in the substitutionary atonement." When it needs to find God in the processes of
nature, the citizen "is told that he who believes in evolution cannot believe in God."

Mathews threw down more gauntlets as he drew boundaries: 5:126
the world needs faith in the divine presence in human affairs "and
is told it must accept the virgin birth of Jesus Christ." It needs
hope for a better world order "and is told to await the speedy
return of Jesus Christ from heaven to destroy sinners, cleanse the
world by fire, and establish an ideal society composed of those
whose bodies have been raised from the sea and earth." Mathews
often wrote as if he were keeping a formal list of the Fundamentals at hand on his desk so he could counter them. For him, the
appalling fact was that dogmatic Christianity no longer appealed
to thousands, no longer regenerated the modern world, and was
never workable.

Modernists were born to hope, and Mathews nourished hopes. 5:127
Christianity, despite predictions, had not passed away. Christians
were finding new power in their religion. An "untheological,
practical, scientific age" was now shaping a religious and moral
Christianity with an intellectual and spiritual power. Missionaries
were building hospitals and founding schools. Mathews did not
mention that they were also to be saving souls. Churches were
building parish houses and becoming community centers. He did
not on that page mention worship. Christian associations were
equipping gymnasiums and establishing hotels. Vice was being
outlawed. War was being denounced. Social service was broadcasting Christian love. Economic justice was being promised.
Denominations were seeking to cooperate. Scientists were redis-
covering God. Statesmen were pleading for the Christian spirit.
In the face of all this, Mathews turned to accusation: the "dogmatists," which could be translated "Fundamentalists," wanted
to impose archaic patterns. "A theology that must be enforced is
a religious Blue Law."

5:128   In Mathews' helpful distinction, two types of mind were struggling with each other, and they displayed competing attitudes toward culture. Enemies of both Catholic and Protestant Modernism saw them as denials of Christianity, not experiments with faith. This approach was "good controversial strategy, but it is not correct." The adversary simply employed this technique: "Group your adversaries together into a party; give that party a name; give that name a bad meaning by attaching to it your own interpretation of its champions; and then attack opponents without discrimination as representing the evils which have been attributed to the name."

5:129   Such dogmatists in the twenties were doing outrageous partisan and unscientific things, such as sending questionnaires which demanded Yes or No answers about "the fundamentals" to pastors and teachers. Mathews granted that opponents to Modernism were sometimes sincere, not simply belligerent or unthinkingly reactive. Yet they misread the intention of Modernist methods. So he italicized what the heart of Modernism was: it "*is the use of the methods of modern science to find, state and use the permanent and central values of inherited orthodoxy in meeting the needs of a modern world.*" It was a phase of the scientific struggle for freedom in thought and belief. Modernists were Christians who accepted "the results of scientific research as data with which to think religiously." And they used their methods of historical and literary science on the texts of the Bible and the religious heritage.

5:130   While extreme Modernism became unpopular during the controversy with Fundamentalists, Modernism itself lived on in more moderate liberalisms. Fewer scholars called themselves Modernist after the controversy. During its moment in the sun it wore many guises. A review of its expressions and professors suggests that overall it was the sincere attempt of leaders to advance the Christian faith in a new age. These Modernists were in their own way Christians who did not want to leave the faith or the church but who could not move back into the scholastic or other worldviews in which they had been brought up.

5:131   The Fundamentalists were no doubt correct in their claim that a poll of denominational memberships had found only a small percentage of the people signed up for Modernism. Neither Modernists nor Fundamentalists won, then, in the Federal Council denominations. The temporary winners were those who worked for inclusiveness, who allowed some diversity and stayed short of final definition. These moderates or mild liberals had become custodians of original-stock Protestantism. They had little time to sit back to count their treasures and weigh their spoils. As we shall see, their close relatives, "realists," neo-orthodox thinkers, would soon produce a second challenge.

The Weapon of Biblical Inerrancy

One task remains: to survey the effects of Fundamentalism on   5:132
some churches which were neither in the Federal Council nor formally in Fundamentalist ranks. Some of these were large in their regions: the Southern Baptist Convention, the southern Presbyterians, the Upper Midwest Lutheran groups, the midwestern Mennonites. The traumas within these churches as a result of the spread of a Fundamentalist ethos produced fissures and fault lines which readied believers for quakes within them, decades later. In each case, the most effective weapon for traditionalist parties was one of the fundamentals, the concept of biblical inerrancy.

These were all somehow conservative denominations; other-   5:133
wise most of them would have been members of the Federal Council, as they were not. But in the twenties conservatism was turning into reaction. The acids of modernity were eating away, and determined leadership wanted to encase the doctrines of their denominations in safe containers. In each family quarrel the reactionary party, alert to even the mildest of compromises on the part of moderate conservatives, encircled these beleaguered moderates as if looking for a sure target. Even where they could not find one, they armed themselves for future battle.

One candidate for their weaponry, dispensational premillenni-   5:134
alism and precise beliefs about the return of Christ, could not well serve. Those who held it were passionate about its centrality, but Fundamentalists disagreed over details of millennial teaching. What emerged therefore was the issue of authority in a world of relativity. The concept of biblical inerrancy best addressed the issue and served most efficiently in the arsenal to be used in intrachurch battles. Inerrancy meant that the original manuscripts of the Bible were accurate on all points of fact, including nature, history, and science. The Bible did not claim inerrancy for itself, but Fundamentalists devised or discovered elaborate philosophical defenses of the idea. How it came to be picked up and then reinforced in the twenties and early thirties is an important element in

the story of schism and reshaping in the Protestant majority between the wars.

5:135   The Southern Baptist Convention was the most obvious case. It numbered 25,000 congregations after World War I. Even its most thoughtful theologian, E. Y. Mullins, sounded triumphalist about postwar prospects. Southern Baptists, he trumpeted, would lead to the reconstruction of the world. "The Baptist conception of the Christian religion contains elements which in the highest degree are adapted to meet the needs of the modern world." In the older civilization of Europe, Christians substituted culture for salvation. "The Germans converted the conception of culture into *kultur*, and Christianity became simply an element in the German *kultur*." Evidently assuming that such culture-Christianity was also a danger in America, Mullins advocated a Baptist approach to life because it promoted salvation, not *kultur*. How completely adapted Southern Baptists were to southern *kultur* was a theme that even the wise Dr. Mullins overlooked.

5:136   Baptists were generally optimistic. To advance their cause, in 1919 the convention adopted the Seventy-Five Million Campaign, to raise $75 million in five years. At the end of an announced Victory Week their accountants reported that these Baptists had pledged an astonishing $92 million. Counting these fiscal eggs as hatched merely because they were laid, writers in the convention *Annual* crowed that that time was "the most momentous period in Baptist history since the Day of Pentecost." Richard H. Edmonds, the lay editor of *Manufacturers' Record* called the campaign the "greatest achievement ever made by any denomination in the world's history." Five years later, however, only $58 million was collected and in the bank. Still, Baptists of the South were undaunted. The Arkansas Baptist convention proceedings all but gloated: "The past five years have marked the greatest spiritual strides in Arkansas and in the South that Baptists or any other religious group have made in the history of Christianity."

5:137   Then it began to rain on the Baptist parade. Clerics enflamed by Fundamentalists began to attack professors. They feared both the taint of Federal Council denominations and some lures to join the council itself. But they focused on biblical authority. Lacking pope and hierarchy and creed, conservative Baptists were used to starting and settling arguments on the basis of their understanding of the Bible which, all agreed, they must preserve from the cancer of European-style biblical criticism. But those who were fearful of modernity or who were in a mood to pick a

fight went out of their way to start some civil wars in that generally protected collection of congregations. To quote the Mississippi state Baptist paper, they saw the Scopes trial as a second
carpetbag invasion. The South had triumphed, and the convention's Home Mission Board spoke expansively: "The South con-
stitutes the nursery, the training ground, the granary, the source
of supplies, indeed, for our conquest in all lands."

Baptists J. Frank Norris and Amzi C. Dixon led charges   5:138
against Southern Baptist leadership. While they could find no true
heretics, they did produce so much smoke that leaders had to
worry about laypeople or pastors shouting "Fire!" The seminary
professors and presidents were quickly forced on the defensive.
In effect they had to respond as if to say, "Look, we're not as
liberal as the enemies accuse us of being," but that was an answer
unsatisfying to reactionaries who had turned anxious or ideological. These wanted absolute assurance about absolute truth through
absolute fealty to an absolutely inerrant Bible. Some moderate
conservatives fought back. Mercer University president Rufus
Weaver did some summarizing in 1932: the Fundamentalists were
unnecessary in the convention. They produced only a "controversial, bitter, and domineering" spirit. Let Baptists settle Baptist
affairs on their own, he argued. In his language, Fundamentalism
was still an outside force working its way into Baptist domain.

Who and what could the Fundamentalists find to attack so ve-   5:139
hemently? As they began scouting for deviation and heresy they
often seemed to be exemplifying a dictum uttered by philosopher
John Dewey in 1922: "Men do not shoot because targets exist,
but they set up targets in order that throwing and shooting may be
more effective and significant." Baptist partisans came to focus
on the most respected articulator, E. Y. Mullins, who did say that
the Bible should be put to critical and scientific tests if it was
permanently to retain its influence as he hoped it would. Mullins
did not like the way premillennialists failed to understand that
"figures of speech, metaphors and all sorts of literary media for
communicating truth" were to be found in the Bible. Over against
their flattening literalism, he wrote that anyone with a good literary sense would have no difficulty with the passages they rendered
controversial. Such responses, of course, would not satisfy Fundamentalists who wanted to attack the Baptist fortress.

J. Frank Norris trained his sights on the Foreign Mission   5:140
Board. James F. Love had to answer for the board and did so
in terms which revealed the conditions of tribal life: "The de-

nomination wants its orthodoxy championed in the name of the denomination and within the denomination." Some denominationalists did fire back. Thus Joe Hankins, a pastor down the block, as it were, in Childress, Texas, answered Norris in Texas-style direct language. The Fundamentalists, conservatives such as Hankins claimed, verged on support of what was called a dictation theory. This notion would turn biblical writers into secretaries for the Holy Spirit. Hankins asked: "If God had to make a phonograph or stenographer out of a man to speak His message, then why did He ever use a man at all? Why did He not do like He did about the Ten Commandments, write them with His own finger?"

5:141   Fracases like these replicated what reached the floor when Southern Baptists met in convention. The most important year was 1925, when the Convention produced a document called "Statement of Baptist Faith and Message." Mullins headed the committee which drafted it and, despite some distracting fundraising duties for his Louisville Seminary and despite his own ill health, he went to Memphis to fight for it. The moderates debating the issue won by 2,259 to 218 and then by 2,103 to 950. Mullins saw the "Statement" to be a conservative but not Fundamentalist document. As such its adoption meant "an open defeat of the Radicals and Extremists," who, he said, wanted to "put the thumb screws on everybody who does not agree in every detail with their statements of doctrine."

5:142   The statement retained the high view of biblical authority but was designed to fend off Fundamentalist attacks. In a sense it represented a departure for Baptists, for it gave off the odor of something creedal, and Baptists always resisted creedal formulas and testing. Mullins, though weary of controversy, had to keep defending the document. Norris never let up on his attack, demanding that Mullins should "cease to disturb the peace of our Southern Baptist Zion." Mullins in turn responded to what was in his eyes a "radical fundamentalist" camp, which was "going over on Catholic ground and leaving the Baptist position" by trying to pin brethren down to stereotyped statements. Doing so was not in the Baptist spirit. The battles fatigued Mullins; he had to be cautious in 1926 and for reasons of health was not even able to attend the annual convention in 1927. But by then, as in the northern denominations, Fundamentalists had overshot; some key figures were fired from their editorial posts or took their causes elsewhere.

Evolution was the controversial theme for many of these fight-   5:143
ers south of the Scopes belt. Crowd-pleasing evangelists could
always attract followings by attacking evolution. Thus Mississippi
revivalist T. T. Martin attacked theistic evolutionists as "Bible-
denying, Christ-dethroning, and soul-destroying." He helped
form an Anti-Evolution League of North America to fight evolution by law and in the public schools. Whenever people of his
party found a Southern Baptist theistic evolutionist, they lunged.
The most popular target was a foremost convention intellectual,
William L. Poteat of Wake Forest University. But Poteat more
than Mullins learned to give as well as he got against the ones he
called "misguided men" who created problems for Christians by
posing false alternatives between Bible and science.

The Baptist battles ended in a draw. No one had scored a   5:144
knockout punch, and the two sides quietly coexisted. But in the
mid-twenties, with the infusion of Fundamentalist-style thinking
and rhetoric, a new element had come into Southern Baptist life.
No matter how many years this party would have to work from
the underground or the edges, it was waiting for a better moment
to strike.

Southern Presbyterianism, the second group, at times qualified   5:145
as a Federal Council denomination and at other times as an isolated one, for the simple reason that in its quest for identity and
mission the membership fought over the council and moved in
and out of membership, and then in again. Officially called the
Presbyterian Church in the United States, it had led a separate
existence from the northern Presbyterians since 1861. Policies
concerning race and secession more than doctrine originally drove
the churches apart. During the Fundamentalist struggles in northern Presbyterianism in the twenties the southerners generally kept
their distance, but their eyes were open. Their profound controversies were to come in the thirties. The evolution battles were
strong especially in North Carolina Presbyterianism, but they led
to no schism.

Still, there were plenty of family quarrels. The *Presbyterian*   5:146
Standard predictably and successfully introduced the inerrancy
issue into its editorials and led the battles in North Carolina, a key
state. Its party began to find what it claimed was Modernism on
the Presbyterian foreign mission field, particularly at the Nanking
(China) seminary. Returning missionary Hugh W. White did not
welcome the presence of northern Presbyterians on the faculty. L.
Nelson Bell, M.D., was also critical of trends. He received sup-

port because he was a layperson. Said one partisan, "It isn't some 'narrow preacher' who is sounding the alarm, but an 'M.D.', a sure enough doctor." The apologist at the Nanking school, Donald W. Richardson, dismissed the charges. "Some men have got modernism on the brain. They got 'bughouse' on the subject." They may have had Modernism on the brain, but they did not yet find enough in the Presbyterian body to turn the denomination from its instinctive conservatism to an embrace of Fundamentalism. Yet inerrancy remained as a potential weapon for traditionalists who wanted to scout for heresy.

5:147   The third major group, the Lutherans, were also at the borders of the Federal Council, though some groups among them were consistently hostile to it. The United Lutheran Church had a cooperative arrangement with it, but all the other Lutheran bodies stayed outside. In the twenties, Lutherans were just beginning to learn to cooperate with each other, so they were in a precarious position when the Fundamentalist controversy came along. Some of them were changing from German or Scandinavian expression to English, adapting to America, taking their first look around at options. Those who viewed the battles knew that they could never be allies of Modernists. Meanwhile, premillennialism and some of the theology derived from Calvin and Zwingli or the Reformed in general put them off Fundamentalism. But they felt more sympathy with Fundamentalism than with Modernism, and began to find the weaponry of biblical inerrancy useful in their arsenal. A mentor whom Lutherans of all parties claimed as their own, Martin Luther, held quite paradoxical and open views of the Bible, which was for him always the authoritative word. However, the seventeenth-century Lutheran dogmatists felt impelled to find philosophical bases for supporting biblical infallibility. The different Lutheran immigrant groups brought competing views of scriptural authority to America. Some heirs of the seventeenth century, it turned out, matched up their teachings on this subject with those of the new Fundamentalists.

5:148   Lutherans had the luxury of doing most of their fighting out of public view. Despite their substantial numbers, most of them were not original-stock Americans, and they did not seem to be central to the Anglo-Saxon Protestant establishment. They did fight each other, however, first across the lines of their separate synods. Thus the large Missouri Synod repudiated what it called unionism, anything smacking of federated church life or of moves toward organic union, unless the cooperating bodies agreed completely with each other. This meant for most Missourians that others must come to agree with their synod, which already possessed the full truth. The United Lutheran Church thus became the liberal enemy. Missouri found the United Lutherans unwilling to import the concept of inerrancy in order to guard their scripture or dogma.

The battles in the twenties occurred around theses or declara-   5:149
tions which, as if on a moment's notice, any Lutheran synod could and would generate. Thus in fateful 1925, leaders of the Iowa and Buffalo synods convened in Minnesota; hence, the name of their product, the Minneapolis Theses. In the climate of that peak year of Fundamentalist-Modernist controversy, they took up the term and concept of inerrancy as they worked to form what five years later became an American Lutheran Conference. It was an anti–United Lutheran Church movement. Norwegian-American Lars Boe made no secret of what he called this "intention to form a kind of protective league over against other Lutherans."

When in 1930 the Iowa, Ohio, and Buffalo synods formed the   5:150
American Lutheran Church, inerrancy, the Fundamentalist agenda topic, was the main point at issue. The joint commissioners of the three uniting synods in 1926 brought in for a possible constitutional phrase the note that the Bible was "the inspired and inerrant Word of God." The most notable Iowa Synod theologian, Michael Reu, who did not believe there were errors in the Bible, also did not believe that such a phrase belonged in the constitution. "Scripture itself does not say that it is inerrant in . . . things that neither directly nor indirectly pertain to faith and life," so Reu would not allow himself to be driven to a position narrower than Scripture itself required, he said. In 1926 he made his case against inerrancy and, to the surprise of many, against merger. But the Ohio Synod leadership held firm on inerrancy, and did what the Southern Baptist firebrands did to men like E. Y. Mullins; they forced those who would not accept their formula to sound only half safe, half sure of biblical authority; certainly they must be weak leaders.

Enter the shadow of explicit Fundamentalism. Iowa Synod   5:151
president C. G. Prottengeier in 1930 kept having to face the charge, as he put it, "that since the Fundamentalist society of the Twin Cities had put the word 'inerrant' on its standard, we dare not fall short of them, but must do likewise." He scorned this tactic and said Lutheranism dared not mimic Fundamentalism. He would not allow a merger that made his Iowa synod look as if it

had been weak and compromising. It must be "completely cleared of the infamous suspicion and the contemptible insinuation that she has modernistic views" just because the synod was wary of the inerrancy formula.

5:152   Test votes, however, put Reu and Prottengeier on the defensive; the Fundamentalist climate was too pervasive. Somehow the drafting committee came up with a constitutional phrase acceptable to Reu, but associated it with a longer phrase in an appendix which he found unacceptable. The delegates voted for the package. Reu still protested that the synods were placing upon Lutheran minds and consciences something that was a deduction from the Bible more than something explicitly taught there. He went along with the action, however. The formula which was favored in the American Lutheran Church pleased few Lutherans outside it. It was too close to Fundamentalism to satisfy the United Lutheran Church but not firm enough to please the Missouri Lutherans on the right. Thus in 1932 the Missouri Synod delegates, in a belligerent spirit at their convention, agreed on a document which they would use in any merger proposals. Combining the seventeenth-century Lutheran scholastic style with the tone made fashionable by anti-Modernists in the Fundamentalist camp, its new *Brief Statement of the Doctrinal Position of the Missouri Synod* said that the Holy Scriptures "contain no errors or contradictions," and were infallible truth even "in those parts which treat of historical, geographical, and other secular matters." Now, like the Fundamentalists, Missouri had a weapon with which to advance the family quarrels in Lutheranism.

5:153   Or one can look, finally, at the formerly pacific Mennonites, who also found nothing like liberalism or Modernism in their body. Yet to John Horsch, a polemical member who became expert at promoting Fundamentalism, even to use a sermonic quotation of Harry Emerson Fosdick would be enough to put a Mennonite minister under suspicion. Horsch generated enough smoke to bring about the temporary closing of the denomination's Goshen College in 1923 and Witmarsum Seminary in 1931. For a while Horsch won an ally in the prominent minister Aaron Augsburger, who had a taste for heresy-hunting but who found little heresy. "If cleaning is a necessity, then let us roll up our sleeves and go at it with our might." Yet Augsburger grew disillusioned with Horsch, and broke with him: "I accept no blame for your unhappy controversy with others."

While Horsch fought on intellectual fronts, he picked up an   5:154
activist ally in evangelist C. F. Derstine, whose move to Canada
in 1925 did not end his influence in the American controversy.
Liberalism was to him a canker of masked unbelief under Satan,
who was disguised as an angel of light. Derstine tried to find this
canker and claimed it was present in Mennonite schools. So he
promoted Fundamentalist Moody Bible Institute in Chicago over
Mennonite schools. Professor Paul E. Whitmer responded from
the Mennonite's Bluffton College in Ohio. Fundamentalist institutions of the Moody sort, he said, "practically all believe in the
efficacy of fight and contention as a method by which to rid this
world of evil. Their dominant method is combative. They use it
lavishly in speech, in writing, in Bible teaching," he complained,
where they contradicted Mennonite pacifist traditions. So, he
went on, they deferred peace "to a future age, leaving us nothing
better than the militarism of paganism to live by."

Still, Horsch and Derstine kept moderate conservatives on the   5:155
run. Attacks on Goshen brought down six presidents in six years.
Yet, however disruptive the Modernist-hunters, they never completely took over and did not cause a schism. They did force Mennonites to spend years in anxiety and paralysis as Fundamentalists
pursued their fellow believers with the armament of inerrancy and
the importation of traditionally or historically non-Mennonite
concerns. The pattern became standard, as family quarrels combined with church quarrels to bring the noise of conflict to the
religious scene in the twenties.

It is not easy to picture the America that might have developed   5:156
had not Protestantism so distracted itself from other business at
hand, including its reign of dominance, by its own family quarrels
in the twenties. Maybe Catholics, Jews, humanists, and others
would have been worse off had Protestantism kept a united front
rather than dividing somewhere down the middle during the decade. What had come of the conflict of the twenties was a deeply,
permanently divided Protestantism. While Fundamentalists became for some decades less visible in many parts of the country,
sent into exile at the margins of culture, forced to rebuild institutions and shoot from distances, it became clear that original-stock
Protestantism—from which both sides derived—no longer presented a single front. It was obvious that the divisive style also
reached the Protestants who had been previously isolated from
main trends by ethnic or geographical separateness. Organized

social-action programs passed into the hands of the inclusive and
federating churches.

5:157   Whoever asked the question, "Will America remain Protestant
and Anglo-Saxon?" now had to ask, "Which kind of Protestant?"
Which kind, which version, which party was bidding for attention? The schism in Protestantism's soul had been too profound to
overlook. If for a moment a skeptic like H. L. Mencken or a
humanist like Walter Lippmann did not call attention to the split,
members of one of the surviving parties in any denomination
would be glad to oblige. They could point the public to the denominational trenches, in those rare moments when they were not
too busy pointing those fingers of accusation and condemnation
at each other. All the while they were splitting up what was left
of a Protestant establishment, leaving it ever less prepared to hold
its place of dominance in American culture in the decades to
come.

6

A Sober Nation and a Warless World

Liberals: Their Chief Preoccupation Is Social Welfare

Against: the 'tango,' scanty and diaphanous women's gar-   6:1
menture, bathing costumes, rouge, lipstick . . . jazz, Sunday
movies, Sunday motor rides, a 'pleasure-mad age,' divorce, the
difficult ways of the young." And "For: longer skirts and sleeves,
the natural complexion, more sedate manners and more defensible
morals, increased church attendance. . . ." These were the "little
crusades" of the twenties that prominent Congregationalist pastor
Gaius Glenn Atkins recalled later. He listed no big crusades, for
example in support of organized labor, even though he was serving in the tense Detroit of industrialist Henry Ford and of Protestant pastor and critic Reinhold Niebuhr, who together represented
both sides of the labor issue. Atkins left out such a grand cause
even though he was himself engaged at least once in an event
involving controversy over labor.

Against: "cigarettes, alcohol, and the slums." These were cru-   6:2
sades in which André Siegfried saw American Protestants "imbued with a missionary spirit that is typically Anglo-Saxon." He
went on to list what, we would have to note, only the liberals
among them were for: "feminism, pacifism, anti-vivisection,

215

Americanization of immigrants, and even the gospel of eugenics and birth control." These were crusades in which at least the group he called Modernists were involved. "Whether an American is a Wilson, a Bryan, or a Rockefeller," added the French visitor, "he cannot leave people alone," but engages in reform and uplift. "His self-satisfaction as a member of God's elect is almost insufferable, and so is the idea that his duty toward his neighbour is to convert, purify, and raise him to his own moral heights." This works best when, as in the Anglo-Saxon case in the United States, there is a belief that "the state is working for the Protestant conception of the Kingdom of Heaven on Earth."

6:3   The two lists of little and big crusades show something of how half of a house divided stayed busy. Both halves of the divided Protestant house found plenty to do. The Fundamentalist leadership, who had just overreached and were defeated in denominational battles, soon specialized in evangelism and promoted individual morality in uncongenial times. The leaders of the moderate-to-liberal party coached their membership to specialize in social welfare as an expression of Christian love and justice and as a chief means of influencing the culture, also in uncongenial times. E. A. Ross set forth theories based on observation of the scene. Both sides, said he, were living out an example of what the sociologist discerned about the aftermath of battles. After a violent encounter, "in case the rival cannot be destroyed one seeks to *withdraw from competition*, just as an army which cannot whip the enemy retires behind fortifications."

6:4   The fortifications in the case of Fundamentalist Protestantisms were their churches, interchurch organizations, Bible colleges, radio stations and religious magazines, and their distinctive styles of religiously reinforced personal and familial living. The Fundamentalists made two great exceptions on the political scene. Seeing the use or nonuse of alcoholic beverages as an issue over which individuals had control, most of them worked to prevent repeal of the Prohibition amendment to the Constitution. Because they feared that the election of a Catholic candidate for the presidency would fundamentally alter the character of God's elect, America, many of them organized politically to oppose the candidacy of Governor Alfred E. Smith in 1928. The Scopes trial in 1925 showed how difficult it would be for Fundamentalists to get their way in national forums of opinion or elections. They appeared to be ever more sectarian in their withdrawal. Ross applied his own theories to religious life, and they match what we here observe: "If the state will not shield her, the church that shrinks from meeting competition builds for herself a citadel within which she can continue her life untroubled by the assaults from the outside world." Continuing her life in this case included the mission of making forays into the surrounding world, chiefly in order to rescue people from it into the sphere of evangelical salvation.

On the other hand, the Federal Council churches and their   6:5
members increasingly retreated from competition in the fields of Fundamentalist, evangelical, pentecostal, and conservative specialization: foreign missions and personal evangelism. Of course, they also wanted very much to grow by bringing in new members. They also did believe in salvation through trust in Jesus Christ, as Modernist Shailer Mathews rightfully insisted. They likewise kept supporting and raising funds for departments of evangelism. But they did not have a sufficiently exclusive theology to move them toward passion for consistent soul-winning. God, they reasoned or intuited, would somehow take care of the people they would not reach and convert. Meanwhile, they did not have a worldview which permitted enjoyment of spiritual fortification or life in citadels.

The federating churches, now coming to be seen as the main-   6:6
stream ones, instead developed other specializations. Sociologist Ross might well have been writing a textbook for them, too. "An institution *eludes competitors by specializing.*" Catholicism also aspired to make its way in the political and social order, as we shall see. It made important contributions, but there were some inhibitions against and limits to their efforts, as the Alfred E. Smith candidacy for president in 1928 revealed. Jews were too few, too localized in a handful of cities, too recent as immigrants, too much excluded by practice and prejudice yet to do much more in groups than to represent their own or interfaith civil interests. Black churches were segregated and their influence was generally confined, since blacks had little access to the larger political process. Fundamentalists and conservative individualists were the only plausible competition, but they would not and could not specialize in working out the social vision that the federated Protestants promoted.

"*Constrained adaptation*" Ross called the forced adjustment   6:7
of religious groups. "Owing to competition among themselves American religious denominations have had forced upon them changes distasteful to the ruling element." Thus he watched churches invent what they and he called "institutional or social"

features, "not because their members all necessarily desire them, but in order to attract . . . the unchurched," and, we add not inappropriately, to serve and hold their place in society. Specifically, Ross added in his writing of 1920: "No doubt the advanced social program of the Federal Council of Churches in Christ [sic] was adopted by most of the Protestant churches reluctantly and only because it was realized that 'something must be done to win back the workingman'."

6:8   Ross's insight may have been a bit too suspicious, even cynical, to satisfy those enthusiastic church leaders who did have a sense of divine mission behind what they were doing. He was not wrong, however, about their specialization or adaptation on the field of competition and conflict. André Siegfried, using the senses of a gifted visitor, connected this mission with what he detected to be "the real sources of American inspiration." These flowed from the Puritan spirit which now lived on in religious Modernism, by which he meant all Protestantism except Fundamentalism and isolationist conservatism. The Calvinist, wrote the man from Catholic France, thinks he must carry out a mission "to purify the life of the community and to uplift the state." Such a Calvinist-turned-modern argued that Christians must take their place in the life of the community, whereas, said their observer, "in former times they withdrew from the world in order to remain pure." This withdrawing was something that only the anti-Modernists among the heirs of Calvinism were now ready to do.

6:9   Because American "Modernists have been so active since the war," Fundamentalists "had to defend themselves with an ardour that was not simply religious." Indeed, the schism within Protestantism in fact was "the very heart of the American religious problem." The Fundamentalists insistently claimed that true Protestants were individualistic, not to be concerned with religion in public life. These Modernists on the other hand, Siegfried observed, did act strictly in line with the Puritan traditions. As with their ancestors, he commented, their "chief preoccupation was moral sincerity and social welfare." Siegfried's Modernists, thus described, considered that Christianity should come first in all affairs of life, personal and social. Believers should adapt to the conditions of their time so that Christianity, as he rephrased it for them, could "fill its appointed role as guiding factor of the community." Such religion *had* to occupy itself with morals and even politics, wrote Siegfried, or it could not possibly justify itself to the conscientious.

As a social critic and skeptic about the way Americans fused   6:10
Christianity with materialism, Siegfried added one more important observation. When the spiritual elite faced social or ethical
problems, he noted, they could not please everybody. The rich
among them, who overwhelmingly did support churches and welfare organizations, consequently claimed the right to dictate political activities to the larger community of the religious. They
reproved leaders if any of them practiced the more revolutionary
doctrines of the New Testament. Its internal critics argued that the
church should not meddle in political matters. If they did thus
intervene, the well off would not contribute funds.

In two pages of *The Faith of Modernism* Shailer Mathews out-   6:11
lined the social approach. "The Modernist Christian believes the
Christian religion will help men meet social as well as individual
needs." Mathews looked at the fortifications and citadels of Fundamentalist faith and said that the believers inside them emphasized rescue from the world, saving of individual souls. Mathews
instead specialized in using the term "social": "Students of society know that the relation of the individual to the social order
involves him in responsibility for social actions as well as liability
to social influences. Therefore, they undertake to transform social
forces for the benefit of the individual."

Mathews was quick to qualify and balance his theme. All their   6:12
stress on the social did not mean that Modernists thought that only
physical salvation was necessary. They simply believed that "the
Gospel is as significant for social forces as for individuals." And
in direct contrast to the stated aims of Fundamentalists, Mathews
went on, "They find little hope in rescue of brands from burning;
they want to put out the fire." Jesus to them was more than the
savior of isolated individuals; he saved people in society. That
was one reason why the Modernist was an object of suspicion.
The dogmatic mind, which Mathews evidently equated with Fundamentalism, was, he charged, almost always to be found among
social reactionaries. Mathews noticed that Modernism in theology
often begot opposition precisely because public-minded Modernists urged reform in economic matters. "In the struggle over economic privilege the Modernist is properly feared as one who takes
Jesus seriously and believes implicitly that his Gospel applies to
wages and war as truly as to oaths, charity and respectability."

The times were not favorable for elites in middle-class   6:13
churches to rouse their members into support of organized labor
or peace causes. Their members could engage in creative foot-

dragging, drift off into the secular culture, or simply oppose them. Parish pastors especially were on the spot. They had to live with a delicate politics relating pulpit to pew. If they accepted the social order as it was they were failing to heed the critical message of their faith. If they rejected the same order too directly the laity reacted. Their position was both precarious and strategic. Professor Shailer Mathews and his colleagues always spoke from the security of their university or seminary teaching posts. Members of denominational boards were also partly shielded from day-to-day contact with laity who reacted so regularly against their suggested or imposed programs. Similarly, editors like those at the *Christian Century* could shape opinion among like-minded leaders and still keep enough subscribers, but they too did not depend on the loyalty of or have direct access to, ordinary church members. Ministers in local congregations were always aware that professors, editors, and bureaucrats worked from safer places than did these frontline warriors. As a writer in the *Christian Century* put it in 1937, for a situation that was even more true in 1927: "Bravely and boldly the professors tell young seminarians to preach a realistic gospel—and wave good-bye to them from their bomb-proof dugouts as the young hopefuls go out to the battle." For the ministers, trench warfare without bomb-proofing was the norm.

6:14   Survey after survey in the twenties found most ministers in congregations not to be as well-poised as celebrities of Fosdick's order were. Most were underpaid, many were underhonored, and some were losing their previous status as being among the few educated cohorts in most local communities. Other professions and professionals increasingly challenged them. As frequently quoted university president Glenn Frank put it, the minister now had to have the qualities of "a medieval saint, a carelessly courageous agitator, an expert in mental hygiene, and the business head of a business corporation"—for thirty dollars a week and a parsonage.

6:15   John Roach Straton, a Fundamentalist who agitated against social Christianity and clergy activism, knew all about that situation when in 1922 he called on lay people to oppose churchly social action. "They outnumber the preachers a hundred to one, and they are the ones who have to pay the bills." Why, Straton was asking, should they subsidize the Federal Council opposition viewpoints? Meanwhile some bias also certainly colored a survey that came from the enemy flank, one made by Jerome Davis, a man of the left who thought in terms of class. Still, there were some data in his finding which give a helpful glimpse of the situation. After having studied 387 church boards, Davis reported that 55 percent of their members were proprietors, managers, or in professional service. Merchants, clerks, and bankers were most frequently elected to church leadership posts, with manufacturers being next most numerous. No wonder, he thought, that they were reluctant to engage in social activities of a reformist character.

Naturally, Davis noted, even if these elites did not represent all   6:16
the membership of their congregations, it was natural that people of talent and power in secular worlds would also be elected in church life. From these church-board positions they would exert disproportionately strong influence on their ministers. "Does it not seem rather probable," Davis asked, that under the class conditions he had just discovered, "the average church will of necessity be a strong supporter of the status quo in business life?" He had another question: since the makeup of the board "is predominantly business and professional, whatever the minister may say about the profit motive on Sunday, will not his board tend to follow the customary rule of profits during the rest of the week?" Of course we must also assume as Davis may not have, that not all these board members agreed with each other or were utterly predictable in their positions on public issues. Still, there are reasons to concur with him that the clergy were in no small measure dependent upon those in the community who, as Davis put it, were least likely to approve criticism of the existing economic order even if the clergy themselves were persuaded that they should seek change. These are cautionary themes to keep in mind lest the word of Siegfried or Mathews on liberal social positioning be taken too naively. One must qualify conclusions by noticing the dynamics of diversity and opposition within the Federal Council and the Modernist ranks.

Labor: The Church Does Not Think Very Much of It

Organized labor, the major social issue, represented problems   6:17
for Protestant leadership. Its membership connoted those "workers of the world" whom the Communists of the epoch urged to unite. The Red Scare showed how uncongenial America at large found such urgings. Catholicism was perceived to be the laborer's church just as Protestantism, by and large, was not. The prewar

Social Gospel had focused on transforming capitalism if not into socialism then into some sort of cooperative order with organized labor having a key part. After the war it was natural to see clerical leadership trying to pick up that Social Gospel and its programs again and to continue the advocacy. And labor was in a mood and moment to make demands while workers wanted support. Organized labor therefore might have become the test of how serious American Protestantism was in its social role.

6:18   More should have happened. In his review of the 1920s, Detroit minister Gaius Glenn Atkins, who had listed the "little crusades" by the churches in the twenties, looked back on the period and commented on the social engagement of the clergy. Atkins perceived a long development which had led to the time when, as he put it, "massed Protestantism became a force to be reckoned with—even in politics." But labor issues were curiously missing from his chronicle of the decade. Atkins took pride in his observing that the recent movements for social engagement in general "naturally developed religious leaders who needed no instruction in political technique from the secular politician." They had learned their way in church life and, though they might not put the pure fear of God into the hearts of legislators, they did, he said, inspire some with a godly fear of the church vote. Churches put to work some of this potential for power in some of the crusades for peace and Prohibition that Atkins cited. But it was much less so, rarely so at all, with labor, where the otherwise politically adept Protestant leaders mustered few church votes.

6:19   Elsewhere around the world organized labor seemed to be in the center of affairs right after the war. The Bolshevik Revolution claimed to have been centered in the cause of workers, while postwar Germany saw unrest based in similar urgencies. During the war organized labor had progressed. Moves that labor made to consolidate gains after the war, however, often suffered from reaction. Small-town, rural, and business-class Protestants were ill-prepared to understand urban-industrial America. Catholics could take care of their own in the labor movement. In selected fields, such as the garment industry, Jews had dominated membership and leadership. A Protestantism which ventured to support labor would not be perceived as simply "taking care of its own."

6:20   Mainstream Protestant leaders knew that these workers were quite alienated from their kind of churches. It was easy to find many labor leaders speaking as Warren S. Stone did in 1924 for the Brotherhood of Locomotive Engineers: "The main reason why the average clergyman does not understand the workers' problems is because he does not associate with the workers." Social class was the barrier; here Stone's instincts matched Jerome Davis's findings: "The prominent members of [the minister's] church and the intimate friends whom he invites to his dinner table are almost invariably persons without any connection and often without any sympathy for organized Labor." Stone could be even more emphatic: "You want to know what labor thinks of the church. I tell you, very frankly, that labor does not think very much of the church, because the church does not think very much of labor."

The original-stock Protestant churches and labor did have wide   6:21
cultural gaps to cross if they wanted to meet. Thus the Methodist *Christian Advocate* was being quite unrealistic when it expressed the thought that Protestant Christianity was admirably effective in the anthracite coal fields. Church leaders wanted to nourish the spiritual life there, it said, because labor often came into collision with what the editor called "the superstition and intense bigotry which the Slavs have brought with them out of centuries of priestly intolerance" in Catholicism. Much of the Protestant concern expressed for labor derived from fear lest organized labor would be too close either to Catholicism or socialism.

The great labor strikes which divided and influenced religious   6:22
forces occurred after World War I and again just before the Crash, in 1919 and 1929. Between these episodes, the age of normalcy was not as propitious a time for dealing with labor issues as was to be the decade of the thirties, with the onset of the Great Depression. The strikes of 1919 revealed and enlarged great cleavages in American society: between labor and management, workers and middle classes, left and right, Protestants and Catholics, prolabor and antilabor Protestants, and various factions of workers. People who inherited Puritan consciences had reason to address the crises in these troubling contexts.

The first great postwar conflict arose over the strike in western   6:23
Pennsylvania steel mills late in 1919. People who worked six twelve-hour days a week in the great heat emitted from the smelter ovens rebelled against low wages and the harsh demands made on them. In September 100,000 steelworkers struck. Eventually 375,000 workers went out. In that climate which was so unfriendly to unions, the strikers, many of them recent immigrants, were soon put down and the strike was broken. After ten weeks the strike was called off. Attention therefore quickly turned to the

walkout of 150,000 textile workers in the Northeast, and then to the unprecedented threat to public order that most citizens saw in a walkout of Boston police. Public sentiment in a time of serenity worked against strikers, and labor soon had to lessen its demands. In this climate, in July of 1920, the Interchurch World Movement issued a report on the great steel strike of 1919. In the religious setting, the report made even more news than the strike.

6:24   The Interchurch World Movement, backed by big business money and bigger clerical dreams, sponsored a 300-page finding on the steel strike. The confident leadership thought it could urge Christian love on all parties and that it could produce a fair-minded report. Few dissented against the notion of such an inquiry. But the resulting *Report on the Steel Strike* and a follow up document *Public Opinion and the Steel Strike* provoked responses which in the end helped devastate the movement. The report found almost nothing to applaud in steel management, scourging it for many violations of human rights and dignity. The drafters countered the antilabor view of the strike presented by the general press, and became an affront to those clergy who were themselves instinctively antilabor. In retrospect, the church investigators still turned out to be on the winning side in the cause, because by 1923, partly as a result of the controversy, U.S. Steel did abandon the twelve-hour workday, as labor had demanded.

6:25   Before that occurred, however, the *Report* stirred up conflict within the churches and enraged steel management, which gave publicity to E. Victor Bigelow's *Mistakes of the Interchurch Steel Report*. Said Bigelow, a minister, "It may be that eight hours is a good standard day for reckoning a unit of toil, but this world would have empty larders and raw comforts if men didn't work more than eight hours in twenty-four." An exuberant partisan of management, Methodist layperson Judge Elbert H. Gary of the United States Steel Corporation, saw to it that hundreds of thousands of Bigelow tracts made the rounds.

6:26   In 1923 came a more formal response, an *Analysis of the Interchurch World Movement Report on the Steel Strike* by Marshall Olds. He argued that steelworkers actually liked to work twelve-hour days. This was good for them because they were foreigners who would waste their long days if they were not on the job. But Judge Gary, for all his wealth and energy and power could not use Bigelow and Olds to complete effect. The public had come to know that there was too much to be said for the strikers and the Interchurch document. Much of the church press came to the defense of those who wrote the reports. The Disciples of Christ's *Christian-Evangelist* exemplified this: "Garyism must go. The workers have a right to be heard." The *Presbyterian Advance* went on: "The fact that a number of men who would be recognized as leaders of various denominations signed such a report should make many of us less ready to accept the view of any one party to a labor controversy and less easily frightened by the cry of Bolshevism."

As a side benefit of the report controversy, some Protestant   6:27
leaders now began to seek and find the company of Catholic and Jewish prolabor forces and to identify with them. In 1923, an interfaith panel boldly held a press conference: "The forces of organized religion in America are now warranted in declaring that this morally indefensible regime of the twelve-hour day must come to an end." On July 6, 1923, it did. In 1927 the *Christian Century* showed where its version of liberal Protestantism stood when its editors had their chance to put in the last word as they wrote an obituary for Judge Gary: "To him money was power, religion was personal, laissez-faire was God-made, and profit was the primary motive in all material enterprise." But by then the issues raised by labor had already been quieted and suppressed, in the spirit of Coolidge-era normalcy.

Now and then progressives would try to stir up more church   6:28
support in local situations. In crucial Detroit, where Henry Ford was the legendary leader of American industry, a Federal Council operative in 1926 attempted to start something when the American Federation of Labor was coming to town for its annual meeting. He wanted two hundred Protestant ministers to invite labor figures to their pulpits during the convention that autumn. A gathering to gain support for the move drew only eighteen attenders. Five of these offered their pulpits, but three of them had to back down when their church boards resisted the move. That left two of two hundred hoped-for pulpits, those of Unitarian Augustus P. Record and Evangelical Reinhold Niebuhr.

A very similar controversy, also in Detroit, came when the   6:29
Young Women's Christian Association invited labor leader William Green to speak. The Y.W.C.A. was concurrently holding a major fund drive, supported by large pledges from Ford, the Fisher Body Company, and S. S. Kresge. When such large donors reacted negatively against the Green invitation, the Y.W.C.A. backed down. Niebuhr and a few other clerics responded in anger and, in a meeting at Congregationalist minister Gaius Glenn At-

kins's own church, worked to patch things up. In the end, eight labor speakers did appear in Protestant pulpits as part of a compensatory gesture. There must have been little sense of triumph. Atkins, as we noted at the beginning of this chapter, does not even bother to mention the event in his memoirs.

6:30   From the secular prolabor front, the *Nation* observed, as the Y.W.C.A. backed off, that "the Protestant pastors of Detroit obviously are not in the habit of choosing their texts from the nineteenth chapter of Matthew," where Jesus told a rich young man, "Go, sell all that Thou hast, and give to the poor." Yet the editors were not surprised by what they called the cowering of the Detroit churches when the nonunion employers cracked the whip. It was, they said, "part and parcel of a long, long history." The new Protestant cathedrals were built not with the pennies of millions, said the editorial, "but with the substantial contributions of the 'substantial' section of the community."

6:31   Few Protestant church people, including liberals, favored labor strikes as a general policy. Many of them were pacifists, and strikes implied the potential of violence or provoked open conflict. Typically, at the time of the steel-strike controversy in 1919 and 1920 John Haynes Holmes, the theologically very liberal New York minister, consistently opposed strikes. To face the issue at all, the Federal Council of Churches leadership had to overcome its own reluctance to support actions which might include violence. Many of its members thought it sufficient if they called for Christian love and benign cooperation between labor and management. The problem was that these gentle techniques did not catch the eye of management or the attention of striking laborers. They found the religious leaders who spoke up for them to be ineffective and unempathic. Quite naturally, the tense and torn supporters in Protestant communions greeted the quieting of labor agitation through the mid-twenties with some relief.

6:32   Protestant reluctance to back labor led some of the more radical figures who in youth had been identified with the church to abandon it and to cease relying on it for support. Among these were Norman Thomas, a former seminarian trained as a Presbyterian minister, but who became the perennial Socialist candidate for president, and Quaker A. J. Muste, a longtime advocate of nonviolence. In 1929 Muste pondered: "In a world built on violence one must be a revolutionary before one can be a pacifist: in such a world, a non-revolutionary pacifist is a contradiction in terms, a monstrosity." Though a pacifist, Muste said that in the end he could not try to dissuade workers from striking, because in these cases the alternative of submission was a far greater evil than the risk of violence. He even argued that Red terrorism in history was itself "a bagatelle compared to the 'white' terrorism of reactionaries." Muste could talk New Testament language. "The question is pertinent as to whether the 'Lord's will' is done by the servant who talks about terrorism and practices very little or by the servant who talks about law and order and practices a vast deal of terrorism."

The noted Methodist pastor and professor Halford E. Luccock   6:33
took his fluent pen to the crusade. It was time for the church at large, Luccock wrote in the downtimes of 1927, to "throw itself recklessly and with a genuinely careless rapture into the struggle for a Christian social order," and, he had to add, into a deadly conflict with all that impedes it. The church, Luccock said, thus "might lose the First Mortgage but it would find a Second Blessing." True, he observed, the tradition against such careless rapture was time-honored and hallowed. The forces against it looked so respectable. But if the church took action, it would soon find such a warmth of fellowship at its hearth that multitudes would be drawn by an irresistible power. One is tempted to add: so he hoped.

Catholics could more conveniently face the issue of organized   6:34
labor. Thanks to the impulse of their Bishops' Program of 1919 and the presence of millions of workers in their membership, they often shamed Protestants in the eyes of those who would back labor. In 1926 during a strike at Passaic, New Jersey, some Protestant ministers wanted to intervene in order to give the workers a hearing. But they had to back off, fearing as they said they did a Communist presence. Finally a set of local churches did ask for a congressional hearing. "Here is the church," wrote the *Christian Century* editors a bit later, "intervening at last in an industrial situation which has compelled the attention of the nation. But what church?" As if mournfully, the editors pointed out that this church was not made up of the congregations of established, original-stock Protestantism.

Only by publishing the long list of churches and movements   6:35
sympathetic to labor can we capture a sense of the editorial. It included the following: "Daily Slovak American, Catholicky sokol, Slovak evangelical union of America, Polish national league, Slovak league, Holy Name Slovak Catholic Church, St. Peter and St. Paul Russian orthodox church, St. Michael's Greek Catho-

lic church, St. Stephen Roman Catholic Hungarian church, St. Stephen Slovak sick benefit society, Petofi workingmen's sick benefit society, Polish democratic club, St. Anton Hungarian club, H. M. and S. society, Slovak Evangelical Lutheran Holy Trinity church, . . . Russian Slovak Union Church, St. Martin society, St. Peter and St. Paul society, Congregation of Three Saints, St. John Russian orthodox society, Russian orthodox St. Nicholaus independent society, Russian national organization, St. Stanislaw Polish society, St. John's Russian church, Slovak all saints society, Russian American citizen club, St. Peter and St. Paul national Polish church, St. Vladimir Russian orthodox society, St. George's Russian orthodox society, Maris [sic] S.S. dei miracoli Italian Catholic church, Ascension Ukrainian church," and, oh yes, one original-stock exception, "St. George's Episcopal church." That equivalent of a Passaic phone-book Yellow Pages list showed the *Christian Century* editors what America was becoming ethnically and revealed to its readers what Protestants of Anglo-Saxon heritage were abandoning.

6:36   Near the end of the decade came the last strikes to upset the churches in the twenties, this time in textile country at and around Gastonia and Elizabethtown, North Carolina. After the experience of failure and frustration on the labor front in the twenties, the cause of workers had become quiet, the movement was breaking apart. It was therefore easy for a revitalized Communist element to take advantage of legitimately aggrieved workers. Once again there was an opening for radicalism, and Communist organizers did arrive to make this strike different from most.

6:37   The appearance of antireligious radicalism characteristic of Communism made it harder than ever for churches in this Bible Belt area to identify with strikers, however just their cause. That conditions in the mills were appalling few could deny. Yet most mainstream churches on the scene were unsympathetic. The ministers did not have the mind of labor in their background, and they had the eye of management in the foreground, in their own pews and vestries. When after two nonviolent weeks Communist agitation produced some mayhem in North Carolina, most workers were caught between company-town capitalism and Communism.

6:38   On April 18 some masked men vandalized strike headquarters with impunity. Then on June 7 in the Communist tent colony someone shot the police chief, an event that nearly led to a lynching. When indictments after the violence were handed down, seven of fifteen charged workers were indeed found to be Communist. The local *Gazette* thereupon editorialized that the blood of the murdered cried out to high heaven for vengeance.

After that violence the doomed strike subsided and the de-   6:39
feated workers went back to the mills, while spiritually worn-out ministers recognized that they had not done well under the national spotlight. It would have been unthinkable for the Baptist, Lutheran, Presbyterian, or Methodist leaders to have spoken up for the strikers, with Communists visible on the scene. Only lower-caste Church of God or Holiness churches found ways through their ministers and lay preachers to work past the Communists and have direct access to the strikers. When early in the strike the Federal Council of Churches sent an agent, Dr. James Myers, to meet with a dozen local ministers, he reported: "The attitudes revealed were defensive, cold, unresponsive to a degree I have never met before in a group of ministers. Evidently they have not yet thought of any connection between the mind of Christ and low wages or night work for women or child labor." Many ministers then and thenceforth stressed the spiritual side of life at Gastonia with new intensity, avoiding reference to the working world of their townsfolk.

In the aftermath, mill management found a way to reward the   6:40
clergy with new status and tasks. Following novel policies that were inaugurated at the end of 1929, all applicants for mill jobs had to bring along a recommendation from their former minister. There was no thick veil over the intent of the practice. The ministers turned out to be screeners of the acceptable. Some relished their task and considered the assignment a proud achievement in the company town. One observed, "When I came, there were whores, bootleggers, and other sorry people aplenty in the village." Then came the new recommendation system. It "has helped to keep out drunkards, whores, whore-mongers, bootleggers, and the like." The *Gazette* followed up in 1930 noting that cooperation between churches and the company in one town had made the church a vital factor in the religious life of the community.

The townsfolk found a ritual way to celebrate the fragile peace.   6:41
The Patriotic Order of the Sons of America brought out its banner for a program uniting church, management, and town against the threat of Communists. "GOD—OUR COUNTRY—OUR ORDER," it read, and followed up this line with "We believe in and practice PATRIOTISM, RELIGION, LOYALTY AND FELLOWSHIP." The Baptist State Convention sent in money and two

young women to assure the future of Baptist work there. The Baptists designed their effort to help offset what the sponsors called the incoming tides of materialism, unbelief, and anti-Americanism that were flowing in ever-increasing volume into these fast-growing industrial centers. The expression of Halford Luccock's "genuinely careless rapture" in a struggle for what he called a Christian social order would have to wait.

Peace: Less Interest than Before

6:42   The cause of peace should not have been hard to promote after World War I, as a war-weary America disengaged from European conflict and as its warriors came home hoping for normalcy and serenity. And in a superficial way, peace remained a popular cause. Yet when approaches to it grew more controversial and when advocates implied any judgment on America or called for any risk to its policies, there were many who expressed reserve or turned antipathetic.

6:43   The first of three incidents involved the League of Nations, which was a political issue in 1919 and 1920. The Federal Council of Churches tried at once to set an optimistic tone of a sort not heard since well before the war began. The council had backed the proposal by Woodrow Wilson for America to take part in forming a League of Nations. Among some, this organization acquired the epithet "the political expression of the Kingdom of God on earth." Yet the Senate rebuffed the dying President Wilson and thwarted this version of the Kingdom, turning down treaties which would have led to American participation in that ill-fated league.

6:44   Through the decade there were numerous efforts to revive the league proposal, to find ways to work with that international organization, or seek other ways to achieve its stated ends. Those who spoke up for international peace organizations had come to be realists, sometimes almost defeatists. After activist Kirby Page wrote a book called *The Sword or the Cross*, Charles Clayton Morrison, editor of the near-pacifist *Christian Century*, wrote Page a letter which captured something of the spirit of the times. "I sometimes think there is less interest in constructive peace than before the war." When Morrison himself faced the enemies of the peace movement, he became mournful: "We have been much more seriously brutalized by the war than we know." The editor

wrote that he could not profitably have signed on as an agent for
Page because sales would be too meager. "Your book will be read
by the esoteric few. The mood of the time is anything but congenial with pacifist doctrine." Morrison, of course, was not the kind
of person who could be permanently deterred by an uncongenial
mood of the times, so he was among those who pressed tirelessly
for causes.

The editor was by no means alone in offering dour assess-   6:45
ments. Sixteen years after the event, the Episcopal Social Gospel
leader Vida Scudder remembered how broken and scattered the
ranks of reformers at her side had become after the war. For her
and her kind of activist, the twenties were simply "those ten ex-
hausted years," the participants the "most discouraged I have
known." In the hard times of the thirties, Scudder remembered as
she described the course of affairs that there had been a worse
type of depression than the economic. It was this worse type that
discouraged those who had worked for what she recalled had once
seemed to be the rising forces of social redemption. She chose a
word often used to describe the letdown: a surging flood of "disillusion," she said, threatened to submerge the idealism and
drown the hopes of the world, and it now threatened her own
hope. She wrote a kind of epitaph on the times: hardly without
exception, the reforms on which such hope and effort had centered had been halted or destroyed. Yet Scudder, being a liberal,
endured through it all.

The Federal Council and the Carnegie-funded Church Peace   6:46
Union, which had succumbed to World War I fever, both counted
on Protestant clergy to support the peace cause. But extra strength
came from the women's groups which especially spoke up, sometimes out of disappointment with what suffragist and prohibitionist leader Carrie Chapman Catt called the timid and incompetent
male leadership of the peace movement. A large number of
women, she thought, were not in the least satisfied with the situation in which they found themselves. That situation simply
meant "carrying out the orders of the men managers of the different peace societies." Many women, especially pacifists in the liberal churches, assumed responsibility through the decade, though
they also found insufficient support in existing denominational
organizations.

The second crusade of the decade, instead of concentrating on   6:47
any leagues of nations, set out simply to outlaw war. As early as
1921 Chicago attorney Salmon O. Levinson began to dream. He

worked with such people as philosopher John Dewey and *Chris-*
tian Century editor Charles Clayton Morrison to help lay the
groundwork for what became the Kellogg-Briand Pact, or the Pact
of Paris, for the outlawry of war. For this cause the Carnegie
people also contributed resources and energy. Thus in March,
1927 the Carnegie representative gained the support of Aristide
Briand, the French foreign minister, to help head such a treaty
effort. Secretary Frank Kellogg at the U.S. State Department was
at first suspicious of the proposal.

6:48   Through it all, the original-stock Protestant churches were enthusiastic supporters of the cause. The Federal Council presented
to the White House 185,333 signatures of members urging Senate
ratification. But it was Morrison who was most strenuously involved. The editor explained that he had first become excited one
night in 1925 at a Fellowship of Reconciliation dinner where a
Quaker explained to him the Friends' mode of reaching consensus. Could not that approach also work in disputes between
nations? With his typical dispatch when an attractive cause came
along, Morrison three weeks after the dinner signed up for a committee to work on proposals for outlawing war. He worked with
familiar churched and churchless liberal names like those of Norman Thomas, Kirby Page, John Haynes Holmes, Halford Luccock, and, of course, the pioneer Salmon O. Levinson himself.
F. Ernest Johnson for the Federal Council was on the scene and
he helped assure that religious voices outnumbered those who
came with other motivations.

6:49   What made the political difference in the eventual acceptance
of the pact was the fact that Kellogg in the course of time had
changed his policy and decided to make the proposal his own. In
1928 the United States submitted a version of a draft treaty to
the nations. Signatories, it said, would bind themselves to turn
against war as an instrument of national policy in their relations
with one another. Eventually sixty-three nations, including the
Soviet Union, signed on. As for executive leadership, President
Coolidge was quite deaf to Protestant peace causes. Finally, in
August 1928, fifteen nations signed the agreement, which the
Senate ratified at the end of Coolidge's term in January 1929. In
the midst of all the peace talk, the Protestants fought each other
over approaches to ending war and over means of selling the subject to their members. Levinson, the Jewish participant, wrote:
"To me it is sickening. If christian [sic] civilization has not
enough brains and morality to cope with war, God help it." God

helped it just enough to get the ineffective pact passed. The day
the pact was signed Morrison cheered, *"Today international war
was banished from civilization."* The Episcopal *Living Church*,
however, was among the more expressive realist voices which began to foresee failure in the whole effort. The pact, it said, was
a "futile gesture, a jumble of high-sounding but meaningless
words." Not many seasons later much of the religious press had
to agree; the pact achieved little if anything.

The third program promoted the idea of a world court designed   6:50
to help arbitrate in cases of international conflicts. This project
appealed to church people because it used the language of justice
and because, tantalizingly, it offered the prospect of settlements
which were to be achieved without force. Such a world court actually had been set up in 1921, and in 1923 even President Harding recommended that America express support for it. It turned
out that court ties to the League of Nations kept the United States
from moving further toward it in the early twenties. By 1926 observers thought that all chance for American participation on any
level had more or less gone, even though the Senate did pass a
half-hearted resolution in support. Little came of the efforts,
again despite much church support. On balance, one has to say,
laypeople in the churches had other things on their minds than
these seemingly remote world organizations. General apathy on
the governmental level did not help the cause. The pro-peace liberal group only found itself solidifying into an ever more sharply
defined and more isolated bloc in the churches. Most of the Protestants instead put energies into what was for them a more attractive, closer-to-home cause.

Prohibition Is the Law and Ought to Be the Law

The third campaign, which this time we can rightfully call a   6:51
crusade, perpetuated efforts to produce a dry America through
support for Prohibition or, better stated for the twenties, for the
campaign against repeal of Prohibition. In the case of labor organization, the standard-brand churches only reluctantly supported
the cause; in the case of work for peace they were divided and
often frustrated; but in the case of Prohibition (as in the instance
of opposition to Catholic Alfred E. Smith's candidacy for President in 1928) they found a cause which drew such massive support from Protestant leadership that one can speak of it as

religious zealotry. Without such leadership there would not have been Prohibition or, after the amendment passed outlawing beverage alcohol, there would have been earlier repeal.

6:52   Prohibition began when the Eighteenth Amendment, backed by the Volstead Act, went into effect in 1919. The government did what it could to stop the liquor trade, but it was powerless in the face of a public that massively circumvented and disdained the laws. Speakeasies became fashionable, as did organized crime. By 1928 pro-repeal "wets" were in charge of the Democratic party, while Protestant church leadership largely lined up for the "dry" cause. The grand anti-repeal crusade, like the anti-Smith campaign, even bridged the cleavages between Fundamentalists and Modernists, conservatives and liberals, activists and those reluctantly involved in politics in the twenties. If the consequence of the disputes within Protestantism had led, as we saw it did, to specialization so that one party involved itself with public issues while the other did not, the party lines did not hold in respect to alcoholic beverages. Church factions which could not even talk with each other about the economic order or the virgin birth of Christ coalesced against the forces of alcohol and against the practices of recent immigrants, ordinarily Catholics, who wanted repeal. Exceptions to the united front were rare, and when they came, they usually had sources outside original-stock Anglo-Saxon church circles.

6:53   The movement against repeal attracted denominations outside the Federal Council. The experience of the huge Southern Baptist Convention illustrates how nonfederating churches which did not see themselves as political turned out to be so in the Prohibition case. This church body was not officially Fundamentalist but it remained staunchly conservative and ordinarily suspicious of the church in politics. True, said Arthur J. Barton, who headed the convention's Social Service Commission, believers must work for reform chiefly through efforts by individuals. This was a very Southern Baptist way to put the case for social engagement. The "salvation of society must be approached through the salvation of the individual." Yet many of the state convention voices, publications, and commissions, had worked corporately in the state legislatures to see to the passing of the prohibitionist Eighteenth Amendment. To fight against the prospect of repeal, the convention's underfunded Standing Committee on Temperance once again began uncharacteristically to cooperate with other churches' agencies against the legally approved use of alcoholic beverages.

During efforts at gaining repeal of Prohibition, temperance groups were
subjected to fierce ridicule, as in this painting by artist Ben Shahn.
(Museum of the City of New York.)

Not all Southern Baptists agreed with Barton when he took   6:54
to this cause with such zest. Thus, whatever the Texas Social
Service Committee thought of Prohibition—the committee liked
it—its members could still be steadfast against churchly public
action. "Social service is temporal and material; the work of the
church is eternal and spiritual. Social service seeks to improve the
housing problems in the slums; the church points to mansions in
the skies." And committee members attempted to draw a line:
while "social service deals in soap as the means to cleanliness;
the church contends for the cleansing through the blood of
Christ." But these hard lines were inevitably shifting. Two years
after this stated rejection of politics, the Georgia Baptist Social
Service Committee repudiated any claim that a transcendental
gospel should isolate Christians and keep them unspotted from
the world. That committee seemed more ready than Barton was
to confront what it called "full Gospel" issues like race relations,
world peace, education, health, and prison reform. Prohibition
had given such forces confidence.

Prohibition in its beginnings was a standard movement of so-   6:55
cial progressivism, aimed at the corporate structures and interests

which promoted liquor. These were seen as exploiters of the vulnerable, victimizers of the poor and defenseless, who planted saloons at the entrances to mines and factories, there to beguile wage earners. When they lured victims and turned them into addicts, they left the families dependent upon society and abandoned these men to helplessness. So one can say that in this case, Southern Baptists lined up with heirs of progressivism.

6:56   Just as it had earlier represented such progressivism, Prohibition could also fire up reactionary and racist forces and bring them into the anti-repeal coalition. For instance, W. B. Crumpton, a worker for the cause in Alabama, admitted that "when the agitation began in earnest in Alabama, it was mainly on account of the negro." Blacks had originally been good farm workers, but "when whiskey was accessible, [they] became utterly unreliable, inefficient and uncontrollable." The documents of the time and place suggest that some of the popularity of Prohibition did come from such impulses. "White women and children, in districts densely populated by the black race," thought Crumpton, "came to be in imminent danger." Riot and bloodshed loomed. If farmers noted this circumstance first, city-folk soon also learned it. "This state of affairs furnished arguments that were irresistible in favor of prohibition, when put before the legislature."

6:57   People like Crumpton knew where the pro-Prohibition votes originated. "Representatives from the white counties, to a man, were ready to come to the rescue of their white brothers in the black belt." Crampton saw himself as much a friend to blacks as an enemy to alcohol, in both cases on his own Baptist terms. "Let the superior race pity the poor negro," he added, for with the help of whites, "it will be easy to free the negro of the curse of the worse [sic] slavery that ever befell any race."

6:58   Southern Baptist Barton's approach led him to national prominence as president of the National Conference of Organizations Supporting the Eighteenth Amendment and chairman of the National Executive Committee of the Anti-Saloon League. There he showed how far the otherwise nonpolitical Southern Baptists could move into legislative action. Barton, it turns out, tacked on to prohibition other causes such as Sunday blue laws and anti-gambling measures. Such policies made him a proudly self-proclaimed progressive. Barton could rightfully say that in the terms of the day, his commission had assumed "advanced positions on all the great social problems affecting human society and government."

One can point rather precisely to the way this change occurred   6:59
by observing the response of the Committee on Temperance and
Social Service as these Southern Baptists first greeted the arrival
of Prohibition in 1920. Few northern liberals could have been
more jubilant over what the committee called this "greatest victory for industrial economy, moral reform and sound governmental policy ever won by any people." But such a victory, these
Baptists said, also demanded vigilance all down the line, if there
was to be law enforcement and general moral advancement. At
that point W. B. Crumpton, the regular blurter of truths, boasted
about what many fellow Baptists might not have wanted to own
up to and which they would have found embarrassing to admit.
"Yes, Baptists are in politics and have been for years against the
mightiest foe of humanity."

Through the years Crumpton pushed the commission and the   6:60
convention to be ever more bold. In 1931 the whole convention
entered the ranks of those who supported single-issue approaches
to politics. Its delegates passed a resolution that went so far as to
say that in both national and state political campaigns, they would
"seek the defeat of any candidate or nominee who may oppose
prohibition regardless of any party affiliations and labels." These
Protestants of the Protestants, who decried Catholic bloc voting,
tried bloc tactics in order to help defeat wet Al Smith and oppose
repeal. Yet on most other issues, the Southern Baptists backed off
and were closer to the Fundamentalists in opposing liberal actions
for social transformation.

Politically engaged Methodism was by far the most active of   6:61
those churches which tried to prevent repeal after it was evident
that law enforcement had broken down and crime was rising in
the 1920s. Many of the Anti-Saloon League pioneers had been
Methodists. The Southern Methodists, usually more reluctant
than their northern counterparts to speak up in matters affecting
legislation, called the league their "approved agency for active,
efficient co-operation with the members of other Churches and
Temperance organizations in the fight against the common
enemy." On all levels, the Southern Methodists said, members
must work so that "officials must be selected who believe in enforcement, not only because prohibition is the law, but because it
ought to be the law." The note of uneasiness was there because
many Americans by then had begun working against its remaining
the law.

Up north the Methodist bishops defended similar actions. One   6:62

said: "We have bad politics because so few people insist upon good politics. The sinner goeth to the primary, and the righteous hold an indignation meeting." Did all this agitation mean a religious call for lobbying? Of course. A Methodist editor wrote that there were lobbies for munitions, tariffs, the poor, aliens, oil, and other causes that were just as "odorous." Meanwhile the church's own lobbying for Prohibition and peace, he complained, was "denounced as an enemy of the republic" while the church was seen as "guilty of working openly for a sober nation and a warless world!" And, he mourned, "the accusers remain at liberty as if they were mentally competent." To advance their position, the Methodists by that time had moved an office close to the United States Capitol in Washington. Their headquarters for promoting the social creed was as near as a nongovernmental building could be to the Capitol grounds. They were happy to be in shouting and even in whispering distance of the halls of power.

6:63   During Prohibition the Methodists were so alert that they even began monitoring the bills for sacramental wine in those churches which, unlike Methodism, used fermented grape juice. They were suspicious of the evident great new attention to the Lord's Supper among Lutherans, Episcopalians, Catholics, and other less pro-Prohibitionist churches. They agitated for ever greater scrutiny of wine sales to churches which used wine. Conveniently, Edwin A. Olson, United States district attorney in the northern district of Illinois, provided evidence for their viewpoint to a Senate committee. In his district, Olson charged, "after prosecution had been commenced against those charged with illegal diversion," orders for sacramental wine in the two years leading up to 1925 dropped from 885,000 to 60,000 gallons.

6:64   To pursue the sacramental wine scandal the Federal Council used its Department of Research and Education to explore the subject and educate the public about it. Who could tell what the legitimate demand for sacramental wine should be? Certainly, thought the department, it could not have been more than 800,000 gallons biennially. Yet from two to three million gallons were being tapped each year in rectories and parsonages and vestries. "Not more than one-quarter of this wine is sacramental—the rest is sacrilegious."

6:65   Almost while no one was looking and while Methodists and others kept counting on women to be in the anti-repeal camp, there developed a pro-repeal group of women, who quickly came to be seen as traitors to the cause. These leaders made clear that

their interest was not in promoting tippling or spreading drunkenness. They wanted instead to promote good and law abiding
citizen life. Previously, they noted, it had been the voices of the
Woman's Christian Temperance Union and the National American
Woman Suffrage Association, with their overlapping interests,
which worked both for the vote and for the proper use of the vote.

Then the lineups of women's power forces began to change　6:66
when in 1929 Mrs. Charles H. Sabin spoke up; her husband was
an officer in the Association against the Prohibition Amendment.
She was known as having an instinct for the jugular, and she used
it. Not lost on pious enemies was the fact that Mrs. Sabin represented not the common folk, nor the middle classes, but the elite
of this elite. Her allies were wealthy, otherwise generally conservative and Republican, though there was among them an admix-
ture of Democrats, of course. The advocates bore names like
Van Rensselaer, du Pont, Sloane, Field, Cudahy, Harriman, and
Roosevelt.

If social causes divided churches as a whole in the tribal twen-　6:67
ties, they also sundered women's solidarity. When society women
formed a Women's Organization for National Prohibition Reform,
they met understandable reaction. Thus in Georgia Dr. Mary Armor fought back against them. She announced that "as to Mrs.
Sabin and her cocktail-drinking women, we will outlive them,
out-fight them, out-love them, out-talk them, out-pray them and
out-vote" them. They may have done all but the last of these. A
dry paper, *The American Independent*, had its own view of these
"wet women, though rich most of them are," who were "no more
than the scum of the earth, parading around in skirts, and possibly
late at night flirting with other women's husbands at drunken and
fashionable resorts."

The doughty Methodist prohibitionist Clarence True Wilson　6:68
also poured vitriol on this "little group of wine-drinking society
women who are uncomfortable under prohibition" and who, he
said, were not by any means reformers. The once solid phalanx
of women's organizations was now broken. Mrs. Sabin's group,
as the rather snobbish description had it, the "largest body of
instructed, knowledgeable women ever let loose in a democracy,"
found enough allies to be effective. Alfred E. Smith, a man in
position to assess such matters after his loss in 1928 summarized
it all: "When women entered the fight for repeal, sanity began to
return to the country."

Prohibition plus chaos associated with law enforcement and　6:69

illegal trafficking endured through the twenties. It took a new president, Democrat Franklin D. Roosevelt, to recommend, in a six-line message to Congress on March 18, 1933, "the passage of legislation for the immediate modification of the Volstead Act, in order to legalize the manufacture and sale of beer and other beverages of such alcoholic content as is permissible under the Constitution." The churches which had won so much in 1919 lost just as much in 1933. They could never after put together the very tense coalition between so many kinds of Protestant voices.

6:70   From sidelines the Missouri Synod of Lutheranism looked on and sneered. Most of its members enjoyed beer and wine, despised activist Methodists, opposed the Social Gospel, and said they were against churchly involvement in political causes. These Lutherans and their kin stood apart from or against most of the rest of the churches. They made news by being so exceptional. Dr. W. H. T. Dau spoke for his fellow Lutherans. He said he could not help noting that, in order to gain votes for their side, Protestants had to work with the Ku Klux Klan. Dau even heard of a bid for the pope's support of "this whole miserable business" of Prohibition, which, he said, should never have been a church issue in the first place. No, the church had greater tasks before it than to be involved in such foolishness.

6:71   In a time halfway between Prohibition and repeal amendments, Dau tried to find a perspective from which to view the strange patterns of alliances and oppositions in this sober cause. The Methodists, Baptists, and some Lutherans, he charged, had made the Volstead Act into a churchly issue. "The worst enemy of Protestantism," he said, "could not have devised a more effectual means for letting Protestants make fools of themselves and then exhibiting them to the world in their plight than this scheme of making America bone-dry with the aid of Protestant churches." Dau could always hope for one happy outcome to this "latest and humiliating episode." That result, he said, might be to "take Protestantism out of politics."

6:72   In Dau's mind, Protestantism was looking ahead to a far greater battle than anti-repeal. He added ominously that this conflict could come soon. Its prosecutors would not have time to waste on the "poor critters" who could not keep away from liquor. Dau did not specify in 1926 what that battle might be. Was he foreseeing and forearming against the candidacy of Catholic Al Smith? And, if so, would even such fierce fighters for political aloofness on the part of Protestants as Missouri Lutherans be able to resist political expression themselves?

The Smith Candidacy: A Real Issue between Catholicism and American Institutions

As for the story of the 1928 candidacy: Calvin Coolidge did   6:73
not choose to run and the Republicans nominated Herbert Hoover. Governor Smith had served effectively in New York through four terms. He had led a coalition of progressives and big-money people, who could help him on the national level. No other Democrat could challenge Smith's popularity across the nation. At the party convention, though the nominators were tentative about the touchy liquor question, Smith as their nominee openly supported repeal. Immediately Republicans and many ordinary Democrats started bringing up charges that there had been ties between Smith and corrupt Tammany Hall, charges that were eagerly heard, especially in the South and the West. It turned out that Smith showed himself to be a less than eloquent and not always informed national candidate. Most analysts agree that 1928 was not a Democratic year in any case. So Smith lost 444 to 87 to Herbert Hoover in the electoral count. The Democratic solid South did not remain solid; much of it went Republican this once. Still, Smith received the largest Democratic popular vote to that date, and as a legacy of the campaign the Democratic cause was not lost for the future.

That should have been that. But Smith was both a wet and a   6:74
Catholic, and those two factors taken together made him religiously interesting to those who were making a last stand for the Protestant and Puritan America that Siegfried had described. It was good strategy for Protestants who did not want to sound anti-Catholic to stress that they were simply antiwet, as some of them indeed were. That is why it is hard to say just how much Smith's Catholicism helped defeat him in the election. The Methodist *Zion's Herald* was not entirely atypical when its editors wrote that 1928 represented an election contest which was "clear cut—prohibition versus the saloon, Tammany versus law and order," while the editors made no mention of the pope.

In any case, by 1928 many original-stock Protestant citizens   6:75
would have agreed with Lutheran W. H. T. Dau: Protestantism

had a greater, or at least a new, battle to fight. Dau's politically inexperienced fellow Missouri Lutherans furnish as strong a case study on this issue as did Southern Baptists on Prohibition. Both bodies claimed to be most distant from participation in the political processes and both were ordinarily most critical of the Federal Council of Churches leadership for being so vocal and active in those processes.

6:76 The Missouri twist was to turn the election into a religious issue and prevent consideration of it as political at all. When a maverick Protestant minister said that there should be no reason to oppose a Catholic president, Dau's colleague in St. Louis, Martin Sommer, wrote an editorial asking, "Is it Jesuitry or Stupidity?" Sommer: "No one can blame Protestants if they warn their people earnestly against the religious errors of Rome and beg their fellow-citizens to vote against any candidate for the Presidency who is a faithful son of the Roman hierarchy." In a book written for the election but published too late to be of help, another colleague, Theodore Graebner, explained why this was so. "The Roman Catholic parishioner, whether oiler on a freight steamer or President of the United States, must acknowledge an authority higher than the federal constitution, higher than any law, the authority of the Pope at Rome." In every case, said Graebner, a Catholic has an Italian, not an American, boss. With so much nonpolitical politicking going on in the dry tree of Missouri leadership, one would expect, and does find, much more in the overt politics of the federated churches.

6:77 The Northern Baptist Convention simply but formally asked its members to support and vote for only such men who would "unequivocally and openly commit themselves to an honest and effective observance and enforcement of the prohibition laws of our country." The delegates could make their point without mentioning any candidate names. The editors of the Baptist *Watchman-Examiner*, on the Fundamentalist heights, declared that they based their opposition to Governor Smith entirely on the fact that he was and always had been the implacable foe of Prohibition.

6:78 The same theme which complicated Missouri Lutheranism also dogged these Baptists. The editors complained that "the Roman Catholic papers insist on lugging in the religious question." It was hard to make one point, against repeal, without being accused of the other connected one, anti-Catholicism. The editors professed not to be interested in politics, only morality. "Let the churches everywhere," they wrote, fight Smith because "there is a great

New York's Governor Al Smith, Democratic candidate for president of the United States, could draw great crowds in 1928, as he did here at Worcester, Massachusetts. But he did not attract enough votes to defeat Herbert Hoover in a campaign marked by strong anti-Catholicism. (AP/Wide World Photos.)

moral issue at stake and because he has deliberately and defiantly taken the wrong side." The Southern Baptist Convention called its opposition to Smith "a sacred covenant and a solemn pledge" in support of candidates who themselves upheld the present order of Prohibition. The delegates also asked whether it was not cunning of Catholics who worked for Mr. Smith because he was a Roman Catholic, to criticize Protestant dry forces which would not support him on the issue of repeal.

6:79   The testimony of the denominations was so consistent on this point that more of their editorials in that period should be filed under "Prohibition" than under "Catholicism." The *American Baptist* urged: "Our very civilization is at stake. As all liquorites are for Smith, why should not all prohibitionists be for Hoover?" Even the more liberal National Council of Congregational Churches, departing from policy, went partisan. "As a Christian," it urged each member, "consider well the moral issues at stake in the coming election, and vote." There was then no question as to how to vote. "The issue," they wrote, "is a straight one as to whether this country wants a 'dry' or a 'wet' President."

6:80   The most dramatic evidence that this one event served as the last gathering for the whole Protestant coalition came from Texas. There J. Frank Norris of Fort Worth's First Baptist Church, who could not even get along with and stay in the Southern Baptist Convention, suddenly and momentarily united with theological moderates who were also opposed to Smith. Among these was the most notable moderate Southern Baptist theologian, Edgar Y. Mullins, whom Norris despised. Baptists and Methodists who never before in their lives had deserted Democratic ranks did so now. Norris himself held the highest banner in 1928: "Texas is the battleground for this, the most titanic struggle in the political, moral and religious life of the nation."

6:81   When a few Baptists sounded less than enthusiastic about taking the church into the struggle, Norris would flail at them. George M. Truett, a prominent Dallas pastor, said he did not want to politicize his pulpit. Norris blasted: "God have mercy on a straddling, compromising, pussyfooting fellow in the ministry who is afraid he will split his church." And how dared the *Baptist Standard* pursue its "policy of compromise and silence?" The noisy forces won out, and after Smith was defeated, Norris claimed for himself much credit, as Hoover carried Texas. Some Hoover supporters themselves gave Norris an engraved watch for his efforts in an event the minister called a "Preacher's Victory." He said of his paper, *The Fundamentalist,* that it had brought down the fire of the Al Smith crowd during the campaign. There were good reasons after the victory, he argued, for Hoover to bring him to his inauguration party, as we have seen that he did. Norris, in turn, said he was glad to see the president kiss the "same Bible that's in every Protestant pulpit" as Hoover took the oath of office. What, Norris asked, would it have meant for America had Smith been there to kiss the Roman Catholic Bible?

While Southern Baptists were not supposed to be accustomed   6:82
to the political stage, in the case of the 1928 election those who
stood back met scorn from extremists. Thus just as he had done
to Pastor George Truett, Norris chided Judge J. B. Combs of
Beaumont, a supporter of Smith who brought a resolution to the
Texas Baptist Convention. Combs's resolution asked for prayers
lest political causes and candidates ever again distract and violate
the integrity of the church. Baptist squared off against Baptist, as
Norris flashed: "One thing must be said about Judas Iscariot, and
to his everlasting credit, after he betrayed his Lord and Master he
had enough self-respect never to return and ask for fellowship
with the disciples and was unwilling for the sun to rise on his
treachery." Combs lacked such self-respect, but saw the sun rise.

Increasingly during the campaign Protestant reservations about   6:83
Smith's Catholicism and the attacks on it came more and more to
the fore. Eventually these vied for prominence with repeal in
strongly Protestant sectors. And increasingly the Catholic press
indulged in expressions of the sort one of the Protestants had described as "cunning"; it did try to fight back. The *Catholic Union
and Times* fingered the webbing of the issues. "Were Herbert
Hoover as dry as the Sahara, as Republican as Mark Twain, but a
Catholic, these dwindling, divided sects [the Protestant churches]
would vote against him to a man." And then it probably overstated the alternative. "Were Al Smith as wet as the Niagara
River, as Democratic as the electorate of Alabama, but a Protestant, these dying embers of the so-called reformation would turn
out in force to put him in Washington."

Commonweal editor Michael Williams in 1932 collected   6:84
samples of the pandemic and pandenominational Protestant anti-
Smith language in a book called *The Shadow of the Pope*. While
Lutherans had not been in the political center-stage as drys, Williams found them now in the company of anti-Catholics. He
quoted a Lutheran official asking a New York crowd: "Shall we
have a man in the White House who acknowledges allegiance to
the autocrat on the Tiber, who hates democracy, public schools,
Protestant personages, individual right, and everything that is essential to independence?" Meanwhile the *Wesleyan Christian Advocate* advanced the typical unassailable logic that Protestants
regularly adduced: "Governor Smith has a constitutional right to
run for President, even though a Catholic. This we confess. And
we have a constitutional right to vote against him because he is a
Catholic," for, it went on, "we are strongly persuaded that Ca-

tholicism is a degenerate type of Christianity which ought everywhere to be displaced with a pure type of Christianity."

6:85   From the Supreme Advocate of the Knights of Columbus, St. Louis alderman Luke Hart, came responses born of his experiences fighting the Klan. Hart knew whereof he spoke before the votes were cast. "However," he said, "win or lose I think Smith's campaign has done much for Catholicity by dragging old man Intolerance out into the broad daylight where the public can have a good look at him." The intra-Christian conflict revolved around the notion of who should run America, and on what terms. What the Catholics called intolerance the Protestants saw as vigilance for liberty. The two elements did not speak the same language, and seemed as far apart as they had been in old nineteenth-century nativist days.

6:86   The most celebrated exchange of the campaign, the rare one that drew Smith out on the subject, involved a noted Protestant Episcopal lawyer, Charles C. Marshall. The attorney used the *Atlantic Monthly* for what was intended to be an urbane put-down of Smith. Marshall raised questions as to how Catholicism in a president might fit into the American republic's patterns. The periodical gave Smith a chance to reply. His argument was very much in the tradition of Catholic responses made during the previous century and a half. While Protestants always seized and publicized rigorous antidemocratic proclamations from Rome, statements which in truth did scourge republican liberties and reject the rights of what Rome called error, American Catholics never had been able to understand what the controversy was all about. Never had Rome flexed muscles to enforce in America the codes or opinions of documents such as an embarrassing *Syllabus of Errors* of 1864. Never had Catholic office holders felt tensions between their two commitments, to church and state. Why could Protestants not understand that?

6:87   Smith belonged to that tradition which refused to see reasons to connect Rome's strictures with the American situation. "I have taken an oath of office in this State nineteen times," he boasted; "I have never known any conflict between my official duties and my religious belief. No such conflict could exist." Just as almost all Catholics would have agreed with Smith's statement, few non-Catholics could see how there would never be a clash between Rome and Washington, the Vatican and the Constitution, on the national level.

As so often, it was Charles Clayton Morrison of the *Christian*   6:88
Century who capsuled the standard-brand Protestant viewpoint.
In a column in October 1928, on the election's eve, that crusading
anti-Catholic wrote that the Protestant should vote against a
Catholic not because the Protestant wanted to restrict religious
freedom or because he was a religious bigot or because he did not
appreciate Catholic ways of worship, or even because he feared
that Al Smith as president would take orders from the pope. Why
would Morrison make that last concession? Simple. "Such a fear
is surely groundless if for no other reason than the fact that the
pope is no fool." Instead, the voter was called to see what the
editor called "a real issue between Catholicism and American
institutions."

Morrison then set out the logic of his position. "The increase   6:89
of Catholic influence in American society threatens certain institutions which are integral to the American system. With a
Roman Catholic in the White House, the influence of the Roman
Catholic system will be enormously increased in American social and political life." This most modest statement of Protestant
fears may also have been one of the most profound in respect to
the question which haunted Protestants: "Will the United States
remain Protestant and Anglo-Saxon?" The voter, said the Protestant editor, would not interfere with Catholic expansion through
what Morrison called normal means of propaganda and growth.
But the liberal editor said that the voter would also not "assist
in its extension by helping to put its representative at the head of
the government." Morrison's neat posing of "our American system" versus "the Roman Catholic system" showed how in this
Protestant mentality Catholicism was not part of the American
system.

It was all well and good for editors of *Commonweal* and the   6:90
Christian Century to fight about their systems, but many politicians felt especially uncomfortable being put on the spot between
camps. Thus Senator George W. Norris was a Progressive from a
very Protestant state, Nebraska. Yet Norris decided to make a
move into the Democratic ranks in 1928 precisely to support Al
Smith. Years later he recalled the cost of the move. Friends of
long standing, in their bigotry, had reacted against that move.
Norris said that these former friends would have "delighted to
cast me into the bottomless pit if the opportunity had presented
itself."

6:91   Norris also brought perspective to the issue of religious violence in the tribal warfare of the twenties. In 1928, "the dominant thing that brought about this bitterness," complained the senator, was religion. He knew all about the noise of conflict in that field. "Religious grievances always do bring bitterness—unreasonable, illogical bitterness." By contrast, the senator located even the wet versus dry issue of Prohibition into a milder zone. "Prohibition brings pointed disagreement, but men do not turn their love of years into hatred because their friends do not agree with them regarding it." One may well accept the verdict of most historians who see and say that religion was not the decisive issue in 1928 and still note with Norris that whenever it was introduced, religion produced the most noise, the deepest passions.

6:92   So at the end of the twenties Protestant America, threatened and internally divided, had survived its own schism and withstood many alien forces. Morrison, observing events in the year 1928, spoke up as well as anyone, one more time, for the idea that Protestants were the real "at home" people while others were immigrants, aliens, foreigners at heart. The editor wrote, with his eye on the president's chair, that Protestants could not look with unconcern "upon the seating of a representative of an alien culture, of a medieval Latin mentality, of an undemocratic hierarchy and of a foreign potentate." Morrison instead saw the 1928 race as the first national election since slavery days which involved "a fundamental organic conviction of the churches."

6:93   The editor, claiming to want to sound tolerant, wrote that he could not fault the Catholics for their own organic conviction. They were promoting their pride and their purposes. Catholics, of course, still occupied a minority position in American culture. They represented what Morrison called "a culture sharply alien to the culture which produced American institutions." They held convictions which challenged what he designated "the most typical features of the American system."

6:94   For Protestants, concern for the obverse side of the organic culture dispute was apparent. This was no casual issue on the part of such Protestants. In historic origin and in organic character their churches were a protest against all that a Catholic president would represent. "The issue is of the very texture of their corporate conviction." It was therefore preposterous, said Morrison, to call anyone a bigot who was intelligent enough to let his vote be determined by "so deep-going a cleavage in social idealism!"

Morrison spoke for Protestants who suffered from many other social cleavages in the decade but who came together this one more time. "In such a situation no power in heaven or in earth can keep the church out of politics. It will go in because it is already in." And so it was.

7

Depression Extremism: Right with a Capital R, Left with a Capital L

No Revival: In This Depression It Is Different

7:1   The stock-market crash which occurred on Wall Street on Black Thursday, October 24, 1929, was part of a cluster of economic events which serves neatly to divide the interwar years in the United States. In almost all conventional reckonings, the period from 1919 to 1929 was one of general economic prosperity. There was good reason for continuing optimism through at least September 3, 1929, when the price of stocks on the New York Stock Exchange reached an all-time high in an autumn of apparent continuing good times. Then in a sudden and unforeseen turn, stock market speculation became frantic on and after Black Thursday, as investors lost confidence in the rapidly rising stock prices. Prices fell as stockholders quickly tried to sell. Panic followed. Many banks closed. America's classic Great Depression had begun, and with it, spiritually, the decade of the thirties also began. Not until World War II, at the turn to the forties, was there sufficient economic and psychological recovery to permit historians to say that the Depression was over.

7:2   Readers do not expect religious historians to provide details on economic history or to advance social scientific theories about events like the Crash or the Depression. But when events of social and political history color virtually every aspect of religious life, those who chronicle American religious history have to help account for these aspects in the piety, spirituality, theology, and churchly programs of citizens. To point to changes does not imply that there were absolute breaks between the themes which dominated the stories of religion in the two decades. The continuities are impressive, and the mind's eye can easily bring them back to view.

In both times Jews and Christians praised the God of Israel and   7:3
tried to bring the meanings of this praise to bear on personal and national life. Devoted Christians were somehow responsive to faith in Jesus Christ and attempted to shape individual, churchly, and public life in the light of that faith. Editors of theological journals published articles by scholars who in their vocations, by the evidence of their products, often seemed oblivious to the activities that marked their own daily struggles for survival and dignity. Believers observed the passages of life with rituals which antedated the Crash by millennia and would outlast the Depression. Congregants found warmth and fellowship in their life together. Believers who faced death using the language of faith which affirmed that they would trust God "though he slay me," did not fall away from faith merely because of economic trauma.

Churches and synagogues, then, were among the centers of   7:4
shared loyalties. This strategic position made it possible for them to represent continuities in troubled times, to be refuges from the worst terrors, and places to help citizens deal with some of their problems. It did not permit them to be exempt from the troubles and problems themselves. To look at the concerns of these institutions is a helpful if neglected way to see how American life held together in Depression times. How capture the flavor of religious life then without distortion because of the mixed benefits of hindsight now? Fortunately there is at hand a retrospect which provides a window on the years, Chicago Theological Seminary Professor Samuel C. Kincheloe's *Research Memorandum on Religion in the Depression*. It allows for a sounding comparable to the one that eleven years earlier the religious census of 1926 provided. The Kincheloe memorandum was chartered by the Social Science Research Council as one of a number of efforts to study Depression effects on various social institutions.

One of the icons of Depression America is Walker Evans' photograph of Bethlehem, Pennsylvania, with idle smokestacks. (Library of Congress.)

7:5   Kincheloe's evidence led him to conclude simply that the churches were surviving but depressed. Numberless reports by others corroborate this. Churches were trying various strategies to fulfil their mission. None worked very well. If people were expecting a national revival of religion to compensate for material decline, this did not appear. "There has been much emphasis on the belief that what society needs is religion," reported Kincheloe, but society evidently did not think so.

7:6   Efforts to promote emotional revivals in the mainstream churches were fruitless. Kincheloe paid little attention to Fundamentalism and the churches of backwoods and bypaths. There tent revivals went on as before. Charismatic healers like California's Aimee Semple McPherson were in their pentecostal prime. Radio preachers were beginning to gather large audiences for revival-type messages. But awakening of a sort that moved beyond that subculture which had always been dependent upon revivalism did not occur. In the broader and public culture, for instance, leaders had hoped that a National Preaching Mission of the Fed-

eral Council of Churches in the autumn of 1936 would help sweep
the country back to God. The mission was a dud. A minister in
one northern city wrote Kincheloe that although congregation after congregation had promoted efforts to revive churches, the response was negligible. Kincheloe expected, and his expectations
were to be met, that these methods would soon be definitely abandoned by what one of the ministers he cited called "all normal
church groups." Fundamentalistic and other historically revival-
istic churches were not "normal."

Public apathy led Kincheloe and others who saw what he saw   7:7
to ask: was the reaction of people to church life different in the
Depression of the 1930s from what it had been in previous periods
of economic depression? "At the beginning of the depression
there was an assumption on the part of some church people that if
the depression continued the country would experience a wave of
revivals." This time nothing happened to match their assumption.
Oh, there were a few signs of what the researcher described as
" 'near religious' " behavior. These included the response to black
leader Father Divine at one end of the spectrum through the recent
invocation of "neighborliness" in speeches by President Franklin
D. Roosevelt or Agriculture Secretary Henry A. Wallace on the
other.

The *churches*, however, had no easy times in the hard times.   7:8
Christian Century editors asked: did people not address this Depression religiously because for once they did not think it occurred under the providence of God? The editorial conclusion:
this may have been "the first time men have not blamed God for
hard times." Despite persistent hopeful predictions, the editors
simply found "no revival of religion." In former times, people
regarded their suffering as due to forces beyond their control,
springing out of the nature of things, and thus evoking religious
attitudes of awe and resignation. Such people then asked whether
humans had offended God. Should they therefore repent? Would
God help them in their helplessness if they would make peace
with him? "But in this depression it is different." America's humanly invented economic system had simply failed it. The Depression was not an act of God like an earthquake, but it was "due
to the failure of human intelligence or the blind power of en-
trenched privilege, or both." The Depression, therefore, was not
something about which one need "get 'religious,' " wrote the editors. Few did.

Against such a framework of inquiry the Social Science Re-   7:9

search Council's team did its digging. They came up with data, not mere impressions about moods. Their findings showed that normal conditions and even slight decline marked the religious institutions of the 1930s. Indeed, America was even growing more secular, which in this memorandum meant that it saw a further diminishing of loyalty to churches. Of course, this also meant some lessening of the power churches needed if they were to instil conflict in society that would promote the Kingdom of God on one hand or resist secularizing moves on the other.

7:10   Ominously, churches were losing their functions to government and nonreligious agencies. Individual church members were themselves strong supporters of these agencies. However, the churches as organizations had begun to "accept the role of spiritual agents rather than leaders or organizers of group care for the needy" in the hour of the needy. Kincheloe hoped to find churches inventing new approaches. He did this by keeping an eye on the scope of their programs and activities. Few studies were available, but the Chicagoan was ready with some tentative suggestions about the changing patterns. He also therewith reminded anyone who cared to notice that churches did not exist merely for public life and conflict. They also had other missions to fill; he spelled some out.

7:11   What did the public activity called worship tell about response to the Depression? In long traditions like those of Roman Catholic, Protestant Episcopal, and certain Lutheran churches, little had changed. The visitor could worship without recognizing from the service that America was in a depression period. However, in what the author so nicely called the churches "of the early American emphasis"—Kincheloe named the Baptist, Congregational, Disciples of Christ, Methodist, and Presbyterian—worshipers would be made very conscious of the times in which they were living, particularly in the periods ministers set aside for announcements and during the sermon. The changes in worship content in such cases became so important, he noticed, that these seemed to alter the very structure of the service itself.

7:12   The times also demanded church cooperation if denominations were to have influence. To his surprise Kincheloe discerned signs of stagnation on the church union front. During the Depression, appeals for Christian union had not lost their fervor, but, the author noted, "it is generally agreed that, for some cause, church unions have not made progress." After a second decade of talk supporting mergers and organic unity, the churches seemed to be stuck with the federating model. Reporters in the twenties and the thirties alike, then, found a gap between the commitment to and rhetoric about Protestant church union on the one hand and on the other the resulting meager progress, countered and then canceled by occasional schisms. It did happen that some mergers were effected in the thirties. The Congregational Church and the Christian Church united in 1931 to produce the Congregational Christian Churches. The Reformed Church in the United States merged with the Evangelical Synod in 1934 to produce the Evangelical and Reformed Church. Northern and southern wings of the Methodist Episcopal Church were to merge in 1939. But these looked like generally timid familial joinings which did not contradict the general view of slowdown.

The Depression also produced more need for welfare services   7:13
than before. Many church workers, however, reported that, progressively, people in need stopped even calling on the churches for help. They felt that church resources were too meager and that their need was so great that they had to rely on government for adequate aid. Churches supplied temporary or what Kincheloe called invisible relief. Many congregations, of course, did perform services admirably. But, the memorandum asked, could and should churches any longer even try to "care for their own," as the saying of the day had it?

As for non-Protestants, many connected the notion of caring   7:14
for their own with a belief about the Mormons in Utah. The Mormons propagated the impression that they kept government aid at a distance and took care of fellow Mormons. Kincheloe added: "Opinions about the real scope and success of the program differ." Protestants were sometimes inspired and goaded by comparisons of their organizations with Catholic and Jewish relief and charity agencies. Protestants seemed too loose in organization to match these. They did make a late, inadequate start to step up efforts in the Depression. There were tense situations, and conflicts rose in those cities where Protestants felt that their welfare institutions were being given closer public scrutiny than were those of Catholics and Jews. New rivalries were developing. Some religious groups rebelled against the "Social Service Party" and even sometimes promoted what they called "givers' strikes."

Might Protestant bodies now be driven to integrate with each   7:15
other in order to address massive human need? Kincheloe found no signs that they had begun to do so. Or should one foresee what he described as "communal conflict on a larger scale than we have

known," in addition to "conflict between church and state" when people argued whether the secular community fund and the government should take up all the welfare work? These were legitimate concerns of believers and of those who monitored their worlds in the Depression. Right under the eyes of American religious leaders a fundamental shift in the definition and direction of churchly energies was occurring. Who knew where it could lead?

7:16　　The memorandum was quick to note that some congregations genuinely kept trying to meet Depression needs by promoting special institutional churches and neighborhood houses. Protestants were divided among themselves: should these agencies use Protestant funds basically to serve their own, or to serve the city's needy no matter who they were? While the churches argued, resources kept declining; Depression-caused fund shortages meant that in the Methodist, Congregational, and Presbyterian churches from 1932 to 1935 there had been real decreases in giving to churches. Still there was relatively less decline for such institutional work than for other churchly purposes in Methodism and Congregationalism. From 1930 to 1935 the decrease in giving to the three churches was 38 percent while the decline in institutional work was only 26%. This creative gap indicated that Christians were making some real efforts to meet physical and not only spiritual needs.

7:17　　As for the secular drift, Kincheloe stressed that it did not always mean the increase of antireligious attitudes. He quoted ethicist John C. Bennett from New York's Union Theological Seminary: secularity merely represented "that characteristic of our world according to which life is organized apart from God as though God did not exist." However one defined it, a new chasm was growing between the church and the remainder of society.

7:18　　What people were trying to convey with the term "secularization," of course, had presumably been a long-term trend. Kincheloe listed seven factors which might have speeded up secularization and four which might have retarded it. Among the latter he applauded a new realism in Protestant theology, which he saw as a reaction to the "tired liberal" ways of overselling progressivism and reform. He thought that realist Reinhold Niebuhr said it well: "adequate spiritual guidance can come only through a more radical political orientation and more conservative religious convictions than are comprehended in the culture of our era."

7:19　　Theological probing was in order. "What did the depression do to this message of the church?" Kincheloe modestly turned aside to let others provide some answers to that question. He asked, "Did the message become more personal or more social? Did it become more sacred or more secular?" And, since people cannot place the various elements of their lives into neat, separate compartments, he also asked, "was the social, political and economic message of the church during the depression more reactionary, conservative, neutral, liberal, or radical?" Kincheloe italicized his thesis: "*The social message of churches during the depression was influenced by the economic status of its [sic] members and by changes or contemplated changes in the economic situation of the membership and constituency.*" Of course.

Kincheloe consistently reinforced his conclusion that depressions did not necessarily promote religion. He quoted with apparent disfavor a sermon preached in a program at a Presbyterian church in Riverside, Illinois, by Alfred A. Waldo. This denominational promoter had urged: "When vast masses of men, as at present, encounter adversity, anxiety and perplexity, they lose confidence in themselves and, if properly led, turn to God." Kincheloe thought Waldo was talking more about the strivings of survivors who remained in the pews than about new prospects who might turn to God and use churches for their odyssey. Once again: no revival was on the way.   7:20

The memorandum relied on statistical summaries for hard data. "In the country as a whole . . . there have not been significant changes in church membership." Some southern bodies such as the Southern Baptist Convention were growing. Already, then, there were sharp increases in the number of members of what still looked like minor Fundamentalist groups. However, rabbis who reported at all said that membership in their congregations had been greatly reduced during the Depression despite efforts to adjust the cost of membership. Across the board, almost necessarily and certainly not surprisingly, financial giving to the churches had declined during the 1930s Depression. Foreboding changes were occurring. Many believers who made up the conventional churches were somehow protected from or chose to shield themselves from the more stark ideologies which attracted and repelled so many in the thirties. But the members of this set were not the only people who counted. Millions of others were dislodged, insecure, desperate. They were ready to listen to strident calls by demagogues who offered simple religious solutions to their problems. Gone were the days of normalcy which President Harding had called for a decade before. This was a time for nostrums.   7:21

The Furthest Right: An Ominous Political Fact

7:22   When secure middles break down and centers do not hold, people turn to right and left. When it came to offering nostrums or promoting agitations, the political, economic, and religious right drew the biggest crowds. In the middle years of the Depression decade, when dictators Hitler and Mussolini, Salazar and Franco and Stalin ruled in Europe, commentator Raymond Gram Swing wrote about the *Forerunners of American Fascism*. Why and how could economic demagogues find any following for their dangerous magic and their illusions? European radicals at least tried to deal with the harsh realities of social and economic class. But in America radicals tried to work simple magic with money. They tried to peddle schemes that would promote cheap money, free silver, or inflation, rather than take on what Swing called "the fundamental conflict of employe against employer."

7:23   In Swing's book, a single quack by himself was not significant. However, the credulity revealed in the American public by such peddlers was. "Now the masses are ready to believe." He set forth as a miniature social law what seemed to apply equally to the storms from the right and from the left in the thirties. "It is dissatisfaction with the attainable which leads to fanaticism and at last to social fury." And, more: "When great masses are ready to believe the impossible, that is an ominous political fact."

7:24   Later Americans looked back on the America of Depression days with nostalgia. They saw a folksy Norman Rockwell nation of small-town churches and schools. In the real world of the thirties, however, Americans confronted a number of ominous political facts. Some of these came from outside the churches and some from within, but in either case they were designed as attractions for religious people. Not content with the sober and undramatic attempts of the churches to meet something of the attainable, or to offer transcendent meaning where immediate goals seemed unattainable, a large public followed leaders who channeled their fanaticisms and furies into the realms of the impossible and the dangerous. Some of these leaders were themselves attracted to or lured by the European ideologies. As often as not they were homegrown independents.

7:25   When World War II broke out and the more drastic panaceas had largely disappeared from view, Harvard sociologist Talcott Parsons appraised the recent far-right movements with their fascist tinges. He was an influential social thinker who always looked for equilibrium in social structures, the kind of balance which became hard to find in the 1930s. What Parsons saw was applicable to the followership of many of the American movements. In such radicalisms "large masses of the 'common people' have become imbued with a highly emotional, indeed often fanatical, zeal for a cause." For our purposes, note: "They are movements, which, though their primary orientation is political, have many features in common with great religious movements in history." These masses needed "sufficiently concrete and stable systems of symbols around which the sentiments of the individual can crystalize." This was especially the case in a time of upsets in the social system, disruptions which disturbed "previously established definitions of the situation, or routines of life, or symbolic associations." On both the religious and political right and left in America there were a number of movements, each of which attracted thousands or even millions of citizens. They became regular subjects of notice in the religious and the secular press. Only one or two of these threatened to prevail, which here means to alter the basic terms of American religious and political life. The rest are important because they illustrate the instability of American existence in the Depression era, the legacy of disturbances in the twenties, and the desire of many religious citizens to experiment, to reach out into experiences borrowed from elsewhere, or from nowhere, which is what Utopia means.

On the American political far right, the most watched extreme   7:26
of the extremes in Europe was of course Germany's National Socialism, Nazism. Because of Nazism's totalitarian anti-Semitism, its recourse to pre-Christian religious symbols, and its attempts to control and use the Catholic and Protestant churches, this German movement had a bearing on religion from its first day through the end of World War II and the death of Hitler. Quite naturally, an international movement like Nazism, which tried to gather loyalties of all pure Aryan folk, targeted other nations with German or "Nordic" populations, or sent agents to do some flaunting of symbols or subverting of anti-Nazi ways. The United States qualified for these endeavors. Yet the American Nazi movement, however chilling it might appear to be when exposed, did not amount to much. While scholars trace Nazi precursor movements in the United States back to the mid-twenties, not until Fritz Kuhn seized power in 1936 was Nazism much of a public movement in America. It was a pathetic rival which never held appeal for church people.

7:27   Toward the end of the times when Nazi activities still were public, before the movement disintegrated under wartime pressures, Congressman Martin Dies headed a House Committee to Investigate Un-American Activities. Dies possessed instincts which usually led him to track movements on the left. He acquired a reputation for free-swinging and irresponsible attacks on persons who did not share his own conservative social philosophy. But he also revealingly threw the Nazi movement up against his own defense of Americanism. Dies called the Nazi party part of Hitler's instigation of treasonable work, and set out to pursue it.

7:28   Many church people could have agreed with his definitions. One must know what Americanism is, he urged, if there is to be a war on un-Americanism. Thus: "It is as un-American to hate one's neighbor [if] he has more of this world's material goods as it is to hate him because he was born into another race or worships God according to a different faith." Then came the positive side: "Americanism is a philosophy of government based upon the belief in God as the Supreme Ruler of the Universe; nazi-ism, fascism, and communism are pagan philosophies of government which either deny, as in the case of the communist, or ignore as in the case of the fascist and nazi, the existence and divine authority of God."

7:29   For Dies as for the more moderate majority of Americans, the contrasts between systems were total. "Since nazi-ism, fascism, and communism are materialistic and pagan, hatred is encouraged. Since Americanism is religious, tolerance is the very essence of its being." Dies himself was never noted for tolerance, and critical citizens were suspicious when he did their defining for them. But such words typified the language which did rule out the German-American Bundists who presented the American face of Hitlerite Germanism.

7:30   The incautious followers of Kuhn during those very years blamed their American hard times on precisely the people Nazis always blamed, the Jews. They claimed there was a Jewish circle in the State Department that was harassing them. "Jewish-Marxist Internationalism," said one tract, "will only lead to war against all nations combating Jewish Domination and Bolshevism." Bund literature depicted Jews as sexual perverts and moneygrubbers. In June of 1937 in Queens, New York, Herman Schwarzmann, the local National Socialist leader, looked for the time to come when America could "wipe out the Jew pigs."

7:31   The Nazis promoted their own bizarre brand of Americanism to counter what they said was Judaism's. Fritz Kuhn aimed past politicians to the people, calling on them to keep a "Free America," which meant a "Gentile America." At a Convention in 1938 one handout read like a violent extension of the milder language the "100 percent Americanists" had used a decade earlier. In an appeal "For a Gentile Controlled America" there was a resolution: "WHEREAS, this Nation was conquered, pioneered and built by White Men, whose Culture, Form of Government and Ideals of Americanism are being undermined and destroyed by an alien minority with an unassimilable code, therefore be it RESOLVED that we demand a socially just, White-Gentile ruled United States." This time the Nazis appealed to religious interests. Not only should there be an attack on "Jewish radio" but the public should also assault the antipatriotic pacifism "in subverted Pulpits," and what was called the "demoralization of Old and Young through de-Christianization of Institutions and Observances."

After 1937 the New York legislature took up the issue of Nazism because the Bund was most strongly represented in its state. State senator John J. McNaboe there detailed how the Friends of the New Germany called both Jews and Catholics "even more vile names than those now used" by their other enemies. People began to ask what exactly was this Bund, which by then was tending to displace the older Friends of the New Germany. The overt Nazi front claimed 20,000 members, but a congressional committee estimated a hard core of only 6,500. It gained only a bit of power by working with other organizations: the Christian Front, Silver Shirts, Christian Mobilizers, the Social Justice Society, and the like. 7:32

By all reckonings the front was truly a ragtag conglomerate whose chief purpose was announced in the Bund circular: "To unite with all Americans defending the Aryan Culture and Code of Ethics upon which this nation was founded." The McNaboe Committee followed Kuhn until the trail took it to the last and biggest rally of the Bund, on George Washington's birthday in 1938. The committee report described how the swastika appeared there next to an American flag, near huge banners: "Wake up America," "Smash Jewish Communism," and "Stop Jewish Domination of Christian America." Plenty of swagger was evident during the Bund's brief season, but when war broke out in Europe in 1939 it was finished. The organization had tried to serve one purpose, in which it largely failed: to collect and unify 7:33

the furthest out and strangest of the misfits on the right. Whether named Friends of the New Germany or the Bund or the Nazi Party, such an organization held up only the most distorting mirror to the old "Christian America" advocates. And it became the extreme next to which everything else looked somewhat, but not always much more, moderate.

Three Leaders: There's Going to Be a Revolution in This Country

7:34   When people overturn planks on the ground, they are likely to find all kinds of slippery silver creatures scurrying around. The mass of the American people who came in contact with them at all treated the German-American Bund and the Black Legion as subjects so remote from the normal patterns of American conflict that they had to be dealt with but not seen as indicative of ordinary discontents, handled as if they were objects from under such a plank. For the circle of those whom one might call more conventional demagogues that were somehow in the American grain, one looks elsewhere. The most explicitly religious among the marginal movements did their best gradually to head toward the centers of power. Because of the religious theme, they drew special attention. The Dies Committee claimed to have located at least two hundred right-wing extremist groups, many of which were at least partly religious.

7:35   The Black Legion, one of these two hundred, was a pathetic regathering of Ku Klux Klan types, who met with the Nazis Bund members at several rallies and made common cause with them. Its program: to keep "the secrets of the order, to support God, the United States Constitution, and the Black Legion in its holy war against Catholics, Jews, Communists, Negroes, and aliens." Up to 40,000 members responded to these religious and racial symbols, purportedly to fight for capitalism and to preserve America from aliens. Civil authorities held the Black Legion responsible for numerous acts of arson, kidnapping, flogging, and murder. It remained too far beyond the spectrum of the plausible to find much continuing acceptance or to deserve much notice.

7:36   Three overlapping movements, each founded by sons of revivalists, were barely less incredible and irresponsible, but they gained sufficient followings to display Depression discontents and demagogueries. First on the borderline of the homegrown schemes of anti-Semitic Christian America and furthest from Christian orthodoxy was the Silver Legion or Silver Shirts. In the Depression depths in 1933 its founder and leader, eclectic religionist William D. Pelley, tried to build on what was left of sympathies for homogeneous America. His roots were Protestant; he was the son of a circuit-riding Methodist preacher. Pelley hoped to see or establish what he called a "Native-Son, Protestant-Christian political machine." Some days he claimed he only wanted to develop a *Christian* commonwealth; at such times he would go light in his criticism of Catholics.

When the Dies Committee later questioned Pelley about the   7:37 claim that about 50 percent of his membership was made up of prime young Catholics, he stood by the false but not insignificant claim. Himself a former anti-Catholic, he came to find reasons to admire and for a time to work with a Catholic, Father Charles E. Coughlin. Pelley drew less than did most of his competitors on old midwestern or southern loyalties and worked chiefly on the West Coast. There he seemed to have most attraction for older, poorer people who bought into his economic program which his tract title called *No More Hunger*. He tried to gain support by claiming that he had located an international Jewish conspiracy. The Dies Committee found him to be simply a "racketeer engaged in mulcting thousands of dollars annually from his fanatical and misled followers."

When Americans paging through histories of demagoguery   7:38 think of extremism, their memories recall the Ku Klux Klan more readily than the Silver Shirts. Yet Pelley's people were at least regionally very visible for a time. They attracted national notice for typifying one response based in Depression discontent. As in several other cases, this movement was an exaggerated version of the 100 percent Christian Americanism that in the twenties had sometimes still passed as semirespectable. In the thirties, with their upheavals, Pelley's call for a 100 percent Christian America sounded and was more ominous. All Jews, Pelley demanded, must for the sake of national purity be cited as permanent aliens in America. They dared not become a nation within a nation. The only way the nation should permit Jews any civil rights would be if they would swear to forswear forever any Jewish allegiance. In a decade when Zionism was becoming increasingly controversial, Pelley also attacked it: a Jew who gave any "moral or financial support to Jewish nationalism operative in this country" must face prosecution for sedition. The leader dreamed of a Protestant utopia, for which there was to be this kind of plank in the Silver Shirt platform: "We are pledged to respect and sustain the sanctity of the Christian Ideal . . . to deify Patriotism and pride of race."

7:39   Pelley was religious, but in such a way that American Protestantism did not have to take responsibility for his synthesis. His biography reveals a sumptuous eclecticism. By 1930 he had prepared himself for his later calling with a visit to Siberia, a brief career in Hollywood, the writing of fiction, and the acting out of dabblings with so many movements that Pelley seemed a fictional creation: Christian Science, atheism, Rosicrucianism, theosophy, New Thought, spiritualism, Darwinism, the occult, the Great Pyramid, telepathy, sexology, metaphysics, Emersonianism, more of conventional Christianity than he or his enemies recognized, and science of the sort later associated with extrasensory perception. As he gathered his movement, Pelley insisted that people could remain in their own denominations; he claimed not to be starting a new sect or cult.

7:40   Pelley and his movement crested early in the decade. By 1931 he was disappointing followers and subscribers, many of whom he called spiritual vagrants because they would not make deep commitments to his ever-changing fabrications. Pelley held on through setbacks until at the time of Hitler's rise he celebrated by forming the Silver Legion to bring the "work of Christ militant into the open." It was his noisy praise of Hitler that brought him notoriety. Pelley reached ever further to gain warrant for his bizarre theories. While he never produced any kind of evidence, the Silver Legionnaire claimed to have known of some missing pages from the diary of an American founder, Charles Cotesworth Pinckney. These fictional pages proved to Pelley's satisfaction that Benjamin Franklin had wanted the Constitutional Convention to ban immigration by Jews. Pelley also credited Franklin himself with using words like "unassimilated" or "vampires" when talking about Jews. Franklin, he claimed, had said that Jews would undermine Christian republicanism, as Jewish influence in Roosevelt's New Deal was threatening to do.

7:41   The Silver Legion of Silver Shirts never ceased to push toward the furthest borders beyond the plausible. International anti-Semitism was Pelley's own best boost, since those who hated Jews on both sides of the Atlantic took their company where they could get it. During his decline, Pelley tried to be original. He invented a utopian economic scheme which he called a Christian Commonwealth, on "native-born Protestant Christian" lines. By this time he was lapsing into nostalgia for rural America, condemning modernism. This movement he defined as the "current practice of being flip, superficial, blasé, hard-boiled, contemptuous of moral values, impudent to parents, sympathetic toward concupiscence, and cynically indifferent to old forms of restraint and moderation."

At one stage Pelley urged a public "oscillation into Puritanism." This scheme helped him and his movement survive for several seasons more, since through and for it he collected donations, sold publications, and found ways to stay ahead of creditors by juggling accounts. In 1935 the law caught up with him and he was convicted of fraud in North Carolina. Pelley summoned energies for one last display, announcing that he would run for president on the Christian party ticket. This race would be in opposition to the "Dutch Jew, Franklin D. Rosenfelt," or "Mr. Rossocampo and his Jew Gang, head of the Great Kosher Administration" and the "first Communist President of the United States." For all his agitation, only in Washington State could Pelley ever get on the ballot to test his strength and make his point; he drew only 1,600 votes. Naturally, he blamed Jews for his troubles.   7:42

It was in 1940 that Martin Dies found it worthwhile to check out Pelley's un-Americanism. Though exposed thus to a different kind of searchlight than the one he knew on the trail, Pelley kept speaking up for America's purity, but finally he attracted charges of sedition in 1942. United States Attorney B. Howard Caughran showed that he could use Pelley's own kind of rhetoric to address him as a Benedict Arnold, an Aaron Burr, someone like Norway's traitor Vidkun Quisling. No murderer, Caughran charged Pelley, "had a blacker heart than you, who tried to murder the country that nurtured you." The heart was black, the Silver Shirts were tarnished, and they disappeared.   7:43

The two main Protestant competitors to Pelley the metaphysician gained much larger followings, on soil more congenial to their movements. The first of these two was Kansan Gerald B. Winrod, another son of a conservative evangelist. Winrod was another agent and victim of Depression confusions who reached out to people like himself. He was ready to attack when Roosevelt came to power in 1933. The evangelist charged the new president with being pro-Jewish and pro-Communist. The new invention to fulfil his purposes was the Defenders of the Christian Faith, a pro-Nazi group inspired when Winrod visited Hitler's Germany in 1934. In the Nazis Winrod identified "Puritanical" objections to   7:44

the excesses of Weimar Germany. These he transferred into express revulsion over practices in immoral America.

7:45   Winrod went two better than Pelley in one respect: he concentrated on anti-Catholic and antiblack themes as well as on the utterly predictable anti-Semitism. Winrod was more informed about church life than were some of his competitors. He regularly monitored the National Conference of Christians and Jews and saw the Federal Council of Churches and liberal Protestant churches as fronts for Communist Jews, or as being Judaized themselves. The Winrod vitriol reached 100,000 subscribers around its own peak and the Depression's depth in 1936.

7:46   The roots of Winrod's movement went back to the mid-twenties, when he associated with fundamentalists like William Bell Riley and evangelists like Billy Sunday. The ambitious newcomer soon came to see himself as a front-rank defender against Modernism. As late as 1935 he was awarded an honorary doctorate from the rather staid Fundamentalist Bible Institute of Los Angeles. Well aware of the reputation that Fundamentalists had for fighting each other, Winrod aspired to unite them all in a movement that would promote conflict against a common foe. The hardworking, handsome publisher and evangelist won the confidence of many, including for a time Pentecostal evangelist Aimee Semple McPherson, who helped give him credibility. But her interests were less of a political sort than his, and she was no hater as he was, so the coalescence soon ended. Winrod in these years still claimed that he wanted to be charitable to rivals and colleagues, lest at every turn they give liberals what he foresaw as otherwise decisive victories. Liberals alone deserved criticism, he thought, but it did not take much to be called a liberal in Winrod's book. He found such foes everywhere: they were running seminaries, mission boards, bureaucracies of denominations—all of them consistently parading as "Angels of Light."

7:47   When Congregationalist lay leader and popular economist Roger Babson rather innocently proclaimed that "more religion—rather than more legislation—is the need of the hour," Winrod twisted it into something more sinister-sounding. He thereupon entered politics in order to do the providing of such religion. As a premillennialist, he looked for signs of the times toward Armageddon and the second coming of Christ. He saw such a sign in the Roosevelt victory of 1932, and for years kept up constant attack on the president in his *The Defender*, which eventually became *The Revealer*. Winrod was also the sort of exception who helps prove a rule. He was one of the few celebrities who was convinced or would convince others that the Depression was not humanly caused. He blamed it on sin, specifically on economic confusion which resulted from denial of the law of God. The crisis, he said, was "first spiritual, then moral, then economic." In other words, modernisms caused the Crash.

While Winrod was promoting his cause he used a range of   7:48
techniques. Sometimes he sounded like an old-time evangelist: "Let revival fires be lighted across the continent! . . . Then, and not until then, every problem, whether it be political or economic, a blight of Socialism or a curse of Communism, will have a rational and permanent solution." Again, he could speak of conspiracy. He circulated old stories about one Adam Weishaupt and his Illuminati, a Bavarian secret society which from its eighteenth-century beginnings was supposed to have survived to influence Marx, Lenin, Trotsky, Stalin, and American Communists. The real change in his movement came later in the 1930s, however. As Pelley had done, so now Winrod muted his anti-Catholicism out of admiration for Father Charles Coughlin, with whom he entered into some alliances.

Winrod peaked politically in 1938, the year he managed to   7:49
gain 53,149 votes in the Republican senatorial primary race in Kansas. While his positions were well known, for the moment of the campaign he made less of his anti-Semitic stance than was usual at the time and sounded less anti-Catholic than before. Now the time had come, Winrod said, when he would befriend a devout Jew and would only oppose the "apostate, atheistic Communist Jew." He explained his defeat as being the result of efforts by Jewish financial interests, but his pro-Nazi positions were becoming too well known for him to retain support. Before long the federal administration in Washington targeted Winrod for observation. When war came in 1941 it put his name first among twenty-eight who were indicted for conspiracy to cause insubordination in the armed forces. The evangelist surrendered in Washington but was never found guilty or sent to prison. Winrod remained convinced of the truth and value of his views and continued his fight against Communism and his attack on Jewish conspiracies until he faded into insignificance.

The other case that was located between the simply out-of-   7:50
bounds Nazi movement and the partly successful Coughlin phenomenon, which meant at the side of Pelley's Silver Legion and Winrod's Defenders, was that of Gerald L. K. Smith. Like Win-

rod, Smith nurtured a distinctively religious following and used that context as a base to reach out politically. Journalist H. L. Mencken, who could spot a rouser when he came near one, thought that Smith was "a rhetorician who was even greater than Bryan," for whom Mencken cherished a disrespectful sort of higher respect.

7:51   Like his two peers, Smith was the son of an evangelist, in this case a Disciples of Christ circuit-rider, and Smith was himself ordained in the Disciples of Christ tradition. He spent his early ministry in Indiana's Ku Klux Klan country, which he found congenial in the years in which he was building up a strong congregation. Thereafter he moved to Shreveport, Louisiana, then promising soil for populist movements, there to start both congregational pulpit and radio ministries. For a time the gleam of Pelley's Silver Shirts attracted him. But he needed a larger scope for his talents, of which he was very conscious. He once told reporters, "Oh, I'm a rabble rouser. Put that down—a rabble rouser. God made me a rabble rouser of and for the right. Better spell that word right with a capital R." Smith was defining his America First party over against Franklin Roosevelt's "rabble rousers of the Left. Spell left with a capital L, will you?"

7:52   As a younger man in the mid-twenties, during the Fundamentalist-Modernist schism that was causing some trouble in the Disciples of Christ, Smith seemed first to be sizing up the sides. For a moment he had once even toyed with Modernism, perhaps as part of a calculation to gain power. It was indeed true that he had once had some more liberal moments. When he first moved to Shreveport in 1929, Smith exchanged pulpits with the rabbi of B'nai Zion Temple. He also made other surprising interfaith gestures of friendliness which in later years he would have had to repudiate if they were brought up against him.

7:53   In the course of Smith's early career he had received some heady liberal accolades, for example from *The Christian Century*. The editors thought they saw him fighting for social justice early in the thirties. All those confusions sorted themselves out for such observers, however, when Smith decided in 1934 to sign on with Governor Huey Long. His waverings over his positions then simply ended. Smith took lessons from this master and sometime senior partner, who held his state of Louisiana as a fiefdom based on extravagant promises in the mid-thirties. Long called his capstone program Share-Our-Wealth. For attempts to make inroads in the religious field he found Smith an attractive ally who could make a pitch for Long's cause among Louisiana's many religious-minded dispossessed.

To get Smith into some focus one must first glimpse Long,   7:54
who denied that he was a demagogue or a Fascist but who to his
critics sounded like both. From William Jennings Bryan, Long
stole and misused a slogan: "Every Man a King." Smith exploited the bond which he saw developing between Long and the
Louisianans: "We do not create a state of mind; we merely discover and recognize a state of mind that has been created by conditions." But that mind needed leaders, and Long and Smith
nominated themselves for roles. Long once said to T. Semmes
Walmsley, the mayor of New Orleans, "There's going to be a
revolution in this country and I'm going to lead it."

Because the popular resident of the White House, Franklin   7:55
Delano Roosevelt, stood in his way while Long sought power, the
Louisianan saw the need to attack the president. But all the plot-
ting ended on September 8, 1935, when an assassin's bullet cut
short his attempts. Now Smith stood ready to inherit Share-Our-
Wealth. It was he who preached the funeral sermon for Long in
front of 125,000 devotees on the capital grounds that September.
For the next few months he made the most of the Long mantle.
But he was an evangelist, not a politician, and the experienced
professionals soon seized that mantle from him, leaving Smith to
more explicitly religious work. The Long lieutenant who outmaneuvered Smith was Seymour Weiss, a Jew; his activity may have
helped inspire the evangelist's anti-Semitism. Smith was ejected
from state power and went looking for new fields of battle.

The Depression climate permitted so many extremist experi-   7:56
ments that he had many choices, but Smith at first seized on a
conservative southern politician, Georgia governor Eugene Talmadge, with whom he shared anti-Roosevelt passion. Smith was
then sermonizing that Roosevelt "gave us the Russian primer and
cursed the Bible." Soon the preacher was attracting so much attention that he threatened to become a rival with whom Talmadge
had to be uncomfortable and he quickly outlasted his welcome in
Georgia. Talmadge dropped him almost instantly. Next he spotted
an opening with the always roving Dr. Francis E. Townsend.
Smith gravitated toward this doctor who offered wild schemes that
were supposed to bring economic benefit to the aged. Townsend
and Smith disagreed with each other constantly, but for practical
reasons they papered over their grievances with each other in the
interest of winning and sharing power. They did merge constitu-

encies, but the fusion was a bad bargain for the more benign Townsend who did not share the rabble rousing skills of which Smith boasted.

7:57   Townsend demands notice of his own. His career rather poignantly demonstrates something of the range that existed between hope and despair during the Depression. While not explicitly religious in his appeal, Townsend liked to remind hearers that he was raised in a Methodist family and he liked to crowd his stage with clergy to give invocations. In his own older age the Long Beach, California, physician devised a scheme whereby all persons over sixty were to get a $200-a-month pension. Townsend proposed the doling out of scrip which by law would have to be spent within a month, thus producing a cycling effect which was supposed to help the economy recover and thrive. While no reputable economist saw anything but hoax or delusion in the scheme, Townsend through his plan claimed to command the sympathy of 30 million people; in various ways it probably did attract several millions.

7:58   Stuart A. A. Rice of the United States Central Statistical Board viewed the situation most appropriately. The Townsendites, he said, were really demanding "a revision of the science of arithmetic by law." Congress had the good sense to undercut Townsend and his program by passing a Social Security Act in 1935. Social Security was a straight political and economic measure, whereas Townsend's approach had become almost religious. In 1936 Smith once appealed to an already standing crowd with a call that the United States should keep on believing in "Santa Claus, Christmas trees, Easter bunny, the Holy Bible, and the Townsend plan." The crowd cheered so long that Smith had to use the Lord's Prayer to quiet them. The combination of "beliefs" Smith evoked that day was rather faithful to what Townsend came to mean.

7:59   This "Messiah on the March," as *Time* magazine called him, arrived on the scene with little perspective on himself or economics and he soon lost the bit he had. In a convention at Chicago in 1935 Townsend had described his plan as the "sole and only hope of a confused and distracted nation." He could relegate a rival to secondary status: "Where Christianity numbered its hundreds in its beginning years, our cause numbers its millions. And without sacrilege we can say that we believe that the effects of our movement will make as deep and mighty changes in civilization as did Christianity itself." Washington snubbed this messiah, and Smith

kept gaining power while Townsend was increasingly discredited
and his cause abandoned. Smith more effectively used religion for
his cause. His program, he said, was just "religion and patriotism," and he would "keep going on that. It's the only way you
can get them really 'het up.' "

Getting them het up became Smith's enduring task after Town-   7:60
send was to slip off his stage as quickly as he had come on to it.
Meanwhile, big-city reporters who found that coverage of conventional churchgoing and pulpiteering was dull by contrast, followed Smith's speeches and reported on his ravings, most of them
extensions of 1920s-style superpatriotic outbursts. "They tell me
I mustn't refer to our sacred flag. . . . They say I must not speak
of our glorious Constitution. . . . They tell me that I cannot quote
from my beloved Bible, which I hold here in my hand." If that
be rabble-rousing, "then I pray to God that He in his wisdom will
make me the greatest rabble-rouser in the land and fit to follow in
the footsteps of Huey Long, who chose me as his great disciple."
Smith, however, increasingly became a problem for old compa-
triots. In one last overtly political move, he formed his own party
in 1937. It attracted only hundreds but he called it The Committee
of One Million to "seize the government of the United States."

Finally, Smith overstepped even the boundaries of his own fol-   7:61
lowers' fantasies and became a victim of the new media of communication. In March 1936, a *March of Time* newsreel showed
him rehearsing postures that reminded everyone of dictators Hitler
and Mussolini. The newsreel camera glimpsed him before a mirror, with pictures nearby of the Nazi and the Fascist who in some
respects served him as his models. Narrator Westbrook Van Voor-
his provided comment on screen: "In Gerald Smith's sweating,
bombastic oratory serious commentators see the making of a fascist dictator." That precise role was not what dreaming American
populists had in mind. Smith's career suffered. When he sued the
March of Time for $5 million, he included in his complaints one
which said that the film made him too vulnerable to approaches
from "sponsors of Hitler and Jew-baiting." He settled for
$4,999,999 less than he had sought, after the damage had been
done. It was too late for Smith to be effective when he finally
began criticizing Hitler and the Bund. He never did suppress his
instinctive anti-Semitism.

Smith found a final postscripted sort of fame in the early 1940s   7:62
when he moved to Detroit and became a radio broadcaster with
the support of Henry Ford, who gave him access to both the Ford

To all but their admirers, these three leaders were demagogues: Dr. Francis P. Townsend, Protestant rabble-rouser Gerald L. K. Smith, and Father Charles E. Coughlin, here in a playful mood after a speech by Coughlin at a Townsend rally in 1936. (UPI/Bettmann Newsphotos.)

home and office. The two men shared dislike for labor unions; they both promoted eccentric interpretations of capitalism and somehow found rapport with each other. But the old extremism remained, and when Smith ran for the Senate in 1942, in a race which garnered him 100,000 Republican primary votes, prominent Detroiters found good reason to put distance between themselves and him. A still later attempt for him to go home again, to Louisiana, was also futile, for Earl Long now wore the Long mantle and bore the right pedigree. The Long following booed Smith off the scene. Smith lasted for years, but fades from our scene as war came. He was left with *The Cross and the Flag*, his World-War-II-era magazine. The Justice Department saw him as seditious when, late in the war, he would write things like: "If we'd herd all Reds and Communists into concentration camps and outlaw about half of the movies and then turn to Christian statesmanship, our problems would be solved." In the end he had nothing but his spewings and a couple tens of thousands of subscribers to show for the efforts that had begun long ago at the edges of the Disciples of Christ circuit.

Coughlin's: A Body of Opinion Shared by Millions of Americans

In the biography of all the other demagogues of the Depres-   7:63
sion, it is the name of Father Charles Coughlin that always shows up and casts them in the shadow. Coughlin was the first American Catholic priest to gain a large following among non-Catholics. That by itself was a significant achievement, given the tradition of anti-Catholic attitudes among the kinds of Protestants who followed him. It equally signified the depth of discontent and the wildness of experimental flailing that was going on among non-Catholics who could virtually overlook Coughlin's Catholicism because of their hunger for the solutions he seemed to offer. No one else so capably gathered the support of the disaffected. But while the priest eventually turned into a pure anti-Semite after having attracted a bit of Jewish support, for a time he attracted Protestant and Catholic malcontents who together hoped for better days. The same Protestants who could resent or fight Catholics on doctrine, could stand side by side with them in Coughlin's partisan efforts or tune in together with them to his radio show.

Canadian-born Charles Coughlin made his way to the Detroit   7:64
diocese in the twenties, to begin what may have looked like ordinary parish work. The young priest chose to make it extraordinary. Archbishop Michael J. Gallagher welcomed the young philosopher and baseball player who was already in his early twenties known as a spellbinding preacher. Gallagher assigned him to a nondescript suburb, Royal Oak, which was just then beginning to boom. The hierarch himself had just returned from Rome, full of enthusiasm for St. Thérèse of Lisieux, "the Little Flower of Jesus," whose canonization he had attended. What better name for the new parish near Detroit than "Little Flower"? Coughlin would build her a shrine.

There was no way to confine Coughlin to one parish. He   7:65
reached out and somehow learned to use radio as his instrument. The priest was to become one of the master broadcasters of the period. After the stock-market crash he learned that he could get

a following by broadcasting explanations about what had gone wrong economically and politically. Only three years into a radio career he located a national audience for Detroit's WJR. His range of crowd-pleasing topics included opposition to birth control, but Coughlin had ambitions beyond Catholicism and the conservative Protestant sphere which that issue attracted.

7:66   What other choices were there for such a would-be leader? The Red Scare was ten years behind him, but he still found some people ready for anti-Communism as they picked up the pieces after the Crash. Coughlin's new theme became "Christ or the Red Fog." Even that topic by itself turned out not to be sufficiently close to home. Any religious figure who wanted to make a mark on the national scene sooner or later had to deal with domestic politics. Coughlin entered the scene attacking the hapless Herbert Hoover during that Republican president's electoral contest with Roosevelt in 1932. After that autumn Coughlin would never leave the political arena, but also never again would he find a plausible candidacy so congenial as Roosevelt's had been early in the Depression.

7:67   Since Coughlin was becoming dependent on the funds that came with letters in response to his programs, he had to have ready replies, and he soon put to work almost 150 clerks to make reply. Not all listeners agreed with him by any means, but the support he received came chiefly from people devastated by the Depression. Even those who despised his message found it hard to turn the priest off, as he held people enthralled with clever furies and a rhetorical charm. He made up in numbers what he lacked in support from the prosperous. One week he walked into a bank with the 22,000 one-dollar-bills which his mail had yielded him in the previous several days. As he became more controversial and when reaction set in during 1931, the Columbia Broadcasting System quietly dropped him. The response to such action was vehement. CBS had second thoughts, but did not quickly act upon them. Nor would the National Broadcasting System pick up such a disruptive character. Coughlin, to his own advantage, therefore developed a personal network and soon outdrew CBS weekly.

7:68   *Fortune* in 1934 found it valid to introduce its readers to "Father Coughlin (pronounced Kawglin)." "They say we never shall see Bryan's like again. They say the people are skeptical and that oratory is dead." But here, said the editor, was Father Coughlin.

"The first fact to absorb about Father Coughlin is his tremendous reputation." He was the biggest thing yet to happen to radio. "If you are thinking of comparing him with other famous radio preachers like . . . Harry Emerson Fosdick, you may as well stop at once; his mail exceeds theirs by at the very least 1,000 to 1."

Somehow, thought *Fortune* editors, the other print media were   7:69
slighting this man Coughlin, so the public at large until then had "underestimated his size as a public man. Today he looms in the nation as a public power." The editors quoted Detroit's Bishop Gallagher: no, he would not silence Coughlin, because he " 'has preached no heresy.' " As for the politics, "one thing is certain: Father Coughlin is no iconoclast." He was, the editor noted, *against* "communism, fascism, socialism, inflation, prohibition, big bankers, and the uneven distribution of wealth," all legitimate Depression-era topics. He had been *for* Christian capitalism, President Roosevelt, and any number of things that Roosevelt stood for, but which *Fortune* did not. "There is no smell of heresy here." In fact, Coughlin was important, judged the magazine, because he had "given his voice to a body of opinion that is shared, in whole or in part, by millions of Americans."

The White House after Roosevelt took over in 1933 momen-   7:70
tarily welcomed Coughlin, who was at first sycophantic toward the new president because he obviously enjoyed access to power. The priest instructed listeners to end their letters to the president, "I love you." Roosevelt was intelligent enough to be wary of the priest, but for a time he found it valuable to cultivate the Detroiter and his national constituency. The Roosevelt advisers, his brain trust, became increasingly nervous, however, whenever Coughlin stepped forward as an administration representative or, as he would wish to be, as a power behind the presidential chair. It was confusing to hear that the New Deal could sometimes be described by Coughlin as "Christ's Deal."

Coughlin substantiated his positions by quoting papal encycli-   7:71
cals in support of justice in the social order. "If I be a demagogue, so must be [Popes] Leo and Pius," said the preacher when he announced that his economic programs did not "exceed the doctrine of Jesus Christ." He also loved to quote his favorite popes in their attacks on unrestrained capitalism and then say something like, "If I am a Socialist for pronouncing that doctrine, so is Pius XI. But we both happen to be Catholic."

Coughlin, untutored, uninformed, incompetent in economics,   7:72

working only on his instincts, began to devise proposals to meet Depression crises. As his followers came to find these plausible and supported them, he increasingly seemed to feel that whatever he invented must be true and workable. For a moment, as when his views in respect to a gold revaluation scheme in 1932–33 coincided with Roosevelt's, he seemed on the way to becoming an insider. When the administration's own scheme disappointed him, Coughlin started attacking internationalist "financial Dillingers," named thus by him after the most notable criminal of the times. These Dillingers were the Warburgs and Rothschilds in Europe. He accused them of hoarding gold, and in late 1933 he started promoting free silver.

7:73   While the younger Coughlin had swung wildly without aiming, later, as he found support whenever he attacked bankers named Warburg or Rothschild, the priest gradually warmed to his own rhetoric and exploited the specific prejudices of his hearers. The turn he took was expensive for his reputation. He did not want to alienate his Jewish supporters. But he had to, because he could not resist lapsing into language which excluded Jews: "Don't forget this is a Christian nation."

7:74   Coughlin had finally found his ideological platform. He even reprinted the *Protocols of the Elders of Zion*, although they had been discredited when Henry Ford used them a decade earlier. "The factuality of the content of the *Protocols* is about us at every turn," he would write even as he had to admit that the factuality of the authorship was more than questionable. He asked paranoiac questions that to some hearers began to sound plausible in Depression times. Thus he asked: "Is it not true that the synagogue of Satan, under the leadership of anti-Christ, has hindered and hampered the activity of the Mystical Body of Christ?" And he went on to ask whether it was also not true that "some unseen force has taken Christ out of government, business, industry, and to a large degree, education?" Was it not true that "a force, over which we Christians seem to have no control, has gained control of journalism, motion pictures, theatres and radio?" In 1938 Coughlin agreed with Nazis that Jews had been behind the Russian Revolution. And yet, "believe me, my friends, it is in all charity," Coughlin said, that he spoke against Jews. He was seeking, he said, "to discover the causes that produced the effect known as Nazis—Nazism—which was evolved to act as a defense mechanism against the incursions of Communism."

While some Methodists, Lutherans, and other Protestants be-   7:75
longed to the original and developing Coughlin constituency,
Catholics, of course, predominated, to the discomfort of priestly
and lay leaders who increasingly found the priest an embarrassment. Hierarchs gradually began to put distance between themselves and the best-known Catholic in America. They thus had to
risk alienating lower-middle-class Irish and German Catholics
who thought Coughlin addressed Depression ills when leaders in
formal channels refused to. Governor Al Smith was one of the
notables who did find courage to attack Coughlin. Boston's William Cardinal O'Connell also thought it proper to back Monsignor
John A. Ryan when that pro–New Deal priest began publicly to
attack Coughlin. Bishop Gallagher in Detroit long remained in his
priest's camp, admiring his intellect, basking in the derived fame,
perhaps sharing some of the economic views, and not ready to
risk angering Coughlin's supporters. Some Catholics enjoyed using Coughlin to get revenge against the upper-class Protestants
whose prejudices they had experienced, whose ways they had envied. Wilfred Parsons, editor of the Jesuit magazine *America* correctly described most partisans in 1935: "The motivation of
Father Coughlin's followers is almost entirely one of hatred."

Eventually Roosevelt had to become the subject of Coughlin's   7:76
hatred, after the priest broke with him in disgust in 1934. On
November 11 of that year Coughlin announced a major new instrument, the National Union for Social Justice. The hearers who
had been an audience were now to become a movement. Their
leader knowingly quoted the very language a pope had used to
start the Crusades: "God wills it!" and asked, "Do you?" It
turned out that on the old western and southwestern Protestant
populist soil Coughlin was relatively weak, but he foresaw good
prospects, he said, if only Protestants would join in forming the
virtual party which he called the Union.

Toward mid-1935 Coughlin claimed 8.5 million supporters   7:77
and in the next half year said he had added 5,267,000 new members. A year later their leader was more realistic and honest, for
then he boasted only 1.6 million "active" members alongside six
million "passive" ones. The actives probably made up the
Union's true constituency and indicated its proper size. Yet this
smaller number of people gave money generously, and because of
their support the priest and leader came to be a feared figure.
Many politicians cowered in the face of the language Coughlin

used in 1936 when he cut all ties to Roosevelt. "Today I humbly
stand before the American public to admit that I was in error.
Despite all the promises, the money changer has not been driven
from the temple." Whereas once his slogan was "Roosevelt or
Ruin!" now it became "Roosevelt and Ruin."

7:78   The Union Party, which for a time rallied Gerald L. K. Smith
and Dr. Townsend, became Coughlin's new instrument. It was in
part the simple product of the priest's hatred for Roosevelt. By
having access to a political party, he could and did run candidates
for the presidency and vice-presidency of the United States, but
found few ready to go on his platform. William Lemke of North
Dakota was the only professional who did. But the support
Coughlin's radio hearers, subscribers, parishioners, and audiences
gave him had turned the priest's head. He predicted that his third
party would "engage the attention of 25,000,000 voters." To promote this notion he chose as Lemke's running mate one Thomas
Charles O'Brien. Hence the Detroiter could sound momentarily
ecumenical. On his team there were now "East and West! Protestant and Catholic, possessing one program of driving the money
changers from the temple." Socialist Norman Thomas, who regularly ran for president, sized up the challenge, calling the team
"two and a half rival messiahs plus one ambitious politician plus
some neopopulists plus a platform which reminds me of the early
efforts of Hitler." As the campaign proceeded, the *Literary Digest* magazine experimented with the new art of poll-taking, but
its surveyors lacked the skill to make room for skewed samples
and biased respondents. That poll consistently found Lemke a serious contender.

7:79   Candidate Roosevelt had reason for being cheerful during the
campaign when he saw many Catholics coming to oppose Coughlin. Charlton Ogburn, a prominent lawyer, informed Roosevelt
that his contacts at the Vatican were telling authorities there to be
on the alert, because, as he put it, of "the harm which Coughlin
is doing to the Church in America by attacking you." And Monsignor John A. Ryan, whose biographer called him *The Right
Reverend New Dealer,* came to lead the clergy attacks on Coughlin. Now in response the priest from the Shrine of the Little
Flower had to take time to speak of the "false" and "despicable"
assertions, the "ugly, cowardly and flagrant calumnies" of his
fellow priest. Ryan called for votes in support of Roosevelt, as
did some bishops. Father Maurice S. Sheehy wrote Roosevelt

concerning this support: "There is a feeling now prevalent among the priests that the priesthood, through Father Coughlin, has betrayed the President, and some extraordinary things are being attempted to offset this betrayal."

Coughlin's campaign oratory exceeded the usual boundaries of   7:80 permitted hyperbole. He told 15,000 North Dakota farmers to prepare to take arms. If Landon or Roosevelt were to be installed in the White House, Coughlin warned, there would be no election in 1940. "Fascism will be here and Communism will be making a bid for power." In Providence, he said that the New Deal was surrounded by atheists, red and pink Communists, and, alluding to Jewish Supreme Court justice Felix Frankfurter, "by 'frankfurters' of destruction." A month later, the radio priest shouted that if Americans voted for Roosevelt, they were voting for "the Communists, the socialists, the Russian lovers, the Mexican lovers, and the kick-me-downers." In September in Brooklyn he saw the battle as being "between the basic principles of Christianity and the old doctrines of paganism," a "struggle for the preservation of Americanism." For a moment Coughlin moderated his excesses, but in a speech at Cincinnati he soon showed he was back in stride: Mr. Roosevelt was "anti-God and a radical." When the press asked a question about where he found America, Coughlin pointed: "We are at the crossroads. One road leads toward fascism, the other toward Communism. I take the road to fascism."

In the face of such stridency, official Catholicism grew ever   7:81 more embarrassed. Protestants who had reserved judgment now used the Coughlin movement to increase the embarrassment. The usually passive Missouri Synod of the Lutheran Church was ordinarily diffident about commenting on current affairs, but even one of its professors and editors charged that "the voice behind that radio priest is the voice of his church." By then Detroit's Bishop Gallagher was finding support of Coughlin to be less attractive than formerly. Rome helped set the climate for moves against him. On September 2, 1936, the Vatican newspaper, *L'Osservatore Romano*, criticized Bishop Gallagher for claiming that the pope approved of Coughlin's activity and then denounced Coughlin. The paper followed up its blast with press releases to international agencies. These stressed that the paper's voice and view were officially Rome's. Gallagher henceforth tried to rein in Coughlin, but with little effect. Eugenio Cardinal Pacelli, the future pope, was sent to America to deal with Coughlin, but even he could not effectively edge the priest out or lead him to fall into silence.

7:82   The mistake politically minded clerics sometimes make is to position themselves where ordinary voters get to express their attitudes. This the public did on November 3, 1936, when a tearful Coughlin was humiliated. In the presidential election, Roosevelt received 22,751,597 votes to Landon's 16,679,583, while Coughlin's candidate Lemke had to settle for less than 2 percent, 892,378. Coughlin responded: "President Roosevelt can be a dictator if he wants to; I hope that God will bless him and the Holy Ghost will inspire him not to misuse his power." Analysts asked what went wrong, not only with the *Literary Digest* poll but with the Lemke candidacy and the party itself. There never had been an electoral constituency; that was clear, and should have been all along. Some anti-Catholic Unionists, for instance, early deserted the new party because it was dominated by a priest. The Unionists only picked up a few upper Midwest rural populist voters. Some aged Townsendites may have remained loyal; no doubt a handful of Huey Long partisans came along for the moment. But electoral rejection of his candidate and program only led Coughlin to turn more extreme. While out scape-goat hunting he invented a Christian Front which turned out to be a near match for the German-American Bund, so far as attitudes toward Nazism was concerned. Gallagher's successor in Detroit, Archbishop Edward Mooney, who had chosen for a while to be tolerant, scrutinized the scene in wartime Washington and found it best to confine the noisy priest to his parish. Coughlin's radio voice was silenced, but he did not change his opinions.

7:83   When the United States entered World War II, his old critics found more reason than ever to focus on Coughlin and his defenses of Nazism, his lack of sympathy for Jews, and his critique of American military power. When the Christian Front people engaged in ruffian-like activities, they made Coughlin look irrelevant, isolated. A period was ending. He more than anyone else, whether in clerical or lay garb, had been the galvanizer of the "right with a capital R." While he would live on to serve the Shrine of the Little Flower for decades, Coughlin was effectively finished except in that parish and in the reminiscences of old haters. What sense could people make of a man with his record who distorted its intent as much as he had in an interview on August 12, 1939, the month before the war. "My purpose," he was saying at the time, was "to help eradicate from the world its mania for persecution, to help align all good men, Catholic and Protestant, Jew and Gentile, Christian and non-Christian, in a battle to stamp out the ferocity, the barbarism and the hate of this bloody era." Winrod and Pelley, Townsend and Smith, and Coughlin most of all, had done their part to promote barbarism and hate. But with the coming of World War II, their chapter effectively had ended. The noise of conflict in American religion had sounded as loudly as it ever would, but the guns of war were louder, and they signified new preoccupations in "this bloody era."

On the Left: The Marxist Federation for Social Strife

If the focus here has been not on mainstream conservatives but on the right with a capital R, those who sensed and exploited the instabilities and disruptions of Depression times, it is only fair to go in search of their counterparts who embodied the left with a capital L. The assumption is this: if the right with a capital R movements tell about one extreme, then left with a capital L movements in balancing them should provide further evidence of the wild religious experimentations of the decade. Who qualifies in this left category? Certainly, in retrospect, the Communist party in the United States reached as far beyond consensus as did Father Coughlin on the right. There were also erratic radicals with wild schemes for reorganizing America through and after class struggles and wars. But none of these provides an exact counterpart because they did not issue in religious mass movements which could attract identifiable millions, as Coughlin's did. They did not use the language of conventional religion to amass mailing lists that ran into the hundreds of thousands of names. The left phases more easily into the orthodox, secular prosocialist schemes and ideology of Depression times than did Winrod's or Smith's extremism phase into unorthodox procapitalist advocacies. Yet the religious and antireligious expressions of the radical left say something about Depression despair and hopes. 7:84

Ten years after the Red Scare which marked the turn to the twenties, the antireligious Communist party was in a woebegone condition at the moment of the Crash and the beginning of the Depression. Its membership seemed to be decreasing constantly. If the party could claim a couple tens of thousands in 1919, it 7:85

could find only 7,545 in 1930. Even in response to hard times, which should have benefited the party, and despite strenuous recruiting, the membership rose only to 9,219 a year later. By the time of the Roosevelt election in 1932 it still had not attracted 10,000, which left it no statistical match for any circuit-riding evangelist's local crowd on any night of the year. In the early New Deal days, when many a conservative hater of Roosevelt and of social planning sniffed around for and claimed to find Communists on the trail all the way to the White House, the party lingered with between only 14,000 and 18,000 adherents nationally. Membership passed through a revolving door; there was little loyalty or endurance. Years into the Depression, leaders could find and boast of at most 26,000 members, a disappointing figure to the dreamers among them.

7:86   Recruits to this Communist party complained of leadership inefficiency, bureaucratic shuffling, low drama, disrespect for members, intrigue, and irrelevance. Most new members disappeared quickly, just as they had joined. The cohort was made up chiefly of the unemployed who had nothing to lose and intellectuals who thought they had everything to gain. Few original-stock Protestants, not enough blacks, and far too few women signed up to satisfy the ideologues and organizers. Leaders were reduced to having to rely on fellow travelers to make their movement sound significant at all. Thus Earl Browder thought that up to a half-million citizens were sympathizers at mid-decade. But they would not join and be counted.

7:87   Communists in Europe expected more than that of the United States by at least 1932, and were puzzled by the enduringly conservative outlook of the American electorate. They saw the new President Roosevelt as anything but radical; Socialist Norman Thomas attracted few votes, while Communist candidate William Z. Foster received almost none. Socialism had been more attractive in its peak year of 1912 than it was in America's economic bottom election year, 1932. Not one in forty American voters deserted the two main parties which fought to control the reconstructed center.

7:88   One must look elsewhere than in the electoral ranks for signs of discontent from the extreme left, for 1932 should have been as congenial an atmosphere for Communist ideas as any year of the century. One did occasionally hear some good words for Moscow from traveling church people. Some religious magazines put the best possible face on Communist repressions of religion and economic experiment in Russia. There was also a literary-intellectual left, but not always of the party stripe: philosopher Sidney Hook, churchman J. B. Mathews, novelist John Dos Passos were typical; they left a mark before reacting and then heading to the right. Many a major campus was hospitable to those who expressed a radical left ethos. However one reckoned, it still took some stretching for *Daily Worker* columnist Eugene Lyons to claim the thirties as "the Red Decade" to follow the twenties as a "Lost Decade" for the cause.

An incident in Catholicism showed how limited was the appeal   7:89
of the radical left in America's largest denomination. Since Communism was strong in the Spanish Loyalist leadership and present among some of its American supporters, there were reasons for Catholic defenders of General Francisco Franco's Fascist Republicans to accuse their opponents of being Communist. This fracas remained confined, for it was a controversy of religious editors, arguments among elites fought out more among interviewees in polls than in any company that was really disruptive. Catholics remained uncertain and divided about Spain. One poll found that 39 percent of the Catholics were pro-Franco, but 30 percent were pro-Loyalist and 31 percent were neutral. At the same time, only 9 percent of the polled Protestants were pro-Franco, but the topic of the Spanish War was not set high on their churchly agenda.

On the rare occasions when a Catholic editorial writer would   7:90
wander with comment into the Spanish no-man's-land, he soon learned that it was hard to make himself clear as to why he spoke up. In 1936 a sober George N. Shuster wrote an editorial criticizing both sides in the Spanish brutality. He voiced not one friendly word for Communism, but questioned whether the church or peasants would fare very well under Franco. His *Commonweal* piece was designed to counter an opening comment in the Jesuit weekly *America*. The editor there had written that "whatever the nature and the policies of the government that would be established after a victory of the Right army, they could not possibly lead to greater disasters than those already perpetrated by the Red Government now in control." If the government in Madrid did prevail, said the Jesuit editors, it "would not stop until the whole of Spain was Sovietized."

Shuster, in turn, argued in 1936 that General Franco would   7:91
only superficially oppose anticlericalism "because Fascism is traditionalistic and there is only Catholic tradition in Spain," but support by the church would be an expensive commitment. On

April 2, 1937, Shuster wrote again. "But shall we also be obliged to record the equally shocking fact that Catholics are ready to ignore the manifest brutality, reactionary political method and intellectual simplicity of the Francoites?" Would the church, indeed, be better off instead with them?

7:92   The response to this article was devastating. All the pro-Franco people had found a target. Shuster summarized: "It now dawned on me that for Catholic New York the world outside the United States was either Communist or Fascist and that therefore they opted for Fascism." Shuster, at the time ready to leave the magazine post for an academic career, peered ahead presciently: "One has only to look around and see that Fascism is rapidly being converted into what has been termed National Bolshevism" in Germany and elsewhere.

7:93   While these notable Catholic weeklies fought and partly neutralized each other, only a few Protestants took up the cause at all. Such editorialists ordinarily minimized the Communism in Spain's Republican coalition, a fact that was itself a sign of how disreputable Communist ties looked even at the peak of Depression reaction. In 1936 the *Christian Century* grumbled when the future Pope Pius XII, Eugenio Cardinal Pacelli, visited America. Would this nation now join hands with an ally "who sees Communism as a peril but who is complacent toward fascism and cooperative with it?"

7:94   Since the Spanish Civil War was and remained distant, one must probe elsewhere for religious support of Communism. The most celebrated controversy in this zone was the trial of the Scottsboro Boys, nine young blacks who were accused of raping two white girls in 1931. They were found guilty and eight were sentenced to death. Black outrage over manifest injustices in that trial was understandable, as was the Communist party effort to exploit the fury. Yet few black churches stepped up front in defense, no doubt out of distaste for the party. In the North, several Federal Council denominations joined the council itself in 1934 and 1935 in calling for a fair trial. Harry Emerson Fosdick even chanced to play a role worth a footnote. On a March evening in 1933 one Ruby Bates, a conscience-stricken visitor, came to confess to the New York minister that her testimony which had helped get the Scottsboro nine in trouble was perjured. Fosdick talked her into retelling the story and witnessing to the truth in her testimony, and then made arrangements for her to return to Birmingham, Alabama, at trial time. In 1937 four of the accused were

An interracial cause célèbre of this period was the Scottsboro Boys case. Here 3,000 marchers parade toward the White House in an effort to bring petitions demanding freedom for black young men who were falsely imprisoned in a rape case. Ruby Bates, who confessed to the Reverend Harry Emerson Fosdick that she had made false charges, is a conspicuous marcher (in light coat). (UPI/ Bettmann Newsphotos.)

released while others were given shorter sentences and paroled. Not until 1966 was evidence revealed which conclusively proved them innocent.

While Communists made the most of the Scottsboro case, 7:95 some church leaders who were anything but pro-Red took it up as an instance of racial injustice. A Scottsboro Defense Committee included Paddock and Holmes, Charles Clayton Morrison, Fosdick, and one of those truly rare people who was friendly to Communist types at the extreme, Episcopalian John Howard Melish. *The Presbyterian Tribune* used the kind of language that characterized moderates in the thirties: "Cases like this do more to undermine our institutions than the efforts of thousands of 'agitators.'" Even some southern papers applauded when the United States Supreme Court brought justice to the complex case and saved the lives of the accused. Such support only enraged the

Communists, who wanted to have the case all to themselves. They were making strenuous efforts to invade black churches, the centers of loyalty among the people they would recruit. But the Scottsboro case, by bringing moderates to an awareness of injustices against blacks and to the cause, helped neutralize Communist party involvement.

7:96   Tireless Communists displayed even more pathos in their effort to link with another black cause, this time one regarded in its time by both whites and mainstream blacks as crackpot. These Communists focused on Father Divine, one of the colorful figures who stood out against the bleak background of the thirties. The Georgia-born man of mystery, probably named George Baker, made his way past some legal scrapes in his native state and some ministry in Baltimore to Sayville, Long Island, where by 1919 he had begun a ministry that would last for decades. In 1933 what he called the Father Divine Peace Mission moved to Harlem, where it served as a cultlike magnet for blacks and some whites who called Divine "God" and who enjoyed the material goods he distributed in difficult times. His weekly newspaper *New Day* popularized his message, one designed to neutralize racial and political tensions. While some communalism was present in Divine's program, he displayed only an utterly naive congeniality toward Communism in Marxist or party senses. The casual character of that confluence did not prevent enemies from trying to fault connections between the movement and the party.

7:97   For several years, into New Deal times, critics of "Communism in the Churches" pointed to Divine's relaxed but real ties to that movement of the left. He and the party made an odd couple: he was God and they were anti-God. He refused even to draw lines between black and white and wanted to abolish class distinctions while they wanted to exploit such distinctions. Divine did think that Communists were friends of his people, for they at least often sided with blacks when white churches would not. And many of them also seemed ready to take lessons from such a crowd-pleaser.

7:98   In a celebrated incident of 1934 the two camps even took part in a parade. In Harlem about three thousand of Father Divine's legions marched in an event led by the Communist-connected American League Against War and Fascism. A reporter for the *New York Times* noted the confusion of causes and styles in the event. The Communists, he noted, were trying to provoke violence while the Divineites were nonviolent. The latter may have served to keep the day peaceful with their chants of "Amen!" Wrote the reporter: "The monotonous chanting of 'Fight-fight-against war—and fascism' in harmony with the marching feet of the Communists was interspersed with hymnists singing 'Keep on praying for the rain—keep on praying for the rain,' a chant of 'Father' Divine's flock." That mixing was clearly no way to run a revolution; not a few Communists scorned others who wanted to engage in such crisscrossing activity.

An intraparty dispute over this pragmatic alliance grew so 7:99 heated that even Earl Browder, who rejected Divine's "fantastic slogans," felt a need to intervene in defense of those who allowed "religious people to march in our parade." He thought the effort showed that Communists could reach the backward masses and eventually help lead these blacks into the revolutionary struggles. And there *were* a few black Communists such as James W. Ford, who attacked those Trotskyites and Socialists who derided the coming together of such disparate forces. Ford admitted too that Divine led "backward undeveloped elements," but then went on to say that there were forward, developed elements in the more conventional black churches, and that they could be reached and needed cultivating. These "little big preachers" were "close to the masses," and, Ford said, they "hate the domination of the big ministers."

Some big "big preachers" also hated. Adam Clayton Powell, 7:100 Jr., an up-and-coming leader at Harlem's Abyssinian Baptist Church, was among those who said he could deal with Elks and Holy Rollers, Republicans or Communists, if they met one test: that of racial equality. Michael Gold, a party leader and writer, held his nose and wrote that while the "united front seems grotesque," this did not mean that it was strategically implausible. He wrote in the neutralizing spirit of Walter Lippmann and Joseph Wood Krutch, secularists who claimed to find more integrity in Fundamentalism than in suave and adaptive liberalism. Thus Gold said, "I see as much sense in Father Divine's cult as in the elaborate and sometimes hypocritical twistings of logic of a John Haynes Holmes," the Modernist who sometimes allied himself with the Socialists.

Tensions between Socialists and Communists divided the left 7:101 as much as the stresses between blacks and whites or Protestants and Catholics helped minimize the efficiency for combat of the Christians in Depression America. When Father Divine noticed the Socialist-Communist sniping that went on above his head and

behind his back, he seemed caught. Naively he defended himself
to New York alderman Lambert Fairchild: "The platform of the
Communist party as we understand it, is the brotherhood of man,
the abolition of war and equal opportunity." This matched the
word of Ben Davis in the *Daily Worker*: "If the progressive features of Divine's program are 'demagogy' and 'petty racketeer-
ing,' then let us have more of such."

7:102   Divine, who set out to please all political parties, added: "Give
me something better than the Communists have and I will endorse
it." As the thirties ended, it was clear to Divine that Communists
also did not give much, so he progressively cut off relations with
them. For now he kept riding his Rolls-Royces and providing ban-
quets or healing for his followers, to the discomfort of the secular
left. The day came when Divine turned explicitly anti-Communist
and when, in turn, Communists denounced the man and the
movement which had, in the end, helped block or divert their
access to black "undeveloped" elements. Those who wanted to
catch Divine in the Communist-in-religion net found nothing to
count on and few to count from his ranks on their list of believers
on the left.

7:103   Socialism was more credible than Communism to some religious leaders. If the Socialists scorned Communists for their flir-
tation with Father Divine, the Communists in their turn fired away
at Socialists for compromise with bourgeois society. Seldom was
this pattern so evident as in the unfolding career of ex-seminarian,
ex-Presbyterian Norman Thomas. His leftism was so genteel that
many nonviolent Protestant leaders regularly voted for him as the
Socialist candidate for President of the United States when they
wanted to express distaste for Republicans or Roosevelt. While
Thomas gave up his clerical orders in 1931, the Union Seminary
graduate kept using on occasion the language of prayer and blessing and evoking the recollection of conversion in his Socialist
meetings.

7:104   Already in the late twenties the Communist *Daily Worker* attacked Thomas from the far left; his Socialist following, it
charged, was in thrall to the "petty capitalist class." When many
Thomas followers found reasons to vote for Al Smith and the
Democrats, Communists did some lumping together of the
forces: "There is no essential difference between what the Rev.
Thomas' party offers and what the also-pious Al. Smith offers
except one will break strikes with protestant incantations, the
other with catholic devotion." And an "Odds and Ends" column

in the *Daily Worker* included satires like this short notice: "LOST—Presbyterian prayer book. Please return to Rev. Norman Thomas, Brickbat Presbyterian Church. Finder will receive reward of benediction worth seventy-five cents." These kinds of evidences show why it was that conservatives who wanted to divide and conquer the left found it divided and eminently conquerable, if not defeated before the fight.

What Communists began in the family quarrel with Socialists   7:105
they carried over to liberal Protestant clergy who were not formal Socialists. The stakes were less high there than in the political movement, but for the *Daily Worker* the clerical targets seemed fatter, so they dipped their pens deeper in acid for these attacks. The Communist writers found, or knew, no reason to keep types of clergy apart in their minds or speech. Whenever they found Fundamentalists and evangelists involved in any sort of scandal, they were gleeful.

Perhaps to the surprise of those not near the left, Communists   7:106
made every effort not to show sympathy for liberals in the churches, liberals who were under fire there for being too anticapitalist. T. J. O'Flaherty was an ex-Catholic turned anticlerical who might as well have served a metropolitan daily as a religion editor, so alert was he to the religion front. In the Fundamentalist-Modernist controversy days, O'Flaherty had written that "the liberal churches put . . . God through a fumigating process and serve him up to suit the tastes of their more advanced customers." Here, in the crisscrossing of American factions, there was a coincidental Communist-Fundamentalist coalition of criticism. If such diatribes would not drive social liberals from even the outer precincts of Communism, then *Daily Worker* atheism had to attempt to create wedges of disdain. One sample of alienating activities occurred when Brooklyn Communists in 1931 chose to parody Christian sacraments with a "red Baptism." They wanted to dramatize the way religious methods were designed to poison the minds of workers.

If the Communists had wished for an intelligent strategy for   7:107
growth in an America that was at least semireligious, they would not have come up with miscalculations such as the Workers' Anti-Religious League which they tried to sell in Manhattan and Harlem. The league's program was as ambitious as its achievement was small. Thus when the league wanted to attack churches for being passive in the Scottsboro Boys case, it instead nudged the public to appraise the examples of actual if tempered churchly

support for this pet Communist cause. Attacking religions did not work in America, a fact which confirmed some Communists in their antireligious and antibourgeois positions and also confirmed much of the rest of America in its notion that Communists were inept misreaders of the character of American society.

7:108   It was not the liberal church leaders, who were durably anti-Communist, but the Communists who had to beat a retreat and revise strategies as the decade developed. Efforts like those of the Young Communist League and the Young Pioneers to stage anti-Christian displays at an "Anti-Christmas Circus" in Cleveland showed how futile were these efforts to import and develop European styles of opposition to religion in an America which stayed friendly to faith even in the Depression. Party leader Michael Gold never got the message. He used the *Daily Worker* for his own protesting incantations to remind readers that "Communism is the irreconcilable foe of religion," and that religion was "spiritual dope," his translation of Karl Marx's more elegant equation of religion with the opium of the people. Though the paper could sometimes say good things about anti-Fascist clergy and might print letters from a rare "Christian Communist," it displayed no ability to make Communism attractive to the churches.

7:109   One of the rare Communists who remained atheist but knew how to cross the line intelligently if still without success was Earl Browder. This executive secretary of the party through the decade came from a long line of Methodist ministers and Unitarian laity, so he knew the language and concerns of people of faith. When Union Seminary students in New York invited Browder to speak in 1935 he gladly accepted. He told them that "we have preachers, preachers active in the churches, who are members of the Communist Party," a claim which was just what the suspicious had thought all along. But he told the students that Communists would not place people who had strong religious beliefs in the most responsible leading positions of the movement. The guest speaker then went on to criticize miracles and supernature, themes which were probably not on the minds of activist seminarians in any case. He again provided a bit of grist for Communist-hunters: "There are churches in the United States where the preachers preach Communism from the pulpits," but, he added, "in a very primitive form, of course." All that finally came of the event were attacks on Union Seminary, new suspicions that there were Communists in the pulpit, and a position in party cross fire for Browder because he had ventured too far.

J. B. Mathews, who had been an enthusiastic Communist early   7:110
in the thirties, was one of the creators of suspicion. A Methodist
who attended strict Asbury College in Kentucky and then went on
to master's degrees in theology in Europe and America, Mathews
returned from missionary efforts in the South Pacific to work in
black colleges in the American South. There, shocked by religious neglect of or prejudice against blacks, he looked for other
outlets for his energies. Also a pacifist, Mathews after 1929
served the Fellowship of Reconciliation; his name turned up in
most of the clerical causes which supported racial justice and nonviolence. He was chair of that American League against War and
Fascism which had momentarily seen Father Divine followers and
Communists in the same ranks.

In 1935 Mathews said he wanted to drop all " 'ifs,' 'ands', or   7:111
'buts' " in his previous defenses of the Soviet Union and, as he
said later, came to be as much a Communist Front man as was
anybody who never joined the party. In the same year he attacked
the Federal Council of Churches as being too bourgeois, much
too captive of the rich. With Fosdickian sentences he derided
Harry Emerson Fosdick for serving the Rockefellers: "Personally,
I dread the thought of collectivism which Russia represents as I
would dread the devil."

Later Mathews took a new job, switched sides again, sidled up   7:112
to the Rockefeller types, and, naturally, was attacked by the Communists even as he attacked them. Mathews soon took his insider's knowledge and his renegade passion and put them to work
against the Communist party and against clerics who held milder
versions of what he had once supported so fanatically. He became
a plum for Congressman Martin Dies, who was scouting for "un-
American" activities, and Mathews became a counsel to the committee when it pursued Communism in 1939.

In that setting he grilled Earl Browder in a scene in which one   7:113
cannot tell whether Browder was exaggerating for effect or mini-
mizing relations between the party and the clergy. Mathews
pressed Browder on his recall of the Union Seminary speech.
Would he now provide the names of Communist party clergy?
Browder said he could, but he would not. Then, under pressure,
the Communist leader admitted that he could not name a single
Catholic priest who was a member, but he claimed to know many
such Catholic laypeople. Under Matthews's questioning about
clergy Communists, Browder finally came up only with an unnamed "Holy Roller in the South." Not a single Methodist, Pres-

byterian, Congregationalist, or Quaker name came to mind. No Unitarian? "No. That is my old church. I have done very little work there." So that left only Baptists, presumably African-Americans, possibly to represent the cohort from which that lonely Holy Roller came. "Those are the only ones that I am sure of." There seemed to be no place for someone to go who would avoid the stigmatizing, jeopardizing character of party support. Since party membership was unattractive and almost out of the question, the choice had to be coalition-building or, in the most prominent institutional form in Depression times, what was called the United Front.

7:114   The United Front was designed to connect liberal clergy and other religious leaders with Communist fronts in a decade when many causes attracted both sets of people. Many of the fronts had international links or counterparts. American clergy always had to be wary, because in many cases Russian influence was dominant and because rank and file American sentiment was so anti-Communist that a misstep or something misspoken in this context could end a career. Ironically, while the fronts were designed to help the workers, it was only elites among Protestants who openly identified with them. Typical among these was the American League against War and Fascism, founded in 1932, a front which became attractive to some blacks and pacifist whites. It was when Communists disrupted a Madison Square meeting of the league in 1934 that Mathews resigned. And the *Christian Century* did its concluding, after the fiasco: "Seldom does contemporary life throw up a better example of the folly of trying to build a better world with no sounder ethic than that of expediency."

7:115   On rare occasions the pursuers of pro-Communist activists might stumble onto a figure like Winifred Chappell, a Methodist who was religiously committed to the Communist vision. She explicitly tried to impart her counsels to young people. In 1934 Chappell, anticipating the revolution that never came, went so far as to use a denominational magazine in order to urge young Methodists to "accept the draft, take the drill, go into the camps and onto the battlefield, or into the munitions factories and transportation work—but sabotage war preparations and war. Be agitators for sabotage."

7:116   Had a Dies Committee already then been active, it would there have found seditious language, but Chappell was not big enough game. In 1935 she joined Union Seminary professor and fellow Methodist Harry F. Ward in sending out eighteen Crisis Leaflets.

These spread the idea, then popular on the extreme left, that "it is increasingly clear that there is no middle ground between accepting the system and abolishing it"—at the precise moment when most Americans were putting energy into occupying and saving the middle ground. The right kept its eye on the Crisis Leaflets more than Methodist Federation members seemed to be swayed by them. The papers of William Randolph Hearst eagerly attacked, as did Methodism's arch-conservatives. They were ready with a name for this agency: "Marxist Federation for Social Strife." The Methodist General Conference as a supervising body looked on, seeming tolerant enough in 1936, but it did insist that the federation letterhead bear the word "Unofficial." The Conference did not need to monitor or chastise the federation. It lost followers during World War II and soon came to be regarded as patently beside the point—as, by then, was Chappell.

On center stage at United Front activities Professor Harry F. Ward played out his acts. In this strategic moment, he was the most important and most consistent cleric on the far left, the only professor who brought some intellectual substance to the bridging efforts, even as he created some embarrassment for more moderate leaders at New York's Union Theological Seminary. He became a passionate defender of things Soviet, and was always the first figure at whom Communist-hunters on clerical soil would point.   7:117

No one knows quite why the British born teacher developed such a passionate distaste for the American economic system in boom times as in bad ones. But he did nurture this revulsion until he expressed a "holy, impersonal hatred against an evil system that is wrecking human society." Nor is it known quite how Ward came to identify the Russian Communist experiment so closely with the ways of Jesus, but in 1931 he confirmed such an identification. In 1934 at the Second Congress of the American League against War and Fascism Ward did some counting. He was glad to see that 25 of 3,332 registered delegates "officially" represented the churches. He gloried in the accounts of league growth, which in 1939 claimed 7,836,691 members even though it probably had only 20,000 actual dues payers. In fact, the league never attracted more than 57 "religious delegates" at any of its five congresses. Only a few clerics were prominent. Some of them, like Harlem's Adam Clayton Powell, withdrew almost as quickly as they joined. Ward was left to keep the pro-Communist torch held high.   7:118

7:119   Professor Ward had already acquired a reputation for extreme leftism in the twenties, but the thirties seemed styled for him. He persistently set out to lead the Methodist Federation for Social Service leftward. The Union Seminary professor gave up on and came to despise old-style progressivisms. He was always sure that the New Deal did not go far enough to meet the problems of unemployment and bad labor conditions. In *Which Way Religion?* Ward employed modern biblical scholarship. He argued that the Bible provided an objective base for social reorganization. His big burden was to explain why in Christian America in the time of Communist progress elsewhere there was no attraction for the masses in a coalition of social Christianity and Communism. Like so many radicals of his day, Ward was an elitist who believed that he must find and develop a latent and talented leadership cadre to bring about revolutionary change.

7:120   The Methodist Federation *Bulletin* became a radical voice under Ward. He used its pages to monitor and comment on strikes, capitalism, domestic legislation, and world Communism. It was, however, no instrument for taking over the world. Few people received or read it, and with its frail base it constantly had to plead for funds and a hearing. Ward also used the paper to demonstrate some vestiges of liberal optimism in the days of disillusionment. Thus in 1933 he wrote, "This year is one in which a page of history has been turned." Liberals might have agreed with that when they drew on their progressive hopes as the New Deal might embody them. No, Ward went on to counter that expectation: "We have definitely entered the period of state capitalism." His *Bulletin* then pushed further. "To realize where this leads one must understand that state capitalism and economic Fascism are synonymous." The best hope in the mass middle class churches, he thought, was to "keep as many of the middle class as possible from going Fascist." For all the stir, even Ward rejected Leninism and, while not a pacifist, he also did not advocate violent revolution or overt class warfare.

7:121   Methodists Ward and Chappell kept looking for plausible and effective fronts for their work. Ward failed with the American League against War and Fascism. Chappell went so far as to work with Charles Foster of the Communist party, with which she identified herself. But almost no one who was so well positioned as they were followed the two in their pattern of uncritical support for the Soviet Union. In 1931 and 1932 Ward went to Russia and returned with enthusiasm for its social program. More important, he thought that in Russia he had learned to nurture a desire to remake a people. Ward never became a careful analyst of Marxist or Stalinist programs, and hard-core practitioners of Communism would have dismissed him as a visionary.

Ward the apologist tried to see the positive side of something like Jesuitism in the Marxist movement. "Communist organization is more like that of a religious order than a political party, also they both seek larger ends than the politicians." But the party was more moderate: "The Jesuits tortured and burned people for the good of their souls, the Communists ask them to live meagerly and discipline them in 'Isolated Communities' for the sake of a nobler society on earth." This, after the Stalinist cruelties were coming to be common knowledge. Ward saw the Jesuits as people who used the state to protect a religion and thus enhance church power. The Communists looked purer to Chappell; they were using the state, as she insisted, to enhance a social ideal.   7:122

Lenin, in Ward's most incredible stretching of things, was turned into an icon, a sort of religious figure. If they had not done so earlier, it was at this point that those who looked for balance between left and right would use the Union Seminary professor as a match or foil for the bizarre rightists, so out of touch with reality did he seem. Ward argued against those—and Union employed several of these—who in the prophetic tradition would see a danger of idolizing or enshrining the party. It was true, said Ward, that "history is full of cases in which a priesthood guarding a sacred truth has become the ruling power and finally more mighty than the truth itself, which it has then corrupted and destroyed." However, the Communist party, he was sure, would never do any thing like this. In fact, so directed was the party that it would one day work itself out of a job; as people grew in intelligence, party leadership would not be needed. "Stalin recognizes this."   7:123

Ward saved his derision for liberals, whom he considered timid. They did not offer what Communism did, the gift of "that which life has not had since the break up of the Middle Ages—a central purpose." The Middle Ages offered him a concept of the organic, of the social and communal living which could absorb the individual. The anthropology which the longtime Methodist was seeking he found in Communism. "It is certain that when the Communist view of man's relation to the cosmos appears it will interpret the universe in social, not personal terms."   7:124

Tracking Ward to the end means finding him unwilling to repudiate the Soviet ways even at the instant of shock and truth, at   7:125

the moment in August 1939, when Hitler and Stalin signed a mutual nonaggression pact. Only hard-core members of the Communist party could stomach that bond, and many of them lost heart, interest, and membership after it. A few United Front traveling fellows like Ward tried to put the best face on the pact, and he attempted to keep his faith blind to reality.

7:126   The league in its further course became increasingly divided, irrelevant, ready to fall apart. One late hurrah occurred on February 1, 1940, at a secret dinner. The league, having given the professor some tributes, listened to his apologies. No, Communists had never dominated the League, but they had been welcome in it. Ward kept making efforts to interpret Communist activities positively, something most Americans would not want to do again until the Second World War, when the Russians were allies. During the thirties, however, Ward played out his role as someone who brought religious perspective to support of much Communist policy and vision. His students and Methodist Federation partners took what they could from him. It is hard to know how many they were or how much they absorbed. Their movement was no match for those of the right, and the effects seemed few, and small.

Socialism: To Transform Capitalism through Non-Warlike Means

7:127   While Communists were scarce, Socialists were more numerous even as they were more moderate. Their position on the left makes them candidates for scrutiny here, even though they operated within the more public spectrum of politics, this time in ways that were analogous to responsible political conservatives of the time. The two best representatives were Kirby Page and Sherwood Eddy. Page mirrored the uncertainties of the age while he reflected the certainties of his own faith. He was secretary of what was then the Quaker Fellowship of Reconciliation and was also a leader in the new Fellowship for a Christian Social Order. He made his name as editor of the socialist-minded *World Tomorrow*. Page served his apprenticeship as a cleric-of-all trades on the conference circuit in the twenties. An economic naïf, he became inexpertly at home with plans for economic reorganization. No one doubted the dedication he brought from the horrors he had seen as a Y.M.C.A. agent with American troops in the war. Page revealed his cast of mind in 1924 when he described disciples in a way that defined his own purpose: "Every follower of Jesus is under obligations to obey the will of God regardless of where it leads and what it costs." Following Jesus meant rejecting war. At the turn of the decade, in *Jesus or Christianity*, Page followed through with the logic of its title. He argued that the world had not yet seen the ideals of Jesus lived out in human society.

Page was realistic where Ward was not; he could even lapse   7:128 into uncharacteristic pessimism. Domestically, he was not a supporter of violence to effect social change, and thus he parted company with the Communists. He had to ask himself, what might pacifists who would follow Jesus, no matter what, have to offer society? He had to say in the thirties that pacifism "is sufficient to demonstrate the *relative* advantages of this strategy [nonviolence] in contrast to revolution through civil war." Page went on: "The fact that the odds are heavily against victory in the effort to transform capitalism through non-warlike means does not invalidate this procedure," since "the barriers to triumph through violent seizure of power are far higher." Page knew the locales of such power in America, but he chose for himself some refuge in a position that was more satisfying within the sects or denominations than in the political order.

To partisan and doctrinaire Socialists, then, Page would look   7:129 only superficially congenial and in the eyes of the Communists his piety would make him seem foolish. At the same time, that piety enraged the right. They had no room for Page's saying something like this: "When the Lord's Prayer is prayed with insight, it becomes a petition for the abolition of capitalism." He was anything but a "Right Reverend New Dealer" like Monsignor John A. Ryan. When church people backed the New Deal, Page thought that their act constituted "betrayal of the basic principles of the Family of God on earth." He saw in it what many have come to see: that Roosevelt's program helped save the order which Page dismissed as capitalist. "Humanized slavery was not ethical," Page wrote, "and reformed capitalism must be recognized as utterly unacceptable to true followers of Jesus' way in life."

Even when it came to polling techniques, Page was naive. In   7:130 1934 he headed a group of clerics who sent a questionnaire to 100,499 ministers, 20,870 of whom stood up to be counted. Of these, 51 percent favored "drastically reformed capitalism," the New Deal being a moderate type of such drastic reform. Approximately 28 percent, or 5,879, chose socialism. Any critic of such polling would know that Page's was a self-selecting and biasing sample. The importance people could attach to this survey was that there *were* at least 5,879 clergy ready to be reckoned as Socialist. That number by itself need not have meant much. In 1932 the Rock River Conference of Northern Methodists in Illinois unanimously endorsed socialist-sounding resolutions. But their critics later pointed out that 86 percent of these delegates confessed to having gone on to vote for Herbert Hoover in that Depression year.

7:131   Sherwood Eddy often came paired with Kirby Page in listings of Protestant leaders who were of Socialist and pacifist bent but who were critics of Soviet Communism. Eddy and Page were obviously of the left, though they did not always deserve the capital L. Eddy, another Y.M.C.A. leader, made the requisite trips to Russia in the 1920s, but was less dazzled than Ward had been. He criticized the "class dictatorship" and the force the Soviets had used to pursue what he named, in their spirit, their "classless society of unbroken brotherhood, what the Hebrew prophets would have called a reign of righteousness on earth."

7:132   After his visit in 1930 Eddy wrote *The Challenge of Russia*, which was then regarded as one of the major surveys of the scene. This book showed him using more pale shades than did Page. The Russians, Eddy said, did not plan first to change human nature; they only would change the social situation. Then they hoped that a whole network of healthy motives could enable both the individual and society to function more effectively than did what he termed "the old capitalist profit motive which had commercialized and debased almost all human relations." So far, so good. But, he admitted, in Russia the individual was lost in the mass. He thought the United States had more of the right idea, but it had never lived into its vision.

7:133   With Page and many other Americans, Eddy cherished an organic vision of life which he saw partly realized overseas. "Russia has achieved what has hitherto been known only at rare periods in history, the experience of almost a whole people living under a unified philosophy of life. All life is focussed in a central purpose," and this Eddy admired. In fact, the vision was, in his eyes, religious. He said that it was impelled "by such powerful and growing motivation that life seems to have supreme significance." Where Eddy stepped back from Ward's brink was to see also the evils of Soviet life as being integral to Communism itself.

7:134   Along with a number of prominent individuals like Page and Eddy, there were also some harder-line leftist editors like Kenneth

Leslie, whose *Protestant Digest* came close to party-lining after 1938. And there were ephemeral groups like the National Religion and Labor Foundation, founded in 1932, and the United Christian Council for Democracy, which was formed in 1936. One must also note some efforts by far leftists to take over or infiltrate churchly movements, some of which were devoted to youth. The plot gets to be standard. Idealistic young people, some of whom had visited Russia, came together to denounce capitalism and Fascism but ended up being overpowered by a Communist presence.

The American Youth Congress best fit that plot. Its first meet-   7:135
ing in 1934 "allowed" some attenders to hold Sunday worship; the Communist faction could be at least grudgingly generous when bargaining was advisable. Word came with the permission: "This did not compromise the Communist youth and yet showed to the masses of religious youth that this was not a unified front against religion but against political reaction." Two years later some church groups came to the congress as groups. The National Council of Methodist Youth was prime among them. Leader of the anti-Communists among Methodist youth was Franklin H. Littell. He and the other reactors were outmaneuvered or overpowered in the meetings, but still Littell and his associates did not by any means acquiesce. The congress never turned out to be a stable or permanent organization. The pact between Stalin and Hitler took away whatever credibility was left, and the congress entirely disappeared.

The American Youth Congress with its Methodist youth in-   7:136
volvement was at least sufficiently suggestive of discontent with capitalism to be taken seriously. If only 123 out of 20,870 respondents in Kirby Page's poll called themselves Communist and if we can turn up only a handful of party members or fellow travelers, this does not mean that capitalism was home free in the New Deal experiment.

Some of the young Methodists passed around pledge   7:137
cards—who signed them? how many did? who knows?—which read: "I surrender my life to Christ. I renounce the Capitalistic system based on economic individualism and the profit motive and give myself to the building of an economic order based on cooperation and unselfishness." It also added, "I believe that the possession of wealth is unbecoming a Christian." One of the cards crossed the desk of a Missouri Synod Lutheran leader who was in the business of defending business and capitalism. He used

it to expose the corruption of liberal Protestantism. The example does reveal how some youth leaders on the left knew how to exploit Methodist piety and youthful discontent.

7:138   Some senior Methodists exemplified the confusions of the day. They were also often in the anticapitalist (though not pro-Communist) churchly vanguard. In 1932 the Northern General Conference bishops, weary of and frightened by economic collapse, called for the replacement of "our present policy of unplanned, competitive industrialism with a planned industrial economy." They settled instead for the New Deal. The present industrial order, agreed the conferees, "is unchristian, unethical and antisocial, because it is largely based on the profit motive which is a direct appeal to selfishness." And in Nashville the *Christian Advocate* editors wrote that "it is a soft and senseless sentimentalism that would ignore the necessity of coercion." The editors said that there were capitalists who were guilty of oppression and injustice toward the weaker members of society, and, said the magazine editors, "a gospel appeal would not reach [them] in a thousand years."

7:139   Such resolutions might not have converted many from the middle, but they did inspire reaction from the right. One sample was *Moscow over Methodism*, a reply of the Reverend Rembert G. Smith. He formed a Methodist League against Communism, Fascism, and Unpatriotic Pacifism. In Chicago on July 29, 1935, the league declared: "We are going to demand a settlement of the status of the Communist-influenced Methodist Federation for Social Service, and of clergymen and church officials who use their positions to preach Socialism and Communism." Members in the two Methodist extremes ended up pouring energies into fighting each other, thus preventing the formation of a Methodist bloc and adding a deep denominational fissure to the American landscape.

7:140   While liberal Protestants stumbled in their confusions, Catholics took their zealous anti-Communism along in a milder crusade against Socialism. Catholics provided huge majorities for the New Deal policies, but the mass of them supported nothing more radical than these. A few right-wing diocesan papers like the *Brooklyn Tablet* did find Communism to be in league with Roosevelt and the New Deal in the 1936 campaign. Reds, urged the editor of that paper, would expect much from Roosevelt after their help. Pius IX satisfied some American Catholic anti-Communists when he told a visitor in 1930 to be careful lest Depression unemployment lead to Communist growth. *Brooklyn Tablet* editor

Patrick Scanlan disagreed with Catholic social liberals when they argued that the method to use for keeping Communism at bay was to reform capitalism. No, he countered, Communism was simply a direct import, "mostly by Russian aliens," who should be deported, after which this Red Peril would end.

The bishops showed more equanimity. In 1938, however, the   7:141
hierarchs felt a need to warn against "the spread of subversive teachings" and "the audacity of subversive action in our country." Fort Wayne's Bishop John F. Noll began to wonder whether the debates over movements on the right and the left were marked by so many strenuous efforts at balance that Communism seemed to be growing more credible in the comparisons. There was, Noll said, "such a vigorous campaign against Fascism in the American press," furthered by numerous organizations of men and women, that the attention of the people had been "at least temporarily withdrawn from the even greater evil of communism."

Little remained of the religious left's defense of Russia after   7:142
the Stalinist pact with Hitler in 1939. There were then few reasons for anyone to remain romantic about Soviet promise. The Communist fronts dwindled. On August 26 that year the American League for Peace and Democracy, in a classic case of bad timing, three days after the pact-signing, tried to collect 5,000 people at a New York rally. Not one-tenth that number came, though the *Daily Worker* claimed that 8,000 marched. Harry F. Ward was not there, and it was left to Thomas L. Harris, who was on his way out of the Episcopal ministry, and to William B. Spofford, Sr., another of the extremely far-left clerics, to speak. Spofford was bewildered by the circumstances, but he did urge hearers to think that Stalin was perhaps being a master strategist. American Civil Liberties Union leader Roger Baldwin and other stalwarts left the league, which met for the last time on February 1, 1940.

Nonreligious Communists like Earl Browder and William Z.   7:143
Foster kept changing their tack to meet the winds, but they saw constant desertion from their ranks. In October, Mike Gold was still trying to claim that there had been less demoralization among fellow travelers than the capitalist press claimed. But the ex-Unitarian minister Granville Hicks, who was known for bringing a Protestant conscience to Communism, told *New Republic* readers in considerable detail why he was deserting the fold entirely. In such literature Communism increasingly came to be "the God that failed." Literary critic Malcolm Cowley wrote that it had been impossible even to keep intact a letterhead for the American

League for Peace and Democracy; the people who owned most names on it had disappeared from the ranks. The Dies Committee pursued "Un-American Activities" undaunted, but had trouble finding enough organizations resembling the American Youth Congress to make tracking efforts worthwhile.

7:144   Unitarian minister John Haynes Holmes of New York managed to be most eloquent even as he was eating crow for his old left commitments. On January 21, 1940, Holmes preached "Why We Liberals Went Wrong on the Russian Revolution." The Russian experience, he said, was "the supreme disillusionment of my life." Holmes added, "I have been deceived, deluded and disgraced—sold out by those I trusted most; and I am as deeply afflicted as I am utterly disgusted by what has happened." He faulted himself and his fellows for not having properly read the signs of the times. Liberals, in their concern to fight economic injustice, he said, had permitted evils to go on which "in our own hearts we knew to be wrong." Sometimes "we" had fallen to doctrines which hold that the end justifies the means. It was the Hitler-Stalin pact which, as Holmes saw it, stripped away the last veils of self-deception from the eyes of liberals, and set them "steadfastly against the cruel and bloody regime which they should have uncovered years before." Now, at last, he concluded, "Russia is forever spewed out of our mouths." Quaker A. J. Muste brought perspective: "Perhaps the immediate lesson for Americans and all Christians to take to heart is that democracy cannot work in harness with either Fascism or Communism." Those therefore had done well, he said, who shut their ears "to the clamor of Coughlinites, Bundists, Kluxers, et al., who seek to pin the label of Communism on anything or anybody they don't like, and also to the clamor of Communists and others who fling the epithet Fascist or Nazi at anyone who differed with them." So he and many like him were free to shut their ears. There were, after all, some other more credible voices which beckoned for a hearing in dark times.

8

The Age of Realism

Religious Realism, Christian Realism, and Realistic Theology

The decisive battles of the Fundamentalist-Modernist civil   8:1
war in the mainstream Protestant denominations ended before the
Depression. The winning Modernist, now called liberal, faction
found no time to enjoy its victory. A second division within the
Protestant house followed at once. This conflict helped keep the
original-stock Protestants from strengthening their claim to be
the privileged people who should define and interpret American
religion in culture. They never fully recovered from the double
blows. The story of this second struggle, familiar in theology
books, is often overlooked in cultural history. The noise of conflict sounded in classrooms and saw print in editorials and books
where the battlers in pulpits, pews, and agencies went to get their
signals. The books demonstrate that American religion in the Depression years was more than a scene of bombast and demagoguery, of extremism from left and right, of microphones and crowds
and statistics. The decade was a period of rare creativity, a time
for ideas and for books which offer a feast for the thoughtful.

Realistic Theology, Professor Walter Marshall Horton of Ober-   8:2
lin proposed to call this new school, in a book title of 1934. Seven

303

years later, *Christian Realism* turned up as a book title by Union Theological Seminary's John Bennett in New York. H. Richard Niebuhr and Reinhold Niebuhr, the American born titans, were at home with the term. So was Paul Tillich, the most profound and celebrated immigrant from the European theological scene, who started making his American mark in the thirties. Catholics and Jews who did not use the term matched the concept. The age of realism had arrived.

8:3   Walter Marshall Horton marked the moment: "The Age of Realism is not ringing with the strains of *Ein' Feste Burg*, nor accompanying the 'march of Progress' with triumphant *Te Deums.*" Horton was being realistic: partisans, he observed, were not singing triumphant songs like "A Mighty Fortress" or always confidently talking to God in the classic Christian hymn of praise. Still, Horton alerted his peers: "A change has come over the spirit of our times, and the old faiths and hopes no longer carry conviction, when stated in the old terms." The old faiths about which this thinker with impeccable liberal traditions and original-stock Protestant lineage spoke, were not antique visions of life. He was referring instead to his own mainstream Protestantism, which was supposed to have triumphed when it routed Fundamentalism. Horton dismissed that controversy on page 1.

8:4   Liberalism, Horton accurately remembered, had until very recently still been self-confident and aggressive. It held that all truth and value belonged in a single harmonious system, and that the Bible and science were mutually consistent parts of it. Liberalism's thinkers contended that the great task of Christian thought was the restating of the Christian gospel in terms acceptable to the modern mind. Fundamentalists took fright at some of the consequences of this attempt. The liberals rejected the Fundamentalists as fossils. Modernists wore the wounds inflicted by Fundamentalists as badges of honor. They were sure it was possible to be at once thoroughly modern and thoroughly Christian. But now, by 1934, the liberal self-assurance was gone.

8:5   Who *was* winning in this partisan warfare? Liberals should have been, but now they were criticizing each other more violently than they did reactionaries. John Bennett as a fellow heir of liberalism put it savagely: "The most important fact about contemporary American theology is the disintegration of liberalism." Indeed, Horton had to say: "The defeat of the liberals is becoming a rout. Harried by the fundamentalists on the right flank and the humanists on the left," as they were in Horton's eyes, liberals had a hard time of it intellectually. They simply kept living off morale left over from their headier days.

Horton slipped into the third person when speaking of liberals: 8:6 "Now their morale has cracked, rebellion and desertion are rife within their ranks." Something profound had gone wrong. But something strong and new was appearing and must continue to prosper. The *Realistic Theology* which Horton discerned and described offered the best hope. And he had to talk in the language of hope both as a confessing Christian and as someone who cared about addressing Western and American civilization.

New voices would offer *realistic* theology? One can hear a 8:7 contemporary of Horton and Bennett protesting: in the midst of the grayness of the Depression and in the shadow of war clouds which were gathering over Europe, how marketable was a religious message which stressed realism? Would not there be a better market for the preaching of promise and illusion, of fantasy and hope, as the escapist cinema of the day was doing? And offer realistic *theology*? How could talk about theology belong to a realistic assessment of the time? Real shakers and movers in the thirties, one thinks, had to be economists and political scientists, arms manufacturers and organizers of bread lines, those concerned with things one could see and touch. Theology belongs to ivied classroom buildings, ivory-towered studies, and unread journals. Theology was the work of one caste of religious professionals, most of whom were exiled to divinity schools at the edges of universities. Theology was about millennia-old texts and issues. Such issues were certainly irrelevant to the present real world.

Decades after original-stock Protestantism lost its place of 8:8 dominance, it is hard to grasp the potential of religious thought in the America of that day. The historian of religion, knowing that not even most church people read theology, has an instinct to be restrained, to be ready to foresee the limits of theology. It would be a distortion to picture Herbert Hoover's cabinet members rising in the morning to see what Oberlin and Union Seminary thinkers were saying, in order to assess their stocks. At high noon, the Roosevelt brain trust would have on its mind the National Recovery Act or the Agricultural Adjustment Administration, not the writings of Swiss theologian Karl Barth or those of the American brothers Reinhold and H. Richard Niebuhr. Toward evening, if a person of culture would choose to curl up with a book, a realistic novel by Willa Cather (on Horton's list as such) or books by people named Hemingway or Faulkner or Steinbeck would be more credible choices than Reinhold Niebuhr's realistic *Moral Man and Immoral Society*. But just as it would be grotesque to oversell the place of theology, it would be folly to underestimate its impact within certain spheres.

8:9   The Hortons and the Bennetts, the Niebuhrs and the Tillichs, meanwhile, aspired to be public theologians. They stood in a tradition which connected ancient texts and traditions with modern life. They employed the language of faith to address a public also beyond the churches. They used their grasp of the word of God to interpret the life of a people. The most profound thinkers functioned almost as novelists or artists do. They offered discernments which might pass by those who encounter only the surface of popular culture. On such a scene, Horton's tract for the times speaks forcefully.

8:10   He told of some thinkers at Yale and Chicago who in 1931 held a symposium on a theme which became a book title, *Religious Realism*. It was an early sign of the trend that quickly advanced. Europeans were also exporting something they called variously crisis theology, theology of the Word, or neoorthodoxy. In postwar Germany, most of all, they reacted fifteen years earlier against romanticism, optimism, and liberalism. The unspeakable horror of pointless trench warfare between 1914 and 1918 and then the unsettled life of the Weimar Republic in the 1920s led serious articulators of progressive humanistic and optimistic Christian thought alike to make an about-face. Imported works by antiliberals such as Karl Barth witnessed to the voice of a transcendent God. This God addressed human affairs in ways that seemed to deny the culture's own frames of reference. There dared be no "triumphant nationality," no "national church," no pride in being of the original stock, among those who listened to such a word. No one could take this God captive.

8:11   The realist reaction came to America with the Depression and the specter of overseas totalitarianisms. To meet the demands of this new age, the moderate Professor Horton expected realists to acknowledge their own liberal roots and retrieve what was good from them. "Quitting the camp of liberalism for the camp of realism," the Oberlin professor worried, could otherwise be merely fashionable and faddish. But they also had to reject much. Liberalism had largely become "politically inept, sociologically shallow, psychologically stupid." Those words provoked at a time when liberals still occupied fashionable pulpits, tenured chairs, and editorial posts in Protestantism.

Horton cited John Bennett, who earlier in 1933 had asked "After Liberalism—What?" Horton sensed in Bennett's essay and elsewhere "a great ground-swell of new life in the general 'realistic' tendency of our times." He pointed also to Paul Tillich and his talk not about *mere* realism but "belief-ful Realism." With the Niebuhrs and so many others, Horton found himself also moving politically to the left but theologically to the right. The movement was toward social radicalism on the one hand and Christian neoorthodoxy on the other. Neoorthodoxy, partly a European import, stressed the transcendence of God, the limits of the human, and the crisis of decision. As he looked both ways, Horton hoped that in that shared tension former conservatives and former liberals might find more in common than they used to expect to find. Of course, the right with a capital R and the left with a capital L would not meet. But many thoughtful people between these camps were looking for a new standard.   8:12

Writers on "realistic theology" or "Christian realism" took pains to define their school. Realism suggests, "above all, a resolute determination to face all the facts of life candidly, beginning preferably with the most stubborn, perplexing, and disheartening ones, so that any lingering romantic illusions may be dispelled at the start." That was only the start; "then, *through* these stubborn facts and not *in spite* of them, to pierce as deep as one may into the solid structure of objective reality, until one finds whatever ground of courage, hope, and faith is *actually* there, independent of human preferences and desires, and so casts anchor in that ground." This condensed language Horton and his cohorts unpacked in books, articles, and sermons; on programs and platforms and political stages, until its brunt came to be easily recognized, its effects felt.   8:13

The noise of conflict increased when the liberals and humanists started to reply. Some charged their colleagues with defeatism; the times demanded hope. What business did Reinhold Niebuhr have in giving new currency to the old concept of original sin? His approach was the last thing that a depressed culture needed. To Horton, such accusations were misinformed. Beyond mere realism, he contended, this camp was seeking "a sure ground of hope, a Gospel for the poor in spirit." Its members were shedding liberal illusions—a favorite word—and did not care if they had   8:14

to borrow terms from older orthodoxy. Let the liberals shed what they carried from yesterday.

8:15   "Yesterday" meant the liberal hour, when Modernists were dominant. Listen to the realists accurately describing the human predicament: They first recognized *the enemy within*, our *finitude* and *ignorance*; no one could get rid of these. Next, they faced *the enemy around*. This included the *self-reproducing power of unjust institutions*. In this context realists could say that in selective ways "Karl Marx is right . . . " about this critique or that. Third, there was *the enemy beyond*. The human predicament related thus to *sin*.

8:16   Realists as well as liberals used events in public life to mark their moves. March 4, 1933, was one of these. Americans that day laid to rest the ghost of indecision and found leadership to help them begin to do something about their plight. That date, the inauguration of Franklin D. Roosevelt, signaled something of note: many realists could work with the New Deal. Horton could find no correlate cheer in churchly activity. "There is every reason to expect a revival of religion in times like these, but somehow it does not come." Hard times did not deliver what people used to expect of them.

8:17   Even March 4, 1933, could not offer utopia to a realist. Against the screen of eternity, Horton went on, "*there is very little in our present social order that naturally suggests the Providence of God.*" It was blasphemy to picture God as one of the well-to-do rulers of the present social system. To do so, cried Horton, was to pave the way for atheistic revolt. Yet religious and political conservatives had committed just such blasphemy when they connected God with normalcy, which they had been doing in the decade of the twenties. Now there must be drastic change in human institutions before the work of God's will and God's providence could be visible. Those forces of God might just possibly be more visible in the energies which would demolish the corrupt social order than in those which would preserve its crumbling institutions.

8:18   To no one's comfort, Horton warned that even in the Depression America had not yet reached bottom. The "bumptious, over-confident spirit of our youthful nation," he said, had to be humbled in some fiery furnace of suffering. Happily, some religious thinkers were turning to the Bible more than to science to get more accurate pictures of human nature and destiny. The age of scientific precision in theology was over at last. The age of social action had arrived. And unless theology could issue in what he termed full-blooded convictions that were at least as capable of inspiring religious fervor and social passion as were the convictions of the Nazis and the Communists, the theologians might as well shut up shop and admit defeat.

Any right-thinking calculator of such odds would have given   8:19
up on the churches. When only the old liberal churches came to mind, the realists were ready to give up. Horton accused the churches: they "have no corporate life, no common consciousness; they are collections of religious individuals, each carrying on his private and peculiar type of commerce with God but occasionally gathering for worship in the same place, where they may listen to some exceptionally gifted preacher air his private religious opinions—after which they go their separate ways as before." Horton dropped his mild manners: liberal church leaders reminded him of stolid Stoics or esoteric Neo-Platonists listening to pagan philosophers, not early Christians assembled for a love feast. From those first Christians, latter-day believers should have learned to leave the world to become members of the new society, not to be mere listeners to sermons. "Modern liberal Protestantism cannot be said, by any stretch of the imagination, to have 'left the world.' " It was *pagan.*

Liberals had taken the central spiritual figure of the culture,   8:20
Jesus, and adapted him to normalcy. The realists posed Jesus over against the times not as a teacher, example, or moralist. They offered what to them was a distinctive account of the basic transaction between God and humans. With the cross of Christ, a permanent change took place in the relations between God and humans. A power that had not been released before was now available. And a new social organism developed over against the forces of darkness. "This social organism *was not here* before." Those were fighting words to Protestant individualists, but Horton and his colleagues were ready for fights. Let them be dismissed as holding medieval Catholic or organismic views of the church; something had to happen, they thought, to restore the biblical picture of churchly solidarity. But the church, as the Oberlin theologian kept reminding anyone who was ready to listen, did not exist for itself. "*It is characteristic of the experience of divine grace to feel the impulse to share it even if the price of sharing is persecution.*"

It would have been arrogant and ignorant, thought Horton, to   8:21
see the church as the *only* channel through which the grace of

God flowed. In a public theology God's message had to impinge on every institution, religious or secular. The church was to bring out "the divine spark in other institutions, other movements, and *other religions.*" The church entered into commerce with all of these, even if the message of full truth was embodied in Jesus Christ. The church, the author argued, entered into commerce with other agencies. Horton could not let all dreams die: "What a burst of flame might come from Nationalism and atheistic Communism if the Christian Church dared to go to Calvary in their midst!"

8:22   The manifestos for realistic theology, just like those for liberalism, sooner or later, and usually sooner, addressed the social order. Even what Christians called "*the foolishness of preaching,*" could at its best serve the common good, argued Horton. Churchly missions and charities helped meet acute forms of human distress. The organized church generated creative spin-offs and orders like the Fellowship of Reconciliation and the Fellowship of Socialist Christians. The church of realist vision and stamp could train politicians not to expect the millennium but to work pragmatically instead in order to help bring in the highest degree of justice.

8:23   To make his strongest point in this context, Horton again reached for italics, just as once he must have all but shouted the words in his lectures at Newton Seminary in 1934: the church's "*proper sphere is precisely the sphere of the mind and will, collective as well as individual; and she is as competent, in a crisis, to convert a nation's soul as to convert an individual's.*" To convert a nation's soul: ten years earlier the liberal theologians were trying to find how to *preserve* Protestant, Anglo-Saxon America, with its privileged churches, and through education to transform it more into the shape of the coming Kingdom of God. They had fought back then against Catholics and all comers, including eventually their own Fundamentalist flank, with the nation's soul at issue. Now a new school of thinkers and agitators was insistent that that fallen soul needed basic conversion.

The Church against the World

8:24   While some of the realists rolled up their sleeves, got their hands dirty, did some sweating, joined organizations, worked to support organized labor, gathered petitions, and ran for public

office—Reinhold Niebuhr was the exemplar on that circuit—
most of them did what theologians and preachers are called to do:
they taught and wrote and spoke. Their world was one of books
which remain available for inspection. No other manifesto captured their spirit as well as a modest blue-covered volume significantly titled *The Church Against the World*.

Of its three authors, Francis Pickens Miller was the layperson.   8:25
He was also the youngest and most angry. A ruling elder in southern Presbyterianism, he was chair of the World Student Christian
Federation. His travels helped him observe militant nationalisms
close up and he used them to measure America in the time after
Senator and then President Harding had spoken of "triumphant
nationality." What did it produce? Miller regarded the modern
versions to be utter denials of the Christian faith. He assailed the
liberalism of the past generation and the conservatism of his own
for supporting religious nationalism in America. In Germany it
took demonic, in America threatening, forms. He charged that
the foremost educators, philosophers, and theologians had here
created the environment for this form of denial of faith. For him,
American Protestantism in the liberal age and the culture of normalcy was culturally as captive as was the German Protestantism
of his time or, ironically, one has to say, as was European Catholicism when the Reformation began. Ironically, that is, if his charge
was in any way true, because in the 1930s these two references
pointed to the least attractive conceivable models of what original-stock American Protestants thought that they themselves were
or wanted to be.

A church against the world, Miller argued, dared not depend   8:26
upon a common Western culture. For that matter, no such coher-
ent culture was even available. Despite what liberals said, "as far
as this century is concerned and the centuries which immediately
follow"—and here came a line that was heretical in the zone of
liberal hopes—"no world culture is emerging or will emerge."
The very notion of one would have sounded simply fantastic, said
the brash young Miller, had it not been associated with the names
of eminent recent Protestant leaders. It is stunning to realize from
his manifesto, representative as it was of the new voices, how
suddenly a hard-won cultural synthesis and dream had been shattered for many Protestant leaders.

The federating churches expected a new world-order, but this   8:27
head of the World Student Christian Federation spoke only of a
forthcoming world disorder. The passions and ambitions of mu-

tually hostile collectivities were developing in 1935. Miller discerned that the main force was "the self-centered nation-state living in fear and jealousy of its neighbors." Mutual dissimilarities and animosities produced the violent accents of the day. Science, technology, and industrialism were no aids for producing order. Japan and Russia, for example, had both invested in technology and turned out to be not convergent but further apart than before.

8:28   Protestantism's witness made it appear exposed and defenseless in the face of national cultures. All realists knew that inherited Protestantism was being destroyed before their eyes. Its proponents huddled for refuge within their national cultures; Miller saw them doing this whenever German, British, and American Christian students convened. Fifty years earlier things may have been different, he thought, but now one set of people had almost no communication with another in the matter of faith. The degradation of Protestantism marked the United States as much as any other Protestant land.

8:29   "Is American Religion Christian?" This question asked by young Miller sounded more devastating in 1935 than it would years later. Until shortly before he asked it, the cultural core of this religion, the dominant brand of Protestantism, had still been arguably intact. Miller, in answering his own question with a "no" was pointing to a self-inflicted wound or inflicting one of his own. He pushed further than his seniors had done, seeming to want to shatter the bonds of common defense of the Protestant culture which someone like André Siegfried thought still held American power as late as 1927.

8:30   Miller knew both the result of the Protestant civil war and the strategy Protestants used to defend their dominance. Perhaps he had causes like Prohibition or opposition to a Catholic candidacy for president in mind when he wrote that there were "bitter family quarrels within the community, but when American Protestantism itself is called in question both fundamentalists and modernists instantly forget their differences and rally to its defense." Too many in both camps still simply assumed the stability of the Protestant foundations. They looked at developments in Germany with a spirit which said "it can't happen here." Yet those Protestant foundations in America were crumbling for the same reasons they did in Europe or anywhere. Degradation, though it appeared to be subtle, was as advanced in the United States as in the situation of any other old national Protestant church.

Three centuries of development had come to an end, said the   8:31
prescient young Protestant of some trends which many at that time
overlooked and which others refused to see for years to come. "A
process which began with a culture molded by religious faith has
ended with a religious faith molded by a national culture." Miller
noted that while the Protestant synthesis was fragmenting, there
were people ready with substitutes for it, none of which were
attractive. He took on the century's most notable public philosopher, John Dewey. Two years earlier that sage had spoken of and
written *A Common Faith*, and Miller had done his homework with
that book. Now he had to address this humanist faith. In brash
young Mr. Miller's eyes, Dewey, "the outstanding liberal of his
generation," was the "high priest of the movement which is preparing the way in the United States for a national religion as opposed to the Christian religion." Could any other Christian realist
be more arrogant or more trenchant than was Miller when he
charged that Dewey's "philosophy and his religion have laid substantial foundations for the American equivalent of the Nazi religion in Germany"? Dewey, under Miller's gaze, had chosen to
replace "conscience" with "imagination" in religion and public
life. In that way he provided what the young man termed the
"humanist's equivalent for the authority which the theist finds
in God."

Imagination could only provide the basis for a common na-   8:32
tional faith or a class faith, never a common universal one. In the
language of the Niebuhrs, Miller observed that such an imagination "invariably reflects the dominant social forces in which the
individual is interested." Thus the normal thing to expect of a
German child was Nazi faith; only through grace might faith in
Christ transcend that corruption. But John Dewey's world, according to Miller, was one in which a philosopher could still see
human beings as naturally good and productive of their own values. Therefore grace had a harder time of it. *A Common Faith*
consequently turned out to be "the very stuff out of which religions like the Nazi religion are eventually compounded." Ten
years earlier even somewhat critical Protestant liberals still had
been courting Dewey, citing him as a partner, taking lessons from
him. Realism exacted its price, at the expense of civility.

The Depression years, then, gave evidence that the time was   8:33
past for developing a cultural synthesis with liberal religion as a
prime component. Realists did carry on conversations with
leaders of the humanist culture, all the way over to the heirs of

Karl Marx, but they wanted to be sure that all contenders knew the terms and the stakes in such dialogue. For Miller, the price was high. Dewey, in that context, summed up what Miller named "the present stage of development of American culture" and, worst of all, thought his young critic, "his influence within the Protestant church is perhaps as great as it is without the church."

8:34   When Miller looked at world Christianity from an American base, he went on to attack Chicago professor Archibald Baker, who wanted to export Dewey's humanism to the world missions field. For Baker, religion was "a phase of cultural development, and missions one aspect of a more general process of culture interpenetration." This idea horrified Miller, who saw how profoundly such a liberal culture conditioned any religious person who allowed himself or herself to be vulnerable to its lures. Miller could overlook obvious foes like religious fundamentalists in order to say that Dewey and Baker merely illustrated "what is perhaps the most significant trend in the contemporary thought of the American Protestant community."

8:35   Even a brusque agitator could provide calming words, and Miller finally used some in order to find a few positive signs of the times. He knew that some heroic Christian groups were trying to go against the trends. With some hope he pointed to worldwide ecumenical conferences at Lausanne, Stockholm, and Jerusalem, where advance guard American Christians met with Christians from elsewhere, people who with them hoped to transcend national faiths. For such gatherings, Christians would be foolish to bring along Dewey's *Common Faith*. The ecumenical ambassadors, as Miller prescribed, had to forgo all interests related to the realization of the special ends of their American national culture. "And paradoxical though it may seem," added Miller, it would be only as American Christians were faithful to the Christian, not the national, frame of reference "that any culture worthy of the name" might survive in America. William Adams Brown's idea of a national church was now in ashes.

8:36   The second author who posed *The Church Against the World* was a recent migrant from Germany, Professor Wilhelm Pauck, now at Chicago Theological Seminary. He used both his European and his professorial credentials to add to Miller's case. Pauck brought the freshness of his own youthful participation in the European movements of crisis theology to fight against the humanism and liberalism in which his generation had been nurtured. Protestant liberals would have united with humanism, but it was to Pauck an enemy more dangerous than any in the past. The current form of humanism was an "atheistic movement which claims to cultivate moral ideals of the same value as those defended by the church." What, then, would serve for rescue from such emphases in America? Pauck addressed the question with a survey of resources. He had arrived too late to take part in the theological controversy of the twenties, but he recognized the parties in the aftermath. This new immigrant took backward glances at the Fundamentalists and regarded them more seriously than did most realists. He found good reason to visit old battlefields.

Pauck chided colleagues who either casually or with fore-   8:37
thought overlooked those intransigent antimoderns. It was "certainly neither sane nor wise intentionally to ignore an existing historical fact." Fundamentalism may have been pushed into the shadows or off to the margins, as many liberals thought, but the existing historical fact was that it still thrived. "The number of Christians who consider themselves members of this group is so remarkably large that it must startle the innocent outsider." Pauck wanted believers to pay attention to these folk who cultivated their Christian traditionalism "with a loyalty as curious as it is admirable." Still, the fundamentalist sections of the church puzzled him because they did not appear to be sufficiently or profoundly disturbed by the fact that, in his words, "the modern world runs along without paying more than slight attention to their voices." They had chosen seclusion from the world, and were getting what they wanted.

If Pauck's half-admiration at this point verged on something   8:38
that sounded like *mere* admiration, it did not prepare readers well for what came next. The ex-German went on vehemently to dismiss the theology of the Fundamentalists. Some people thought their movement might be able and willing to face the spiritual crisis of the day. In Pauck's accusation, their single method was wholly negative and thus inadequate. Such a charge must have surprised liberals and humanists who had good reason to think of *The Church Against the World* as purely negative. But Pauck defined the situation differently. Fundamentalism's method "consciously ignores the fact of crisis and suggests to the church that it continue in its tested course of the past while resolutely refusing to consider the causes and forces which have produced the modern critical conditions." Pauck's eyes were open to the power of Fundamentalism, but he bridled when he saw how it missed the point and engaged in false advertising. And Pauck, like Miller,

would insist that he spoke dialectically and that along with criticism he had a positive intention.

8:39   With Fundamentalism disposed of, Pauck took with realist zest to his own attack on humanism and Protestant Modernism. Humanists, who represented what Pauck called secularized religion, received only a moment's notice. They left out of their thinking the one element which could break the circle of human self-preoccupation: God. Frankly, because humanism ignored the most profound human problem, the *why* of existence, it could not even be a candidate for meeting the crisis. Church worriers had foreseen secular thought as their great rival, but it had consistently failed.

8:40   Optimistic liberalism, however, was an entirely different candidate for rivalry. Pauck brought with him from Germany the kind of eyes which led him to notice how liberal theologies were matters of practice in the privileged churches. He summarized the main movements of the decade past. In pursuit of the Kingdom of God, he pointed his finger, "certain American churches consider themselves to be integral parts of society," and thus to be agents in "the cause of a holy society." Well and good, but along the way they had become captive of social scientists, sociologists, and social planners. They let others set the agenda for the church. Where was God in all this?

8:41   Modernism, Pauck's code word for liberal Protestantism as preached in those privileged churches, failed in the present crisis. It talked about God, but, the professor said, it had lost God. Just as tellingly, he went on, Modernism "thought and acted on the basis of the existent church," as if it were able to take that church for granted. True, in its apology and defensiveness the church would still always go back to Jesus, and its leaders could still point to the church as a reasonably healthy and strong institution. But Modernism always and only ended with a search, a quest, and never with a bold witness. It offered no defense against the crisis of religion in a time when no one could any longer take the survival and role of the church for granted. Once again, the old idea of a "national church" was doomed.

8:42   H. Richard Niebuhr, of the Yale Divinity School, was the third critic who posed *The Church Against the World*. A towering ethical thinker and a theologian who, many said, outclassed his better-known brother, Reinhold, when it came to formal thought, he was the son of a Missouri pastor in the Evangelical and Reformed traditions. The German background of his church and his training at its Elmhurst College and Eden Theological Seminary in that tradition meant that Niebuhr was never quite so at home as were many of his colleagues who were of the original-stock heritage represented by Yale. He and his brother also drew on some different resources than did Protestant leaders in most of the standard churches with their English backgrounds. Thus H. Richard found European Continental thought especially congenial, and brought an angle of vision half-way toward Pauck's in respect to the American religious environment.

In H. Richard Niebuhr's early major book, often thought of as   8:43
a classic and certainly a pioneering effort to bring social scientific thought to bear on American theology, he placed the accent on *The Social Sources of Denominationalism.* In that work of 1929 Niebuhr displayed familiarity with environmental influences on the faith along with a readiness to remain some distance from the mainstream of Protestantism. He had seen the shamefully divided and warring American denominations, as he described them, progressively turning over to others the tasks of developing effective morale and providing moral structure in society. But these other forces also turned out not to have much depth. They placed too heavy a premium on material acquisition or success and on national and racial prestige. Such churches almost inevitably adopted what appeared to Niebuhr to be a style identified with "the psychologically more effective morale of the national, racial, and economic groups with which they are allied."

As he looked on, Niebuhr came to describe these churches   8:44
more as cheerleaders than as players: they usually joined in the "'Hurrah' chorus of jingoism, to which they add the sanction of their own 'Hallelujah.'" In just a few lines Niebuhr reviewed their tribal experience in the twenties. Such churches abandoned Christian ethics as they excluded the Orientals from the privileges enjoyed by Occidental racial groups. They especially created disabilities for the Negro. Their leaders also engaged "in the fulsome praise of the superior qualities of Nordic tribes," and thus showed themselves "no less contrary to the ideals of the Nazarene and to the spirit of community he founded" than any one else.

Now in 1935 Niebuhr pleaded for the cultural independence of   8:45
the church. He added attacks on two more subjects: capitalism and industrialism, both of which could easily become idolatries. Private ownership of property had its place, but in the present

system, Niebuhr deduced, "no antithesis could be greater than that which obtains between the gospel and capitalist faith." Jesus in his proclamation posed faith in God over against the god Mammon. In a charge that positioned Niebuhr and the realists at a far remove from the world of Bruce Barton or Roger Babson, he concluded that Protestantism in America bowed down to Mammon. As for what had come of Harding's "triumphant nationality" and William Adams Brown's "national church," things had gone astray. Modern nationalism regarded the nation itself "as the supreme value, the source of all life's meaning, as an end-in-itself and a law to itself." A note of cheer somehow broke through: Niebuhr discerned the beginning of a revolt in the church against "the 'world' of contemporary civilization and against the secularized church."

8:46   In 1935 he saw this revolt to be still an infant movement, often emotional, confused, and guilty of making the wrong alliances with partners outside the church. Niebuhr was wary of those who simply allied the faith with radical movements on the left or the right, those who found salvation in either Christian socialism or Christian nationalism. Christians who made such alliances had to be in conflict with each other. Niebuhr knew all about family quarrels and civil wars. "For if it is a frequent experience that common antagonism is confused with common loyalty, it is also well known that allies are prone to fight among themselves because of their variant interests." Niebuhr called instead only for common "loyalty to God and to Jesus Christ."

8:47   The Yale professor revisited these themes in a book two years after he published the essay in *The Church Against the World*; this one turned out to be a classic interpretation of *The Kingdom of God in America*. In it Niebuhr paid less attention than he had in 1929 to analysis based on social class and spent more energies on witness to God and to Jesus Christ in American history. He started right off by quoting once more, and making a kind of text of, André Siegfried's view of Protestantism as America's "only national religion." Niebuhr then went on to reduce talk about American Catholicism to one bibliographical footnote. He spoke of Judaism not at all. There was no trace of reference to John Dewey's "common faith," no citing of American public religion, no reference to humanism. Remarkably, even to the Fundamentalists Niebuhr gave notice in less than one line.

8:48   Instantly, instead, he lunged for the Protestant core culture.

"American Christianity and American culture," Niebuhr was bold to say, "cannot be understood at all save on the basis of faith in a sovereign, living, loving God." For that reason—and here he sounded like Francis Pickens Miller jabbing at John Dewey— "apart from God and his forgiveness nationality and even Christianity particularized in a nation become destructive rather than creative." The theologian knew, of course, that Christianity was not purely spiritual; religious witness had to be institutionalized. Such an organizational trend was necessary, inevitable, but also a costly reality. And just as inevitably one found it accompanied by nationalization. Citizens then directed attention to lures of the nation and thus to themselves, therewith turning "from aggression and confession to defense and apologetic." The old and still valid idea of a chosen people of God now, he said, became corrupted into a chosen nation concept. At this point he scored the idolatry of the Anglo-Saxon race and the rise of religious imperialism.

On his final pages Niebuhr presented a condensed realist interpretation of contemporary America. Alas, "to be reconciled to God now meant to be reconciled to the established customs of a more or less Christianized society." Christianity became the new protector of the social mores. Even revivalism was then the mere instrument to enforce the prevailing standards; witness the activity that had issued in Prohibition. Meanwhile, moralism degenerated into a belief in progress. "The life now lived in the land of promise was regarded as the promised life," he charged, while America refused to turn God's judgment on itself.   8:49

It was left to Niebuhr in this book to lead the attack on the liberal flank of the Protestant establishment and to try to provide the definitive obituary for the untroubled liberalism of his time. Liberal faith had begun dynamically, Niebuhr was fair enough to admit. With it had first come creative revolts against both fatalism and biblicism, and then against mechanized revivals and otherworldliness. He was also careful to say that not all liberalism was naively optimistic, as rash critics all too readily charged. At its best, liberal optimism was rooted in the Christian gospel. Even its doctrine of progress began with biblical impulses and momentum before it became culturally corrupted.   8:50

In the face of all this, liberalism lost out in the struggle with realism because its conception of the Kingdom, mourned Niebuhr, who was at home in liberalism, "involved no discontinuities, no crises, no tragedies or sacrifices, no loss of all things, no   8:51

cross and resurrection." It deified humans and humanized God. "Evolution, growth, development, the culture of the religious life, the nurture of the kindly sentiments, the extension of humanitarian ideals and the progress of civilization took the place of Christian revolution." Then came Niebuhr's most famous line about liberalism: in it "A God without wrath brought men without sin into a kingdom without judgment through the ministrations of a Christ without a cross."

8:52   This heir of liberalism was not finished with his word of judgment on its latter-day representatives. Niebuhr's was a story about the decline and fall of liberalism in an American Protestantism which had trouble getting the message. Liberalism had become ever less evangelical—less biblical, gospel-centered, "saving"— and ever more thoughtlessly adapted to secular culture. "The liberal children of liberal fathers needed to operate with ever diminishing capital." Near the end, "it was not God who ruled, but religion who ruled a little, and religion needed God for its support." Even nearer the time of its recent demise, liberalism glibly identified human values with the divine, "proclaimed the glad tidings of progress and hallowed man's moral efforts though they led to civil, international and class war." In the very end liberalism became as conservation-minded, as defensive, as orthodoxy had ever been. It guarded religion carefully as a tender plant which required protection against the blighting frost of a scientific world.

8:53   No Fundamentalist could have cut so surgically or worked so effectively as did Niebuhr. Liberalism's late defenders, he concluded, "were thankful for every sop which men of science threw their way and for every kind word which the mighty, in universities and halls of government, ventured on [liberalism's] behalf." The movement of the Kingdom of God in America "had apparently come to a stop." Since the author was a Christian and therefore had to have hope, he did point to some signs of recovery. These he designated "indications of a spiritual unrest which might become the seed plot of new life." In these movements—presumably including something like Christian realism, which he did not name—he found growing interest in the more profound Christian doctrines and traditions. In them were signs that many recognized that "there was no way toward the coming kingdom save the way taken by a sovereign God through the reign of Jesus Christ."

Immoral Man and Even More Immoral Society

Reinhold Niebuhr, the brother of H. Richard Niebuhr, was also   8:54
a professor, but his title connected him with *applied* Christianity,
as New York's Union Theological Seminary would have it. He
also had a desk, but this Niebuhr at the same time possessed a
railroad map, a set of invitations to campuses and interest groups,
some denominational assignments, a gown for the pulpit and a
passion for the circuit, a journalist's typewriter, the ear of politicians, and a holy vocation to look up from that desk and participate in the public world. Christian realism or realistic theology
came to public notice chiefly through this Niebuhr, who was the
century's most influential native-born American theologian.

By the thirties, Niebuhr was a seasoned thinker. Already in   8:55
1916 he was precociously writing for the *Atlantic Monthly*, not
usually an outlet for not fully mature theologians, or for any theologians for that matter. In 1923 the liberal *Christian Century*,
which was also to be the first journal to publish his brother in
1925, began disseminating the first of a constant flow of Reinhold's pieces. He was the magazine's joy and pride at first, though
its editors always treated him gingerly. Later, after a conflict over
pacifism before World War II, he became its nemesis. Niebuhr
meanwhile wrote hundreds of articles for other magazines, religious and secular, plus a stream of books which made him the
dominating American religious thinker in the middle third of the
century.

Reinhold Niebuhr spent much of the twenties in a Detroit pas-   8:56
torate, where he worked with Catholics and Jews and against
Henry Ford and industrialists who, he thought, took advantage of
workers. The young pastor there polished preaching skills and
learned to deal with the needs of ordinary believers. He also began writing on national affairs. In 1928 Pastor Niebuhr moved to
Union Theological Seminary in New York, where he spent his
years in or near that chair of Applied Christianity. From there
Niebuhr also launched, just before World War II, a realist rival to
the liberal *Christian Century*. The new magazine, *Christianity
and Crisis*, became a vivid symbol of the second transdenomina-
tional cleavage in Protestant power forces and outlooks during the
two interwar decades. Niebuhr also became a Socialist party candidate for Congress in 1930. He consistently blended his politics
with a theological vision which combined some heritage of liberal

theology with European critical traditions. Such a hurried biographical sketch evokes the pace but does not provide opportunity
to capture the character of the man. Contemporaries were awed
by his energy, his rhetoric, his ability to see to the heart of issues,
and his impulse to take risks.

8:57   In 1927 Niebuhr published his first book, *Does Civilization
Need Religion?* This early book only anticipated the one which
altered American religious history, the decisive work of the new
Christian realism, *Moral Man and Immoral Society*, which appeared in 1932. In his first book, Niebuhr, signing off as a pastor,
asked himself questions about the possible relevance of religion
to the lives of people like his members. One can still detect in its
pages some idealism, traces of an outlook Niebuhr was soon to
scorn in himself and others. He also still carried much of the
impetus of the older Social Gospel; though he was soon to shatter
its liberal premises, he never lost admiration for much of the reform it generated.

8:58   It was evident that Niebuhr identified, however uneasily, with
the Federal Council brand of churches and their causes during the
twenties. As he became increasingly ill at ease with those he
thought of as bourgeois churches, he sometimes still looked back
wistfully on the old sphere of Protestant dominance, because at
least it had provided some sort of base for the call to conscience,
the word of judgment, and responsible argument. The old times
had given the churches access to the ear of the nation. But by the
end of the 1920s, it was clear to him that many leaders who made
decisions in the society were no longer deferential just because
someone had the title "Reverend" before his name. The church
had become a liability, not an asset, for someone who wished to
address society. As Niebuhr made his subsequent moves, however, he did not abandon or shroud the Christian message but
made an effort to find a base where he could get a hearing for it,
an arena where he could apply it, as he often felt he could not
among those he called the semi-pagans who filled church pews.

8:59   When Niebuhr commuted to the political scene he did not call
himself a realist, a word which never did become an official party
label. (Ironically a ticket on which he once ran for office was
called the Liberal party!) He found himself instead at home with
socialist groups, though he made relatively little of any identification with the word "socialist." In 1928 Niebuhr publicly supported Socialist Norman Thomas for president and in due course
joined socialist political groups. By then he had also become in-

fluenced by the crisis thinking of Karl Barth and other Europeans who carried on a war with liberal theology in the name of a God who was "Wholly Other." Niebuhr was never a conventional neo-orthodox thinker, never a disciple of Karl Barth, partly because he was a very independent thinker who never too easily fit in anywhere. But the theology called Niebuhrian focused on Barthian themes such as the transcendence of God, renewed attention to human sin, divine judgment, and the need to address a world in want.

While Niebuhr was not a card-carrying partisan of the left with a capital L, he certainly belonged with "small l" leftists, and overtly drew upon the thinker they regarded as their mentor, Karl Marx. Niebuhr for a time called himself a Marxist, but later emphatically distanced himself, having never been an orthodox Marxist either. His Marx was the thinker who analyzed class society, not the provider of triggers for violent revolution. Niebuhr readily translated Marxian categories into themes which could be congenial to the Christian gospel as he interpreted it. These led him to what friend and foe alike called his prophetic stance. He noticed that this outlook, rooted in the Hebrew Scriptures, matched some major Marxian ideas. His new colleague at Union Seminary, Paul Tillich, a refugee from Hitler, also informally tutored Niebuhr in German-style religious socialism. By 1932 Niebuhr was writing editorials which explicitly invoked Marx. However, he was convinced that Marxism by itself could not substantively address America. Christian interpretations of society which were informed by Marx might do so. Niebuhr would preach them, and he did. **8:60**

Moral Man and Immoral Society marked his major turn. One line about the title is almost as famous as the title itself. Niebuhr liked to say that he should have called it *Immoral Man and Even More Immoral Society*. In his book he blasted away at perfectionism, idealism, liberalism. He spoke of Marxism also as one more illusion, a myth, however useful it was as a practical instrument. He could take Marxism apart, at the same time standing in awe of and being skeptical about key portions. Thus he took a central Marxist doctrine and said of it that it was "more than a doctrine. It is a dramatic, and to some degree, a religious interpretation of proletarian destiny." Marxists, he noted, claimed to possess a complete philosophy of history. They held to what he called an apocalyptic vision. Christian realism, thought Niebuhr, could make tense but helpful pragmatic alliances with such Marxism. **8:61**

8:62   Niebuhr did his own qualifying of this prospect several years later. In a few sentences he strung together a number of words ending in "ism" to show he had been looking for a lever with which to counter some regressive forces. He said he had "used Marxist collectivism to counter liberal individualism, Marxist catastrophism to counter liberal optimism, and Marxist determinism to challenge liberal moralism and idealism." He took Marxist and other notions which argued that the collective life of humans could achieve perfect justice and said of the whole idea that it was a "very valuable illusion for the moment," because unless people had a "sublime madness in the soul," such as that notion inspired, it would be hard to work for at least half-way measures of justice. Niebuhr was half-supporting Marxism as a critical tool and then criticizing it because of its usefulness by ignoble regimes. When he looked at one realization of Marxism in Soviet Communism he described it as "a new religion. Its virtues and its vices are the virtues and vices of religion." After Niebuhr toured Russia in 1930, he came back aware more than before of the way Communism had come to take the place of religion in the lives of people there.

8:63   By 1932, after turning his Marxist analysis on both liberal and conservative politicians, Niebuhr for a second time supported candidate Norman Thomas, which meant he was very public about his Socialist tie. Such a connection was not as suspect then as it might have been years later, for this was a time when thousands of Protestant clergy could blithely and without explanation call themselves socialists. At mid-decade when Niebuhr became an editor of the religiously socialist *World Tomorrow*, he even entered into some intraparty battles. He and his colleagues next invented still another periodical, *Radical Religion*, to rally others for the cause. His name was on any number of Popular Front letterheads. In the first half of the thirties, Niebuhr often took stands opposing preparation for war, positions of the sort he had to reverse a couple of years later. Gradually he loosened and let go of his ties to overtly and militantly Marxist fronts, having appeared at times to be more of an apologist for the Soviet experiment than he wished. Always he was more of an explicitly Christian participant in the social crisis than any orthodox Marxist could comprehend.

8:64   Conservatives in the church could always point to these Marxist socialist connections as signs that Niebuhr and his kind were subverting capitalism and thus America. The more cautious and moderating leaders at Union Seminary, however, often saw their colleague from a different perspective. There he played a strategic role. They hoped Niebuhr would talk sense to student radicals who were only too ready to follow Harry F. Ward into Marxist dogmatism. *Time* magazine watched the process from the beginning, having seen Niebuhr as "one of Socialism's ablest, most trustworthy advocates."

More effectively than any other minister, Niebuhr kept his base   8:65 in distinctive Christianity while he cultivated ties to humanists. Thus at a banquet on October 2, 1932, John Dewey joined others in honoring Niebuhr—something they would not likely have done for the likes of young Francis Pickens Miller or all those other critics of Dewey. But Niebuhr could and did continue to attack this philosopher, too, for believing that adequate moral and social pedagogy would bring social problems to solution. He found Dewey platitudinous on such subjects; the philosopher, he said, underestimated the place of human self-interest and of conflict. "Conflict," wrote Niebuhr, "is inevitable, and in this conflict power must be challenged by power." Such words in *Moral Man and Immoral Society* were virtual taunts designed to draw out the secular community, where liberalism had more enduring power than in the churches.

His contentions with Dewey and the educators reveal how Nie-   8:66 buhr thought Christian realism plus Marxism might effect change. The pedagogues, said the theologian, believed that experimental procedures could produce human good without issuing in conflict. Christians and Marxists when they were in classic form knew that they would then meet only in a somewhat artificial contest. "Contending factions in a social struggle require morale; and morale is created by the right dogmas, symbols and emotionally potent oversimplifications." The industrial workers would never win freedom through the experimental procedures of educators. They needed energy to contest the power of the strong.

Just as he could criticize progressive educators as naive, Nie-   8:67 buhr challenged even more the regular run of sociologists. They tended to see social conflict as a mere result of a clash between kinds of behavior patterns. Their credo and policy would call them to authorize a social scientist to provide a better pattern, and all could be well. Not at all, said Niebuhr. Self-interest, not ignorance, was at the root of conflict. At times he could momentarily listen to social scientists who promoted accommodation between parties. Yes, he agreed, that kind of technique sometimes worked. But then the prophetic Christian and the heretical Marxist in him would ask, "But will a disinherited group, such as the Negroes for instance, ever win full justice in society in this fashion?" Quoting sociologist Howard Odum, Niebuhr noted that most blacks had to regard the potential of violence as being necessary, "'until broader principles of education and cooperation can be established.'" Niebuhr did not even share the progressivism implied in that line: he thought conflict would never end because self-interest would not.

8:68   Still, believing that Christians should be put to the most severe tests and that judgment must begin at home, Niebuhr showed that he was only warming up on educators and sociologists as he went on to attack the modern religious idealists who tagged along with them. Too many liberal church leaders in the thirties, he thought, still employed the language of compromise and accommodation between unequal forces, in contests where one party had everything to lose. Thus he read progressive churchman Justin Wroe Nixon making the point that no impassable gulf existed between certain prominent capitalists and socialists. Niebuhr protested: there *was* such a gulf, and no one could pretend it away. Moralists like Nixon failed to understand what Niebuhr called "the brutal character of the behavior of all human collectives, and the power of self-interest and collective egoism in all inter-group relations." The liberal moralists' hope also was in education and what they professed to see as a developing purer religion.

8:69   In such a context Niebuhr recalled and took swipes at the ideology behind the ineffective Kellogg-Briand Peace Pact. It showed how liberal Christians had been living under the illusion that all social relations were being brought progressively under the law of Christ. Never shy about naming names, including those of friends and colleagues, Niebuhr here attacked not only Nixon but even the venerable William Adams Brown for this "moral confusion of liberal Christianity." Let liberals humanize social life within the limits they had to learn were theirs. Niebuhr saw in both such secular and religious liberalisms some survivals of the illusions and sentimentalities of the Age of Reason and the credos of nineteenth century progressive humanism. He, in turn, wrote from the perspective of a disillusioned generation which was barely saved from cynicism by a Christian social understanding and moved to attempt change by a philosophy of history informed in part by encounter with the Marxist myth.

The Union Seminary preacher often shocked hearers and   8:70
readers by transgressing one liberal assumption: he was open to
the possible exercise of violence in struggles between classes and
interests. He knew about and regularly commented on the noise
of conflict. Niebuhr often sounded like and even cited sociologist
E. A. Ross on resentment: it was "merely the egoistic side of the
sense of injustice." As such it was "not valueless and wholly
evil." When such resentment was totally absent, this could be a
sign that there was a lack of social intelligence or moral vigor.
Thus those blacks who resented injustice could make a larger contribution than did those who suffered injustice passively, without
expressing emotions. Of course, the more that people could purge
the egoistic impulse from their resentment, the better an instrument of social justice it would become.

Niebuhr, a master of irony, might well have mused in later   8:71
years about the irony of his own captivity to some illusions in this
period. On the one hand he had an almost mystical vision of what
the poor, the oppressed, the workers, and the blacks might rise
to, and on the other hand he had to support elites who did much
of the deciding for these groups. The professor often worked to
help outcasts find access to better living conditions without showing much worry about what bourgeois life would do to them if
they some day reached comfortable circumstances. In sum, his
major book showed Niebuhr standing "between the times," as
theologians then liked to talk of their period. He made enemies
on both sides of the central conflicts of the day. But since Fundamentalists had never been part of movements linked with him, it
was liberals who felt most betrayed and were most angered by his
changes.

Efforts to discern why Niebuhr was so consistent in his attack   8:72
on liberalism lead one eventually to an understanding of how he
conceived of conflict. The pursuit of justice always had to involve
competition and conflict, a fact which liberals seldom granted. As
people worked for just ends they would not find it possible to
come to a stage which saw the partisans move permanently beyond conflict. There would only be changes in the balance of
power, shifting alliances, new circumstances eliciting new combat. To progressives all this was a chilling vision. On these terms
Niebuhr produced shock by saying that Marxism could be helpful
when people tried to find meaning in the midst of chaos. The
divide was deep and total. Marxism "is superior to liberal Chris-

tianity because Christian liberalism is spiritually dependent upon bourgeois liberalism and is completely lost when its neat evolutionary process toward an ethical historical goal is suddenly engulfed in a social catastrophe." The thirties represented such social catastrophe. Liberalism could never cope with it.

8:73   Niebuhr continued through all his politicking to be a theologian; *Moral Man and Immoral Society* was not his rite of passage out of the church. He stayed, and kept company with other theologians while he delved into the deeper themes of Christian thought. Jesus, not Marx, was always central to his reflection. In mid-decade Niebuhr in *The Interpretation of Christian Ethics* dealt with the concept of sin, which he kept reintroducing to public debate. Sin was not just a part of the biological makeup of humans. It was "an inevitable fact of human existence, the inevitability of which is given by the nature of man's spirituality. It is true in every moment of existence, but it has no history." And Christians must work with sin.

8:74   Such a Niebuhrian theme was a total assault on the legacy of the half century of liberalism which characteristically put limits on talk about limits and which all but named it a sin to make so much of sin. Niebuhr saw sin everywhere. When he directed his insight to the national scene, he saw enmity among people only grow worse. "The collective life of mankind promises no . . . hope of salvation," as nations and cultures kept hoping to find it, "for the very reason that it offers men the very symbols of pseudo-universality which tempt them to glorify and worship themselves as God."

8:75   His book on ethics gave Niebuhr still another opening to probe the liberal tradition and to attack more contemporaries. He found the roots of liberal optimism in figures like Thomas Jefferson and, overall, in the eighteenth century Age of Reason. The liberal churches converted this moralistic utopianism to their own purposes. Among these churches Niebuhr observed only "the substitution of sentimental illusions for the enervating pessimism of orthodoxy." Thus the Union professor chided Chicago Modernist Shailer Mathews for having said: " 'The impulse to get justice is not evangelical; the impulse to give justice is.' " To Niebuhr, this was a strikingly naive picture of the political problem. Mathews, he said, had learned nothing in twenty years despite the catastrophes of the time. Mathews still interpreted Christianity as "the preaching of a moral ideal, which men do not follow, but which they ought to." Unvarying and always false refrains came Niebuhr's way whenever he heard the liberal church approach politics with the word that "love and co-operation are superior to conflict and coercion, and that therefore they must be and will be established." His assault on the dominant form of Protestantism was constant and total.

Some other Christian realists, colleague John Bennett among   8:76 them, worried lest the talk about original sin might lead to determinism and would cause believers to turn passive. In the last season before World War II came to involve America, Bennett, in the preface to his *Christian Realism*, took on the extremes in this debate. Realism, he said, was originally designed to avoid the illusions of both the optimists and the pessimists. Bennett believed that "the liberal optimism of the past generation and the theologians who deduce their view of human possibilities from a dogma of original sin which goes beyond the evidence are both wrong." Clearly he was implicating his friend Niebuhr, who worked down the hall from him at Union. Original sin was simply a presupposition for Niebuhr. He needed no evidences. Would such a concept of the human produce passivity, Bennett asked? Niebuhr's best argument that such need not be the case was his own career, to which he could point as a refutation of the charges or implications of his friend and colleague Bennett.

Reinhold Niebuhr never seemed to care how close to home he   8:77 got with his attacks on liberals. He almost seemed to be picking fights, not out of a thirst for combat but to make his points. So, though he was very much in the company of the federating churches, he criticized the congresses on politics sponsored by the Federal Council. "If the liberal Church had had less moral idealism and more religious realism its approach to the political problem would have been less inept and fatuous."

The Union Seminary theologian was equally abrupt in dealing   8:78 with people he in some respects and other contexts admired. Even when he spoke of Bishop Francis J. McConnell, a friend and associate from Detroit days, Niebuhr had to say that this Methodist demonstrated what Niebuhr charged was "the final bankruptcy of the liberal Christian approach to politics." Also, E. Stanley Jones might be Niebuhr's ideal of the great liberal missionary, but a new book by Jones showed a "complete lack of relevance to the political and economic problems of the hour." And the irrelevance of Jones was, in Niebuhr's phrase, "perfectly typical of liberal Christian thought as a whole." Liberal Christian literature, he said, "abounds in the monotonous reiteration of the pious hope that people might be good and loving, in which case all the nasty business of politics could be dispensed with." Liberals, who could never change a corrupt world, could only adapt to it.

8:79   One theologian whose political views Niebuhr could generally support was Paul Tillich, whose *Religious Situation* was translated by Niebuhr in 1932. Tillich's work was a corrective to Christian liberalism, an analysis which Niebuhr thought could not possibly have been written in America. He knew it would offend many liberal, semiradical and unreligious radical Americans. Their nation, said Niebuhr just one month after Roosevelt was elected president, was "still too thoroughly immersed in the illusions and superstitions of liberal, middle-class culture to appreciate just what Tillich is trying to do."

8:80   In Tillich Niebuhr found laudable belief-ful realism, the attitude in which "the religious tension between time and eternity, between the absolute and the relative," was maintained. It stood over against both beliefless realism and idealism. The *Religious Situation* would serve Niebuhr in the decade ahead as he and Tillich and the other realists had to come to terms with the catastrophe that was happening in Europe and the war, preparation for which once more divided the factions in the Federal Council kinds of Protestant churches, and not in them alone. Whether or not realism ever came to be the prevailing position—almost certainly it did not—it had removed all possibility of a united non-Fundamentalist Protestantism being privileged as an American establishment. Why take original-stock Protestantism seriously if twice in two decades its house divided and its leaders could not agree on visions of God or country or self? But were there other candidates? Was Catholicism poised to make its move into dominance? Curiously, a movement parallel to Protestant realism showed how divided Catholicism was when it came to prescribing for society in crisis.

Love in Action Is a Harsh and Dreadful Love

8:81   Across the gulf in Catholicism all the key partisan terms were different. Some who called themselves religious idealists held realistic views of the world. But they tried different strategies and used different names for addressing the problems of the day. Not all of them took refuge from the public scene or were nostalgic about liberal recent pasts. The thirties also saw the rise of some religious radicalisms which fit no preexisting American molds. They may not have issued from people as well positioned as Niebuhr, Bennett, and Tillich were to challenge conventional Christian liberalisms. Yet they worked effectively within other huge American subcommunities, of which none were as large as Roman Catholicism. American Catholicism had not by then developed a notable intellectual tradition. In Depression times the conflict over approaches to the social order on realist grounds were as often moved by activism as they were by reflective considerations. The Catholic response which throws most light on the course of events in the decade was that of the Catholic Worker movement, its leaders Peter Maurin and Dorothy Day, but activist Day most of all.

This appearance of social and spiritual radicalism in American   8:82
Catholic history contrasted in almost every important respect with the Protestant realist turns toward various radicalisms. Walter Marshall Horton, John Bennett, Francis Miller, and the Niebuhr brothers inherited long traditions of social activism, whose legacies they set out to rework, revise, or reject. In their immediate past were the Social Gospel and theological liberalism, both of which were matches for progressive and liberal humanist trends in the larger culture. In their longer and immediate pasts alike were obvious and still powerful American cultural heritages: their Protestant ancestors had been running the country in many of its aspects, and they now had had to take a new stand on how to carry on this custodianship, if carry it on was something they should do at all.

The Catholic experience was quite different. The Catholics   8:83
who massed in great cities demonstrated considerable political brawn and finesse until they came to dominate many of them. But the opposition to Alfred E. Smith's presidential candidacy in 1928 showed how far Catholics still were from being at the center of national power when the Depression came. The United States was still in many ways religiously a Protestant nation, and it did not take an André Siegfried to tell Catholics what all of them sensed about this fact. All they needed to do was look at who was in Who's Who, where frequency of listings indicated the prestige and influence of groups from which its subjects came. Few Catholics were included. They could next look at the state universities and private non-Catholic colleges only to find few Catholics in positions of influence in science or the arts. Few Roman Catholics were wealthy or experienced enough to engage in large-scale phi-

lanthropy. The boards of large corporations were made up of people from original-stock Protestant backgrounds. If Protestants were busy trying to learn how to retain status, or how gracefully or grudgingly to yield their hold on the nation, Catholics were still producing credentials to show that they belonged and had a right to share authority and influence.

8:84   Not that Catholics found their America an uncongenial place. They did not agree with or even understand how their non-Catholic neighbors might ever have found them suspect. If anything, the long record of Catholicism's engagement with the United States was one of an intense patriotism and nationalism which would have disturbed the authors of *The Church Against the World* had they ever cared to notice it. Catholics really belonged and felt they belonged in the United States. But before World War I they were not able to show this with as much security as they demonstrated in New Deal times. Now some of them could even question some basic assumptions of national life and the economy as Protestants in the Social Gospel era could and did.

8:85   When the Crash of 1929 occurred, when the Great Depression devastated the American labor force, much of it Catholic, church leaders with vision found opportunity to borrow or develop almost any kind of social philosophy as long as it was not incompatible with orthodoxy. And they could offer many kinds of programs, though not without meeting political opposition—Catholics came in all kinds of stripes, most of them not friendly to social radicalism—without being doctrinally suspect. It was in this context that the Catholic Worker movement developed. It became a subject of public interest on May 1, May Day, of 1933, just months after Franklin D. Roosevelt became president. This was a time of great social unrest, a period when terms like crisis and catastrophe, words favored by Protestant realists, gained immediate resonance among publics. But that May Day had its own prehistory in the biography and vocation of one of its two leaders, Dorothy Day, and in the philosophy called personalism, imported from France.

8:86   What Marxism was to the Christian realists, this personalism was to the Catholic radicals. That is, it offered an instrument for criticism of the existing economic patterns and an impetus to change, even if it was not completely understood or applicable in America and even if its importers did not follow it all the way. Personalism would have been hard to follow even in the hands of clear-minded intellectuals. Neither co-founder Peter Maurin nor Dorothy Day claimed to be, were thought of as, or were such.

The fact that the philosophy was vague, however, did not mean that it was without influence; since Maurin, Day, and their colleagues believed that they were living by it, this outlook became part of an American event.

Not that personalism was full blown, waiting to be exported   8:87
from France to nations where social radicalism might be in order. Not that Maurin and Day spent their hours reading personalist philosophers and looking for a laboratory. In a way, just the opposite occurred: they adopted ways of living the Catholic life and improvised programs for meeting need—and then went shopping for rationales to serve as their guides and legitimators. Personalism served as well as any for these. Maurin, Day's mentor, through much of his career published a stream of what he called "Easy Essays," and he recommended "Books to Read." His essays quoted the books he recommended, and these were often of this French school.

Emmanuel Mounier and his personalist journal *L'Esprit* were   8:88
prime in France during the time in the 1930s when the Catholic Worker movement developed in America. Mounier through his career focused on Western bourgeois civilization with a consistency to match Niebuhr's critique, though without the comparable rigor of analysis. His was a philosophy of action which permitted French Catholics to remain faithful and orthodox, which meant, among other things, non-Marxist, while achieving some of the same ends as Marxists sought. There was a utopian tinge to such thought. Mounier, no less than the Marxists or the Christian realists, worked for a replacement of the existing economic order while attacking the present middle-class civilization.

The startling difference between personalism and Protestant   8:89
Christian realism was in the accent on Christian love in the former, on justice in the latter. The Niebuhrians, given to the preaching of love and grace in many contexts, feared that in liberal hands the concept of love sentimentalized and thus benumbed social classes, which needed conflict to effect change. Mounier, and with him Jacques Maritain and other intellectuals of influence, believed that the love which God in Christ brought to humans could change individuals and then society. This was a reversal of the realist program, which attacked structural evil, social sin, though without letting "moral man" or "immoral man" off the hook.

The redeemed person would "put on Christ" and move out of   8:90
the study and into the streets, there to set love to work and in that

way to bring about justice. En route, the corrupt and selfish manners of bourgeois civilization would be exposed and countered. The approach had therefore to be nonviolent in a time when most Christians kept allowing for violence in those cases where other approaches to change all failed and when justice was out of reach. Peter Maurin often spoke of "building the new within the shell of the old." He called upon Catholics to be "announcers of a new social order and not denouncers of the old."

8:91   To speak in these terms makes the philosophical background sound too ordered, too neat, too directly influential. Maurin and Day raided other systems of thought as well. Jacques Maritain, a French thinker who spent much time in America, came to be an enduring influence. Maritain was everything that Mounier was not: precise, clear, focused, almost dogmatic. His work was regularly on Maurin's reading lists and he came to speak at Catholic Worker gatherings. Maritain articulated Catholic social philosophies which were congruent with papal teaching and were at home in the modern world.

8:92   The Russians were still another influence. From Dostoyevsky's *The Brothers Karamazov* came words on love which sounded realist and became something of a life motto for Day: "Love in action is a harsh and dreadful thing compared to love in dreams." Active love, he had said, was "labour and fortitude." And another Russian, the Orthodox philosopher Nicolai Berdyaev, taught Maurin and Day to mistrust progress and to criticize the rationalism of the Enlightenment, two more themes they shared with the Protestant realists. With Berdyaev in mind, they attacked professionalism and the professors' ways of analyzing reality without acting in it. From such sources they fashioned bases for their own action.

8:93   Peter Maurin was a disheveled, mystical French Catholic who made his way via Canada to the United States in 1911, where he did low-scale odd jobs. He worked and slept where he could, took no pains to fit in to the society of the twenties, and fed himself intellectually by reading at the New York Public Library or wherever there were good books and shelter. Always vague about the details of his personal life, he would change the subject when it was brought up and would then engage in discourse about Catholic ways of living. He came mysteriously into Dorothy Day's life as a figure who looked like a "bum." But it became clear at once that he could hold people in thrall as he delivered his endless cryptic monologues. It was apparent that he was especially capable of addressing the homeless and poor who were part of the Catholic Worker movement's endeavors. He spent little time criticizing the church, and generally ignored its institutional patterns. Given to voluntary poverty, Maurin lived a critique of bourgeois society more than he articulated it. In the 1930s in the anarchic style he favored, he was most responsible for Maryfarm, the Catholic Worker's rural outpost.

Dorothy Day came to the movement of Catholic radicalism   8:94
through a route that had long involved her with the left with a capital L, but always the secular left. Born into an Episcopalian family but having grown up relatively casual about religion, she went to the University of Illinois and soon drifted off into Communist-front groups and the radical literary set, back in the years of the Red Scare. As a child she had discovered some Christian classics, to whose central themes she was later to return, but for a time novels by socialists Upton Sinclair and Jack London engrossed her. In the course of these years, the religious fonts dried up in her as she made her way before World War I through the Bohemia of Greenwich Village. She was soon writing, making a name for herself in socialist magazines like *Call* and *New Masses*.

A physically beautiful person with a strong presence, Day also   8:95
plunged into love affairs with writers, and for a short time was especially close to dramatist Eugene O'Neill, in 1917 and 1918. She became pregnant by a lover and had an abortion. Then she married a man of many marriages, and almost immediately divorced him. She subsequently wrote an inferior autobiographical novel, which she later repudiated. Day then took up with and loved a man with whom she entered a common-law marriage and had a child, Tamar Teresa. By now, with religious stirrings growing ever stronger within her, she had Tamar baptized. When Day herself converted to Catholicism in 1927, the man left her. She was henceforth on her own, with her troubled self, her child, and the church she would serve almost obsessively but in her own way for the decades to come.

In the twenties, while Dorothy Day was still poised between   8:96
Communism and Catholicism, she shared the left's criticism of most Christianity. "The Marxists, the I.W.W.'s, who looked upon religion as the opiate of the people . . . were the ones who were eager to sacrifice themselves here and now, thus doing without now and for eternity the good things of the world which they were fighting to obtain for their brothers," wrote Day. Could she sustain her social passion in the church of which she was now a

traditionalist sort of member? She spent several years addressing that question and finding ways to live out her new vocation. When Peter Maurin came into her life, she began to envision some ways. Observing Depression poverty, she watched the government being apparently helpless in the face of it. It was the Depression which began to give plausibility to John A. Ryan's call for a social program to meet human need. The Depression was also the occasion which permitted Catholic weeklies like *America* and *Commonweal* to engage in criticism of a sort earlier Catholic organs were reluctant to offer. It prepared the climate which made possible the audience for people like Charles E. Coughlin on the Catholic right with a capital R. And between December 1932 and May 1933, its effects led Maurin and Day to plan their own address to the situation.

8:97   The best idea Maurin had was to produce a Catholic newspaper that would aim for the attention of the unemployed workers, of whom there were millions that bleak winter. Day was a journalist, and her faith in the press led her to develop some plans. On May Day in New York's Union Square, where the unemployed, radicals, and anyone who would talk or listen, doze or read, gathered, Maurin and Day descended with the first issue of their penny paper. To the surprise of everyone, the *Catholic Worker* attracted a readership at once. The first issue was limited to a printing of 2,500, but by 1935 circulation reached 65,000 and at the end of the thirties would climb to 185,000. The paper, which attracted first rate artists and writers, soon articulated a social vision derived in part from the personalists and the favored Russian thinkers, and in another part from the Bible—Day's old Protestant upbringing tilted her that way—while there was also a mixture of elements from hit-or-miss social and intellectual experiments.

8:98   The *Catholic Worker* became more than a newspaper. Soon it was also a movement which spawned the institution of round-table discussions, lectures, and, most important, houses of hospitality for the poor. As these spread nationally they attracted Catholics who were ready to adopt voluntary poverty and examples of direct action to help the victims of the Depression and also, Day would say, of bourgeois civilization. The *Catholic Worker* included news of the labor movement. Day's own articles also made mention of labor leaders like John L. Lewis or Harry Bridges, priests who favored workers, and the intransigence of manufacturers and management. Day also provided a personal column which reflected a combination of traditional Catholic

piety and radical social action to match the combination of neoorthodoxy and social critique in people like Reinhold Niebuhr.
The leaders were so loyal to the church that Day insisted she
would abandon the *Catholic Worker* if New York's Francis Cardinal Spellman told her to do so. The charismatic but not always easy-to-live-with Dorothy Day became the teacher, mentor,
spiritual guide, and casual administrator of the Catholic Worker
movement and houses, always encouraging self-help among the
adherents on the local levels.

Her old Greenwich Village bohemian friends and Communist   8:99
associates, puzzled by Day's spirituality, were offended by her
Catholicism. Most stopped seeing her. They might well have
shared her critique of the church. "I loved the Church for Christ
made visible. Not for itself, because it was so often a scandal to
me. Romano Guardini said the Church is the Cross on which
Christ was crucified; one could not separate Christ from His
Cross, and one must live in a state of permanent dissatisfaction
with the Church." She was appalled by "the scandal of business-
like priests, of collective wealth, the lack of a sense of responsibility for the poor, the worker, the Negro, the Mexican, the
Filipino, and even the oppression of these . . ." But the old secular radical admirers would not follow her after she stated her "and
yet": "And yet the priests were the dispensers of the Sacraments,
bringing Christ to men . . ." Such loyalty meant that priests and
laypeople were free to support Day and join the Catholic Worker
cause without meeting official harassment by bishops and other
authorities.

The Worker movement, which centered on the notion of vol-   8:100
untary cooperation, originally had no specific program. It was,
said Day, an organism rather than an organization. She acknowledged that she constantly improvised programs and policies.
Those who enjoyed the houses of hospitality were expected to join
in their upkeep, in gathering donations, in serving food, in tending to needs. Those close to the scene were not romantic about
the results of *Catholic Worker* idealism. There were dropouts,
moral failures, controversies, wearinesses expressed about the
relative anarchy, and losses of focus. Yet in Depression times
Catholics, and not only they, began to find in the controversial
approach of Maurin and Day an alternative to the helplessness of
the government and the remoteness of many in the intellectual and
religious communities. People who had wearied of capitalism but
could not endure Communism's atheism were attracted by the at-

tachment to gospel simplicity. It was this literalist perfectionism in attempts to live out the gospel that made it hard for Catholic conservatives to dismiss the Catholic Worker movement while they rejected simple ideological leftism.

8:101   The approach of Christian openness meant that the movement attracted all kinds of radicals, reformers, drifters, and fanatics. Day sometimes grew depressed about these. "There are," she said in an inventory, "followers of seemingly every lost cause and believers in every path to world brotherhood" in Depression America. She added: "Hardest to deal with are those who have gone entirely 'off the deep end'," adding, "and whose poor brains have collapsed completely. They will follow you around for hours laying out some fantastic panacea for the social order." There were always some of these in the Worker's midst. One participant, Stanley Vishnewski, had difficulty dealing with the attraction: "Sometimes it seemed that the CW had the rejects of every religious order in the country." He reduced the problem to epigram. "The Catholic Worker consists of saints and martyrs, and the martyrs are those who have to live with the saints." Day was given to epigrams when she set out to stress the positive side of the movement. Criticizing those who misused Jesus' saying that "The poor you always have with you," she retorted: "This class structure is of our making, not His." Yes, "there will always be His poor, but there need not be so many."

8:102   Official Catholicism did not depend upon or defend the Catholic Worker. The leadership made attempts to alleviate Depression era problems through Catholic progressive interactions with New Dealers, to whom Monsignor John A. Ryan was attracted and on whose administrators he put constant pressure. *America* and *Commonweal* chose support of Roosevelt as the best course, as did Cardinals Patrick Hayes of New York and William O'Connell of Boston. Roosevelt, returning the favors, brought Catholics into his administration and councils as no president before him had. The secular press, through it all, kept up its suspicions. Thus *American Mercury* editors thought they saw a Catholic front in the movement of workers. They believed it to be significant, they said, "of the attempt to re-fortify the Church, to win back wavering proletarians seduced by famine and Communism," more than "the emergence of a paper called the *Catholic Worker*." Not being able to make sense of the "odd" linking of traditionalist spirituality and social radicalism, such editors thought that the hand of the conservative church must be behind the movement. Most wildly, it announced concerning Dorothy Day the "open secret that she carries on her work with the approval of the Cardinal."

Maurin and Day were politically inept and uninterested in, if   8:103
not disdainful of, ordinary legislative processes. But they could not support labor without becoming involved with politics. The Catholic Worker people, strongly supporting the Child Labor Amendment, joined John A. Ryan in doing so. Clearly, they were not working with the approval of the cardinals. The New York archdiocese, for one, vehemently opposed that amendment. Bishops and cardinals saw it as an interference in the sacred sphere of the family and parental rights and an expansion of governmental surveillance and outreach. And when Catholic Worker pickets were in the same lines as Communist supporters of strikes, many hierarchs could hardly resist moving in against Day. But Maurin answered when Catholics invoked patriotism against such identifications with labor: "When people see Red, it is useless to present to them the Red, White and Blue."

The real test case of who worked with whose approval came in   8:104
the Spanish Civil War, which we have seen was a volatile issue among Catholics. *Commonweal* lost heavily when it supported the Republic against Catholic Franco and the Loyalists. What would the *Catholic Worker* do? Whoever had been reading it would know in advance: it would ask America and its Catholics to keep their distance, remain neutral, and try to find ways to barter for peace. Day's evangelical perfectionism and biblical literalism had led her to absolute pacifism, a position that would cost her dearly when World War II came. In 1937, however, it was still a permissible luxury in respect to a transatlantic war. John LaFarge, S.J., an editor of *America* and an earlier friend of the Catholic Worker, on that occasion turned on the movement, charging it with utopianism and irresponsibility. Was it appropriate for the movement as a movement to call itself Catholic? There was, he wrote, "a vast difference between some individual freelance layman" on one hand and "that of a multitude of groups engaged in active works all over the country," and this difference concerned representativeness. Yet even LaFarge considered the Catholic Workers to be "humble and holy," and he trusted them to think responsibly.

The issue of how Catholic was the Catholic Worker movement   8:105
could easily be settled so far as relation to church power was concerned. All its leadership professed and intended to act in accord with obedience to the authority of the church, even while testing

its limits and patience. Of course, it was disturbing to anyone who rejected the movement's gospel perfectionism, its course of voluntary poverty, and its criticism of an economic system into which most of official Catholicism had bought. How Catholic was it? Never did it attract the loyalty or notice of many thousands of Catholics, who chose the church's general support of New Deal policies as its way of entree into politics. It is not likely that most Catholic workers had heard of the movement. Yet in Depression times it was a significant alternative to ordinary Catholicism, Protestant realism, or the apathy and sullenness into which so many lapsed.

8:106   Few people could have been less interested in seeking majority acceptance or in counting noses than Peter Maurin and Dorothy Day. They were content to sell their penny paper, keep their houses of hospitality open, pray, debate ways of life and live out some inconveniencing ones, and be free. Perhaps only times as upsetting and chaotic as the Depression would have created the opening for an alternative like this, one whose effects would last well beyond World War II. And, while Day would have shunned the noun "realism," she would argue that harsh and dreadful love was more realistic than was mere talk about justice, or permitting injustice to prevail. Thus Day could say: "There is always a great need of idealists who uphold the ideal rather than the practical." She continued her response to a critic: "Without them men would not strive so high. Little by little it can be found that the ideal works and is practical, and then men are surprised." Such an approach belonged well in what Horton had called "An Age of Realism," a Depression-era and, in its way, now post-Protestant America.

9

The Entire Social and Political Field

A Society Riven by a Dozen Oppositions

T he Depression disaster which befell America in the 1930s   9:1
predictably brought with it conflict over religious interpretations
and strategies of action. The gulfs between the parties were broad,
the fissures deep. Inherited from the twenties were some wars of
each faction against all, and these could get worse when there
were fewer spoils over which to fight. Those who sought refuge
from conflict in religion, then, had reason to be disappointed in
the thirties. Those who recognize that religion does not only con-
sole but that it can also irritate, goad, and even kill will find not
less but more drama in the second interwar decade.

Religion, we have just remarked, can "even kill." Yet in this   9:2
period religious factions in the United States never killed. This
was an astounding fact, if one views it against the whole religious
past or against twentieth-century patterns elsewhere. While the
newspapers on any day in the twentieth century might record
scenes of murderous tribal conflict based partly in race and ethnicity but also charged with religious passion, we noted in the
American twenties only four such killings across religious lines
or by groups motivated by desires to serve God. This despite the

intensity of convictions held by many believers on any number of subjects.

9:3   Occasions and impulses for killing abounded. Of course, seeking to measure conflict by monitoring the amounts of bloodshed and the numbers of corpses would evidence a bizarre set of tastes when one deals with American religion. Armed violence is not the most significant effort in this case. In the United States, varying kinds of stakes brought forth differing schemes of struggle: these included verbal violence, legal pressure, organizational harassments, and the sort of rhetoric which can produce great psychological or spiritual distress but little physical violence.

9:4   Even so, it is valid to speculate about the American genre of conflict. Why in the tribal twenties had the tribes not shot at each other? Several explanations come to mind. A first response is to be based in replies to the question, If there is shooting, at whom would or could one shoot? True, there were some concentrations of people who could have become targets: Native Americans on reservations, blacks in slums, Jews in ghettos. But in general there were too many dispersals of people from their tribes; there was too much diffusion of populations. One could not point and shoot a gun in a holy war without recognizing the danger of catching a relative or neighbor in the cross fire.

9:5   The nature of the American polity suggests an additional explanation. This constitutional and representative republic provided factions with ways to address and neutralize each other. James Madison's tenth and fifty-first Federalist Papers, written in 1787 and 1788 when the states were debating the ratification of the Constitution, are of help here. Madison anticipated situations such as the interwar scene because he wanted to show how in a great republic as opposed to a small one, coalitions of factions could block or blunt each other's goals. In this constitutional pattern, the framers set out to solve the classic problem of religion by removing religion from the official center of public life. Religion became what many called a "private affair." When religion turned public, as it so often did in these decades, the larger public saw this turn as being exceptional, intrusive, temporary, a circumstance that needed thwarting.

9:6   A third answer to the question about the absence of bloodshed draws on elements to which people like André Siegfried pointed. For all their sectarian divisions, Americans, he said, were united in *real* or more fundamental faiths such as the religions of nationalism or materialism, "the real power that aids assimilation" in

America. Sectarian killing would disrupt the progress of these. Such commitments, which some would call semisecular or pseudoreligious, always worked to undercut or intersect specific ethnic or orthodox religious commitments. Why shoot at other sects or factions, if the act of doing so slows down or confuses the hopes for national stability and personal success?

Fourth, in any general accounting for the character of effective   9:7
American religious conflict, it would be foolish to underestimate the measures of tolerance based on conviction which Americans did develop toward each other much of the time. Some visitors like Alexis de Tocqueville, a century earlier, had indeed attributed this tolerance to religious indifference. America, they thought, was secular enough and apathetic enough to let values like neighborliness or the common good motivate citizens more than the dogmas or practices which from time immemorial had led their ancestors to persecute and kill. The efforts of agencies like the newly patented National Conference of Jews and Christians to bring interfaith amity or the Federal Council of Churches to promote Protestant concord served somewhat to counter the violent impulses.

In this retrospect we will consult for a last time sociologist   9:8
E. A. Ross to introduce one more explanation—his most helpful and important one—for the peculiar American way of helping reduce conflict or making it creative, and then supplement that with an insight of public philosopher Walter Lippmann. Ross made his American readers aware that the chief oppositions which occur in societies are between individuals, sexes, ages, races, nationalities, sections, classes, and political parties. To these he added the locations he never isolated but which are most relevant in our context: "and religious sects."

Ross elaborated: "Several such oppositions may be in full   9:9
swing at the same time, but the more numerous they are, the less menacing is any one." In that context the sociologist noted what has emerged from our story but which we have not defined or stressed about religious factions or the religious dimension in factions: "Every species of conflict interferes with every other species in society at the same time, save only when their lines of cleavage coincide; in which case they reinforce one another."

In Ross's specific and appropriate illustration, a strain may de-   9:10
velop along the line between Christians and Jews. But if a similar strain appears along a different line in the same society, for example between employers and workmen, he wrote, "the religious

opposition will be less intense." Jewish bosses and Jewish work-men will be estranged from each other, as will Christian bosses from Christian workmen. On each side, some Jews and Christians will find they are "in the same boat" and will sympathize with each other across lines of faith. This in fact they did, both in domestic and international issues in the thirties.

9:11   The insight that, at least for these times, best illumines Ameri-can polity and life follows. "These various oppositions in society are like different wave series set up on opposite sides of a lake, which neutralize each other if the crests of one meet the troughs of the other, but which reinforce each other if crest meets crest while trough meets trough." The sociologist could well have been describing his contemporary America: "A society, there-fore, which is riven by a dozen oppositions along lines running in every direction, may actually be in less danger of being torn with violence or falling to pieces than one split along just one line. For each new cleavage contributes to narrow the cross clefts, so that one might say that society *is sewn together* by its inner conflicts." The result, said Ross, was "not such a paradox after all if one remembers that every species of collective strife tends to knit to-gether with a sense of fellowship the contenders on either side."

9:12   As with factions, so with individuals in interwar America. The development of mass media such as radio, cinema, and popular magazines and newspapers made individuals aware of the differ-ing commitments, practices, and passions of the many other kinds of citizens. Similarly, the patterns of affiliation in America pro-duced what we might call the pluralistic personality, which differs from the type reinforced by tribalism. Walter Lippmann observed this emergence most acutely and made it part of his respected public philosophy. The effect of modern civilization, of which America was perhaps the best example, wrote the pundit, was "the dissolution of the bonds which bound one man to another." Modern civilization dissolved psychological bonds and helped break up clannishness and personal dependence. This dissolving, Lippmann added, resulted from the diversification of the interests of men and women alike.

9:13   Lippmann liked to contrast the modern condition with the past. Life back in what he called the ancestral order was simpler, con-tained within narrower limits, and with far greater unity in the activity of each individual than contemporary existence allowed. Simple allegiance to the chief of the tribe, he said, would unite the tasks or the people's acts of worshiping. Not now. "In the modern world this synthesis has disintegrated and the activities of a man cannot be directed by a simple allegiance." Of course, sects could still try to do this directing. The Fundamentalists, by organizing and isolating a way of life complete with their own separate radio stations, Bible schools, denominations, and publishing ventures, were "come-outers" who tried to maintain synthesis and simple allegiances.

Such was not the case with, among others, the more exposed   9:14
Protestants of the federating churches, and more and more Catholics and Jews coming out of their ghettos. Lippmann spoke eloquently of such citizens at the places where the lines of societal cleavage coincided. He was describing personal life along what Ross called the "dozen oppositions along lines running in every direction," the spiritual "cross clefts." To illustrate, Lippmann used the masculine pronoun for a series that was even then applicable to both sexes. Thus: "Each man finds himself the center of a complex of loyalties. He is loyal to his government, he is loyal to his state, he is loyal to his village, he is loyal to his neighborhood. He has his own family. He has his wife's family. He has his church. His wife may have a different church." This citizen may be an employer or employee, who must be loyal to his corporation, or trade union, or professional society. He buys and sells in different markets, is a creditor and debtor and shareholder in several industries. He belongs to a political party, to clubs, to a social set. "The multiplicity of his interests makes it impossible for him to give his whole allegiance to any person or to any institution."

Of course, Lippmann knew, this web of commitments mixed   9:15
with loose affiliations represented a problem for ancestral orders, tribes, and sects, because, as he said, "these allegiances are partial. Because a man has so many loyalties each loyalty commands only a segment of himself." The citizen expresses these loyalties through institutions which reveal a "criss-crossing of loyalties." This circumstance was what Lippmann thought constituted modern society as pluralistic.

In these decades America was realizing how pluralistic it had   9:16
become. This change began to put mainstream churches at a disadvantage. They had to compete against both the new ideological forces and intense religious groups which tried at high cost to remain unassimilated. They did not want to be diffused, and wanted to resist erosion. For the mainstream groups, "to live and let live" became the ethos. People of affairs learned what Lippmann called "the necessity of not pressing any claim too far,"

and of "conducting matters so that there is some kind of harmony in a plural society." This was their great contribution to civil peace, bargained for at the cost of some loss to their own self-interests. The Fundamentalist minority in the twenties and thirties could keep on pressing their claims at whatever cost to civil society. So could radical factions of left and right. For most others, life during the Depression decade was one that ordinarily attracted only semicommitments and shared loyalties, if at some expense to their groups while at some profit to those who sought social peace in the most tense times.

9:17   By the mid-thirties, in the face of great tests which we shall forthwith describe, it was ever more clear that congregations and denominations, for all their internal conflicts, were coming to be among the agencies through which conflict could be directed into ever less dangerous channels. The Great Depression produced the deepest crisis in society since the 1860s. In the nineteenth century the mixture of denomination plus creed plus region plus race had led to deeper cleavages in society and to war. Southern *versus* Northern Baptist, Methodist, and Presbyterian groups produced opposite justifications for the War Between the States, while white *versus* black Methodists or Baptists in the South reinforced the separate and warring camps in respect to slavery.

9:18   Now in the fourth decade of the twentieth century conflict between people in competing economic and social classes once again had increased. The ideological right and left thereupon had their best chance in the century to demolish each other. For but one illustration: differing attitudes toward European and Asian totalitarianisms threatened to sunder society. For another: economic disorder led citizens to be tempted to extremes embodied in fascisms and communisms overseas. But there were so many cross-cleavages of the sort which Ross described and so many crisscrossings of loyalty, as Lippmann pictured them, that some measure of common national and spiritual life survived.

A Culture of Cross-Clefts and Crisscrossings

9:19   We have resisted all temptations to turn this story into an almanac of denominations, a program of equal time for all movements. Instead, the place of groups in the public argument has determined the plot. The thesis that trauma was preoccupying the cultural center leads to the discovery that potential disruptions

from "outsiders," "marginal groups," and others did not disturb
society at large or even come to public notice. Six illustrations
will show how various movements were neutralized and accom-
modated. The first is a simple story with a bearing on the future:
the case of the first Muslims in America. An observer with acute
eyes would expect to watch Muslims serving as an irritant in
a Protestant or Christian or Judeo-Christian culture between the
wars. There were some adherents of Islam in the United States.
Yet if the concentration was to be on public religion, on the sort
which made news, this observer would need *very* acute eyes.
Halfway between the wars when C. Luther Fry reported on
American "churches," he noticed Mormons and Jews but not
Muslims. Most of the earliest American Arabs, from Syria and
Lebanon in particular, came unoffensively as converts to Christianity. In 1911 sociologist Louise Houghton found ten Catholic
and eighteen Protestant churches with Syrian pastors and, presumably, Syrian members. There were no mosques, though she
spotted nine small Muslim "religious bodies," three of them
Druze and, in Sioux City, Iowa, a Shi'ite community—which she
did not list as Muslim!

The Immigration Restriction acts of 1921 and 1924 were de-   9:20
signed to keep out people like Muslims, but a few were gathering
in one large urban area, Detroit; one rural setting, Ross, North
Dakota; and two small cities, Michigan City, Indiana, and Cedar
Rapids, Iowa. In the Detroit area they adapted existing structures
for religious purposes, but probably the first structure built to be
a mosque was in a town with fewer than one hundred people,
Ross, North Dakota, in 1929. So effective were its builders at
crisscrossing and adapting activities that most of them took on the
religious colors of their neighbors and turned Lutheran. The
mosque was bulldozed in 1978, and only a cemetery remains.
More durable was a mosque built in Cedar Rapids, Iowa, in 1934,
for a friendly group who held joint dinners with St. George Orthodox Church. The Quaker of Quaker Oats, whose silos and
whose odors dominated the scene, could look down on signs of
concord, not conflict. Muslims were too small, too adapted, to
scandalize.

Issues of language, ethnicity, geographical isolation, and con-   9:21
stant internal feuding kept the Eastern Orthodox Christians from
living up to the potential for visibility their numbers implied.
Hundreds of thousands of them lived and worshiped in America.
They were ordinarily all but unrecognized as a public presence,

as a set of disputants in the cultural forum, even if their bishops regularly made calls at the White House. Fry also gave no account of these Orthodox. Prevented, as the Muslims were, from seeding America with a sizable immigrant population after 1924, they spent their energies in internal disputes as they came to terms with, variously, Greek monarchism, the Russian Revolution, or issues of identity and leadership in America. This they did strenuously and noisily, so noisily that sometimes they did make news, in one instance contributing a rare dead body to the scene of religious rivalries. To most Americans, the Greeks would have priority among these churches. In 1922 the Greek Archdiocese of North and South America was canonically authorized under Alexander, an unfortunate archbishop who reigned over chaos. His great distraction was a set of battles between pro- and anti-monarchist forces in Greece, with the royalists having only a small but fanatic faction in America. So intense did battles between factions become that police sometimes had to be stationed in churches during worship to ward off violence.

9:22   Historians of Orthodoxy speak of the interwar period as a time of "The Civil War within the Church," a conflict so intense that it drained Orthodoxy of energies which might have gone into the making of a bigger mark in American religion and culture. The war had to be fought under dreadful circumstances, since the Greek community suffered much from the Depression. Its people rejected most of the ideological lures which drew European counterparts into far left and right movements—Marxism was not popular in the Greek community. At the same time, many kept expressing loyalty to Greece and, in some cases, to its royal family. The clergy represented that tie most of all.

9:23   The new patriarch appointed to succeed the failed Alexander in 1930, Athenagoras, brought some measure of peace. A popular leader who was greeted with enthusiasm upon his arrival in 1931, he had to face the disorder of parishes which were used to ignoring or rejecting orders from anywhere but within their own parishes. He paid respects to President Herbert Hoover, worked to become known in Washington, and settled in for his difficult task. By 1936 he had made the rounds of the parishes and spoke in generally optimistic terms. Yet devastating divisions threatened. Athenagoras found some who betrayed the church, he charged, "by becoming Jehovah's Witnesses and followers of other heresies. Others have no patriot feelings or preach sermons of division and hatred among the people, distorting the truth, scandalizing the Faith and the conscience of the faithful." So eager was he to be a man of the people and a parish visitor that he disdained pomp, rode subways, and traveled so much that some critics were reduced to finding no more fault than that he was away from his desk too much.

Athenagoras soon found, however, that his efforts at reform provoked violent reaction. As he worked to centralize power, he offended not only many of the laity but also clergy, some of whom had entered the ordained priesthood upon payment of fees and in order to earn a living from it. They treated parishes as their own possessions. A new element entered the scene when a Russian Orthodox archbishop Apollinarius ordained Greek lay Americans into the priesthood, a violation of Orthodox practice and canon law. Athenagoras rejected their religious "variety stores," as they began to appear in the New York area. These clergymen, he charged, were "people who trade religion for material profit." His attacks on them led to the building up of his corps of enemies.   9:24

The Russians and the priestly variety store clerks were less his problem than was a formal group of dissidents who gathered around a rival in 1933 and 1934, Archimandrite Christophoros Contogeorge, who led a faction opposed to centralization and the ordering of leadership. In the Clergy-Laity Congress in Chicago late in October of 1933 this element led insulting and almost violent disruptions. As Athenagoras saw it, "they opened drains and sewers and, with their hands, scattered everything that was filthy. . . . They were matricidal as they turned against our Mother Church with cynical piety and bitter tongues." A schism did result, as did a sequence of appeals to the Ecumenical Patriarchate and the courts of law. Contogeorge kept his little faction going for years, and won some skirmishes, but his movement eventually faded after having tested the boundaries of civility in Orthodoxy. The entire struggle went on, however, without drawing much notice outside Greek and, because of jurisdictional rivalries, other ethnic Orthodoxies.   9:25

Athenagoras, who had his battles with other Orthodox leadership, constantly worked to urge his church to represent a common face. In a letter to Orthodox leadership in March 1941, he complained of Orthodox invisibility caused in part, he was sure, by the infighting. Although it was "the Orthodox Church of Christ and although our Christians here exceed the five million mark," he wrote, it "is still, officially, 'the forgotten Church in America.'" The members had failed to make Orthodoxy "known   9:26

to the American Government, churches of other denominations, intellectuals and to the American public in general." A sad by-product of this forgottenness was the inability of the Orthodox to find "the means to defend our Faith against any kind of proselytism"; it lost members to aggressive sects. The public debate about religion in culture went on as if Orthodoxy, busy with schism, did not exist.

9:27   The Greek situation was mirrored in other Orthodox ethnic communities. Thus the Romanian Orthodox Episcopate of America was troubled from the day of Bishop Policarp's arrival in Detroit in June 1935. He was cheered when he was greeted by Romanian speakers; his first impression was: "Thus the Romanians had resisted Americanization." But their ability to use the language of the old country did not mean that these eager greeters of a long-awaited bishop still had their hearts in Romania. He saw himself as the rescuer of people from the embrace of "sectarians"—who were also always on Athenagoras's mind—Jews, Catholics, and others. He intended to be a firm and aggressive leader, but he overestimated the time his Americanized followers would be deferential and he underestimated their willingness to oppose him at all points and to continue their battles with each other and with him while showing no respect at all. He was noted for having said, "I take you as I found you, but from now on there will be order." There wasn't. The people who did look back to Europe perpetuated old regional battles: they were Transylvanians, Banateni, Macedonians, Bukovinians, before they were Romanians and after they were Americans. Others fought over which calendar to use, since some still held to the Julian calendar. Never did he get his Romanian church to be of one mind, and he beat a retreat to his old home. In July 1939, at the Detroit train station where crowds had greeted him four years earlier, he left, with no one to wish him well.

9:28   The Armenian Orthodox had the most violent internal life, and one of the rare deaths connected with organized religion occurred in their camp. In this instance as in the other Orthodox scenes, Old World loyalties again turned out to be more volatile than homegrown schisms. Archbishop Leon Tourian, head of the Armenian Orthodox Church, was leading worship in New York just before Christmas in 1933. In front of two hundred congregants, four assassins stabbed him, having moved past his armed bodyguard with such swiftness that no one saw the act itself. The incident resulted from conflict at the Century of Progress Exposition in Chicago the previous summer. At that scene Tourian had rejected the old Armenian flag and insisted on the hammer and sickle of the Soviet Union, of which Armenia had been forced to become a part. In August he was assaulted at a picnic in Massachusetts, the hammer and sickle again being the issue. Still, despite the recall of the Red Scare, the presence of the red flag, and the shedding of blood, the Armenian incident had little effect on the public at large. It only reflected a division which permanently divided the Armenian worshipers in the United States. Orthodoxy was seen as fighting European battles on American soil, as off by itself from the rest of the American scene.

Some Orthodox leaders tried to bring the various national 9:29 churches together, but they only increased the conflict by doing so. Aftimios Ofiesh, elected in 1916 to head the Russian mission in America, met opposition from the first day. After the next year the Russian Revolution complicated Orthodox Church life in America; while his rivals promoted Syrian Orthodox ties, Aftimios wanted to keep Russian ones, but this became impossible. He made many efforts through the twenties to consolidate his position against rivals as leader of Middle Eastern Orthodoxy in America and by 1927 was making bold proposals, which only met bolder opposition and were condemned by many colleagues in the sphere of Russian orthodoxy in 1930. But when he married in 1933, against canons for Orthodox bishops, he lost almost all support. His rivals all failed to persuade a majority to follow them, and drifted off, some also to marry. Ethnic rivalries fueled these personal conflicts, and the idea of an Orthodox Church in America remained only a dream. The Orthodox, for all their ability to fight, fought each other and canceled out their potential to clash with non-Orthodox.

That the Mormons had indeed been moving out of the zone of 9:30 public dismissal toward a situation of some acceptance resulted from the fact that the public believed pro-Mormon elements of the popular press more than they believed the federal officials on the scene. It must also be said that Mormon public relations were more effective. A third illustration of neutralization appears in connection with a group that found a way to win commendation where long it had been only condemned. The Mormons met all the terms of original-stock America; though some Scandinavian and other European converts immigrated to the Mormon kingdom in and around Utah, most Latter-day Saints bore New England names and should always have "fit in." Certainly they stood for many of the virtues and cherished the artifacts that small-town American Protestantism enjoyed. But they were heirs of America's most-hated religion in nineteenth century times, and their separate revelation and self-chosen segregation from much of the rest of America continued to set them apart. During the 1920s they dropped most of the vestiges of their cooperative styles of economic life. But the Depression helped them move into a new status in American life. They sought and gained the reputation of "taking care of their own," and thus many conservative Americans who resisted the New Deal measures, to say nothing of socialism, found themselves taking a new look at the Mormons.

9:31   The Church of Jesus Christ of Latter-day Saints had reasons to sort out its economic attitudes. A communal economic program belonged to its past, and some Depression-era leaders wanted to connect Mormon efforts to "take care of their own" with that past. In 1939 J. Reuben Clark, Jr., the Mormon emissary to the Republican party, felt it important to caution that there was a growing sentiment that Communism and the Mormon program, the United Order, were virtually the same thing. "I am informed that ex-bishops, and indeed bishops, who belong to communistic organizations, are preaching this doctrine." It is highly unlikely that any Mormon bishop belonged to anything communistic with a capital "C"; anything that verged on a welfare economy looked communistic to Clark. Ten years later Joseph A. Geddes remarked on the Mormon transition of the New Deal years: "Having given up the utopian struggle and having re-entered American society, the reunion was so thorough-going that in economic matters religious leadership espoused the cause and became a bulwark of the existing capitalistic system, giving it sanction by example and precept."

9:32   Such an espousal was at a far remove from the Mormon past or Christian realism of the new day during the New Deal. But the church and its membership were in transition, picking their way, during the Depression. Some Latter-day Saints did admit to Mormon dependency. Thus Gordon Taylor Hyde, a Salt Lake City bishop, wrote a letter to a Senate candidate who had chided people for their employment on public works projects: "It is my opinion, and that of many other Bishops, that without the aid of the present government relief projects it would be impossible to care for the unemployed members of our church." But such voices were hardly heard in a climate which produced many who welcomed publicity about a people who took care of their own. The *Reader's Digest* was simply the most widely read: "A year and a half ago," the editors wrote in 1937, "84,460 Mormons, about one-sixth of the entire church membership, were on direct relief. Today none of them are. The church is taking on its own. . . . Within a year every one of the 84,460 Mormons was removed from the government relief rolls all over the country." The myth was set in the public mind, and at least one religious group found the Depression fate a means of access to public accessibility.

The most agitated Roosevelt agent was Dean R. Brimhall of   9:33
the Works Projects Administration, who met with Mormon leadership at Salt Lake City in 1936. While the Mormons made much of "taking care of their own," Brimhall was unconvinced. A year later he made a point of the fact that only six of the forty-eight states had a "higher load" of Emergency Works Program cases than Utah. He called the notion of Mormon self-administered welfare "propaganda" and "fictitious." The Mormon leadership in 1938 in an official policy statement admitted: "The Church has not yet made any effort, or pretended to make any effort to take members from governmental work projects." Brimhall was angry that such announcements did not square with the voice of Utah politics during the New Deal. Thus during the 1936 campaign a Republican adviser boasted: "All Mormons were off relief. National publicity immediately followed. . . . At last someone had shown that 'it could be done' without governmental aid."

The Mormons had several interests. First, of course, was the   9:34
face of human need, the suffering brought on by the Depression. Second was a theological theme which matched the old Puritan ethos that still marked Protestant America: people should not be on "the dole"; they must, if they are able-bodied, be productive workers. This meant that government or church, preferably church, should find opportunities for work, and this the Latter-day Saints certainly strove hard to provide. President Roosevelt joined them in opposing the dole; he saw that it contributed to "spiritual and moral disintegration." The Mormon-owned *Deseret News* warned people to make preparation: "where no preparation has been made, suffering, difficulties, and bloodshed are not remote possibilities." The result of the efforts left the truth somewhere between the public relations imagery of a people who "take care of their own" and the criticisms of Brimhall. A plan

for welfare established by the church was a sincere effort, but it
never succeeded in helping Mormon believers get off the rolls of
those who benefited from government intervention.

9:35   Some of the idea of "taking care of their own" was motivated
by Heber Jeddy Grant, who was the seventh Prophet of Mormonism, from 1918 to 1945. Grant despised Roosevelt, believed that
the New Deal was "one of the most serious conditions" that confronted him and that there was evidence that many Saints "almost
worship" Roosevelt. Only church leaders should be so revered.
Yet Grant could not control all the Mormons; the *Deseret News*,
owned by the church but a public paper, generally supported Roosevelt, as did most of the Mormon faithful.

9:36   A fourth case resulted from the fact that the church in question
posed no new issues. Some of the historic irritants to mainstream
denominations and nonreligious Americans had made their point
or were in civilly quiescent stages between the wars. The Church
of Christ, Scientist, had by no means won the battle for full acceptance, and still had to work to get legal guarantees for its practitioners, but the pattern had been earlier set and no new *causes
célèbres* occurred at this time. Meanwhile the *Christian Science
Monitor* won increasing respect for the movement. Thus a church
whose theology all the others rejected and which they did not
regard as part of the ecumenical Christian orbit became increasingly acceptable in the cultural mainstream.

9:37   The best illustration of both cross-clefts and neutralizing,
though unexpected, partnerships, was Seventh-day Adventism,
often poised with Christian Science, Mormonism, and Jehovah's
Witnesses as a fourth born-in-America religious movement. It
stayed alert on the front of church and state. The "crisscrossing"
pattern of religious interactions pointed to by E. A. Ross and Walter Lippmann was certainly in operation in this case: Adventists,
to protect Saturday worship and to oppose the legal support of
Sunday as a day of rest, shared sympathies with Jews, who held
a similar position. Together they opposed "blue laws" in state
after state, and thereby extended the zone of religious liberties or,
as some would have it, despite the Adventists' own intense reli-
giosity, they contributed to the further secularization of American
customs and practices. *Liberty*, the magazine of its Religious Liberty Association, became recognized far beyond Adventism for
its call for religious liberty.

9:38   The most public Adventist intrusion—from the point of view
of a group that did not see itself as politically active—occurred

when President Roosevelt named Myron C. Taylor as his personal representative to the Vatican in 1939. Adventists had long prophesied that the "beast of Rome" foretold in the biblical Apocalypse, now living in the Church of Rome, would make alliances with the United States government. The *Liberty* editor warned that the Taylor appointment, if carried out, would "force Senators and Congressmen to take notice of an issue which is repugnant to the ideals and the consciences of Americans who believe in a separation of church and state." He attacked the Catholic clergy for "artful maneuvering." In the spring of 1940 the church disseminated two million tracts protesting the planned move. General Conference president J. L. McElhany tried a different tack: he wrote to Roosevelt assuring him that support for his efforts at making peace would be much more forthcoming from the churches if the Taylor appointment were withdrawn. Such noisy activity would have stamped Adventism as a political church, were it not for the fact that its voice was only part of a huge chorus which issued from almost all forms of non-Catholic faith in 1939 and 1940. So Adventism, through its protests, also did not disrupt the civil peace as it might have in isolation.

The legal tradition and Anglo-Saxon patterns of liberty made room for the least compromising sect. This fifth people was self-segregated as the sect which had a theology to condemn everyone else and a way which led everyone else to condemn them. This was the Jehovah's Witnesses, increasingly polyglot and multiethnic, but still largely made up of poorer people of original stock. They professed to be nonpolitical and antipolitical, and had suffered for their convictions in World War I, when, seen as unpatriotic, some of them were deprived of civil liberties. In an editorial in 1929 the leadership expounded on earthly government and America, Satan's organizations, demanding loyalty only to God's organization as they saw the Jehovah's Witnesses movement to be. They thought it reasonable to picture that Paul in the Bible was directing loyalty only to "the powers possessed and exercised in God's organization, and not to those that are exercised in Satan's organization."   9:39

In Depression times the struggle meant to Joseph Franklin Rutherford, successor to founding pastor Charles Tazewell Russell as the leader, a forthcoming battle of Armageddon between labor and capital. But he did not treat this metaphorically, as the Christian realists did. This was to be a literal battle between the religion, politics, and economy of "Satan's organization" and   9:40

Jehovah's followers in their sect. This outlook kept them in constant jeopardy before the law and in the public eye. If there was any group at which other religious people in America were still tempted to shoot, it would have been the Witnesses.

9:41 The members of the sect, with official leadership, did all they could to promote reaction, particularly from Catholics, the worst agents of Satan. They tested American law more than any other group, and by doing so, all but forced the United States Supreme Court to extend interpretations of the scope of American civil liberties. In 1935 Judge Rutherford began criticizing as an act of idolatry the practice of saluting the American flag. The larger public began to do what it could to trip up the offending and offensive Witnesses. In November of 1935 two children of Witness Walter Gobitis, instructed by their parents to refuse to salute the flag in school, resisted that salute. They were expelled. Their father sued to have the action repealed. The next year over a thousand Witnesses were arrested in flag salute cases. Finally in 1940 in a precedent-shattering case, *Minersville School District v. Gobitis*, the Court, with but one dissent, ruled against the Witnesses, partly under the influence of a grateful Jewish immigrant, Justice Felix Frankfurter. Never in this period did religiously founded mob violence threaten so much. Witnesses were castrated, imprisoned, abducted, exiled from their homes, disgraced. Finally the attorney general had to act to protect them. The *Christian Century* was one of many liberal church organs that spoke up passionately for a sect it had to despise. Not until 1943 did the Court reverse itself and protect the Witnesses' practice of religious freedom.

9:42 The *Gobitis* case, teamed with another Jehovah's Witness incident decided two weeks earlier in favor of the Witnesses, *Cantwell v. Connecticut*, were of epochal significance in Constitutional history. For the first time the Supreme Court, using the Fourteenth Amendment, assured that First Amendment liberties would be protected in all the states. Before that time support of the amendment had been up to state and local authorities, and the pattern of support was very irregular. Since that time there have been endless arguments about the Court decisions on religion, and some scholars have disagreed with such a use of the Fourteenth Amendment, but ironically it was the antinational Jehovah's Witnesses who did most to nationalize religious freedom cases.

9:43 The *Cantwell* decision was based on incidents relating to interfaith conflict of a sort that was almost unheard of outside the Je-

hovah's Witnesses orbit. All through the 1930s the sect engaged
in practices which collided with local authorities and laws forbid-
ding certain practices of selling literature and making noise in
public places. The American Civil Liberties Union, a secular organization, took up the cause of Witness liberties. Jesse Cantwell,
in the most public case, insisted on playing a phonograph record
which, the Court said, embodied "a general attack on all organized religious systems as instruments of Satan and injurious to
man; it then singles out the Roman Catholic Church for strictures
couched in terms which naturally would offend not only persons
of that persuasion, but all others who respect the honestly held
religious faith of their fellows." But Cantwell represented "no
clear and present menace to public peace and order." He was
home free, free to be offensive and uncivil, free to attack Catholics and other religionists.

In 1920 George Santayana published an essay which the Jeho-   9:44
vah's Witness cases twenty years later well illustrate and which
throws light on the way conflict came to be addressed: "English
Liberty in America." On the one hand in English America there
were "pensive or rabid apostles of liberty," seeking liberty only
for themselves; like these Witnesses, they brought "vehement defiance of anybody who might ask them, for the sake of harmony,
to be a little different." By themselves they could not produce or
keep a republic. Here the other side of English liberties came into
play. The legal tradition was based on this English liberty which
is "co-operative, because it calls only for a partial and shifting
unanimity among living men." Thus "absolute liberty and English liberty are incompatible," but Americans found a way to
assure an ever larger zone of freedoms to individuals and groups
while finding civil ways to compromise for the good of the whole.
Such a resolution could never be complete or comforting;
America was to remain tense about religious liberties ever after
the Supreme Court began to build on these Jehovah's Witnesses
cases.

A final instance of neutralized potential disrupters brings   9:45
strange company to the circle of outsiders, the religious humanists
in the left wing of Unitarianism or those who came to humanism
independently. They would have felt ill at ease and not at home
with Islam and Orthodoxy, Mormons and Jehovah's Witnesses,
but they also represented challenges to the mainstream culture yet
were not disruptive. Unitarians, of course, were from the mainstream; a century earlier they had parted with Congregationalism.

Orthodox Christianity repudiated their doctrine, but Unitarian social status, as evidenced by the frequency of appearance of Unitarian names in *Who's Who*, was unchallenged. They were original-stock Americans who were well-positioned to influence the culture. Yet as a denomination they were small, barely visible on the screen of Catholics, Baptists, and black Christians.

9:46   Unitarians of the past had been theists, but around the turn of the century one element began to feel kinship with the Free Religious Association, Ethical Culture, and other religious or ethical movements which were nontheistic. This developing humanist flank was not always opposed to witness to God, but it was opposed to metaphysics, to making God integral to religion, and they found the concept of God potentially and, as the historical record showed them, often actually limiting to human imagination and freedom. Since the "100 percent Americans" put God along with country among their highest sources of value, a religious movement dealing with non-God could have been expected to have sent rioters into the streets in front of humanist agencies. Nothing of the sort happened: Unitarians seemed to be elitist philosophers more than worshipers. They were out of sight and out of mind to all but polemicists. The humanist movement within Unitarianism was seen, among those who noticed it, to be a tempest within a remote denomination, not an upset in American culture.

9:47   The Unitarian side of the humanist fusion is often seen as the result of activity by three ministers raised in Protestant orthodoxy who became reactors against it. They were Charles Frances Potter, ex-Baptist from New York and, more significantly—for Unitarian humanism was a midwestern movement—John H. Dietrich, ex-Reformed, then in a Minneapolis Unitarian congregation, and Curtis W. Reese, ex–Southern Baptist, but then a Unitarian minister in Des Moines. A former Catholic priest, William L. Sullivan, is often listed with the other patriarchs. Dietrich and Reese met at a Des Moines convention in 1917, found that they had both been preaching humanism, and determined to press their case. They found company among other ministers, philosophers, and lay leaders all through the twenties. Leading Boston-area Unitarians opposed them, but the opposition was not of a militant sort, and many Unitarians found themselves in a middle position, tolerant of the "No-God" option.

9:48   Humanism was later to suffer for having been overidentified with optimistic outlooks such as pre–World War I Protestant liberalism in general shared. Thus in 1927 Reese introduced *Humanist Sermons* with the notice that the humanist feels that "personal and social values should speed ahead." The humanist "finds no compensation in unfolding cosmic purposes, no cosmic compensation for the dead scattered over a thousand battlefields nor for the living dead in a million homes." Instead, the humanist would "speed up" the processes of human development. "Man is capable of achieving things heretofore thought impossible. It but remains for religion to place human responsibility at the heart of its gospel."

While humanists were coming to prominence and in some   9:49
places predominance among Unitarians, a body of philosophers, some of them Unitarian, were on a convergent track. Charles Lyttle, scanning this scene, pointed to titles such as Max Otto's *Natural Laws and Human Hopes* (1926), Harry Elmer Barnes's *The Twilight of Christianity* (1929), Walter Lippmann's *Preface to Morals* (1929), and Roy W. Sellars's *Religion Coming of Age* (1928) as a crowding of a publishing market late in the twenties. One or two of these—Lippmann's most notably—departed from the optimistic "speed up" impulse and spoke of modernity as working its "acids," as creating a spiritual wasteland, a forlorn scene. When the Depression came, humanism took on a more realistic turn, as did much of Protestant orthodoxy.

The special year for humanist emphasis was 1933, when the   9:50
Depression was deepest. Dietrich published a tract for the American Unitarian Association which described religious humanism not as atheistic but as a movement which "simply ignores the existence of God." Therefore "its whole program is based on the assumption of an indifferent universe." There humans must carve out their own destiny. Supernatural religion was the enemy. "Two ideas are here in conflict: on the one hand, man organizing and directing his own life, on the other, professing to believe that a deity orders it for him."

In 1933 Reese's successor in Western Conference Unitarian-   9:51
ism, the Reverend Raymond B. Bragg, teamed with philosopher Sellars, the main drafter, to compose a "Humanist Manifesto," which fourteen ministers—thirteen Unitarian and one Universalist—signed along with a rabbi, eleven professors, and numerous independent writers and thinkers. They issued the manifesto to an un-waiting world, which ignored it as the humanists would ignore God. Decades later Fundamentalists looked back on the manifesto as the issuance of a creed of official anti-God religion which be-

came privileged in American life, but in its time Fundamentalists paid no attention, press notice was small, and outside the circles of philosophy and one denomination, few paid notice.

9:52   Significantly, while Unitarianism had for decades made room for people of humanist outlook, the new, more vocal humanist party felt especially at home after the election to the presidency of their denomination in 1937 of Frederick May Eliot, who was friendly to the humanist cause. What external response there was came not from Catholics and Fundamentalists but from a few religious liberals within and outside Unitarianism. Thus the *Christian Century* made light of the manifesto's fifteen points, rather snidely suggesting that one was so jejune that it must have been "lifted bodily from some sophomore's term paper." It attacked philosopher John Dewey, the most notable signer, for the "incredible" act of lending his name to the creed. The editors were most vehement in their opposition to the notion that "man is at last becoming aware that he alone is responsible for the realization of the world and his dreams." No, humans were becoming aware that the man-made social order was breaking down because the Cosmic Partner was being ignored. On this front, the *Christian Century* sounded like the Christian Realists of the decade.

9:53   Curtis Reese was sure that humanists were "entering into the consciousness of increasing numbers of people," but he overestimated his count. Union Seminary president Henry Sloane Coffin, another liberal, knew why there was no surge: "Their incapacity to recognize the perils to their cause in some of the trends of economic development and to embody their own ideals in the industrial system has helped to bring about their present weakness." And Max Otto who, with Clarence Darrow and John Haynes Holmes, refused to sign, saw it in market terms: "Humanism . . . cannot be 'sold' to people." [This] "'Manifesto' will serve no sufficient purpose." Liberals found it unrealistic, conservatives ignored it, ethicists found it too intellectual, but most people found it not at all.

9:54   Religious humanism lived on noninstitutionally in the thought of a number of leaders, most notably John Dewey, the Columbia University scholar who was the most important public philosopher of his age. Dewey, reared in moderate New England Congregationalism, had long left its creeds behind but was not averse to using the terms "religious" and "God" if he had his own opportunity to define them. One year after the Humanist Manifesto he published a short book, *A Common Faith*, which critics thought was a rehash of old Deweyan views but which, through the decades, has come to stand as a convenient summary of his outlook on religion. Because he was the preeminent theorist behind public education in the mid-century decades, his views on religion in society, culture, and schools acquired some institutional importance and, decades later, would serve as grist for debates about humanism in education.

The John Dewey of the 1930s completely ruled out supernaturalism and any notion of a transcendent God. He was opposed to religion being expressed through denominational life, and favored a religious outlook in all of life. This meant that there was no room for creeds but only for experience. He felt that science and religiousness on these terms were not incompatible, though many colleagues took him to task for what they regarded as a lapse into sentimentalism. Dewey thought it important to profess that the democratic process itself was spiritual or religious, and needed propagating as such—under whatever terms—in the schools. Of course, he would not close the churches; they had an aesthetic and social function, and their symbols and rites might still reinforce human values. "In that way the churches would indeed become catholic." 9:55

Dewey never pretended that his use of the term "God" would mean a cease-fire between himself and the supernaturalists who made up the vast majority of the American public. "I cannot understand how any realization of the democratic ideal as a vital moral and spiritual ideal in human affairs is possible without surrender of the conception of the basic division to which supernatural Christianity is committed." He ended the book on an uncharacteristically belligerent note as he defended a humanist religious outlook as containing "elements for a religious faith that shall not be confined to sect, class, or race. Such a faith has always been implicitly the common faith of mankind. It remains to make it explicit and militant." That was a challenge which liberals at the *Christian Century* and realists like Reinhold Niebuhr took up. The public must have regarded it, if it regarded it at all, as the kind of thing philosophers in a secular culture talk about. Decades were to pass before mass movements of opposition would find in Dewey and secular humanism the agents of conspiracy against religious America. Fundamentalists and modernists, liberals and realists, Catholics and Protestants kept each 9:56

The leading "Christian realist" Protestant theologian in his prime: Reinhold Niebuhr of Union Theological Seminary. (Ursula B. Niebuhr Collection.)

Monsignor John A. Ryan was both the most persistent Catholic articulator of a progressive social action program and a highly visible defender of conservative Catholic views on church and state. (Catholic University of America Archives.)

other in their figurative gunsights, while humanism was an expression of elites, one more evidence that America needed God and not an argument why it did not.

Catholicism: Right Reverend New Dealing

9:57   Catholics and Protestants had the scene pretty much to themselves. Their opposition was now entering a new stage. The Depression called forth new urgency about the social and political realm, and the noise of conflict between these two rivals, if it did not disappear, was background sound to disputes within the communities over the public order. Through the Depression and as war in Europe and Asia approached, both communions had new agendas. In the New Deal era, Catholic social thought and action came into their own. The original-stock Protestantism which had fought to retain dominance in culture during the twenties, now twice torn within, kept yielding ground as the new needs and opportunities brought other peoples and faiths into prominence. Catholicism was well poised precisely because so many members of organized labor were also members of the Catholic church. Catholic thought had been positioned since 1919 to deal with the place and rights of labor. The New Deal meant a new era.

Franklin D. Roosevelt, an Episcopalian, was ready to step into the role of leading what we might call the nation's public religion. This meant that he needed to count on and had to be friendly to Catholics, and he was. He had a cousin who had converted to Catholicism and had become an archbishop, and Roosevelt knew many close friends and coworkers who were Catholic. He simply had not been bred to be suspicious of Catholics in their churches or as politicians, and he was savvy enough to use the votes of Catholics or anyone else whose support would not lose him other backing.   9:58

Those who knew him well found Roosevelt to be theologically unsophisticated, accepting of the Christian creeds, if in a relaxed way, and incapable of letting theological confusion or controversy derail him. In March 1935 he uttered a response about religion which was as typical as it was rare: "In the dim distant past," he said of his foreparents, "they may have been Jews or Catholics or Protestants. What I am more interested in is whether they were good citizens and believers in God. I hope they were both." He of course strongly supported Catholic Democrat Al Smith in the 1928 campaign. If any American brought up Smith's Catholicism as an excuse to vote against the governor in intolerant spirit, Roosevelt responded: "I say solemnly to that man or woman, 'May God have mercy on your miserable soul!'"   9:59

It became clear between 1928 and 1932 that at least many powerful New York Catholics were promoting Roosevelt as a presidential candidate. Smith for a time challenged Roosevelt, but professional politicians sensed a better chance with Roosevelt and began to side with him against Smith, "one of their own." Monsignor John A. Ryan, who came to be called "Right Reverend New Dealer," feared revivals of anti-Catholicism, so he was glad to see Roosevelt make progress. Many of Roosevelt's inner circle were Catholic: James A. Farley, James M. Curley of Boston, and many others were in the front ranks. After he outpaced Smith, Roosevelt had to woo Catholics and he did so enthusiastically,   9:60

though with mixed effects. Eventually Smith came to campaign for Roosevelt, an act that helped Democrats in the closing of their ranks.

9:61   Roosevelt in the course of time learned how to neutralize residual Catholic opposition, though he risked alienating some Protestant supporters while doing so. Ryan, a reluctant backer at first, became positive and public about helping the campaign in quiet ways in response to friendly gestures by Roosevelt, who on occasion quoted papal encyclicals favorably. We have seen that Father Charles E. Coughlin, if later to Roosevelt's embarrassment, was a strong and early supporter, and he brought votes. Insofar as one can isolate Catholic populations, as in northern industrial counties where they overwhelmingly predominated, it was clear that these had largely moved into the Roosevelt and Democratic camps. Yet few observers spoke of a Catholic bloc vote, given the ambiguities of the motives voters express, the inefficiency of polling devices in 1932, and the fact that the Depression led so many people to try something fresh, like a New Deal.

9:62   After the election of 1932, Ryan and his cohorts, the manifest leaders of Catholic social action, were ready to put to work the bishops' program. Never did these Catholics show that they felt any strain between their politics and their theology. An encyclical which Roosevelt had quoted in 1932, Pope Pius XI's *Quadragesimo Anno*, also gave them encouragement, because it criticized the unrestrained capitalism which leaders felt had helped produce the Crash and the Depression in Hoover's years. Moderate and liberal Catholics could even say that they could call upon official, highest-level support for their views, and thus put the many conservative or at least unexperimental Catholics on the defensive.

9:63   The National Catholic Welfare Conference in Washington was the voice of the hierarchy, even if not all hierarchs agreed with all its positions. Also key was Father Francis J. Haas of the National Catholic Conference of Social Work, a gifted and powerful priest who very publicly moved into the New Deal camp and brought a constituency with him. So were leaders of the National Conference of Catholic Charities, which met in Omaha during October of the campaign year of 1932. Often such leaders and groups only cried out against Depression-era injustices and evils, but there seemed to be no way to do so without sounding anti-Hoover, anti-Republican, and pro-Roosevelt. Criticizing capitalism eventually came to be a constant, almost safe strategy. Father James M. Gillis in the Paulist *Catholic World* sounded much like the radical

Protestants: there were, he contended, "mad incongruities" in the economy of the day, and they were not accidental but "inherent in the capitalist system."

Within a month after Roosevelt took over, William Cardinal   9:64
O'Connell of Boston began to show a friendliness which other bishops also displayed. Various hierarchs came out with endorsements which Roosevelt could well have used in his second campaign in 1936, especially in those cases when politically he had to disappoint Catholics and some of them turned on him. The voluntary organizations of Catholicism, and thus the representatives of broad elements of the citizenry, climbed on the bandwagon and helped provide a constituency of a sort Protestant liberals were not sure they could muster to back their New Deal policy support.

Commonweal editors best summarized the state of affairs: "All   9:65
Catholics who desire to give practical effect to the principles of Social Justice laid down by Pope Pius XI" would follow Roosevelt's lead, because such efforts could "make the teachings of Christ apply to the benefit of all." Some Catholics wanted to claim that it was American Catholicism, not Protestant liberalism and Social Gospel people, who had made the religious preparations for the new way. When Roosevelt started naming Catholics to the cabinet and other high offices, the bonds of the church grew thicker. John A. Ryan and Francis J. Haas began to be called on regularly for advice and were given consultative posts. Certainly, American Catholics had never been so well positioned in policymaking as they were with the coming of the New Deal.

Not that everything in the Democratic administration was a   9:66
matchup for Catholic positions and policies. For one thing, many Catholic leaders were more critical of capitalism than the candidate had been. Critic after critic in the social-action camp sounded at least as radical as Reinhold Niebuhr in attacking the status quo. Thus Michael O'Shaughnessy blamed "human greed, the uncontrolled profit motive, the inordinate desire for gain" and similar factors for the Crash and the Depression. Cincinnati's Archbishop John T. McNicholas preached that "the comparatively small group possessing fabulous wealth and exercising the enormous influence wealth confers" was immorally distant from those who could not get "the very food and shelter necessary to keep body and soul together." At the other extreme, some voiced worries about the growth of big government. *America*'s Father Paul Blakely, S.J., warned that the government was "so ignorant and

corrupt that we should hesitate long before using it, even as a club." But such critics stood little chance in a Catholic populace which felt the need to do something governmental to meet Depression needs.

9:67   To follow Catholics in their support of specific policies such as the National Recovery Administration, the Agricultural Adjustment Administration, and other experiments, is hardly necessary here, so hand-in-glove did church proposal and political policy tend to be. Fairly early on Father Coughlin began to find fault with these policies, but he would be impossible to contain permanently by any political movement which he did not run. Many bishops openly asked their members to line up with New Deal programs which many Protestants and some Catholic conservatives thought of as socialistic. On the other hand, some Catholics claimed that the New Deal was not going as far as papal encyclicals, for example, in support of organized labor.

9:68   The pope, of course, did not command assent to the New Deal (militant Protestants always charged that American Catholics took all their political signals from Rome) and Catholics were free to do their own interpreting of it. For example, the National Recovery Administration and other programs met resistance among conservatives. Negative reaction came from one largely midwestern movement, the Central-Verein, which supported a kind of medieval Catholic guild system for labor. One leader of the Verein, P. Kenkel, called the NRA "State Socialism," and with a sense of balance expressed the thought that it gave too much power to big companies at the expense of small business. Another leader, L. S. Herron, used the Verein's house organ to agree: the program would "strengthen the position of capitalistic industry and still further intrench monopoly."

9:69   Meanwhile more conventionally conservative types, among them the editor of the San Francisco diocesan paper, the *Monitor*, thought the policy could "very deftly be turned into an American brand of Communistic state." All the debate turned out to be beside the point. The Supreme Court struck down the scheme, an act which caused many politically active Catholics to react in everything from disappointment to rage, but all knew that protest was futile, since all nine judges agreed on the measure's unconstitutionality. The social activists scurried to find other ways to keep the spirit of the encyclicals alive in the New Deal during hard times.

The labor issue which profoundly divided the Catholic forces   9:70
was the Child Labor Amendment, which needed support of ten
more states to take effect in 1932. Catholic leadership kept insisting that it opposed the exploiting of child labor but even more it
opposed government intervention into intimate spheres of life like
the family. Some critics said that child labor was no longer a
problem, a position which almost everyone later came to agree
departed from the facts. Cardinal O'Connell was one of the
strongest opponents of congressional involvement with child labor. It would, he charged, "Russianize American parents and nationalize American children." Massachusetts, where O'Connell
and Catholicism were powerful, failed to ratify the amendment.
As the controversy continued, Roosevelt consulted pro-amendment Catholics in an effort to neutralize the antagonists. He
mentioned that Catholic opposition was straining relations with
Protestants, whose leadership tended to favor the cause. John A.
Ryan, strongly pro-amendment, thereupon began downplaying
the extent of Catholic opposition, and an interfaith flap failed to
develop. Ryan himself put new efforts into support of the plan,
and rallied some Catholic voluntary organizations.

While Roosevelt and the New Deal experienced some difficult   9:71
times with Catholic leadership, for the most part the administration's prolabor record put it first in the hearts of Catholic workers
and, with them, of most politically minded clerics. Still, various
issues nagged. Some hierarchs were put off by the way the administration had dealt, or failed to deal with, Mexican anticlericalism
in the mid-thirties. At least one leader, Oklahoma's Bishop Francis C. Kelley, worked for the Republican challenger, Alfred M.
Landon, in 1936. Al Smith, always concerned as he was about
big government, astonished everyone by moving to support Republican Landon, but—one must by now say "of course"—
carried few voters with him.

For all the developing ties, as years passed, more and more   9:72
Catholics found elements in the New Deal programs with which
to disagree, and began to share their concern over threats from
big government. Father Coughlin became suddenly very public
about his charges that Communists were powerful in government,
and that may have pulled away some of his still large populist
following. Roosevelt, however, had to worry more about the way
charges of his being leftist would alienate Catholics. He became
very vocal about distancing himself from anything that smelled

Communist. Eventually some of the bishops began to be expressive about the recklessness of Coughlin's charges. In the encounter Roosevelt probably gained from the attacks. The bishops showed their support of the president, however muted and compromised it had to be.

9:73 　　Catholic capitalists like Philadelphia's John B. Kelly and Boston's Joseph P. Kennedy started calling Roosevelt the rescuer of capitalism itself, and their support helped him. Roosevelt, said Kennedy, was "a God-fearing ruler who has given his people an increased measure of social justice." The Roosevelt landslide of 1936 left no room for doubt where the huge Catholic electorate had put its energies. Ryan thought that 70 percent or more of the clergy were with Roosevelt, and opinion polls, though still not too reliable or sophisticated, confirmed high support among the laity. Both Roosevelt and Catholics came away with bonuses after four years characterized more frequently by alliances than by opposition.

9:74 　　When the newly reelected Roosevelt made an effort to pack the Supreme Court in order to have his way in his program, Catholics were divided. Monsignor Ryan saw reasons to speak of necessity for action and backed the president, but the *Brooklyn Tablet*'s Patrick Scanlan, usually anti-Roosevelt, grew more so: the plan would be the end of democracy, the beginning of dictatorship. The Court did not get packed, Catholic division on the issue had not sundered the church; but now enemies of Roosevelt had found the range and felt more free than before to criticize. The *Tablet* stepped up attacks. Recognition of Soviet Russia was a perennial issue which agitated the Catholic community, and fear of Bolshevism led to retreat from efforts to effect the bishops' program of 1919 in more detail and extent.

9:75 　　The new situation was curious, because through the thirties Protestantism with its middle-class base more often than not stayed with Republicanism against Roosevelt while Catholics provided New Deal support. Meanwhile, some Protestant elites, the realists and Socialists in particular, who always found public forums even where they had small constituencies, drew attacks from Catholics who accused them of being too far left. Most Catholic energies, however, went into internal concerns, into finding a Catholic course. It took moderating figures to speak for Catholicism against its own extremes. Thus Father John A. O'Brien was much in line when he said that "the only effective warfare" against Communism was not agitation but the acts of "sanitizing our social and industrial order," making it conformable to laws of justice and the needs of the poor.

John A. Ryan, by his stance combining traditionalist views of   9:76
Catholic relations to the state and progressivist social-action policies, drew fire from both sides. He was both the central figure and the most confusing one on two battlefronts. He could support restrictions on child labor, a living wage, and other causes he shared with liberal Protestants, and then provide the best cannon target to Protestants who feared Catholic assaults on the Constitution. It was in 1922 that Ryan first coedited *The State and the Church*. Liberals never forgot his contention in that book that "the State should officially recognize the Catholic religion as the religion of the commonwealth," though, of course, it was not in position to do so in America.

Could a Catholic like Ryan be too expressive on such subjects?   9:77
The most controversial point came when in his text, speaking of non-Catholic thought, he wrote: "Error has not the same rights as truth." Warily Ryan included the line that in a perfect political order non-Catholic groups would be limited in their rights. The Catholic state "could logically tolerate only such religious activities as were confined to the members of the dissenting group." Lines like that had hurt Al Smith in 1928, and kept Ryan at some distance from non-Catholics with whom he might otherwise have had natural alliances through the thirties.

When he picked up a new coeditor and revised the book in   9:78
1940 as *Catholic Principles of Politics*, Ryan only slightly compromised on the offending sentences, throwing in an occasional "apparently" to soften the most encroaching theme. Prewar Protestants thus found a fresh distraction, fighting off this putative or potential Catholic assault on their liberties. Ryan did not back down. Protestants "are wrong," he insisted; "we are right. And error has not the same rights as truth." How could he change basically in the years after he first uttered that truth in 1922? Catholic truth was changeless. Whenever, in the years following, Protestants wanted to point out the dangers of Catholicism, they would cite the notorious "Ryan and Boland" text, as they codenamed it, for examples of dangers. If such contentions could appear in the green tree of Catholic New Deal liberalism, think what could happen in the dry tree of conservatism!

All through the years of Ryan's predominance, Catholics were   9:79
emulating Protestants in one tactic: they certified their credentials as true Americans, *the* true Americans, so that they could provide

criticism and offer programs. They had no difficulty showing the public that they were extremely anti-Communist. But they also wanted to be extreme in defense of Americanism against secularism. In 1927 André Siegfried turned in his report on America as a Protestant nation, premier Catholic historian Peter Guilday placed himself in a long succession which did not end in the thirties. Guilday wrote that "to understand the Catholic Church in America, one must see how naturally and integrally the spiritual allegiance of its members knits into their national allegiance so as to round each other out." Like the Protestants, argued one apologist on whom he reported, the founders of America on the model of Jefferson produced a nation that was "Catholic in philosophical principle." After Al Smith lost his election, editor James Gillis consoled Smith's followers with the assurance that Catholics had found themselves "more in harmony with true Americanism than . . . were [those] who deny us the right to be American."

9:80   In the thirties, especially during the crusade against Communism, Catholics wanted to be seen as the preeminent American purists. In 1938 the bishops even proclaimed a "Catholic Crusade for Christian Democracy." Father Francis X. Talbot in *America* sounded the old call to Catholicism for staying with "the Constitutional and the traditional Americanism that made the country what it was before 1914." That year represented a curious time for Catholics to think of as good old days, for their situation was certainly better-off when Talbot was writing than it was in 1914. But Talbot had a special case to make for the thirties as a time of decline and fall. Now there were "devastating changes coming over American civilization," thanks to the fact that American liberals were being infected with "un-American ideas" while the American proletariat, as he called it, was being mobilized for redress. Along with many establishment Protestants, Catholics attacked the public schools for being godless and secularist, though Catholics came up with unacceptable plans for what to do about this circumstance. Whatever else happened, Catholics were not going to be seen as the second-best Americans.

9:81   In 1939 as war in Europe threatened, Roosevelt engaged in an action which enraged Protestants and other Americans, delighted Catholics, and divided the two communities. The president named Myron C. Taylor, a Protestant, his "personal representative" at the Vatican. The United States had no diplomatic relations there but its government found strategic reasons to locate an ear and a voice in Rome. Roosevelt, having consulted New York's potent Francis Cardinal Spellman, was also seeking to keep positive ties with domestic Catholicism. His motives were thoroughly mixed, but the conflict that ensued had clear religious party lines.

Roosevelt may have underestimated the nearly unanimous expression of passionate Protestant reaction to this move which played up to Catholicism. A reporter asked the president what Taylor would do at Rome. "He will get up in the morning, eat his breakfast and go through the normal functions of a human being in a post of that kind." Roosevelt, on Taylor's demand, gave him ambassadorial status. Omaha's Bishop James H. Ryan responded with, "Say what you will about some of the domestic policies of President Roosevelt, when it comes to the field of foreign affairs he is easily the outstanding statesman of the contemporary world." And young Monsignor Fulton Sheen was even more lavish: this appointment was "the first concrete recognition any great nation in modern times has given to the spiritual and moral foundations of peace."   9:82

The Federal Council of Churches wanted Roosevelt to withdraw the appointment, but it was a latecomer to the opposition which was more noisily voiced by denominations like the Methodists and Baptists, who were at home in political debate, and even by Lutherans, who were less so. The *Christian Century* was almost frantic; no event of this European war year received so much passionate attention from the editors who, for a moment again, were back in alliance with the also vigorously protesting Fundamentalists. Soon Seventh Day Adventists, Lutherans, Baptists, and others who did not usually ring doorbells together were calling at the White House. Roosevelt did not satisfy the callers, but he quieted them by talking about the personal and temporary character of the appointment. It was to become merely an irritant, not a *cause célèbre*, for the next ten years.   9:83

As war came, only the Catholic Worker camp voiced pacifist sentiments of the sort Protestants had long heard. For most of Catholicism, World War II was both tragic and in its own way a holy war. Like Niebuhr, Catholic leaders portrayed Hitler in demonic terms, and Nazism in catastrophic language. When the bishops gave theological support to the war effort, Roosevelt returned their favor: America would win the war and then put its energies into "the establishment of an international order in which the spirit of Christ shall rule the hearts of men and of nations."   9:84

9:85   In responding to such language and action, Bishop A. J. Muench of Fargo condensed the whole issue for Catholics: "When a government speaks with the voice of authority, it speaks with the voice of God." And San Antonio's Bishop Robert E. Lucey sounded just like the Niebuhrians, though more jingoist in his lead-in when he said that America was to "redeem the Christian Church from oppression and to salvage what is left of Western Civilization." The fissures between Catholics and Protestants, so deep in the twenties and still threatening in the thirties, could be temporarily crossed over or overlooked on the landscape after December 7, 1941, when a war demanding common action held the highest priority. For four years new preoccupations helped citizens momentarily transcend old differences.

The Search for a New Strategy in Protestantism

9:86   All the changes in Jewish, Catholic, and the rest of American religious life in the public order necessarily meant some adjustment in the still dominant Protestant order and approach. Still, most of the Protestant reordering occurred along party lines that developed independently of the challengers around it. In this reordering was an example of "cross-currents" and a "crisscrossing of loyalties" that would have taken place whether or not there had been any non-Protestants around. Fundamentalism was finding its way, generally out of the spotlight. Realists were coming to be the most heard articulators. But the public voice and action came chiefly from the Federal Council of Churches, the denominational bureaucracies and convention delegates, and others who were more expressive of the now beleaguered liberal and moderate position. Here we will collapse the two into "liberal," which had outlasted the Fundamentalist challenge and which was only chastened or turned revisionist when realists spoke up. They remain in the spotlight through the New Deal years and into the time of the Second World War.

9:87   John Bennett spoke for chastened liberals: "Now many of us are left with a feeling of theological homelessness." Walter Marshall Horton saw irony squared in the situation: "The liberal theology has now fallen beneath the same sentence of doom which it so often pronounced upon older systems of theology: O irony of ironies, its 'thought-forms' have become 'outmoded'!" He went further: "The thoroughness with which liberalism did its work has been its undoing; having completely assimilated the characteristic ideas of a particular era in history, it was foredoomed to perish with the passing of the era." Yet in embattled condition it still had to speak and act.

The voices of a professor, a bishop, a bureaucrat, an editor, and a pastor suggest something of the liberal response. First, University of Chicago professor Edwin E. Aubrey prepared an opinionated but still fair-minded report, *Present Theological Tendencies*. He at once gave a neat turn to the chiding from Horton when he noted that "reactions against the involvements of theology in the *Zeitgeist* are themselves modernistic," and belong to a newer *Zeitgeist*.　9:88

The book opened with the reflexive line: "The Western world has become acutely conscious of the culture problem which it faces because of the collapse of its economic structure." But Aubrey contended that the cultural collapse produced the economic one, and not vice versa. Philosopher John Dewey, poet Carl Van Doren, and humanist Joseph Wood Krutch appeared as witnesses to the fact that humanism was also not able to provide direction. "Not only have we lost faith in the puritan virtues but we have lost faith also in the democratic pattern of social life."　9:89

Aubrey did agree with the Christian realists that industry, government, science, and religious institutions alike were failing the citizens. But Aubrey showed how devoted liberals were to the intimate patterns of life when, in their tradition, he concentrated on the family, that institution which had long formed "the congenial environment of traditional Christian theology." As Aubrey looked at it now, contrasting the old-style woman with the new woman, he foresaw basic changes in the momentous transformation of family life. "When woman's place was in the home, this was a very busy home indeed." Now her tasks had taken her out of the family circle to a public world of work where she must gain a livelihood. The Depression pitifully revealed that the family was becoming ever less self-sufficient, ever more dependent on economic forces outside it. Now it was at the mercy of external conditions.　9:90

More disruption was evident in the accompanying change in sexual roles. The professor noted that "the new woman has helped to fashion a new sex-morality"; now the "old foundations of family life seem to be dissolving in a confusing bewilderment which besets the young people of today." Liberal Protestant thinkers were as concerned with the stability, and now the instability,　9:91

of the home as were conservatives. The crisis of social forms hit both sides equally hard. On what could liberals count in the future?

9:92   The important point Aubrey set out to make, one that colors most liberal talk in the period was this: Modernists, and now liberals after them, were self-correcting, self-adjusting people. They employed critical methods more than they invented conclusions. For instance, if once they had been too individualistic, they by now had become self-critical about their assumptions. At the same time, as they moved toward promoting collective social life, they did this with their sense of criticism intact. Modernists no less than realists displayed their alertness to change when they objected to the identification of modern Christianity with democracy and when they criticized the institutions of the church. Aubrey fired: "Only an ascetic Christianity can remain fixed; an institutional, and hence social, Christianity of a church must be emancipated from absolutism." The Hortons and Niebuhrs, he thought, should not be surprised to see liberal adaptation going on; such changes occurred in order to continue the constant purpose which dictated them. "This common purpose is the basis of [the Modernist's] adherence to the historic church." The Depression years and those before World War II can be seen as a history of liberal self-correction and adjustment of course.

9:93   If the professor could pay attention to the family, a bishop would naturally keep his eye on the congregation and the forms of the church and on lay concerns in general. Bishops had to be practical as well as pastoral. Some of the reformed liberals among them busied themselves with recovery. As powerful as any among them in the Federal Council of Churches orbit was St. Louis Methodist Episcopal bishop Ivan Lee Holt, who even served as a president of the council. In mid-Depression times he outlined a liberal program in *The Search for a New Strategy in Protestantism*. Professors could find refuges, but leaders like Holt acted in the smell and sound of battle.

9:94   Naturally, he began by speaking of "the hopes and disappointments of Liberalism." Had he not done so, he would have had to surrender his credentials as an alert leader. Line 1 is of note in all such books: "There is great confusion in Protestantism." Holt sided with Fosdick and Aubrey and anyone else who was self-critical about Modernism's having overdone adjustment to the times, to sentimentalism, human-centeredness, and ethical loss. After all the devastations he quickly had to ask: "Is Protestantism a spent force?" This, less than a decade after André Siegfried and other observers were still seeing it as the only national religion in America.

World Protestantism was certainly in retreat; look at life in the   9:95
Nazi regime of Germany. Factionalism paralyzed it in Great Britain. In the United States? In the First World War the Protestant church had been practically an agency of the state. No more. Not too long ago people dreamed, if not of one, then of but two Protestant churches, one liberal and the other conservative. Such merging did not happen. Nothing came of such hopes, and nothing would during the Depression. In the hard times, Holt had to turn to another front. Was a *third* schism ahead? "Economic issues are responsible for most decided differences of opinion, and there is danger of division over these issues in many Protestant denominations." Holt sounded weary: "Social hopes of this generation have not been realized. We do not have a warless world; we do not have a Christian state; we do not have a kingdom of God on earth." Such failures, he knew, all worked to weaken the Social Gospel. And Fundamentalism exploited the situation with some success.

Holt respected realist Reinhold Niebuhr, but he misread him: 9:96
"Through disillusionments, which have come to him and others," said Holt of Niebuhr, "he has reached the conclusion that religion has not the resources for the transformation of society." Somehow he thought that the author of *Moral Man and Immoral Society* had decided to concentrate on individual salvation alone. So he could not help much. Nor could the solutions of neoorthodox Karl Barth, the neomedievalism of the University of Chicago's Mortimer Adler, or the individualistic moralism of what was then called Buchmanism or the Oxford Group movement, "religion in evening clothes." The various strategies of these contenders canceled each other out. A question remained: "Which road shall we take to a New Reformation, to a reinvestment of the Protestant Church with power and influence?"

Economics, ecumenism, and missions, three of our chapter   9:97
subjects, represented the central Depression-era concerns of the Federal Council. As a bishop, Holt kept in mind the kind of burden that would elude catastrophic thinkers like Reinhold Niebuhr: the problem of church indebtedness in hard times. The churches had lost standing in the business world; this disturbed leaders though it was hardly an item that would unsettle critics of bourgeois church life. Second, it was clear that churchly resources

were too thin to permit churches to play a large role in human relief, such as in solving unemployment crises. "How much it would have added to the influence of the Church if it had been able to meet these needs of those who look to it for help!" First the church could not stop a world war. Now it offered little help in economic crisis, so its prestige was still further lowered and the strength of its influence questioned even more frequently.

9:98   Even modest Federal Council efforts to address wrongs brought it threats from lay members who would withhold contributions because their ministers were concerned with economic issues. Church assemblies were torn with bitter strife over the establishment of some Christian programs of social action. After such an observation, the politically minded reformer engaged in the kind of gesture that would win little sympathy from a Niebuhr, a Day: he sympathized with people of wealth and employers who were also distressed. His heart went out in sympathy to them when they got no sympathy from their ministers. "It is not an unusual thing to hear that some business man has withdrawn from the membership of the church," demoralized by pulpit criticism. The situation was getting so heated that the larger Protestant churches appeared ready to divide not over theological but over economic questions. That would be "a real calamity; it may have to come, but it will be a real calamity."

9:99   Holt rejected Kirby Page's call that "a revolution must come and the Church must be a leader in the revolution, though it is to be a peaceful revolution." Holt said no; "The only revolution which succeeds quickly is a bloody revolution." Liberals like himself who worked for a cooperative commonwealth in a cooperative world were getting to be regarded as reactionary and that was cause for complaint. The bishop was sure that 75 percent of the laity would be opposed to such cooperative dreams, since in their thinking *cooperative* was synonymous with *communistic*. A circular sent weekly to business people crossed his desk. The September 28, 1935, issue charged: "The Federal Council of Churches of Christ is the most hypocritical of the subversive organizations. . . . It is said to be largely financed by communistic radicals." If this was said of the safe Federal Council, what, then, of Christian realism and radicalism?

9:100   More than the Catholic church, Protestantism was squeezed between those who dismissed it as the defender of the status quo and those who feared it as communistic. Holt thought living in this vise was one of the most difficult problems the church had ever faced. He saw no way out of the dilemma in Depression America other than to take the route which the Niebuhrs would have said was a relapse into generality and pious individualism. They would agree with him that the churches had to bring specifically religious approaches to the issue. They shared his sense that humanisms had little to offer. Holt cited Irving Babbitt, prime humanist of the twenties: "Unless there is a reaffirmation of the truths of the inner life in some form—religious or humanistic—civilization is threatened at the base." What could that mean?

The second element in Protestant recovery strategy called for churches to work for a larger fellowship of nations and of working people, as well as for racial solidarity. Of course, Holt regretted the failure of America to take part in the League of Nations, which at that very moment, was failing even to force Mussolini to make terms after the Italian-Abyssinian war. The bishop was well aware of the disillusionment of those who had dreamed that the Kellogg-Briand peace pact would work, as it had not. As for working people, Russia brought improvements to them, but at terrible cost. Class warfare engendered hatred, so the policy of uniting class against class could not work. The efforts to develop racial solidarity schemes were worst of all. Hitler wanted to unite the Aryans, but again, at what cost! All the racial schemes were hopeless: some of their own leaders urged the Negroes of the United States to stand together. The Japanese were promoting a separatistic union of the colored races. Some people of English descent were suggesting that Great Britain and the United States should unite for world supremacy. On this issue, the new generation offered little hope: the youth aped their parents. 9:101

As for religious understanding, Holt knew that no sooner might someone advance the cause than he or she would be challenged by anyone who knew the true story of the divisive influence of religions: Jewish, Mohammedan, Christian, Catholic, Protestant—these were names for warring parties, not for agencies of unity. Even closer to home, Protestant denominations, Holt confessed, set family against family, brother against sister, father against son. Still, a liberal had to find ways to express hope: "Religion may unite while religions divide." 9:102

A few good signs were in sight. The Federal Council of Churches was protesting the treatment of Jews in Germany. Catholics and Protestants in Germany were friendlier to each other than they had ever been. Holt himself had attended the elevation of a priest to the rank of monsignor, a rare experience for 9:103

a Protestant in the 1930s, and on occasion he led services involving Jews and Catholics. In Hawaii he could point to the way religions beyond Judaism and Christianity joined in works of amity. Given such precedents, why could not people of good will hold an international conference of religions in the interest of world peace?

9:104   Third, the churches in the Federal Council core of Protestantism were revising their concepts of mission. Holt still and emphatically considered missionary work to be an element in the liberal Protestant program. He brought back from a tour of Asian and Pacific missions some hope for a new approach. Far from being imperial about Western missions, he wanted churches elsewhere to develop their own talents, ways, and resources and he promoted two-way communication between churches of East and West. Here as often Holt voiced the kind of hope that Niebuhr and the realists dismissed as liberal dreaming: "The peace of the world will depend on the quality of our Christianity in the United States. We can have peace if we are Christian enough."

9:105   His was the Federal Council strategy: the language of old piety about being consecrated to God survived. Holt wanted missions to be efficient, in order to minimize duplication in the programs of the cooperating churches. Of course, there must be "a union or closer federation of Protestant churches." There it was, bluntly out on the table: otherwise in disunion "the Protestant world will disintegrate." There was no fear of bigness when agencies united for peace and reform. As had his predecessors in the twenties, Holt wavered: was union or federation better for the United States? Without doubt, the Protestant churches in the past had made greater gains through their divisions than they could have made as a united church. These diverse churches reached different sections of the country and appealed to different temperaments. But for the present evils, Protestantism needed the power of a united voice. "We have come to the time when we need to think and act together; in federations we too often think together and then act separately."

9:106   The self-correcting and self-adjusting character of liberalism was evident also among thoughtful bureaucrats. The most poised of them was F. Ernest Johnson, executive secretary of the Federal Council, keeper of its social agenda conscience, and a more careful strategist than Holt. Johnson held to the liberal and progressivist outlook but was capable of picking up some impetus from Niebuhr and the realists. At mid-decade in *Church and Society* he made his own proposals for the elements of a social philosophy to serve organized Christianity. Like Holt, he felt the squeeze of the churchly right and left. "Every shot reaches a mark," he concurred, as he also responded to the left's charge that the church supported the economic status quo. Yet Protestantism gave "hostages to an admittedly unchristian social order"; it was, as the left, charged, "a first cousin to capitalism."

If true, said Johnson, these charges left Protestantism precariously situated. He heard as well the conservatives in pew and pulpit who charged from the right that churchly "humanitarianism becomes humanism, and hence anti-Christian," and that therefore churches should not specialize in humanitarianism. He agreed with most observers that, by and large, "the social and the theological conservatives in our American churches are the same people." Theological conservatism undergirded laissez-faire economics. Against it, the Social Gospel could not make much headway. There was little reason to disagree with Johnson's view of the squeeze.

9:107

Johnson honestly faced the problems of the Federal Council approach. Then, as before and later, there was always a question: for whom and to whom did council figures speak? Johnson: "A liberal takes his life in his hands to say this, but I believe it needs to be said" that the social programs and declarations of social faith of the various church groups, while he agreed with them in almost every detail, spoke only for minorities in the church. It was "no more than wishful thinking" on the part of leaders to picture themselves as representative of whole church bodies. These minorities, of course, had been important within the church, but they dared not be identified as being it.

9:108

Johnson did agree with the realists' charges that denominational resolutions on economic issues were generally ineffective. He quoted the *Christian Century* editor Paul Hutchinson on the ambiguity of Protestant leadership: " 'The astonishing thing to me is to meet so many young clergymen who think they can take [a socially revolutionary position] and yet remain on terms of pleasant social intercourse with church members whose whole manner of life is dependent on the continued operation of the profit motive.' " Protestantism's inevitable and necessary jousting between pulpit and pew, its politics based on everything from the financial support of churches to personal bonds between pastor and people, were among the factors which prevented it from developing a prophetic or critical outlook that had much effect.

9:109

9:110   Johnson showed his liberal side when he asked Christians to
rebuild using the notion of progress. The dream died hard: the
task was "to make the structure of society itself Christian, to realize in the world the ideals of the Kingdom." Johnson could find
no clear supportive scripture, but said that "the teachings of Jesus, *in a continuing world*," made such a theme unescapable. If
Jesus were living in the modern world, "his gospel would inevitably take on a more definitely social form, for the social gospel,
rightly understood, is Jesus' ideal of life applied to the structure
of a continuing society."

9:111   At that precise point Johnson the liberal parted company with
the Christian realists. He said that Niebuhr, in his psychological
analysis, always assigned too much to the demonic. Modern psychology ("the James-Lange theory of the emotions") also contradicted Niebuhr. Its proponents argued: "We do not fight because
we get angry, but get angry because we fight." The Social Gospel, in Johnson's eyes, was an adaptation of the James-Lange
theory. Niebuhr, he went on, overlooked the fact that the social
milieu helps determine what human nature was expected to be.
On point after point one sees Johnson, as was the way with reformed liberals, playing politics between the progressives like
Morrison and Holt on one side and the realists like Niebuhr on
the other, to the satisfaction of no one.

9:112   Still another precarious poise needed treatment. When churches
acted in the social, economic, and political orders, what happened
to the cherished American notion of the separation of church and
state? As a Protestant, Johnson had to believe in such separation.
Yet he also wanted to realize the dream of the whole church shaping the whole society. This included criticism of "man's other
religion," nationalism. The phrase was that of Chief Justice
and good Baptist Charles Evans Hughes. In the recently much-
debated *Macintosh* case in the Supreme Court, Hughes defended
the idea that the state in the end cannot claim ultimate control of
life over against the demands of God. "One cannot speak of religious liberty, with proper appreciation of its essential and historic
significance, without assuming the existence of a belief in supreme allegiance to the will of God." Americans were too ready
to buy the theory that the state had absolute control in the secular
order and that churches were purely spiritual. Absolute state sov-
ereignty seemed to be winning.

9:113   Here the Federal Council man was pessimistic. "The great in-
dictment of religion is not that it has failed to exalt the authority

of the church as against the state, as an abstract principle, but that it has done so little to transform society by enthroning spiritual sanctions in the affairs of men." In Depression times and with war looming, too many placed a premium upon the exercise of collective force, wrote Johnson; as a result, the state grew ever more dominant while the church was submissive.

Johnson has kept his place on this scene so long because in both his puzzlements and criticisms he almost perfectly stated the dilemma that liberal Protestantism was facing in the years when it was surrendering its old position of dominance without being ready to abandon the scene simply to secularists. For instance, just as Aubrey focused on the family and Holt on the congregation, Johnson paid attention to another intimate institution, the key public one for the shaping of America: its elementary and secondary schools. But squabbling religionists, jealous of their own views, were edging each other out produced a strange conjunction of "sectarian interests, bent on having no religion taught [in a school] if it cannot be their own, and the secular portion of the community, saying, 'A plague on *all* your houses'." — 9:114

At this time the dominant sort of Protestants, while losing position, did want to have influence in the schools, however complex that topic was: "There is a deep desire to maintain a place for religion in education, coupled with a fear that it will get out of bounds." Almost all religious communities would be happy, he thought, if there could be some religious teachings in public schools. Deep down in their hearts Protestants no more than Catholics wanted secularism. When critics accused liberals of secularizing the schools, Johnson had no ready response, but he could give a partial answer. He was ready also to say "that it is a badge of mutual ineptitude that Protestants, Catholics, and Jews should have found no way to combat the common foe, antisocial secularism, except to remove from our most influential institutions for character building the resources of spiritual living that we hold in common." From such scenarios it is evident that the mid-thirties was a time of passage from leftover traces of dominating mainstream Protestantism toward a pluralist and more secular style. The Federal Council man posed the issue perfectly. — 9:115

Again and again Johnson returned to this theme which haunted the Federal Council, the *Christian Century*, and other custodians of what remained from the years of liberal Protestant dominance. "No modern-minded Protestant wants to see a return to ecclesiastical control either of education or of other state functions." — 9:116

Yet, he thought, they also all opposed the "secularist attitude which separates the doing of the routine work of life—in business, politics, education and elsewhere—entirely from the pursuit of spiritual values." What such Protestants were unable to do was to depict a satisfying approach to such values in a society over which they had ever less control.

9:117   After the schools, it all came down to politics and religion. Johnson tried to lighten the debate; he said he craved a sense of humor for Methodists and Catholics alike as they accused each other of being in politics. They both were. With most Protestants Johnson believed that Catholics had the advantage on that scene because they lived under a central authority, had more discipline, and expressed unanimity. How little he knew about their actual situation! Meanwhile, Protestants should envy this posture, Johnson said, for it put a church "in position, not to dominate, but to play a part in forming the value judgments of its members."

9:118   Johnson had to admit three years after repeal of Prohibition that even though it lacked Catholic power, Protestantism sometimes overstepped boundaries. Prohibition had been a cause for organized Protestantism. It failed because the larger public rejected the imposition of such a program of whose value it had not been persuaded. Protestant churches thereafter came to look selfish and sectarian. It was wrong and ruinous when only minorities in the Protestant churches tried to hold enough power to support Prohibition. Johnson regretted that the leadership failed to reconstruct the mood of their own people.

9:119   If the church was not a mere pressure group, Johnson had a harder time saying exactly what he thought it should be. What did it mean when he italicized: the church's business was to deal with every vital issue "*and to move forward in the entire political and social field when we have a group conscience that will support the action we propose to take*." The Protestant radicals, he feared, were too impatient. They were unwilling to train and educate a generation. Of course, he never did expect unanimous agreement on issues, but there could be action where there was substantial accord. Niebuhrians, of course, always smiled condescendingly at the notion that education would bring bourgeois believers to a place where they would vote for undercutting the very system off which they lived. But Johnson kept insisting that, barring unpredictable social catastrophe, the church still would do best through faith in gradual means.

Finally, there was no way for the Federal Council executive to   9:120
avoid the mid-Depression theme: if education does not work,
what form of social conflict was appropriate? Niebuhr may have
overstated the case for demonism behind the urge to battle others,
Johnson declared, but of course there *was* something close to the
demonic in the story of resistance to change. He cited Andrew
Meiklejohn as he spoke for scientists to young liberal ministers:
"'You people made a great mistake when you let the devil go.
You will have to get him back again.'" Liberal theology had gone
astray by trying cheerfully to resolve all reality into a simple division between the good and the potentially good. This approach,
Johnson agreed, was unrealistic. Individualism in religion was
also of no help. "Social radicals continually condemn liberalism
for this blindness to the realities of group conflict. In large measure they are right." But, he added, the radicals then go too far in
their insistence that conflict must grow in intensity until it issues
in a prefigured catastrophe. Back and forth: now it was time again
for Johnson to agree: radicals were right to criticize the romantic
liberalism which was equivalent to reactionism.

The usual test case was industrial conflict. When the church   9:121
tried to profess neutrality between labor and management, it
threw its weight to the strongest battalions, the owners of industries. Whenever the issue of social and economic class came up,
Christians rightly condemned Communism for its religious fervor
about the inevitability of conflict, but then they so often looked
away. On an even more troubling issue, when war loomed, he
regretted to say, "the Christian conscience seems to undergo little
strain in making a complete moral accommodation to it. That is
to say, a moratorium is declared on the Ten Commandments."
What to do? For all his turning and twisting, Johnson was in the
end consistent as a liberal: he vaguely trusted vague education
while resisting the more drastic approaches.

What did the leaders of the Federal Council of Churches do?   9:122
Domestically they came to support the general scope of Roosevelt's New Deal social program. Internationally, they feared a
drift toward war and therefore opposed programs of armament
and military readiness. To state this, after recalling the Council
record in the twenties, is to point to a certain tiredness in the
approach. The Fundamentalists were a dramatic voice as they
took refuge in individualism and sectarianism. So were the realists, with their radicalism on the other hand.

9:123   Liberals had been at first wary of Roosevelt, but they warmed to him even when their lay members did not. Thus C. Oscar Johnson, president of the Northern Baptist Convention, took advantage of the location of his convention's meeting in Washington in 1933 to call on the president. The churchman is said to have said to Roosevelt: "'Baptists are back of you 96.8 percent. We cannot go the other 3.2 percent.'" Significantly, 3.2 percent was the permitted alcoholic content of beer as Prohibition was nearing its end. Yet Oscar Johnson's ability to cut his percentages thus showed that bygones could become bygones.

9:124   The *Christian Century* provided still another way of monitoring liberal churchly relations to the Depression and the New Deal. This magazine, which called itself undenominational after it cut ties to its Disciples of Christ origins, made weekly critical comment on New Deal measures. With Johnson it retained a commitment to the ideal of cultural dominance by the right Protestants. But all decade long it found its shaping power diminished because it was distracted by the battle with Christian realism. Before Roosevelt took charge as president—the editors had backed Hoover—they sounded much like Johnson: "What is needed is a moral awakening among those now in control of the industrial machine." Too late, said the realists like Niebuhr, a regular contributor who disturbed the peace of his editors.

9:125   Neither the council nor the *Christian Century* could remain forums for the more radical church leadership, which was ready for violent conflict in the name of religion and justice. As for socialism, they saw little power in actions when denominations passed mild resolutions which favored socialist measures but which no one who knew their membership took seriously. Meanwhile, radicals not closely associated with denominational policy and quite critical of it kept inventing socialist publications or movements of their own including *World Tomorrow, Radical Religion*, along with numerous familiar "fellowships" and "leagues."

9:126   While the *Christian Century* was never uncritical, radicals charged its sort of liberals with collusion when the federated church movements appeared too comfortable with Roosevelt. They remembered how in 1932 candidate Roosevelt had tried to win favor in some circles and neutralize others by saying he was "as radical as the Federal Council." The new president spoke at its silver anniversary gathering in 1933. The council returned the favors. Its *Information Bulletin* regularly promoted support for New Deal measures. Not all constituents, of course, welcomed such support. The lay membership of the churches which made up the council regularly voted against Roosevelt and the Democrats.

No one knew better than pastors the need for liberal self-   9:127
correction and self-adjustment. How choose from the tens of thousands of frontline ministers who were caught between all these forces? One will find many expressions like the one of Methodist pastor W. K. Anderson of Johnstown, Pennsylvania, whose people should have been as likely as any to be ready for change: "The social gospel is in the amazing and tragic predicament of being identified with the New Deal, by haters of the New Deal," and thus the New Deal actually set back some Social Gospel causes. "The social gospel is no longer riding the crest of the wave; it is not now being listened to nonchalantly by laymen. No one needs to be told that we are in a serious backwash of reaction in favor of the old-time religion and against the interpretation of Christianity in international and, particularly, in economic terms." Anderson was accurate and prescient: "So the Church is in the anomalous position of having preached the desirability of many things which are coming to actuality, and of now being in danger of mourning their arrival instead of welcoming them with a paean of victory." The closer the two forces became, the less did substantive distinctiveness mark liberal churches over against the general society. C. C. Morrison and F. Ernest Johnson could argue that this closeness only demonstrated the positive power of the church to influence and even reshape society. Their opponents charged that this coalition only showed how much liberal Protestantism had capitulated to the culture.

Anderson was significant because he could voice the concerns   9:128
of the ministers in their figurative trenches; he did not have the luxury of professors, editors, or bureau heads who fired from safer command posts. Pastor Anderson did not want to give up entirely on the Social Gospel. He simply spoke up for preachers who were puzzled over how to advocate it and win or retain any following. "First, there must be polite but unyielding insistence upon the right of the social interpretation to a place in Christian propaganda." But, "second, the wise prophet of social righteousness will possess an attitude of tolerance," which, he considered, few ideologues were ready to display. The impatient preacher of social ideals neglected the people who seemed to be on the receiv-

ing end. "As a consequence, he alienates his constituency, which knows the individual aspect of the gospel, by trying to lead them into a field which they think is foreign to their religion."

9:129   Continuing his attack, Anderson could not resist taking a swipe: "Many of the radical school keep dinning social reform into the ears of Christians *ad nauseam*, and then wonder why they meet with stolid unresponsiveness." The gospel, he reminded readers, was more than social reform, and anyone going into ministry merely to use the church as a social instrument would meet defeat. "After all, church members have a right to expect of their minister something more than social agitation." They need comfort, encouragement, guidance, and inspiration. "The man who tries to preach without knowing anything else than prohibition, or the wider distribution of wealth, or the problems of peace, is bound to end up in cynical disappointment and self-pitying martyrdom."

9:130   The Reverend Mr. Anderson spoke for thousands of Social Gospel ministers whose vantages in their pulpits led them to be discontented with those realists and radicals who had no congregations and who felt free blithely to promote causes and techniques which laity could not connect with their faith in Christ. Many Christian leaders were now advocating force in order to attain desired social ends, feeling that reason and love were too slow to serve as instruments of change. What Anderson called "this baneful influence of communistic philosophy upon Christian thought" had no doubt stirred the forces of conservatism to militant opposition. So he was there figuratively at the side of Johnson, relying on education and persuasion, but while doing so he was caught between forces over which his kind had little control. Still, he chose to speak with measured hope, in spite of everything.

9:131   The pressure of those who would change society by force—Anderson must have had in mind the Niebuhrians and the Harry F. Ward types—and the dire situation of America was pulling some centrists further to the left. Even the *Christian Century* read the lesson of the elections of 1934 and the character of Roosevelt as leading toward the left. As for artificial capitalism, the president "is the capitalist's best friend. But he is also the socialist's best friend." Overall, "the step from the Roosevelt system to a true and candid socialization of the economic system would be a much easier one to take than is generally recognized." He chose not to go as far as the left leadership of the church, but much further than the middle-class laity wanted the New Deal to go. Only the ideologues had it easy in the thirties, and they did not have to run seminaries and journals, bureaus and congregations. Those who did remained tense through the decade.

A Corruption of Civilization Which Has Sworn to Destroy

In 1939 a European war broke out, one that from its first day   9:132
was called World War II and which in 1941 was to draw America into the conflict that took fifty million lives. The story of that war awaits our third volume. An account of Jewish adjustments in a time when anti-Semitism was a demonic factor in the Nazi onslaught and when Reform Jews virtually completed their adoption of Zionism also belongs to that story. The narrative of what the war did to lessen the noise of conflict between American parties also must wait. Yet the forthcoming war colored debate among all Americans in the thirties. Thus the final pre–World War II test of the tensions between the liberal and realist visions came as conflict in Europe and the Pacific threatened, and Roosevelt kept promoting preparedness for war. In the 1930s, at a time when many Protestants were taking vows against war, one in five Congregationalist ministers who were polled, clergy in the liberal mainstream, responded that they were ready to "renounce war and all its works and all its ways and to refuse to support, sanction, or bless it." Among 10,000 Baptist members who took pains to respond to the survey, over one-fourth said they would refuse service in any and all wars. Eight years before the European war began, socialist Kirby Page received 19,000 ministerial responses to a poll in the isolationist *World Tomorrow*. Among these, 10,000 clerics said that as individuals they could never sanction war. In 1934 the figure of the disapprovers climbed to 13,000 out of 21,000 respondents. The percentages meant little, because those polled made up a self-selective group. The very mass of answers was what was most impressive. Pacifism was not risky or rare or a marginal theme in those years. But as Japan invaded Manchuria, Italy moved into Ethiopia, the Spanish Civil War posed Communism versus a kind of Fascism, liberal pacifists found their community ever more torn.

At mid-decade Reinhold Niebuhr was still trying to avoid the   9:133
issue of international war, so deep were his old commitments against it. But he had already endorsed the potential use of vio-

lence in class conflict on Marxist lines. He could hardly be consistent now if he opposed violence against evils as great as those that Hitler and Mussolini posed. He toyed for a little while with isolationist positions, but could not remain content with them. It was cheap heroics, Niebuhr thought, to say from the vantage of a protected America "that a war would be better than such a capitulation before Nazi terror," when commenting on a famed appeasement meeting at Munich in 1938 which made it look as if European allies might capitulate to Hitler. After Munich that note disappeared. In 1938 Niebuhr worked with John C. Bennett and some people he had often chided as being liberal, among them William Adams Brown, Justin Wroe Nixon, and future Union Seminary president Henry Pitney Van Dusen, to sign up for preparedness and in support of the allies.

9:134   In his writings on war Niebuhr rang the changes again on the themes of "immoral man in even more immoral society," a situation in which one had to make decisions when none were promising or good. The Christian Century kept pressing Niebuhr to be clearer than he wanted to be about alternatives between pacifism and intervention. Niebuhr during those prewar seasons kept resisting the call for intervention, despite such pressures; he clearly had not worked out scenarios that would take him through all the confusions of 1940 and 1941.

9:135   Charles Clayton Morrison at the Christian Century, on the other side, called tirelessly for peace conferences and experiments at reconciliation, while Hitler was making his advances and Japan threatened. Much criticized for seeking settlement apart from conflict when it seemed too late, Morrison generally agreed, but said that he was using language that was useful long before still another war would start after the impending one. By then he had pushed himself to the limit and resorted to defeatist language and sarcasm. Still, even at the end of 1941, in an issue of the magazine which was being edited while Japan was attacking Pearl Harbor, a Ministers No War Committee could rally Social Gospel figures like the magazine's Paul Hutchinson and his editorial colleague, Yale professor Halford Luccock, along with prominent ministers. Many such clergy also formed a Churchmen's Campaign for Peace through Mediation. Few of these groups lasted long after Pearl Harbor.

9:136   Reinhold Niebuhr nettled Morrison most. Almost no act better symbolized the break between the liberals who had dominated in the twenties and the realists who came to power in the Depression years than Niebuhr's break with the *Christian Century* to form a rival Christian realist outlet, *Christianity and Crisis*. This act sealed the split within Federal-Council-type Protestantism which was showing up on any number of other issues as well. During the stir, Harold E. Fey of the Fellowship of Reconciliation, who was later to become the *Christian Century* editor, paid grudging tribute to Reinhold Niebuhr, the man whom Fey and his colleagues had to treat as an apostate and renegade from the peace cause. Niebuhr, admitted Fey, had had "more influence than any other man in leading the church into another repudiation of its mission in compromise with the state on the war issue." The old alliance from Kellogg-Briand days was by then forever broken. That Niebuhr had changed his view was a secret no one, least of all Niebuhr himself, wanted to guard. *Why* he changed was the important issue.

Even after the switch, Niebuhr could never wholly abandon his   9:137
grudging admiration for pacifists as prophets and sectarians. He simply at first and then vehemently later insisted that these dissidents could not speak for a whole society or represent all the interests of a culture. He argued: let pacifists go their way, being "frankly irresponsible in the social struggle as the best ascetics of Christian history were." Let some citizens and believers regard the problem of social justice as something that did not concern them directly. As he voiced these words, Niebuhr progressively heightened his tone of condescension: pacifists, he came to say, were missing the point. Let *us* get on with real life in the real world, he seemed to be saying to people inside the growing realist circle.

In time Niebuhr came to use some of the most bitter language   9:138
of his career against Charles Clayton Morrison and the Fellowship of Reconciliation people who were not utterly pacifist but who were also very reluctant to see America intervene in World War II. Niebuhr knew he had to answer those who wondered how he could speak so much for a God whose ways transcended those of foolish nations. He did so by urging that Hitler and Nazism were "an incarnation of evil more diabolical than anything mankind has yet experienced." Evil actions called forth new rules of the game. "Here is a corruption of civilization which has sworn to destroy our civilization—a civilization which, with all its imperfections, tolerated the Christian faith and was slowly but surely responding to the demands of the Christian ethic."

By December 7, 1941, and the Japanese attack on Pearl Harbor   9:139

which triggered America's actual entry into the war, Niebuhr had not yet joined the company of Protestant leaders like Henry Pitney Van Dusen who was openly calling for intervention in the war in Europe. Months before, numbers of Methodist and Episcopal bishops, especially from the South, called for the United States to rescue Britain and civilization. The language of crusades started being voiced in the pulpits. Niebuhr opposed such terms because the concept of holy war always struck him as idolatrous. He did not think it possible or theologically proper to revisit Woodrow Wilson's kind of World War I idealism. He could only see fighting the impending war as a negative task, a burden.

9:140   In the end Niebuhr's attitude has to be described as one of acquiescence to the necessity of fighting. He was apparently invoking persistent themes in his theology: humans do not know enough about the future to speak strongly about what Providence wants. Yet they are held responsible in the world and are called to act. If they are Christians, they have a particular vocation and insight. Faith in the grace of Jesus Christ alone, he wrote, could "disclose the actual facts of human existence. It alone can uncover the facts because it alone has an answer for the facts which are disclosed." This kind of language always looked like desperate retreat, in the sight of anti-Niebuhrians, but for Niebuhr himself it was his most profound resource. That faith also made it difficult for him to be as capable a leader against the pacifists and isolationists as he might have been, but its expression provided a tinge of moderation in the bitter polemics of the pre-war year or two. Then, when Japan attacked Pearl Harbor, facts and events took over and the Niebuhrians moved quickly to support prosecution of the war that Morrison came to call "an unnecessary necessity." A new day for America, American religion, and religious conflict came with the sound of the bombs.

Conclusion:
After Conflict,
Toward Consensus

Suddenly, after Pearl Harbor and the beginning of United States involvement in World War II, the noise of conflict in public religion quieted. Not that Americans came to agreement on matters spiritual. Just as throughout the interwar period of conflict there were agents of concord, so during the next quarter-century agents of disagreement between camps of believers endured. Protestants formed an anti-Catholic organization of note and protested the appointment of an ambassador to the Vatican by President Harry S. Truman. Some of them opposed the election of John F. Kennedy, a Catholic, to the presidency. "McCarthyism" blighted religion at mid-century. Religion often reinforced racism. Denominations remained internally divided.

Despite those inevitable signs of conflict, however, a new vocabulary emerged. From the beginning of World War II into the mid-sixties one heard words like these: consensus, dialogue, ecumenism, interfaith, church unity, integration, collegiality, conciliarism, merger. There were phrases to accompany these words: "global village," "spaceship earth," "the American century," "world federalism." Believing citizens formed local, state, regional, national, and world councils of churches to promote amity and common faith and purpose. Supporters attached religious symbols to the causes of the United Nations and other international organizations. They began to work for equality of sexes *and integration of races. Whereas for decades only revivalists had talked about revival, now observers spoke of constant if ever-changing revivals of interest in religion across the national board. They saw these awakenings as promoters of national unity.*

In the mid-fifties a Jewish sociologist and theologian, Will Herberg, tried to discern an implicit pattern within pluralism: Protestants, Catholics, and Jews, he saw, enjoyed separate identities. But they all reinforced a common civic faith in "the American Way of Life." Historian Sidney E. Mead began to talk of a "religion of the Republic," born with the nation almost two hundred years before, but still serving to unite people who were divided in their separate denominations. A president after mid-century, Dwight D. Eisenhower, invoked faith in faith itself and convoked solemn assemblies of citizens to support American religion in general.

The new times, as we shall see in the next volume in this history, produced new problems for people of faith. Jesuit Father John Courtney Murray asked, "How much pluralism and what kinds of pluralism can a pluralist society stand?" and "How much unity and what kind of unity does a pluralist society need in order to be a society at all?" Critics of scholars who observed "consensus" argued that the notion of consensus obscures the necessary conflicts which victims of society need to win their rights. Yet during that next quarter-century centripetal forces countered the centrifugal ones which had dominated between the wars while convergences replaced divergences in American public religion.

The major events of the period suggest reasons why these changes occurred. During the Second World War, a war much believed in, it was necessary for citizens to unite against external enemies. During the early years of the Cold War, it was natural that presidents would join clerics in calling for a united "Christian crusade against atheistic communism." The years of postwar prosperity, as couples raised large families of children to nurture in faith, changed residence (e.g., to suburbia) and built churches and synagogues, sought peace of mind or peace of soul, promoted racial integration, and pursued new idealisms on new frontiers, were not appropriate times for accentuating old hostilities.

Through all the changes, however, the legacy of the interwar years of conflict remained. Original-stock Protestantism had begun to be disestablished, and was being progressively dislodged from its place of unique privilege, though few realized by 1965 how insecure this old center of national faith had become. Its disappearance from a stage of simple dominance, from a scene of "cultural hegemony," its inability any longer to "run the show," left a void. Long-time dissenting and marginal religious groups found it ever more difficult to use the oppressing Other, white and especially mainstream Protestantism, as a foil, an instrument which could help them keep their own identities and find their own missions. The way this Protestantism yielded and came to share place with other forces turned out to have been relatively graceful: we have noted few dead bodies along the way. The conflict was chiefly rhetorical, though the preceding pages have shown how violent the rhetoric had been.

Only with the gift of hindsight can a reader late in the twentieth century see how much disintegration had occurred in the white Protestant empire and, with it, the old-stock Protestant hegemony. This is not to say that people of this stock did not retain positions of power late in the century: they still had easiest access to elite status in, for example, the business world. But in literature, the arts, athletics, entertainment, national government, and fields of moral prescription they yielded, not to any single rival but to a new pluralism which looked chaotic to many. And where their power did survive, it seemed less directed by mainstream Protestant churchly norms. America had no center, or it had many centers—which amounted to much the same thing.

Never again could Protestants overcome their own schism between modernist-liberal-moderate and fundamentalist-conservative-zealous flanks and thus never again could they present a united front against all comers. The old moderate liberalism never seemed so credible again after the assaults of Christian realists. But the original-stock Americans were not the only ones who faced the later years of the century with ranks divided. In the cases of Catholicism, Orthodoxy, Judaism, and other religious complexes, divisions within these cohorts were often henceforth more nagging than were differences across the boundaries of churches and other faith groups. In these respects Americans lived with decisive heritages of the years of interwar conflict.

Whatever else came with the changes from a time of conflict to a time of consensus, religion itself, both of public and private sorts, survived in a putatively secular century and nation. Individuals and groups employed religion to heat up nonreligious conflict and they expressed their religion in ways that produced conflict in the nonreligious arena. In both cases, they thereby paid respects to the power of religion to reach and express the deepest of human needs, the most profound sources of individual and social life. In the years ahead, they were to pay those respects in a different way. They then employed religion to promote otherwise nonreligious concord and they expressed their religion in ways that produced concord in the otherwise nonreligious spheres of national life.

Those who might criticize reporters between the interwar years for stressing the "picturesque" character of conflict and a historian like me who reported on their reports, will find that new subject matter calls forth different stresses and preoccupations. My acquaintance with the sources and recall of the events between 1941 and 1965 suggests that while the picturesqueness of these earlier conflicts, what Alfred Lord Tennyson might call "old, unhappy far-off things and battles long ago," found some parallel in events of the later period, newer, more happy, nearer things brought drama of their own as Americans went seeking a new spiritual center.

Between the wars, in 1927 a foreign visitor and in 1937 a notable theologian still observed that Protestantism was America's "only national religion." They were right. In 1931 the United States Supreme Court for a last time said of Americans that "we are a Christian people," and in a sense and on the Court's terms, that was still right. However, after the wars, in 1952, a Court decision broadened the observation and the concept to "we are a religious people," and again, in a sense and on the Court's terms, that was true. Through it all the United States was also a secular society, of a sort. John Courtney Murray argued properly that Americans were "entering a new era." It calls for another book, one which necessarily deals with "pluralism" and "consensus" in modern American religion during that new era.

Notes

Chapter One

1:1. Milton, *Paradise Lost*, VI, 259.

1:2. Ibid., VI, 91, 92, 257, 259.

1:3. Martin E. Marty, *Pilgrims in Their Own Land: 500 Years of Religion in America* (Boston: Little, Brown, 1984), chap. 17, "A Season of Conflicts;" see especially 374.

1:4. See *The New Shape of American Religion* (New York: Harper and Brothers, 1959); *Second Chance for American Protestants* (New York: Harper and Row, 1963); *Righteous Empire: The Protestant Experience in America* (New York: Dial Press, 1970); *Protestantism* (New York: Holt, Rinehart and Winston, 1972); *Modern American Religion*, volume 1, *The Irony of It All, 1893–1919* (Chicago: University of Chicago Press, 1986).

1:5. See the organization of chapters in *Pilgrims in Their Own Land*, which suggests what I see these decisive earlier events to have been.

1:6. Garry Wills, *Reagan's America: Innocents at Home* (Garden City, N.Y.: Doubleday, 1987), chap. 40, "Greenfield Village on the Potomac," 371–77, relates the themes of illusion and nostalgia to the time of President Ronald Reagan, who evoked myths connected with Henry Ford and the 1920s; see also chap. 6, "Depression," 55–63, to see how events and images of that period got revised in the former president's memory.

1:7. All these contentions, related specifically to the times, were superimposed on longer-term divisions which will not receive treatment in this book, for example between North and South, as evidenced in efforts around 1924 and (successfully) in 1939 to unite northern and southern Methodist Episcopal churches; Frederick E. Maser, "The Story of Unification, 1874–1939," in Emory Stevens Bucke, ed., *The History of American Methodism*, 3 vols. (Nashville: Abingdon, 1964), 3: 407–78, especially 448, on Bishop Warren A. Candler.

1:8. Cultural histories come closer to including religious symbolization; for a fairly typical example, see Warren I. Susman, *Culture as History: The Transformation of American Society in the Twentieth Century* (New York: Pantheon, 1984), which has generous chapters on the interwar period; and chap. 9, "Culture and Civilization: the Nineteen-Twenties," 105–21, and "The Culture of the Thirties," 150–83.

1:9. For an accounting of religious-cultural-ethnic-national nexuses in warfare today, see Harold Isaacs, *Idols of the Tribe* (New York: Harper and Row, 1975).

1:10. Access to the argument appears in a varied literature: e.g., John P. Diggins, *The Lost Soul of American Politics: Virtue, Self-Interest, and the Foundations of Liberalism* (New York: Basic Books, 1984); William Lee Miller, *The First Liberty: Religion and the American Republic* (New York: Alfred A. Knopf, 1985); A. James Reichley, *Religion in American Public Life* (Washington, D.C.: The Brookings Institution, 1985); Mark A. Noll, *One Nation Under God? Christian Faith and Political Action in America* (San Francisco: Harper and Row, 1988); Harold O. J. Brown, *The Reconstruction of the Republic* (Milford, Mich.: Mott Media, 1981); Robert Booth Fowler, *A New Engagement: Evangelical Political Thought, 1966–1976* (Grand Rapids, Mich.: Eerdmans, 1983); Alasdair MacIntyre, *After Virtue* (Notre Dame, Ind.: University of Notre Dame Press, 1981); Richard P. McBrien, *Caesar's Coin: Religion and Politics in America* (New York: Macmillan, 1987); George Will, *Statecraft and Soulcraft: What Government Does* (New York: Simon and Schuster, 1983).

1:11. Alexander Hamilton, John Jay, and James Madison, *The Federalist: A Commentary on the Constitution of the United States Being a Collection of Essays Written in Support of the Constitution Agreed upon September 17, 1787, by the Federal Convention* (Washington, D.C.: Robert B. Luce, 1976); "The Federalist No. 2," 9; Charles Hodge, "Anniversary Address," *The Home Missionary* 2 (June 1, 1829): 17–19; the quote is on page 18.

1:12. T.S. Eliot, *After Strange Gods* (London: Faber and Faber, 1934), 18–20.

1:13. Essays in support of the pluralist thesis appear in Martin E. Marty, *Religion and Republic: The American Circumstance* (Boston: Beacon, 1987); see, e.g., 3–6, 34–36, 238–39.

1:14. On the sheer amount and force of often-overlooked religion in contemporary American life, see ibid., chap. 1, "Rediscovery: Discerning Religious America," 11–30.

1:15. An updating of cultural history themes is "Extending the Reach of American Cultural History: A Retrospective Glance and a Prospectus," chap. 5, in Michael Kammen, *Selvages and Biases: The Fabric of History in American Culture* (Ithaca, N.Y.: Cornell University Press, 1987), 118–53.

1:16. James L. Axtell, *The European and the Indian: Essays in the Ethnohistory of Colonial North America* (New York: Oxford University Press, 1981), 6, cited by Kammen, *Selvages and Biases*, 125; Kammen refers to a relative congruity among recent historians in their definition or location of the controversial term "culture" by reference also to the work of Daniel Walker Howe and Alan Trachtenberg.

1:17. Jacques Barzun, "Cultural History as a Synthesis," in Fritz Stern, ed., *The Varieties of History, from Voltaire to the Present* (New York: Meridian Books, 1956), 393, cited by Kammen, *Selvages and Biases*, 149. Kammen also refers to Johann Huizinga on inexactness.

1:18. Paul Crawford, "The Farmer Assesses His Role in Society," in Paul H. Boase, ed., *The Rhetoric of Protest and Reform 1878–1898* (Athens: Ohio University Press, 1980), 102–3; see accompanying references in Marty, *The Irony of It All*, 12, 323.

1:19. Dominick LaCapra, *History and Criticism* (Ithaca, N.Y.: Cornell University Press, 1985), 36; see chap. 1, "Rhetoric and History," 15–44.

1:20. Georg Simmel, *Conflict*, trans. Kurt H. Wolff (New York: The Free Press, 1955); see also the influential exegesis and elaboration of Simmel by Lewis Coser, *The Functions of Social Conflict* (New York: The Free Press, 1956).

1:21. Simmel, *Conflict*, 17–18, 34, 47, 93.

1:22. Ibid., 96–97, 35, 98–99.

1:23. I have deliberately avoided elaborating on "cultural hegemony" as outlined by Antonio Gramsci for two reasons: (1) it would take us into Marxian contexts which would not illumine this story and arguments largely irrelevant to this narrative; (2) Gramsci stresses the " 'spontaneous' consent given by the great masses of the population to the general direction imposed on social life by the dominant fundamental group," an assertion sometimes borne out by the American conditions and sometimes not. The two religiously attractive features of Gramscian theory are: (1) it does urge one to locate "the dominant fundamental group," something which turns out to be easy and important to do in America in this period, and (2) it makes much of rhetoric and the way elites attract followers. For an introduction to the issue, see T. J. Jackson Lears, "The Concept of Cultural Hegemony: Problems and Possibilities," *American Historical Review* 90 (June 1985): 567–93; and Antonio Gramsci, *Selections from the Prison Notebooks*, ed. and trans. Quintin Hoare and Geoffrey Nowell Smith (New York: International Publishers, 1971), 12.

1:24. Two samples of later literature on outcomes are Robert Wuthnow, *The Restructuring of American Religion* (Princeton: Princeton University Press, 1988); and Wade Clark Roof and William McKinney, *American Mainline Religion: Its Changing Shape and Future* (New Brunswick, N.J.: Rutgers University Press, 1987.)

1:25. John Milton Cooper, Jr., "Modernism and Other Modern Isms," in *New York Times Book Review*, Jan. 4, 1987.

1:26. Robert T. Handy, *A Christian America: Protestant Hopes and Historical Realities* (New York: Oxford University Press, 1971); Robert T. Handy, "The American Religious Depression," *Church History* 29 (1960): 3–16; Joel Carpenter, "Fundamentalist Institutions and the Rise of Evangelical Protestantism," *Church History* 49 (March 1980): 62–75. I could not have written this book in anything like its present form without at least the following additional works: Paul A. Carter, *The Decline and Revival of the Social Gospel: Social and Political Liberalism in American Protestant Churches* (Ithaca, N.Y.: Cornell University Press, 1954); William R. Hutchison, ed., *Between the Times: The Travail of the Protestant Establishment in America, 1900–1960* (Cambridge: Cambridge University Press, 1989); Donald B. Meyer, *The Protestant Search for Political Realism, 1919–1941* (Berkeley: University of California Press, 1960); Robert Moats Miller, *American Protestantism and Social Issues, 1919–1939* (Chapel Hill: University of North Carolina Press, 1958); Ferenc Morton Szasz, *The Divided Mind of Protestant America, 1880–1930* (Tuscaloosa: University of Alabama Press, 1982); for Catholicism, especially William M. Halsey, *The Survival of American Innocence: Catholicism in an Era of Disillusionment 1920–1940* (Notre Dame, Ind.: University of Notre Dame Press, 1980); David J. O'Brien, *American Catholics and Social Reform: The New Deal Years* (New York: Oxford University Press, 1968); to my knowledge, there is no synthetic work on Jewish religion which focuses on this period.

1:27. See Martin E. Marty, "The American Religious History Canon," *Social Research* 53:3 (Autumn 1986): 513–28. On the outsider, see R. Laurence Moore, *Religious Outsiders and the Making of Americans* (New York: Oxford University Press, 1986). Moore was writing at a time when the outsiders—Mormons, Fundamentalists, blacks, Adventists, and others—were subjects of far more historiographical curiosity and endeavor than were "insiders" of the Protestant mainstream.

1:28. There are beginnings to address deficiencies in Virginia Lieson Brereton, "United and Slighted: Women as Subordinated Insiders," in Hutchison, *Between the Times*, chap. 7, 143–67. Significantly, while the book covers the period from 1900 to 1960, Brereton has to concentrate on the final decade or two in that period.

1:29. Michael A. Meyer, *Response to Modernity: A History of the Reform Movement in Judaism* (New York: Oxford University Press, 1988), 296. The reference to "twenties" and "thirties" prompts a comment: many historians criticize thinking by such decades: they are artificial, not well defined, and so on. The reader can see that in this case the demarcating makes sense: there is a very different national and religious ethos from 1919 to 1929 and then from 1930 to 1941, and it would be inaccurate not to treat the differences as the religious movements proceed through time.

1:30. See J. Elliot Ross, "Courtesy at Columbia," *Commonweal* 3:131 (Feb. 20, 1929): 449.

1:31. See Isaacs, *Idols of the Tribe*, for contrasting stories of militant tribalism around the world.

1:32. Marty, *The Irony of It All*, 6–7.

1:33. See John Headley, *Luther's View of Church History* (New Haven: Yale University Press, 1963), 1–19, especially 4, 6; on 46 he cites Luther from the Weimar edition, 50:385.

1:34. This Luther quotation is fugitive. Professor Hans Hillerbrand of Duke University, a noted Luther scholar, who, along with so many other scholars, has heard the phrase cited and sees it as representative, has notified the author that it "must be an inaccurate conflation of two passages from Luther's writings in the *Weimar Ausgabe*, vol. 18, 702:22ff and 709:14–28, which, in fact, improves on Luther." Hillerbrand "checked this with Martin Brecht, the living Luther encyclopedia, and he concurs."

Chapter Two

2:1. Harding explained his use of "normalcy," perhaps a corruption of "normality," in the *New York Times*, July 21, 1920, 7. The speech is reprinted in Frederick E. Scortemeier, ed., *Rededicating America: Life and Recent Speeches of Warren G. Harding* (Indianapolis: Bobbs-Merrill, 1920), 223.

2:2. Frederick Lewis Allen, *Only Yesterday* (New York: Bantam, 1959; 1st ed. 1931), 30.

2:3. For Harding's explanation, see Robert K. Murray, *The Harding Era: Warren G. Harding and His Administration* (Minneapolis: University of Minnesota Press, 1969). John Higham, *Strangers in the Land: Patterns of American Nativism 1860–1925* (New York: Atheneum, 1975; 1st ed., 1955), 264, named his chapter 10 "The Tribal Twenties"; other historians have adopted the designation. See also Thomas Hobbes, *Leviathan* (London: Printed for Andrew Crooke, at the Green Dragon in St. Paul's Church-yard, 1651), 64.

2:4. Loren Baritz, ed., *The Culture of the Twenties* (Indianapolis: Bobbs-Merrill, 1970), is a well-introduced anthology reflecting the spirit of the literary community.

2:5. Robert S. Lynd and Helen Merrell Lynd, *Middletown: A Study in American Culture* (New York: Harcourt and Brace, 1929). Their subsequent volume was *Middletown in Transition: A Study in Cultural Conflicts* (New York: Harcourt and Brace, 1937). The *New York Times* reporter is quoted by Theodore Caplow et al., eds., *All Faithful People: Change and Continuity in Middletown's Religion* (Minneapolis: University of Minnesota Press, 1983), 17. *All Faithful People* was part of a follow-up study whose existence demonstrates the hold *Middletown* continues to have on students of American life and underscores the reasons for ʃ choice.

2:6. Caplow et al., *All Faithful People*, 14, 32–33, 39–40, discuss the secular bias of the Lynds.

2:7. Lynd and Lynd, *Middletown in Transition*, 318.

2:8. Ibid., 390; chap. 23, "Religious Observances," 371–409.

2:9. Ibid., 407, 488.   2:10. Ibid., 492–93.

2:11. Ibid., 315, 321.   2:13. Ibid., 333.
2:12. Ibid., 322, 331–32.   2:14. Ibid., 333–34.
2:15. On localism and cohesion, see ibid., chap. 28, "Things Making and Un-making Group Solidarity," 478–95.
2:16. Ibid., 369–70.
2:17. E. O. Watson, ed., *Year Book of the Churches 1924–25* (Baltimore: J. E. Stohlmann, 1924); the census report is covered in C. Luther Fry, *The U.S. Looks at Its Churches* (New York: Institute of Social and Religious Research, 1930); Samuel McCrea Cavert, ed., *Twenty Years of Church Federation: Report of the Federal Council of the Churches of Christ in America 1924–1928* (New York: Federal Council of Churches of Christ in America, 1929).
2:18. Watson, *Year Book of the Churches*, 22–23, 395; Robert W. Lynn and Elliott Wright, *The Big Little School: 200 Years of the Sunday School* (Birmingham, Ala.: Religious Education Press, 1980; 1st ed., 1971), is the only history of the Sunday school that carries the account into the twentieth century.
2:19. Watson, *Year Book of the Churches*, 398.
2:20. On the meaning and role of denominations in American history, see Russell E. Richey, ed., *Denominationalism* (Nashville: Abingdon, 1977).
2:21. Denominations are classified by Watson, *Year Book of the Churches*, 395–400.
2:22. Ibid., 404.
2:23. Ibid. Watson relied on the Federal Census, and provided comparative data for 1890, 1906, 1919, and 1921–23.
2:24. Ibid., 13–14, 395.   2:26. Ibid., 395, 397, 32.
2:25. Ibid., 19–22, 92.   2:27. Ibid, 34–43.
2:28. R. W. Burchfield, ed., *A Supplement to the Oxford English Dictionary* (Oxford: Clarendon Press, 1972), vol. 1, *A-G*, 905, gives 1935 as the earliest citation for "ecosystem" and quotes *New Statesman*, March 28, 1963, for definition: "The unit of ecology is the ecosystem, which includes the plants and animals occurring together plus that part of their environment over which they have an influence."
2:29. Ibid., 76–77, 142.
2:30. Ibid., 299–301.
2:31. Ibid., 344–45, 354, 355–72.
2:32. Ibid., 368–72; the quotation is from 371.
2:33. See Fry, *The U.S. Looks at Its Churches*, 1–5, for discussion of United States Census data; see also Kevin Christiano, *Religious Diversity and Social Change: American Cities, 1890–1906* (Cambridge: Cambridge University Press, 1987), chap. 2, " 'Numbering Israel': United States Census Data on Religion," 22–48.
2:34. Fry, *The U.S. Looks at Its Churches*, 1–3, summarizes statistics.
2:35. Ibid., 2–3, on the South, Jews, and Mormons.
2:36. Ibid., 9, 14, 11, on women and blacks.
2:37. Ibid., 45.   2:39. Ibid., 50.
2:38. Ibid., 45–46, 49.   2:40. Ibid., 52.
2:41. On the concept of "center and periphery," especially as employed in the writings of Edward Shils, see Liah Greenfeld and Michel Martin, "The Idea of the 'Center': An Introduction," in Greenfeld and Martin, eds., *Center: Ideas and Institutions* (Chicago: University of Chicago Press, 1988), viii–xxii; on "periphery" or "margin," see R. Laurence Moore, *Religious Outsiders and the Making of Americans* (New York: Oxford University Press, 1986).

2:42. Matthew Fox, *Religion USA: An Inquiry into Religion and Culture by Way of Time Magazine* (Dubuque, Iowa: Listening Press, 1971), by its citations, gives book-length evidence of the way the most influential weekly favored mainstream denominations.

2:43. Cavert, *Twenty Years of Church Federation*, 5.

2:44. Ibid.   2:47. Ibid., 29, 34.

2:45. Ibid., 9–11.   2:48. Ibid., 11–12.

2:46. Ibid.   2:49. Ibid., 15–16, 17–18.

2:50. Elias P. Sanford, *Origin and History of the Federal Council of Churches of Christ in America* (Hartford, Conn.: S. S. Scranton Co., 1916), 251.

2:51. For autobiographical details, see William Adams Brown, *A Teacher and His Times: A Story of Two Worlds* (New York: Charles Scribner's Sons, 1940); 60–67, 273–95, depict his involvements with Yale.

2:52. William Adams Brown, *The Church in America: A Study of the Present Conditions and Future Prospects of American Protestantism* (New York: Macmillan, 1922), 177.

2:53. Ibid., 350.

2:54. Ibid., 256–57.   2:56. Ibid., 3–4, 349.

2:55. Ibid., 271–72.   2:57. Ibid., 3–5.

2:58. On the philosophy of life implied by the word "still," see Gerhard Ebeling, *The Nature of Faith* (Philadelphia: Muhlenberg, 1961), 174; Brown also uses it in *The Church in America*, 6.

2:59. Brown, *The Church in America*, 27–31.

2:60. Ibid., 27–28.   2:62. Ibid., 115, 44.

2:61. Ibid., 29–31.   2:63. Ibid., 79–80, 269–72.

2:64. On the role of popular heroes in the twenties, see Warren I. Susman, *Culture As History: The Transformation of American Society in the Twentieth Century* (New York: Pantheon, 1973), chap. 8, "Culture Heroes: Ford, Barton, Ruth," 105–21.

2:65. For a discussion of the career of Conwell, see Daniel W. Bjork, *The Victorian Flight: Russell Conwell and the Crisis of American Individualism* (Washington, D.C.: University Press of America, 1979).

2:66. W. S. Crosby, "Acres of Diamonds," *The American Mercury* 14:53 (May 1928): 104–13; see especially 104.

2:67. For critical comment by Babson, see "The Competitive System and the Mind of Jesus," *The Christian Century* 38 (May 26, 1921): 8–10.

2:68. Roger W. Babson, *Religion and Business* (New York: Macmillan, 1921); and idem, *New Tasks for Old Churches* (New York: Macmillan, 1922).

2:69. Babson, *Religion and Business*, 140, 181.

2:70. Ibid., chap. 10, "The Interchurch Movement," 126–42; on denominational fights, 8.

2:71. Ibid., 198.

2:72. See Susman, *Culture As History*, 122–33; Leo P. Ribuffo, "Jesus Christ as Business Statesman: Bruce Barton and the Selling of Corporate Capitalism," *American Quarterly* 33 (1981): 206–31; James Nuechterlein, "Bruce Barton and the Business Ethos of the 1920's," *South Atlantic Quarterly* 76 (1977): 293–308. The quotation is from Bruce Barton, *A Young Man's Jesus* (Boston: The Pilgrim Press, 1914), 71.

2:73. Allen, *Only Yesterday*, 127–28.

2:74. Ibid., 128, 127, 126.

2:75. Bruce Barton, *The Man Nobody Knows* (Indianapolis: Bobbs-Merrill, 1925), 177, 8–9.

2:76. Quoted from a tongue-in-cheek article of Barton's by Susman, *Culture As History*, 123.

2:77. Barton, *The Man Nobody Knows*, 179–80.

2:78. See n. 83.

2:79. C. Luther Fry, "The Reported Religious Affiliations of the Various Classes of Leaders Listed in *Who's Who*, 1930–31 edition," in Herman C. Weber, ed., *Year Book of American Churches, 1933* (New York: Round Table Press, 1933), 311–14.

2:80. See the important essay, William R. Hutchison, "Protestantism as Establishment," in William R. Hutchison, ed., *Between the Times: The Travail of the Protestant Establishment in America, 1900–1960* (New York: Cambridge University Press, 1989), 3–16. See also Brown, *The Church in America*, 144–55.

2:81. The sermons appear in Charles Clayton Morrison, *The American Pulpit* (New York: Macmillan, 1925). For the list of preachers, see *The Christian Century* 41 (Dec. 4, 1924): 1572; (Dec. 11, 1924): 1605; (Dec. 25, 1924): 1673.

2:82. See Edwin S. Gaustad, "The Pulpit and the Pews," in Hutchison, *Between the Times*, 21–47, especially 23–26.

2:83. See Mark A. Mathews, "The Virgin Birth of Christ," and Ernest Fremont Tittle, "Evolution and Religion"; and Morrison, *The American Pulpit*, 215–26, 341–51.

2:84. Gaustad cites the layperson; see Hutchison, *Between the Times*, 30.

2:85. Ellis J. Hough, "Terrors of the Protestant Ministry," *Presbyterian Advance* 40 (January 30, 1930): 18. See chap. 6, "The Changing Ministry: A Study in Clerical Self-Respect," in Paul Carter, *The Decline and Revival of the Social Gospel: Social and Political Liberalism in American Protestant Churches 1920–1940* (New Haven: Archon Press, 1971), 70–84.

2:86. Glenn Frank, "A Layman Looks at the Ministry," *Christian Advocate* 104 (February 21, 1929): 232–34. The quotation is on 234.

2:87. See Carter, *The Decline and Revival of the Social Gospel*, 78, and a summary of Kelly in *Homiletic Review* 88 (September 1924): 181ff. Heywood Broun was quoted in *Churchman* 139 (January 12, 1929): 25.

2:88. Quoted by Carter, *The Decline and Revival of the Social Gospel*, 82–83; see Halford E. Luccock, "Preaching in an Age of Disillusion," *Baptist* 10 (March 9, 1939): 316ff.

2:89. Halford E. Luccock, "The Church Nobody Knows," *Christian Advocate* 102 (October 20, 1927): 1263.

2:90. Ibid.

2:91. The best biography is Robert Moats Miller, *Harry Emerson Fosdick: Preacher, Pastor, Prophet* (New York: Oxford University Press, 1985); references to relations with Niebuhr passim.

2:92. *Social Service Bulletin*, June 1921, quoted by Robert Moats Miller in *American Protestantism*, 32; Reinhold Niebuhr, "How Adventurous Is Dr. Fosdick?" *The Christian Century* 44 (January 6, 1927): 17–18.

2:93. Niebuhr, "How Adventurous?"

2:94. Ibid.

2:95. From a sermon preached in 1920, quoted by R. M. Miller, *Harry Emerson Fosdick*, 452–53.

2:96. From correspondence quoted in ibid., 465–66.

2:97. Ibid.

2:98. On the religious role of presidents, see Richard G. Hutcheson, Jr., *God in the White House: How Religion Has Changed the Modern Presidency* (New York: Macmillan,

1988); and Richard V. Pierard and Robert D. Linder, *Civil Religion and the Presidency* (Grand Rapids, Mich.: Zondervan, 1988). Coolidge goes unmentioned, and there are few references to Harding and Hoover.

2:99. Samuel Hopkins Adams, *Incredible Era: The Life and Times of Warren Gamaliel Harding* (Boston: Houghton Mifflin, 1939), 194.

2:100. Herbert Hoover, *The Memoirs of Herbert Hoover: The Cabinet and the Presidency, 1920–1933* (New York: Macmillan, 1952), 56.

2:101. The speech is in C. Bascom Slemp, *The Mind of the President: As Revealed by Himself in His Own Words* (New York: Doubleday, Page, 1926), 274.

2:102. Merlin Gustafson, "President Hoover and the National Religion," *Journal of Church and State* 16:1 (Winter 1974): 87–88. See Hoover's letter to *American Lutheran* 13:10 (October 1930): 1.

2:103. These references are from an address on "Religious Tolerance" delivered August 11, 1928, and an interview with Preston Wolfe, cited by Martin L. Fausold, *The Presidency of Herbert C. Hoover* (Lawrence: University Press of Kansas, 1985), 1.

Chapter Three

3:1. *Attorney General A. Mitchell Palmer on Charges Made against Department of Justice by Louis F. Post and Others, Hearings before the Committee on Rules, House of Representatives* (Washington, D.C.: U.S. Government Printing Office, 1920), 157–58; see also the standard history of the Red Scare, Robert K. Murray, *Red Scare: A Study in National Hysteria, 1919–1920* (Minneapolis: University of Minnesota Press, 1955), 79.

3:2. U.S. Congressional Record (1924) 68:1: 5865, 5868–69; and Benjamin B. Ringer, *"We the People" and Others: Duality and America's Treatment of Its Racial Minorities* (New York: Tavistock, 1983), 801–2.

3:3. The reference to the Protestant element is cited in Michael Williams, *The Shadow of the Pope* (New York: Whittlesey House, 1932), 134–35.

3:4. Edward Alsworth Ross, *The Principles of Sociology* (New York: Century, 1920); Georg Simmel, *Conflict*, trans. Kurt H. Wolff (New York: The Free Press, 1955), and *The Web of Group-Affiliations* (New York: The Free Press, 1955).

3:5. See Ross, *The Principles of Sociology*, 160, 179; he quoted Charles Cooley, *Human Nature and the Social Order* (New York: Charles Scribner's Sons, 1902), 238. Ross slightly misquotes; Cooley used a comma, not a semicolon, and has "our self," not "ourself." Mitford M. Mathews, ed., *A Dictionary of Americanisms on Historical Principles* (Chicago: University of Chicago Press, 1951), defines the *hundred-percenter* as one who is "volubly, often offensively, patriotic," and provides two illustrations dated 1928.

3:6. Ross, *The Principles of Sociology*, 179–80, 176, 165; the emphasis on *religion* is mine.

3:7. Ibid., 178.

3:8. For statistics as of 1926, see C. Luther Fry, *The U.S. Looks at Its Churches* (New York: Institute of Social and Religious Research, 1930), pp. 18–29.

3:9. André Siegfried, trans. H. H. Hemming and Doris Hemming, *America Comes of Age: a French Analysis* (New York: Harcourt and Brace, 1927).

3:10. Catholic reviewers often criticized Siegfried's book because of his accent on Protestantism at a time when Catholics were trying to establish their claims in American history. Some critics complained about his criticisms of American materialism. Charles A. Beard thought that the book had "neither the flatulent philosophy" of Alexis de Tocqueville nor "the arid banality" of James Lord Bryce. But he was outraged that Siegfried criticized American Fundamentalists for superstition while defending Catholicism, which Beard found to be superstitious and illiberal. See Charles A. Beard, "A Frenchman on America," *New Republic* 51 (June 8, 1927): 75. Most reviews were highly favorable. H. L. Mencken began, "This book is so good that it seems almost incredible." The Baltimore journalist especially agreed with Siegfried's views of Puritan Protestant influence. See H. L. Mencken, "A Frenchman Takes a Look," *The Nation* 124 (May 11, 1927): 533.

3:11. Siegfried, *America Comes of Age*, 3.

3:12. Ibid., 7–8; Siegfried speaks of "100 per cent Americans" on 102.

3:13. Ibid., 12, 14.   3:16. Ibid., 34–36.

3:14. Ibid., 19–21, 33.   3:17. Ibid., 46–47, 48–53.

3:15. Ibid., 33, 35–36, 39–45.   3:18. Ibid., 129, 146.

3:19. For the standard history, see Murray, *Red Scare*.

3:20. For a setting of the scene, see ibid., chap. 1, "The Contemporary Scene," 3–17.

3:21. See Mary Harris Jones, *The Autobiography of Mother Jones*, ed. Mary Field Parton (Chicago: Charles H. Kerr, 1972), which reprints the original of 1926.

3:22. Quoted in a portrait of Mother Jones in Judith Nies, *Seven Women: Portraits from the American Radical Tradition* (New York: Viking Press, 1977), 105.

3:23. The *Continent* headline is quoted in Robert Moats Miller, *American Protestantism and Social Issues 1919–1939* (Chapel Hill: University of North Carolina Press, 1958), 187; see also 188 for the Baptist reference, and *Annual of the Northern Baptist Convention* (1921): 220–21.

3:24. The membership estimates are from Murray, *Red Scare*, 53; on Williams, see Ralph Lord Roy, *Communism and the Churches* (New York: Harcourt and Brace, 1960), 20.

3:25. On Williams, see Murray, *Red Scare*, 46.

3:26. See Miller, *American Protestantism*, 258–59; *Herald and Presbyter* 90 (Feb. 19, 1919): 5; *Presbyterian Advance* 20 (Sept. 18, 1919): 5.

3:27. For a portrait of Palmer see Murray, *Red Scare*, chap. 12, "The Quaker and the Ark," 190–209.

3:28. Stanley Coben, *A. Mitchell Palmer: Politician* (New York: Columbia University Press, 1963), 215; on the Union of Russian Workers, see Murray, *Red Scare*, 196.

3:29. Quoted by Murray, *Red Scare*, 208; *Literary Digest* 64 (Jan. 3, 1920): 14, quotes the *New York Evening Mail* and italicizes "Soviet"; *Saturday Evening Post* 192 (Feb. 7, 1920): 28.

3:30. See David H. Bennett, *The Party of Fear: From Nativist Movements to the New Right in American History* (Chapel Hill: University of North Carolina Press, 1988), 193; William T. Ellis, "The Fighting Quaker of the Cabinet," *American Review of Reviews* 61 (January 1920): 35–38; *Annual Report of the Attorney General of the United States for 1920* (Washington, D.C.: U.S. Government Printing Office, 1920), 172–81; Charles S. Thomas, "The Evils in Our Democracy," *Forum* 61 (January 1919): 44–52.

3:31. Bennett, *The Party of Fear*, quotes Palmer on "autocrats."

3:32. For the nicknames and the decline of Palmer, see ibid., 196; on 196 Bennett also quotes Harding from the *New York Times*, May 2, 1920; see also *Saturday Evening Post* 196 (Mar. 22, 1924): 28.

3:33. For an introduction to that literature, see Murray, *Red Scare*, 92, n. 15.

3:34. Joseph M. McShane, S.J., *"Sufficiently Radical": Catholicism, Progressivism, and the Bishops' Program of 1919* (Washington, D.C.: Catholic University of America

Press, 1986), details this program; see especially chap. 4, "The Genesis and Contents of the Bishops' Program of Social Reconstruction," 136ff.

3:35. John Tracy Ellis, *The Life of James Cardinal Gibbons*, 2 vols. (Milwaukee: Bruce Publishing Co., 1952), 1: 541, cites the Mason letter to Gibbons and tells of the absence of a response in the NAM files.

3:36. See John A. Ryan, *Social Doctrine in Action: A Personal History* (New York: Harper and Brothers, 1941), 147.

3:37. See William G. McLoughlin, Jr., *Billy Sunday Was His Real Name* (Chicago: University of Chicago Press, 1955), 276, 278.

3:38. Ibid., 278, 281.

3:39. Ibid., 282; *Western Recorder* (Sept. 2, 1920): 8. Robert Moats Miller, who quotes this, *American Protestantism*, 187, adds that this Kentucky Southern Baptist paper positively compared Benedict as a patriot, Nero as a gentleman, and Judas Iscariot as a Christian to Lenin.

3:40. See Miller, *American Protestantism*, 40–44, for Protestant reactions; *Zion's Herald* 101 (July 4, 1923): 849; (July 11, 1923): 897.

3:41. Roy, *Communism and the Churches*, 70–77, refers to *The Christian Century*'s critically balanced attitude.

3:42. *The Christian Century* 44 (Dec. 8, 1927): 1448.

3:43. *Baptist* 10 (July 6, 1929): 872–73.

3:44. Ibid.

3:45. *The World Tomorrow* 3 (January 1920): 3.

3:46. Ibid., 2 (March 1919): 79.

3:47. William Montgomery Brown, *Communism and Christianism* (Galion, Ohio: Bradford-Brown Educational Co., 1921), especially 16; see also William Montgomery Brown, *My Heresy* (New York: John Day, 1926); for the Brown story, see Roy, *Communism and the Churches*, 21–28.

3:48. Brown, *Communism and Christianism*, p. 30.

3:49. For the nativist context of immigration restriction, see John Higham, *Strangers in the Land: Patterns of American Nativism 1860–1925* (New Brunswick, N.J.: Rutgers University Press, 1963; 1st ed., 1955), chap. 9, "Crusade for Americanization," 234–63.

3:50. See Arthur Mann, *The One and the Many: Reflections on the American Identity* (Chicago: University of Chicago Press, 1979), chap. 5, "The Melting Pot," 97–124; Mann's references to Israel Zangwill's play, *The Melting Pot*, and to literature about the subject are particularly rich.

3:51. The most convenient summary of U.S. policy on immigration is William S. Bernard, "Immigration: History of U.S. Policy," 486–95, in Stephen Thernstrom, ed., *Harvard Encyclopedia of American Ethnic Groups* (Cambridge: Harvard University Press, 1980).

3:52. On Japanese exclusion (which did allow for the entrance of "ministers of religion"), see C. Bascom Slemp, *The Mind of the President: As Revealed by Himself in His Own Words* (Garden City, N.Y.: Doubleday, Page, 1926), 47–48, 215–17.

3:53. Ibid., 218–25.

3:54. Theodore Abel, *Protestant Home Missions to Catholic Immigrants* (New York: Institute of Social and Religious Research, 1933), viii.

3:55. Ibid., 103–4.

3:56. On Jews, see Higham, *Strangers in the Land*, 309, citing *Hearings: Emergency Immigration Legislation* (Senate Committee on Immigration, 66 Cong., 3d Sess., Washington, D.C.: U.S. Government Printing Office, 1921), 10. On Episcopalian centrality, see

Leighton Parks, *The Crisis of the Churches* (New York: Charles Scribner's Sons, 1922), 54, 111–13; Robert T. Handy, *A Christian America: Protestant Hopes and Historical Realities* (New York: Oxford University Press, 1971), 199, poses this against "cruder" Ku Klux Klan language.

3:57. Howard B. Grose, *The Incoming Millions* (New York: Fleming H. Revell, 1906); "What Shall the United States Do about Immigration?" *Missions* (March 1922): 143; see also "The Check on Immigration," *Missions* 14 (September 1923): 467. For a full account of Baptist views, see Lawrence B. Davis, *Immigrants, Baptists, and the Protestant Mind in America* (Urbana: University of Illinois Press, 1973), 185–91.

3:58. Northern Baptist Convention *Minutes* (1925), 166–67; see Davis, *Immigrants, Baptists and the Protestant Mind*, 186–90, for a fuller account of Baptist change.

3:59. *91st Annual Report, American Baptist Home Mission Society* (1923), 26; Davis, *Immigrants, Baptists and the Protestant Mind*, 190.

3:60. Robert Moats Miller, *Harry Emerson Fosdick: Preacher, Pastor, Prophet* (New York: Oxford University Press, 1985), 442–44, cites Fosdick from letters and archival material.

3:61. Theodore Lothrop Stoddard, *Scientific Humanism* (New York: Charles Scribner's Sons, 1926), 173–74; Stoddard, *The Rising Tide of Color Against White Supremacy* (New York: Blue Ribbon Books, 1920), 220; Stoddard, *The Revolt Against Civilization: The Menace of the Under Man* (New York: Charles Scribner's Sons, 1922), 220. A summary of racist books from 1920 to 1924 is in Thomas F. Gossett, *Race: The History of an Idea in America* (Dallas: Southern Methodist University Press, 1963), chap. 15, "Racism in the 1920's," 370–408.

3:62. Albert E. Wiggam, *The New Decalogue of Science* (Indianapolis: Bobbs-Merrill, 1923), 110–11.

3:63. Wiggam, *The New Decalogue*, 17–18; the "Bolshevists" item is quoted by Higham, *Strangers in the Land*, 306, from Grant correspondence of 1918.

3:64. California State Board of Control, *California and the Oriental* (Sacramento, Calif.: State Printing Office, 1920), 13; V. S. McClatchy, *The Germany of Asia. Sacramento Bee* (pamphlet), 4. This pamphlet and three others are reprinted in, V. S. McClatchy, ed., *Four Anti-Japanese Pamphlets* (New York: Arno Press, 1978)); see Benjamin B. Ringer, *"We the People" and Others: Duality and America's Treatment of Its Racial Minorities* (New York: Tavistock, 1983), 787, 782.

3:65. For an account of Buddhism in this period, see Tetsuden Kashima, *Buddhism in America: The Social Organization of an Ethnic Religious Institution* (Westport, Conn.: Greenwood Press, 1977), chap. 2, "Buddhism Among the Japanese to the Time of the Oriental Exclusion Act," 11–28. On statistics, see S. Frank Miyamoto, *Social Solidarity Among the Japanese in Seattle* (Seattle: University of Washington Press, 1984), 99–104; on "Buddha Loves Me," see Roger Daniels, *Asian America: Chinese and Japanese in the United States Since 1850* (Seattle: University of Washington Press, 1988), 171; Daniels gives an excellent overview.

3:66. V. S. McClatchy, "Japanese in the Melting Pot: Can They Assimilate and Make Good Citizens?" *Annals of the American Academy of Political and Social Science* 93 (1921): 31–32.

3:67. *U.S. Congressional Record* (1924) 68:1: 5681; see Ringer, *"We the People,"* 800.

3:68. U.S. Congressional Record (1924) 68:1: 5742; and Ringer, *"We the People,"* 807–8.

3:69. Ibid.

3:70. John B. Trevor, "An Analysis of the American Immigration Act of 1924," *International Conciliation*, no. 202 (September 1924): 5.

3:71. For an introduction to the Klan in the 1920s, see Arnold S. Rice, *The Ku Klux Klan in American Politics* (Washington, D.C.: Public Affairs Press, 1962). See also Ross, *The Principles of Sociology*, 160, 179.

3:72. The two major contemporaneous analyses stressed religious ties throughout: John Moffatt Mecklin, *The Ku Klux Klan: A Study of the American Mind* (New York: Harcourt and Brace, 1924); and Stanley Frost, *The Challenge of the Klan* (Indianapolis: Bobbs-Merrill, 1923).

3:73. Mecklin, *The Ku Klux Klan: A Study of the American Mind*, 174–80, provides a lengthy personal witness on these themes by an informant in the Klan. All the extensive testimonies match this spiritual theme. See also Siegfried, *America Comes of Age*, 132–33.

3:74. Robert S. Lynd and Helen Merrell Lynd, *Middletown: A Study in Contemporary American Culture* (New York: Harcourt and Brace, 1929), 481.

3:75. For a pictorial interpretation, see Dwight W. Hoover, *Magic Middletown* (Bloomington: Indiana University Press, 1986), chap. 6, "The Klan in Muncie," 96–107.

3:76. For the statistics, see Hoover, *Magic Middletown*, 97.

3:77. Ibid., 98–99.

3:78. Ibid.

3:79. Ibid.

3:80. For a popular narrative of Klan revival, see William Peirce Randel, *The Ku Klux Klan: A Century of Infamy* (Philadelphia: Chilton, 1965), chap. 11, "The Klan Revived," 182–216.

3:81. Randel, *The Ku Klux Klan: A Century of Infamy*, 186, reproduces one of these catechisms.

3:82. The four aspects are in a pamphlet circulated by the Ku Klux Klan, *Ideals of the Ku Klux Klan* (Atlanta: n.p., 1923), 3–4. See Rice, *The Ku Klux Klan in American Politics*, 20–21, also for Evans citation.

3:83. Evans is quoted by Rice, *The Ku Klux Klan in American Politics*, 20–21.

3:84. Ibid., 22.

3:85. Ibid., 24.

3:86. Blaine Mast is quoted by Randel, *The Ku Klux Klan: A Century of Infamy*, 188.

3:87. See *Shreveport Journal* (May 15, 1924) and *Colonel Mayfield's Weekly* (Houston, Dec. 8, 1923); see Charles C. Alexander, *The Ku Klux Klan in the Southwest* (Lexington: University of Kentucky Press, 1965), 88, 90.

3:88. Michael Williams, *The Shadow of the Pope* (New York: Whittlesey House, 1932), 134.

3:89. Ibid., 135.

3:90. Hiram Evans, "The Klan's Fight for Americanism," in *North American Review* 223:8 (1926): 49.

3:91. Hiram Wesley Evans, "The Klan: Defender of Americanism," *Forum* 74:6 (December 1925), 807–08.

3:92. *Northwest Christian Advocate* 97 (Dec. 14, 1922): 1565; *Baptist* 2 (April 23, 1921): 358; *The Christian Century* 42 (Oct 1, 1925): 1225; for more on Protestantism and the Klan, see Robert Moats Miller, *American Protestantism*, 137–46.

3:93. The *World* attacked the "Forged Oath of Treasonable and Murderous Obligations," in 62 (Sept. 14, 1921): 1; see also Kenneth T. Jackson, *The Ku Klux Klan in the City, 1915–1930* (New York: Oxford University Press, 1967), 11–12; see also *NCW News*

Sheet 3 (Feb. 5, 1923): 1; and Christopher Kauffman, *Faith and Fraternalism: The History of the Knights of Columbus 1882–1982* (New York: Harper and Row, 1982), 278.

3:94. On Powell, see Jackson, *The Ku Klux Klan in the City*, 194–95.

3:95. Ben Olcott is quoted in ibid., 202; Olcott was recorded in Executive Department Proclamation, State of Oregon, May 13, 1922, Salem, Oregon.

3:96. For the full Oregon story of Olcott and the legislation, see Jackson, *The Ku Klux Klan in the City*, 201–7.

3:97. Robert T. Miller and Ronald B. Flowers, *Toward Benevolent Neutrality: Church, State, and the Supreme Court* (Waco, Texas: Markham Press Fund of Baylor University Press, 1977, 1982, 1987), cite "Pierce v. Society of the Sisters of the Holy Name of Jesus and Mary," 458–60. The quotation is on 460.

3:98. Black and Mahoney are quoted by Rice, *The Ku Klux Klan in American Politics*, 17, 24.

3:99. M. A. King of Lincoln Klavern, quoted by Emerson H. Loucks, *The Ku Klux Klan in Pennsylvania: A Study in Nativism* (Harrisburg, Pa.: The Telegraph Press, 1936), 120, 39; see also Mecklin, *The Ku Klux Klan: A Study of the American Mind*, 13, 37.

3:100. Mecklin, *The Ku Klux Klan: A Study of the American Mind*, 13, 14.

3:101. For estimates of Klan size, see Rice, *The Ku Klux Klan in American Politics*, 12.

3:102. On scandals in the Klan, see Randel, *The Ku Klux Klan: A Century of Infamy*, 196–97.

3:103. On the decline of the Klan, see Rice, *The Ku Klux Klan in American Politics*, chap. 8, "Disrepute and Decline," 92–107.

3:104. Charles P. Sweeney, "Bigotry Turns to Murder," *The Nation* 113 (August 31, 1921): 232.

3:105. Ibid.

3:106. Ibid.

Chapter Four

4:1. André Siegfried, trans. H. H. Hemming and Doris Hemming, *America Comes of Age: A French Analysis* (New York: Harcourt and Brace, 1927), 33, 1, 3, 9.

4:2. Ibid., 135, 130. (The emphasis is mine.)

4:3. E. A. Ross, *The Principles of Sociology* (New York: Century, 1920), 159–60. (Again, the emphasis is mine.)

4:4. Georg Simmel, trans. Kurt H. Wolff, *Conflict* (New York: The Free Press, 1955), 17–18, 34.

4:5. For a narrative of Native American life leading up to the Wounded Knee massacre, see Dee Brown, *Bury My Heart at Wounded Knee: An Indian History of the American West* (New York: Holt, Rinehart and Winston, 1971); there are informative essays in Clyde A. Milner II and Floyd A. O'Neil, *Churchmen and the Western Indians 1820–1920* (Norman: University of Oklahoma, 1985); for the larger context, see Henry Warner Bowden, *American Indians and Christian Missions: Studies in Cultural Conflict* (Chicago: University of Chicago Press, 1981), especially chap. 7, 198–221.

4:6. The Constitution quote is from Charles F. Wilkinson, *American Indians, Time, and the Law: Native Societies in a Modern Constitutional Democracy* (New Haven: Yale University Press, 1987), 12, 140–41. Wilkinson cites the Commerce Clause, U.S. Constitution, Article I, Sec. 8, Clause 3; Benjamin B. Ringer, *"We the People" and Others: Duality and American's Treatment of Its Racial Minorities* (New York: Tavistock, 1983), 137–38.

Francis Paul Prucha, *American Indian Policy in Crisis: Christian Reformers and the Indian, 1865–1900* (Norman: University of Oklahoma Press, 1976), 64, cites *Cherokee Nation v. Georgia* 5 Peters 1 (1831); 6 Peters 515 (1832); see also 5 Peters 17 (1831).

4:7. Ringer, *"We the People" and Others*, 143–4, on the Dawes Act. He cites U.S. Statutes at Large, 1887, XXIV: 390.

4:8. Ibid., 145–46. Ringer quotes from Felix S. Cohen, *Handbook of Federal Indian Law* (Albuquerque: University of New Mexico Press, 1942), 28.

4:9. See Ringer, *"We the People" and Others*, 147, on the Indian Reorganization Bill. He cites Cohen, *Handbook of Federal Indian Law*, 84.

4:10. E. O. Watson, ed., *Year Book of the Churches 1924–25* (Baltimore, Md.: J. E. Stohlmann, 1924), 358, 363.

4:11. Samuel McCrea Cavert, ed., *Twenty Years of Church Federation: Report of the Federal Council of the Churches of Christ in America 1924–1928* (New York: Federal Council of Churches, 1929), 118–19.

4:12. Walter M. Camp, "The Condition of Reservation Indians," was submitted on June 8, 1920 to Malcolm McDowell, secretary of the Board of Indian Commissioners. The typescript is in the Edward Ayer Collection in Chicago's Newberry Library. See Frederick E. Hoxie, *A Final Promise: The Campaign to Assimilate the Indians, 1880–1920* (Lincoln: University of Nebraska Press, 1984), 239–44; the quoted words are from Camp's report, 5–8, 13–14.

4:13. For background, see Omer C. Stewart, *Peyote Religion* (Norman: University of Oklahoma Press, 1987), especially chaps. 8 and 9, "Efforts to Pass a Federal Law," and "An International Church and the Further Spread of Peyotism on the High Plains," 213–64.

4:14. James S. Olson and Raymond Wilson, *Native Americans in the Twentieth Century* (Urbana: University of Illinois Press, 1984), 95–99; on Collier, see Stewart, *Peyote Religion*, 231–32.

4:15. Robert M. Kvasnicka and Herman J. Viola, *The Commissioners of Indian Affairs, 1824–1977* (Lincoln: University of Nebraska Press, 1979), 259–60.

4:16. John Collier, *From Every Zenith: A Memoir and Some Essays on Life and Thought* (Denver: Sage Books, 1963), 126.

4:17. Ibid.

4:18. James Weldon Johnson, *Along This Way* (New York: Viking Press, 1935), 341; for the larger context, see William M. Tuttle, Jr., *Race Riot: Chicago in the Red Summer of 1919* (New York: Atheneum, 1970).

4:19. See Nathan I. Huggins, *Harlem Renaissance* (New York: Oxford University Press, 1971); there is comment on churches in Florette Henry, *Black Migration: Movement North 1900–1920* (Garden City, N.Y.: Doubleday, 1975), 186–87.

4:20. See David M. Reimers, *White Protestantism and the Negro* (New York: Oxford University Press, 1965), chap. 3, "The North Compromises," 51–83.

4:21. Ibid., chap. 4, "The Churches Edge Forward," 84–108, discusses the trends in the twenties and thirties.

4:22. Siegfried, *America Comes of Age*, 108, 100.

4:23. Ibid., 106.

4:24. Benjamin Elijah Mays and Joseph William Nicholson, *The Negro's Church* (New York: Institute of Social and Religious Research, 1933), 14, 96.

4:25. On Methodist statistics, see Harry V. Richardson, *Dark Salvation: The Story of Methodism As It Developed among Blacks in America* (Garden City, N.Y.: Doubleday, 1976), 253; the Olivet Baptist story is in *Facts and Figures* (no imprint), a pamphlet in the Papers of the Chicago Commission on Race Relations at the Illinois State Archives in Springfield; and in S. Mattie Fisher, "Olivet as a Christian Center," *Missions* 10 (March 1919): 199–202, cited by Tuttle, *Race Riot*, 98–99.

4:26. See Benjamin Mays, *Born to Rebel* (New York: Charles Scribner's Sons, 1971); Samuel Kelton Roberts, "Crucible for a Vision: The Work of George Edmund Haynes and the Commission on Race Relations, 1922–1947," (Ph.D. diss., Columbia University, 1974).

4:27. George Edmund Haynes, *The Trend of the Races* (New York: Council of Women for Home Missions and Missionary Education Movement of the United States and Canada, 1922), 82, 86, 15. On the South in general, see Wilma Dykeman and James Stokely, *Seeds of Southern Change* (Chicago: University of Chicago Press), 273–75; David Reimers, *White Protestantism*, 84–93, reports on the various commissions on race relations.

4:28. On the controversy over Race Relations Sunday, see Reimers, *White Protestantism*, 91.

4:29. *Woman's Home Missions* 39 (August 1922): 9; (December 1924): 4; *Annual Report of the Woman's Missionary Council of the Methodist Episcopal Church, South* (1919–20), 29, 179–80; *Annual Report of the Department of Woman's Work of the Presbyterian Church in the U.S.* (1931); see also Reimers, *White Protestantism*, 88–91, which reports in detail on women's activities.

4:30. *Journal of the General Conference of the Methodist Episcopal Church, South* (1922), 356, discusses lynching; on clergy evasion, see Arthur Raper, *The Tragedy of Lynching* (Chapel Hill: University of North Carolina Press, 1933), 22–23, 71–72, 82, 335–36. Prominent Methodist Bishop Warren A. Candler opposed federal activity against lynching in "Mistaken Advocates of Mischievous Measures," *Southern Christian Advocate* 87 (March 29, 1923): 4; the action of Methodist women is discussed in *Annual Report of the Woman's Missionary Council of the Methodist Episcopal Church, South* (1920–21), 32.

4:31. *Annual Report of the Northern Baptist Convention* (1929), 153; (1926), 168–69.

4:32. I. A. Newby, *Jim Crow's Defense: Anti-Negro Thought in America, 1900–1930* (Baton Rouge: Louisiana State University Press, 1965), 88–99. Theodore D. Bratton, *Wanted—Leaders! A Study of Negro Development* (New York: Department of Missions and Church Extension, 1922).

4:33. Theodore D. Bratton, *Wanted—Leaders! A Study of Negro Development*, 215, 220, 223; also see Theodore D. Bratton, "Race Cooperation in Church Work," in James E. McCulloch, ed., *Battling for Social Betterment, Southern Sociological Congress, Memphis, Tennessee, May 6–10, 1914* (Nashville: Southern Sociological Congress, 1914), 145–53. Newby, *Jim Crow's Defense*, cites Bratton on "savage morality."

4:34. Lankford is in *Congressional Record*, 67th Congress, 2d Session (January 18, 1922), 1371; E. H. Randle, *Characteristics of the Southern Negro* (New York: Neale Publishing, 1910), 116.

4:35. Robert Edwin Smith, *Christianity and the Race Problem* (New York: Fleming H. Revell, 1922), 41, 138.

4:36. George Mallison, *Color at Home and Abroad* (Boston: Christopher, 1929), 117, 128; Newby, *Jim Crow's Defense*, 83–109, is the best survey of attitudes; he assesses that the cited works were more representative than directly influential.

4:37. W. E. B. Du Bois wrote to Joseph B. Glenn, St. Joseph's Mission, Richmond, Va., in *The Crisis* 30 (July 1925): 121.

4:38. John LaFarge, *The Catholic Viewpoint on Race Relations* (Garden City, N.Y.: Hanover House, 1956), 62–63, cites the plaint of Federated Colored Catholics. See Newby, *Jim Crow's Defense*, 105–8, for elaboration of the Catholic story.

4:39. Benjamin Elijah Mays and Joseph William Nicholson, *The Negro's Church*, 180, 289; consult Mays and Nicholson for data on black churches in the period.

4:40. Two introductions to Garvey are Randall K. Burkett, *Garveyism as a Religious Movement* (Metuchen, N.J.: Scarecrow Press, 1978), and Judith Stein, *The World of Marcus Garvey: Race and Class in Modern Society* (Baton Rouge: Louisiana State University Press, 1986).

4:41. For the United Negro Improvement Agency program, see Amy Jacques-Garvey, ed., *The Philosophy and Opinions of Marcus Garvey*, 2 vols. (London: Frank Cass and Co., 1967), 2: 126.

4:42. Robert A. Hill, ed., *Marcus Garvey and the Universal Negro Improvement Association Papers*, 5 vols. (Berkeley: University of California Press, 1983), 1: 41, 42, 120.

4:43. Stein, *The World of Marcus Garvey*, chap. 4, "The Black Star Line," 89–107, tells the story of Garvey's venture.

4:44. Amy Jacques-Garvey, *The Philosophy and Opinions of Marcus Garvey*, 2: 98, 101; this is a quotation from a speech at Carnegie Hall, August 1, 1924.

4:45. For relations between Garvey and Du Bois, see Stein, *The World of Marcus Garvey*, 213–17.

4:46. The declaration is quoted by Gayraud S. Wilmore, *Black Religion and Black Radicalism: An Interpretation of the Religious History of Afro-American People* (Maryknoll, N.Y.: Orbis, 1983), 148. See also Amy Jacques-Garvey, *The Philosophy and Opinions of Marcus Garvey*, 2: 135–40.

4:47. Quoted in Amy Jacques-Garvey, *Garvey and Garveyism* (Kingston: United Printers, 1963), 133–34.

4:48. Ibid.

4:49. Stein, *The World of Marcus Garvey*, chap. 4, "The Politics of Mail Fraud," 186–208, details the mail-fraud incident.

4:50. James Weldon Johnson, *Black Manhattan* (New York: Alfred A. Knopf, 1930), 255; the speech is in *Negro World* 10:2 (February 19, 1921): 4.

4:51. Burkett, *Garveyism as a Religious Movement*, 88–89, 95, 111–13, details the founding of the African Orthodox Church; *Negro World* 11:21 (January 7, 1922): 4, prints the words of rejection of McGuire.

4:52. Stein, *The World of Marcus Garvey*, 158–70, tells the story of the Klan venture; see *New York World*, August 15, 1922; June 27, 1922.

4:53. On the meeting with Clarke, see Stein, *The World of Marcus Garvey*, 154–59.

4:54. *New York World*, February 18, July 15, Sept. 24, 1922, reproduces words of Garvey defending his actions with Clarke.

4:55. For Randolph, see Theodore Kornweibel, Jr., *No Crystal Stair: Black Life and the Messenger, 1917–1928* (Westport, Conn.: Greenwood Press, 1975), 136. William Pickens is cited from a letter to Garvey on July 24, 1922, by Stein, *The World of Marcus Garvey*, 164.

4:56. On Eason's murder, see Stein, *The World of Marcus Garvey*, 171–85.

4:57. Ibid., chap. 13, "Garvey and Pan-Africanism: the Last Years," 248–272, appraises Garvey's final years.

4:58. Siegfried, *America Comes of Age*, 25.

4:59. Ibid., 25–27.

4:60. Ibid., 26.   4:62. Ibid., 27.

4:61. Ibid., 26–27.   4:63. Ibid., 28.

4:64. On the historic confusion between "Protestant America and American Protestants," see Charles H. Anderson, *White Protestant Americans: From National Origins to Religious Group* (Englewood Cliffs, N.J.: Prentice-Hall, 1970), especially 13–32, 97–111.

4:65. Claris Edwin Silcox and Galen M. Fisher, *Catholics, Jews and Protestants: A Study of Relationships in the United States and Canada* (New York: Harper and Brothers, 1934), 1–2.

4:66. Ibid., 2.   4:69. Ibid., 20–22.

4:67. Ibid., 19.   4:70. Ibid., 20–21.

4:68. Ibid.   4:71. Ibid., 21–22.

4:72. Ibid., 14, provides statistics on Jews in America in this period.

4:73. Numbers of these movements incorporated the concepts of "Good Will" and "Brotherhood." See, for instance, James E. Pitt, *Adventures in Brotherhood* (New York: Farrar, Straus, 1955), especially chap. 1, "The Advance Guard of Good Will," 7–39.

4:74. For the earliest efforts, see John A. Hutchison, *We Are Not Divided: A Critical and Historical Study of the Federal Council of the Churches of Christ in America* (New York: Round Table, 1941), 138–40.

4:75. On Straus, see Pitt, *Adventures in Brotherhood*, 20–32; Roger W. Straus, "The Good Will Movement in the United States During the Year 5691," *Jewish Telegraphic Agency*, Sept. 11, 1931, is quoted by Benny Kraut in "A Wary Collaboration: Jews, Catholics, and the Protestant Goodwill Movement," in William R. Hutchison, *Between the Times: The Travail of the Protestant Establishment in America, 1900–1960* (New York: Cambridge University Press, 1989), 197–98; see the whole essay, 193–230.

4:76. See Everett R. Clinchy, *All in the Name of God* (New York: John Day, 1934).

4:77. A full-length attack on liberal and modernist approaches to missions by an early fundamentalist is John Horsch, *The Modernist View of Missions* (Scottdale: Fundamental Truth Depot, 1920).

4:78. Quoted from minutes of the North American Section of the International Missionary Council's Committee on the Christian Approach to the Jews, Nov. 9, 1934, Presbyterian Historical Society, as cited by Benny Kraut, "A Wary Collaboration: Jews, Catholics, and the Protestant Goodwill Movement," in Hutchison, ed., *Between the Times*, 201. On Mott, see *B'nai B'rith Magazine* 45 (1931): 190.

4:79. Kraut in Hutchison, ed., *Between the Times*, 210, cites a letter from Rush Rhees to Isidor Singer, Oct. 3, 1929, in the Singer Papers, AJA.

4:80. See Kraut, in Hutchison, ed., *Between the Times*, 193–230, for details of practical cooperation.

4:81. Garry Wills, *Reagan's America: Innocents at Home* (Garden City, N.Y.: Doubleday, 1987), chap. 40, "Greenfield Village on the Potomac," 371–77, relates Ford to the impulse to keep America simple and discusses Ford's interest in the *Protocols of Zion*.

4:82. On references to Bolshevik influences, see Seymour Martin Lipset and Earl Raab, *The Politics of Unreason: Right Wing Extremism in America, 1790–1970* (New York: Harper and Row, 1970), 135; Marshall is quoted in Harry Schneiderman, ed., *The American Jewish Yearbook 5686* (Philadelphia: Jewish Publication Society of America, 1925), 27: 458.

4:83. On Taft, Wilson, and the Federal Council of Churches, see Henry L. Feingold, *Zion in America: The Jewish Experience from Colonial Times to the Present* (New York: Twayne, 1974), 270.

4:84. On Fordlandia, see ibid., 270.

4:85. On discrimination at universities, see Heywood Broun and George Britt, *Christians Only: A Study in Prejudice* (New York: Vanguard, 1931), 72–124.

4:86. Lewis S. Gannett, "Is America Anti-Semitic?" *The Nation* 116: 330–31

(1923); the reference to Schechter is in Charles Reznikoff, ed., *Louis Marshall: Champion of Liberty: Selected Papers and Addresses*, 2 vols. (Philadelphia: Jewish Publication Society of America, 1957), 1: 257.

4:87. Reznikoff, *Louis Marshall*, 1: 266–67, cites a letter from Marshall to A. C. Ratchefsky, Boston, June 17, 1922; see also Morton Rosenstock, *Louis Marshall, Defender of Jewish Rights* (Detroit: Wayne State University Press, 1965), 252.

4:88. Naomi Cohen, *Not Free to Desist: The American Jewish Committee 1906–1966* (Philadelphia:; Jewish Publication Society of America, 1972), 458–59, reports on a three-volume mimeographed work by J. V. Thompson et al., 1934, "A Study of Jew-Christian Relationships as Found in Official Church School Materials."

4:89. For the general story, see Melvin I. Urofsky, *American Zionism from Herzl to the Holocaust* (Garden City, N.Y.: Anchor Press, 1975).

4:90. On Christian Zionism, see Yaakov Ariel, "American Premillennialism and Its Attitudes towards the Jewish People, Judaism and Zionism, 1875–1925" (Ph.D. diss., University of Chicago, 1986); Timothy Weber, *Living in the Shadow of the Second Coming: American Premillennialism, 1875–1982* (Chicago: University of Chicago Press, 1987); David A. Rausch, *Zionism within Early American Fundamentalism 1878–1918* (New York: Edwin Mellen, 1979).

4:91. Urofsky, *American Zionism*, 129, cites Brandeis from the *Baltimore American*, September 16, 1914.

4:92. For surveys of Jewish denominations, see Marc Lee Raphael, *Profiles in American Judaism: The Reform, Conservative, Orthodox, and Reconstructionist Traditions in Historical Perspective* (New York: Harper and Row, 1984); Moshe Davis, *The Emergence of Conservative Judaism: The Historical School in 19th Century America* (New York: Burning Bush, 1963); Michael A. Meyer, *Response to Modernity: a History of the Reform Movement in Judaism* (New York: Oxford University Press, 1988).

4:93. Stephen S. Wise wrote to Robert Kesselman, May 8, 1930, quoted by Carl Herman Voss, ed., *Stephen S. Wise, Servant of the People* (Philadelphia: Jewish Publication Society of America, 1969), 167–68.

4:94. On Schechter and Conservatism, see Samuel Halperin, *The Political World of American Zionism* (Detroit: Wayne State University Press, 1961), 101–7; Israel Goldstein, *Toward a Solution* (New York: G. P. Putnam's Sons, 1940), 165–93; on Orthodoxy, see Abraham J. Karp, *Haven and Home: A History of the Jews in America* (New York: Schocken, 1985), 258–59: Karp quotes Baruch Meir Klein, *Sha'alu Sh'lom Yerushalayim* (New York, 1917), and on "our brothers—our foes," *Ha-Ivri* 7: 42 (November 16, 1917): 1.

4:95. Quoted by David Polish, *Renew Our Days: The Zionist Issue in Reform Judaism* (Jerusalem: World Zionist Organization, 1976), 144.

4:96. *Yearbook of the Central Conference of American Rabbis* 30 (1920): 169.

4:97. Newman is cited in Fred Rosenbaum, *Architects of Reform: Congregational and Community Leadership: Emanu-El of San Francisco, 1849–1980* (Berkeley, Calif.: Western Jewish History Center, 1980), 103; Hyman G. Enelow's 1929 address is cited by Raphael, *Profiles in American Judaism*, 41. See also Enelow's "Palestine and the Jews," in *The Allied Countries and the Jews: A Series of Addresses* (New York: Temple Emanuel-El, Block Publishing Co., 1918), 73.

4:98. See Karp, *Haven and Home*, chap. 10, "After the Armistice," 247–74, for an overview; on reform, Meyer, *Response to Modernity*, 296, writes that "the years between the world wars were not an exciting time for American religion" and then provides many stories of excitements in Judaism in chap. 8, "Reorientation," 296–334.

4:99. Philip Gleason, "American Identity and Americanization," in Stephen Thernstrom, ed., *Harvard Encyclopedia of American Ethnic Groups* (Cambridge: Harvard

University Press, 1980), 43–47, strenuously points to the neglected racist aspect of Kallen's "cultural pluralism."

4:100. See, for instance, Horace M. Kallen, *Secularism Is the Will of God* (New York: Twayne, 1954).

4:101. For elaborations of his vision, see Horace M. Kallen, *Culture and Democracy in the United States* (New York: Boni and Liveright, 1924), and *Judaism at Bay: Essays toward the Adjustment of Judaism to Modernity* (New York: Bloch, 1932).

4:102. Kallen, *Culture and Democracy*, 179; and Kallen, *The Structure of Lasting Peace* (Boston: Marshall Jones Co., 1918), 31.

4:103. See Kallen, *Culture and Democracy*, 124–25, for his picture of America as a "democracy of nationalities" showing a "multiplicity in unity."

4:104. Kallen, *Judaism at Bay*, 32; *Culture and Democracy*, 125.

4:105. Kallen, *Culture and Democracy*, 226.

4:106. Raphael, *Profiles in American Judaism*, 179–94, offers an overview of Reconstructionism. See also Mordecai Kaplan, "The Way I Have Come," in Ira Eisenstein and Eugene Kohn, eds., *Mordecai M. Kaplan: An Evaluation* (New York: Reconstructionist Foundation, 1952), 311.

4:107. Eisenstein and Kohn, eds., *Mordecai M. Kaplan*, 320, 311; on the Society for the Advancement of Judaism, see Emanuel S. Goldsmith and Mel Scult, eds., *Dynamic Judaism: The Essential Writings of Mordecai M. Kaplan* (New York: Schocken, 1985), 9–12.

4:108. Mordecai M. Kaplan, *Judaism as a Civilization*, (New York: (Macmillan, 1934), 328.

4:109. Ibid., 328–29.

4:110. Mordecai M. Kaplan, *The Religion of Ethical Nationhood: Judaism's Contribution to World Peace* (New York: Macmillan, 1970), 156, on the Torah.

4:111. Kaplan, *Judaism as a Civilization*, 78, on Catholics and Jews.

4:112. Bernard Drachman, "An Examination of Professor Mordecai M. Kaplan's Views on Judaism," *Jewish Forum* 4 (February 1921): 724–29, 731; Kaplan responded in *Morgen Journal*, Jan. 16, 1921; see Richard Libowitz, *Mordecai M. Kaplan and the Development of Reconstructionism* (New York: Edwin Mellen, 1983), 98–100.

4:113. Mordecai Kaplan, "Toward a Reconstruction of Judaism," *Menorah Journal* 13 (April 1927): 119; *Proceedings of the Rabbinic Assembly of America* 2 (1928): 131–33.

4:114. On the Zionism issue as a matter of conflict within Reform Judaism, see Horward R. Greenstein, *Turning Point: Zionism and Reform Judaism* (Chico, Calif.: Scholars Press, 1981), chap. 4, "Advocates and Adversaries: The Inner Conflict Over Zionism," 73–100.

4:115. James M. Gillis, "Out of the Shadows into the Light," editorial, *Catholic World* 123 (August 1926): 691.

4:116. Mementos of the period reflect the triumphalism; see for example *XXVIII International Eucharistic Congress, June 20–24, 1926 Chicago, Ill.* (Chicago: The XXVIII International Eucharistic Congress, Inc., 1926).

4:117. Bernard Fay, "Catholic America," *Living Age* 335 (September 1928): 53–56.

4:118. Ibid., 53.

4:119. Ibid., 56.

4:120. Ibid.

4:121. *New World* (April 23, 1920): 4; James O'Donnell Bennett, *The Eucharistic Congress as Reported in the Chicago Tribune* (Chicago: Chicago Tribune, 1926), 18; *Christian Century* 43 (June 17, 1926): 767.

4:122. William M. Halsey, *The Survival of American Innocence: Catholicism in an Era of Disillusionment 1920–1940* (Notre Dame, Ind.: University of Notre Dame Press, 1980), provides an overview of the period.

4:123. Siegfried, *America Comes of Age*, 23–24.

4:124. Ibid., 48, 51–53.

4:125. Silcox and Fisher, *Catholics, Jews and Protestants*, 33.

4:126. On the period as one of unreason, see Lipset and Raab, *The Politics of Unreason*, chap. 4, "The Bigoted Twenties," 110–49.

4:127. Silcox and Fisher, *Catholics, Jews and Protestants*, 23–24, 26.

4:128. On the National Catholic Welfare Council, see Elizabeth McKeown, *War and Welfare: American Catholics and World War I* (New York: Garland, 1988), chap. 5, 165–200; Kraut in Hutchison, ed., *Between the Times*, 212, tells of the American Committee on the Rights of Religious Minorities.

4:129. Silcox and Fisher, *Catholics, Jews and Protestants*, chap. 9, "Cooperation," 305–49, describes these interfaith efforts.

4:130. *The Promotion of True Religious Unity*, encyclical letter of His Holiness Pope Pius XI, issued Jan. 6, 1928; the quote is on 11 (Washington, D.C.: National Catholic Welfare Council, 1928).

4:131. J. Elliot Ross, "Courtesy at Columbia," *Commonweal* 9 (February 20, 1929): 449.

4:132. John Tracy Ellis, *The Life of James Cardinal Gibbons*, 2 vols. (Milwaukee: Bruce, 1952), 2:298, describes the mood at Gibbons' jubilee; see also his word to the American episcopate of April, 1919, cited in *The Catholic World* 109 (July 1919): 440.

4:133. On the bishops' program, see Joseph M. McShane, S.J., *"Sufficiently Radical": Catholicism, Progressivism, and the Bishops' Program of 1919* (Washington, D.C.: Catholic University of America Press, 1986).

4:134. Daniel Tobin, "Can the Church Be Led Back to the Humble Carpenter of Nazareth?" 62–66, and James H. Maurer, "Has the Church Betrayed Labor?" 29–36 (quotation on 34), in Jerome Davis, ed., *Labor Speaks for Itself on Religion: A Symposium of Labor Leaders Throughout the World* (New York: Macmillan, 1929); see also McShane, *Sufficiently Radical*, 239–82.

4:135. Winfred E. Garrison, *Catholicism and the American Mind* (Chicago: Willett, Clark and Colby, 1928), 7.

4:136. Ibid., 141, 181; see also all of chap. 8, "Legends of Catholic Toleration," 159–71, and chap. 9, "Promotion and Propaganda," 172–206.

4:137. John F. Moore, *Will America Become Catholic?* (New York: Harper and Brothers, 1931), 4–5.

4:138. Ibid., 16, 40.

4:139. Ibid., 229, 238, 242.

4:140. For background to the controversy, see Ferenc Morton Szasz, *The Divided Mind of Protestant America, 1880–1930* (University, Ala.: University of Alabama Press, 1982).

Chapter Five

5:1. Bernard Clausen, "Why Quarrel?" *Baptist* 5 (July 5, 1924): 546.

5:2. F. M. Goodchild, "The Fundamentalists and the Bible," *Watchman-Examiner* 13 (Oct. 22, 1925): 1362.

5:3. E. A. Ross, *The Principles of Sociology* (New York: Century, 1920), 161.

Ross also made reference to the work of Georg Simmel on conflict, citing his "The Sociology of Conflict," Part I; *American Journal of Sociology* 9:4 (January 1904): 490–525.

5:4. Leo P. Ribuffo, *The Old Christian Right: The Protestant Far Right from the Great Depression to the Cold War* ((Philadelphia: Temple University Press, 1983), picks up the story of the Fundamentalist extreme from this period through the next decades. An accounting of the late twentieth-century controversies awaits volume four in the present work.

5:5. Alfred North Whitehead, *Adventures of Ideas* (New York: Macmillan, 1933), 205. On the declining significance of denominationalism in much of the century, see Robert Wuthnow, *The Restructuring of American Religion: Society and Faith Since World War II* (Princeton: Princeton University Press, 1988), chap. 5, 71–99.

5:6. On the concept of "center and periphery," especially as employed in the writings of Edward Shils, see "The Idea of the 'Center:' An Introduction," by Liah Greenfeld and Michel Martin, in Liah Greenfeld and Michel Martin, eds. *Center: Ideas and Institutions* (Chicago: University of Chicago Press, 1988), viii–xxii; on "periphery" and "margin," see R. Laurence Moore, *Religious Outsiders and the Making of Americans* (New York: Oxford University Press, 1986). (See identical note 41 in Chapter 1 of this volume.)

5:7. Ferenc Morton Szasz, *The Divided Mind of Protestant America, 1880–1930* (University, Ala.: University of Alabama Press, 1982), best describes how biblical criticism and evolution came to be two predominant themes behind the controversy, and provides valuable historic insight into the background of the battles.

5:8. The most satisfying general introduction to Fundamentalism is George M. Marsden, *Fundamentalism and American Culture: The Shaping of Twentieth-Century Evangelicalism 1870–1925* (New York: Oxford University Press, 1980); see also the bibliographical essay, "The Evangelical Tradition in America," by Leonard I. Sweet, in Sweet, ed. *The Evangelical Tradition in America* (Macon, Ga.: Mercer University Press, 1984), 1–112.

5:9. On *The Fundamentals* see Marsden, *Fundamentalism and American Culture*, 118–23.

5:10. Curtis Lee Laws, "Fundamentalism in the Northern Convention," *Watchman-Examiner* 10 (June 15, 1922): 745.

5:11. Ibid., 8 (July 1, 1920): 834.

5:12. The correspondent is quoted in an editorial, "Baptists and Fundamentalists," *Watchman-Examiner* 8 (July 22, 1920): 925; see also W. B. Riley, "The Buffalo Convention and Brotherly Love," *Baptist* 7 (August 7, 1920): 977.

5:13. Some moderate Fundamentalists joined the stereotypers in criticism, and formed a National Association of Evangelicals in 1941; see Louis Gasper, *The Fundamentalist Movement* (The Hague: Mouton, 1963), 25–31.

5:14. The element of Fundamentalism that best expressed its competitive worldview was premillennialism; the most extensive accounting of it is Ernest R. Sandeen, *The Roots of Fundamentalism: British and American Millenarianism 1800–1930* (Chicago: University of Chicago Press, 1970).

5:15. William Bell Riley, "What Is a Fundamentalist?" in *Christian Fundamentalist* 3 (December 1929): 445; Frances C. Blanchard, *The Life of Charles Albert Blanchard* (New York: Fleming H. Revell, 1932), 73, shows a typical use of the "come-outer" language.

5:16. Walter Lippmann, *American Inquisitors* (New York: Macmillan, 1928), 63.

5:17. Ibid., 65–66.

5:18. On choice of doctrines, see Gasper, *The Fundamentalist Movement*, 2–3, 10–13, 41–42; and Sandeen, *The Roots of Fundamentalism*, xiv–xv, 251–53.

5:19. On the preference for "the literal," see James Barr, *Fundamentalism* (Philadelphia: Westminster, 1978), 40–55.

5:20. Isaac M. Haldeman, *A King's Penknife* (New York: Frances Emory Fitch, 1929), 152–53.

5:21. For Baptist statistics, see C. Luther Fry, *The U.S. Looks at Its Churches* (New York: Institute of Social and Religious Research, 1930), 132. See table XXIV.

5:22. In the account of the Northern Baptist Convention battle, I have drawn upon and gained access to sources through Roland T. Nelson, "Fundamentalism and the Northern Baptist Convention," (Ph.D. diss., University of Chicago, 1964); see 119–23 on the formation of the Northern Baptist Convention. Harding was described as a "pillar in the local Baptist church," but was not notably active nationally; see Robert S. Alley, *So Help Me God: Religion and the Presidency, Wilson to Nixon* (Richmond, Va.: John Knox Press, 1972), 43–46.

5:23. On the theological leadership in the convention, see Robert G. Torbet, *A History of the Baptists* (3d. ed., Valley Forge, Pa.: Judson, 1963), 425–36.

5:24. Nelson, *Fundamentalism and the Northern Baptist Convention*, 515, lists the participants; reference to the journals is in chap. 12, "The Jousting of the Journals," 337–41.

5:25. Editorial, "We Are on the March," *Baptist* 2 (July 9, 1921): 717; editorial, "Fundamentalism Is Very Much Alive," *Watchman-Examiner* 9 (July 28, 1921): 941; editorial, "*The Baptist* on a Rampage," idem, (Aug. 4, 1921): 973.

5:26. Editorial, "*The Outlook* Should Look Out," *Watchman-Examiner* 9 (Jul. 21, 1921): 906; editorial, "*The Times* and Fundamentalism," idem, 11 (Jun. 7, 1923): 709; Algernon Crapsey, "The Shame of the Churches," *Nation* 118 (Jan 16, 1924): 53–54.

5:27. Editorial, "The Theological Controversy," *Watchman-Examiner* 11 (Sept. 27, 1923): 1229.

5:28. Editorial, "A Liberal Estimate of Modernists," *Watchman-Examiner* 14 (Apr. 29, 1926): 530; the *Western Recorder* is cited from the *Baptist* 10 (Apr. 13, 1929): 472.

5:29. The paraphrase of Riley on Luther is in Stewart G. Cole, *The History of Fundamentalism* (New York: Harper and Brothers, 1931), 233.

5:30. Harry Emerson Fosdick, "Shall the Fundamentalists Win?" in *The Christian Work* 102 (June 10, 1922): 716–19, 722.

5:31. Ibid., 14; Harry Emerson Fosdick, *The Living of These Days* (New York: Harper and Brothers, 1956), 156, cites the author's earlier comment on Collier.

5:32. John Roach Straton, *Religious Searchlight* (New York: Calvary Baptist Church, 1922), 1.

5:33. Cited by Fosdick in *The Living of These Days*, 155–56.

5:34. Nelson, *Fundamentalism and the Northern Baptist Convention*, builds his story around these successive Convention meetings; for a listing of sites and dates, see 128–29.

5:35. Ibid., 154–55, reprints speculation by Laws that 95 percent of the people agreed with the Fundamentalists, while Riley put the figure at 85 percent and the *Watchman-Examiner* at 75 to 90 percent.

5:36. I. M. Haldeman, *Why I Am Opposed to the Interchurch World Movement* (New York: n.p., n.d.), 31.

5:37. *Baptist Fundamentals: Addresses Delivered at the Pre-Convention Conference at Buffalo, June 21 and 22, 1920* (Philadelphia: Judson, 1920), vi; *Watchman-Examiner* 8 (July 1, 1920): 834; *New York Times*, June 26, 1920, 6; W. B. Riley, "The Buffalo Convention and Brotherly Love," *Baptist* 7 (August 7, 1920): 977.

5:38. F. L. Anderson, Letter in "What Our Readers Are Thinking," *Watchman-Examiner* 10 (July 27, 1922): 955.

5:39. On the Treat gift, see editorial, "Dean Mathews Criticizes," *Watchman-Examiner* 9 (June 16, 1921): 741.

5:40. On Straton and Bertha Henshaw, see Nelson, *Fundamentalism and the Northern Baptist Convention*, 274–80.

5:41. On the battle over educational institutions, see ibid., chap. 7, "The Scrutiny of the Schools," 181–222. For Shields, see *Gospel Witness* (May 31, 1923), cited in ibid., 392.

5:42. Charles H. Fountain, *The Denominational Situation: Should Our Schools Be Investigated?* (Plainfield, N.J.: n.p., 1921).

5:43. For responses of the schools, see Nelson, *Fundamentalism and the Northern Baptist Convention*, 195–200.

5:44. See Robert A. Ashworth, "The Fundamentalist Movement among the Baptists," *Journal of Religion* 4 (November 1924): 621, for the quotation from the communication to the Fundamentals Council, December 1921.

5:45. Editorial, "The Religious Ku-Klux," *Christian Register* 101 (Feb. 23, 1922): 170; the *Boston Herald* is cited in A. C. Dieffenbach, *Religious Liberty: The Great American Illusion* (New York: William Morrow, 1927), 80; editorial, Carleton College and the Baptists," *Watchman-Examiner* 16 (Nov. 22, 1928).

5:46. *Baptist* 6 (Sept. 26, 1925): 1016. This appeared in the *Seattle Times*.

5:47. Editorial, *Christian Fundamentalist* 1 (April 1928): 19.

5:48. Timothy Weber, *Living in the Shadow of the Second Coming: American Premillennialism 1875–1982* (Chicago: University of Chicago Press, 1987), chap. 4, "The Perfect Solution," 82–104, discusses the mixed record of premillennialists in respect to reform.

5:49. On nationalism, see Marsden, *Fundamentalism and American Culture*, chap. 15, "Four Views, *Circa* 1910," gives background to views of transforming nationalism.

5:50. John Roach Straton, *Fighting the Devil in Modern Babylon* (New York: Stratford, 1929), ii.

5:51. Editorial, *Watchman-Examiner* 7 (Sept. 18, 1919): 1315; *Western Recorder* (Oct. 2, 1919), 8.

5:52. Editorial, "The Sacco-Vanzetti Excitement," *Christian Fundamentalist* 1 (Oct. 1927): 4.

5:53. On the consequences of the controversy for Fundamentalists, see Marsden, *Fundamentalism and American Culture*, chap. 21, "Epilogue: Dislocation, Relocation, and Resurgence, 1925–1940, " 184–98.

5:54. See Norman F. Furniss, *The Fundamentalist Controversy, 1918–1931* (New Haven: Yale University Press, 1954), chap. 9, "The Northern Presbyterians," 127–41.

5:55. An uncritical biography is Ned Stonehouse, *J. Gresham Machen: A Biographical Memoir* (Grand Rapids, Mich.: Eerdmans, 1955).

5:56. John Gresham Machen, *Christianity and Liberalism* (New York: Macmillan, 1923); and *The Virgin Birth of Christ* (Harper and Brothers, 1930).

5:57. A profile of Machen is in C. Allyn Russell, *Voices of American Fundamentalism: Seven Biographical Studies* (Philadelphia: Westminster, 1976), chap. 6, "J. Gresham Machen: Scholarly Fundamentalist," 135–62, and especially 146–50; for his self-description see *The Presbyterian* 97 (July 7, 1927): 8.

5:58. Stonehouse, *J. Gresham Machen: A Biographical Memoir*, 85.

5:59. Machen, "The So-called Child Labor Amendment," *The New Republic* (Dec. 31, 1924): 6.

5:60. On Woman Suffrage, see Russell, *Voices of American Fundamentalism*, 147.

5:61. For general background, see S. A. Grave, *The Scottish Philosophy of Common Sense* (Oxford: Clarendon Press 1960).

5:62. J. Gresham Machen, "History and Faith," *Princeton Theological Review* 13 (July, 1915): 337–51 (quotation on 338); and Machen, *Christianity and Liberalism*, 70, 73–74.

5:63. Machen, *Christianity and Liberalism*, 48–49; for reference to his unwillingness to attend the association meeting, see Russell, *Voices of American Fundamentalism*, 143.

5:64. See Machen, *Christianity and Liberalism*, 159–60, for his views of the radical difference between Fundamentalism and liberalism.

5:65. Ibid., 1–2.   5:68. Ibid., 17, 52, 159–60, 180.
5:66. Ibid., 2–6.   5:69. Ibid., 179.
5:67. Ibid., 7–15, and especially 15.

5:70. Among numerous studies of Princeton as a bastion, see John C. Vander Stelt, *Philosophy and Scripture: A Study in Old Princeton and Westminster Theology* (Marlton, N.J.: Mack, 1978).

5:71. Machen wrote of this in a letter to Reid Dickson, March 10, 1925; Russell, *Voices of American Fundamentalism*, 152–53, cites it.

5:72. On the founding of Westminster as the new bastion, see Russell, *Voices of American Fundamentalism*, 156, and the *New York Times*, Sept. 26, 1929, for Machen's boasts about the school.

5:73. There is a profile of Macartney in Russell, *Voices of American Fundamentalism*, 190–211.

5:74. Furniss, *The Fundamentalism Controversy*, 131–34.

5:75. Ibid., 136–37.

5:76. Ibid., 139–41; Russell, *Voices of American Fundamentalism*, 155–56.

5:77. Russell, *Voices of American Fundamentalism*, 156–57.

5:78. *God Hath Spoken: Twenty-five addresses delivered at the World Conference of Christian Fundamentals* (Philadelphia: World Conference of Christian Fundamentals, 1919), 7–8.

5:79. *The Presbyterian* 90 (Jan. 8, 1920): 3; see Marsden, *Fundamentalism and American Culture*, 159.

5:80. Quoted by Marsden, *Fundamentalism and American Culture*, 161; also see William Jennings Bryan, *In His Image* (New York: Fleming H. Revell, 1922), 94.

5:81. Robert W. Cherny, *A Righteous Cause: The Life of William Jennings Bryan* (Boston: Little, Brown, 1985), chap. 8, "The Final Battle: Crusade Against Evolution," 157–82, is one among many fair accountings of Bryan's odyssey to the evolution cause.

5:82. William Jennings Bryan, *In His Image*, 121–34, develops themes involving the "brutishness" of evolution.

5:83. Editorial, "Will Christian Taxpayers Stand for This?" *Moody Monthly* 23 (May 1923): 409; on *The King's Business*, see Marsden, *Fundamentalism and American Culture*, 209; M. E. Dodd, "Three Questions Concerning Modernism," is cited by Willard B. Gatewood, Jr., *Controversy in the Twenties: Fundamentalism, Modernism, and Evolution* (Nashville: Vanderbilt University Press, 1969), 6.

5:84. Jon H. Roberts, *Darwinism and the Divine in America: Protestant Intellectuals and Organic Evolution, 1859–1900* (Madison: University of Wisconsin Press, 1988); chaps. 5, 6, 7 have detailed discussions of pro-evolution Protestant thought.

5:85. Ibid.; chaps. 2, 4, 8 elaborate on the anti-evolution arguments before 1900.

5:86. *Southern Baptist Convention Annual 1922*, 35; Edmund D. Soper is quoted from the Charlotte *News and Observer* in Willard B. Gatewood, Jr., *Preachers, Pedagogues and Politicians: The Evolution Controversy in North Carolina 1920–1967* (Chapel Hill: University of North Carolina Press, 1966), 193.

5:87. Watson Davis, "Latest Phase of Evolution Controversy," *Current History* 25 (March 1927): 859.

5:88. James R. Moore, *The Post-Darwinian Controversies: A Study of the Protestant Struggle to Come to Terms with Darwin in Great Britain and America 1870–1900* (Cambridge: Cambridge University Press, 1979), does much with military metaphors; this virtual anthology of quotations is from 74–75.

5:89. Out of the vast literature on the Scopes trial, one item of special background interest is John T. Scopes and James Presley, *Center of the Storm: Memoirs of John T. Scopes* (New York: Holt, Rinehart and Winston, 1967).

5:90. See Ray Ginger, *Six Days or Forever? Tennessee v. John Thomas Scopes* (Boston: Beacon Press, 1958), for one of many accounts.

5:91. André Siegfried, trans. H. H. Hemming and Doris Hemming, *America Comes of Age: A French Analysis* (New York: Harcourt and Brace, 1927), 61–62, quoted Bryan.

5:92. Ibid., 62.

5:93. Paolo E. Coletta, *William Jennings Bryan*, vol. 3, *Political Puritan* (Lincoln: University of Nebraska Press, 1969), 208–14, discusses the violent character of Bryan's rhetoric on this one issue. Samples are from Bryan, "A Very Present Help in Trouble," in *Commoner* (Nov. 1921): 8–9; "Bryan Upholds the Bible," in the Rochester, New York, *Democrat and Chronicle*, Nov. 5, 1921; "Darwinism in the Public Schools," *Commoner* (Jan. 1923): 1–2; for the epithets, see Coletta, *William Jennings Bryan*, 3: 212.

5:94. William Jennings Bryan, *In His Image*, 106. For the reference to the paycheck, see Coletta, *William Jennings Bryan*, 3: 229, quoting a letter from Bryan to Mayor John F. Hylan, New York City, June 12, 1923.

5:95. Coletta, *William Jennings Bryan*, 3: 238, discusses Bryan's loneliness in the Dayton venture.

5:96. Ibid., 214, reproduces a letter from Sunday to Bryan, June 19, 1922; idem, 216, quotes Eggleston to Bryan, Feb. 28, 1922; and, idem, Governor Charles H. Brough to Bryan, Mar. 9, 1922.

5:97. Siegfried, *America Comes of Age*, 58.

5:98. Ibid., 58–59.

5:99. Shailer Mathews, "Ten Years of Protestantism," *North American Review* 217 (May 1923): 577–93, is a full-length critique; see also "The Crusade against Darwinism," *New York Times Book Review and Magazine* (Mar. 5, 1922): 5; and "Bryan in Dayton, Calls Scopes Trial Duel to the Death," *New York Times*, July 8, 1925, 1, 6.

5:100. On premillennial dispensationalism, see James Barr, *Fundamentalism* (Philadelphia: Westminster, 1978), 191–207; A. C. Gaebelein, *Our Hope* 31 (January 1925): 654; J. Frank Norris is quoted in William Henry Smith, *Modernism, Fundamentalism, and Catholicism* (Milwaukee: Morehouse, 1926), 42.

5:101. See Weber, *Living in the Shadow of the Second Coming*, 204–15.

5:102. I use "philosophy of history" in the substantive, not the analytic, sense; for definition, see Arthur Danto, *Analytic Philosophy of History* (Cambridge: Cambridge University Press, 1965), chap. 1, "Substantive and Analytical Philosophy of History," 1–16.

5:103. On the rural-urban and northern-southern issue, see Sandeen, *The Roots of Fundamentalism*, xi–xii.

5:104. *Atlanta Constitution*, May 8, 1947.

5:105. J. Frank Norris, *The Gospel of Dynamite: Messages that Resulted in Over 700 Conversions. Delivered to the Largest Congregations in America, Including the Recent Sermon, The Fear of Death and How to Overcome It* (n.p., n.d.), 168.

5:106. From an interview with Homer Ritchie, June 8, 1970; see Russell, *Voices of American Fundamentalism*, 27; on Norris's Zionism, see idem, 27–28.

5:107. Quoted by John Franklyn Norris, *Inside History of First Baptist Church, Fort Worth; and Temple Baptist Church, Detroit. Life Story of J. Frank Norris* (n.p., n.d.), 194.

5:108. *The Fundamentalist* 3 (Feb. 1, 1929).

5:109. Russell, *Voices of American Fundamentalism*, 40, quotes minutes of Baptist conventions.

5:110. For a typical newspaper account, see the *New York American*, Jan. 28, 1927; for a brief report, see Russell, *Voices of American Fundamentalism*, 35–36.

5:111. For an assessment of the impact on Norris, see E. Ray Tatum, *Conquest or Failure? A Biography of J. Frank Norris* (Dallas, Tex.: Baptist Historical Foundation, 1966), 211–16.

5:112. *Christian Advocate* 95 (June 10, 1920): 791, reprints address of Bishop Berry at closing session of the General Conference, Des Moines, Iowa, May 27, 1920.

5:113. Robert Leet Patterson, "The Church of To-Morrow," *Open Court* 34 (June 1920): 327.

5:114. Harry Emerson Fosdick, *Christianity and Progress* (New York: Fleming H. Revell, 1922), 177–78, 175.

5:115. Dieffenbach is quoted in Harry Emerson Fosdick, *The Living of These Days: An Autobiography* (2d. ed., New York: Harper and Row, 1967), 166.

5:116. Henry Nelson Wieman, *The Wrestle of Religion with Truth* (New York: Macmillan, 1927), 3.

5:117. An apology for evangelical liberalism is found in Henry Pitney Van Dusen, *The Vindication of Liberal Theology* (New York: Charles Scribner's Sons, 1963).

5:118. Shailer Mathews, *New Faith for Old* (New York: Macmillan, 1936), 196–97.

5:119. Shailer Mathews, *The Faith of Modernism* (New York: Macmillan, 1924), 142, 154–55.

5:120. Ibid., 166–67.

5:121. Editorial, "Fundamentalism and Modernism: Two Religions," *The Christian Century* 41 (Jan. 3, 1924): 5–6.

5:122. Ibid., 77–78.	5:126. Ibid.
5:123. Ibid., 82–83.	5:127. Ibid., 13–14.
5:124. Ibid., 3.	5:128. Ibid., 20.
5:125. Ibid., 9–10.	5:129. Ibid., 21, 23, 29.

5:130. See the assessment of the demise of Modernism by William R. Hutchison, *The Modernist Impulse in American Protestantism* (Cambridge: Harvard University Press, 1976), 298–311.

5:131. Ibid., 289–98, discusses the neo-orthodox challenge to latter-day Modernism. See Chapter 8 of the present book as well.

5:132. Two helpful guides are James J. Thompson, Jr., *Tried As By Fire: Southern Baptists and the Religious Controversies of the 1920s* (Macon, Ga.: Mercer University Press, 1982), and Milton J. Rudnick, *Fundamentalism and the Missouri Synod: A Historical Study of Their Interaction and Mutual Influence* (St. Louis: Concordia Publishing House, 1966).

5:133. On the search for enemies in patterns of conflict, see Lewis A. Coser, *The Functions of Social Conflict* (New York: Macmillan, 1956), 48–55, citing John Dewey, Georg Simmel, and others.

5:134. See Timothy P. Weber, "The Two-Edged Sword: The Fundamentalist Use of the Bible," in Nathan O. Hatch and Mark A. Noll, eds., *The Bible in America: Essays in Cultural History* (New York: Oxford University Press, 1980), 101–20.

5:135. E. Y. Mullins, "Baptist Theology in the New World Order," *Review and Expositor* 17 (October 1920): 405–7; on the period, see James J. Thompson, Jr., *Tried As By Fire*, 3–14.

5:136. See Thompson, *Tried As By Fire*, 19; *Southern Baptist Convention Annual* (1920), 50; Edmonds wrote in the Richmond, Va., *Religious Herald*, Jan. 8, 1920, 11; see also the *Proceedings of the Arkansas State Baptist Convention* (1924), 74–75.

5:137. See *Southern Baptist Convention Annual* (1924), 319; also Thompson, *Tried As By Fire*, 70, 72.

5:138. Thompson, *Tried As By Fire*, 80, cites a typescript of Feb. 5, 1932, by Rufus Weaver, "The Baptist Opportunity in a Scientific Age"; see also ibid., 77–78.

5:139. John Dewey, *Human Nature and Conduct* (New York: Holt, 1922), 226; E. Y. Mullins, *Christianity at the Cross Roads* (New York: George H. Doran, 1924), 185; Thompson, *Tried As By Fire*, 98, quotes Mullins writing to T. O. Mabry, June 7, 1923.

5:140. For the Love-Norris encounter, see Thompson, *Tried As By Fire*, 154–58; Love had written in the Richmond, Va., *Religious Herald*, Jan. 3, 1924, 4; Thompson, *Tried As By Fire*, 94–95, discusses Hankins, who wrote to R. R. Cumbie, Dec. 14, 1929.

5:141. Mullins wrote to Livingston Johnson, July 3, 1925; see William E. Ellis, *"A Man of Books and a Man of the People:" E. Y. Mullins and the Crisis of Moderate Southern Baptist Leadership* (Macon, Ga.: Mercer University Press, 1985), 190–91. The *Annual of the Southern Baptist Convention* (1925), 76, reports on the votes.

5:142. On "Zion," see the *Searchlight*, June 25, 1925; Mullins responded in the *Searchlight*, Apr. 16, 1926; see also Ellis, *A Man of Books and a Man of the People*, 193.

5:143. T. T. Martin, *Hell and the High Schools: Christ or Evolution, Which?* (Kansas City, Mo: Western Baptist Publishing, 1923), 31; Thompson, *Tried As By Fire*, 108, 128, 131, discusses the controversy and on 120–21 cites William L. Poteat's typescript of a Phi Beta Kappa oration at the University of the South, June 9, 1930.

5:144. Ellis, *A Man of Books and a Man of the People*, 195–210, carries the story through the Great Depression; the story of the Fundamentalist victories in the convention late in the century will appear in volume 4 of the present work.

5:145. The best telling of the Southern Presbyterian story is Ernest Trice Thompson, *Presbyterians in the South*, vol. 3, *1890–1972* (Richmond, Va.: John Knox Press, 1973).

5:146. *Presbyterian Standard* 65 (Feb. 20, 1924): 1; 65 (May 14, 1924): 1; Thompson, *Tried As By Fire*, 316–23, reports on the evolution controversy; see L. Nelson Bell, "The Bible Union of China," *Presbyterian Standard* 63 (Oct. 25, 1922); Donald W. Richardson, "Modernism on the Church Mission Field," *Presbyterian of the South* (Aug. 30, 1922): 2–3.

5:147. The best mapping of Lutherans in these decades is a chart inside the cover of E. Clifford Nelson, *Lutheranism in North America 1914–1970* (Minneapolis: Augsburg Publishing House, 1972).

5:148. On inerrancy in one synod see Milton L. Rudnick, *Fundamentalism and the Missouri Synod*; Richard C. Wolf, *Documents of Lutheran Unity in America* (Philadelphia: Fortress Press, 1966), 328–78, documents inter-Lutheran efforts in these decades.

5:149. Nelson, *Lutheranism in North America*, 78–83, discusses the controversy; see Lars W. Boe, "The Church and Its Work," *Lutheran Herald* 17 (June 27, 1933): 592.

5:150. *Constitution and By-laws for the Evangelical Lutheran Synod of America: Rules and Regulations for the Synodical Boards and Recommendations of the Joint Commission* (Columbus, Ohio: Lutheran Book Concern, 1926), 8; Frederick W. Meuser, *The Formation of the American Lutheran Church: A Case Study in Lutheran Unity* (Columbus, Ohio: The Wartburg Press, 1958), 186, quotes a letter from Reu to C. C. Hein, May 28, 1926.

5:151. Meuser, *The Formation of the American Lutheran Church*, 212, quotes Prottengeier from a letter of May 31, 1927.

5:152. For the votes, see *Minutes of the Evangelical Lutheran Synod of Iowa and Other States* (1928), 22; Meuser, *The Formation of the American Lutheran Church*, 228, reproduces Reu's sentiments from penciled notes on the back of a half-sheet carbon copy which is part of the Merger Convention minutes. For Missouri, see "Brief Statement of the Doctrinal Position of the Missouri Synod," *Concordia Theological Monthly* 2 (May 1931): 401–16.

5:153. Some of these conflicts are features in Willard H. Smith, *Mennonites in Illinois* (Scottdale, Pa.: Herald Press, 1983), chap. 12, "Strain, Stress, Liberalism and Fundamentalism," 303–44, especially 322–23, where Augsburger is cited for writing Horsch, May 17, 1920.

5:154. Whitmer wrote Derstine Apr. 21, 1920; see W. H. Smith, *Mennonites in Illinois*, 310–12.

5:155. Ibid., 329–34.

5:156. Ibid., 333, carries the Mennonite story into the 1930s and beyond.

5:157. See Hutchison, *The Modernist Impulse*, 282–87, for Lippmann's dismissal of Modernism.

Chapter Six

6:1. Gaius Glenn Atkins, *Religion in Our Times* (New York: Round Table, 1932), 166.

6:2. André Siegfried, trans. H. H. Hemming and Doris Hemming, *America Comes of Age: A French Inquiry* (New York: Harcourt and Brace, 1927), 35, 34.

6:3. E. A. Ross, *The Principles of Sociology* (New York: Century, 1920), 211.

6:4. Ibid., 212. On fundamentalist successes in the figurative backcountry and out of the spotlight after the defeats of the mid-twenties, see Joel Carpenter, "Fundamentalist Institutions and the Rise of Evangelical Protestantism," *Church History* 49 (March 1980): 62–75.

6:5. John A. Hutchison, *We Are Not Divided: A Critical and Historical Study of the Federal Council of the Churches of Christ in America* (New York: Round Table, 1941), 271–85, is a half-hearted and wary treatment of evangelism in the context of the more prominent Federal Council of Churches agenda.

6:6. Ross, *The Principles of Sociology*, 217.

6:7. Ibid., 213–15.

6:8. Siegfried, *America Comes of Age*, 33–34.

6:9. Ibid., 39–40.

6:10. Ibid., 40–41.

6:11. Shailer Mathews, *The Faith of Modernism* (New York: Macmillan, 1924), 32.

6:12. Ibid.

6:13. Quoted by Robert Moats Miller, *American Protestantism and Social Issues, 1919–1939* (Chapel Hill: University of North Carolina Press, 1958), 115–16.

6:14. Quoted from *Christian Advocate* 104 (Feb. 21, 1929): 234, by Paul A. Carter, *The Decline and Revival of the Social Gospel: Social and Political Liberalism in American Protestant Churches, 1920–1940* (Hamden, Conn.: Archon, 1971; 1st ed., 1956).

6:15. Carter, *The Decline and Revival of the Social Gospel*, 63, quotes John

Roach Straton, "Let the Laymen Organize," *The Faith* (formerly the *Fundamentalist*) 2 (Mar. 22, 1925): 9; see also Jerome Davis, "A Study of Protestant Church Boards of Control," *American Journal of Sociology* 38 (November 1932): 418.

6:16. Davis, "Protestant Church Boards of Control," 431.

6:17. "The Churches and Labor" in the interwar decades, takes up the largest single portion, Part III, of Robert Moats Miller's entire canvass of issues; see *American Protestantism*, 203–87. Donald B. Meyer, *The Protestant Search for Political Realism, 1919–1941* (Berkeley: University of California Press, 1960), gives it proportionately almost as much space, as in chap. 4: "The Faces of Power: Labor," 76–106.

6:18. Atkins, *Religion in Our Times*, 145.

6:19. For a discussion of labor involvement as a "one-generation phenomenon," see Henry L. Feingold, *Zion in America: The Jewish Experience from Colonial Times to the Present* (New York: Hippocrene, 1974), 158–78, 262–63.

6:20. Warren S. Stone, "Possible Cooperation Between the Churches and Labor," *Zion's Herald* 102 (Apr. 16, 1924): 493–94 ; see Donald B. Meyer, *The Protestant Search*, chap. 4, "The Faces of Power: Labor," 76–106, for a systematic treatment of the issue; see also Miller, *American Protestantism*, Part III: "The Churches and Labor," 203–90.

6:21. *Christian Advocate* 94 (June 5, 1919): 710; Edwin D. Mouzon, D.D., Bishop of the Methodist Episcopal Church, South, "Translating the Church into Our National Life," *Christian Advocate* 95 (Apr. 8 1920): 482–83.

6:22. On the decline of labor interests in the later 1920s, see Joseph G. Rayback, *A History of American Labor* (New York: The Free Press, expanded edition, 1966), chap. 21, "A Decade of Decline," 290–313.

6:23. On the strikes, see Rayback, *A History of American Labor*, 286–87; and Interchurch World Movement, *Report on the Steel Strike of 1919* (New York: Harcourt and Brace, 1920).

6:24. Eldon G. Ernst, *Moment of Truth for Protestant America: Interchurch Campaigns Following World War One* (Missoula, Mont.: Scholars Press, 1972), 128–32, details the background of the report. Meyer, *The Protestant Search*, discusses the report and its aftermath, 58–63.

6:25. E. Victor Bigelow, *Mistakes of the Interchurch Steel Report* (n.p., n.d.), 20; see Miller, *American Protestantism*, 212.

6:26. See Marshall Olds, *Analysis of the Interchurch World Movement Report on the Steel Strike* (New York: Da Capo Press, 1971; first publication was New York: C. P. Putnam's Sons, The Knickerbocker Press, 1923); Olds is cited by Miller, *American Protestantism*, 212; *Christian-Evangelist* (Aug. 5, 1920): 762; *Presbyterian Advance* 21 (Aug. 12, 1920): 4; also see Miller, *American Protestantism*, 214.

6:27. *Federal Council Bulletin* 6 (June–July 1923): 5; *The Christian Century* 44 (Sept. 8, 1927): 1039–40.

6:28. Meyer, *The Protestant Search*, 82–84, recounts the Detroit incident.

6:29. Editorial, *The Nation* 123 (Oct. 20, 1926): 387–88.

6:30. Ibid.

6:31. John Haynes Holmes, *World Tomorrow* 3 (June 1920): 174–75; see also Henry J. Cadbury, *World Tomorrow* 3 (May 1920): 131–35.

6:32. A. J. Muste, "Pacifism and Class War," in Devere Allen, ed., *Pacifism and the Modern World* (Garden City, N,Y.: Doubleday, Doran, 1929), 96–97, 99.

6:33. Halford E. Luccock, "The First Fine Careless Rapture," *World Tomorrow* 10 (December 1927): 491.

6:34. *The Christian Century* 43 (June 3, 1926): 701.

6:35. Ibid.

6:36. A classic account is Liston Pope, *Millhands and Preachers: A Study of Gastonia* (New Haven: Yale University Press, 1942).

6:37. On Communist involvement at Gastonia, see ibid., 239–52.

6:38. *Gastonia Gazette*, June 8, 1929.

6:39. Pope, *Millhands and Preachers*, 279, cites James Myers from a manuscript, "Field Notes on Textile Strikes in the South," 5.

6:40. See ibid., 323; and *Gastonia Gazette*, Sept. 30, 1930.

6:41. Pope, *Millhands and Preachers*, 326, quotes an advertisement in the *Gastonia Gazette*, Sept. 30, 1930; *Annual of the Baptist State Convention of North Carolina* (1930), 58–59.

6:42. For background to this period, see Peter Brock, *Pacifism in the United States: From the Colonial Era to the First World War* (Princeton: Princeton University Press, 1968), chap. 23, "The Reemergence of Nonsectarian Pacifism," 889–919. For the period itself, see Charles Chatfield, *For Peace and Justice: Pacifism in America, 1914–1941* (Knoxville: University of Tennessee Press, 1971).

6:43. On League of Nations, see Miller, *American Protestantism*, 319–24; and *Report of Special Meeting of the Federal Council of Churches* (1919), 9.

6:44. Chatfield, *For Peace and Justice*, 91, cites a letter from Morrison to Page, Jan. 12, 1920.

6:45. Vida Scudder, *On Journey* (New York: E. P. Dutton, 1937), 300.

6:46. Charles de Benedetti, "Alternative Antiwar Strategies of the Thirties," in Charles Chatfield, ed., *Peace Movements in America* (New York: Schocken, 1973), 66–67; a letter from Carrie Chapman Catt to Lucia Ames Mead, Jan. 9, 1924, Box 6, Lucia Ames Mead Papers, Swarthmore College Peace Collection.

6:47. Chatfield, *For Peace and Justice*, 102–6, tells of the effort to outlaw war.

6:48. *The Christian Century* 45 (Sept. 6, 1928): 1070.

6:49. Chatfield, *For Peace and Justice*, 103–6, cites Salmon O. Levinson to Kirby Page, Dec. 31, 1925; *Living Church* (August 11, 1928): 484.

6:50. Chatfield, *For Peace and Justice*, 102–6, discusses the World Court debate.

6:51. On Protestantism in Prohibition, see Miller, *American Protestantism*, 18–19, 48–62; and Joseph R. Gusfield, *Symbolic Crusade: Status Politics and the American Temperance Movement* (Urbana: University of Illinois Press, 1963), 107, 117–18.

6:52. On Fundamentalist-Modernist cooperation against Repeal, see Ferenc Morton Szasz, *The Divided Mind of Protestant America* (University, Ala.: University of Alabama Press, 1982), 64–65.

6:53. John Lee Eighmy, *Churches in Cultural Captivity: A History of the Social Attitudes of Southern Baptists* (Knoxville: University of Tennessee Press, 1972), 81, 93–108, details Southern Baptist participation; See A. J. Barton, "The Baptist Stand on Prohibition," *Religious Herald* 106 (Jan. 19, 1933): 4; *Biblical Recorder* (Oct. 24, 1934): 1.

6:54. *Annual, Texas Baptist Convention* (1920), 80; *Minutes, Georgia Baptist Convention* (1927), 30.

6:55. By the 1920s Prohibition was no longer a "progressives' " cause as it had been; see Richard Hofstadter, *The Age of Reform: From Bryan to F.D.R.* (New York: Vintage, 1955), 288–93.

6:56. See George Kelsey, *Social Ethics Among Southern Baptists 1917–1969* (Metuchen, N.J.: Scarecrow Press, 1973), 144–46; Kelsey cites W. B. Crumpton, "Pity the Poor Negro," *Alabama Baptist* 48 (Feb. 13, 1918): 7.

6:57. Crumpton, "Pity the Poor Negro," 7.

6:58. Eighmy, *Churches in Cultural Captivity*, 96–97, comments on Barton's career; see also *Annual of the Southern Baptist Convention* (1933), 116.

6:59. *Annual of the Southern Baptist Convention* (1920), 94; W. B. Crumpton, "Baptists in Politics," *The Alabama Baptist* 57 (Jan. 26, 1926): 8.

6:60. A. J. Barton, "The Baptist Stand on Prohibition," *Religious Herald* 106 (Jan. 19, 1933): 4.

6:61. Robert Moats Miller discusses Prohibition and Methodism in Emory Stevens Bucke, ed., *The History of American Methodism*, 3 vols. (Nashville: Abingdon, 1964), 3: 329–43; *The Daily Christian Advocate, Methodist Episcopal Church, South* (May 19, 1926): 104; *Journal of the General Conference of the Methodist Episcopal Church, South* (1926), 292.

6:62. *Journal of the General Conference of the Methodist Episcopal Church* (1924), 187; editorial, "The Chicago Tribune and the Churches," *Northwestern Christian Advocate* (Feb. 7, 1929): 124; see Miller in Bucke, ed., *The History of American Methodism*, 3: 335–36.

6:63. *National Prohibition Law*, Hearings before the Subcommittee of the Judiciary, United States Senate, 69th Congress, 1st Session, 2 vols. (Washington, D.C.: Government Printing Office, 1926), 2: 1229.

6:64. Ibid., 1: 386.

6:65. See Grace C. Root, *Women and Repeal* (Harper and Brothers, 1934), for the insiders' story of the emergence of pro-Repeal women.

6:66. For a Prohibitionist attack on Mrs. Sabin and the Woman's Organization for Prohibition Reform, see Fletcher Dobyns, *The Amazing Story of Repeal: An Expose of the Power of Propaganda* (5th ed., Evanston, Ill.: Signal Press, 1974; 1st ed., 1940), 105–19.

6:67. Andrew Sinclair, *Era of Excess: A Social History of the Prohibition Movement* (New York: Harper and Row, 1964), 343, quotes Mary Armor, the *New York Tribune*, June 18, 1930; Root, *Women and Repeal*, 110, quotes the *American Independent*.

6:68. From the Woman's Organization for Prohibition Reform "Declaration of Principles," quoted by Dobyns, *The Amazing Story of Repeal*, 107.

6:69. For a very critical review of the campaign for Repeal from the viewpoint of the Women's Christian Temperance Union, see ibid., 179–82.

6:70. W. H. T. Dau, *Theological Monthly* 6 (March 1926): 78–79.

6:71. Ibid.

6:72. Ibid.

6:73. Allan J. Lichtman, *Prejudice and the Old Politics: The Presidential Election of 1928* (Chapel Hill: University of North Carolina Press, 1979), details the incident.

6:74. *Zion's Herald* (Nov. 14, 1928): 1455–56.

6:75. See Myron A. Marty, *Lutherans and Roman Catholicism* (Notre Dame, Ind.: University of Notre Dame Press, 1968), 115–18.

6:76. *Lutheran Witness* 45 (Nov. 2, 1926): 360; Theodore M. Graebner, *The Pope and Temporal Power* (Milwaukee: Northwestern Publishing House, 1929), 132.

6:77. *Annual of the Northern Baptist Convention* (1928), 21: 198.

6:78. *Watchman-Examiner* 21 (Oct. 4, 1928): 1259; ibid., (Aug. 30, 1928): 1095; *Annual of the Southern Baptist Convention* (1924), 116.

6:79. Robert Moats Miller, *American Protestantism*, 48–58, argues that Prohibition was a more prominent issue than Catholicism, 57; he quotes the *American Baptist*; see also *Watchman-Examiner* 16 (Oct. 25, 1928); *Minutes of the National Council of Congregational Churches* (1929), 70–71; *Congregationalist* (July 19, 1928): 69.

6:80. *Fundamentalist* 2 (Jan. 20, and Jan. 22, 1928).

6:81. *Fundamentalist* 2 (Mar. 2, Mar. 16, Apr. 13, July 20, Aug. 17, and Aug. 31, 1928), features Norris against Smith; Norris is cited in Jeanne Bozzell McCarty, *The Struggle for Sobriety: Protestants and Prohibition in Texas: 1919-1935* (El Paso: University of Texas at El Paso Press, 1980), 16. For the Hoover incident, see *Fundamentalist* 2 (Nov. 9, 1928); see also McCarty, *The Struggle for Sobriety*, 19; the inauguration incident is in *Fundamentalist* 3 (Mar. 8, Mar. 15, 1929).

6:82. *Baptist General Convention of Texas, Proceedings*, (1928), 18 and 113-14; for Norris's responses, see *Fundamentalist* 2 (Nov. 16, Nov. 23, 1928).

6:83. Miller, *American Protestantism*, 59, quotes the *Nashville Christian Advocate* (Nov. 2, 1928): 1380, which, in turn, quoted the Catholic paper.

6:84. Michael Williams, *The Shadow of the Pope* (New York: Whittlesey House, 1932), 195, 192.

6:85. Luke E. Hart wrote to John F. Martin, Nov. 3, 1928; quoted by Christopher Kauffman, *Faith and Fraternalism: The History of the Knights of Columbus* (New York: Harper and Row, 1982), 286.

6:86. "Catholic and Patriot: Governor Smith Replies," in the *Atlantic Monthly* 139 (May 1927): 721-28.

6:87. Ibid., 722.

6:88. *The Christian Century* 45 (Oct. 11, 1928): 1218.

6:89. Ibid.

6:90. From a letter by George W. Norris to John F. Cordeal, Nov. 13, 1928, quoted in Lichtman, *Prejudice and the Old Politics*, 40; chap. 3, "Catholics versus Protestants," 40-76, carries a cogent, statistically based argument and refutation of the opinions in earlier books that religion was a minor theme in the Smith defeat.

6:91. Ibid.

6:92. Charles Clayton Morrison, "The Religious Issues," *The Christian Century* 45 (Oct. 18, 1928): 1252.

6:93. Ibid.

6:94. Ibid.

Chapter Seven

7:1. The literature on the Depression is vast; two popular social histories provide a sense of day to day life as background to the religious story: J. C. Furnas, *Stormy Weather: Crosslights on the Nineteen Thirties, an Informal Social History of the United States 1929-1941* (New York: Putnam, 1977), and Edward Robb Ellis, *A Nation in Torment: The Great American Depression 1929-1939* (New York: Coward-McCann, 1970).

7:2. Pioneering essays on the religious dimension of the Depression are Robert T. Handy, "The American Religious Depression, 1925-1935," *Church History* 29:1 (March 1960): 3-16; and Joel Carpenter, "Fundamentalist Institutions and the Rise of Evangelical Protestantism," *Church History* 49:1 (March 1980): 62-75. Handy saw the spiritual depression preceding the economic one; Carpenter stresses the selective character of the religious depression: fundamentalism was beginning to prosper and change. Handy's periodization helps show that not all the "breaks" came with the Crash.

7:3. Works like Catherine L. Albanese, *America: Religions and Religion* (Belmont, Calif.: Wadsworth, 1981); and Peter W. Williams, *Popular Religion in America: Symbolic Change and the Modernization Process in Historical Perspective* (Englewood Cliffs, N.J.: Prentice-Hall, 1980), by their accent on the "ordinary," "popular," and "social," focus on dimensions of religious life which the present work by its choice of topic and approach neglects.

7:4. Samuel C. Kincheloe, *Research Memorandum on Religion in the Depression*, Bulletin 33 (New York: Social Science Research Council, 1937).

7:5. Ibid., 93.

7:6. Ibid., 94.

7:7. Ibid., 94, 95.

7:8. Ibid., 95–96, citing *The Christian Century* 52 (Sept. 18, 1935): 1168–70.

7:9. See the citation in ibid., 89, of Robert S. Lynd and Helen M. Lynd, *Middletown in Transition* (New York: Harcourt and Brace, 1937), 306, on secularization of welfare work.

7:10. Ibid.

7:11. Ibid., 92.   7:14. Ibid., 107, 104–5.

7:12. Ibid., 102–3.   7:15. Ibid., 105.

7:13. Ibid., 103–7.   7:16. Ibid., 109.

7:17. Ibid., 45–46; Kincheloe also cites Bennett's *Christianity and Our World* (New York: Association, 1936), 1.

7:18. Ibid., 42; Reinhold Niebuhr, *Reflections on the End of an Era* (New York: Charles Scribner's Sons, 1934), ix.

7:19. Kincheloe, *Research Memorandum on Religion in the Depression*, 59–61.

7:20. Ibid., 1.

7:21. Ibid., 6, vii.

7:22. Raymond Gram Swing, *Forerunners of American Fascism* (New York: Julian Messner, 1935), 131.

7:23. Ibid., 131–32.

7:24. Introductions to the right-wing extremist tradition—later references will deal with the left—include Seymour Martin Lipset and Earl Raab, *The Politics of Unreason: Right-Wing Extremism in America, 1790–1970* (New York: Harper and Row, 1970), and David H. Bennett, *The Party of Fear: From Nativist Movements to the New Right in American History* (Chapel Hill: University of North Carolina Press, 1988). Both give generous attention to the interwar period.

7:25. Talcott Parsons, *Essays in Sociological Theory* (New York: The Free Press, 1954), 125–27. Reflections on the limits and the continuing influence of demagoguery are in David H. Bennett, *Demagogues in the Depression: American Radicals and the Union Party 1932–1936* (New Brunswick, N.J.: Rutgers University Press, 1969), "Epilogue: Yesterday's Radicals and American History," 293–309.

7:26. From the extensive literature on the subject, one singles out Klaus Scholder, *The Churches and the Third Reich*, vol. 1, *Preliminary History and Time of Illusions 1918–1934* (Philadelphia: Fortress Press, 1987), and vol. 2, *The Year of Disillusionment: 1934 Barmen and Rome* (Philadelphia: Fortress Press, 1988). Scholder, who did not live to complete the work, includes excellent bibliographies on Nazism and religion. Sander A. Diamond, *The Nazi Movement in the United States 1924–1941* (Ithaca, N.Y.: Cornell University Press, 1974), gives the movement the most extensive coverage.

7:27. Diamond, *The Nazi Movement*, 308, quotes U.S. House of Representatives, Special Committee to Investigate Un-American Activities and Propaganda in the United States, *Hearings*, 76th Congress, 1st Session (Washington, D.C.: Government Printing Office, 1939) 7: 1.

7:28. U.S. House of Representatives, *Investigation of Un-American Propaganda Activities in the United States, Report No. 2*, 76th Congress, 1st Session (Washington, D.C.:

Government Printing Office, 1939); "What Are Un-American Activities?" Section A., "Americanism Defined," 10–11; see Diamond, *The Nazi Movement*, 309.

7:29. Diamond, *The Nazi Movement*, 309.

7:30. Ibid., 316, quotes a handout of the Anti-Defamation League of B'nai B'rith citing a Nazi attack and, 68, a statement of Hermann Schwarzmann on the Ordnungs-Dienst, Queens, New York, June 17, 1937.

7:31. Ibid., 317–18, quotes "Which Way America?" and "For a Gentile Controlled America," from the pamphlet collection of the Anti-Defamation League of B'nai B'rith in New York.

7:32. Gustavus Myers, *History of Bigotry in the United States* (New York: Random House, 1943), 382, cites *History and Organization of the German-American Bund* (State of New York: Report of Joint Legislative Committee, 1939), *Legislative Document No. 98*, 303.

7:33. *Legislative Document No. 98*, 1363; cited by Myers, *History of Bigotry*, 383.

7:34. Lipset and Raab, *The Politics of Unreason*, 171–73, analyze Gallup polling surveys assessing the power of this kind of group; see also *Investigation of Un-American Activities in the United States*, 76th Congress, 3rd Session, *House Report No. 1476* (Washington, D.C.: Government Printing Office, 1939), xx.

7:35. The quotation is from an oath quoted by Lynn Dolgin, "The Black Legion: A Study of American Nativism during the 1930s," a seminar paper at the University of Michigan, 1967, 16; see Lipset and Raab, *The Politics of Unreason*, 157; see also Morris Janowitz, "Black Legions on the March," in Daniel Aaron, ed., *America in Crisis: Fourteen Crucial Episodes in American History* (New York: Alfred A. Knopf, 1952), 306–10.

7:36. Pelley is quoted in Donald S. Strong, *Organized Anti-Semitism in America* (Washington, D.C.: American Council on Public Affairs, 1941), 52.

7:37. William D. Pelley, *No More Hunger* (Asheville, N.C.: Pelley Publishers, 1939), details the program; for the boast about Catholic followers and the Dies Committee reference, see Donnel Byerly Portzline, "William Dudley Pelley and the Silver Shirt Legion of America" (Ph.D. diss., Department of Education, Ball State University, Muncie, Ind., 1965), 158, 109.

7:38. See Myers, *History of Bigotry*, 406, quoting *Pelley's Weekly*, Sept. 5, 1934.

7:39. Leo Ribuffo, *The Old Christian Right: The Protestant Far Right from the Great Depression to the Cold War* (Philadelphia: Temple University Press, 1983), 52–57, traces Pelley's pilgrimage.

7:40. Pelley, "People Have Queer Notions about the Psychic Senses," *New Liberator* 1 (June–October 1930): 61–62; "People Hold Queer Ideas about a Spiritual Movement," *Liberation* 4 (July 22, 1933): 1–3; Ribuffo, *The Old Christian Right*, 56–57, includes more anti-Semitic references and the announcement of Pelley's movement: "Did Benjamin Franklin Say This about the Hebrews?" *Liberation* (Feb. 3, 1934); see Ribuffo, *The Old Christian Right*, 59.

7:41. Ribuffo, *The Old Christian Right*, 69, gives details of Pelley's later career including the attack on Modernism, citing "Cogitations" in *Pelley's Weekly* 2 (July 1, 1936): 6, 8.

7:42. Ibid., 72, reproduces the Puritan reference and discusses Pelley's presidential campaign; the references to Roosevelt are quoted by David H. Bennett, *The Party of Fear*, 246.

7:43. See Ribuffo, *The Old Christian Right*, 198, quoting the *Indianapolis Star*, Aug. 6, 1942.

7:44. Ralph Lord Roy, *Apostles of Discord: A Study of Organized Bigotry and Disruption on the Fringes of Protestantism* (Boston: Beacon Press, 1953), 28–29.

7:45. Ibid., 27–28.

7:46. On denominational conflict, see "Revising Denominationalism," *Defender* 4 (July 1929): 6; *Wichita Beacon*, Nov. 11, 1937; for anti-Modernism, see Gerald B. Winrod, *Three Modern Evils* (Wichita: Defender Publishers, 1932), 17; biographical details are in Ribuffo, *The Old Christian Right*, 80–93.

7:47. "Babson Speaks," *Defender* 5 (January 1931): 1; "Items," *Defender* 6 (January 1932): 2; and *Defender* 7 (June 1932): 2; on Modernism, see Ribuffo, *The Old Christian Right*, 105.

7:48. Gerald B. Winrod, *Communism and the Roosevelt Brain Trust* (Wichita: Defender Publishers, 1933), 24–25; Gerald B. Winrod, *Adam Weishaupt: Human Devil* (Wichita: Defender Publishers, 1935); Ribuffo, *The Old Christian Right*, 116, discusses the way Winrod moderated his anti-Catholicism.

7:49. Ribuffo, *The Old Christian Right*, 124, reports on the senatorial campaign as covered in newspapers and comments on Jews in tracts or in flyers from the Winrod campaign, now in the Kansas Historical Society; see 127 for the trial and 129–31 for the postwar career.

7:50. Glen Jeansonne, *Gerald L. K. Smith: Minister of Hate* (New Haven: Yale University Press, 1988), is the most complete biography. H. L. Mencken is quoted by Milton Crane, ed., *The Roosevelt Era* (New York: Boni and Gaer, 1947), 192.

7:51. For the rabble-rousing quotation, see Walter Davenport, "The Mysterious Gerald Smith," *Collier's* 113:10 (Mar. 4, 1944): 15.

7:52. Ribuffo, *The Old Christian Right*, 133–34, deals with the momentary liberal phase of Smith's career.

7:53. "Honor for 'Social Gospel' Preacher," *Christian Century* 50 (Aug. 9, 1933): 1019; Jeansonne, *Gerald L. K. Smith*, 45, discusses the Long-Smith relationship.

7:54. Huey Long, *Every Man a King* (Chicago: Quadrangle, 1964), 297; *New Republic* 82:1054 (Feb. 13, 1935): 15; David H. Bennett, *Demagogues of the Depression*, quotes Long's comment on revolution.

7:55. Bennett, *Demagogues of the Depression*, 130, describes the funeral; 131–33 describes the rivalry with Weiss.

7:56. The reference to Roosevelt is in *Time* 27:6 (Feb. 10, 1936): 17.

7:57. For a report on a Townsend meeting, see "Townsendism: Old Time Religion," *New York Times Magazine* (Mar. 8, 1936): 5, 25.

7:58. Stuart A. Rice, "Is the Townsend Plan Practical?" in *Vital Speeches of the Day* (Jan. 27, 1936): 264; Ribuffo, *The Old Christian Right*, 144, quotes the "Santa Claus" reference from the *New York Times*, July 20, 1936.

7:59. *Time* 27:22 (June 1, 1936):9–10; *Time* 26:19 (November 4, 1935): 20. Herbert Harris, "That Third Party," *Current History* 45:1 (October 1936): 84, quotes "het up."

7:60. Heywood Broun, "Broun's Page," *The Nation* 143:8 (Aug. 22, 1936): 213; on the committee, see *New York Times*, Oct. 18, 1936, "Long Ally Now Heads a Drive against Reds," 32; Oct. 20, 1936, "G. L. K. Smith Plans New Organization," 7.

7:61. *March of Time*, "The 'Lunatic Fringe,'" Motion Picture, Sound, and Video Branch, National Archives, as reported on by Raymond Fielding, *The March of Time, 1935–1951* (New York: Oxford University Press, 1978), 159–61; for the "Jew-baiting" reference, see Ribuffo, *The Old Christian Right*, 146.

7:62. On the ties to Ford, see Ribuffo, *The Old Christian Right*, 154–57; on the

Long campaign, see Thomas Martin, *Dynasty: The Longs of Louisiana* (New York: G.P. Putnam's Sons, 1960), 179. Harnett Thomas Kane, *Louisiana Hayride: The American Rehearsal for Dictatorship 1928-1940* (New York: Morrow, 1941), 447; see also House Committee on Un-American Activities, *Investigation of Gerald L. K. Smith* (Washington, D.C.: Government Printing Office, 1946), 21.

7:63. Of special interest is Louis B. Ward, *Father Charles E. Coughlin: An Authorized Biography* (Detroit: Tower Publications, 1933).

7:64. On the parish assignment, see Charles J. Tull, *Father Coughlin and the New Deal* (Syracuse: Syracuse University Press, 1965), 2-3.

7:65. On WJR, ibid.

7:66. On "Red Fog," see Ward, *Father Charles E. Coughlin*, 59-60.

7:67. "Father Coughlin (pronounced Kawglin)," *Fortune* 9:2 (February 1934): 34, tells of the dollar bills.

7:68. Ibid.

7:69. Ibid.

7:70. David H. Bennett, *Demagogues of the Depression*, 38, describes Coughlin's instructions to his followers; see also "Coughlin Assails Smith's Gold Views," *New York Times*, Nov. 27, 1933; see Ward, *Father Charles E. Coughlin*, 252. "Christ's Deal" is quoted in Bennett, *Demagogues of the Depression* (Bennett cites the *New York Times*, Nov. 27, 1933), 41.

7:71. Ward, *Father Charles E. Coughlin*, 252, quotes Coughlin on demagoguery; Charles E. Coughlin, *The New Deal in Money* (Royal Oak, Mich.: The Radio League of the Little Flower, 1933), 7, 107-8.

7:72. A. B. Magil, "Can Father Coughlin Come Back?" *The New Republic* 87:1125 (June 24, 1936): 197.

7:73. David H. Bennett, *Demagogues of the Depression*, 52, cites Coughlin, *Driving Out the Money Changers* (Royal Oak, Mich.: The Radio League of the Little Flower, 1931).

7:74. Tull, *Father Coughlin*, 196 and 198, quotes *Social Justice* (Nov. 21 and Nov. 28, 1938).

7:75. Wilfred Parsons, "Father Coughlin and Social Justice," *America* 3:6 (May 18, 1935): 129-31.

7:76. Tull, *Father Coughlin*, 61, reports that Coughlin announced the formation of the National Union for Social Justice; David H. Bennett, *Demagogues of the Depression*, 69, cites Coughlin, *A Series of Lectures on Social Justice, 1935-1936* (Royal Oak, Mich.: The Radio League of the Little Flower, 1936), 18-22.

7:77. For the "active" and "passive" definitions, see "Lemke Promises a Remade Nation; Coughlin Stricken," *New York Times*, Aug. 17, 1936; "A Third Party," *Vital Speeches* 87 (June 1, 1936): 614.

7:78. On the Union party, see "Coughlin Says Third Party is Near; Hints at Support of Candidate," *New York Times*, June 17, 1936; *Detroit News*, June 17, 1936; Charles E. Coughlin, "A Third Party," *Vital Speeches of the Day* 2:20 (July 1, 1936): 615; for Norman Thomas, see "Thomas Ridicules New Lemke Party," *New York Times*, June 21, 1936; Norman Thomas, *After the New Deal, What?* (New York: Macmillan, 1936), 2, 5-6, 143, 203.

7:79. David H. Bennett, *Demagogues of the Depression*, 223-25, covers anti-Coughlin Catholicism; he cites a letter from Charlton Ogburn to Roosevelt, Sept. 10, 1936, and one from Maurice S. Sheehy to Margaret Le Hand, Oct. 5, 1936; Ryan and Coughlin exchanges are reported on in "Mgr. Ryan Backs Roosevelt, Attacks Father Coughlin," *New York Times* Oct. 9, 1936; "Father Coughlin Denounced by Father Ryan," *The Nation* 143:16

(Oct. 17, 1936): 434; Charles E. Coughlin, *An Answer to Father Coughlin's Critics* (Royal Oak, Mich. The Radio League of the Little Flower, 1940), 44; "Ryan-Coughlin Controversy," *Commonweal* 24:26 (Oct. 23, 1936): 597–98.

7:80. Tull, *Father Coughlin*, 138–39, on campaigning in North Dakota and Providence; "Debt 'Repudiation' Urged on Farmers in Coughlin Threat," *New York Times*, July 27, 1936, 1, 7 (quotation is on 7); "Coughlin Attacks Roosevelt as Red," *New York Times*, Aug. 3, 1936, 8. David H. Bennett, *Demagogues of the Depression*, 228–29, 230, cites the *New York Times*, Sept. 7, 1936, Sept. 12, 1936, and Sept. 13, 1936. Bennett also cites "Coughlin's Bullets," in *Time* 28:14 (Oct. 5, 1936), 33. See also *New Masses* 20:2 (Oct. 6, 1936): 10.

7:81. Campaign reports quoted here include "Catholics Chided on Coughlin Stand," *New York Times*, Aug. 2; "Coughlin Rebuked by Vatican Paper," Sept. 3; "New Coughlin Rebuke Issued from Vatican," Sept. 10; "Coughlin's Ticket Quits in the State," Oct. 10, 1936; "Coughlin in the Papal Doghouse," *New Republic* 88:138 (Sept. 23, 1936): 182–83; *The Nation* 143:16 (Oct. 17, 1936): 434; see David H. Bennett, *Demagogues of the Depression*, 254–57.

7:82. See David H. Bennett, *Demagogues of the Depression*, 263. Bennett cites Dale Kramer, "The American Fascists, *Harpers Magazine* 191:9 (Sept. 1940): 390; and "Prophets," *Newsweek* 8:18 (Nov. 14, 1936).

7:83. Tull, *Father Coughlin*, 211–12, cites Edward Doherty, "Is Father Coughlin Anti-Semitic?" *Liberty* (Aug. 12, 1939).

7:84. David H. Bennett, *Demagogues of the Depression*, and most books on Depression-era extremism focus on the right, because of its mass followings; the left worked more through individuals, cells, or the small Communist party.

7:85. Earl Browder, *Report to the 8th Convention* (New York: Workers Library Publishers, 1934), 81, offers statistics.

7:86. Earl Browder, "New Steps in the United Front," *Communist* 14 (November 1935): 1010, is a complaint about how sectarian party strife kept it small; see also Browder, *Report to the 8th Convention*, 81, 98.

7:87. A durable brief review of the Roosevelt campaign is William E. Leuchtenberg, *Franklin D. Roosevelt and the New Deal 1932–1940* (New York: Harper and Row, 1963), chap. 1, "The Politics of Hard Times," 1–17, and bibliography on the election, 356.

7:88. Eugene Lyons, *The Red Decade: The Stalinist Penetration of America* (Indianapolis: Bobbs-Merrill, 1941); see also Harvey Klehr, *The Heyday of American Communism: The Depression Decade* (New York: Basic, 1984).

7:89. These figures are cited by Hugh Jones Parry, "The Spanish Civil War" (Ph.D. diss., University of Southern California, 1949), 373.

7:90. "Perils of a Communist Victory in Spain," *America* (Aug. 8, 1936): 420.

7:91. See *Commonweal* 24 (Aug. 28, 1936): 414; and "Some Reflections on Spain," *Commonweal* 25 (Apr. 2, 1937): 626.

7:92. From a speech at Massachusetts Institute of Technology, May 24, 1969, a retrospect of the controversy, quoted by Rodger Van Allen, *The Commonweal and American Catholicism: The Magazine, The Movement, The Meaning* (Philadelphia: Fortress Press, 1974), 64; see also *Commonweal* 25 (Apr. 23, 1937), 716–17.

7:93. "Cardinal Pacelli's Vacation," *The Christian Century* 53 (Oct. 14, 1936): 1352–54 (quotation is on 1354).

7:94. On the Bates incident, see Robert Moats Miller, *Harry Emerson Fosdick: Preacher, Pastor, Prophet* (New York: Oxford University Press, 1985), 264.

7:95. *Presbyterian Tribune* (Apr. 18, 1935): 4. Robert Moats Miller, *American*

Protestantism and Social Issues, 1919–1939 (Chapel Hill: University of North Carolina Press, 1958), 178–80; and Ralph Lord Roy, *Communism and the Churches* (New York: Harcourt, Brace, 1960), 50–53, detail the Scottsboro case.

7:96. On Father Divine, see Robert Weisbrot, *Father Divine and the Struggle for Racial Equality* (Urbana: University of Illinois Press, 1983), and Kenneth E. Burnham, *God Comes to America: Father Divine and the Peace Mission Movement* (Boston: Lambeth, 1979).

7:97. See Weisbrot, *Father Divine*, 148–52 and 211–12, for relations between Divine and Communists.

7:98. *New York Times*, Aug. 5, 1934, "Red Rally Dimmed by Harlem Fervor," covered the Madison Square rally; see also Weisbrot, *Father Divine*, 149.

7:99. *The Communist* 14 (February 1935): 171; James W. Ford, "The United Front in the Field of Negro Work," *The Communist* 14 (February 1935): 171–72.

7:100. Adam Clayton Powell, Jr., *Marching Blacks: An Interpretive History of the Rise of the Black Common Man*, rev. ed. (New York: Dial, 1973), 68; see Roy, *Communism and the Churches*, 55, on Father Divine.

7:101. Weisbrot *Father Divine*, 151, cites correspondence between Lambert Fairchild and Orol Wiltshire, Oct. 24 and Oct. 26, 1935, as quoted in *Spoken Word* (Nov. 2, 1935): 23; for Ben Davis, see *Daily Worker* (Feb. 11, 1936): 2.

7:102. Quoted in the Fairchild exchange by Weisbrot, *Father Divine*, 151.

7:103. On Communist scorn for Thomas, see Roy, *Communism and the Churches*, 37–38.

7:104. *Daily Worker* (June 1, 1928): 6, and (Nov. 2, 1927): 6; and Roy, *Apostles of Discord*, 37–38.

7:105. Roy, *Communism and the Churches*, 54–57, discusses antireligious activities of the Communist party.

7:106. *Daily Worker* (June 20, 1925), as cited by Roy, *Communism and the Churches*, 41; and *Daily Worker* (May 20, 1931): 2.

7:107. On the Workers' Anti-Religious League, see *Daily Worker* (Sept. 25, 1931): 2.

7:108. Roy, *Communism and the Churches*, 57–61, tells the story of Communism's improvised later views of religion; on Cleveland, see *Daily Worker* (Jan. 1, 1932): 2; Gold is in *Daily Worker* (June 15, 1935): 7.

7:109. Roy, *Communism and the Churches*, 58–59, cites Earl Browder, *Religion and Communism* (New York: Workers Library, 1935).

7:110. Ibid., 248–51, provides biographical material on Mathews.

7:111. J. B. Mathews and R. E. Shallcross, *Partners in Plunder: The Cost of Business Dictatorship* (New York: Covici Friede, 1935), 329–42, includes this attack on Fosdick; on his 1935 speech, see *Daily Worker* (Feb. 27, 1953), and Roy, *Communism and the Churches*, 249.

7:112. Roy, *Apostles of Discord*, 60–63, provides background to the Dies Committee hearing.

7:113. *Investigation of Un-American Propaganda Activities in the United States*, Hearings before a Special Committee on Un-American Activities, House of Representatives, 76th Congress, 1st Session on H. Res. 282, vol. 7 (Sept. 6, 1939): 4457.

7:114. *The Christian Century* 51 (Mar. 7, 1934): 339.

7:115. Winifred L. Chappell, "A Decision Must be Made," *Epworth Herald* 45 (Mar. 3, 1934): 132.

7:116. On "no middle ground," see *The Social Service Bulletin* 25 (March 1935); see also *Social Questions Bulletin* 26 (May 1936) 21; ibid. (May 1936), 2, quotes opposition. Note the change of the *Bulletin* name.

7:117. Roy, *Communism and the Churches*, 89–90, provides background on Ward.

7:118. Ward is quoted from *The Social Service Bulletin* 22 (Dec. 15, 1932): 3–4; see Roy, *Communism and the Churches*, 91, for statistics.

7:119. Harry F. Ward, *Which Way Religion?* (New York: Macmillan, 1931).

7:120. Ward is cited by Donald B. Meyer, *The Protestant Search for Political Realism, 1919–1941* (Berkeley and Los Angeles: University of California Press, 1960), 187.

7:121. Roy, *Communism and the Churches*, 84–97, discusses the American League Against War and Fascism.

7:122. Harry F. Ward, *In Place of Profit: Social Incentives in the Soviet Union* (New York: Charles Scribner's Sons, 1933), 239.

7:123. Ibid., 427–28.

7:124. Ibid., 96–97, 456.

7:125. Roy, *Communism and the Churches*, 144–45, discusses the Hitler-Stalin pact and its influence on figures like Ward.

7:126. Ibid., 147, tells about the dinner.

7:127. Kirby Page and Sherwood Eddy, *The Abolition of War* (New York: George H. Doran, 1924), 92; see also Kirby Page, *Jesus or Christianity?* (Garden City, N.Y.: Doubleday, 1929).

7:128. Kirby Page, *Must We Go to War?* (New York: Farrar and Rinehart, 1937), 264.

7:129. Kirby Page, *Individualism and Socialism: An Ethical Survey of Economic and Political Forces* (New York: Farrar and Rinehart, 1933), 311; Kirby Page, *Living Triumphantly* (New York: Farrar and Rinehart, 1934), 46.

7:130. Robert Moats Miller, *American Protestantism*, 101, presents findings of the poll; 113–14 tell of Rock River resolutions.

7:131. George Sherwood Eddy, *The Challenge of Russia* (New York: Farrar and Rinehart, 1931), 20.

7:132. George Sherwood Eddy, *Russia Today: What Can We Learn From It?* (New York: Farrar and Rinehart, 1934), 119, 170.

7:133. Ibid., 177.

7:134. Roy, *Communism and the Churches*, 281–90, comments on the career of Leslie.

7:135. Gil Green, "Growth of the United Front among the Youth in America Described," *Daily Worker* (Sept. 28, 1935): 5, reports on the permission to worship.

7:136. Roy, *Communism and the Churches*, 97–106, tells the story of the American Youth Congress.

7:137. Quoted by Theodore M. Graebner, *The Business Man and the Church: An Economic Study* (Clinton, S.C.: 1942), 10, as cited by Miller in *American Protestantism*, 68.

7:138. *Journal of the General Conference of the Methodist Episcopal Church* (1932): 652–55; see Robert Moats Miller, *American Protestantism*, 66; *The Daily Christian Advocate*, The Methodist Episcopal Church (May 24, 1932): 594; the *Nashville Christian Advocate* (Oct. 20, 1933): 1318.

7:139. Smith is quoted in *Social Questions Bulletin* (May 1936): 2; see also Roy, *Communism and the Churches*, 295.

7:140. "The Catholic Vote" in *Brooklyn Tablet* (Aug. 1, 1936); and Patrick Scanlan, "From the Managing Editor's Desk," ibid., Feb. 8, 1936, and July 4, 1936, are samples of *Tablet* criticism cited by David J. O'Brien, *American Catholics and Social Reform: The New Deal Years* (New York: Oxford University Press, 1968), 61; see 82 for Pius IX's counsel; see also Scanlan, "From the Managing Editor's Desk," *Tablet* (July 26, 1930).

7:141. Raphael M. Huber ed., *Our Bishops Speak* (Milwaukee: Bruce Publishing Co., 1952), 100; Bishop John F. Noll, "Introduction," James A. Vaughn, ed., *Our Modern Social and Economic Order* (Huntington, Ind.: Our Sunday Visitor, 1939), n.p.; see David J. O'Brien, *American Catholics and Social Reform*, 4.

7:142. See *Daily Worker* (Aug. 27, 1939): 1–2; *New York Herald Tribune*, Oct. 29, 1939.

7:143. For Gold, see *Daily Worker* (Oct. 30, 1939): 7; Hick's resignation letter is in *The New Republic* 100 (Oct. 4, 1939): 244–45. Harvey Klehr, *The Heyday of American Communism*, 401, tells the Cowley letterhead story.

7:144. John Haynes Holmes, "Why We Liberals Went Wrong on the Russian Revolution," Series 1939–40, No. 8, published by Community Church in New York City and cited by Roy, *Communism and the Churches*, 151–52. A. J. Muste wrote in *The Presbyterian Tribune* 54 (Sept. 14, 1939): 9.

Chapter Eight

8:1. On the creativity of theologians in this period in the large context, see Sydney E. Ahlstrom, *A Religious History of the American People* (New Haven: Yale University Press, 1972), chap. 55, "Neo-Orthodoxy and Social Crises," 932–48.

8:2. Walter Marshall Horton, *Realistic Theology* (New York: Harper and Brothers, 1934); John C. Bennett, *Christian Realism* (New York: Charles Scribner's Sons, 1941); the Niebuhrs and Tillich will be introduced below.

8:3. Horton, *Realistic Theology*, 88; William R. Hutchison, *The Modernist Impulse in American Protestantism* (New York: Oxford University Press, 1976), 294–95, 304–5, characterizes Horton as a leader of "moderate neoorthodoxy."

8:4. Horton, *Realistic Theology*, 1–2.

8:5. Ibid., 2; *The Christian Century* 50:45 (Nov. 8, 1933): 1403–6.

8:6. Horton, *Realistic Theology*, 2.

8:7. On the realistic and escapist aspects of intellectual life in the thirties, see Warren I. Susman, *Culture as History: The Transformation of American Society in the Twentieth Century* (New York: Pantheon, 1984), chap. 9, "The Culture of the Thirties," 150–83.

8:8. Horton, *Realistic Theology*, 12, includes illustrations by the author of figures from literature, politics, and philosophy.

8:9. For my attempt to locate "public theology" in a particular instance, in this case that of Reinhold Niebuhr, see Martin E. Marty, *Religion and Republic: The American Circumstance* (Boston: Beacon Press, 1987), chap. 5, "Interpretation: The Classic Public Theologian," 95–122.

8:10. Ibid., 14–15.

8:11. Ibid., 15, 38.

8:12. Horton, *Realistic Theology*, ix.

8:13. Ibid., 38.

8:14. Ibid., 42.

8:15. Ibid., 75–78.

8:16. Ibid., 89.

8:17. Ibid., 90.

8:18. Ibid., 95–96.

8:19. Ibid., 120–22.

8:20. Ibid., 137, 150.

8:21. Ibid., 151.

8:22. Ibid., 176.

8:23. Ibid., 187–88.

8:24. H. Richard Niebuhr, Wilhelm Pauck, and Francis P. Miller, *The Church Against the World* (Chicago: Willett, Clark, 1935).

8:25. Ibid., 73–74, 81–82.

8:26. Ibid., 91.

8:27. Ibid., 91.

8:28. Ibid., 100.

8:29. Ibid.

8:30. Ibid., 100–102.

8:31. Ibid., 102, 106–7.

8:32. Ibid., 108, 111.

8:33. Ibid., 112.

8:34. Ibid., 113, 115.

8:35. Ibid., 119.

8:36. Ibid., 32–38.

8:37. Ibid., 32.

8:38. Ibid., 37.

8:39. Ibid., 38–47.

8:40. Ibid., 47–57, is an extended discussion of Modernism, with some affirmations but ending with a critique of its doctrine of God; see especially 53.

8:41. Ibid., 57–59.

8:42. On H. Richard Niebuhr's theology, see Paul Ramsey, ed., *Faith and Ethics: The Theology of H. Richard Niebuhr* (New York: Harper and Row, 1957); James W. Fowler, *To See the Kingdom: The Theological Vision of H. Richard Niebuhr* (Nashville: Abingdon, 1974); Donald E. Fadner, *The Responsible God: A Study of the Christian Philosophy of H.Richard Niebuhr* (Missoula, Mont.: Scholars Press, 1975); Douglas F. Ottati, *Meaning and Method in H. Richard Niebuhr's Theology* (Washington, D.C.: University Press of America, 1982).

8:43. H. Richard Niebuhr, *The Social Sources of Denominationalism* (New York: Holt, 1929), 22.

8:44. Ibid., 22, 9.

8:45. Niebuhr, Pauck, and Miller, *The Church Against the World*, 130, 133, 141.

8:46. Ibid., 143, 152–53.

8:47. H. Richard Niebuhr, *The Kingdom of God in America* (New York: Harper and Brothers, 1937), 17, 182.

8:48. Ibid., xvi, 178–79.

8:49. Ibid., 181, 183.

8:50. Ibid., 184–93, has an extended discussion of liberalism in theology and religion.

8:51. Ibid., 191–93.

8:52. Ibid., 193–96.

8:53. Ibid., 196–98.

8:54. Richard Fox, *Reinhold Niebuhr: A Biography* (New York: Pantheon, 1985), is the most detailed biography of Niebuhr. D. B. Robertson, *Reinhold Niebuhr's Works: A Bibliography* (rev. ed., Washington, D.C.: University Press of America, 1983), provides access to the enormous corpus of writings by and about Niebuhr.

8:55. Fox, *Reinhold Niebuhr: A Biography*, 72–75, tells of Niebuhr's early relations with *The Christian Century*.

8:56. Ibid., chap. 6, "A State of Joy and Pain," 111–41, details the early career of Niebuhr at Union.

8:57. Reinhold Niebuhr, *Does Civilization Need Religion?* (New York: Macmillan, 1927); and *Moral Man and Immoral Society* (New York: Charles Scribner's Sons, 1932).

8:58. Fox, *Reinhold Niebuhr: A Biography*, 49–50, 241–42, 255, comments on Niebuhr's relations to the Federal Council of Churches in different phases of his career.

8:59. On Niebuhr's socialist involvements, see Paul Merkley, *Reinhold Niebuhr: A Political Account* (Montreal: McGill-Queen's University Press, 1975), 54–55, 93–96; see 70–77 for comment on Karl Barth.

8:60. Fox, *Reinhold Niebuhr: A Biography*, 160–65 and 257–59, tells of Niebuhr's changing relations with Tillich.

8:61. Ibid., 136–47, tells of the original impact of Niebuhr's book; see also Merkley, *Reinhold Niebuhr: A Political Account*, 83–87. R. Niebuhr, *Moral Man and Immoral Society*, 154, has the reference to Marxism as religion.

8:62. "Communism and the Clergy," *The Christian Century* (Aug. 19, 1953):

937; R. Niebuhr, *Moral Man and Immoral Society*, 277; "The Religion of Communism," *Atlantic Monthly* (April 1931): 462.

8:63. On Norman Thomas, *World Tomorrow* and *Radical Religion*, see Merkley, *Reinhold Niebuhr: A Political Account*, 96–99.

8:64. *Time* 17 (May 11, 1931): 25.

8:65. On the banquet, see Fox, *Reinhold Niebuhr: A Biography*, 135; R. Niebuhr, *Moral Man and Immoral Society*, xv.

8:66. R. Niebuhr, *Moral Man and Immoral Society*, xv.

8:67. Ibid., xvii–xix; see also Howard W. Odum, *Man's Quest for Social Guidance* (New York: Holt, 1927).

8:68. R. Niebuhr, *Moral Man and Immoral Society*, xx.

8:69. Ibid., xxi–xxii.

8:70. Ibid., 249–50.

8:71. William R. Hutchison, ed., *Between the Times: The Travail of the Protestant Establishment in America, 1900–1960* (New York: Cambridge University Press, 1989), vii, takes the concept of "Between the Times" from European thought to cover the whole period.

8:72. Reinhold Niebuhr, *Reflections on the End of an Era* (New York: Charles Scribner's Sons, 1934), 135.

8:73. Reinhold Niebuhr, *An Interpretation of Christian Ethics* (New York: Harper and Brothers, 1935), 90.

8:74. Ibid., 89.

8:75. Ibid., 169, 172–76; Niebuhr commented on Shailer Mathews, *The Gospel and Modern Man* (New York: Macmillan, 1910), 23, 255; Shailer Mathews, *Christianity and Social Process* (New York: Harper and Brothers, 1934) chap. 6, especially 177.

8:76. John C. Bennett, *Christian Realism* (New York: Charles Scribner's Sons, 1941), x.

8:77. R. Niebuhr, *An Interpretation of Christian Ethics*, 178–79.

8:78. Ibid., 179–81, 196–97, 187.

8:79. See Niebuhr's review of Paul Tillich, *The Religious Situation* (New York: Holt, 1932), in *The World Tomorrow* 15 (Dec. 21, 1932): 596.

8:80. Ibid.

8:81. See Mel Piehl, *Breaking Bread: The Catholic Worker and the Origin of Catholic Radicalism in America* (Philadelphia: Temple University Press, 1982). On the tardy development in the twentieth century of an American Catholic intellectual tradition, see Margaret Mary Reher, *Catholic Intellectual Life in America: A Historical Study of Persons and Movements* (New York: Macmillan, 1989), chaps. 5 and 6.

8:82. Enough has been said about Protestant styles; it is instructive to compare them through American history with Catholic approaches. An instrument for that is David J. O'Brien, *Public Catholicism* (New York: Macmillan, 1989). For this period, see chap. 7, "Social Catholicism," 158–94. On the lack of a strong intellectual tradition before mid-century, see Margaret Mary Reher, *Catholic Intellectual Life in America*, especially chap. 6, "The Path to Pluralism, 1920–1985," 91–141.

8:83. For background to this period and these themes, see William M. Halsey, *The Survival of American Innocence: Catholicism in an Era of Disillusionment 1920–1940* (Notre Dame, Ind.: University of Notre Dame Press, 1980); Dorothy Dohen, *Nationalism and American Catholicism* (New York: Sheed and Ward, 1967); Mary T. Hanna, *Catholics and American Politics* (Cambridge: Harvard University Press, 1979); David J. O'Brien, *American Catholics and Social Reform* (New York: Oxford University Press, 1968).

8:84. Dohen, *Nationalism and American Catholicism*, provides ample evidence of Catholic loyalty to the nation and interest in its destiny and mission.

8:85. On the personalist background, see John Hellman, *Emmanuel Mounier and the New Catholic Left, 1930–1950* (Toronto: University of Toronto Press, 1981), and Joseph Amato, *Mounier and Maritain: A French Catholic Understanding of the Modern World* (University, Ala.: University of Alabama Press, 1975).

8:86. Piehl, *Breaking Bread*, 116–17, discusses the Catholic Worker movement's appropriation of personalism.

8:87. Ibid., 60–64, 102–3, describes Maurin's "Easy Essays."

8:88. William D. Miller, *A Harsh and Dreadful Love: Dorothy Day and the Catholic Worker Movement* (New York: Liveright, 1973), chap. 1, "The Radical Idea of the Catholic Worker Movement," 3–16, introduces the philosophy, based in part on personalism, which motivated the movement.

8:89. The Miller book title—*A Harsh and Dreadful Love*—suggests the accent on love, quite appropriately.

8:90. Miller, *A Harsh and Dreadful Love*, 6–7, quotes Maurin on the positive features of the new social order.

8:91. See Bernard Doering, "Jacques Maritain's Friendship with Dorothy Day," *New Oxford Review* 52:10 (December 1985): 16–23.

8:92. Miller, *A Harsh and Dreadful Love*, 7–13; and Piehl, *Breaking Bread*, 72–73, comment on the Russian influence.

8:93. William D. Miller, *Dorothy Day: A Biography* (San Francisco: Harper and Row, 1982), chap. 9, "The Gentle Personalist," 227–48, tells much of what can be known of Maurin.

8:94. Piehl, *Breaking Bread*, 3–16; and Miller, *Dorothy Day*, chap. 3, "The Journalist," 54–86, discuss Day's earlier career.

8:95. The novel is Dorothy Day, *The Eleventh Virgin* (New York: Boni, 1924).

8:96. On Marxists, see Dorothy Day, *The Long Loneliness* (New York: Harper and Row, 1952), 63.

8:97. See Nancy L. Roberts, *Dorothy Day and the Catholic Worker* (Albany: State University of New York Press, 1984), for a full accounting of the *Catholic Worker* and Day as journalist.

8:98. Piehl, *Breaking Bread*, 60–62, 74–75, and 96–97, treats round-table and houses of hospitality; 93 quotes Day on Spellman.

8:99. Day, *The Long Loneliness*, 149–50.

8:100. Piehl, *Breaking Bread*, 95–102, is the source for this account of Catholic Worker movement self-description.

8:101. Ibid., 107–9.

8:102. Lester P. Eliot, "Troubles of American Catholicism," *American Mercury* 34 (March 1935): 275.

8:103. *Catholic Worker* 2 (December 1934): 3; see also Dorothy Day, *From Union Square to Rome* (Silver Spring, Md.: Preservation of the Faith Press, 1938), 140.

8:104. John LaFarge, S.J., "Some Reflections on the Catholic Worker," *America* 57 (June 26, 1937): 275; "Catholic Workers," *America* 57 (July 24, 1937): 371.

8:105. For an appraisal of the Catholic impact of the movement, see Piehl, *Breaking Bread*, chap. 7, "Catholic Spiritual Radicalism in America," 241–50.

8:106. *Catholic Worker* 1 (April 1934): 3.

Chapter Nine

9:1. Polarities in cultural expression provide parallels to religious tensions; the very titles of books suggest the climate: Leo Gurko, *The Angry Decade* (New York: Dodd, Mead, 1947); Frederick R. Benson, *Writers in Arms: The Literary Impact of the Spanish Civil War* (New York: New York University Press, 1967); Harold Clurman, *The Fervent Years: The Story of the Group Theatre and the Thirties* (New York: Hill and Wang, 1957); Morgan Himelstein, *Drama Was a Weapon: The Left-Wing Theatre in New York 1929–1941* (New Brunswick, N.J.: Rutgers University Press, 1963); Isabel Leighton, ed., *The Aspirin Age, 1919–1941* (New York: Simon and Schuster, 1949); Jack Salzman and Barry Wallenstein, eds., *Years of Protest: A Collection of American Writing of the 1930s* (New York: Pegasus, 1967).

9:2. On the death-dealing aspects of religion, see René Girard, trans. Patrick Gregory, *Violence and the Sacred* (Baltimore: Johns Hopkins University Press, 1977); and Nicolas G. Onuf, *Reprisals: Rituals, Rules, Rationales* (Princeton: Princeton University Press, 1974), on the extensive literature on concepts such as crusades in Christianity, jihads in Islam, and the like.

9:3. Two examples of literature discussing the spiritual toll are Caroline Bird, *The Invisible Scar: The Great Depression and What It Did to American Life, from Then Until Now* (New York: David McKay, 1966); and Studs Terkel, *Hard Times: An Oral History of the Great Depression* (New York: Pantheon, 1970).

9:4. On regionalization and diffusion of immigrant groups, see Ramond D. Gastil, *Cultural Regions of the United States* (Seattle: University of Washington Press, 1975); Wilbur Zelinsky, *The Cultural Geography of the United States* (Englewood Cliffs, N.J.: Prentice-Hall, 1973); and Donald K. Fellows, *A Mosaic of America's Ethnic Minorities* (New York: Wiley, 1972).

9:5. Alexander Hamilton, James Madison, John Jay, *The Federalist: A Commentary on the Constitution of the United States Being a Collection of Essays Written in Support of the Constitution Agreed Upon September 17, 1787, by The Federal Convention* (Washington, D.C.: Robert R. Luce, 1976), 53–62, 335–41; John Murray Cuddihy, *No Offense: Civil Religion and Protestant Taste* (New York: Seabury Press, 1978), comments on the premium placed on civility and the need to keep religions from being abrasive in America.

9:6. André Siegfried, trans. H. H. Hemming and Doris Hemming, *America Comes of Age: A French Analysis* (New York: Harcourt and Brace, 1927), 52.

9:7. George Wilson Pierson, *Tocqueville in America* (Garden City, N.Y.: Doubleday, 1959), 70, 99, 139, 203, 322; and Alexis de Tocqueville, *Journey to America* (Garden City, N.Y.: Doubleday, 1971), 15, 132, 290, 395, include comments relevant to the "indifference" and tolerance theme.

9:8. Edward Alsworth Ross, *The Principles of Sociology* (New York: Century, 1920), 164.

9:9. Ibid.

9:10. Ibid.

9:11. Ibid., 165.

9:12. Walter Lippmann, *A Preface to Morals* (New York: Macmillan, 1929), 267.

9:13. Ibid., 268.

9:14. Ibid.; and Ross, *The Principles of Sociology*, 165.

9:15. Lippmann, *A Preface to Morals*, 269.

9:16. Ibid., 269, 271.

9:17. On the decline of the denomination as a base for conflict, see Robert Wuthnow, *The Restructuring of American Religion* (Princeton: Princeton University Press, 1988), chap. 5, "The Declining Significance of Denominationalism," 71–99. Wuthnow regards the denominations as having played a different role before World War II.

9:18. This understanding differs from conflict theories which follow radical and Marxian lines. For comment on alternatives, see William Appleman Williams, *The Contours of American History* (Cleveland: World, 1961), chap. 4, "The Transformation of Reality and the Inception of New Ideas," especially, "The New Deal as the Convergence and Consolidation of Old Traditions—Noblesse Oblige and Reform, Syndicalism and Expansion," 439–50; Howard Zinn, *The Politics of History* (Boston: Beacon Press, 1970), chap. 7, "The Limits of the New Deal," 118–36; the informal comments on Marxist interpretations by William E. Leuchtenberg, in John A. Garraty, *Interpreting American History: Conversations with Historians*, 2 vols. (New York: Macmillan, 1970), 2: 191–92.

9:19. C. Luther Fry, *The U.S. Looks at Its Churches* (New York: Institute of Social and Religious Research, 1930). See also Louise Houghton, "The Syrians in the United States," *Survey* 26, nos. 1–4 (1911): 480–95, 647–65, 786–802, 957–68.

9:20. On the early mosques, see Gregory Orfalea, *Before the Flames: A Quest for the History of Arab Americans* (Austin: University of Texas Press, 1988), 95–96, 165–276, and, for Cedar Rapids, 262–65.

9:21. Peter Kourides, *The Evolution of the Greek Orthodox Church in America and Its Present Problems* (New York: Cosmos Greek-American Printing Co., 1959), 8, bewails the schism among the Greeks.

9:22. Theodore Saloutos, *The Greeks in the United States* (Cambridge: Harvard University Press, 1964), 299–309, tells of the early thirties; on the opposition to Marxism, see 332.

9:23. The quotation from Athenagoras's visitation of 1936 and the account of his critics appear in George Papaioannou, *From Mars Hill to Manhattan: The Greek Orthodox in America under Patriarch Athenagoras* (Minneapolis: Light and Life Publishing Co., 1976), 75–76.

9:24. Peter Kourides, *The Evolution of the Greek Orthodox Church in America and Its Present Problems*, 10–1; Athenagoras attacked noncanonical clergy in an encyclical of March 2, 1933; see Papaioannou, *From Mars Hill to Manhattan*, 101–2.

9:25. See Papaioannou, *From Mars Hill to Manhattan*, 102–13; he quotes a special report by Athenagoras to Patriarch Photius, Sept. 16, 1934. The quotation is on 103.

9:26. Ibid., 173.

9:27. Gerald J. Bobango, *The Romanian Orthodox Episcopate of America: The First Half Century, 1929–1979* (Jackson, Mich.: Romanian-American Heritage Center, 1979), 85, 90, 95, 97ff., 120; the quotations are on 90, 95.

9:28. *New York Times*, Dec. 25, 1933; Dec. 26, 1933.

9:29. This narrative depends upon seminar papers by Frederick C. Rogers, who at the time of my writing was developing a thesis for a Ph.D. dissertation on the subject; most of the materials are in archives, and the general story awaits a telling by Rogers and others. Yet the points are already established that ethnicity and the Russian Revolution's repercussions were barriers to Orthodox unity.

9:30. "Taking Care of Their Own" is even a chapter title in Robert Mullen, *The Latter-Day Saints: The Mormons Yesterday and Today* (Garden City, N.Y.: Doubleday, 1966), 203–13.

9:31. Clark is quoted by Thomas F. O'Dea, *The Mormons* (Chicago: University of Chicago Press, 1957), 254; see also Joseph A. Geddes, *Institution Building in Utah* (Logan: Faculty Association, Utah State Agricultural College, 1949), 14.

9:32. Marc A. Rose, "The Mormons March Off Relief," *Reader's Digest*

30:182 (June 1937): 43–44; see also John Heinerman and Anson Shupe, *The Mormon Corporate Empire* (Boston: Beacon Press, 1985), 187.

9:33. Heinerman and Shupe, *The Mormon Corporate Empire*, has a very critical treatment of Mormon economics and politics; their account is based upon access to the Brimhall papers. The book is dedicated to Dean R. Brimhall. See especially 182–87.

9:34. These quotations from *Deseret News* and private correspondence are cited in Leonard J. Arrington and Davis Bitton, *The Mormon Experience: A History of the Latter-day Saints* (New York: Alfred A. Knopf, 1979), 273.

9:35. Grant is quoted in Robert Gottlieb and Peter Wiley, *America's Saints: The Rise of Mormon Power* (New York: Putnam's, 1984), 69–70.

9:36. On Christian Science's efforts at accommodation and, on occasion, its culturally near-mainstream character in the preceding years, see Stephen Gottschalk, *The Emergence of Christian Science in American Religious Life* (Berkeley: University of California Press, 1973).

9:37. Adventist history in this interwar period was colored by impressions gathered from a polemical work, Clara Endicott Sears, *Days of Delusion: A Strange Bit of History* (Boston: Houghton Mifflin, 1924); more fair-minded was Mahlon Ellsworth Olsen, *History of the Origin and Progress of Seventh-day Adventists* (Washington, D.C.: Review and Herald Publishing Assn., 1926); most historical research has concentrated on the origins of Millerism and Adventism in the mid-nineteenth century.

9:38. C. S. Longacre, "The President's Representative to the Vatican," *Liberty* (Third Quarter, 1940): 16–19.

9:39. Barbara Grizzuti Harrison, *Visions of Glory: A History and Memory of Jehovah's Witnesses* (New York: Simon and Schuster, 1978), 177, quotes *The Watchtower* (1929), 164.

9:40. Harrison, *Visions of Glory*, 179.

9:41. An account appears in ibid., 188–92; for the *Gobitis* ruling, see *Minersville School District v. Gobitis, 310 U.S. 586 (1940)* in John T. Noonan, Jr., *The Believer and the Powers That Are: Cases, History, and Other Data Bearing on the Relation of Religion and Government* (New York: Macmillan, 1987), 247–50.

9:42. *Cantwell v. Connecticut 310 U.S. 696 (1940)* is reprinted by Noonan, *The Believers and the Powers That Are*, 234–38.

9:43. Ibid.

9:44. George Santayana, *Character and Opinion in the United States* (New York: Charles Scribner's Sons, 1920), 218, 232–33.

9:45. A convenient recent history and set of biographical sketches is found in David Robinson, *The Unitarians and the Universalists* (Westport, Conn.: Greenwood Press, 1985).

9:46. See "The Reaction to Humanism," Robinson, ibid., 150–57.

9:47. On the Western character of the movement, see a history by one of its proponents, Charles H. Lyttle, *Freedom Moves West: A History of the Western Unitarian Conference 1852–1952* (Boston: Beacon Press, 1952), chap. 14, "Western Freedom for Religious Humanism," 238–58.

9:48. Quoted in ibid., 252.

9:49. Ibid., 252–53.

9:50. Quoted in ibid., 254.

9:51. The manifesto is reprinted in David Parke, ed., *The Epic of Unitarianism: Original Writings from the History of Liberal Religion* (Boston: Starr King, 1957), 138–42.

9:52. "The Humanist Manifesto," *The Christian Century* 50 (June 7, 1933): 743–45.

9:53. Curtis Reese, *The New Humanist* 6 (1933): 39; Henry Sloane Coffin, "Can Liberalism Survive?" *Religion in Life* 4 (1935): 196; Max C. Otto, *The New Humanist* 6:3 (May–June 1933): 33. For a whole account of the movement, see William Schultz, "Making the Manifesto" (D.Min. diss., Meadville/Lombard Theological School, Chicago, 1975).

9:54. John Dewey, *A Common Faith* (New Haven: Yale University Press, 1934); for a defense of the book against critics who found it unimportant, see Robert T. Roth, *American Religious Philosophy* (New York: Harcourt, Brace, and World, 1967), 99, n. 30.

9:55. Dewey, *A Common Faith*, 82.

9:56. Ibid., 84, 87.

9:57. David O'Brien, *American Catholics and Social Reform: The New Deal Years* (New York: Oxford University Press, 1968), best summarizes the complex of actions.

9:58. George Q. Flynn, *American Catholics and the Roosevelt Presidency 1932–1936* (Lexington: University of Kentucky Press, 1968), 1–3, comments on Roosevelt's religion.

9:59. On his ancestors, see Samuel Rosenman, ed., *The Public Papers and Addresses of Franklin D. Roosevelt*, 2 vols. (New York: Random House, 1938), 4: 96. Flynn, *American Catholics and the Roosevelt Presidency*, 5, quotes Roosevelt on the 1928 election.

9:60. Flynn, *American Catholics and the Roosevelt Presidency*, 5–8, accounts for the days when Roosevelt was beginning to pick up Catholic backing.

9:61. On papal references, see Rosenman, *The Public Papers*, 1: 778. The biography of Ryan is Francis L. Broderick, *Right Reverend New Dealer: John A. Ryan* (New York: Macmillan, 1961).

9:62. See Flynn, *American Catholics and the Roosevelt Presidency*, 23–24, on *Quadragesimo Anno*.

9:63. Haas receives biographical treatment in Thomas E. Blantz, C.S.C., *A Priest in Public Service: Francis H. Haas and the New Deal* (Notre Dame, Ind.: University of Notre Dame Press, 1982). Gillis wrote in *Catholic World* 133 (May 1931): 231–32.

9:64. William Henry Cardinal O'Connell, *Recollections of Seventy Years* (Boston: Houghton Mifflin, 1934), 98, 379, 228; see also *Boston Pilot*, May 6, 1933, 1; and *Brooklyn Tablet*, April 8, 1933, 2, for his attitudes to Roosevelt.

9:65. *Commonweal* 17 (Nov. 16, 1932): 58.

9:66. Michael O'Shaughnessy, "Greed is the Witch," *Commonweal* 18 (Nov. 4, 1931): 9–11; Archbishop John T. McNicholas, "Justice and the Present Crisis," *Catholic Mind* 29 (Oct. 22, 1931): 473–81; Paul L. Blakely, S.J., "The Marriage Encyclical and Wages," *America* 44 (Jan. 24, 1931): 384–86. (As cited by David O'Brien, *American Catholics and Social Reform*, 48–49.)

9:67. One of the best ways to trace Catholic action in the New Deal era is to follow the career of strategically placed Father Francis J. Haas. See Blantz, *A Priest in Public Service*. For an excellent introduction which provides the larger context for American Catholic social thought, see David O'Brien, *Public Catholicism* (New York: Macmillan, 1989).

9:68. Flynn, *American Catholics and the Roosevelt Presidency*, 94–96, reviews criticisms, especially by Catholic conservatives.

9:69. *San Francisco Monitor*, July 29, 1933, 1; Aug. 19, 1933, 1; see also Flynn, *American Catholics and the Roosevelt Presidency*, 96.

9:70. Ibid., 109–11, presents O'Connell's opposition to the Child Labor Amendment; on Russianizing American children, see the *Boston Pilot*, Feb. 23, 1935, 1.

9:71. Flynn, *American Catholics and the Roosevelt Presidency*, 196, comments on Kelley's work for Landon.

9:72. Ibid., 202–34, follows the Coughlin roles during the Roosevelt campaign.

9:73. Kennedy was quoted in the *New York Times*, Oct. 25, 1936, 33.

9:74. For samples, see the *Brooklyn Tablet*, Feb. 13, 1937, and March 13, 1937; see also Gillis, "The President Slips One Over," *Catholic World* 145 (May 1937): 129.

9:75. John A. O'Brien, "Fighting for Social Justice," *Commonweal* 26 (May 28, 1937): 119. Cited in David O'Brien, *American Catholics and Social Reform*, 93.

9:76. John A. Ryan and Moorhouse F. X. Millar, *The State and the Church* (New York: Macmillan, 1922), 34.

9:77. Ibid., 36, 38.

9:78. Broderick, *Right Reverend New Dealer*, 248, quotes Ryan writing to Daniel E. Lawler, Jan. 13, 1942.

9:79. Peter Guilday, "The Catholic Church in the United States," *Thought* 1 (June 1926): 7; William F. Sands, "The Return of the New Deal," *Catholic Digest* 1 (May 1937): 1–7; James Gillis, *This Our Day: Approvals and Disapprovals* (New York: Paulist Press, 1933), 141; see David O'Brien, *American Catholics and Social Reform*, chap. 9, "Catholicism and Americanism," 212–27, for a summary.

9:80. See O'Brien, *American Catholics and Social Reform*, 217–18, on the crusade; Francis X. Talbot, "Catholicism in America," in Harold E. Stearns, ed., *America Now* (New York: Charles Scribner's Sons, 1938), 530, 534, 540.

9:81. George Q. Flynn, *Roosevelt and Romanism: Catholics and American Diplomacy, 1937–1945* (Westport, Conn.: Greenwood Press, 1976), 106–15, tells of the appointment.

9:82. Roosevelt is quoted from a press conference of Dec. 26, 1939, by Flynn, *Roosevelt and Romanism*, 108; for the Ryan quote, and the words of a Fulton Sheen telegram (Dec. 24, 1939), ibid., 110; Wilfred Parsons, "The Pope, the President and Peace," *Thought* 15 (March 1940): 5–8.

9:83. Flynn, *Roosevelt and Romanism*, 111, tells of Federal Council of Churches actions; see also Myron A. Marty, *Lutherans and Roman Catholicism* (Notre Dame, Ind.: University of Notre Dame Press, 1968), 112–13.

9:84. Flynn, *Roosevelt and Romanism*, 216, quotes Roosevelt.

9:85. Ibid., 188, quotes the bishops of Fargo and San Antonio, from National Catholic Welfare Conference wire services.

9:86. Note that despite the generic term "Protestant" in both book titles, the authors treat only Federal Council of Churches type organizations in the pioneering historical works on Protestantism in this era: Donald B. Meyer, *The Protestant Search for Political Realism, 1919–1941* (Los Angeles: University of California Press, 1960), and Robert Moats Miller, *American Protestantism and Social Issues 1919–1939* (Chapel Hill: University of North Carolina Press, 1958). Both show little curiosity about "sectarian," fundamentalist, pentecostal, and evangelical denominations.

9:87. John C. Bennett, "After Liberalism—What?" *The Christian Century* 50 (Nov. 8, 1933): 1403; Walter Horton, *Realistic Theology* (New York: Harper and Brothers, 1934), 5.

9:88. Edwin Ewart Aubrey, *Present Theological Tendencies* (New York: Harper and Brothers, 1936), 45–46.

9:89. Ibid., 3, 7.

9:90. Ibid., 10.

9:91. Ibid.

9:92. Ibid., 54.

9:93. Ivan Lee Holt, *The Search for a New Strategy in Protestantism* (Nashville: Cokesbury Press, 1936).

9:94. Ibid., 15.

9:95. Ibid., 22, 32–33.

9:96. Ibid., 33–44, 47.

9:97. Ibid., 48–53.

9:98. Ibid., 53.

9:99. Ibid., 60, 62.

9:100. Ibid., 65–66, 82.

9:101. Ibid., chap. 3, "Efforts for a Larger Fellowship," 85-117, especially 85-86, 89-90.

9:102. Ibid., 100.

9:103. Ibid., 100-102, 105-14, discuss Hawaii.

9:104. Ibid., chap. 4, "A New Approach to the Christian World Mission," 118-55, especially 154.

9:105. Ibid., 157, 185.

9:106. Frederick Ernest Johnson, *The Church and Society* (Nashville: Abingdon, 1935), 12, 10.

9:107. Ibid., 16.

9:108. Ibid., 86.

9:109. Ibid., 31, citing Paul Hutchinson, *The Ordeal of Western Religion* (New York: Houghton Mifflin, 1933), 63.

9:110. Ibid., 60-61.

9:111. Ibid., 67-68.

9:112. Ibid., 112-16.

9:113. Ibid., 122.

9:114. Ibid., 124-25.

9:115. Ibid., 124-26.

9:116. Ibid., 126.

9:117. Ibid., 128.

9:118. Ibid., 123-33.

9:119. Ibid., 136.

9:120. Ibid., 166-68.

9:121. Ibid., 171.

9:122. See Paul Carter, *The Decline and Revival of the Social Gospel: Social and Political Liberalism in American Protestant Churches 1920-1940* (Hamden, Conn.: Archon Press, 1971 edition), chap. 10, "Legacy: The Social Gospel in 1929," 125-40, locates the movement.

9:123. Carter, *The Decline and Revival of the Social Gospel*, 167, rediscovered the Johnson anecdote; see also *The Christian Century* 50 (June 7, 1933): 761.

9:124. On Roosevelt and Hoover, see *The Christian Century* 48 (Mar. 22, 1931): 336; 49 (Sept. 21, 1932): 1126-28; 48 (Nov. 9, 1931): 1766-67.

9:125. On the invention of socialist Christian magazines and movements, see Meyer, *The Protestant Search*, 172-78.

9:126. Roosevelt was quoted in the *New York Times* (Oct. 3, 1932), 2; see "The Churches and the New Deal," *Federal Council Bulletin* 16 (Sept. 1933): 3-4; and (Oct. 1933): 6-7; Donald S. Meyer, *The Protestant Search for Political Realism* (Berkeley: University of California, 1960), quotes Roosevelt on how the council collects evidences of FCC and New Deal congruence, 314-16.

9:127. W. K. Anderson, "The Dilemma of the Socially-Minded," *Religion in Life* 8 (Winter 1939): 49-60, especially 51-52.

9:128. Ibid., 55-57.

9:129. Ibid., 57-58.

9:130. Ibid., 60.

9:131. "An Evolutionary Revolution," *The Christian Century* 51 (Jan. 17, 1934): 78-80.

9:132. Cyrus R. Pangborn, "Free Churches and Social Change: A Critical Study of the Council for Social Action of the Congregational Christian Churches of the United States" (Ph.D. diss., Columbia University and Union Theological Seminary, 1951), deals with the Congregational survey; Carter, *The Decline and Revival of the Social Gospel*, 205, also cites J. Milton Yinger, *Religion in the Struggle for Power* (Durham, N.C.: Duke University Press, 1946), chap. 6, on pledges. The poll is in *World Tomorrow* 14 (May 1931): 138-54, ibid., 17 (May 10, 1934): 222-56. Devere Allen, ed., *Pacifism in the Modern World* (Garden City, N.Y.: Doubleday, Doran, 1928), 17, comments on the difficulty of envisioning "redemptive force."

9:133. *Radical Religion* 3 (Fall 1938): 2.

9:134. Meyer, *The Protestant Search*, 376–81, discusses the latter-day pressures by *The Christian Century* on Niebuhr and his colleagues.

9:135. Morrison's editorial after Pearl Harbor appeared in *The Christian Century* 58 (Dec. 17, 1941): 1565–67; Meyer, *The Protestant Search*, 376–81, discusses the magazine's many editorials against impending war.

9:136. *The Christian Century* 57 (Mar. 6, 1940): 325.

9:137. Reinhold Niebuhr, "Japan and the Christian Conscience," *The Christian Century* 54 (Nov. 10, 1937): 1390–91.

9:138. Ibid.; see also Niebuhr, "America's Last Chance," *Christianity and Crisis* (July 14, 1941): 1–2.

9:139. Meyer, *The Protestant Search*, 360–61, discusses the formation of a group which signed a statement on "America's Responsibility in the Present Crisis."

9:140. Reinhold Niebuhr, "Christian Moralism in America," *Radical Religion* 5 (Winter 1940): 16–20.

Index

Note: In a book on modern American religion the words "modern," "American," and "religion" appear too frequently to be indexed; so do terms for some major clusterings such as "Christian," "Catholic," and "Protestant."

445